THE CRICKETERS' WHO'S WHO 2000

N.N.

THE CRICKETERS' WHO'S WHO 2000

Introduction by
JOHN STEPHENSON

Edited by
CHRIS MARSHALL

Statistics by
RICHARD LOCKWOOD

Portraits photographed or researched by
BILL SMITH

Queen Anne Press

QUEEN ANNE PRESS
a division of Lennard Associates Limited
Mackerye End, Harpenden, Herts AL5 5DR

Published in association with
The Cricketers' Who's Who Limited

First published in Great Britain 2000

© The Cricketers' Who's Who Limited

British Library Cataloguing in Publication is available

ISBN 1 85291 620 6

Typeset in Times and Univers Condensed
Editor (for Queen Anne Press): Kirsty Ennever
Quiz compiled by Chris Marshall
Cover design by Paul Cooper

Printed and bound by
WBC Book Manufacturers, Bridgend

PICTURE ACKNOWLEDGEMENTS

Cover photographs by Allsport
(main picture)
Shane Warne
(inset, left to right)
David Sales, Chris Schofield, Alamgir Sheriyar, Vikram Solanki

The publishers would also like to thank several new county players
for providing their own photos and Roger Wootton, Neil Doody,
Allsport and the *Express and Echo*, Exeter for additional portraits.

CONTENTS

NO ONE DOES MORE TO PROTECT CRICKET'S MOST VALUABLE ASSETS

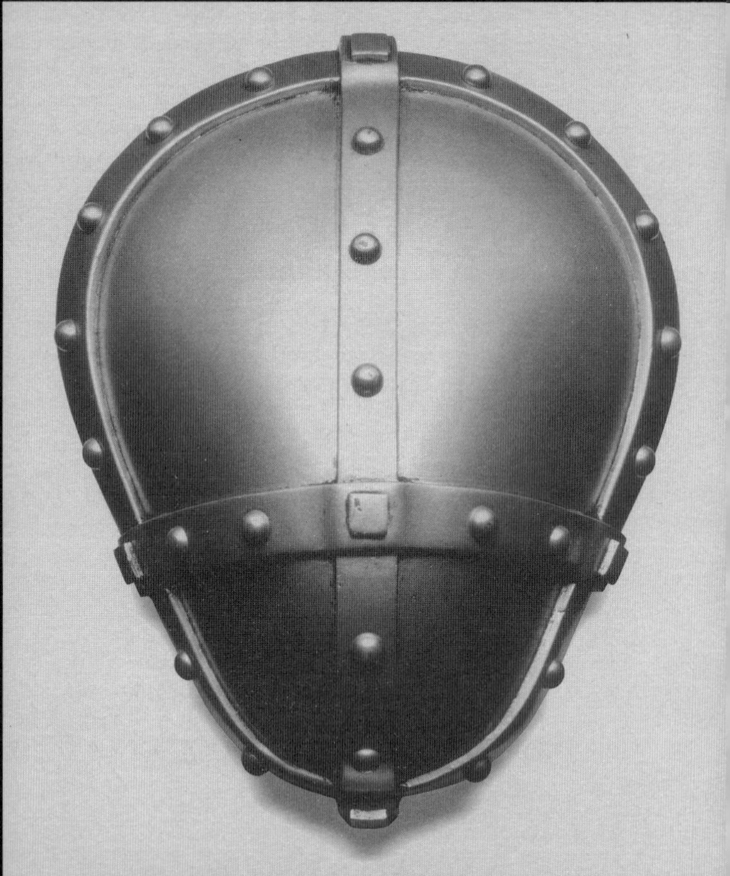

There seem to be annual changes to the structure of county cricket, but one thing always remains the same – there have to be players to play the game. The Professional Cricketers' Association has 100% membership of all the professionals playing county cricket and, as such, we consider our endorsement of *The Cricketers' Who's Who* to be a natural and important partnership. It is the true foundation of every new cricket season. It is the ultimate reference point for the players' records and statistics as well as their opinions on the state of the game. Believe me, it is read as much by the players as it is by the supporters!

The first cricket season of the new century brings with it a fresh format to our oldest domestic competition, the county championship. There are two divisions and higher stakes. Teams will fight to the wire for valuable promotion spots and hearts will be broken in the battle to avoid relegation. We also welcome back the Benson and Hedges Cup, which has been reinstated after a season of the Super Cup version. It will be interesting to see if Gloucestershire can build on their one-day triumphs of 1999, despite being in the second division of the PPP County Championship. Who knows what new innovations Bob Woolmer will introduce to lift Warwickshire back onto the winners' podium that they occupied so often in the last decade?

We also have some new exciting overseas stars in the county game to add to the summer's appeal, capped off with England's calypso contest with the West Indies, and Test matches against Zimbabwe for the first time on English soil. What's more, the one-day internationals are being taken further afield, which will, I'm sure, be met with enormous enthusiasm in Durham, Canterbury, Cardiff and Bristol. Enjoy *The Cricketer's Who's Who* and good luck to all the players this summer.

David Graveney
Chief Executive

The NatWest Series

NatWest Trophy

NatWest England Under 19's

NatWest Development of Excellence

NatWest Media Centre

We don't like cricket. We love it.

National Westminster Bank Plc. Registered Number 929027 England. Registered Office: 41 Lothbury, London EC2P 2BP

INTRODUCTION

At the time of writing, the first signs of a winter coming to its end are starting to show. Most of the cricketers in the pages that follow will have already been in the indoor nets for a month, and the anticipation of a fresh start will be within them. Those players fortunate enough to be touring with England will be experiencing different emotions. Their challenge will be to shrug off the fatigue of a winter of unremitting, high-octane international cricket. To report back to one's county after the sweet caress of Cape Town and the adventure of Harare can sometimes be the hardest test of temperament. It can be easy to forget the bread and butter when you get used to something rather more exotic.

The ECB in their wisdom will spare most of those playing regular international cricket the mythological 'drudgery' and 'grind' of the county circuit, when central contracts are introduced for the first time this summer. These will keep our best players fresh and prepared and not allow them to be tainted by the 'mediocrity' of county cricket. If you took this idea to its logical conclusion, county cricket (and its exponents) should be abolished, such is the harm done to our national game by it. But no, there is a lot that is good about the county game, and the majority of our Test players would prefer to be playing in it than not.

In the early 1990s Graham Gooch set the example of how to approach playing for your county in between Tests. Nasser Hussain has followed his lead and provides an excellent role model in the few games that he is available for Essex. Likewise, when Steve Waugh and Justin Langer play state cricket they inevitably end up scoring hundreds, such is their commitment to every single match that they play. Their dedication is never diluted and that can come only from within. One should never underestimate the pressures of playing for one's country, especially in this era, but county cricket and the great fraternity associated with it will be richer for the support and commitment of the best players, current and former, that it has produced over the years.

I am keenly aware that our domestic game has its faults and is responsible for many of the poor performances of our national team. I do, however, make no apology for trying to defend an institution to which I have given 17 years of my life. For example, the charms of festival cricket are undeniable. I am not one for nostalgia or traditions, but playing a county game during the Cheltenham Festival or the Canterbury Week is indeed a pleasure and an experience. This is the core of county cricket. Cricket played on outgrounds is of utmost importance in that it takes cricket to every corner of the country and provides variety and interest to the players and public alike. The pitches are invariably better than any that one will find at our Test venues, and the cricket played is always entertaining.

The matches that truly stand out in my mind have all taken place during these festival weeks, where the crowds are big and the surfaces have tested to the full the techniques of batsman and bowler alike. Southend will turn, Cheltenham will bounce, and this is where you learn how to adapt. The absence of any truly flat Test match pitches in recent years makes it even more important for our players to learn a correct technique. Inconsistent bounce has been the blight on many of our pitches for some years now – one does not mind a pitch that seams and turns, as long as the bounce is consistent. The close monitoring of pitches this season should bring an improvement in the way wickets are prepared, in particular with regard to how they play on the first morning of a match. And the improvement of pitches should remain a priority because if you hear it once you will hear it a million times – good pitches produce good players who produce good cricket...

The introduction of promotion and relegation has already proved a success in regard to intensity and interest. Whether this in turn will provide a better England team is an unknown, but we must give it a chance. For the Hampshire team last season, striving to stay in the top nine provided a focus that would not have been there in previous years. To stay in the first division next year requires a team to be sixth in the country, and to do that a team not only has to win a lot of games but also draw a few with credit against the very best in the competition.

I felt that last season county cricket had at last got it about right. The balance of cricket played was good, and an encouraging number of young players were coming through. It was a brave decision by the selectors to pick

Michael Vaughan on class rather than weight of runs, and I believe it will not be long before a couple of other young batsmen from Yorkshire, such as Matthew Wood, follow him. The peculiar demands of playing for Yorkshire seem to nurture the kind of temperament that is suited for Test cricket.

Witnessing at first hand what Gordon Lord and Hugh Morris are trying to achieve with the National Coaching Scheme gives me a great feeling of optimism for the future. The Level III course that I attended at Lilleshall is designed to equip every 'advanced' coach with an holistic approach to coaching. As a result of this, the younger players especially are benefiting from personal development programmes that cover not just the technical side of their game but also the tactical, physical, mental and lifestyle management sides. This should bring them into line with their Australian counterparts.

Coaches at county level are also being encouraged to use this approach. There are, unfortunately, not many English coaches left in county cricket, such is our predilection for overseas exotica. It does worry me that we have such an inferiority complex. English coaches should not be filling only the 2nd XI coach's role (which is in itself a very important one), they ought to be taking up the majority of jobs around the counties. We have just as much if not more expertise in this country, so let's use it. My hope is that once this current craze passes, the new skills that many coaches are being equipped with will start to filter through and result in better prepared cricketers.

To put all of this into perspective, let us not forget the tragic deaths of three great players during the past few months, all of whom have graced the pages of this publication in recent years. Malcolm Marshall, Phil Carrick and Sylvester Clarke were all very fine performers who made county cricket their life. The game will be much worse off without them around.

Whatever level of cricket you play, it is always important to remember that it is only a game and to have fun. Good luck to every supporter of English cricket and every player (and umpire) in this book for the first season of a new century.

John Stephenson
February 2000

IT'S THE NEW GAME IN TOWN

cricnet.com

Where else can you go from minor county and county board details to club cricket news and information in a heartbeat? When you want to know where past players are **cricnet.com** will let you know. Coaching clinics, tips and trivia contests. If there is a player injury we will know it before the doctor has a look. Rain in the offing? We'll tell you days before you open the umbrella.

And, speaking of games, care to place a wager? **cricnet.com** will have all the latest and most up to date spreads. Check out our records, trends and historical data before calling or visiting your bookmaker. Analysis, previews and predictions from the nation's best.

Go shopping, send a postcard, bid for an item, get a cricket screensaver, win an autographed photo of your favourite bowler or batsman and order tickets for the next match. You'll find it all on the web site that is the newest game in town.

And, it's not just cricket! Follow European basketball and your favourite team from here to Italy, the NBA, America's NFL, the top tennis and golf tournaments, Formula One, football results and quite a bit more. Click, click and stay where you are. The new game in town has it all. If you don't see it let us know and we will be on it straightaway.

cricnet.com is as good as being there, often better. Come see what all the others have tried to be.

cricnet.com
Come see what cricket is all about.

THE PLAYERS

THE COUNTY CHAMPIONSHIP QUIZ

Throughout the book there are 100 quiz questions referring to the history of the county championship from 1890 when it was officially constituted. The answers can be found on page 768.

Editor's Notes

The cricketers listed in this volume include all those who played for a first-class county at least once last season, in any form of cricket, and all those registered (at the time of going press) to play for the 18 first-class counties in 2000, even those who have yet to make a first-team appearance. All statistics are complete to the end of the last English season (One-Day Internationals to the end of the World Cup). Figures about 1000 runs and 50 wickets in a season refer to matches in England only. All first-class figures include figures for Test matches which are also extracted and listed separately. One-Day 100s and One-Day five wickets in an innings are for the English domestic competitions and all One-Day Internationals, home and abroad. Career records include 'rebel' tours to South Africa. In the interests of space separate season statistics for 1999 are not given for those whose appearances in first-class cricket or One-Day competitions were only for teams other than the county to which they are now registered, i.e. universities, Board XIs, minor counties etc (World Cup excepted). These appearances are however reflected in their career statistics and reference is made in the Extras section to the team for which they played.

The following abbreviations apply: *means not out; All First – all first-class matches; 1-day Int – One-Day Internationals; 1-day Lge – National League (including former Sunday leagues); NatWest – NatWest Trophy; B&H – Benson and Hedges Cup (including the Super Cup). The figures for batting and bowling averages refer to the full first-class English list for 1999, followed in brackets by the 1998 figures. Inclusion in the batting averages depends on a minimum of six completed innings, and an average of at least 10 runs; a bowler has to have taken at least 10 wickets. A bowler's strike rate refers to balls bowled per wicket taken. The Stop press category is a home for highlights of closeseason tours etc. These highlights are not reflected in the statistics in this edition.

Readers will notice occasional differences in the way the same kind of information is presented. This is because it has been decided to follow the way in which the cricketers themselves have provided the relevant information.

Each year in *The Cricketers' Who's Who*, in addition to those cricketers who are playing during the current season, we also include the biographical and career details of those who played in the previous season but retired at the end of it. The purpose of this is to have, on the record, the full and final cricketing achievements of every player when his career has ended.

A book of this complexity and detail has to be prepared several months in advance of the cricket season, and occasionally there are recent changes in a player's circumstances or the structure of the game which cannot be included in time. Many examples of facts, statistics and even opinions which can quickly become outdated in the period between the actual compilation of the book and its publication, months later, will spring to the reader's mind, and I ask him or her to make the necessary commonsense allowance and adjustments.

Chris Marshall, March 2000

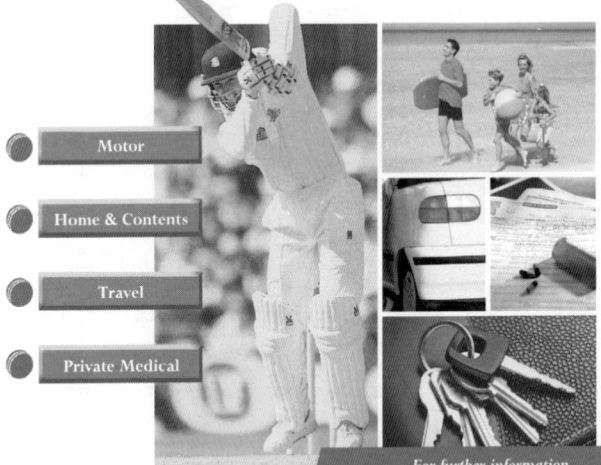

ADAMS, C. J.   Sussex

Name: Christopher John Adams
Role: Right-hand bat, right-arm medium
bowler, slip fielder, county captain
Born: 6 May 1970, Whitwell, Derbyshire
Height: 6ft **Weight:** 13st 7lbs
Nickname: Grizzly
County debut: 1988 (Derbyshire),
1998 (Sussex)
County cap: 1992 (Derbyshire),
1998 (Sussex)
One-Day Internationals: 2
1000 runs in season: 4
1st-Class 50s: 48
1st-Class 100s: 24
1st-Class 200s: 2
1st-Class catches: 225
One-Day 100s: 13
One-Day 5 w. in innings: 1
Place in batting averages: 81st av. 32.96 (1998 32nd av. 41.92)
Place in bowling averages: 113th av. 33.30
Strike rate: 72.00 (career 90.82)
Parents: John and Eluned (Lyn)
Wife and date of marriage: Samantha Claire, 26 September 1992
Children: Georgia Louise, 4 October 1993; Sophie, 13 October 1998
Family links with cricket: Brother David played 2nd XI cricket for Derbyshire and
Gloucestershire. Father played for Yorkshire Schools and uncle played for Essex 2nd XI
Education: Tapton House School; Chesterfield Boys Grammar School; Repton School
Qualifications: 6 O-levels, NCA coaching awards, Executive Development Certificate
in Coaching and Management Skills
Off-season: England tour to South Africa and Zimbabwe
Overseas tours: Repton School to Barbados 1987; England NCA North to N Ireland 1987;
England to South Africa and Zimbabwe 1999-2000
Overseas teams played for: Takapuna, New Zealand 1987-88; Te Puke, New Zealand
1989-90; Primrose, Cape Town, South Africa 1991-92; Canberra Comets 1998-99
Cricketers particularly admired: Ian Botham, Dean Jones, Graham Gooch
Young players to look out for: Steve Harmison, Graeme Swann, James Kirtley,
Robin Martin-Jenkins
Other sports played: Football ('mad on it'), golf
Other sports followed: Football (Arsenal FC)
Relaxations: 'My kids'
Extras: Beat Richard Hutton's 25-year-old record for most runs scored in a season at
Repton. Represented English Schools U15 and U19, MCC Schools U19 and, in 1989,

England YC. Took two catches as 12th man for England v India at Old Trafford in 1990. Set county records for the fastest century by a Derbyshire batsman (57 mins) and the highest score in the Sunday League (141*). Whittingdale Young Player Award 1992. Played for an England XI in the Cricket Max tournament in New Zealand in 1997. Was released by Derbyshire at the end of the 1997 season and after much speculation joined Sussex for 1998 as captain. Was selected to represent England in the cancelled World Super Max 8s originally scheduled to take place in Perth in October 1998. Sussex Player of the Year 1998 and 1999. Set individual one-day record score for Sussex of 163 (off 107 balls) v Middlesex in the National League at Arundel 1999; the innings included nine sixes, a Sussex Sunday/National League record. CGU Player of the Month July/August 1999. Signed a six-year contract with Sussex in 1999

Opinions on cricket: 'A genuine lack of quality practice facilities. A genuine lack of time for quality practice. A genuine lack of quality pitches. Other than that it's a great game!'

Best batting: 239 Derbyshire v Hampshire, Southampton 1996

Best bowling: 4-29 Derbyshire v Lancashire, Derby 1991

Stop press: Made Test debut in the first Test v South Africa at Johannesburg, November 1999

1999 Season

	M	Inns	NO	Runs	HS	Avge	100s	50s	Ct	St	O	M	Runs	Wkts	Avge	Best	5wl	10wM
Test																		
All First	17	31	2	956	130	32.96	1	5	23	-	120	28	333	10	33.30	3-37	-	-
1-day Int																		
NatWest	2	2	0	52	51	26.00	-	1	1	-	13	0	61	0	-		-	-
B & H	2	2	1	161	88	161.00	-	2	1	-	10	0	53	1	53.00	1-41	-	
1-day Lge	15	15	5	798	163	79.80	2	5	9	-	44.2	3	202	12	16.83	3-22	-	

Career Performances

	M	Inns	NO	Runs	HS	Avge	100s	50s	Ct	St	Balls	Runs	Wkts	Avge	Best	5wl	10wM
Test																	
All First	190	313	23	10561	239	36.41	26	48	225	-	2543	1530	28	54.64	4-29	-	-
1-day Int	2	2	0	28	25	14.00	-	-	2	-							
NatWest	21	20	5	936	129*	62.40	4	5	9	-	96	76	1	76.00	1-15	-	
B & H	37	34	5	1191	138	41.06	2	9	14	-	84	74	1	74.00	1-41	-	
1-day Lge	149	142	25	4642	163	39.67	7	30	78	-	650	590	23	25.65	5-16	1	

ADAMS, J. H. K.   Hampshire

Name: James Henry Kenneth Adams
Role: Left-hand opening bat, left-arm medium bowler
Born: 23 September 1980, Winchester
Height: 6ft 1in **Weight:** 13st 7lbs
Nickname: Jimmy, Griz, Jimma
County debut: No first-team appearance
Parents: Jenny and Mike
Marital status: Single
Family links with cricket: 'Dad played for Kent Young Cricketers. Brothers Ben and Tom played/playing for Hampshire YC'
Education: Twyford Prep School; Sherborne School; University College, London
Qualifications: 9 GCSEs, 3 A-levels
Career outside cricket: Student
Off-season: 'I am going to Australia (Adelaide) to play some district cricket for Woodville'

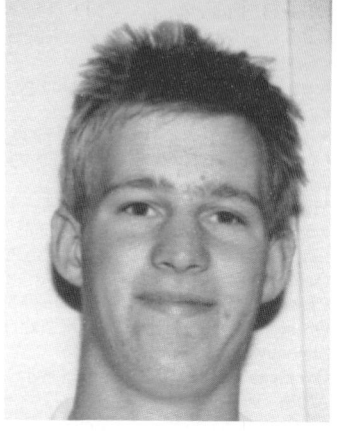

Overseas tours: West of England to West Indies 1995; Sherborne School to Pakistan
Overseas teams played for: Woodville, Adelaide 1999-2000
Cricketers particularly admired: 'Dad', Alan Rowe, 'and on the famous side, Tendulkar, Walsh'
Young players to look out for: 'Brothers Tom and Ben (if he bothers to play again) and a lot of good young Hampshire players'
Other sports played: Hockey (Dorset age group when 14), football
Other sports followed: Football (Aston Villa)
Relaxations: 'Other sports and relaxing at home'
Extras: Played in Lombard World Cup (U15)
Opinions on cricket: 'Club cricket needs to reach a higher average level and the club cricketers need to be pushed harder.'
Stop press: Called up as an injury replacement for England U19 tour to Sri Lanka for Youth World Cup

---

1. Which was Durham's first season in the first-class County Championship and who was their captain that season?

ADAMS, K.   Kent

Name: Kristian Adams
Role: Right-hand bat, left-arm medium-fast swing bowler
Born: 26 November 1976, Cleethorpes
Height: 5ft 11in **Weight:** 12st
Nickname: Grizzle, Grizzly, The Crab
County debut: No first-team appearance
Parents: Marianne and Kevin
Marital status: 'Girlfriend Vickie'
Education: Thrunscoe Junior School; Lindsey Comprehensive; Lindsey Sixth Form
Qualifications: 10 GCSEs
Career outside cricket: Professional barman
Off-season: 'Spending winter of 2000 in Zimbabwe'
Overseas tours: MCC A to East and Central Africa 1998
Cricketers particularly admired: Darren Gough, Chris Cairns, Wasim Akram
Young players to look out for: Irfan Shah, James Hockley, John Inglis
Other sports played: All sports ('becoming very accustomed to touch rugby!!')
Other sports followed: Football ('I support Grimsby Town – unfortunately!!')
Injuries: Out for two weeks with pulled intercostal muscle
Relaxations: 'Enjoying beating Saggers and Hockley on the PlayStation, then letting them buy me a drink at "Churchills" in Canterbury'
Extras: On MCC Young Cricketers ground staff 1997-99. Leading wicket-taker for Kent 2nd XI 1999. On one-year contract for 2000 season
Opinions on cricket: 'Start giving youth a chance at international level. It's the only way to bring on the teenagers who at U19 level seem to be world class.'

ADSHEAD, S. J.   Leicestershire

Name: Stephen John Adshead
Role: Right-hand bat, wicket-keeper
Born: 29 January 1980, Worcester
Height: 5ft 9in **Weight:** 12st
County debut: No first-team appearance
Parents: David and Julie
Marital status: Single

Family links with cricket: Father played and brother plays club cricket
Education: Bridley Moor HS, Redditch
Off-season: Playing in South Africa
Overseas teams played for: Fish Hoek, Cape Town 1998-99; Witwatersrand Technical, Johannesburg 1999-2000
Cricketers particularly admired: Alec Stewart
Other sports played: Football
Other sports followed: Football (Nottingham Forest)
Relaxations: Coarse fishing and scuba diving
Extras: Averaged 90 for Worcester U19 in county U19 competition in 1998, in which Worcestershire reached the semi-finals. Played a few games for Worcestershire 2nd XI. Played for Herefordshire in Minor Counties 1999

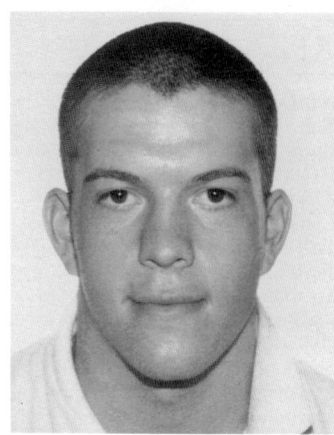

1999 Season (did not make any first-class or one-day appearances)

Career Performances

	M	Inns	NO	Runs	HS	Avge	100s	50s	Ct	St	Balls	Runs	Wkts	Avge	Best	5wI	10wM
Test																	
All First																	
1-day Int																	
NatWest	2	2	0	41	22	20.50	-	-	2	2							
B & H																	
1-day Lge																	

2. Before Surrey achieved the feat in 1999, which was the last county to finish the County Championship unbeaten and when?

AFZAAL, U.   Nottinghamshire

Name: Usman Afzaal
Role: Left-hand bat, slow left-arm bowler
Born: 9 June 1977, Rawalpindi, Pakistan
Height: 6ft **Weight:** 12st
Nickname: Uzzy, Saeed
County debut: 1995
1st-Class 50s: 17
1st-Class 100s: 3
1st-Class catches: 26
Place in batting averages: 109th av. 29.57
(1998 139th av. 29.40)
Strike rate: 98.33 (career 99.08)
Parents: Mohammed and Firdaus
Marital status: Single
Family links with cricket: Uncle Raja
played for PCC 'and scored many runs'.
Brother Aqib plays for England U15. Brother
Kamran played for Nottinghamshire U15,
U17 and U19 and for NAYC; now playing at club level
Education: Blue Bell Hill; Manvers Pierrepont Comprehensive; South Notts College;
Open University
Qualifications: NCA coaching certificate plus computer course
Career outside cricket: Is 50 per cent shareholder in a printing business
Off-season: 'Spending time with family and my girlfriend, and working hard on my
cricket game'
Overseas tours: England U19 to West Indies 1994-95, to Zimbabwe 1995-96;
Nottinghamshire to South Africa
Overseas teams played for: Victoria Park, Perth
Cricketers particularly admired: Sachin Tendulkar, Saeed Anwar, Uncle Raja
Young players to look out for: Younger brother Aqib
Other sports played: Indoor football, squash
Other sports followed: Football (Manchester United and Brazil – Ronaldo)
Relaxations: Following religion, listening to Indian music, reading
Extras: Played for England U15 against South Africa and, in 1994, for England U17
against India. Broke the U16 bowling record in the Texaco Trophy. 'Broke the back
garden indoor record!' Won young Denis Compton Award
Opinions on cricket: 'Believe in yourself and give 100 per cent. Great game!'
Best batting: 109* Nottinghamshire v Derbyshire, Derby 1998
Best bowling: 4-101 Nottinghamshire v Gloucestershire, Trent Bridge 1998

1999 Season

	M	Inns	NO	Runs	HS	Avge	100s	50s	Ct	St	O	M	Runs	Wkts	Avge	Best	5wI	10wM
Test																		
All First	16	30	2	828	104	29.57	1	6	4	-	49.1	8	198	3	66.00	1-17	-	-
1-day Int																		
NatWest																		
B & H																		
1-day Lge	5	5	1	186	83 *	46.50	-	2	2	-	0.5	0	4	0	-		-	-

Career Performances

	M	Inns	NO	Runs	HS	Avge	100s	50s	Ct	St	Balls	Runs	Wkts	Avge	Best	5wI	10wM
Test																	
All First	64	113	10	2673	109 *	25.95	3	17	26	-	3468	2027	35	57.91	4-101	-	-
1-day Int																	
NatWest	3	2	1	39	26 *	39.00	-	-	1	-	66	57	0	-		-	-
B & H	2	2	1	132	78	132.00	-	2	-	-							
1-day Lge	15	11	2	230	83 *	25.55	-	2	5	-	224	191	8	23.87	2-25	-	

ALDRED, P.   Derbyshire

Name: Paul Aldred
Role: Right-hand bat, right-arm medium bowler
Born: 4 February 1969, Chellaston, Derby
Height: 5ft 10in **Weight:** 12st
Nickname: Aldo
County debut: 1995
County cap: 1999
50 wickets in a season: 1
1st-Class 50s: 1
1st-Class 5 w. in innings: 5
1st-Class 10 w. in match: 1
1st-Class catches: 23
Place in batting averages: 282nd av. 8.13 (1998 235th av. 15.83)
Place in bowling averages: 26th av. 21.26 (1998 137th av. 46.33)
Strike rate: 43.52 (career 60.21)
Parents: Harry (deceased) and Lynette
Marital status: Single
Family links with cricket: Father played local cricket

Education: Chellaston and Curbar Primary School; Lady Manners, Bakewell, Derbyshire

Qualifications: 'None to worry about!'

Career outside cricket: Builder

Overseas teams played for: Bentley CC, Melbourne 1994-95

Cricketers particularly admired: Ian Botham, Viv Richards, Phillip DeFreitas

Young players to look out for: Ben Spendlove, Ian Blackwell

Other sports played: Played hockey for Derbyshire U16, U19, U21 and full squad

Other sports followed: Rugby, golf

Relaxations: Any sports (golf, fishing, rugby), 'having a drink with friends'

Extras: 'Had the great opportunity to play against New Zealand with the England NCA team in 1994 which was a great day.' Played for Derbyshire U21 hockey team at the age of 15. Awarded county cap 1999 after taking ten wickets in match v Lancashire in August; his season included a spell of 27 wickets in three matches

Opinions on cricket: 'Players should be looked after more in the off-season to enable them to train more intensely. 2nd XI games should be played more like the first-class game – i.e. over four days.'

Best batting: 83 Derbyshire v Hampshire, Chesterfield 1997

Best bowling: 7-101 Derbyshire v Lancashire, Derby 1999

1999 Season

	M	Inns	NO	Runs	HS	Avge	100s	50s	Ct	St	O	M	Runs	Wkts	Avge	Best	5wI	10wM
Test																		
All First	12	17	2	122	29 *	8.13	-	-	4	-	362.4	85	1063	50	21.26	7-101	5	1
1-day Int																		
NatWest	2	1	0	17	17	17.00	-	-	-	-	16	0	52	3	17.33	3-40	-	
B & H																		
1-day Lge	9	6	2	70	39 *	17.50	-	-	-	-	61	3	294	9	32.66	2-19	-	

Career Performances

	M	Inns	NO	Runs	HS	Avge	100s	50s	Ct	St	Balls	Runs	Wkts	Avge	Best	5wI	10wM
Test																	
All First	39	51	9	497	83	11.83	-	1	23	-	5841	2985	97	30.77	7-101	5	1
1-day Int																	
NatWest	5	3	1	21	17	10.50	-	-	1	-	236	151	7	21.57	4-30	-	
B & H	6	2	1	31	24 *	31.00	-	-	-	-	264	214	7	30.57	3-53	-	
1-day Lge	45	22	8	174	39 *	12.42	-	-	6	-	1554	1451	35	41.45	4-41	-	

ALLEYNE, D.   Middlesex

Name: David Alleyne
Role: Right-hand bat, wicket-keeper
Born: 17 April 1976, York
Height: 5ft 11in
County debut: 1999 (one-day)
Marital status: Single
Family links with cricket: Father played for
Northampton Exiles
Education: Enfield Grammar; Hertford
Regional College; City and Islington College;
London Cricket College
Qualifications: Senior cricket coaching
award
Career outside cricket: Within the leisure
sector
Overseas teams played for: Stratford,
Inglewood, New Zealand
Young players to look out for: Carl
Greenidge
Other sports played: Golf, football, judo, swimming
Other sports followed: Football (Liverpool FC)
Relaxations: Good restaurants, reading and music
Extras: Has played for Winchmore Hill CC. Represented Middlesex Colts U11 to
U17, Middlesex Schools U14 and U15, Middlesex Cricket Board. Played football for
Middlesex U15 and U16 and for Enfield Borough U16
Opinions on cricket: 'More time on preparation.'

1999 Season

	M	Inns	NO	Runs	HS	Avge	100s	50s	Ct	St	O	M	Runs	Wkts	Avge	Best	5wI	10wM
Test																		
All First																		
1-day Int																		
NatWest																		
B & H																		
1-day Lge	1	1	0	13	13	13.00	-	-	2	1								

Career Performances

	M	Inns	NO	Runs	HS	Avge	100s	50s	Ct	St	Balls	Runs	Wkts	Avge	Best	5wI	10wM
Test																	
All First																	
1-day Int																	
NatWest																	
B & H																	
1-day Lge	1	1	0	13	13	13.00	-	-	2	1							

ALLEYNE, M. W.   Gloucestershire

Name: Mark Wayne Alleyne
Role: Right-hand bat, right-arm medium
bowler, cover fielder, occasional
wicket-keeper, county captain
Born: 23 May 1968, Tottenham
Height: 5ft 11in **Weight:** 13st 7lbs
Nickname: Boo-Boo
County debut: 1986
County cap: 1990
Benefit: 1999
One-Day Internationals: 4
1000 runs in a season: 6
50 wickets in a season: 1
1st-Class 50s: 63
1st-Class 100s: 15
1st-Class 200s: 1
1st-Class 5 w. in innings: 6
1st-Class catches: 213
1st-Class stumpings: 2
One-Day 100s: 4
One-Day 5 w. in innings: 3
Place in batting averages: 163rd av. 24.00 (1998 50th av. 38.35)
Place in bowling averages: 138th av. 43.47 (1998 116th av. 34.08)
Strike rate: 95.73 (career 62.83)
Parents: Euclid Clevis (deceased) and Hyacinth Cordeilla
Marital status: Single
Family links with cricket: Brother played for Gloucestershire 2nd XI and Middlesex
YCs. Father played club cricket in Barbados and England
Education: Harrison College, Barbados; Cardinal Pole School, East London
Qualifications: 6 O-levels, NCA Senior Coaching Award, volleyball coaching
certificate

Off-season: England A tour to Bangladesh and New Zealand; England tour to South Africa and Zimbabwe (one-day series)

Overseas tours: England YC to Sri Lanka 1986-87 and Australia 1987-88; England A to Bangladesh and New Zealand 1999-2000 (captain); England to Australia (CUB Series) 1998-99, to South Africa and Zimbabwe 1999-2000 (one-day series)

Cricketers particularly admired: Gordon Greenidge, Viv Richards

Other sports followed: Football, volleyball, athletics

Relaxations: Watching films and sport; listening to music

Extras: In 1986 became youngest player to score a century for Gloucestershire. In 1990 also became the youngest to score a double hundred for the county. Graduate of Haringey Cricket College. Cricket Select Sunday League Player of the Year 1992. In 1992 struck then highest Sunday League score for Gloucestershire (134*). Appointed Gloucestershire captain for the 1997 season. Played for an England XI in the Cricket Max tournament in New Zealand in 1997. Was selected to captain England in the cancelled World Super Max 8s originally scheduled to take place in Perth in October 1998. Scored 112 in the B&H Super Cup final v Yorkshire at Lord's 1999, winning the Man of the Match award. Leading all-rounder in the single-division four-day era of the County Championship with 6409 runs (av. 32.53) and 216 wickets (av. 31.18) 1993-99

Best batting: 256 Gloucestershire v Northamptonshire, Northampton 1990

Best bowling: 6-64 Gloucestershire v Surrey, The Oval 1997

Stop press: Man of the Match in One-Day International v South Africa at East London February 2000 (53, 3-55 and a catch to dismiss Jonty Rhodes)

1999 Season

	M	Inns	NO	Runs	HS	Avge	100s	50s	Ct	St	O	M	Runs	Wkts	Avge	Best	5wl	10wM
Test																		
All First	17	29	1	672	76	24.00	-	3	20	-	367	109	1000	23	43.47	3-36	-	-
1-day Int																		
NatWest	5	4	0	46	18	11.50	-	-	2	-	44.4	3	140	11	12.72	4-14	-	
B & H	3	3	1	153	112	76.50	1	-	3	-	26	4	82	4	20.50	2-30	-	
1-day Lge	16	16	2	407	91	29.07	-	2	8	-	114	8	457	17	26.88	3-29	-	

Career Performances

	M	Inns	NO	Runs	HS	Avge	100s	50s	Ct	St	Balls	Runs	Wkts	Avge	Best	5wl	10wM
Test																	
All First	254	421	40	12100	256	31.75	16	63	213	2	19039	9825	303	32.42	6-64	6	-
1-day Int	4	4	1	76	38 *	25.33	-	-	-	-	90	58	3	19.33	3-27	-	
NatWest	34	28	4	524	73	21.83	-	1	12	-	1365	852	36	23.66	5-30	1	
B & H	51	43	9	812	112	23.88	1	1	24	-	2089	1507	47	32.06	5-27	1	
1-day Lge	206	188	40	4441	134 *	30.00	3	19	80	-	6665	5604	183	30.62	5-28	1	

ALTREE, D. A.   Warwickshire

Name: Darren Anthony Altree
Role: Right-hand bat, left-arm
fast medium bowler
Born: 30 September 1974, Rugby
Height: 5ft 11in **Weight:** 12st
Nickname: Bobby, Bobster, Dazzler
County debut: 1996
1st-Class catches: 1
Strike rate: (career 78.75)
Parents: Tony and Margaret
Marital status: Single
Education: Ashlawn School, Rugby;
carpentry
Career outside cricket: Coil operator
Off-season: 'Rehab!'
Overseas tours: Warwickshire U19 to Cape
Town 1992-93; Warwickshire to South Africa
1997, 1998, to Zimbabwe 1998
Overseas teams played for: Avendale, Cape Town 1994-95
Cricketers particularly admired: Dennis Lillee, Allan Donald
Young players to look out for: 'Billy'
Other sports followed: Football (Coventry)
Relaxations: Music, socialising
Extras: Took two 2nd XI hat-tricks in 1996
Best batting: 2* Warwickshire v Durham, Edgbaston 1998
Best bowling: 3-41 Warwickshire v Pakistan, Edgbaston 1996

1999 Season

	M	Inns	NO	Runs	HS	Avge	100s	50s	Ct	St	O	M	Runs	Wkts	Avge	Best	5wI	10wM
Test																		
All First																		
1-day Int																		
NatWest	1	1	0	6	6	6.00	-	-	-	-	5	1	13	0	-		-	-
B & H																		
1-day Lge																		

Career Performances

	M	Inns	NO	Runs	HS	Avge	100s	50s	Ct	St	Balls	Runs	Wkts	Avge	Best	5wI	10wM
Test																	
All First	5	7	3	2	2*	0.50	-	-	1	-	630	420	8	52.50	3-41	-	-
1-day Int																	
NatWest	1	1	0	6	6	6.00	-	-	-	-	30	13	0	-		-	-
B & H																	
1-day Lge																	

AMIN, R. M.   Surrey

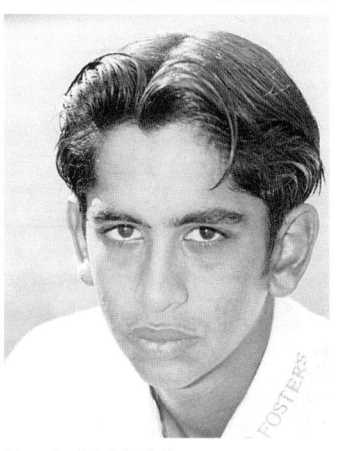

Name: Rupesh Mahesh Amin
Role: Right-hand bat, slow left-arm bowler
Born: 20 August 1977, Clapham
Height: 5ft 11in **Weight:** 10st 7lbs
Nickname: Idi, Plug
County debut: 1997
1st-Class catches: 3
Strike rate: 67.33 (career 88.35)
Parents: Mahesh and Aruna
Marital status: Single
Family links with cricket: Father played club cricket
Education: Stanford Middle School; Riddlesdown High School; John Ruskin Sixth Form; Croydon College
Qualifications: 8 GCSEs, 3 A-levels
Overseas teams played for: Manly Warringah District CC, Sydney 1997-98
Cricketers particularly admired: Saqlain Mushtaq, Sachin Tendulkar
Young players to look out for: Alex Tudor
Other sports played: Snooker
Other sports followed: Football (Liverpool), snooker (Ronnie O'Sullivan), boxing (Prince Naseem Hamed)
Relaxations: Going to cinema, eating good food, going out and seeing places
Extras: Played for Croydon District U15 side that won Hobbs Trophy against London Schools
Best batting: 12 Surrey v Leicestershire, The Oval 1998
Best bowling: 4-87 Surrey v Somerset, The Oval 1999

1999 Season

	M	Inns	NO	Runs	HS	Avge	100s	50s	Ct	St	O	M	Runs	Wkts	Avge	Best	5wI	10wM
Test																		
All First	3	3	2	6	3*	6.00	-	-	1	-	101	45	190	9	21.11	4-87	-	-
1-day Int																		
NatWest																		
B & H																		
1-day Lge																		

Career Performances

	M	Inns	NO	Runs	HS	Avge	100s	50s	Ct	St	Balls	Runs	Wkts	Avge	Best	5wI	10wM
Test																	
All First	10	13	7	31	12	5.16	-	-	3	-	1767	714	20	35.70	4-87	-	-
1-day Int																	
NatWest																	
B & H																	
1-day Lge	2	0	0	0	0	-	-	-	1	-	48	43	2	21.50	2-43	-	

ANDERSON, R. S. G.   Essex

Name: Ricaldo Sherman Glenroy Anderson
Role: Right-hand bat, right-arm medium-fast bowler
Born: 22 September 1976, Hammersmith, London
Height: 5ft 10in **Weight:** 11st 11lbs
Nickname: Ricky
County debut: 1999
50 wickets in a season: 1
1st-Class 5 w. in innings: 2
1st-Class catches: 5
Place in batting averages: 281st av. 8.16
Place in bowling averages: 60th av. 25.46
Strike rate: 45.40 (career 45.40)
Parents: Heather and Junior
Marital status: Single
Education: Lyon Park School; Alperton High School; Barnet College; NWL College; London Cricket College
Qualifications: 6 GCSEs, BTEC National in Engineering
Overseas tours: Middlesex U16 to Jersey

Overseas teams played for: Coronation CC, South Africa 1996-97
Cricketers particularly admired: Malcolm Marshall, Stuart Law, Carl Hooper
Young players to look out for: James Foster
Other sports followed: Football (Liverpool)
Relaxations: Music
Extras: Took 50 first-class wickets in his first season 1999
Best batting: 44 Essex v Kent, Canterbury 1999
Best bowling: 5-36 Essex v Middlesex, Southend 1999

1999 Season

	M	Inns	NO	Runs	HS	Avge	100s	50s	Ct	St	O	M	Runs	Wkts	Avge	Best	5wl	10wM
Test																		
All First	15	20	2	147	44	8.16	-	-	5	-	378.2	84	1273	50	25.46	5-36	2	-
1-day Int																		
NatWest																		
B & H																		
1-day Lge	7	5	1	25	10	6.25	-	-	-	-	44.2	2	241	4	60.25	3-32	-	

Career Performances

	M	Inns	NO	Runs	HS	Avge	100s	50s	Ct	St	Balls	Runs	Wkts	Avge	Best	5wl	10wM
Test																	
All First	15	20	2	147	44	8.16	-	-	5	-	2270	1273	50	25.46	5-36	2	-
1-day Int																	
NatWest																	
B & H																	
1-day Lge	7	5	1	25	10	6.25	-	-	-	-	266	241	4	60.25	3-32	-	

3. Which Glamorgan batsman scored three centuries in successive Championship innings, including two in the match v Northants at Abergavenny, in 1997?

ARCHER, G. F.   Nottinghamshire

Name: Graeme Francis Archer
Role: Right-hand bat, right-arm
'very medium'
Born: 26 September 1970, Carlisle, Cumbria
Height: 6ft **Weight:** 13st 7lbs
Nickname: Bunka
County debut: 1992
County cap: 1995
1000 runs in a season: 1
1st-Class 50s: 27
1st-Class 100s: 10
1st-Class catches: 127
One-Day 100s: 2
Place in batting averages: 168th av. 23.51
(1998 117th av. 28.13)
Strike rate: (career 75.21)
Parents: Christopher William and
Jean Elizabeth
Marital status: Single
Family links with cricket: Father played for Carlisle in N Lancashire League; brother
Neil plays in the S Cheshire Alliance League
Education: King Edward VI High School; Stafford College
Qualifications: 3 O-levels, City & Guilds and BTEC National Diploma in Leisure
Management, NCA Senior Coaching Award
Career outside cricket: 'Anyone got any ideas?'
Off-season: 'Looking for employment'
Overseas teams played for: Hutt District, Wellington, New Zealand 1991-92; Hutt
Valley representative side 1991-92; Old Collegians, Christchurch, New Zealand
1994-96; Lancaster Park, Christchurch 1997-98
Cricketers particularly admired: Graeme Hick, Ian Botham, Derek Randall, Chris
Cairns and Jimmy Adams
Young players to look out for: Guy Welton
Other sports played: Golf ('badly'), 'bit of squash', played badminton for
Staffordshire juniors
Other sports followed: Football (Carlisle United and Newcastle United), rugby
(Lutterworth RFC), squash and badminton, ice hockey (Nottingham Panthers)
Injuries: Wrist and ankle injuries
Relaxations: Spending time with good friends; music, videos, cinema, photography
Extras: Scored 200* in a 15 (8-ball) over match for Walsall U18s. Awarded the
A.A.Thompson Fielding Prize by The Cricket Society in 1990. Made 2nd XI debut for
Notts in 1987 aged 15. Played for Staffordshire in 1990-91. Rapid Cricketline Player

of the Month April/May 1994. Benson and Hedges Gold Award against Northants 1998. Released by Notts at end of 1999 season

Opinions on cricket: 'It's all well and good bringing in two divisions, but cricket clubs have taken it on themselves to produce sub-standard pitches to gain results. How on earth are we going to produce Test cricketers, batsmen to stay at the crease for two days, bowlers to bowl teams out on flat Test pitches? Having said that, the Test pitches for this summer have been a shambles. Second team cricket should be played on first-class grounds. Less overs in the day. Thirty minutes for tea.'

Best batting: 168 Nottinghamshire v Glamorgan, Worksop 1994
Best bowling: 3-18 Nottinghamshire v Hampshire, Southampton 1996

1999 Season

	M	Inns	NO	Runs	HS	Avge	100s	50s	Ct	St	O	M	Runs	Wkts	Avge	Best	5wI	10wM
Test																		
All First	15	28	1	635	132	23.51	1	2	27	-								
1-day Int																		
NatWest	2	2	0	13	8	6.50	-	-	2	-								
B & H																		
1-day Lge	12	12	3	346	75 *	38.44	-	3	5	-								

Career Performances

	M	Inns	NO	Runs	HS	Avge	100s	50s	Ct	St	Balls	Runs	Wkts	Avge	Best	5wI	10wM
Test																	
All First	100	179	14	5354	168	32.44	10	27	127	-	1053	648	14	46.28	3-18	-	-
1-day Int																	
NatWest	11	9	0	132	39	14.66	-	-	5	-	30	17	1	17.00	1-17	-	
B & H	11	10	1	370	111 *	41.11	1	2	2	-	113	117	1	117.00	1-34	-	
1-day Lge	78	71	12	1434	104 *	24.30	1	6	29	-	240	234	9	26.00	2-16	-	

4. Which cricketer tops the list for the number of County Championship appearances in a career?

ATHERTON, M. A. Lancashire

Name: Michael Andrew Atherton
Role: Right-hand bat, leg-break bowler
Born: 23 March 1968, Manchester
Height: 6ft **Weight:** 13st 5lbs
Nickname: Athers, Dread
County debut: 1987
County cap: 1989
Benefit: 1997 (£307,000)
Test debut: 1989
Tests: 86
One-Day Internationals: 54
1000 runs in a season: 7
1st-Class 50s: 91
1st-Class 100s: 46
1st-Class 200s: 2
1st-Class 5 w. in innings: 3
1st-Class catches: 222
One-Day 100s: 11
Place in batting averages: 17th av. 44.46 (1998 42nd av. 39.72)
Strike rate: (career 83.15)
Parents: Alan and Wendy
Marital status: Single
Family links with cricket: Father played club cricket
Education: Briscoe Lane County Primary; Manchester GS; Downing College, Cambridge
Qualifications: 10 O-levels, 3 A-levels; BA (Hons) (Cantab)
Off-season: England tour to South Africa
Overseas tours: England YC to Sri Lanka 1986-87, to Australia 1987-88; England A to Zimbabwe 1989-90; England to Australia 1990-91, to India and Sri Lanka 1992-93, to West Indies 1993-94, to Australia 1994-95, to South Africa 1995-96, to India and Pakistan (World Cup) 1995-96, to Zimbabwe and New Zealand 1996-97, to West Indies 1997-98, to Australia 1998-99, to South Africa 1999-2000
Cricketers particularly admired: Allan Border
Young players to look out for: 'This year, Schofield at Lancs and Stevens at Leicester looked good bets for the future'
Other sports followed: Golf, squash, football
Injuries: Recurring back injury
Relaxations: 'Decent novels (Heller, Kundera, etc.), good movies, food and wine, travelling, most sports, music'
Extras: In 1987 was first player to score 1000 runs in his debut season since Paul Parker in 1976. Became youngest Lancastrian to score a Test century (151 v NZ at

Trent Bridge in 1990); second Lancastrian to score a Test century at Old Trafford (138 v India in 1990). First captained England U19 aged 16. One of *Wisden*'s Five Cricketers of the Year 1991. Selected for England tour to New Zealand and also England A tour to Bermuda and West Indies in 1991-92 but ruled out of both through injury. Appointed England captain in 1993. Cornhill England Player of the Year 1994. Voted England's Player of the Series against the West Indies in 1995. Hit 185 not out in the second Test against South Africa in Johannesburg in 1995-96 series. The innings lasted 645 minutes and was the fourth longest by an Englishman in Test matches. Passed Peter May's long-standing record of most Tests as England captain against Australia during the Ashes campaign in 1997. Relinquished England captaincy after 1997-98 Test series v West Indies. Was England's Man of the Series v South Africa 1998. Captained MCC v Rest of the World in the Diana, Princess of Wales Memorial Match at Lord's in July 1998. Run of 62 consecutive Test matches ended when he pulled out of the Test v Sri Lanka at The Oval 1998. Selected for England's 1999 World Cup squad but forced to withdraw ahead of Coca-Cola Cup tournament in Sharjah in April 1999 because of back injury

Opinions on cricket: 'Restructuring of the county game is a must if England are to prosper. Any chance of the ECB grasping the nettle?'

Best batting: 268* Lancashire v Glamorgan, Blackpool 1999

Best bowling: 6-78 Lancashire v Nottinghamshire, Trent Bridge 1990

Stop press: Awarded England contract (Band A) for 2000

1999 Season

	M	Inns	NO	Runs	HS	Avge	100s	50s	Ct	St	O	M	Runs	Wkts	Avge	Best	5wI	10wM
Test	2	4	0	133	64	33.25	-	1	1	-								
All First	9	15	2	578	268 *	44.46	1	2	4	-								
1-day Int																		
NatWest	1	1	0	61	61	61.00	-	1	-	-								
B & H																		
1-day Lge	7	6	2	244	95 *	61.00	-	3	1	-								

Career Performances

	M	Inns	NO	Runs	HS	Avge	100s	50s	Ct	St	Balls	Runs	Wkts	Avge	Best	5wI	10wM
Test	90	167	6	6178	185 *	38.37	12	38	59	-	408	302	2	151.00	1-20	-	-
All First	288	501	44	18927	268 *	41.41	48	91	222	-	8981	4733	108	43.82	6-78	3	-
1-day Int	54	54	3	1791	127	35.11	2	12	15	-							
NatWest	28	28	2	1007	115	38.73	2	7	9	-	188	154	6	25.66	2-15	-	
B & H	60	59	5	1952	121 *	36.14	3	12	34	-	252	228	7	32.57	4-42	-	
1-day Lge	97	94	8	3143	111	36.54	4	18	30	-	216	248	7	35.42	3-33	-	

ATHEY, C. W. J. Worcestershire

Name: Charles William Jeffrey Athey
Role: Right-hand bat, occasional right-arm medium bowler, occasional wicket-keeper
Born: 27 September 1957, Middlesbrough
Height: 5ft 10in **Weight:** 12st 7lbs
Nickname: Bumper, Wingnut, Ath
County debut: 1976 (Yorkshire), 1984 (Gloucestershire), 1993 (Sussex), 1999 (one-day, Worcestershire)
County cap: 1980 (Yorkshire), 1985 (Gloucestershire), 1993 (Sussex)
Benefit: 1990 (Gloucestershire)
Test debut: 1980
Tests: 23
One-Day Internationals: 31
1000 runs in a season: 13
1st-Class 50s: 126
1st-Class 100s: 55
1st-Class catches: 429
1st-Class stumpings: 2
One-Day 100s: 11
One-Day 5 w. in innings: 1
Strike rate: (career 100.20)
Parents: Peter and Maree

Wife and date of marriage: Janet Linda, 9 October 1982
Family links with cricket: 'Father played league cricket in North Yorkshire and South Durham League for 29 years, 25 of them with Middlesbrough, and has been President of Middlesbrough CC since 1975. Brother-in-law Colin Cook played for Middlesex, other brother-in-law (Martin) plays in Thames Valley League. Father-in-law deeply involved in Middlesex Youth cricket'
Education: Linthorpe Junior; Stainsby Secondary School; Acklam Hall High School
Qualifications: 4 O-levels, some CSEs, NCA coaching certificate
Overseas tours: England YC to West Indies 1975-76; England to West Indies 1980-81, to Australia 1986-87, to Pakistan, Australia and New Zealand 1987-88; England B to Sri Lanka 1985-86; unofficial English XI to South Africa 1989-90; MCC to Bahrain 1994-95, to Bangladesh 1999-2000 (as coach); BSI World Cup, India 1994-95
Cricketers particularly admired: 'Too many to mention, but those with enthusiasm for the game'
Other sports followed: Most sports, especially football (Middlesbrough FC)
Relaxations: Gardening, sport and military history
Extras: Played for Teesside County Schools U16 at age 12. Played for Yorkshire Colts

1974. Played football for Middlesbrough Schools U16 and Junior XI. Offered but declined apprenticeship terms with Middlesbrough FC. Captain of Gloucestershire in 1989. Suspension for playing in South Africa in 1990 was remitted in 1992. 'Scored four hundreds in four innings for Gloucestershire CCC.' Passed 25,000 first-class runs with his 138 not out against Somerset at Taunton in 1997 and retired at the end of the season. Is coach at Worcestershire and played one National League game in 1999 because of injuries to current players

Best batting: 184 England B v Sri Lanka XI, Galle 1975-86
Best bowling: 3-3 Gloucestershire v Hampshire, Bristol 1985

1999 Season

	M	Inns	NO	Runs	HS	Avge	100s	50s	Ct	St	O	M	Runs	Wkts	Avge	Best	5wI	10wM
Test																		
All First																		
1-day Int																		
NatWest																		
B & H																		
1-day Lge	1	1	1	22	22 *	-	-	-	-	-	-							

Career Performances

	M	Inns	NO	Runs	HS	Avge	100s	50s	Ct	St	Balls	Runs	Wkts	Avge	Best	5wI	10wM
Test	23	41	1	919	123	22.97	1	4	13	-							
All First	467	784	71	25453	184	35.69	55	126	430	2	4810	2674	48	55.70	3-3	-	-
1-day Int	31	30	3	848	142 *	31.40	2	4	16	-	6	10	0	-	-	-	-
NatWest	53	52	9	1860	115	43.25	2	14	22	-	199	168	1	168.00	1-18	-	-
B & H	84	79	11	2551	118	37.51	1	20	34	1	478	364	16	22.75	4-48	-	
1-day Lge	270	259	24	7526	121 *	32.02	7	47	97	-	913	857	30	28.56	5-35	1	

5. Which non-wicketkeeping fielder took ten catches
(and scored two 100s) in the match between Gloucestershire and Surrey
at Cheltenham in 1928?

AUSTIN, I. D. — Lancashire

Name: Ian David Austin
Role: Left-hand bat, right-arm medium bowler
Born: 30 May 1966, Haslingden, Lancs
Height: 5ft 10in **Weight:** 14st 7lbs
Nickname: Oscar, Bully
County debut: 1986
County cap: 1990
One-Day Internationals: 9
1st-Class 50s: 20
1st-Class 100s: 2
1st-Class 5 w. in innings: 6
1st-Class 10 w. in match: 1
1st-Class catches: 35
One-Day 5 w. in innings: 1
Place in batting averages: 194th av. 20.83 (1998 180th av. 21.25)
Place in bowling averages: (1998 57th av. 26.38)
Strike rate: 86.00 (career 65.83)
Parents: Jack and Ursula
Wife and date of marriage: Alexandra, 27 February 1993
Children: Victoria, 28 January 1995; Matthew, 26 January 1998
Family links with cricket: Father opened batting for Haslingden CC
Education: Haslingden High School
Qualifications: 4 O-levels, NCA coaching certificate
Overseas tours: NAYC to Bermuda 1985; Lancashire to Jamaica 1986-87, 1987-88, to Zimbabwe 1988-89, to Tasmania and Western Australia 1989-90, 1990-91; England to Bangladesh (Wills International Cup) 1998, to Sharjah (Coca-Cola Cup) 1998-99
Overseas teams played for: Maroochydore, Queensland 1987-88, 1991-92; Randwick, Sydney 1990-91
Cricketers particularly admired: Ian Botham, Hartley Alleyne
Young players to look out for: Andrew Flintoff
Other sports followed: Football (Burnley), golf
Relaxations: Golf, and listening to music
Extras: Set amateur Lancashire League record for highest individual score (147*). Broke Lancashire CCC record for most wickets in the Sunday League in 1991. Scored quickest first-class century in 1991 off authentic bowling (64 balls). Man of the Match in the 1996 Benson and Hedges final and the NatWest semi-final. Lancashire Player of the Year for 1997. Played for an England XI in the Cricket Max tournament in New Zealand in 1997. Man of the Match in the 1998 NatWest final. One of *Wisden*'s Five

Cricketers of the Year 1999. Represented England in the 1999 World Cup. Granted a benefit for 2000
Best batting: 115* Lancashire v Derbyshire, Blackpool 1992
Best bowling: 6-43 Lancashire v Sri Lanka A, Old Trafford 1999

1999 Season

	M	Inns	NO	Runs	HS	Avge	100s	50s	Ct	St	O	M	Runs	Wkts	Avge	Best	5wI	10wM
Test																		
All First	5	8	2	125	45 *	20.83	-	-	2	-	129	29	443	9	49.22	6-43	1	-
1-day Int	2	0	0	0	0	-	-	-	-	-	18.4	1	66	3	22.00	2-25	-	
NatWest	3	2	0	17	13	8.50	-	-	1	-	30	2	120	5	24.00	2-43	-	
B & H	1	1	0	23	23	23.00	-	-	-	-	10	1	37	1	37.00	1-37	-	
1-day Lge	12	3	1	21	10	10.50	-	-	-	-	96.3	18	288	15	19.20	4-15	-	

Career Performances

	M	Inns	NO	Runs	HS	Avge	100s	50s	Ct	St	Balls	Runs	Wkts	Avge	Best	5wI	10wM
Test																	
All First	123	172	37	3778	115 *	27.98	2	20	35	-	17117	8010	260	30.80	6-43	6	1
1-day Int	9	6	1	34	11 *	6.80	-	-	-	-	475	360	6	60.00	2-25	-	
NatWest	31	22	9	343	97	26.38	-	2	3	-	2019	1151	42	27.40	3-14	-	
B & H	57	37	9	608	80	21.71	-	2	11	-	3298	2126	71	29.94	4-8	-	
1-day Lge	181	109	44	1154	48	17.75	-	-	33	-	7489	5444	201	27.08	5-56	1	

6. Who was Essex's overseas player when they won the
County Championship in 1992?

AVERIS, J. M. M. Gloucestershire

Name: James Maxwell Michael Averis
Role: Right-hand bat, right-arm
fast-medium bowler
Born: 28 May 1974, Bristol
Height: 5ft 11in **Weight:** 13st 2lbs
Nickname: Fish, Buster, Avo
County debut: 1994 (one-day),
1997 (first-class)
1st-Class 5 w. in innings: 1
1st-Class catches: 2
Strike rate: 54.25 (career 87.61)
Parents: Michael and Carol
Marital status: Single
Family links with cricket: 'Dad and
grandfather played'
Education: Bristol Cathedral School;
University of Portsmouth; St Cross College,
Oxford University

Qualifications: 10 GCSEs, 3 A-levels, BSc (Hons) Geographical Science, DipSoc (Oxon)
Career outside cricket: 'Open to offers'
Off-season: 'Playing rugby and working until Christmas, then playing cricket in South Africa'
Overseas tours: Bristol Schools to Australia 1990-91; Gloucestershire to Zimbabwe 1997, to South Africa 1999; Bristol RFC to South Africa 1996; Oxford University RFC to Japan and Australia 1997
Cricketers particularly admired: Courtney Walsh, David Lawrence, Ian Botham
Young players to look out for: Mark Wagh, Rob Cunliffe
Other sports played: Rugby (Bristol RFC – first-team debut 1994; Oxford University – Blue 1996)
Other sports followed: Football (Liverpool FC)
Injuries: Out for eight to nine weeks with rib injury
Relaxations: 'Anna Jago, music, fitness, travel'
Extras: Double Oxford Blue in 1996-97. Captain of South West U21 rugby in 1995
Opinions on cricket: 'The PCA is a terrific idea and is doing very well for its members.'
Best batting: 42 Oxford University v Sussex, The Parks 1997
Best bowling: 5-98 Oxford University v Hampshire, The Parks 1997

1999 Season

	M	Inns	NO	Runs	HS	Avge	100s	50s	Ct	St	O	M	Runs	Wkts	Avge	Best	5wI	10wM
Test																		
All First	3	5	2	40	18 *	13.33	-	-	-	-	72.2	16	261	8	32.62	3-42	-	-
1-day Int																		
NatWest																		
B & H																		
1-day Lge	6	5	3	5	5 *	2.50	-	-	-	-	39	6	158	5	31.60	3-17	-	

Career Performances

	M	Inns	NO	Runs	HS	Avge	100s	50s	Ct	St	Balls	Runs	Wkts	Avge	Best	5wI	10wM
Test																	
All First	14	22	7	322	42	21.46	-	-	2	-	2278	1492	26	57.38	5-98	1	-
1-day Int																	
NatWest																	
B & H																	
1-day Lge	13	8	5	8	5 *	2.66	-	-	1	-	486	395	13	30.38	3-17	-	

AYMES, A. N.   Hampshire

Name: Adrian Nigel Aymes
Role: Right-hand bat, wicket-keeper
Born: 4 June 1964, Southampton
Height: 6ft **Weight:** 13st
Nickname: Aymeser, Adi, Keeps
County debut: 1987
County cap: 1991
1st-Class 50s: 31
1st-Class 100s: 7
1st-Class catches: 425
1st-Class stumpings: 35
Place in batting averages: 61st av. 35.95
(1998 59th av. 35.90)
Strike rate: (career 56.00)
Parents: Michael and Barbara
Wife and date of marriage: Marie,
14 November 1992
Children: Lucie, 9 November 1994
Family links with cricket: 'Brother bowled at me in the drive'
Education: Shirley Middle; Bellemoor Secondary; Hill College
Qualifications: 4 O-levels, 1 A-level, 1 AO-level, NCA coaching award

Career outside cricket: Building sites, selling cricket equipment
Off-season: Training, fitness, 'getting Derek Kenway to his true fighting weight'
Overseas tours: Hampshire CCC to Isle of Wight 1992, to Portugal 1993, to Guernsey 1994, to Anguilla 1997
Cricketers particularly admired: Robin Smith, Chris Smith, Peter Haslop, 'and all the Hursley Park players that made us so successful in the late 1970s-early 1980s'
Young players to look out for: Derek Kenway ('if you can still see him'), Graeme Swann
Other sports followed: Football (Arsenal FC, Southampton FC, 'and all other Hampshire football sides')
Relaxations: Spending time with friends and family; training
Extras: Half century on debut v Surrey; equalled club record of 6 catches in an innings and 10 in a match. Hampshire Exiles Young Player of the Year 1990. Was quickest wicket-keeper to 100 dismissals and 1000 runs in the Sunday League. Promoted to bat at number 5 in 1998, made 450 runs in first four Championship games, including two 100s and two 50s. Granted a benefit for 2000; his benefit year got under way at Hambledon with a 13-over game, the opening delivery of which was bowled a few seconds after midnight on 1 January 2000
Opinions on cricket: 'If pitches are reported, the Board have to be strong enough to dock points, otherwise it is a waste of time having pitch inspectors. Good pitches breed good players. Still a great game.'
Best batting: 133 Hampshire v Leicestershire, Leicester 1998
Best bowling: 2-135 Hampshire v Northamptonshire, Southampton 1998

1999 Season

	M	Inns	NO	Runs	HS	Avge	100s	50s	Ct	St	O	M	Runs	Wkts	Avge	Best	5wl	10wM
Test																		
All First	18	27	5	791	115 *	35.95	2	5	51	2	1	0	1	0	-	-	-	-
1-day Int																		
NatWest	2	1	1	2	2 *	-	-	-	4	-								
B & H	1	1	0	1	1	1.00	-	-	-	-								
1-day Lge	13	10	3	105	34	15.00	-	-	6	1								

Career Performances

	M	Inns	NO	Runs	HS	Avge	100s	50s	Ct	St	Balls	Runs	Wkts	Avge	Best	5wl	10wM
Test																	
All First	181	266	67	6316	133	31.73	7	31	425	35	168	318	3	106.00	2-135	-	-
1-day Int																	
NatWest	21	10	3	244	73 *	34.85	-	2	34	2							
B & H	37	23	7	305	46 *	19.06	-	-	37	9							
1-day Lge	139	101	41	1451	60 *	24.18	-	3	123	33							

BAILEY, R. J.   Derbyshire

Name: Robert John Bailey
Role: Right-hand bat, off-spin bowler
Born: 28 October 1963, Biddulph,
Stoke-on-Trent
Height: 6ft 3in **Weight:** 14st 7lbs
Nickname: Biff, Nose Bag
County debut: 1982 (Northants)
County cap: 1985 (Northants)
Benefit: 1993 (Northants)
Test debut: 1988
Tests: 4
One-Day Internationals: 4
1000 runs in a season: 13
1st-Class 50s: 104
1st-Class 100s: 40
1st-Class 200s: 4
1st-Class 5 w. in innings: 2
1st-Class catches: 260
One-Day 100s: 9

Place in batting averages: 66th av. 35.38 (1998 66th av. 34.50)
Strike rate: 114.00 (career 80.16)
Parents: Marie, father deceased
Wife and date of marriage: Rachel, 11 April 1987
Children: Harry John, 7 March 1991; Alexandra Joy, 13 November 1993
Family links with cricket: Brother plays for Betley in the North Staffs and South Cheshire League
Education: Biddulph High School
Qualifications: 6 CSEs, 1 O-level, NCA advanced cricket coach
Career outside cricket: Managing Director of Rob Bailey Ceramics, promotional ceramics business. 'Also sales rep, delivery and packaging for the company!'
Off-season: 'As above!'
Overseas tours: England to Sharjah 1984-85 and 1986-87, to West Indies 1989-90; Northants to Durban 1991-92, to Cape Town 1992-93, to Zimbabwe 1994-95; Singapore Sixes October 1994
Overseas teams played for: Rhodes University, South Africa 1982-83; Uitenhage, Melbourne 1983-84, 1984-85; Fitzroy, Melbourne, 1985-86; Gosnells, Perth 1987-88
Other sports followed: Football (Stoke City)
Relaxations: Walking, and drinking at the local village pub
Extras: Played for Staffordshire. Played for Young England v Young Australia 1983. Selected for cancelled tour of India 1988-89. Was youngest Northamptonshire player to score 10,000 runs. Won three consecutive NatWest Man of the Match Awards 1995.

Took over the Northamptonshire captaincy in 1996 season and held post until the end of the 1997 season. In 1999 v Gloucestershire, passed 20,000 first-class runs for Northamptonshire, becoming only the sixth player to do so. Left Northamptonshire at end of 1999 season and has joined Derbyshire for 2000

Best batting: 224* Northamptonshire v Glamorgan, Swansea 1986
Best bowling: 5-54 Northamptonshire v Nottinghamshire, Northampton 1993

1999 Season

	M	Inns	NO	Runs	HS	Avge	100s	50s	Ct	St	O	M	Runs	Wkts	Avge	Best	5wI	10wM
Test																		
All First	14	23	2	743	113 *	35.38	1	3	9	-	19	1	51	1	51.00	1-4	-	-
1-day Int																		
NatWest																		
B & H																		
1-day Lge	6	5	0	117	43	23.40	-	-	1	-	3	0	20	0	-		-	-

Career Performances

	M	Inns	NO	Runs	HS	Avge	100s	50s	Ct	St	Balls	Runs	Wkts	Avge	Best	5wI	10wM
Test	4	8	0	119	43	14.87	-	-	-	-							
All First	347	584	84	20601	224 *	41.20	44	104	260	-	8978	4790	112	42.76	5-54	2	-
1-day Int	4	4	2	137	43 *	68.50	-	-	1	-	36	25	0	-	-	-	
NatWest	47	47	12	1575	145	45.00	1	10	18	-	654	407	16	25.43	3-47	-	
B & H	69	66	10	2626	134	46.89	4	19	19	-	390	260	3	86.66	1-1	-	
1-day Lge	229	214	34	6386	125 *	35.47	4	41	60	-	1360	1311	39	33.61	3-23	-	

BAILEY, T. M. B.   Northamptonshire

Name: Tobin Michael Barnaby Bailey
Role: Right-hand bat, wicket-keeper
Born: 28 August 1976, Kettering
Height: 5ft 10in **Weight:** 12st 6lbs
Nickname: Bill, Mad Dog, Scruff
County debut: 1996
1st-Class catches: 11
1st-Class stumpings: 1
Parents: Terry and Penny
Marital status: Single
Family links with cricket: 'Step-dad watches a lot'
Education: Bedford School; Loughborough University
Qualifications: 3 A-levels

Overseas tours: Bedford to South Africa 1994
Cricketers particularly admired:
Jack Russell, Mike Atherton, Alan Knott
Young players to look out for:
Michael Davies
Other sports played: Hockey and tennis
(both for Beds at youth level)
Other sports followed: Rugby (Bedford
RFC), football (Leicester City FC)
Relaxations: 'Sleeping in the winter,
drinking and spending time with friends'
Extras: Bedfordshire Young Player of the
Year in 1995. Northants County League
Young Player of the Year in 1995.
Holmwoods Schools Cricketer of the Year.
Played for England Schools U19 and was a
reserve for the England U19 tour to
Zimbabwe. Won the BUSA cricket cup with
Loughborough in 1996

Best batting: 31* Northamptonshire v Lancashire, Northampton 1996

1999 Season

	M	Inns	NO	Runs	HS	Avge	100s	50s	Ct	St	O	M	Runs	Wkts	Avge	Best	5wI	10wM
Test																		
All First	5	4	0	33	24	8.25	-	-	5	1								
1-day Int																		
NatWest																		
B & H																		
1-day Lge	3	1	0	10	10	10.00	-	-	2	-								

Career Performances

	M	Inns	NO	Runs	HS	Avge	100s	50s	Ct	St	Balls	Runs	Wkts	Avge	Best	5wI	10wM
Test																	
All First	9	8	1	81	31 *	11.57	-	-	11	1							
1-day Int																	
NatWest																	
B & H	10	8	1	97	52	13.85	-	1	5	7							
1-day Lge	6	1	0	10	10	10.00	-	-	6	1							

BALL, M. C. J.   Gloucestershire

Name: Martyn Charles John Ball
Role: Right-hand bat, off-spin bowler,
slip fielder
Born: 26 April 1970, Bristol
Height: 5ft 9in **Weight:** 12st 8lbs
Nickname: Benny
County debut: 1988
1st-Class 50s: 8
1st-Class 5 w. in innings: 8
1st-Class 10 w. in match: 1
1st-Class catches: 155
One-Day 5 w. in innings: 1
Place in batting averages: 179th av. 22.20
(1998 157th av. 23.68)
Place in bowling averages: 146th av. 55.61
(1998 119th av. 34.50)
Strike rate: 122.76 (career 80.57)
Parents: Kenneth Charles and Pamela Wendy

Wife and date of marriage: Mona, 28 September 1991
Children: Kristina, 9 May 1990; Alexandra, 2 August 1993; Harrison, 5 June 1997
Education: Stanshawes Court; King Edmund Secondary School, Yate; Bath College
of Further Education
Qualifications: 6 O-levels, 2 A-levels, advanced cricket coach
Career outside cricket: Working in Gloucestershire CCC marketing department
Off-season: As above, plus 'trying to improve my golf'
Overseas tours: Gloucestershire to Namibia 1991, to Kenya 1992, to Sri Lanka 1993,
to Zimbabwe 1996, 1997, to South Africa 1999; MCC to New Zealand 1998-99
Overseas teams played for: North Melbourne, Australia 1988-89; Old Hararians,
Zimbabwe 1990-91
Cricketers most admired: Ian Botham, Vic Marks, David Graveney, Courtney Walsh
Young players to look out for: 'Kim Barnett, Jack Russell', Ben Gannon
Other sports played: Football (AFC Horton)
Other sports followed: 'Follow all sports', football ('religious Man City fan')
Injuries: 'Sporadic rest until NatWest final, having sustained broken finger in B&H Super
Cup final'
Relaxations: Golf, music, 'and reintroducing myself to my wife and children after six
months of the summer not being around'
Extras: Represented county schools at football, rugby and cricket. Played for Young
England against Young New Zealand in 1989. Produced best bowling figures in a
match for the Britannic County Championship 1993 season – 14-169 against Somerset
Opinions on cricket: 'Commentators who used to play the game should stop slagging

England off and get behind them. We do play too much cricket! It is not a coincidence that Glos won both NatWest and B&H but came bottom of the Championship whilst Surrey easily won the Championship yet were poor in the one-day competitions – we cannot perform at optimum every day for so many matches.'

Best batting: 71 Gloucestershire v Nottinghamshire, Bristol 1993
Best bowling: 8-46 Gloucestershire v Somerset, Taunton 1993

1999 Season

	M	Inns	NO	Runs	HS	Avge	100s	50s	Ct	St	O	M	Runs	Wkts	Avge	Best	5wI	10wM
Test																		
All First	12	19	4	333	70 *	22.20	-	1	11	-	266	69	723	13	55.61	3-38	-	-
1-day Int																		
NatWest	5	3	1	12	5 *	6.00	-	-	5	-	23.1	1	97	2	48.50	1-15	-	
B & H	3	2	0	4	2	2.00	-	-	1	-	29	2	117	3	39.00	3-39	-	
1-day Lge	13	10	3	71	23 *	10.14	-	-	7	-	84.2	3	365	17	21.47	5-42	1	

Career Performances

	M	Inns	NO	Runs	HS	Avge	100s	50s	Ct	St	Balls	Runs	Wkts	Avge	Best	5wI	10wM
Test																	
All First	133	207	37	3156	71	18.56	-	8	155	-	19498	9233	242	38.15	8-46	8	1
1-day Int																	
NatWest	17	10	3	96	31	13.71	-	-	11	-	805	533	13	41.00	3-42	-	
B & H	29	18	1	153	28	9.00	-	-	12	-	1518	1016	26	39.07	4-23	-	
1-day Lge	111	80	29	630	36 *	12.35	-	-	36	-	3772	3135	86	36.45	5-42	1	

7. How many counties took part in the 1890 County Championship, the first since the competition was officially constituted?

BANES, M. J.　　　　　　　　　　　　Kent

Name: Matthew John Banes
Role: Right-hand bat (top three), right-arm medium/off-spin bowler
Born: 10 December 1979, Pembury
Height: 5ft 9in **Weight:** 12st
Nickname: Banesy, Bano
County debut: 1999
1st-Class 50s: 1
1st-Class catches: 1
Parents: Christopher and Jane Ann
Marital status: Single
Education: Holmewood House Prep School; Tonbridge School
Qualifications: 10 GCSEs, 4 A-levels
Off-season: Durham University ('1st year')
Overseas tours: Tonbridge School to Australia 1996-97
Cricketers most admired: Mike Atherton, Viv Richards
Other sports played: Hockey (Tunbridge Wells 1st XI), rugby, golf
Other sports followed: Football
Relaxations: Good films, good books
Extras: Set record for most centuries (11 in career) for Tonbridge School 1st XI. Set record for career run aggregate (approx 3100) for Tonbridge School 1st XI. Made first-class debut v New Zealand at Canterbury 1999, scoring 53. Played in Old Tonbridgians side that won *The Cricketer* Cup 1999
Opinions on cricket: 'More time needs to be devoted to training and technical enhancement (i.e., less matches) so as to be able to compete consistently with the better international teams due to improved county standard.'
Best batting: 53 Kent v New Zealand, Canterbury 1999

1999 Season

	M	Inns	NO	Runs	HS	Avge	100s	50s	Ct	St	O	M	Runs	Wkts	Avge	Best	5wI	10wM
Test																		
All First	2	4	0	60	53	15.00	-	1	1	-								
1-day Int																		
NatWest																		
B & H																		
1-day Lge																		

Career Performances

	M	Inns	NO	Runs	HS	Avge	100s	50s	Ct	St	Balls	Runs	Wkts	Avge	Best	5wI	10wM
Test																	
All First	2	4	0	60	53	15.00	-	1	1	-							
1-day Int																	
NatWest																	
B & H																	
1-day Lge																	

BARNETT, K. J.   Gloucestershire

Name: Kim John Barnett
Role: Right-hand bat, leg-break bowler
Born: 17 July 1960, Stoke-on-Trent
Height: 6ft **Weight:** 13st 7lbs
Nickname: The Vicar of Dibley (Dobley)
County debut: 1979 (Derbyshire),
1999 (Gloucestershire)
County cap: 1982 (Derbyshire),
1999 (Gloucestershire)
Benefit: 1993 (Derbyshire, £37,056)
Test debut: 1988
Tests: 4
One-Day Internationals: 1
1000 runs in a season: 15
1st-Class 50s: 142
1st-Class 100s: 51
1st-Class 200s: 4
1st-Class 5 w. in innings: 3
1st-Class catches: 265
One-Day 100s: 12
One-Day 5 w. in innings: 2
Place in batting averages: 113th av. 29.08 (1998 18th av. 47.26)
Strike rate: 121.50 (career 75.20)
Parents: Derek and Doreen
Wife: Janet
Children: Michael Nicholas, 24 April 1990; Christina, 11 June 1996
Family links with cricket: 'Father local sportsman, mainly football'
Education: Ipstones C of E; Leek High School, Staffs
Qualifications: 7 O-levels
Career outside cricket: Bank clerk
Off-season: Training

Overseas tours: English Schools to India 1977-78; England YC to Australia 1978-79; England B to Sri Lanka 1985-86 (vice-captain); unofficial English XI to South Africa 1989-90
Overseas teams played for: Boland 1980-81, 1982-83
Cricketers particularly admired: Eddie Barlow, Gordon Greenidge
Young players to look out for: Kevin Dean
Other sports followed: Football (Stoke City FC), golf, horse racing
Relaxations: Golf and horse racing
Extras: Played for Northamptonshire 2nd XI when aged 15, Staffordshire and Warwickshire 2nd XI. Became youngest captain of a first-class county when appointed in 1983. One of *Wisden*'s Five Cricketers of the Year 1989. Banned from Test cricket after joining tour to South Africa, suspension remitted in 1992. Relinquished Derbyshire captaincy at the end of the 1995 season. Leading century-maker and run-scorer in all competitions in the history of Derbyshire cricket. Left Derbyshire in 1998-99 off-season and joined Gloucestershire for 1999. Awarded Glos cap 1999
Opinions on cricket: 'We will not produce enough bowlers for the Test arena until we produce pitches that encourage the fast bowlers and leg spinners etc., not just the batsmen.'
Best batting: 239* Derbyshire v Leicestershire, Leicester 1988
Best bowling: 6-28 Derbyshire v Glamorgan, Chesterfield 1991

1999 Season

	M	Inns	NO	Runs	HS	Avge	100s	50s	Ct	St	O	M	Runs	Wkts	Avge	Best	5wI	10wM
Test																		
All First	15	26	1	727	125	29.08	2		4	15	-	40.3	6	134	2	67.00	2-52	-	-
1-day Int																		
NatWest	5	5	0	262	98	52.40	-	2	-	-	3	0	12	0	-		-	-
B & H	3	3	0	93	65	31.00	-	1	-	-								
1-day Lge	15	15	0	337	57	22.46	-	1	7	-	27	0	140	6	23.33	4-29	-	

Career Performances

	M	Inns	NO	Runs	HS	Avge	100s	50s	Ct	St	Balls	Runs	Wkts	Avge	Best	5wI	10wM
Test	4	7	0	207	80	29.57	-	2	1	-	36	32	0	-	-	-	-
All First	446	728	69	26283	239 *	39.88	55	142	265	-	13989	6999	186	37.62	6-28	3	-
1-day Int	1	1	0	84	84	84.00	-	1	-	-							
NatWest	49	47	3	1688	113 *	38.36	2	11	17	-	736	496	24	20.66	6-24	2	
B & H	88	79	5	2842	115	38.40	4	20	33	-	540	356	13	27.38	3-52	-	
1-day Lge	292	280	43	8131	131 *	34.30	6	44	98	-	1729	1525	55	27.72	4-25	-	

BARRETT, K. A. O. Surrey

Name: Kevin Andrew Owen Barrett
Role: Left-hand bat, right-arm medium bowler
Born: 16 November 1975, Swansea
Height: 6ft **Weight:** 10st 10lbs
Nickname: Snickers, Wop
County debut: No first-team appearance
Parents: Derek and Sheila
Marital status: Single
Family links with cricket: Father played club cricket for various sides, including Pontarddulais, Hambledon and Yorkshire Nomads

Education: Stoke Bishop C of E Primary School; Edgarley Hall (Millfield junior school); Millfield School; Durham University
Qualifications: 9 GCSEs, 5 A-levels, BA (Hons) Economics
Career outside cricket: International banking/accountancy
Off-season: 'Two months working for Singer & Friedlander Investment Management (London); two and a half months playing grade in Sydney'
Overseas tours: West of England Schools U15 to Trinidad and Tobago 1990-91; Millfield School to Sri Lanka 1993-94
Overseas teams played for: Randwick, Sydney 1997-98
Cricketers particularly admired: Graham Gooch, Mark Waugh
Young players to look out for: Dean Cosker, Chris Read
Other sports played: Football ('local amateur football in Devon')
Other sports followed: Football (West Ham), Canadian ice hockey (Edmonton Oilers)
Injuries: Out for a total of about four weeks with a broken finger and an inflamed disc in the lower back
Relaxations: Cycling, running; watching West Ham; watching gangster/Mob films; philately
Extras: Represented England U14, Wales U19 and Prime Minister's XI. Played for Devon 1997 and 1998, including one NatWest match v Yorkshire 1997. Was in Devon's MCC Trophy winning side at Lord's 1998. Qualified FA referee
Opinions on cricket: 'More emphasis placed on training to improve playing performance – too many fixtures during the domestic season.'

1999 Season (did not make any first-class or one-day appearances)

Career Performances

	M	Inns	NO	Runs	HS	Avge	100s	50s	Ct	St	Balls	Runs	Wkts	Avge	Best	5wI	10wM
Test																	
All First																	
1-day Int																	
NatWest	1	1	0	3	3	3.00	-	-	-	-							
B & H																	
1-day Lge																	

BASE, S. J. Derbyshire

Name: Simon John Base
Role: Right-hand bat, right-arm fast-medium bowler
Born: 2 January 1960, Maidstone
Height: 6ft 3in **Weight:** 14st 7lbs
Nickname: Basey, Moose Man
County debut: 1986 (Glamorgan), 1988 (Derbyshire)
County cap: 1990 (Derbyshire)
50 wickets in a season: 1
1st-Class 50s: 2
1st-Class 5 w. in innings: 16
1st-Class 10 w. in match: 1
1st-Class catches: 60
Strike rate: (career 54.57)
Parents: Christine and Peter (deceased)
Wife and date of marriage: Louise Anne, 23 September 1989
Children: Christopher Peter Elliot, 15 December 1991
Family links with cricket: Grandfather played
Education: Fish Hoek Primary School; Fish Hoek High School, Cape Town
Qualifications: High School Matriculation, refrigeration and air conditioning technician
Overseas tours: England XI to Holland 1989
Overseas teams played for: Western Province B 1982-83; Boland 1986-89; Border 1989-94 (all South Africa)
Cricketers particularly admired: Graham Gooch, Graeme Pollock, Mike Procter, Richard Hadlee, Malcolm Marshall
Other sports followed: Most other sports

Relaxations: Spending time with family, swimming, windsurfing
Extras: Re-registered by Derbyshire in 1999 because of injuries to current players
Best batting: 58 Derbyshire v Yorkshire, Chesterfield 1990
Best bowling: 7-60 Derbyshire v Yorkshire, Chesterfield 1990

1999 Season

	M	Inns	NO	Runs	HS	Avge	100s	50s	Ct	St	O	M	Runs	Wkts	Avge	Best	5wl	10wM
Test																		
All First	1	2	1	25	17	25.00	-	-	-	-	10	3	34	0	-	-	-	-
1-day Int																		
NatWest																		
B & H																		
1-day Lge																		

Career Performances

	M	Inns	NO	Runs	HS	Avge	100s	50s	Ct	St	Balls	Runs	Wkts	Avge	Best	5wl	10wM
Test																	
All First	134	172	36	1551	58	11.40	-	2	60	-	21175	11397	388	29.37	7-60	16	1
1-day Int																	
NatWest	3	2	0	6	4	3.00	-	-	1	-	156	124	3	41.33	2-49	-	
B & H	15	9	3	53	15 *	8.83	-	-	-	-	870	629	15	41.93	3-33	-	
1-day Lge	92	36	9	184	31	6.81	-	-	26	-	3903	2871	115	24.96	4-14	-	

8. Prior to Durham's admission, which county had most recently
joined the County Championship and which was their first season?

BATES, J. J. Sussex

Name: Justin Jonathan Bates
Role: Right-hand bat, off-spin bowler
Born: 9 April 1976, Farnborough, Hants
Height: 6ft **Weight:** 11st 7lbs
County debut: 1996 (one-day), 1997 (first-class)
1st-Class 50s: 1
1st-Class 5 w. in innings: 4
1st-Class catches: 12
Place in batting averages: 211th av. 19.00 (1998 284th av. 7.71)
Place in bowling averages: 105th av. 32.36 (1998 12th av. 19.50)
Strike rate: 76.90 (career 64.25)
Parents: Barry and Sandra
Marital status: Single
Family links with cricket: Father played club cricket and brother Christian played for Sussex Young Cricketers. Cousin Alan Igglesden played for Kent and England
Education: St Mark's Primary School; Warden Park Secondary School; Hurstpierpoint College
Qualifications: 8 GCSEs, 3 A-levels, senior coaching award
Career outside cricket: Freelance graphic designer
Overseas tours: Sussex YC to India 1990-91, to Barbados 1992-93, to Sri Lanka 1994-95
Cricketers particularly admired: Carl Hooper, Saqlain Mushtaq
Other sports followed: Golf and rugby
Relaxations: Reading, computing and music
Opinions on cricket: 'Second XI championship cricket should be played over four days and not three.'
Best batting: 57 Sussex v Hampshire, Southampton 1999
Best bowling: 5-67 Sussex v Northamptonshire, Northampton 1998

1999 Season

	M	Inns	NO	Runs	HS	Avge	100s	50s	Ct	St	O	M	Runs	Wkts	Avge	Best	5wl	10wM
Test																		
All First	6	10	0	190	57	19.00	-	1	2	-	141	46	356	11	32.36	5-154	1	-
1-day Int																		
NatWest	1	1	0	2	2	2.00	-	-	1	-	6.2	1	36	0	-		-	-
B & H																		
1-day Lge	1	1	0	2	2	2.00	-	-	1	-	8	0	24	0	-		-	-

Career Performances

	M	Inns	NO	Runs	HS	Avge	100s	50s	Ct	St	Balls	Runs	Wkts	Avge	Best	5wI	10wM
Test																	
All First	17	26	2	357	57	14.87	-	1	12	-	2827	1154	44	26.22	5-67	4	-
1-day Int																	
NatWest	1	1	0	2	2	2.00	-	-	1	-	38	36	0	-	-	-	-
B & H																	
1-day Lge	6	6	2	20	8	5.00	-	-	4	-	162	165	3	55.00	2-42	-	

BATES, R. T.   Nottinghamshire

Name: Richard Terry Bates
Role: Right-hand bat, off-spin bowler, slip fielder
Born: 17 June 1972, Stamford, Lincs
Height: 6ft 1in **Weight:** 13st
Nickname: Blaster, Blast, Batesy, Roland
County debut: 1993
1st-Class 5 w. in innings: 1
1st-Class catches: 18
Strike rate: (career 97.58)
Parents: Terry and Sue
Wife and date of marriage: Suzanne, 16 March 1996
Children: Jack
Family links with cricket: Father works for ECB; played club cricket for Bourne CC
Education: Abbey Road Primary School, Bourne; Bourne Grammar School; Stamford College for Further Education
Qualifications: 8 GCSEs, BTEC in Business and Finance, NCA Advanced Coach
Overseas tours: Lincolnshire Colts (U19) to Australia 1989-90; Notts CCC to Johannesburg April 1997 and 1998
Overseas teams played for: Redwood CC, Blenheim, New Zealand 1991-92
Cricketers particularly admired: Ian Botham, Derek Randall, Viv Richards
Young players to look out for: Matt Dowman
Other sports played: Football, squash
Other sports followed: 'Watch all sports on TV. Travel to Anfield to watch Liverpool'
Relaxations: 'Eating out, good films, travelling to Anfield, having a beer with mates, walking my dogs and spending as much time as I can with my wife when not cricketing'
Extras: Released by Notts at end of 1999 season

Opinions on cricket: '1. Not enough days off to relax. 2. Too much cricket dampens enthusiasm. 3. First it was the dinosaur; spin bowlers will be next!'
Best batting: 34 Nottinghamshire v Worcestershire, Worcester 1996
Best bowling: 5-88 Nottinghamshire v Durham, Chester-le-Street 1995

1999 Season

	M	Inns	NO	Runs	HS	Avge	100s	50s	Ct	St	O	M	Runs	Wkts	Avge	Best	5wI	10wM
Test																		
All First	1	1	0	0	0	0.00	-	-	-	-	13	0	83	0	-	-	-	-
1-day Int																		
NatWest																		
B & H																		
1-day Lge	1	0	0	0	0	-	-	-	-	-	5	0	29	0	-	-	-	

Career Performances

	M	Inns	NO	Runs	HS	Avge	100s	50s	Ct	St	Balls	Runs	Wkts	Avge	Best	5wI	10wM
Test																	
All First	33	48	12	450	34	12.50	-	-	18	-	4879	2520	50	50.40	5-88	1	-
1-day Int																	
NatWest	6	5	2	17	11	5.66	-	-	4	-	329	241	4	60.25	2-32	-	
B & H	9	6	1	61	27	12.20	-	-	4	-	491	331	10	33.10	3-21	-	
1-day Lge	55	27	7	161	28 *	8.05	-	-	21	-	1834	1575	49	32.14	3-30	-	

BATSON, N. E.   Worcestershire

Name: Nathan Evan Batson
Role: Right-hand (No. 3) bat, off-spin bowler
Born: 24 July 1978, Stanford-le-Hope
Height: 6ft 2in **Weight:** 12st 6lbs
Nickname: Bats, Curly, Penfold, Bish
County debut: 1998
1st-Class 50s: 1
1st-Class catches: 5
Place in batting averages: 201st av. 20.11
Parents: Ann and Jon
Marital status: Single
Family links with cricket: 'Dad plays for, and is chairman of, Billericay CC in Essex. Mother runs Billericay CC!'
Education: Sunnymede Junior School; Billericay Senior School; Mayflower County High

Qualifications: 9 GCSEs, 1 A-level, coaching certificates to senior level
Career outside cricket: Coaching
Overseas teams played for: Old Wilsonians, Harare, and Zimbabwe Academy 1999
Cricketers particularly admired: Robin Smith, Desmond Haynes
Young players to look out for: Vikram Solanki
Other sports played: Golf and most racquet sports
Other sports followed: Football (Spurs)
Relaxations: Most sports and all kinds of music
Extras: Scored 194 on debut for Worcestershire 2nd XI. Released by Worcs at end of 1999 season
Opinions on cricket: '2nd XI cricket should be played on the same grounds with same time span and conditions as first-class cricket to prepare young players better when they step up.'
Best batting: 72 Worcestershire v Sri Lanka A, Worcester 1999

1999 Season

	M	Inns	NO	Runs	HS	Avge	100s	50s	Ct	St	O	M	Runs	Wkts	Avge	Best	5wI	10wM
Test																		
All First	5	10	1	181	72	20.11	-	1	5	-								
1-day Int																		
NatWest																		
B & H																		
1-day Lge																		

Career Performances

	M	Inns	NO	Runs	HS	Avge	100s	50s	Ct	St	Balls	Runs	Wkts	Avge	Best	5wI	10wM
Test																	
All First	8	16	1	231	72	15.40	-	1	5	-							
1-day Int																	
NatWest																	
B & H																	
1-day Lge																	

BATT, C. J.   Middlesex

Name: Christopher James Batt
Role: Left-hand bat, left-arm fast bowler
Born: 22 September 1976, Maidenhead
Height: 6ft 4in **Weight:** 13st
Nickname: Batman, Batty, Nora, Closet
County debut: 1998
1st-Class 5 w. in innings: 2
1st-Class catches: 2
Strike rate: (career 43.97)
Parents: Clive and Julia
Marital status: Single
Education: Wessex County Primary School,
Cox Green, Maidenhead; Cox Green
Comprehensive School, Maidenhead
Qualifications: 9 GCSEs
Career outside cricket: Gym instructor;
personal fitness instructor/trainer
Overseas tours: Berkshire U19 to Australia
1994; Berkshire U23 to Barbados 1996
Overseas teams played for: Motueka, New Zealand 1998-99
Cricketers particularly admired: Richard Hadlee, Dermot Reeve, Graham Thorpe
Young players to look out for: 'Chris Batt!', Jared Payne, Mason Pillon
Other sports played: Golf (U15 Berkshire Schools champion), football
(Berkshire U16)
Other sports followed: Football (Everton), golf, rugby
Relaxations: Playing golf, 'socialising with friends and women!'
Extras: Local cricket team is Boyne Hill. Colt of the Year 1992 and 1994. Also
member of Julian Cup winning team (senior) in 1993, 1994, 1995 and 1996
Opinions on cricket: 'Too many 2nd XI players not having enough aspirations to
further their careers. Compared to overseas teams we are not as strong mentally and
competitively.'
Best batting: 43 Middlesex v Warwickshire, Lord's 1998
Best bowling: 6-101 Middlesex v Nottinghamshire, Trent Bridge 1998

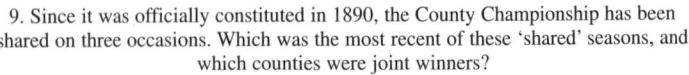

9. Since it was officially constituted in 1890, the County Championship has been
shared on three occasions. Which was the most recent of these 'shared' seasons, and
which counties were joint winners?

1999 Season

	M	Inns	NO	Runs	HS	Avge	100s	50s	Ct	St	O	M	Runs	Wkts	Avge	Best	5wI	10wM
Test																		
All First																		
1-day Int																		
NatWest																		
B & H																		
1-day Lge	2	1	1	8	8 *	-	-	-	-	-	17	0	64	3	21.33	2-33	-	

Career Performances

	M	Inns	NO	Runs	HS	Avge	100s	50s	Ct	St	Balls	Runs	Wkts	Avge	Best	5wI	10wM
Test																	
All First	10	14	2	150	43	12.50	-	-	2	-	1451	946	33	28.66	6-101	2	-
1-day Int																	
NatWest	1	1	0	0	0	0.00	-	-	-	-	48	37	1	37.00	1-37	-	
B & H																	
1-day Lge	4	1	1	8	8 *	-	-	-	-	-	156	111	6	18.50	3-26	-	

BATTY, G. J. Surrey

Name: Gareth Jon Batty
Role: Right-hand bat, off-spin bowler
Born: 13 October 1977, Yorkshire
Height: 5ft 11in **Weight:** 12st
Nickname: Batts, Ian Dowie, Yorkshire Git
County debut: 1997 (Yorkshire),
1998 (one-day, Surrey),
1999 (first-class, Surrey)
Strike rate: 63.00 (career 48.00)
Parents: David and Rosemary
Marital status: Single
Family links with cricket: 'Dad is Yorkshire
coach; brother played for Yorkshire and
Somerset'
Education: Cullingworth First; Parkside
Middle; Bingley Grammar
Qualifications: 9 GCSEs, BTEC in Art/
Design
Career outside cricket: 'Batty Independent Traders'
Overseas tours: England U15 to South Africa 1993; England U19 to Zimbabwe
1995-96, to Pakistan 1996-97

Cricketers particularly admired: 'Everyone in my team'
Young players to look out for: Ben Grange, Asa Firth, Sam Cummins
Other sports played: Rugby union (Bradford and Bingley), golf
Other sports followed: Rugby (West Hartlepool RFC)
Relaxations: 'Meditation, to be at one with myself'
Extras: National U15 bowling award. Made first-class debut for Yorkshire v Lancashire 1997 in non-Championship match. Joined Surrey for 1998. Played for Weybridge side that won Surrey Championship 1999; scored 201* for Weybridge v Spencer 1999
Opinions on cricket: 'Not old enough to comment on such a controversial question.'
Best batting: 25* Surrey v Sri Lanka A, The Oval 1999
Best bowling: 2-45 Surrey v Sri Lanka A, The Oval 1999

1999 Season

	M	Inns	NO	Runs	HS	Avge	100s	50s	Ct	St	O	M	Runs	Wkts	Avge	Best	5wl	10wM
Test																		
All First	1	2	1	36	25 *	36.00	-	-	-	-	21	2	58	2	29.00	2-45	-	-
1-day Int																		
NatWest																			
B & H																			
1-day Lge	5	5	1	34	23	8.50	-	-	1	-	32	1	162	2	81.00	1-33	-	

Career Performances

	M	Inns	NO	Runs	HS	Avge	100s	50s	Ct	St	Balls	Runs	Wkts	Avge	Best	5wl	10wM
Test																	
All First	2	4	1	54	25 *	18.00	-	-	-	-	192	128	4	32.00	2-45	-	-
1-day Int																	
NatWest																		
B & H																		
1-day Lge	8	8	2	87	37	14.50	-	-	2	-	324	271	4	67.75	1-32	-	

BATTY, J. N.   Surrey

Name: Jonathan Neil Batty
Role: Right-hand bat, wicket-keeper
Born: 18 April 1974, Chesterfield
Height: 5ft 10in **Weight:** 11st 7lbs
Nickname: Batts, Lizard, Nora, Mutant
County debut: 1997
1st-Class 50s: 5
1st-Class catches: 106

1st-Class stumpings: 16
Place in batting averages: 148th av. 25.26
(1998 183rd av. 20.64)
Parents: Roger and Gill
Marital status: Single
Family links with cricket: Father played for
Nottinghamshire Schools and played a good
standard of club cricket
Education: Repton School; Durham
University (St Chad's); Keble College,
Oxford
Qualifications: 10 GCSEs, 4 A-levels, BSc
(Hons) in Natural Sciences, Diploma in
Social Studies
Off-season: Playing club cricket in Perth,
Australia
Overseas tours: Repton School to Holland
1990; MCC to Bangladesh 1996
Overseas teams played for: Mount Cawley CC, Perth 1997-2000
Cricketers particularly admired: David Gower, Bruce French, Alec Stewart
Young players to look out for: David Roberts, Stephen Peters, Alex Tudor
Other sports followed: Football (Nottingham Forest), rugby union (Leicester Tigers)
and squash
Injuries: Fractured eye socket and broken nose when struck in face by bouncer
Relaxations: Going to the cinema, listening to music and reading
Extras: Oxford Blue in 1996. Has also played Minor Counties cricket for Oxfordshire
Opinions on cricket: '2nd XI games should be played on 1st XI wickets.'
Best batting: 64 Surrey v Sri Lanka A, The Oval 1999

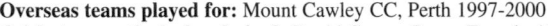

1999 Season

	M	Inns	NO	Runs	HS	Avge	100s	50s	Ct	St	O	M	Runs	Wkts	Avge	Best	5wI	10wM
Test																		
All First	15	20	5	379	64	25.26	-	1	49	7	2	1	9	0	-	-	-	-
1-day Int																		
NatWest																		
B & H																			
1-day Lge	11	9	1	72	19	9.00	-	-	13	1								

Career Performances

	M	Inns	NO	Runs	HS	Avge	100s	50s	Ct	St	Balls	Runs	Wkts	Avge	Best	5wl	10wM
Test																	
All First	46	58	12	1126	64	24.47	-	5	106	16	42	40	0	-	-	-	-
1-day Int																	
NatWest	1	1	0	1	1	1.00	-	-	-	-							
B & H	10	8	3	83	26 *	16.60	-	-	9	-							
1-day Lge	27	23	7	254	40	15.87	-	-	23	6							

BELL, I. R. Warwickshire

Name: Ian Ronald Bell
Role: Right-hand bat, occasional right-arm medium bowler
Born: 11 April 1982, Coventry
Height: 5ft 10in **Weight:** 11st 8lbs
County debut: 1999
1st-Class catches: 2
Parents: Terry and Barbara
Marital status: Single
Family links with cricket: Brother has played England U14
Education: Princethorpe College, Rugby
Off-season: England U19 tour to Malaysia and Sri Lanka
Overseas tours: England U19 to New Zealand 1998-99, to Malaysia and (Youth World Cup) Sri Lanka 1999-2000; Warwickshire to South Africa 1999-2000
Cricketers particularly admired: Michael Atherton, Steve Waugh
Other sports played: Football (was at Coventry City School of Excellence), rugby
Other sports followed: Football (Aston Villa)
Relaxations: Golf
Extras: Played for England U14, U15, U16, U17 and U19. Scored first international century (115) v New Zealand U19 in Alexandra 1998-99. Player of the Series for England U19 v New Zealand U19 'Test' series 1998-99. Scored 190 v Northants 2nd XI and 140 v Glos 2nd XI 1999. Represented England U19 in one-day and 'Test' series v Australia U19 1999

1999 Season

	M	Inns	NO	Runs	HS	Avge	100s	50s	Ct	St	O	M	Runs	Wkts	Avge	Best	5wI	10wM
Test																		
All First	1	1	0	0	0	0.00	-	-	2	-								
1-day Int																		
NatWest	1	1	0	10	10	10.00	-	-	-	-	0.3	0	2	0	-		-	-
B & H																		
1-day Lge																		

Career Performances

	M	Inns	NO	Runs	HS	Avge	100s	50s	Ct	St	Balls	Runs	Wkts	Avge	Best	5wI	10wM
Test																	
All First	1	1	0	0	0	0.00	-	-	2	-							
1-day Int																	
NatWest	1	1	0	10	10	10.00	-	-	-	-	3	2	0	-		-	-
B & H																	
1-day Lge																	

BELL, M. A. V. Surrey

Name: Michael Anthony Vincent Bell
Role: Right-hand bat, left-arm fast-medium bowler
Born: 19 December 1967, Birmingham
Height: 6ft 2in **Weight:** 13st 2lbs
Nickname: Belly, Nelly, Breezer
County debut: 1992 (Warwickshire), 1998 (one-day, Surrey)
1st-Class 5 w. in innings: 3
1st-Class catches: 8
One-Day 5 w. in innings: 2
Strike rate: (career 61.46)
Parents: Vincent and Adelheid
Marital status: Single
Family links with cricket: Father played cricket mainly for Mitchells & Butler in the Birmingham League. An uncle played a few games for Jamaica
Education: Bishop Milner Comprehensive; Dudley Technical College
Qualifications: 5 O-levels, City and Guilds in Recreation and Leisure Parts 1 & 2
Career outside cricket: Casino croupier, worked with the PE staff at Earls High School

and also worked in the corporate hospitality department at EMP plc for two years

Overseas tours: BWIA to Barbados and Trinidad & Tobago 1989; John Morris's Madcap CC to Australia 1992

Overseas teams played for: Swanbourne, Perth 1986-87; Norwood, Melbourne 1989-90; Phoenix, Perth 1992-93; Sunshine Heights 1993-94

Cricketers particularly admired: Dennis Lillee, Viv Richards, Michael Holding, Imran Khan, Wasim Akram, Shane Warne

Other sports followed: Any sport played by the best in that particular field

Relaxations: 'Golf (although I'm no Calvin Peete), good movies and going to a hot country before winter sets in'

Extras: Played in World Cup warm-up game only in 1999. Released by Surrey at end of 1999 season

Opinions on cricket: 'When are the batsmen going to be prevented from taking the initiative over the bowlers and get limited to, for instance, one extra-cover drive – on the up – per over ... and when will a cow jump over the moon!'

Best batting: 30 Warwickshire v Nottinghamshire, Trent Bridge 1997

Best bowling: 7-48 Warwickshire v Gloucestershire, Edgbaston 1993

1999 Season (did not make any first-class or one-day competition appearances)

Career Performances

	M	Inns	NO	Runs	HS	Avge	100s	50s	Ct	St	Balls	Runs	Wkts	Avge	Best	5wl	10wM
Test																	
All First	20	23	10	109	30	8.38	-	-	8	-	3012	1565	49	31.93	7-48	3	-
1-day Int																	
NatWest	1	0	0	0	0	-	-	-	-	-	53	41	2	20.50	2-41	-	
B & H	3	0	0	0	0	-	-	-	1	-	90	59	2	29.50	2-34	-	
1-day Lge	19	10	4	70	16	11.66	-	-	2	-	804	661	28	23.60	5-19	2	

BENJAMIN, J. E.   Surrey

Name: Joseph Emmanuel Benjamin

Role: Right-hand bat, right-arm fast-medium bowler

Born: 2 February 1961, Christchurch, St Kitts, West Indies

Height: 6ft 2in **Weight:** 12st 7lbs

Nickname: Boggy, Moon Man

County debut: 1988 (Warwickshire), 1992 (Surrey)

County cap: 1993 (Surrey)

Test debut: 1994

Tests: 1

One-Day Internationals: 2

50 wickets in a season: 3
1st-Class 5 w. in innings: 17
1st-Class 10 w. in match: 1
1st-Class catches: 25
Place in batting averages: (1998 279th av. 9.50)
Place in bowling averages: (1998 74th av. 28.45)
Strike rate: 102.00 (career 58.54)
Parents: Henry and Judith
Marital status: Single
Education: Cayon High School, St Kitts; Mount Pleasant, Highgate, Birmingham
Qualifications: 4 O-levels
Career outside cricket: Landscape gardener, store manager
Overseas tours: England to Australia 1994-95

Overseas teams played for: Prahran, Melbourne 1992-93
Cricketers particularly admired: Imran Khan, Viv Richards, Malcolm Marshall
Other sports followed: Rugby, squash, football
Relaxations: Music, going to the cinema, reading
Extras: Played for Staffordshire. Released by Warwickshire at the end of the 1991 season and signed up by Surrey for 1992. Surrey Player of the Year in 1993. Released by Surrey at end of 1999 season
Best batting: 49 Surrey v Essex, The Oval 1995
Best bowling: 6-19 Surrey v Nottinghamshire, The Oval 1993

1999 Season

	M	Inns	NO	Runs	HS	Avge	100s	50s	Ct	St	O	M	Runs	Wkts	Avge	Best	5wl	10wM
Test																		
All First	2	2	0	9	5	4.50	-	-	1	-	17	2	78	1	78.00	1-31	-	-
1-day Int																		
NatWest	2	0	0	0	0	-	-	-	-	-	15.5	2	69	2	34.50	2-48	-	
B & H																		
1-day Lge	5	3	2	19	16 *	19.00	-	-	1	-	32	3	154	7	22.00	2-33	-	

Career Performances

	M	Inns	NO	Runs	HS	Avge	100s	50s	Ct	St	Balls	Runs	Wkts	Avge	Best	5wI	10wM
Test	1	1	0	0	0	0.00	-	-	-	-	168	80	4	20.00	4-42	-	-
All First	126	145	43	1161	49	11.38	-	-	25	-	22658	11588	387	29.94	6-19	17	1
1-day Int	2	1	0	0	0	0.00	-	-	-	-	72	47	1	47.00	1-22	-	
NatWest	23	10	5	69	25	13.80	-	-	3	-	1307	809	24	33.70	4-20	-	
B & H	30	7	5	33	20	16.50	-	-	9	-	1776	1175	34	34.55	4-19	-	
1-day Lge	112	48	23	225	24	9.00	-	-	19	-	4737	3472	114	30.45	4-44	-	

BETTS, M. M. Durham

Name: Melvyn Morris Betts
Role: Right-hand bat, right-arm medium-fast bowler
Born: 26 March 1975, Sacriston
Height: 5ft 11in **Weight:** 12st 9lbs
Nickname: Betsy
County debut: 1993
County cap: 1998
1st-Class 50s: 1
1st-Class 5 w. in innings: 9
1st-Class 10 w. in match: 1
1st-Class catches: 14
Place in batting averages: 291st av. 6.11 (1998 263rd av. 12.27)
Place in bowling averages: 86th av. 29.15 (1998 31st av. 22.10)
Strike rate: 52.55 (career 48.94)
Parents: Melvyn and Shirley
Wife and date of marriage: Angela, 3 October 1998
Children: Chloe Grainger
Family links with cricket: Father and uncle played for local club, Sacriston
Education: Fyndoune Comprehensive
Qualifications: 9 GCSEs, plus qualifications in engineering and sports and recreational studies
Off-season: 'Relaxing with the new baby'
Overseas tours: England U19 to Sri Lanka 1993-94; England A to Zimbabwe and South Africa 1998-99; Durham CCC to South Africa 1995
Cricketers particularly admired: Graham Gooch, David Boon, Jon Lewis
Young players to look out for: Nicky Peng, Chris Hewitson
Other sports followed: Football (Newcastle United FC)
Injuries: Groin injury

Relaxations: 'Local pub with friends outside of cricket'
Extras: Played for England U19 in home series against India in 1994
Opinions on cricket: 'More time off to keep fitness high and to work on cricketing skills. First-class pitches need to improve.'
Best batting: 57* Durham v Sussex, Hove 1996
Best bowling: 9-64 Durham v Northamptonshire, Northampton 1997

1999 Season

	M	Inns	NO	Runs	HS	Avge	100s	50s	Ct	St	O	M	Runs	Wkts	Avge	Best	5wI	10wM
Test																		
All First	7	11	2	55	19*	6.11	-	-	4	-	175.1	41	583	20	29.15	4-34	-	-
1-day Int																		
NatWest																		
B & H																		
1-day Lge	12	9	3	73	15	12.16	-	-	2	-	90.3	2	482	15	32.13	4-39	-	

Career Performances

	M	Inns	NO	Runs	HS	Avge	100s	50s	Ct	St	Balls	Runs	Wkts	Avge	Best	5wI	10wM
Test																	
All First	57	87	19	765	57*	11.25	-	1	14	-	8859	5416	181	29.92	9-64	9	1
1-day Int																	
NatWest	6	5	1	38	14	9.50	-	-	1	-	402	328	9	36.44	3-33	-	
B & H	9	6	3	47	20*	15.66	-	-	1	-	421	282	11	25.63	2-26	-	
1-day Lge	43	31	15	173	21	10.81	-	-	7	-	1831	1557	50	31.14	4-39	-	

10. F. S. Trueman took three Championship hat-tricks.
What was unusual about them?

BEVAN, M. G. Sussex

Name: Michael Gwyl Bevan
Role: Left-hand bat, slow left-arm bowler,
county vice-captain
Born: 8 May 1970, Canberra, Australia
County debut: 1995 (Yorkshire),
1998 (Sussex)
County cap: 1995 (Yorkshire),
1998 (Sussex)
Test debut: 1994-95
Tests: 18
One-Day Internationals: 114
1000 runs in a season: 2
1st-Class 50s: 59
1st-Class 100s: 38
1st-Class 200s: 2
1st-Class 5 w. in innings: 1
1st-Class 10 w. in match: 1
1st-Class catches: 94
One-Day 100s: 5

One-Day 5 w. in innings: 1
Place in batting averages: (1998 11th av. 55.00)
Place in bowling averages: (1998 118th av. 34.36)
Strike rate: (career 71.22)
Wife: Tracy
Education: Australian Cricket Academy
Off-season: Playing for New South Wales and Australia
Overseas tours: Australia to Sharjah 1994, to Pakistan 1994-95, to India and Pakistan
(World Cup) 1995-96, to Sri Lanka 1996-97, to India 1996-97, to South Africa 1996-
97, to England 1997, to New Zealand 1997-98, to India and Sharjah 1997-98,
to Pakistan and Bangladesh 1998-99 (one-day series), to West Indies 1998-99 (one-day
series), to UK, Ireland and Holland (World Cup) 1999, to Sri Lanka 1999 (one-day
series), to Zimbabwe 1999 (one-day series)
Overseas teams played for: South Australia 1989-90, New South Wales 1990 –
Extras: In 1990-91 he became the first player to score a century in five successive
Sheffield Shield matches. Made 82 on his Test debut against Pakistan in Karachi,
1994-95. Played for Rawtenstall in the Lancashire League in 1993 and 1994. Joined
Yorkshire in 1995 and was appointed county vice-captain for the 1996 season. Was
part of Australian tour of England in 1997. Joined Sussex for 1998 and was appointed
vice-captain. Averaged 106.00 in the 1998-99 Australian first-class season. Was in
Australia's 1999 World Cup winning side and did not play county cricket that season.
Has returned to Sussex as overseas player and vice-captain for 2000

Best batting: 203* New South Wales v Western Australia, Sydney 1993-94
Best bowling: 6-82 Australia v West Indies, Adelaide 1996-97
Stop press: Named in Australia squad for one-day series v New Zealand 1999-2000

1999 Season

	M	Inns	NO	Runs	HS	Avge	100s	50s	Ct	St	O	M	Runs	Wkts	Avge	Best	5wI	10wM
Test																		
All First																		
1-day Int	10	8	3	264	65	52.80	-	2	2	-	18	1	81	1	81.00	1-26	-	
NatWest																		
B & H																		
1-day Lge																		

Career Performances

	M	Inns	NO	Runs	HS	Avge	100s	50s	Ct	St	Balls	Runs	Wkts	Avge	Best	5wI	10wM
Test	18	30	3	785	91	29.07	-	6	8	-	1285	703	29	24.24	6-82	1	1
All First	161	269	48	12059	203 *	54.56	40	59	94	-	7264	4371	102	42.85	6-82	1	1
1-day Int	114	101	40	3748	108 *	61.44	3	26	41	-	1634	1339	32	41.84	3-36	-	
NatWest	9	9	2	396	91 *	56.57	-	4	2	-	177	129	4	32.25	2-47	-	
B & H	13	12	5	762	95 *	108.85	-	9	1	-	144	123	1	123.00	1-25	-	
1-day Lge	40	38	9	1435	103 *	49.48	2	10	12	-	631	557	32	17.40	5-29	1	

BICKNELL, D. J. Nottinghamshire

Name: Darren John Bicknell
Role: Left-hand opening bat, slow left-arm bowler
Born: 24 June 1967, Guildford
Height: 6ft 4in **Weight:** 14st
Nickname: Denzil
County debut: 1987 (Surrey)
County cap: 1990 (Surrey)
Benefit: 1999 (Surrey)
1000 runs in a season: 6
1st-Class 50s: 60
1st-Class 100s: 30
1st-Class 200s: 2
1st-Class catches: 78
One-Day 100s: 7
Place in batting averages: 96th av. 31.50
Strike rate: (career 53.56)

Parents: Vic and Valerie

Wife and date of marriage: Rebecca, 26 September 1991

Children: Lauren Elizabeth, 21 October 1993; Sam, 9 November 1995; Emily, 16 December 1997

Family links with cricket: Brother Martin plays

Education: Robert Haining County Secondary; Guildford County College of Technology

Qualifications: 8 O-levels, 2 A-levels, senior coaching award

Career outside cricket: Account manager for Courage Brewery

Off-season: 'Finishing off the benefit year'

Overseas tours: Surrey to Sharjah 1988, 1989, to Dubai 1990, to Perth 1995; England A to Zimbabwe and Kenya 1989-90, to Pakistan 1990-91, to Bermuda and West Indies 1991-92

Overseas teams played for: Coburg, Melbourne 1986-87

Cricketers particularly admired: Mark Taylor, Steve Waugh, Malcolm Marshall, Courtney Walsh

Young players to look out for: Alex Tudor, Ian Ward

Other sports played: Football, golf

Other sports followed: Football (West Ham United)

Relaxations: Golf; 'spending time with my family'

Extras: Shared county record third-wicket stand of 413 with David Ward v Kent at Canterbury in 1990 – both made career bests. Surrey Batsman of the Year four times. Hit the fastest hundred of the year in 1990. Has left Surrey and joined Notts for 2000

Opinions on cricket: 'Too much cricket, and the standard of pitches is as poor as I can remember. Too much unnecessary slagging off by the media. We are human and we are trying!'

Best batting: 235* Surrey v Nottinghamshire, Trent Bridge 1994

Best bowling: 3-7 Surrey v Sussex, Hove 1996

1999 Season

	M	Inns	NO	Runs	HS	Avge	100s	50s	Ct	St	O	M	Runs	Wkts	Avge	Best	5wI	10wM
Test																		
All First	11	17	1	504	115	31.50	2	1	3	-								
1-day Int																		
NatWest																		
B & H																		
1-day Lge	6	6	1	123	62	24.60	-	1	-	-								

Career Performances

	M	Inns	NO	Runs	HS	Avge	100s	50s	Ct	St	Balls	Runs	Wkts	Avge	Best	5wI	10wM
Test																	
All First	211	369	35	13200	235 *	39.52	32	60	78	-	1232	789	23	34.30	3-7	-	-
1-day Int																	
NatWest	20	20	4	778	135 *	48.62	1	5	1	-							
B & H	33	32	3	1241	119	42.79	2	9	12	-							
1-day Lge	103	100	14	3061	125	35.59	4	18	24	-	36	39	2	19.50	1-11	-	

BICKNELL, M. P. Surrey

Name: Martin Paul Bicknell
Role: Right-hand bat, right-arm fast-medium bowler
Born: 14 January 1969, Guildford
Height: 6ft 4in **Weight:** 15st 4lbs
Nickname: Bickers
County debut: 1986
County cap: 1989
Benefit: 1997
Test debut: 1993
Tests: 2
One-Day Internationals: 7
50 wickets in a season: 8
1st-Class 50s: 14
1st-Class 5 w. in innings: 29
1st-Class 10 w. in match: 2
1st-Class catches: 73
One-Day 5 w. in innings: 2

Place in batting averages: 80th av. 33.23 (1998 176th av. 21.65)
Place in bowling averages: 13th av. 18.95 (1998 20th av. 20.61)
Strike rate: 46.11 (career 53.07)
Parents: Vic and Valerie
Wife and date of marriage: Loraine, 29 September 1995
Children: Eleanor, 31 March 1995; Charlotte, 22 July 1996
Family links with cricket: 'Brother plays, but with no luck'
Education: Robert Haining County Secondary
Qualifications: 2 O-levels, NCA coach
Career outside cricket: 'Golf bandit'
Off-season: Golf, holidaying, training, 'as little work as possible!'
Overseas tours: England YC to Sri Lanka 1986-87, to Australia 1987-88; England A to Zimbabwe and Kenya 1989-90, to Bermuda and West Indies 1991-92, to South

Africa 1993-94; England to Australia 1990-91

Cricketers particularly admired: Paul Allott, Graeme Fowler, Michael Henderson, Ian Botham

Young players to look out for: Jason Ratcliffe – 'for his possible elevation to the England team as the all-rounder'

Other sports played: Golf

Other sports followed: All sports – mainly golf and football (Leeds United)

Injuries: Out for two weeks with a calf strain

Relaxations: 'Making and spending money'

Extras: Was youngest player to play for Surrey since David Smith. His figures of 9 for 45 were the best for the county for 30 years. One of four players on stand-by as reserves for England's World Cup squad 1991-92. Surrey Supporters' Player of the Year 1993, 1999. Surrey Players' Player of the Year 1997, 1998, 1999. Took 700th first-class wicket v Gloucestershire at The Oval 1999. Took 7-30 in National League v Glamorgan at The Oval 1999. Scored 432 runs to go with his 71 wickets in Surrey's Championship winning season 1999

Opinions on cricket: '1. Why if county cricket is so poor do so many overseas players want to play it? 2. Why is it that so many of these stars perform poorly if county cricket is not up to their usual standard? 3. Why is it that all of our overseas players complain that there is too much cricket played in this country but nothing ever gets done? 4. Why are all the important decisions to do with our cricket made by people who only have their county bank balances to think about? 5. How many more one-day competitions can we play in one season? Whatever happened to the idea that less cricket would help raise the standard? Come to think of it whatever happened to *Raising the Standard*?

'Could someone please explain to me why the Surrey team of 1999 were so unpopular among various sections of the press for being "brash, arrogant, aggressive, confident and cocky", which apparently is "not the done thing" at county level? However, most of England's opponents over the past five years all have these attributes and are applauded for it.

'The standard of pitches in this country needs some very close scrutiny. Surely we cannot go on with the present system of teams being able to prepare whatever they like, and then blaming poor batting to escape punishment by the pitch inspectors. Either we centrally contract the groundsmen, or the penalties for bad pitches should be more rigidly enforced.

'How much more knocking of the game can there be? Can it really help a young player coming into the England team today to know that if he bowls poorly or plays a bad shot the media are going to crucify him? Congratulations to Channel 4 on their coverage so far. It is so refreshing to hear someone being positive for a change.'

Best batting: 88 Surrey v Hampshire, Southampton 1992

Best bowling: 9-45 Surrey v Cambridge University, Fenner's 1988

1999 Season

	M	Inns	NO	Runs	HS	Avge	100s	50s	Ct	St	O	M	Runs	Wkts	Avge	Best	5wI	10wM
Test																		
All First	15	17	4	432	69	33.23	-	3	5	-	545.4	157	1346	71	18.95	4-32	-	-
1-day Int																		
NatWest	4	1	0	2	2	2.00	-	-	-	-	36	7	144	3	48.00	2-32	-	
B & H	1	1	1	11	11 *	-	-	-	-	-	10	0	42	0	-		-	-
1-day Lge	9	9	4	33	16	6.60	-	-	-	-	68	7	304	15	20.26	7-30	1	

Career Performances

	M	Inns	NO	Runs	HS	Avge	100s	50s	Ct	St	Balls	Runs	Wkts	Avge	Best	5wI	10wM
Test	2	4	0	26	14	6.50	-	-	-	-	522	263	4	65.75	3-99	-	-
All First	213	253	63	3844	88	20.23	-	14	73	-	40656	19091	766	24.92	9-45	29	2
1-day Int	7	6	2	96	31 *	24.00	-	-	2	-	413	347	13	26.69	3-55	-	
NatWest	35	18	8	197	66 *	19.70	-	1	15	-	2175	1241	46	26.97	4-35	-	
B & H	52	28	12	289	43	18.06	-	-	10	-	3011	2004	80	25.05	4-38	-	
1-day Lge	156	77	39	577	57 *	15.18	-	1	33	-	6607	4767	187	25.49	7-30	2	

BISHOP, I. E.   Surrey

Name: Ian Emlyn Bishop
Role: Right-hand bat, right-arm fast-medium bowler
Born: 26 August 1977, Taunton
Height: 6ft 2in **Weight:** 11st
Nickname: Bish
County debut: 1996 (Somerset), 1999 (Surrey)
1st-Class catches: 4
Strike rate: 94.80 (career 103.20)
Parents: Brian and Jane
Marital status: Single
Family links with cricket: Both father and brother play club cricket
Education: Parkfield Primary School, Taunton; Castle Secondary School, Taunton; SCAT, Taunton
Qualifications: GCSEs
Cricketers particularly admired: Darren Gough, Chris Lewis, Alec Stewart
Young players to look out for: Andy Harris, Marcus Trescothick
Other sports followed: Football (Liverpool FC)

Relaxations: Sport and socialising with friends
Extras: Played for Devon in 1998. Joined Surrey for 1999
Best batting: 7* Surrey v Middlesex, Lord's 1999
Best bowling: 2-45 Surrey v Derbyshire, Derby 1999

1999 Season

	M	Inns	NO	Runs	HS	Avge	100s	50s	Ct	St	O	M	Runs	Wkts	Avge	Best	5wI	10wM
Test																		
All First	4	5	4	7	7*	7.00	-	-	3	-	79	14	249	5	49.80	2-45	-	-
1-day Int																		
NatWest	1	1	1	0	0*	-	-	-	-	-	5	0	33	0	-		-	-
B & H																		
1-day Lge	8	6	5	23	15*	23.00	-	-	-	-	64.1	7	243	11	22.09	4-34	-	

Career Performances

	M	Inns	NO	Runs	HS	Avge	100s	50s	Ct	St	Balls	Runs	Wkts	Avge	Best	5wI	10wM
Test																	
All First	5	7	4	11	7*	3.66	-	-	4	-	516	278	5	55.60	2-45	-	-
1-day Int																	
NatWest	2	2	2	1	1*	-	-	-	-	-	72	60	0	-		-	-
B & H																	
1-day Lge	8	6	5	23	15*	23.00	-	-	-	-	385	243	11	22.09	4-34	-	

BISHOP, J. E.   Essex

Name: Justin Edward Bishop
Role: Left-hand bat, left-arm fast opening bowler
Born: 4 January 1982, Bury St Edmunds
Height: 6ft **Weight:** 12st 5lbs
Nickname: Bish, Bash, Basher
County debut: 1999
Strike rate: 86.00 (career 86.00)
Parents: Keith and Anne
Marital status: Single
Family links with cricket: 'Father plays for Bury St Edmunds CC and played for Suffolk in his youth'
Education: Ickworth Park Primary School, Bury St Edmunds; Horringer Court Middle School; County Upper School, Bury St Edmunds
Qualifications: '10$\frac{1}{2}$ GCSEs'
Career outside cricket: Studying ('last year')

Off-season: England U19 tour to Malaysia and Sri Lanka for Youth World Cup; studying
Overseas tours: England U19 to Malaysia and (Youth World Cup) Sri Lanka 1999-2000
Cricketers particularly admired: Wasim Akram, Mark Ilott
Young players to look out for: Tim Phillips, Mark Wallace, John Sadler
Other sports played: Football (Suffolk U15; Bury Town U18), golf
Other sports followed: Football (Ipswich Town FC)
Injuries: Knee tendon injury; no time off
Relaxations: 'Watching Ipswich win and/or Norwich lose'
Extras: Opening bowler for England U15 1997
Opinions on cricket: 'The new league structure will enable the game to become even more competitive towards the end of the season.'
Best batting: 17 Essex v Sri Lanka A, Chelmsford 1999
Best bowling: 2-89 Essex v Sri Lanka A, Chelmsford 1999

1999 Season

	M	Inns	NO	Runs	HS	Avge	100s	50s	Ct	St	O	M	Runs	Wkts	Avge	Best	5wI	10wM
Test																		
All First	2	1	0	17	17	17.00	-	-	-	-	43	7	180	3	60.00	2-89	-	-
1-day Int																		
NatWest																			
B & H																			
1-day Lge	1	1	0	1	1	1.00	-	-	-	-	3	0	24	0	-		-	-

Career Performances

	M	Inns	NO	Runs	HS	Avge	100s	50s	Ct	St	Balls	Runs	Wkts	Avge	Best	5wI	10wM
Test																	
All First	2	1	0	17	17	17.00	-	-	-	-	258	180	3	60.00	2-89	-	-
1-day Int																	
NatWest																		
B & H																			
1-day Lge	1	1	0	1	1	1.00	-	-	-	-	18	24	0	-		-	-

BLACKWELL, I. D.　　　　　　　Somerset

Name: Ian David Blackwell
Role: Left-hand bat, slow left-arm bowler
Born: 10 June 1978, Chesterfield
Height: 6ft 2in **Weight:** 15st
Nickname: Blackie, Albert, Sidewinder,
Purple Pip, Ragger
County debut: 1997 (Derbyshire)
1st-Class 50s: 4
1st-Class 5 w. in innings: 1
1st-Class catches: 12
Place in batting averages: 154th av. 24.78
(1998 250th av. 14.11)
Place in bowling averages: 143rd av. 49.58
(1998 123rd av. 37.42)
Strike rate: 125.08 (career 98.25)
Parents: John and Marilyn
Marital status: Engaged to Clare
Family links with cricket: Father plays
for Derbyshire Over 50s

Education: Old Hall Primary School; Manor Secondary School; Brookfield
Community School
Qualifications: 8 GCSEs, 1 A-level, NCA senior coaching award
Career outside cricket: Labourer/coach
Off-season: 'Planning to play club in Australia'
Overseas teams played for: Delacombe Park CC, Melbourne, Australia 1997
Cricketers particularly admired: Phillip DeFreitas, Jamie Cox, Dermot Reeve,
Paul Jarvis, Adrian Rollins, AJ Harris, Robin Weston, Ben Spendlove
Players to look out for: Zach Spendlove, Andy Caddick, Matthew Bulbeck,
Peter Bowler, Rob Turner, Joel Griffiths, Marcus Trescothick
Other sports played: Football, tennis, golf, table tennis
Other sports followed: 'West Country skittles'
Injuries: Out for two months with groin, ankle and back injuries
Relaxations: Computing, socialising
Extras: Played for Derbyshire from the age of eight through to the 2nd XI. Set record
for number of balls lost (7) in a score of 213 not out at Bolsover, which included 23
fours and 15 sixes and equalled the Bassetlaw League 1A record. Left Derbyshire at
end of 1999 season and has joined Somerset for 2000 on a three-year contract
Opinions on cricket: 'Pitches should be run and made by the ECB. This would stop
counties producing assisting pitches for certain bowlers/batters. Good cricket wickets
are needed for players to improve and progress to international level. Then maybe
England as a country will compete with the rest of the world.'

Best batting: 62* Derbyshire v Worcestershire, Kidderminster 1999
Best bowling: 5-115 Derbyshire v Surrey, The Oval 1998

1999 Season

	M	Inns	NO	Runs	HS	Avge	100s	50s	Ct	St	O	M	Runs	Wkts	Avge	Best	5wl	10wM
Test																		
All First	10	16	2	347	62*	24.78	-	2	6	-	250.1	69	595	12	49.58	3-30	-	-
1-day Int																		
NatWest	2	2	1	3	2*	3.00	-	-	-	-	19	3	69	3	23.00	2-34	-	
B & H																		
1-day Lge	9	9	2	262	97	37.42	-	2	2	-	59.5	3	250	12	20.83	3-17	-	

Career Performances

	M	Inns	NO	Runs	HS	Avge	100s	50s	Ct	St	Balls	Runs	Wkts	Avge	Best	5wl	10wM
Test																	
All First	25	39	2	652	62*	17.62	-	4	12	-	2751	1346	28	48.07	5-115	1	-
1-day Int																	
NatWest	3	3	1	7	4	3.50	-	-	-	-	150	102	3	34.00	2-34	-	
B & H	5	4	1	46	27	15.33	-	-	2	-	30	38	0	-	-	-	
1-day Lge	21	19	2	457	97	26.88	-	3	5	-	491	379	17	22.29	3-17	-	

BLAIN, J. A. R. Northamptonshire

Name: John Angus Rae Blain
Role: Right-hand bat, right-arm
fast-medium bowler
Born: 4 January 1979, Edinburgh
Height: 6ft 2in **Weight:** 13st 7lbs
Nickname: Blainey, Haggis
County debut: 1997
1st-Class catches: 2
One-Day 5 w. in innings: 1
Strike rate: (career 156.00)
Parents: John and Elma
Marital status: Single
Education: Eastfield Primary School;
Penicuik HS; Jewel and Esk Valley College
Qualifications: 8 GCSEs, 1 A-level, HNC
Leisure and Recreation, basic cricket
coaching certificate

Career outside cricket: 'Maybe some coaching but no other career'
Off-season: 'At home; maybe 1-2 months in New Zealand coaching'
Overseas tours: Scotland U19 to Holland (International Youth Tournament) 1994-95, to Bermuda (International Youth Tournament) 1997, to South Africa (Youth World Cup; captain) 1997-98; Scotland to Denmark (European Championships) 1996, to Malaysia (ICC Trophy) 1997, to Malaysia (Commonwealth Games) 1998; Northants CCC to Zimbabwe 1997
Overseas teams played for: New Plymouth Old Boys, New Zealand 1998-99; Taranaki Cricket Association, New Zealand 1998-99
Cricketers particularly admired: Allan Donald, Steve Waugh, David Ripley
Young players to look out for: Mark Powell, Michael Davies, David Sales
Other sports played: Football (schoolboy forms with Hibernian and Falkirk, making youth and reserve team appearances), golf
Other sports followed: Football (Hibernian FC)
Injuries: Out for three months with a back injury
Relaxations: Listening to music, going out for a drink, going back to Scotland to spend time with family; watching football, going to the gym
Extras: Was youngest ever player to play for Scotland national side at 17 years and 114 days. Played for Scotland in the Benson and Hedges and NatWest competitions. Made his first-class debut for Scotland against Ireland in 1996. Captained Scotland U19 at U19 World Cup in South Africa. Took 5 for 24 on Sunday League debut for Northants against Derbyshire. Represented Scotland in the 1999 World Cup, taking ten wickets and finishing top of the strike rate chart for the tournament
Opinions on cricket: 'The two divisional set-up has been a beneficial move for the game. More to play for and more competitiveness. Young players in the game expect things on a plate too quickly once a small achievement or some success is gained. There is no substitute for hard work.'
Best bowling: 1-18 Northamptonshire v Worcestershire, Northampton 1997

1999 Season

	M	Inns	NO	Runs	HS	Avge	100s	50s	Ct	St	O	M	Runs	Wkts	Avge	Best	5wI	10wM
Test																		
All First																			
1-day Int	5	5	1	15	9	3.75	-	-	1	-	37.1	1	210	10	21.00	4-37	-	
NatWest																			
B & H																			
1-day Lge																			

11. Which county won the 1990 Championship and who was their captain?

Career Performances

	M	Inns	NO	Runs	HS	Avge	100s	50s	Ct	St	Balls	Runs	Wkts	Avge	Best	5wI	10wM
Test																	
All First	3	1	0	0	0	0.00	-	-	2	-	312	208	2	104.00	1-18	-	-
1-day Int	5	5	1	15	9	3.75	-	-	1	-	223	210	10	21.00	4-37	-	
NatWest	1	0	0	0	0	-	-	-	1	-	66	56	2	28.00	2-56	-	
B & H	3	2	1	14	10 *	14.00	-	-	-	-	90	140	3	46.66	2-82	-	
1-day Lge	3	0	0	0	0	-	-	-	1	-	144	110	7	15.71	5-24	1	

BLAKEY, R. J. Yorkshire

Name: Richard John Blakey
Role: Right-hand bat, wicket-keeper
Born: 15 January 1967, Huddersfield
Height: 5ft 10in **Weight:** 11st 4lbs
Nickname: Dick
County debut: 1985
County cap: 1987
Benefit: 1998
Test debut: 1992-93
Tests: 2
One-Day Internationals: 3
1000 runs in a season: 4
1st-Class 50s: 74
1st-Class 100s: 9
1st-Class 200s: 2
1st-Class catches: 627
1st-Class stumpings: 48
One-Day 100s: 3
Place in batting averages: 147th av. 25.33 (1998 177th av. 21.33)
Strike rate: (career 63.00)
Parents: Brian and Pauline
Wife and date of marriage: Michelle, 28 September 1991
Children: Harrison Brad, 22 September 1993
Family links with cricket: Father played local cricket
Education: Woodhouse Primary; Rastrick Grammar School
Qualifications: 4 O-levels, Senior NCA Coach
Career outside cricket: Started own leisure company
Overseas tours: England YC to West Indies 1984-85; Yorkshire to Barbados 1986-87, to Cape Town 1990-91; England A to Zimbabwe and Kenya 1989-90, to Pakistan 1990-91; England to India and Sri Lanka 1992-93
Overseas teams played for: Waverley, Sydney 1985-87; Mt Waverley, Sydney

1987-88; Bionics, Zimbabwe 1989-90
Cricketers particularly admired: Martyn Moxon, Dermot Reeve, Ian Botham, Alan Knott
Other sports followed: All
Relaxations: All sports, particularly golf and squash, eating out, drawing, photography
Extras: Established himself in Huddersfield League. Made record 2nd XI score – 273* v Northamptonshire 1986. Yorkshire's Young Player of the Year 1989. Made Test debut in second Test against India at Madras, February 1993. He was awarded a citation by the International Committee for Fair Play in 1995, the only cricketer among the 25 winners worldwide
Best batting: 221 England A v Zimbabwe, Bulawayo 1989-90
Best bowling: 1-68 Yorkshire v Nottinghamshire, Sheffield 1986

1999 Season

	M	Inns	NO	Runs	HS	Avge	100s	50s	Ct	St	O	M	Runs	Wkts	Avge	Best	5wI	10wM
Test																		
All First	17	31	4	684	123	25.33	1	4	41	-								
1-day Int																		
NatWest	4	4	4	20	10 *	-	-	-	2	-								
B & H	3	2	1	26	14	26.00	-	-	6	-								
1-day Lge	16	15	6	226	34 *	25.11	-	-	26	6								

Career Performances

	M	Inns	NO	Runs	HS	Avge	100s	50s	Ct	St	Balls	Runs	Wkts	Avge	Best	5wI	10wM
Test	2	4	0	7	6	1.75	-	-	2	-							
All First	292	467	71	12496	221	31.55	11	74	627	48	63	68	1	68.00	1-68	-	-
1-day Int	3	2	0	25	25	12.50	-	-	2	1							
NatWest	33	26	10	418	75	26.12	-	2	36	2							
B & H	55	47	12	1023	80 *	29.22	-	6	53	3							
1-day Lge	183	163	37	4476	130 *	35.52	3	24	166	30							

BLANCHETT, I. N.   Middlesex

Name: Ian Neale Blanchett
Role: Right-hand bat, right-arm fast-medium bowler
Born: 2 October 1975, Melbourne, Australia
Height: 6ft 4in **Weight:** 14st 3lbs
Nickname: Blanchy, Noisy, 'and other descriptive names created by uni housemates based around being very clumsy'
County debut: 1997 (one-day), 1998 (first-class)

1st-Class catches: 2
Strike rate: 60.00 (career 89.14)
Parents: Edward Arthur Blanchett and Susan
Anne Billows
Marital status: Single
Family links with cricket: 'Uncle Steve
played for Surrey YC when he was younger –
a long time ago!'
Education: Feltwell Primary, Norfolk;
Methwold High School, Norfolk; Downham
Market High School; Luton University
Qualifications: 8 GCSEs, 2 A-levels, 'in
process of completing a Health
Science/Leisure degree'
Cricketers particularly admired:
Ian Botham, Graham Gooch
Young players to look out for: Owais Shah,
Aaron Laraman, James Hewitt, Tim Walton,
Kevin Innes
Other sports followed: Football (Norwich City), snooker, swimming
Extras: Voted Player of the Year four times successively by his club in Norfolk.
Awarded a special achievement prize in the 1994 NAYC Cambridge Festival. Released
by Middlesex at end of 1999 season
Opinions on cricket: 'It gets better every day. More day/night cricket is a must.'
Best batting: 18 Middlesex v Worcestershire, Uxbridge 1998
Best bowling: 2-38 Middlesex v Glamorgan, Lord's 1998

1999 Season

	M	Inns	NO	Runs	HS	Avge	100s	50s	Ct	St	O	M	Runs	Wkts	Avge	Best	5wI	10wM
Test																		
All First	1	2	1	11	6	11.00	-	-	1	-	20	1	116	2	58.00	2-64	-	-
1-day Int																		
NatWest																		
B & H																		
1-day Lge	1	1	0	1	1	1.00	-	-	-	-	4	0	34	2	17.00	2-34	-	

12. Which wicket-keeper made the most Championship dismissals
from 1993, when the four-day Championship began, to the end of the
single-division era in 1999?

Career Performances

	M	Inns	NO	Runs	HS	Avge	100s	50s	Ct	St	Balls	Runs	Wkts	Avge	Best	5wI	10wM
Test																	
All First	5	6	1	36	18	7.20	-	-	2	-	624	423	7	60.42	2-38	-	-
1-day Int																	
NatWest																	
B & H	2	0	0	0	0	-	-	-	-	-	42	56	1	56.00	1-44	-	
1-day Lge	10	5	2	19	9 *	6.33	-	-	4	-	312	294	4	73.50	2-34	-	

BLEWETT, G.S. Yorkshire

Name: Gregory Scott Blewett
Role: Right-hand bat, right-arm medium bowler
Born: 28 October 1971, Adelaide
Height: 6ft **Weight:** 11st
Nickname: Blewy
County debut: 1999
Test debut: 1994-95
Tests: 34
One-Day Internationals: 32
1st-Class 50s: 48
1st-Class 100s: 22
1st-Class 200s: 4
1st-Class 5 w. in innings: 1
1st-Class catches: 98
Place in batting averages: 98th av. 31.19
Strike rate: 80.00 (career 79.26)
Parents: Bob and Shirley
Wife and date of marriage: Jodie, 26 June 1998
Family links with cricket: Father played for South Australia
Education: Angaston Primary School, Adelaide; Prince Alfred College, Adelaide
Overseas tours: Australia U19 to England 1991, to Sri Lanka; Australia to New Zealand 1994-95, to West Indies 1994-95, to South Africa 1996-97, to England 1997, to India 1997-98, to West Indies 1998-99, to Sri Lanka 1999, to Zimbabwe 1999
Overseas teams played for: South Australia 1991-92 –
Cricketers particularly admired: Greg Chappell, Gordon Greenidge, Viv Richards
Other sports played: Golf
Other sports followed: Australian Football League (Adelaide Crows)
Relaxations: Eating and sleeping
Extras: Was due to play for Middlesex in 1997 but was selected for Ashes tour. Was the only Australian to make 1000 Test runs in 1997 calendar year. Holds the

unenviable record of being the first Australian to be out for 99 twice in Test cricket. In 1998-99, made 1175 first-class runs (av. 146.86 and including five 100s and a 200) before Christmas in the Australian season, breaking David Hookes' record of 1163 set in 1982-83. In the course of achieving this feat he became only the sixth Australian to score four consecutive first-class 100s; against the England tourists, he scored 143 for South Australia and 169* and 213* in one match for Australia XI. Averaged 118.70 in full Australian first-class season 1998-99. Vice-captain of South Australia. Joined Yorkshire as overseas player for 1999 season; released by Yorkshire at end of 1999 season

Best batting: 268 South Australia v Victoria, Melbourne 1993-94
Best bowling: 5-29 Australian XI v West Indies, Hobart 1996-97
Stop press: Selected for Australia's tour of New Zealand 1999-2000

1999 Season

	M	Inns	NO	Runs	HS	Avge	100s	50s	Ct	St	O	M	Runs	Wkts	Avge	Best	5wI	10wM
Test																		
All First	12	23	2	655	190	31.19	1	2	5	-	66.4	13	212	5	42.40	2-16	-	-
1-day Int																		
NatWest	3	3	0	83	77	27.66	-	1	1	-	16.4	0	57	7	8.14	4-18	-	
B & H	3	3	0	84	71	28.00	-	1	-	-	3	0	23	0	-	-	-	
1-day Lge	11	11	0	178	48	16.18	-	-	6	-	25.1	0	116	4	29.00	1-14	-	

Career Performances

	M	Inns	NO	Runs	HS	Avge	100s	50s	Ct	St	Balls	Runs	Wkts	Avge	Best	5wI	10wM
Test	34	59	2	2003	214	35.14	4	11	37	-	1184	578	11	52.54	2-9	-	-
All First	131	229	15	9851	268	46.03	26	48	98	-	7134	3615	90	40.16	5-29	1	-
1-day Int	32	30	3	551	57 *	20.40	-	2	7	-	749	646	14	46.14	2-6	-	
NatWest	3	3	0	83	77	27.66	-	1	1	-	100	57	7	8.14	4-18	-	
B & H	3	3	0	84	71	28.00	-	1	-	-	18	23	0	-	-	-	
1-day Lge	11	11	0	178	48	16.18	-	-	6	-	151	116	4	29.00	1-14	-	

13. Against whom and at which ground did Graeme Hick amass his 405* for Worcestershire in 1988?

BLOOMFIELD, T. F. Middlesex

Name: Timothy Francis Bloomfield
Role: Right-hand bat, right-arm
fast-medium bowler
Born: 31 May 1973, Ashford
Height: 6ft 3in **Weight:** 14st
Nickname: Nice, BT, Frank
County debut: 1997
1st-Class 5 w. in innings: 4
1st-Class catches: 3
Place in batting averages: 273rd av. 10.00
Place in bowling averages: 99th av. 30.51
(1998 85th av. 30.00)
Strike rate: 48.45 (career 45.91)
Parents: Richard (deceased) and Pauline
Education: Halliford Secondary School
Qualifications: GCSEs
Overseas tours: Berkshire U25 to Barbados
Cricketers particularly admired:
Ian Botham, Viv Richards, Angus Fraser
Other sports followed: Football (Liverpool)

Extras: Has also played for Sussex 2nd XI and Berkshire
Opinions on cricket: 'We play too much cricket. The powers-that-be need to be more
forward thinking.'
Best batting: 20* Middlesex v Sussex, Hove 1998
Best bowling: 5-36 Middlesex v Glamorgan, Cardiff 1999

1999 Season

	M	Inns	NO	Runs	HS	Avge	100s	50s	Ct	St	O	M	Runs	Wkts	Avge	Best	5wI	10wM
Test																		
All First	11	17	9	80	17*	10.00	-	-	1	-	266.3	45	1007	33	30.51	5-36	1	-
1-day Int																		
NatWest	1	1	1	7	7*	-	-	-	-	-	3	0	18	0	-	-	-	
B & H																		
1-day Lge	7	2	1	11	10	11.00	-	-	2	-	57	0	288	6	48.00	2-45	-	

Career Performances

	M	Inns	NO	Runs	HS	Avge	100s	50s	Ct	St	Balls	Runs	Wkts	Avge	Best	5wI	10wM
Test																	
All First	23	30	16	121	20 *	8.64	-	-	3	-	3122	1925	68	28.30	5-36	4	-
1-day Int																	
NatWest	4	2	1	7	7 *	7.00	-	-	-	-	168	123	2	61.50	1-25	-	
B & H	2	0	0	0	0	-	-	-	-	-	84	90	0	-	-	-	
1-day Lge	18	4	1	27	15	9.00	-	-	4	-	744	613	18	34.05	2-8	-	

BOON, D. C. Durham

Name: David Clarence Boon
Role: Right-hand bat, right-arm medium
bowler, county captain
Born: 29 December 1960, Launceston,
Tasmania
County debut: 1997
County cap: 1998
Test debut: 1984-85
Tests: 107
One-Day Internationals: 181
1000 runs in a season: 2
1st-Class 50s: 114
1st-Class 100s: 65
1st-Class 200s: 3
1st-Class catches: 283
One-Day 100s: 6
Place in batting averages: 77th av. 33.56

(1998 36th av. 40.96)
Strike rate: 30.00 (career 82.78)
Overseas teams played for: Tasmania, 1978-99
Overseas tours: Young Australia to Zimbabwe 1982-83; Australia to England 1985,
1989 and 1993, to New Zealand 1985-86, 1989-90, 1992-93, to India 1986-87,
to Pakistan 1988-89, 1994-95, to West Indies 1990-91, 1994-95, to Sri Lanka 1992-93,
to South Africa 1993-94, to India and Pakistan (World Cup) 1986-87
Extras: Captain of Tasmania 1992-93 – 1998-99. With Geoff Marsh, formed
Australia's most successful opening pair since Bill Lawry and Bobby Simpson.
Dropped from the Test series for poor form against England in 1986-87, he came back
to win the International Cricketer of the Year the following season. Was the leading
run-scorer in the series against West Indies 1988-89, and followed that with a
successful tour of England in 1989. Made his highest Test score against New Zealand
at Perth in 1989-90, but had the rest of the season ruined by a knee injury. Recovered

to score over 500 runs in successive series against England and India, now batting at No. 3. Returned to opening against the West Indies in 1991-92, scoring 490 runs at an average of over 60. Also one of the world's finest close to the wicket fieldsmen. Retired from Test cricket in 1995-96. Agreed to play for Gloucestershire in the 1995 season, but withdrew through injury and his overseas berth was taken by Javagal Srinath. Joined Durham as captain for the 1997 season. Retired from first-class cricket at end of 1999 season to become Tasmania's marketing and special events co-ordinator

Best batting: 227 Tasmania v Victoria, Melbourne 1983-84
Best bowling: 2-18 Durham v Kent, Darlington 1997

1999 Season

	M	Inns	NO	Runs	HS	Avge	100s	50s	Ct	St	O	M	Runs	Wkts	Avge	Best	5wl	10wM
Test																		
All First	16	27	2	839	139	33.56	1	7	8	-	5	1	17	1	17.00	1-17	-	-
1-day Int																		
NatWest	1	1	0	51	51	51.00	-	1	-	-								
B & H																		
1-day Lge	13	12	0	334	66	27.83	-	3	3	-								

Career Performances

	M	Inns	NO	Runs	HS	Avge	100s	50s	Ct	St	Balls	Runs	Wkts	Avge	Best	5wl	10wM
Test	107	190	20	7422	200	43.65	21	32	99	-	36	14	0	-		-	-
All First	350	585	53	23413	227	44.00	68	114	283	-	1159	702	14	50.14	2-18	-	-
1-day Int	181	177	16	5964	122	37.04	5	37	45	-	82	86	0	-		-	-
NatWest	4	4	1	217	80 *	72.33	-	3	1	-							
B & H	8	7	1	225	103	37.50	1	1	3	-							
1-day Lge	41	39	3	1023	76	28.41	-	6	11	-	90	90	2	45.00	2-44	-	

14. Which all-rounder topped the Notts batting and bowling averages in their Championship winning season of 1987?

BOSWELL, S. A. J.   Leicestershire

Name: Scott Antony John Boswell
Role: Right-hand bat, right-arm
fast-medium bowler
Born: 11 September 1974, Fulford, York
Height: 6ft 4in **Weight:** 14st 2lbs
Nickname: Bossy, Joey, Grandad
County debut: 1995 (one-day, Northants),
1996 (first-class, Northants),
1999 (Leicestershire)
1st-Class 5 w. in innings: 1
1st-Class catches: 4
Strike rate: 55.20 (career 67.88)
Parents: Tony and Judy
Marital status: Single
Education: Ebor Prep School; Pocklington
School; Wolverhampton University
('Wolly Poly')
Qualifications: 9 GCSEs, 3 A-levels 'and
hopefully BSc (Hons) in Sports Studies'
Career outside cricket: Studying
Overseas tours: Northamptonshire to Zimbabwe 1998
Overseas teams played for: Hutt Valley, New Zealand 1994-95; Koeburg CC,
South Africa 1997-98
Cricketers particularly admired: Richard Hadlee ('for his dedication')
Young players to look out for: Graeme Swann, Mike Davies
Other sports played: Rugby ('toured Zimbabwe in '92 with school')
Other sports followed: Football (York City), rugby (York)
Relaxations: Watching TV, socialising and spending time with friends
Extras: Attended Dennis Lillee's Pace Foundation in India 1996. Released by
Northamptonshire at end of 1998 season and joined Leicestershire for 1999. Made
Championship debut for Leics against his former county at Northampton 1999
Opinions on cricket: 'Read my dissertation!'
Best batting: 35 Northamptonshire v Leicestershire, Northampton 1997
Best bowling: 5-94 Northamptonshire v Worcestershire, Northampton 1997

---

15. In a match at Derby in 1922, W.G. Quaife and B.W. Quaife appeared in the
Warwickshire line-up, while the Derbyshire side included W. Bestwick and
R. Bestwick. How were the Quaifes related and how were the Bestwicks related?

1999 Season

	M	Inns	NO	Runs	HS	Avge	100s	50s	Ct	St	O	M	Runs	Wkts	Avge	Best	5wI	10wM
Test																		
All First	2	4	1	39	15	13.00	-	-	-	-	46	9	214	5	42.80	3-71	-	-
1-day Int																		
NatWest																		
B & H																		
1-day Lge	2	1	1	0	0*	-	-	-	-	-	13	0	57	2	28.50	2-37	-	

Career Performances

	M	Inns	NO	Runs	HS	Avge	100s	50s	Ct	St	Balls	Runs	Wkts	Avge	Best	5wI	10wM
Test																	
All First	15	20	6	166	35	11.85	-	-	4	-	1833	1226	27	45.40	5-94	1	-
1-day Int																	
NatWest																	
B & H	10	6	1	24	14	4.80	-	-	1	-	536	485	6	80.83	3-39	-	
1-day Lge	6	2	1	2	2	2.00	-	-	-	-	216	161	5	32.20	2-37	-	

BOWEN, M. N. Nottinghamshire

Name: Mark Nicholas Bowen
Role: Right-hand bat, right-arm
medium bowler
Born: 6 December 1967, Redcar
Height: 6ft 1in **Weight:** 14st
Nickname: Bully, Jim, Bert
County debut: 1991-92 (Northamptonshire),
1996 (Nottinghamshire)
1st-Class 5 w. in innings: 7
1st-Class 10 w. in match: 1
1st-Class catches: 15
Place in batting averages: 272nd av. 10.00
(1998 215th av. 17.75)
Place in bowling averages: 48th av. 23.56
(1998 71st av. 28.22)
Strike rate: 42.81 (career 59.18)
Parents: Keith
Wife and date of marriage:
Lesley, 11 October 1997
Family links with cricket: 'My father was a big influence and has always had a keen
interest in the game'

Education: St Mary's Junior School, Redcar; Sacred Heart Secondary School, Redcar; St Mary's Sixth Form College, Middlesbrough; Teesside Polytechnic, Middlesbrough
Qualifications: 8 O-levels, 3 A-levels, BSc (Hons) in Chemical Engineering
Career outside cricket: Chemical engineer
Off-season: British Nuclear Fuels – working as production support engineer
Overseas tours: Northamptonshire to Durban 1992, to Cape Town 1993; Christians in Sport to Zimbabwe 1994-95; Nottinghamshire CCC to Johannesburg 1997, 1998, 1999
Cricketers particularly admired: Ian Botham, Dennis Lillee, Viv Richards
Young players to look out for: 'Good ones'
Other sports played: Golf, hockey (played for Durham County), football
Other sports followed: Rugby, football (Middlesbrough FC)
Relaxations: 'Watching TV, DIY, cycling, walking, and a good pint of ale'
Extras: Made debut for Northants first team in Natal on 1991-92 tour to South Africa before playing in the 2nd XI. Released by Northamptonshire at the end of the 1995 season and joined Nottinghamshire for the start of the 1996 season
Opinions on cricket: 'Two divisions is a good start, but pitches need to improve.'
Best batting: 32 Nottinghamshire v Northamptonshire, Northampton 1997
Best bowling: 7-73 Nottinghamshire v Somerset, Taunton 1998

1999 Season

	M	Inns	NO	Runs	HS	Avge	100s	50s	Ct	St	O	M	Runs	Wkts	Avge	Best	5wI	10wM
Test																		
All First	11	21	8	130	19	10.00	-	-	2	-	264	53	872	37	23.56	5-66	1	-
1-day Int																		
NatWest	1	1	0	4	4	4.00	-	-	1	-	9	1	32	3	10.66	3-32	-	
B & H																		
1-day Lge	8	3	1	24	22 *	12.00	-	-	2	-	51.5	0	293	7	41.85	4-46	-	

Career Performances

	M	Inns	NO	Runs	HS	Avge	100s	50s	Ct	St	Balls	Runs	Wkts	Avge	Best	5wI	10wM
Test																	
All First	63	86	26	734	32	12.23	-	-	15	-	10595	5717	179	31.93	7-73	7	1
1-day Int																	
NatWest	4	3	2	12	8 *	12.00	-	-	2	-	180	129	6	21.50	3-32	-	
B & H	5	3	1	10	9	5.00	-	-	-	-	265	194	5	38.80	2-40	-	
1-day Lge	56	24	12	206	27 *	17.16	-	-	12	-	2161	1936	60	32.26	4-29	-	

BOWLER, P. D.   Somerset

Name: Peter Duncan Bowler
Role: Right-hand opening bat, occasional
off-spin bowler, occasional wicket-keeper
Born: 30 July 1963, Plymouth
Height: 6ft 2in **Weight:** 13st 10lbs
Nickname: Tom
County debut: 1986 (Leicestershire),
1988 (Derbyshire), 1995 (Somerset)
County cap: 1989 (Derbyshire),
1995 (Somerset)
1000 runs in a season: 8
1st-Class 50s: 78
1st-Class 100s: 32
1st-Class 200s: 3
1st-Class catches: 166
1st-Class stumpings: 1
One-Day 100s: 5
Place in batting averages: 11th av. 49.00
(1998 132nd av. 26.30)
Strike rate: 29.50 (career 97.33)
Parents: Peter and Etta
Wife and date of marriage: Joanne, 10 October 1992
Children: Peter Robert, 21 September 1993; Rebekah, 25 August 1995
Education: Scots College, Sydney, Australia; Daramalan College, Canberra, Australia;
Nottingham Trent University
Qualifications: Australian Year 12 certificate, LLB
Cricketers particularly admired: Gus Valence, Rob Jeffery, Bill Carracher,
Phil Russell
Young players to look out for: Matthew Bulbeck, Nick Boulton
Other sports followed: Rugby union
Relaxations: Family and reading
Extras: First Leicestershire player to score a first-class century on debut (100* v
Hampshire 1986). Moved to Derbyshire at end of 1987 season and scored a hundred
on his debut v Cambridge University in 1988. First batsman to 2000 runs in 1992,
finishing equal leading run-scorer (2044) with Mike Roseberry of Middlesex.
Derbyshire Player of the Year 1992. Signed a five-year contract with Somerset starting
in 1995. Took over the Somerset captaincy mid-season 1997 after Andy Hayhurst was
released. Relinquished captaincy after 1998 season. Passed 5000 runs in
Sunday/National League, v Durham 1999. Granted a benefit for 2000
Best batting: 241* Derbyshire v Hampshire, Portsmouth 1992
Best bowling: 3-25 Somerset v Northamptonshire, Taunton 1998

1999 Season

	M	Inns	NO	Runs	HS	Avge	100s	50s	Ct	St	O	M	Runs	Wkts	Avge	Best	5wl	10wM
Test																		
All First	17	27	8	931	149	49.00	4	-	8	-	9.5	2	12	2	6.00	2-4	-	-
1-day Int																		
NatWest	5	5	0	147	48	29.40	-	-	1	-								
B & H																		
1-day Lge	11	10	0	356	86	35.60	-	4	3	-								

Career Performances

	M	Inns	NO	Runs	HS	Avge	100s	50s	Ct	St	Balls	Runs	Wkts	Avge	Best	5wl	10wM
Test																	
All First	247	427	43	15158	241 *	39.47	35	78	166	1	3212	2009	33	60.87	3-25	-	-
1-day Int																	
NatWest	24	24	0	700	111	29.16	1	3	11	-	36	26	0	-	-	-	-
B & H	50	49	1	1449	109	30.18	2	11	21	1	309	182	5	36.40	1-15	-	
1-day Lge	182	176	19	5246	138 *	33.41	2	43	70	1	308	323	8	40.37	3-31	-	

BRIDGE, G. D.   Durham

Name: Graeme David Bridge
Role: Right-hand bat, slow left-arm bowler
Born: 4 September 1980, Sunderland
Height: 5ft 8in **Weight:** 11st 3lbs
Nickname: Bridgey, Sydney
County debut: 1999
1st-Class catches: 1
Strike rate: 264.00 (career 264.00)
Parents: Anne and John
Marital status: Single
Education: Ryhope Junior School;
Southmoor
Qualifications: 4 GCSEs
Off-season: England U19 tour to Malaysia
and Sri Lanka
Overseas tours: England U19 to New
Zealand 1998-99, to Malaysia and (Youth
World Cup) Sri Lanka 1999-2000
Cricketers particularly admired: Phil Tufnell, David Boon
Young players to look out for: Ian Bell, Mark Wallace, Richard Dawson
Other sports followed: Football (Sunderland AFC)

Relaxations: Listening to music and reading
Extras: Represented England U19 in the one-day series v Australia U19 1999
Opinions on cricket: 'Tea should be longer than 20 minutes.'
Best batting: 6 Durham v Surrey, The Oval 1999
Best bowling: 1-60 Durham v Surrey, The Oval 1999

1999 Season

	M	Inns	NO	Runs	HS	Avge	100s	50s	Ct	St	O	M	Runs	Wkts	Avge	Best	5wI	10wM
Test																		
All First	1	2	0	11	6	5.50	-	-	1	-	44	12	110	1	110.00	1-60	-	-
1-day Int																		
NatWest	3	2	1	24	15	24.00	-	-	1	-	27	0	123	1	123.00	1-49	-	
B & H																		
1-day Lge																		

Career Performances

	M	Inns	NO	Runs	HS	Avge	100s	50s	Ct	St	Balls	Runs	Wkts	Avge	Best	5wI	10wM
Test																	
All First	1	2	0	11	6	5.50	-	-	1	-	264	110	1	110.00	1-60	-	-
1-day Int																	
NatWest	3	2	1	24	15	24.00	-	-	1	-	162	123	1	123.00	1-49	-	
B & H																	
1-day Lge																	

BRIMSON, M. T.   Leicestershire

Name: Matthew Thomas Brimson
Role: Right-hand bat, slow left-arm bowler
Born: 1 December 1970, Plumstead, London
Height: 6ft **Weight:** 11st 12lbs
Nickname: Brimmo, Doogie
County debut: 1993
County cap: 1998
1st-Class 50s: 1
1st-Class 5 w. in innings: 3
1st-Class catches: 11
Place in batting averages: 261st av. 12.70 (1998 248th av. 14.37)
Place in bowling averages: 108th av. 32.66 (1998 65th av. 27.30)
Strike rate: 79.20 (career 72.72)
Parents: David and Jennifer
Wife and date of marriage: Lyn, 29 December 1993

Children: Poppy Lilian, 14 July 1996; Holly, 25 October 1998

Family links with cricket: Brother played a bit in Kent League and South Thames League

Education: St Joseph's Preparatory School, Blackheath; Chislehurst and Sidcup Grammar School, Sidcup; Van Mildert College, Durham University; Leicester University

Qualifications: 8 O-levels, 3 A-levels, BA (Hons) Geography, PGCE (Secondary) Geography, senior cricket coaching award

Career outside cricket: Teaching

Off-season: Finishing off PGCE course

Overseas tours: Kent Schools U17 to Singapore and New Zealand 1987-88; Leicestershire to Bloemfontein 1994, 1995, to Potchefstroom 1996, to Durban 1997, to Barbados 1998, to Sri Lanka 1999

Cricketers particularly admired: Derek Underwood, Ian Botham

Young players to look out for: Ashley Wright

Other sports played: Golf and tennis

Other sports followed: Football (Charlton Athletic)

Injuries: Out for two weeks with tendonitis of shoulder; for two weeks with chickenpox

Relaxations: 'Family life is great'

Extras: Was on the Kent staff in 1991, Rapidline 2nd XI Player of the Month, July 1995, Leicestershire CCC Player of the Month, June 1998

Opinions on cricket: 'Groundsmen to be directly contracted to ECB and told to prepare best pitches possible. Four-day cricket to be midweek and all one-day games to be weekends or midweek floodlit.'

Best batting: 54* Leicestershire v Warwickshire, Edgbaston 1998

Best bowling: 5-12 Leicestershire v Sussex, Leicester 1996

1999 Season

	M	Inns	NO	Runs	HS	Avge	100s	50s	Ct	St	O	M	Runs	Wkts	Avge	Best	5wI	10wM
Test																		
All First	14	16	6	127	36*	12.70	-	-	2	-	316.5	98	784	24	32.66	5-51	1	-
1-day Int																		
NatWest	2	2	2	6	4*	-	-	-	1	-	15	2	47	1	47.00	1-23	-	
B & H	1	1	1	2	2*	-	-	-	-	-	5	0	26	0	-	-	-	
1-day Lge	4	3	1	2	2	1.00	-	-	-	-	18	2	69	4	17.25	2-24	-	

Career Performances

	M	Inns	NO	Runs	HS	Avge	100s	50s	Ct	St	Balls	Runs	Wkts	Avge	Best	5wI	10wM
Test																	
All First	66	66	27	459	54 *	11.76	-	1	11	-	9018	4069	124	32.81	5-12	3	-
1-day Int																	
NatWest	7	3	2	15	9	15.00	-	-	1	-	406	184	7	26.28	3-34	-	
B & H	10	3	1	2	2 *	1.00	-	-	3	-	449	324	8	40.50	2-36	-	
1-day Lge	24	7	5	19	12 *	9.50	-	-	4	-	915	668	28	23.85	3-23	-	

BROWN, A. D. Surrey

Name: Alistair Duncan Brown
Role: Right-hand bat, off-spin bowler,
'wicket-keeper only when Batts fails to play
the hook properly'
Born: 11 February 1970, Beckenham
Height: 5ft 10in **Weight:** 13st
Nickname: Lordy
County debut: 1992
County cap: 1994
One-Day Internationals: 13
1000 runs in a season: 5
1st-Class 50s: 31
1st-Class 100s: 21
1st-Class 200s: 1
1st-Class catches: 143
1st-Class stumpings: 1
One-Day 100s: 10
One-Day 200s: 1

Place in batting averages: 9th av. 51.22 (1998 15th av. 49.33)
Parents: Robert and Ann
Wife and date of marriage: Sarah, 10 October 1998
Family links with cricket: Father played for Surrey Young Amateurs in the 1950s
Education: Cumnor House School; Caterham School; 'David Ward's card school for
the technically gifted'
Qualifications: 5 O-levels, NCA Senior Coach
Career outside cricket: 'Actor, thespian and all round good egg'
Off-season: Jury service ('subsequently not selected for a trial – no change there
then!'); painting and decorating
Overseas tours: England Six-a-side to Singapore 1993, 1994, 1995, to Hong Kong
1997; England to Sharjah 1997-98 (Champions Trophy), to Bangladesh (Wills
International Cup) 1998-99

Overseas teams played for: North Perth, Western Australia 1989-90
Cricketers particularly admired: Ian Botham, Viv Richards
Players to look out for: 'Nadeem Shahid, who went missing just after the Northants game'
Other sports played: Golf, football, snooker, 'winner of the Lanzarote Open Pool Championship 1990'
Other sports followed: Football (West Ham United), rugby league (London Broncos)
Relaxations: 'Watching Jason Ratcliffe play football and Nadeem Shahid comb his hair'
Extras: Scored three of the eight fastest centuries of the 1992 season (71, 78 & 79 balls). Awarded Man of the Match for 118 against India in the third One-Day International 1996. Played for England in the 1997 Hong Kong Sixes competition in which England finished runners-up to Pakistan. Recorded the highest-ever score in the Sunday League with 203 off 119 balls against Hampshire at Guildford in 1997 and received an individual award at the PCA Dinner for that achievement. Scored 72-ball 100 v Northamptonshire to become joint winner (with Carl Hooper) of the EDS Walter Lawrence Trophy for the fastest first-class 100 of the 1998 season. Scored 31-ball 50 v South Africa in the Texaco Trophy match at Headingley 1998, the fastest 50 in the history of the Texaco Trophy; his score of 59 won him the Man of the Match award. Took over as wicket-keeper for Surrey v Glamorgan at The Oval 1999 after injury to Jon Batty, taking two catches and a stumping
Opinions on cricket: 'Two divisions is a must for competitive cricket. More floodlit cricket and whatever gives the game more appeal to the public.'
Best batting: 265 Surrey v Middlesex, Lord's 1999

1999 Season

	M	Inns	NO	Runs	HS	Avge	100s	50s	Ct	St	O	M	Runs	Wkts	Avge	Best	5wI	10wM
Test																		
All First	17	26	4	1127	265	51.22	4	2	31	1	26	3	80	0	-		-	-	-
1-day Int																		
NatWest	4	4	1	80	39 *	26.66	-	-	2	-								
B & H	1	1	0	5	5	5.00	-	-	-	-								
1-day Lge	15	15	0	403	105	26.86	1	-	7	-	25.5	0	141	3	47.00	1-20	-	

Career Performances

	M	Inns	NO	Runs	HS	Avge	100s	50s	Ct	St	Balls	Runs	Wkts	Avge	Best	5wI	10wM
Test																	
All First	125	198	19	7791	265	43.52	22	31	143	1	492	258	0	-		-	-	-
1-day Int	13	13	0	333	118	25.61	1	1	6	-							
NatWest	22	19	2	486	72	28.58	-	2	5	-							
B & H	38	38	6	1248	117 *	39.00	1	6	10	-							
1-day Lge	137	132	4	4031	203	31.49	9	15	39	-	155	141	3	47.00	1-20	-

BROWN, D. R. Warwickshire

Name: Douglas Robert Brown
Role: Right-hand bat, right-arm
fast-medium bowler
Born: 29 October 1969, Stirling, Scotland
Height: 6ft 2in **Weight:** 14st 2lbs
Nickname: Bullets, Hoots
County debut: 1992
County cap: 1995
One-Day Internationals: 9
50 wickets in a season: 2
1st-Class 50s: 20
1st-Class 100s: 1
1st-Class 5 w. in innings: 11
1st-Class 10 w. in match: 3
1st-Class catches: 57
One-Day 5 w. in innings: 1
Place in batting averages: 123rd av. 27.75
(1998 101st av. 30.04)
Place in bowling averages: 72nd av. 27.57 (1998 83rd av. 29.78)
Strike rate: 53.73 (career 47.66)
Parents: Alastair and Janette
Wife and date of marriage: Brenda, 2 October 1993
Children: Lauren, 14 September 1998
Education: St John's Primary, Alloa; Alloa Academy; West London Institute of Higher
Education (Borough Road College)
Qualifications: 9 O-Grades, 5 Higher Grades, BEd (Hons) Physical Education,
NCA Advanced Coach
Career outside cricket: PE teacher
Overseas tours: Scotland XI to Pakistan 1988-89; England VI to Hong Kong 1997;
England A to Kenya and Sri Lanka 1997-98; England to Sharjah (Champions Trophy)
1997-98, to West Indies 1997-98 (one-day series), to Bangladesh (Wills International
Cup) 1998
Overseas teams played for: Primrose, Cape Town 1992-93; Uredenburg Salohana,
Cape Town 1994; Eastern Suburbs, Wellington 1995-96; Wellington, New Zealand
1995-96
Cricketers particularly admired: 'Everyone who gives 100 per cent for the team's
cause'
Young players to look out for: Tony Frost
Other sports played: Golf
Other sports followed: Football (Alloa Athletic), 'most sports'
Relaxations: Golf, music, 'time with Lauren'

Extras: Played football at Hampden Park for Scotland U18. Played first-class and B&H cricket for Scotland in 1989, and played again for Scotland against Ireland in 1992. Played for England in the 1997 Hong Kong Sixes competition in which England finished runners-up to Pakistan. Played for the victorious England side in Sharjah in 1997 and was called up to the England A tour of Kenya and Sri Lanka after the promotion of Chris Silverwood to England's tour of the West Indies following the withdrawal of Darren Gough through injury. Scored maiden first-class century v Northants on 15 April 1999; it was the earliest 100 in a Championship season, a distinction previously held by N.M.K. Smith's century v Durham on 17 April 1998

Opinions on cricket: 'Still a great game.'

Best batting: 142 Warwickshire v v Northamptonshire, Edgbaston 1999

Best bowling: 8-89 First-Class Counties v Pakistan A, Chelmsford 1997

1999 Season

	M	Inns	NO	Runs	HS	Avge	100s	50s	Ct	St	O	M	Runs	Wkts	Avge	Best	5wI	10wM
Test																		
All First	16	25	1	666	142	27.75	1	3	13	-	232.5	57	717	26	27.57	7-66	1	-
1-day Int																		
NatWest	1	1	0	19	19	19.00	-	-	-	-	5	2	18	2	9.00	2-18	-	
B & H	2	2	1	63	49	63.00	-	-	-	-	14.2	2	64	1	64.00	1-34	-	
1-day Lge	16	13	2	106	26	9.63	-	-	4	-	82	3	400	17	23.52	3-34	-	

Career Performances

	M	Inns	NO	Runs	HS	Avge	100s	50s	Ct	St	Balls	Runs	Wkts	Avge	Best	5wI	10wM
Test																	
All First	98	152	16	3523	142	25.90	1	20	57	-	13488	7135	283	25.21	8-89	11	3
1-day Int	9	8	4	99	21	24.75	-	-	1	-	324	305	7	43.57	2-28	-	
NatWest	13	12	1	248	67	22.54	-	2	1	-	570	362	9	40.22	2-18	-	
B & H	25	19	2	544	62	32.00	-	4	8	-	1247	836	24	34.83	5-31	1	
1-day Lge	88	75	11	1210	78 *	18.90	-	5	23	-	2736	2113	79	26.74	4-42	-	

16. Who registered his 100th first-class century by scoring 311* for Worcestershire v Warwickshire at Worcester in the 1982 County Championship?

BROWN, J. F.   Northamptonshire

Name: Jason Fred Brown
Role: Right-hand bat, off-spin bowler
Born: 10 October 1974,
Newcastle-under-Lyme
Height: 6ft **Weight:** 11st 7lbs
Nickname: Fish
County debut: 1996
1st-Class 5 w. in innings: 4
1st-Class 10 w. in match: 1
1st-Class catches: 4
Place in batting averages: (1998 298th
av. 3.00)
Place in bowling averages: (1998 30th
av. 22.00)
Strike rate: 89.50 (career 58.45)
Parents: Peter and Cynthia
Wife: Samantha
Education: St Josephs RC School,

Stoke-on-Trent; St Margaret Ward RC School, Stoke-on-Trent
Qualifications: 9 O-levels, Level 1 coach's course
Off-season: Working
Overseas tours: Kidsgrove League U18 to Australia 1990; Northants CCC to
Zimbabwe
Overseas teams played for: North East Valley, Dunedin, New Zealand
Cricketers particularly admired: John Emburey, Carl Hooper
Young players to look out for: Mark Powell, John Blain
Other sports played/followed: Golf, football
Relaxations: Music, videos, walking the dog ('Spike')
Extras: Represented Staffordshire at all junior levels and Staffordshire in Minor
Counties. Once took 10 for 16 in a Kidsgrove League game against Haslington U18
playing for Sandyford Under 18. Played for Staffordshire in the 1995 NatWest
competition
Best batting: 16* Northamptonshire v Durham, Northampton 1997
Best bowling: 6-53 Northamptonshire v Somerset, Taunton 1998

---

17. Which England batsman captained Worcestershire to their
first County Championship in 1964?

1999 Season

	M	Inns	NO	Runs	HS	Avge	100s	50s	Ct	St	O	M	Runs	Wkts	Avge	Best	5wI	10wM
Test																		
All First	1	1	0	8	8	8.00	-	-	-	-	29.5	8	64	2	32.00	2-64	-	-
1-day Int																		
NatWest																		
B & H																		
1-day Lge																		

Career Performances

	M	Inns	NO	Runs	HS	Avge	100s	50s	Ct	St	Balls	Runs	Wkts	Avge	Best	5wI	10wM
Test																	
All First	16	21	10	51	16 *	4.63	-	-	4	-	3215	1505	55	27.36	6-53	4	1
1-day Int																	
NatWest	1	0	0	0	0	-	-	-	-	-	72	72	1	72.00	1-72	-	
B & H																	
1-day Lge	1	0	0	0	0	-	-	-	-	-	42	26	4	6.50	4-26	-	

BROWN, M. J. Middlesex

Name: Michael James Brown
Role: Right-hand bat, right-arm off-spin bowler, occasional wicket-keeper
Born: 9 February 1980, Burnley
Height: 6ft **Weight:** 11st 4lbs
Nickname: Weasel, Weak, Richie Rich
County debut: 1999
1st-Class catches: 2
Parents: Peter and Valerie
Marital status: Single
Family links with cricket:
Father played for Burnley CC (Lancashire League) 1968-75 and 1979-98 and Lancashire 2nd XI 1970-72. Also played for Southgate CC 1976-78, winning National Club Knockout in 1977. Brother David plays for Lancashire Schools U16

Education: Rosehill Junior School, Burnley; Queen Elizabeth's Grammar School, Blackburn; Durham University
Qualifications: 10 GCSEs, 4 A-levels
Off-season: Studying Economics and Politics at Durham University

Overseas teams played for: Western Province CC, Cape Town 1998-99
Cricketers particularly admired: Dale Benkenstein, Justin Langer
Young players to look out for: Ed Joyce, James Anderson, David Brown
Other sports played: Golf, football
Other sports followed: Football (Burnley FC)
Injuries: Out for one week with shoulder injury; for two weeks with ankle injury
Relaxations: Listening to music
Extras: Opened batting for Burnley CC in Lancashire League 1995-98. Lancashire League Under-25 Batsman of the Season 1997, 1998. Represented Lancashire Schools at U11, U13, U15 and U17 level 1989-97. Represented Lancashire U19 Federation 1997-98. Played for Lancashire 2nd XI 1997-98. Represented ECB U19 A v Pakistan U19 in two one-day games 1998
Opinions on cricket: 'Too much cricket and not enough time for quality practice. More performance-based pay/salary to ensure every player stays on top of his game.'
Best batting: 24* Middlesex v Cambridge University, Fenner's 1999

1999 Season

	M	Inns	NO	Runs	HS	Avge	100s	50s	Ct	St	O	M	Runs	Wkts	Avge	Best	5wl	10wM
Test																		
All First	2	3	2	48	24 *	48.00	-	-	2	-								
1-day Int																		
NatWest																		
B & H																		
1-day Lge																		

Career Performances

	M	Inns	NO	Runs	HS	Avge	100s	50s	Ct	St	Balls	Runs	Wkts	Avge	Best	5wl	10wM
Test																	
All First	2	3	2	48	24 *	48.00	-	-	2	-							
1-day Int																	
NatWest																	
B & H																	
1-day Lge																	

BROWN, S. J. E.   Durham

Name: Simon John Emmerson Brown
Role: Right-hand bat, left-arm medium-fast bowler, gully fielder
Born: 29 June 1969, Cleadon Village, Sunderland
Height: 6ft 3in **Weight:** 13st
Nickname: Chubby

County debut: 1987 (Northamptonshire), 1992 (Durham)
County cap: 1998 (Durham)
Test debut: 1996
Tests: 1
50 wickets in a season: 6
1st-Class 50s: 2
1st-Class 5 w. in innings: 31
1st-Class 10 w. in match: 2
1st-Class catches: 39
One-Day 5 w. in innings: 2
Place in batting averages:
269th av. 10.66
Place in bowling averages: 41st av. 22.98
Strike rate: 45.23 (career 52.88)
Parents: Ernest and Doreen
Marital status: Single
Education: Cleadon Village Junior School;
Boldon Comprehensive, Tyne & Wear; South Tyneside Marine and Technical College
Qualifications: 6 O-levels, qualified electrician
Career outside cricket: Electrician
Overseas tours: England YC to Sri Lanka 1986-87, to Australia (Youth World Cup) 1987-88; MCC to Bahrain 1994-95
Overseas teams played for: Marist, Christchurch, New Zealand
Cricketers particularly admired: John Lever, Ian Botham, Dennis Lillee
Young players to look out for: Steve Harmison
Other sports played: Golf
Injuries: Out for two weeks with a groin injury
Relaxations: Playing golf
Extras: Offered basketball scholarship in America. Durham Supporters' Player of the Year 1992. Durham Player of the Year 1994. Took 6-25 v Worcestershire at Chester-le-Street 1999 in his first Championship match since September 1997
Best batting: 69 Durham v Leicestershire, Durham University 1994
Best bowling: 7-70 Durham v Australians, Durham University 1993

1999 Season

	M	Inns	NO	Runs	HS	Avge	100s	50s	Ct	St	O	M	Runs	Wkts	Avge	Best	5wl	10wM
Test																		
All First	15	23	8	160	29 *	10.66	-	-	3	-	475	112	1448	63	22.98	6-25	5	-
1-day Int																		
NatWest	1	1	0	8	8	8.00	-	-	-	-	10	2	31	1	31.00	1-31	-	
B & H																		
1-day Lge	4	2	0	4	4	2.00	-	-	2	-	26	3	138	2	69.00	1-30	-	

Career Performances

	M	Inns	NO	Runs	HS	Avge	100s	50s	Ct	St	Balls	Runs	Wkts	Avge	Best	5wI	10wM
Test	1	2	1	11	10 *	11.00	-	-	1	-	198	138	2	69.00	1-60	-	-
All First	140	195	58	1650	69	12.04	-	2	39	-	25279	14194	478	29.69	7-70	31	2
1-day Int																	
NatWest	11	7	3	20	8	5.00	-	-	1	-	700	481	19	25.31	5-22	1	
B & H	20	8	4	38	12	9.50	-	-	4	-	1091	654	28	23.35	6-30	1	
1-day Lge	76	36	12	156	18	6.50	-	-	17	-	3255	2724	81	33.62	4-20	-	

BRUNNSCHWEILER, I.   Hampshire

Name: Iain Brunnschweiler
Role: Right-hand bat, wicket-keeper
Born: 10 December 1979, Southampton
Height: 6ft **Weight:** 12st 7lbs
Nickname: Brunchy
County debut: No first-team appearance
Parents: Arthur and Joan
Marital status: Single
Family links with cricket: 'They mostly
dislike it!'
Education: Highfield C of E; King Edward
VI School, Southampton
Qualifications: 9 GCSEs, 3 A-levels, ECB
Level 1 cricket coaching award, UEFA Part B
football coaching award
Off-season: Grade cricket in Australia
Overseas tours: England U17 to Bermuda
1997; King Edward VI School to South
Africa 1998
Overseas teams played for: Belmont DCC, Newcastle, NSW 1998-99
Cricketers particularly admired: Robin Smith, Adi Aymes, Jack Russell, Ian Healy
Young players to look out for: Damien Sharazi, James Adams, Lawrence Prittipaul,
Charlie van der Gucht
Other sports played: Football (Southampton Youth), hockey, rugby
Other sports followed: Football (Southampton FC)
Injuries: Out for latter half of 1998-99 Australian season with broken jaw requiring
two titanium plates
Relaxations: *FIFA 2000* on PlayStation, kickboxing
Extras: 'Jaw was broken in practice game at Belmont by Jamie Heath, who has this
season broken into NSW's 1st XI and taken first-class wicket of Justin Langer
(Western Australia)'

Opinions on cricket: 'The introduction of floodlight games with music and fireworks is great, increasing enthusiasm and crowd numbers for the game. First-class/Test cricket should stay the same.'

BRYAN, R. B.   Middlesex

Name: Russell Barnaby Bryan
Role: Right-hand bat, right-arm medium-fast bowler
Born: 14 February 1981, Maidstone
Height: 6ft 2in **Weight:** 12st
County debut: No first-team appearance
Parents: Ann and Andrew
Marital status: Single
Family links with cricket: 'Father has played club cricket for 30-odd years and is still playing'
Education: Shebbear Primary School; Shebbear College; Brunel University
Qualifications: 10 GCSEs, 3 A-levels
Career outside cricket: Student
Off-season: University
Cricketers particularly admired: Darren Gough, Mark Ramprakash, Ian Botham, Allan Donald, Shoaib Akhtar, Justin Langer
Other sports played: Football, rugby, squash
Other sports followed: Football (Tottenham Hotspur FC)
Relaxations: Music, football, computer games, socialising
Extras: Represented Devon at U17 and U19 level in teams that reached both Texaco finals in 1998
Opinions on cricket: 'Don't get long enough for tea.'

1999 Season (did not make any first-class or one-day appearances)

Career Performances

	M	Inns	NO	Runs	HS	Avge	100s	50s	Ct	St	Balls	Runs	Wkts	Avge	Best	5wl	10wM
Test																	
All First																	
1-day Int																	
NatWest	1	0	0	0	0	-	-	-	-	-	24	21	0	-	-	-	-
B & H	.																
1-day Lge																	

BULBECK, M. P. L. Somerset

Name: Matthew Paul Leonard Bulbeck
Role: Left-hand bat, left-arm
medium-fast bowler
Born: 8 November 1979, Taunton
Height: 6ft 4in **Weight:** 12st 10lbs
Nickname: Bully
County debut: 1998
50 wickets in a season: 1
1st-Class 50s: 1
1st-Class 5 w. in innings: 3
1st-Class 10 w. in match: 1
1st-Class catches: 3
Place in batting averages: 48th av. 37.85
Place in bowling averages: 79th av. 28.54
(1998 10th av. 19.03)
Strike rate: 50.07 (career 41.95)
Parents: Paul and Carolyn
Marital status: Single
Family links with cricket: Father plays for local club. Sister plays women's cricket
for same club
Education: Bishops Hall Primary School; Castle School; Taunton School; Richard
Huish College
Qualifications: 8 GCSEs
Overseas tours: West of England U15 to West Indies; Somerset U16 to South Africa;
England U19 to New Zealand 1998-99
Cricketers particularly admired: Wasim Akram, Andy Caddick
Young players to look out for: Matthew Gitsham (Somerset U16)
Other sports played: Football (goalkeeper), golf (12 handicap)
Other sports followed: Football (Manchester United), rugby union (Bath RFC)
Relaxations: 'Going out for a drink with Dougie'
Extras: Went to Madras Pace Foundation and was coached by Dennis Lillee and Jeff
Thomson in September 1997. Represented England U19 in one-day and 'Test' series
v Australia U19 1999
Opinions on cricket: 'Should get longer for tea.'
Best batting: 76* Somerset v Durham, Chester-le-Street 1999
Best bowling: 5-45 Somerset v Northamptonshire, Northampton 1999

1999 Season

	M	Inns	NO	Runs	HS	Avge	100s	50s	Ct	St	O	M	Runs	Wkts	Avge	Best	5wI	10wM
Test																		
All First	15	15	8	265	76 *	37.85	-	1	1	-	425.4	101	1456	51	28.54	5-45	3	1
1-day Int																		
NatWest																		
B & H																		
1-day Lge	7	2	0	6	5	3.00	-	-	1	-	38	3	195	4	48.75	4-40	-	

Career Performances

	M	Inns	NO	Runs	HS	Avge	100s	50s	Ct	St	Balls	Runs	Wkts	Avge	Best	5wI	10wM
Test																	
All First	23	26	14	406	76 *	33.83	-	1	3	-	3482	2065	83	24.87	5-45	3	1
1-day Int																	
NatWest																	
B & H																	
1-day Lge	7	2	0	6	5	3.00	-	-	1	-	228	195	4	48.75	4-40	-	

BURNS, M.   Somerset

Name: Michael Burns
Role: Right-hand bat, right-arm medium bowler, occasional wicket-keeper
Born: 6 February 1969, Barrow-in-Furness
Height: 6ft **Weight:** 13st
Nickname: George, Ashley, Butch, Onslow
County debut: 1991 (Warwickshire), 1997 (Somerset)
County cap: 1999 (Somerset)
1st-Class 50s: 16
1st-Class 100s: 2
1st-Class catches: 76
1st-Class stumpings: 7
One-Day 100s: 1
Place in batting averages: 69th av. 35.19 (1998 129th av. 26.47)
Strike rate: 85.71 (career 90.00)
Parents: Robert and Linda, stepfather Stan
Wife and date of marriage: Carolyn, 9 October 1994
Children: Elizabeth, 12 January 1997
Family links with cricket: 'Grandfather was a great back-garden bowler'

Education: Walney Comprehensive; Barrow College of Further Education
Qualifications: 'Few CSEs, couple of GCEs', qualified fitter at VSEL in Barrow, coaching award
Career outside cricket: 'Would like to get involved in sports marketing'
Off-season: 'Working at the club; possibly going to Tasmania after Christmas'
Overseas teams played for: Gill College, South Africa 1991-92; Motueka, Nelson, New Zealand 1992-93; Alex CC, Harare
Cricketers particularly admired: Andy Caddick, Allan Donald
Young players to look out for: Matthew Bulbeck
Other sports played/followed: Rugby league ('had trials for Barrow RLFC and Carlisle RLFC') and golf
Relaxations: Golf, food. 'Just bought a new house, so a little bit of DIY'
Extras: Played for Cumberland 1989-90. Had a trial with Glamorgan, went to La Manga with Lancashire junior side 1984. Player of the Tournament at Benson and Hedges Thailand International Cricket Sixes in 1989. Left Warwickshire and joined Somerset for the 1997 season. Scored maiden first-class 100 (109) v Leicestershire at Taunton 1999. Awarded Somerset cap in 1999
Opinions on cricket: 'Clubs preparing slow, low wickets that are too flat should be docked points or put on report, as these are just as bad for the game as "ropey" wickets on which 15 wickets might fall in a day. These wickets are no preparation for Test cricket. I'm sure batsmen and bowlers would prefer wickets with pace and bounce, and it would also sort out the batters with better techniques who may progress on to Test cricket. These slow, low wickets are also very, very boring to play on, and I presume to watch, and seem to be the only wickets I get to bowl on.'
Best batting: 109 Somerset v Leicestershire, Taunton 1999
Best bowling: 2-18 Somerset v Kent, Taunton 1997

1999 Season

	M	Inns	NO	Runs	HS	Avge	100s	50s	Ct	St	O	M	Runs	Wkts	Avge	Best	5wI	10wM
Test																		
All First	19	27	1	915	109	35.19	2	5	11	-	100	18	365	7	52.14	2-46	-	-
1-day Int																		
NatWest	5	5	1	136	52 *	34.00	-	1	3	-	4	0	15	1	15.00	1-12	-	
B & H																		
1-day Lge	16	16	1	318	52	21.20	-	2	5	-	33.2	0	183	8	22.87	2-14	-	

18. In 1972, the top three in the Hampshire batting averages were a South African and two West Indians. Name them.

Career Performances

	M	Inns	NO	Runs	HS	Avge	100s	50s	Ct	St	Balls	Runs	Wkts	Avge	Best	5wI	10wM
Test																	
All First	63	99	4	2515	109	26.47	2	16	76	7	1080	704	12	58.66	2-18	-	-
1-day Int																	
NatWest	11	11	3	295	84 *	36.87	-	2	5	-	60	42	1	42.00	1-12	-	
B & H	17	15	0	486	95	32.40	-	5	7	2	148	125	7	17.85	3-18	-	
1-day Lge	78	72	7	1326	115 *	20.40	1	6	42	9	705	653	25	26.12	4-39	-	

BURNS, N. D. Leicestershire

Name: Neil David Burns
Role: Left-hand bat, wicket-keeper
Born: 19 September 1965, Chelmsford
Height: 5ft 10in **Weight:** 12st
Nickname: Burnsie, Ern, George
County debut: 1986 (Essex),
1987 (Somerset)
County cap: 1987 (Somerset)
1st-Class 50s: 26
1st-Class 100s: 5
1st-Class catches: 316
1st-Class stumpings: 32
Parents: Roy and Marie
Wife and date of marriage: Susan,
26 September 1987
Family links with cricket: Father played
club cricket for Finchley CC; brother Ian
captained Essex U19 and plays for
Chelmsford, MCC and Stock Exchange
Education: Mildmay Junior; Moulsham High School
Qualifications: 6 O-levels, advanced cricket coach
Career outside cricket: Neil Burns Company Ltd (NBC), specialising in sports
marketing and PR
Overseas tours: England YC to West Indies 1984-85; Essex to Barbados 1985-86;
Christians in Sport to India 1989-90
Overseas teams played for: Northerns/Goodwood, Cape Town 1984-87 and 1992;
Western Province B 1985-86
Cricketers particularly admired: Alan Knott, Bob Taylor, Rod Marsh, Graham
Gooch, Allan Border, Graeme Pollock, David Gower
Other sports followed: Most sports but particularly soccer (West Ham)
Relaxations: Watching/playing sport, reading newspapers, relaxing at home

Extras: Former schoolboy footballer with Tottenham Hotspur and Orient. Once took a hat-trick of stumpings off Nasser Hussain's leg-breaks for Essex U11 v Berkshire U11. Took eight stumpings in match v Kent 2nd XI at Dartford in 1984. Joined Somerset in 1987 after spending four years at Essex. Scored maiden first-class 100 v former county at Chelmsford 1988. Set one-day record of four stumpings in an innings v Kent in Sunday League 1991. Stumped Mike Roseberry off a wide bowled by Ken MacLeay at Lord's in 1992. Retired in 1994. Has also played for Bucks. Has joined Leicestershire for 2000 on a one-year contract
Best batting: 166 Somerset v Gloucestershire, Taunton 1990

1999 Season (did not make any first-class or one-day appearances)

Career Performances

	M	Inns	NO	Runs	HS	Avge	100s	50s	Ct	St	Balls	Runs	Wkts	Avge	Best	5wl	10wM
Test																	
All First	156	234	52	5349	166	29.39	5	26	316	32	3	8	0	-	-	-	-
1-day Int																	
NatWest	20	16	3	224	51	17.23	-	1	22	7							
B & H	32	25	9	441	51	27.56	-	1	29	6							
1-day Lge	103	81	22	1056	58	17.89	-	3	103	17							

BUTCHER, G. P. Surrey

Name: Gary Paul Butcher
Role: Right-hand middle-order bat, right-arm medium bowler
Born: 11 March 1975, Clapham, South London
Height: 5ft 9in **Weight:** 12st
Nickname: Butch
County debut: 1994 (Glamorgan), 1999 (Surrey)
1st-Class 50s: 10
1st-Class 100s: 1
1st-Class 5 w. in innings: 1
1st-Class catches: 18
Place in batting averages: 153rd av. 24.87 (1998 135th av. 25.91)
Place in bowling averages: (1998 78th av. 29.00)
Strike rate: 63.00 (career 59.35)
Parents: Alan and Elaine

Marital status: Girlfriend Roz

Family links with cricket: Brother Mark plays for Surrey and England. Father Alan played for Surrey, England, and captained Glamorgan. Uncle Ian played for Gloucestershire and Leicestershire. Uncle Martin played for Surrey

Education: Cumnor House Prep School, South Croydon; Riddlesdown Comprehensive; Heath Clark College

Qualifications: 5 GCSEs, BTEC 1st Diploma in Leisure Studies, badminton coaching award, cricket coaching award

Career outside cricket: 'Varies from off-season to off-season'

Off-season: Playing and training in Perth, Western Australia

Overseas tours: England U18 to Denmark 1993; England U19 to Sri Lanka 1993-94; Glamorgan to Zimbabwe 1995, to Pretoria 1996, to Jersey 1998

Overseas teams played for: Northern Natal, South Africa 1995-96; Hawkesbury Hawks, Sydney 1996-97

Cricketers particularly admired: Brian Lara, Malcolm Marshall, Viv Richards, Curtly Ambrose, Michael Holding, Steve Waugh, David Gower

Young players to look out for: Carl Greenidge

Other sports played: Football

Other sports followed: Football (Liverpool FC)

Relaxations: Music, playing bass guitar, spending time with friends

Extras: Took wicket with first ball on Sunday League debut 1994. Won Glamorgan's Most Improved Player Award 1996. Nominated for Young Player of the Year award 1996. Released by Glamorgan at end of 1998 season and joined Surrey for 1999. Played in two Championship-winning sides in three years (Glamorgan 1997; Surrey 1999)

Opinions on cricket: '1999 was a good year for competitive cricket in the Championship and CGU, although it is clear that a majority of pitches that are played on are woeful, so players are finding it harder to improve.'

Best batting: 101* Glamorgan v Oxford University, The Parks 1997

Best bowling: 7-77 Glamorgan v Gloucestershire, Bristol 1996

1999 Season

	M	Inns	NO	Runs	HS	Avge	100s	50s	Ct	St	O	M	Runs	Wkts	Avge	Best	5wl	10wM
Test																		
All First	5	8	0	199	70	24.87	-	2	2	-	21	4	77	2	38.50	1-19	-	-
1-day Int																		
NatWest																		
B & H																		
1-day Lge	6	6	2	119	34 *	29.75	-	-	1	-	13.3	0	103	1	103.00	1-27	-	

Career Performances

	M	Inns	NO	Runs	HS	Avge	100s	50s	Ct	St	Balls	Runs	Wkts	Avge	Best	5wI	10wM
Test																	
All First	45	66	10	1556	101 *	27.78	1	10	18	-	3324	2187	56	39.05	7-77	1	-
1-day Int																	
NatWest	4	3	1	77	48	38.50	-	-	-	-	-	120	122	4	30.50	2-33	-
B & H	13	10	3	58	17	8.28	-	-	1	-	199	172	4	43.00	2-21	-
1-day Lge	40	32	7	436	47	17.44	-	-	4	-	671	786	16	49.12	4-32	-

BUTCHER, M. A. Surrey

Name: Mark Alan Butcher
Role: Left-hand bat, right-arm medium bowler
Born: 23 August 1972, Croydon
Height: 5ft 11in **Weight:** 13st
Nickname: Butch, Baz
County debut: 1991
Test debut: 1997
Tests: 22
1000 runs in a season: 5
1st-Class 50s: 48
1st-Class 100s: 13
1st-Class 200s: 1
1st-Class catches: 128
Place in batting averages: 37th av. 39.88
(1998 94th av. 30.90)
Place in bowling averages: 64th av. 26.17
Strike rate: 63.52 (career 64.19)
Parents: Alan and Elaine
Wife and date of marriage: Judy, 4 October 1997
Children: Alita, 1999
Family links with cricket: Father Alan played for Glamorgan, Surrey and England
and is now coach with Surrey; brother Gary played for Glamorgan and is now with
Surrey; uncle Ian played for Gloucestershire and Leicestershire; uncle Martin played
for Surrey
Education: Cumnor House School; Trinity School; Archbishop Tenison's, Croydon
Qualifications: 5 O-levels, senior coaching award
Career outside cricket: Singer, guitar player
Off-season: Touring South Africa with England
Overseas tours: England YC to New Zealand 1990-91; Surrey to Dubai 1990 and
1993, to Perth 1995; England A to Australia 1996-97; England to West Indies 1997-98,
to Australia 1998-99, to South Africa 1999-2000

Overseas teams played for: South Melbourne, Australia 1993-94; North Perth 1994-95
Cricketers particularly admired: Ian Botham, David Gower, Viv Richards, Larry Gomes, Graham Thorpe, Alec Stewart, Michael Holding
Other sports followed: Football (Crystal Palace)
Relaxations: Music, playing the guitar, novels, wine
Extras: Played his first game for Surrey against his father's Glamorgan in the Refuge Assurance League at The Oval, the first-ever match of any sort between first-class counties in which a father and son have been in opposition. Made his maiden Test century v South Africa at Headingley in 1998, earning the Man of the Match award. Captained Surrey during Adam Hollioake's absence on World Cup duty 1999. His 259 v Leicestershire 1999 was the highest score by a left-hander at Grace Road and the fourth highest individual score recorded there overall. Captained England in third Test v New Zealand at Old Trafford 1999, deputising for Nasser Hussain who missed the match through injury. Performed with his star-studded Mark Butcher Band at the PCA awards dinner, Royal Albert Hall, September 1999
Opinions on cricket: 'Four-day games are constantly over in two and a half days because home teams understandably use their home advantage. Until surfaces are made to some specification that is centrally controlled, the situation will get worse. You can't produce great cricketers on crap surfaces.'
Best batting: 259 Surrey v Leicestershire, Leicester 1999
Best bowling: 4-30 Surrey v Lancashire, The Oval 1999

1999 Season

	M	Inns	NO	Runs	HS	Avge	100s	50s	Ct	St	O	M	Runs	Wkts	Avge	Best	5wl	10wM
Test	3	6	0	86	33	14.33	-	-	3	-	12	2	45	1	45.00	1-25	-	-
All First	16	28	1	1077	259	39.88	2	4	15	-	180	49	445	17	26.17	4-30	-	-
1-day Int																		
NatWest	4	4	1	98	54	32.66	-	1	-	-	11	1	69	2	34.50	1-15	-	
B & H	1	1	0	2	2	2.00	-	-	-	-	5	0	15	0	-		-	-
1-day Lge	12	12	0	323	44	26.91	-	-	4	-	30	3	142	2	71.00	1-7	-	

Career Performances

	M	Inns	NO	Runs	HS	Avge	100s	50s	Ct	St	Balls	Runs	Wkts	Avge	Best	5wl	10wM
Test	22	43	1	1087	116	25.88	2	4	21	-	264	128	1	128.00	1-25	-	-
All First	126	222	16	7753	259	37.63	14	48	128	-	6163	3302	96	34.39	4-30	-	-
1-day Int																	
NatWest	15	15	3	476	91	39.66	-	4	7	-	282	196	5	39.20	2-57	-	
B & H	23	19	4	366	67	24.40	-	1	7	-	480	396	7	56.57	3-37	-	
1-day Lge	73	60	13	1121	85 *	23.85	-	3	25	-	1717	1571	37	42.45	3-23	-	

BYAS, D.   Yorkshire

Name: David Byas
Role: Left-hand bat, right-arm medium
bowler, county captain
Born: 26 August 1963, Middledale, Kilham
Height: 6ft 4in **Weight:** 14st 7lbs
Nickname: Bingo, Gadgett
County debut: 1986
County cap: 1991
1000 runs in a season: 5
1st-Class 50s: 75
1st-Class 100s: 23
1st-Class 200s: 1
1st-Class catches: 291
One-Day 100s: 5
Place in batting averages: 127th av. 27.34
(1998 91st av. 31.18)
Strike rate: (career 91.00)
Parents: Richard and Anne

Wife and date of marriage: Rachael Elizabeth, 26 October 1990
Children: Olivia Rachael, 16 December 1991; Georgia Elizabeth, 30 December 1993;
Benjamin, 1997
Family links with cricket: Father played local league
Education: Kilham Primary School; Lisvane School, Scarborough; Scarborough
College
Qualifications: 1 O-level (Engineering)
Career outside cricket: Partner in family farming business
Off-season: Farming
Overseas teams played for: Papatoetoe, Auckland 1988-89
Cricketers particularly admired: David Gower, Viv Richards, Ian Botham
Young players to look out for: Matthew Wood, Anthony McGrath, Matthew
Hoggard, Ryan Sidebottom
Other sports played: Hockey ('way back in my youth')
Other sports followed: Most other sports
Relaxations: 'Gardening and eating out with my wife and family. Spending time with
the family'
Extras: Became youngest captain (aged 21) of Scarborough CC in 1985. Broke John
Hampshire's Sunday League record with 702 runs in 1994, which had stood since
1976. Runner-up in the Sunday League averages 1994. Played hockey for Young
England (U21) in the European Cup in Portugal. Captain of Yorkshire since 1996.
Granted a benefit for 2000
Opinions on cricket: 'I believe that the two division system is excellent. However, to

win, you should be rewarded with the points of last year [1998] – too big a reward for drawing a game. Pitches have got to improve all over the country.'

Best batting: 213 Yorkshire v Worcestershire, Scarborough 1995
Best bowling: 3-55 Yorkshire v Derbyshire, Chesterfield 1990

1999 Season

	M	Inns	NO	Runs	HS	Avge	100s	50s	Ct	St	O	M	Runs	Wkts	Avge	Best	5wI	10wM
Test																		
All First	17	34	2	875	95	27.34	-	8	24	-								
1-day Int																		
NatWest	4	4	1	170	72	56.66	-	2	2	-								
B & H	3	3	1	134	104 *	67.00	1	-	-	-								
1-day Lge	16	16	2	417	87	29.78	-	2	9	-								

Career Performances

	M	Inns	NO	Runs	HS	Avge	100s	50s	Ct	St	Balls	Runs	Wkts	Avge	Best	5wI	10wM
Test																	
All First	235	399	35	12949	213	35.57	24	75	291	-	1092	719	12	59.91	3-55	-	-
1-day Int																	
NatWest	29	27	3	820	73 *	34.16	-	8	19	-	18	23	1	23.00	1-23	-	
B & H	45	42	4	1206	116 *	31.73	2	5	12	-	283	155	5	31.00	2-38	-	
1-day Lge	189	183	27	4775	111 *	30.60	3	25	67	-	529	463	19	24.36	3-19	-	

---

19. For how many seasons did W.S. Surridge captain Surrey in the 1950s and how many Championships did the county win under his leadership?

CADDICK, A. R.   Somerset

Name: Andrew Richard Caddick
Role: Right-hand bat, right-arm
fast-medium bowler
Born: 21 November 1968, Christchurch,
New Zealand
Height: 6ft 5in **Weight:** 14st 13lbs
Nickname: Des, Shack
County debut: 1991
County cap: 1992
Benefit: 1999
Test debut: 1993
Tests: 25
One-Day Internationals: 9
50 wickets in a season: 6
100 wickets in a season: 1
1st-Class 50s: 5
1st-Class 5 w. in innings: 42
1st-Class 10 w. in match: 11
1st-Class catches: 51
One-Day 5 w. in innings: 3

Place in batting averages: 220th av. 18.38 (1998 206th av. 18.94)
Place in bowling averages: 23rd av. 20.87 (1998 14th av. 19.82)
Strike rate: 50.36 (career 49.38)
Parents: Christopher and Audrey
Wife and date of marriage: Sarah, 27 January 1995
Children: Ashton Faye, 24 August 1998
Education: Papanui High School, Christchurch, New Zealand
Qualifications: Qualified plasterer and tiler
Career outside cricket: Plasterer and tiler
Off-season: England tour to South Africa and Zimbabwe
Overseas tours: New Zealand YC to Australia (Youth World Cup) 1987-88, to
England 1988; England A to Australia 1992-93; England to West Indies 1993-94,
to Zimbabwe and New Zealand 1996-97, to West Indies 1997-98, to South Africa and
Zimbabwe 1999-2000
Cricketers particularly admired: Dennis Lillee, Richard Hadlee, Robin Smith,
Jimmy Cook
Players to look out for: Nasser Hussain, Nick Knight, Marcus Trescothick
Other sports followed: 'Mostly all'
Relaxations: Golf
Extras: Rapid Cricketline Player of the Year 1991. Whyte and Mackay Bowler of the
Year 1997. Took 105 first-class wickets in 1998 season. Leading wicket-taker in the

single-division four-day era of the County Championship with 422 wickets (av. 22.48) 1993-99

Opinions on cricket: 'Due to the structure change in all forms of county cricket, it's great to see competitive cricket still being played in September.'

Best batting: 92 Somerset v Worcestershire, Worcester 1995

Best bowling: 9-32 Somerset v Lancashire, Taunton 1993

Stop press: Returned 7-46, his best Test figures, in South Africa's first innings of the third Test at Durban, December 1999; shared Man of the Match award with Gary Kirsten. Awarded England contract (Band A) for 2000

1999 Season

	M	Inns	NO	Runs	HS	Avge	100s	50s	Ct	St	O	M	Runs	Wkts	Avge	Best	5wI	10wM
Test	4	6	0	126	45	21.00	-	-	5	-	174.1	62	412	20	20.60	5-32	1	-
All First	17	23	5	331	45	18.38	-	-	7	-	763.5	249	1900	91	20.87	8-113	5	-
1-day Int																		
NatWest	5	2	1	1	1	1.00	-	-	2	-	50	12	141	7	20.14	3-21	-	
B & H																		
1-day Lge	13	7	3	32	13*	8.00	-	-	1	-	105	19	325	12	27.08	3-16	-	

Career Performances

	M	Inns	NO	Runs	HS	Avge	100s	50s	Ct	St	Balls	Runs	Wkts	Avge	Best	5wI	10wM
Test	25	39	4	417	45	11.91	-	-	13	-	5655	2806	94	29.85	6-65	6	-
All First	145	190	36	2485	92	16.13	-	5	51	-	31308	15859	634	25.01	9-32	42	11
1-day Int	9	5	4	35	20*	35.00	-	-	2	-	522	398	15	26.53	3-35	-	
NatWest	21	11	4	29	8	4.14	-	-	4	-	1280	677	41	16.51	6-30	2	
B & H	21	14	8	124	38	20.66	-	-	4	-	1203	829	30	27.63	5-51	1	
1-day Lge	87	33	11	258	39	11.72	-	-	14	-	3765	2784	109	25.54	4-18	-	

20. Who were the first winners of the officially constituted County Championship in 1890?

CARBERRY, M. A.   Surrey

Name: Michael Alexander Carberry
Role: Left-hand bat, right-arm off-spin
bowler
Born: 29 September 1980, Croydon
Height: 6ft **Weight:** 12st 7lbs
Nickname: Carbs
County debut: No first-team appearance
Parents: Maria and Neville
Marital status: Single
Family links with cricket: 'My dad played
league cricket during the 1970s and 1980s'
Education: Winterbourne Boys School; St
John Rigby RC College
Qualifications: 10 GCSEs, 1 AS-level
Off-season: England U19 tour to Malaysia
and to Sri Lanka for the Youth World Cup
Overseas tours: Surrey U17 to South Africa
1997; England U19 to New Zealand 1998-99,
to Malaysia and (Youth World Cup) Sri Lanka 1999-2000

Cricketers particularly admired: Alec Stewart, Ricky Ponting, Graham Thorpe,
Brian Lara, Saurav Ganguly
Young players to look out for: Carl Greenidge, Michael Gough, Gareth Batty,
Paul Franks
Other sports played: Basketball, football
Other sports followed: Football (Tottenham Hotspur)
Relaxations: 'Listening to music, going nightclubbing with my friends, playing for
my dad's team (Old Castletonians) on a Sunday'
Extras: Second schoolboy to score a century for Croydon U13 since Ali Brown.
Scored century (126*) for ECB U18 v Pakistan U19 at Abergavenny 1998. Scored his
first Surrey 2nd XI century v Lancashire. Represented England U19 in one-day and
'Test' series v Australia U19 1999, scoring 50 in the third 'Test' at Chester-le-Street.
Played for Surrey Board XI in 1999 NatWest
Opinions on cricket: 'Putting young players onto the full international stage and
sticking with them. Allowing young players to play their natural game at the top level
and working on their weaknesses. Getting the more senior players to work alongside
younger players, so that they are passing on their knowledge.'

Career Performances

	M	Inns	NO	Runs	HS	Avge	100s	50s	Ct	St	Balls	Runs	Wkts	Avge	Best	5wl	10wM
Test																	
All First																	
1-day Int																	
NatWest	2	2	0	23	19	11.50	-	-	-	-							
B & H																	
1-day Lge																	

CARPENTER, J. R. Sussex

Name: James Robert Carpenter
Role: Left-hand bat, slow left-arm bowler
Born: 20 October 1975, Birkenhead
Height: 6ft 1in **Weight:** 13st
Nickname: Carps
County debut: 1997
1st-Class 50s: 2
1st-Class catches: 5
Place in batting averages: (1998 252nd av. 13.87)
Strike rate: (career 129.00)
Parents: John and Jo
Marital status: Single
Family links with cricket: Father played Minor Counties cricket for Cheshire
Education: Gayton Primary School; Birkenhead School
Qualifications: 9 GCSEs and 4 A-levels
Off-season: Playing in Sydney after Christmas
Overseas teams played for: Randwick CC, Sydney, Australia 1996-99
Cricketers particularly admired: Ian Botham, Allan Border, Steve Waugh
Young players to look out for: Brett Lee (Mosman CC, New South Wales), Jamie Keggin (Bootle CC), Adam Warren
Other sports played: Played county schools rugby for Cheshire and schoolboy football with Liverpool FC. Had schoolboy forms with Everton and trials with Bolton Wanderers. Played football for Runcorn FC in Vauxhall Conference
Relaxations: Golf and 'lying on Coogee beach, Sydney, in the off-season'
Extras: Captained MCC Young Professionals at Lord's. *Daily Telegraph* Bowling Award. Awarded the Wetherall Trophy by the Cricket Society for the year's

outstanding schoolboy cricketer. Leading catcher in AXA League for 1998 season

Opinions on cricket: 'Two divisions makes the cricket more competitive and more exciting for the public. More floodlit cricket should be encouraged to attract younger audience.'

Best batting: 65 Sussex v Nottinghamshire, Trent Bridge 1998
Best bowling: 1-50 Sussex v Nottinghamshire, Hove 1997

1999 Season

	M	Inns	NO	Runs	HS	Avge	100s	50s	Ct	St	O	M	Runs	Wkts	Avge	Best	5wI	10wM
Test																		
All First																		
1-day Int																		
NatWest	1	1	0	55	55	55.00	-	1	-	-								
B & H	2	2	0	56	45	28.00	-	-	-	-								
1-day Lge	14	9	3	183	64 *	30.50	-	2	4	-								

Career Performances

	M	Inns	NO	Runs	HS	Avge	100s	50s	Ct	St	Balls	Runs	Wkts	Avge	Best	5wI	10wM
Test																	
All First	12	22	0	375	65	17.04	-	2	5	-	129	81	1	81.00	1-50	-	-
1-day Int																	
NatWest	1	1	0	55	55	55.00	-	1	-	-							
B & H	5	5	1	101	45	25.25	-	-	1	-							
1-day Lge	32	25	7	419	64 *	23.27	-	3	19	-	6	15	0	-		-	-

CASSAR, M. E.   Derbyshire

Name: Matthew Edward Cassar
Role: Right-hand bat, right-arm medium bowler, occasional wicket-keeper
Born: 16 October 1972, Sydney, Australia
Height: 6ft **Weight:** 13st 7lbs
Nickname: Chachie
County debut: 1994
1st-Class 50s: 8
1st-Class 100s: 1
1st-Class 5 w. in innings: 1
1st-Class catches: 13
One-Day 100s: 3
Place in batting averages: 214th av. 18.71 (1998 121st av. 27.23)
Place in bowling averages: 91st av. 29.57 (1998 143rd av. 61.40)
Strike rate: 51.78 (career 57.06)

Parents: Edward and Joan
Wife and date of marriage: Jane, 5 October 1996
Family links with cricket: Wife, Jane, is the England Women's wicket-keeper
Education: Punchbowl Primary School, Sydney; Sir Joseph Banks High School, Sydney; Manchester Metropolitan University
Qualifications: School certificate and senior coaching award
Off-season: 'Playing for Petersham/Marrickville in Sydney; working hard on my game and fitness'
Overseas teams played for: Petersham/Marrickville, Sydney 1988-95, 1999-2000
Cricketers particularly admired: Jane
Young players to look out for: Adrian Rollins, Ian Blackwell, Robin Weston, Trevor Smith, 'and me'
Other sports played: Golf, squash, tennis
Other sports followed: Football (Derby County)
Relaxations: Playing social sports, listening to music, going to the cinema
Extras: Played for New South Wales Colts
Opinions on cricket: 'To improve the standard of pitches, groundsmen should be employed by the ECB and not the counties. I like the new two-divisional structure, as I think it does produce more competitive cricket. One overseas player per team is the right balance, because whilst playing with and against the best players in the world is of great benefit, I would hate to see cricket go the same way as football has in this country.'
Best batting: 121 Derbyshire v Sussex, Horsham 1998
Best bowling: 5-51 Derbyshire v Essex, Chelmsford 1999

---

21. Which two batsmen scored unbeaten double centuries in compiling a then world record second-wicket stand of 465* for Warwickshire v Gloucestershire at Edgbaston in 1974?

1999 Season

	M	Inns	NO	Runs	HS	Avge	100s	50s	Ct	St	O	M	Runs	Wkts	Avge	Best	5wI	10wM
Test																		
All First	14	24	3	393	42	18.71	-	-	5	-	164	34	562	19	29.57	5-51	1	-
1-day Int																		
NatWest	1	1	0	57	57	57.00	-	1	-	-	7	1	31	1	31.00	1-31	-	
B & H																		
1-day Lge	14	14	0	377	109	26.92	2	1	6	-	61.4	1	338	11	30.72	4-31	-	

Career Performances

	M	Inns	NO	Runs	HS	Avge	100s	50s	Ct	St	Balls	Runs	Wkts	Avge	Best	5wI	10wM
Test																	
All First	41	67	9	1462	121	25.20	1	8	13	-	2568	1585	45	35.22	5-51	1	-
1-day Int																	
NatWest	6	6	1	175	90 *	35.00	-	2	-	-	78	63	1	63.00	1-31	-	
B & H																	
1-day Lge	29	28	3	760	134	30.40	3	3	11	-	448	434	14	31.00	4-31	-	

CATTERALL, D. N. Worcestershire

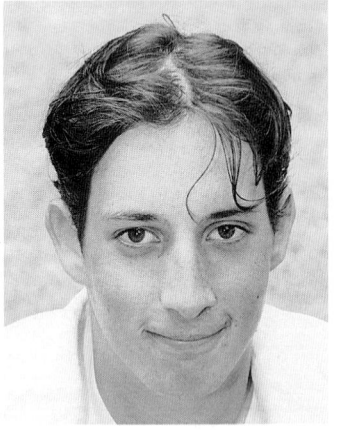

Name: Duncan Neil Catterall
Role: Right-hand bat, right-arm
medium-fast bowler
Born: 19 September 1978, Preston
Height: 5ft 11in **Weight:** 12st 2lbs
Nickname: Cats
County debut: 1998
1st-Class 50s: 2
Strike rate: 55.20 (career 70.80)
Parents: David and Christine
Marital status: Single
Family links with cricket: Brother plays and
father played for Leyland DAF in the
Northern League
Education: Horncliffe School, Blackburn;
Queen Elizabeth's Grammar School,
Blackburn; Loughborough University
Qualifications: 11 GCSEs and 4 A-levels
Off-season: Playing for Manly CC in Australia
Overseas tours: Queen Elizabeth's Grammar School to Australia, December 1996
Overseas teams played for: Manly CC, Sydney 1999-2000

Cricketers particularly admired: Steve Waugh
Young players to look out for: Kabir Ali
Other sports followed: Football (Preston North End)
Injuries: Out for three weeks with a broken finger; for six weeks with a side strain
Relaxations: Music, socialising
Extras: Represented England Schools U19 in 1998
Opinions on cricket: 'Night cricket needs to be increased to bring in more crowds and generate interest.'
Best batting: 60 Worcestershire v Middlesex, Worcester 1999
Best bowling: 2-16 Worcestershire v Essex, Chelmsford 1999

1999 Season

	M	Inns	NO	Runs	HS	Avge	100s	50s	Ct	St	O	M	Runs	Wkts	Avge	Best	5wI	10wM
Test																		
All First	2	3	0	132	60	44.00	-	2	-	-	46	10	185	5	37.00	2-16	-	-
1-day Int																		
NatWest																		
B & H																			
1-day Lge	4	1	0	0	0	0.00	-	-	-	-	30	2	125	2	62.50	2-35	-	

Career Performances

	M	Inns	NO	Runs	HS	Avge	100s	50s	Ct	St	Balls	Runs	Wkts	Avge	Best	5wI	10wM
Test																	
All First	3	4	0	132	60	33.00	-	2	-	-	354	216	5	43.20	2-16	-	-
1-day Int																	
NatWest																	
B & H																	
1-day Lge	7	3	1	16	11 *	8.00	-	-	1	-	258	175	3	58.33	2-35	-	

22. Who captained Yorkshire to their first County Championship in 1893?

CAWDRON, M. J. Gloucestershire

Name: Michael John Cawdron
Role: Left-hand bat, right-arm
medium-fast bowler
Born: 7 October 1974, Luton
Height: 6ft 3in **Weight:** 13st 7lbs
Nickname: Muscles
County debut: 1995 (one-day),
1999 (first-class)
1st-Class 5 w. in innings: 3
1st-Class catches: 1
Place in batting averages: 223rd av. 18.00
Place in bowling averages: 7th av. 16.62
Strike rate: 38.18 (career 38.18)
Parents: William and Mandy
Marital status: Single
Family links with cricket: Father and
brother played local village cricket
Education: Cheltenham College
Qualifications: 10 GCSEs, 3 A-Levels, NCA coaching award
Overseas tours: West of England U14 to Holland; Cheltenham College to Zimbabwe
1992; Gloucestershire YC to Sri Lanka 1993-94; Gloucestershire Gypsies to
Zimbabwe 1994-95; Gloucestershire Gypsies to Cape Town 1997; Christians in Sport
to Zimbabwe 1998
Cricketers particularly admired: Ben Gannon – 'the world's best lodger!!'
Young players to look out for: S. Pope
Other sports followed: Rugby, hockey, rackets, clay-pigeon shooting, golf
Relaxations: Cinema, videos, eating and going out with friends
Extras: Winner of the *Daily Telegraph* Regional Bowling Award 1993. Captain of
MCC Schools and ESCA U19, 1993. 'Made 50 off 32 balls on Sunday League debut
against Essex at my old school' (Cheltenham College). Scored 42 and took 5-35 on
first-class debut, v Hampshire at Bristol 1999; went on to take two more five-wicket
hauls in his next two Championship games
Opinions on cricket: 'Twelve-month contracts would be of great benefit to those
players who do not wish to winter abroad, as work opportunities are not secure, as
other employers are not eager to take on people on such a temporary basis.'
Best batting: 42 Gloucestershire v Hampshire, Bristol 1999
Best bowling: 5-35 Gloucestershire v Hampshire, Bristol 1999

1999 Season

	M	Inns	NO	Runs	HS	Avge	100s	50s	Ct	St	O	M	Runs	Wkts	Avge	Best	5wl	10wM
Test																		
All First	6	9	2	126	42	18.00	-	-	1	-	101.5	30	266	16	16.62	5-35	3	-
1-day Int																		
NatWest	5	2	2	0	0 *	-	-	-	1	-	36	0	184	6	30.66	4-34	-	
B & H	2	1	1	2	2 *	-	-	-	-	-	13.1	1	80	3	26.66	3-42	-	
1-day Lge	8	5	2	23	11 *	7.66	-	-	1	-	46	2	225	10	22.50	4-17	-	

Career Performances

	M	Inns	NO	Runs	HS	Avge	100s	50s	Ct	St	Balls	Runs	Wkts	Avge	Best	5wl	10wM
Test																	
All First	6	9	2	126	42	18.00	-	-	1	-	611	266	16	16.62	5-35	3	-
1-day Int																	
NatWest	5	2	2	0	0 *	-	-	-	1	-	216	184	6	30.66	4-34	-	
B & H	5	2	2	7	5 *	-	-	-	-	-	205	183	10	18.30	4-28	-	
1-day Lge	22	14	5	177	50	19.66	-	1	3	-	714	595	16	37.18	4-17	-	

CHAPMAN, S.   Durham

Name: Steven Chapman
Role: Right-hand middle-order bat, slow left-arm bowler
Born: 2 October 1971, Crook, County Durham
Height: 6ft 4in **Weight:** 16st 5lbs
Nickname: Chappie, Dr Chaplaw
County debut: 1998
1st-Class catches: 3
Strike rate: 84.00 (career 258.00)
Parents: Elizabeth and Roy
Marital status: Single
Family links with cricket: Parents are keen spectators. No playing relatives.
Education: Crook Primary; Willington Parkside Comprehensive
Qualifications: 9 GCSEs, senior cricket coach
Career outside cricket: Groundsmanship (cricket/football)
Overseas teams played for: Roodepoort, Johannesburg 1993; Riversdale, Trinidad 1994; Hallam, Melbourne 1996-99

Cricketers particularly admired: Jimmy Adams, Clint Yorke (Trinidad),
Mark Taylor, Paul Furby (Bishop Auckland)
Young players to look out for: Gary Peatt, Chris Hewison (Durham Academy)
Other sports played: Chung do kwan, taekwondo
Other sports followed: Football (Man Utd, Middlesbrough)
Relaxations: Languages, reading
Extras: Plays for Bishop Auckland CC. Released by Durham at end of 1999 season
Opinions on cricket: 'World Cup every two years.'
Best batting: 32 Durham v Glamorgan, Cardiff 1999
Best bowling: 1-49 Durham v Glamorgan, Cardiff 1999

1999 Season

	M	Inns	NO	Runs	HS	Avge	100s	50s	Ct	St	O	M	Runs	Wkts	Avge	Best	5wl	10wM
Test																		
All First	2	4	1	67	32	22.33	-	-	3	-	14	1	60	1	60.00	1-49	-	-
1-day Int																		
NatWest																			
B & H																			
1-day Lge	1	1	0	30	30	30.00	-	-	1	-	5	0	22	1	22.00	1-22	-	

Career Performances

	M	Inns	NO	Runs	HS	Avge	100s	50s	Ct	St	Balls	Runs	Wkts	Avge	Best	5wl	10wM
Test																	
All First	3	6	1	80	32	16.00	-	-	3	-	258	139	1	139.00	1-49	-	-
1-day Int																	
NatWest																	
B & H																	
1-day Lge	3	3	0	47	30	15.66	-	-	2	-	114	114	3	38.00	2-57	-	

CHAPPLE, G.   Lancashire

Name: Glen Chapple
Role: Right-hand bat, right-arm medium-fast bowler
Born: 23 January 1974, Skipton, Yorkshire
Height: 6ft 2in **Weight:** 12st 7lbs
Nickname: Chappy, Boris, Boomor, Cheeky
County debut: 1992
50 wickets in a season: 2
1st-Class 50s: 6
1st-Class 100s: 1
1st-Class 5 w. in innings: 10

1st-Class catches: 33
One-Day 5 w. in innings: 4
Place in batting averages: 149th av. 25.12
(1998 208th av. 18.80)
Place in bowling averages: 134th av. 40.16
(1998 26th av. 21.40)
Strike rate: 84.50 (career 57.31)
Parents: Eileen and Michael
Marital status: Single
Family links with cricket: Father played in
Lancashire League for Nelson and was a
professional for Darwen and Earby
Education: West Craven High School;
Nelson and Colne College
Qualifications: 8 GCSEs, 2 A-levels
(Geography and Economics)
Overseas tours: England U18 to Canada
1991; England YC to New Zealand 1990-91,
to Pakistan 1991-92, to India 1992-93; England A to India 1994-95,
to Australia 1996-97
Cricketers particularly admired: Dennis Lillee, Robin Smith
Other sports followed: Football (Liverpool), golf
Relaxations: 'Watching films, cinema, music, socialising'
Extras: Set record for fastest century in first-class cricket (21 minutes; against
declaration bowling) v Glamorgan at Old Trafford 1993. Man of the Match in the 1996
NatWest final against Essex after taking 6 for 18
Best batting: 109* Lancashire v Glamorgan, Old Trafford 1993
Best bowling: 6-48 Lancashire v Durham, Stockton 1994

1999 Season

	M	Inns	NO	Runs	HS	Avge	100s	50s	Ct	St	O	M	Runs	Wkts	Avge	Best	5wI	10wM
Test																		
All First	13	18	2	402	83	25.12	-	2	2	-	338	92	964	24	40.16	5-92	1	-
1-day Int																		
NatWest	2	1	0	7	7	7.00	-	-	1	-	18	1	73	3	24.33	3-41	-	
B & H	1	1	0	11	11	11.00	-	-	-	-	4	0	33	0	-		-	-
1-day Lge	12	3	0	24	12	8.00	-	-	5	-	86.2	4	433	12	36.08	3-34	-	

Career Performances

	M	Inns	NO	Runs	HS	Avge	100s	50s	Ct	St	Balls	Runs	Wkts	Avge	Best	5wI	10wM
Test																	
All First	101	138	43	2070	109 *	21.78	1	6	33	-	16162	8376	282	29.70	6-48	10	-
1-day Int																	
NatWest	15	8	1	20	7	2.85	-	-	5	-	804	581	23	25.26	6-18	2	
B & H	21	9	5	37	11	9.25	-	-	5	-	1072	844	26	32.46	5-7	1	
1-day Lge	77	27	11	179	43	11.18	-	-	17	-	2916	2349	81	29.00	6-25	1	

CHERRY, D. D.　　　　　　　　　Glamorgan

Name: Daniel David Cherry
Role: Left-hand bat, right-arm
medium bowler
Born: 7 February 1980, Newport
Height: 5ft 9in **Weight:** 13st
Nickname: Rhino, Banners
County debut: 1998
Parents: David and Elizabeth
Marital status: Single
Family links with cricket: Dad is a qualified
coach and played club cricket
Education: Feltonfleet Prep School,
Cobham, Surrey; Tonbridge School, Kent;
University of Wales, Swansea
Qualifications: 10 GCSEs, 3 A-levels
Career outside cricket: Student
Off-season: 'University'
Overseas tours: Tonbridge School to
Australia 1996-97
Cricketers particularly admired: Michael Atherton, Graham Thorpe,
Steve James
Young players to look out for: Wayne Law, Mark Wallace, David Harrison,
Simon Jones
Other sports played: Rugby, rackets (Public Schools doubles champion)
Other sports followed: Rugby (Wales), football (Everton)
Relaxations: Listening to music, reading; 'drinking and cavorting at university, *Daily
Telegraph* crosswords (with help of Owen Parkin)'
Extras: Played for ECB U19 XI v Pakistan U19 1998
Opinions on cricket: '2nd XI cricket should be played on first-class grounds.'
Best batting: 11 Glamorgan v Derbyshire, Cardiff 1998

1999 Season (did not make any first-class or one-day appearances)

Career Performances

	M	Inns	NO	Runs	HS	Avge	100s	50s	Ct	St	Balls	Runs	Wkts	Avge	Best	5wl	10wM
Test																	
All First	1	1	0	11	11	11.00	-	-	-	-							
1-day Int																	
NatWest																	
B & H																	
1-day Lge																	

CHILTON, M. J.   Lancashire

Name: Mark James Chilton
Role: Right-hand top-order bat, right-arm
medium bowler
Born: 2 October 1976, Sheffield
Height: 6ft 3in **Weight:** 12st 8lbs
Nickname: Chill, Chinny, Prof
County debut: 1997
1st-Class 50s: 4
1st-Class 100s: 2
1st-Class catches: 21
One-Day 5 w. in innings: 1
Place in batting averages: 103rd av. 30.62
(1998 130th av. 26.33)
Strike rate: 75.00 (career 129.00)
Parents: Jim and Sue
Marital status: Single
Family links with cricket: Father played
local cricket
Education: Brooklands Primary School; Manchester Grammar School; Durham
University
Qualifications: 10 GCSEs, 3 A-levels, BA (Hons) Business Economics, senior
coaching award
Off-season: 12-month contract at Lancashire
Overseas tours: Manchester Grammar School to Barbados 1993-94, to South Africa
1995-96; Durham University to Zimbabwe 1997-98
Cricketers particularly admired: Alec Stewart, Michael Atherton
Young players to look out for: Stuart Adamson, Jon Humphreys
Other sports played: Golf, tennis
Other sports followed: Football (Manchester United)

Relaxations: Music ('any type'), eating out, 'a good video'
Extras: Represented England U14, U15, U17. Played for North of England v New Zealand U19 in 1996. Awarded England U15 Batsman of the Year in 1992. Played for British Universities in 1997 Benson and Hedges Cup, winning the Gold Award against Sussex. Played for Lancashire in the first day/night game held in Britain. Awarded 2nd XI cap 1998. Scored maiden first-class century (106*) v Cambridge University at Fenner's on 9 April 1999, setting new record for the earliest ever 100 in a first-class cricket season in this country; followed up with maiden Championship century v Northants at Old Trafford 1999
Opinions on cricket: 'The new 12-month contracts at Lancashire are a good thing. They allow players to consider other options apart from cricket.'
Best batting: 106* Lancashire v Cambridge University, Fenner's 1999
Best bowling: 1-1 Lancashire v Sri Lanka A, Old Trafford 1999

1999 Season

	M	Inns	NO	Runs	HS	Avge	100s	50s	Ct	St	O	M	Runs	Wkts	Avge	Best	5wl	10wM
Test																		
All First	18	30	3	827	106 *	30.62	2	4	21	-	25	9	62	2	31.00	1-1	-	-
1-day Int																		
NatWest	2	2	0	71	50	35.50	-	1	-	-	7	0	42	2	21.00	1-20	-	
B & H	1	1	0	25	25	25.00	-	-	-	-								
1-day Lge	7	7	0	141	44	20.14	-	-	1	-	11	0	65	4	16.25	3-41	-	

Career Performances

	M	Inns	NO	Runs	HS	Avge	100s	50s	Ct	St	Balls	Runs	Wkts	Avge	Best	5wl	10wM
Test																	
All First	22	37	3	994	106 *	29.23	2	4	21	-	258	133	2	66.50	1-1	-	-
1-day Int																	
NatWest	3	3	0	112	50	37.33	-	1	2	-	42	42	2	21.00	1-20	-	
B & H	11	11	1	297	56	29.70	-	2	4	-	369	316	14	22.57	5-26	1	
1-day Lge	13	12	0	192	44	16.00	-	-	2	-	174	170	7	24.28	3-41	-	

CLAPP, D. A.   Sussex

Name: Dominic Adrian Clapp
Role: Right-hand bat, right-arm medium bowler
Born: 25 May 1980, Southport, Merseyside
Height: 6 ft **Weight:** 13st 7lbs
Nickname: Hans, Poppa, Gruber
County debut: No first-team appearance
Parents: Adrian and Sarah

Marital status: Single
Family links with cricket: Brother plays for his local club side, Broadwater
Education: Sompting Abbotts Prep School; Lancing College; Worthing Sixth Form College
Qualifications: 6 GCSEs, 1 A-level, Level 1 and 2 cricket coach
Career outside cricket: Coaching/journalism
Off-season: 'Working hard on my fitness; also working on my technique in the nets; touring with Sussex Martlets to Australia in February 2000'
Overseas tours: Sussex U14 to Jersey 1994; Lancing College to Australia 1996; Sussex U19 to Barbados 1997
Cricketers particularly admired: Jacques Kallis, Steve Waugh, Brian Lara, Mike Atherton, Chris Adams, Richard Montgomerie, Ricky Ponting
Young players to look out for: Ian Bell, Matthew Prior
Other sports played: Tennis (Sussex U10, U11, U12), golf, two-touch football
Other sports followed: Football (Tottenham Hotspur), rugby, golf, tennis, athletics, boxing
Relaxations: 'Reading newspapers, magazines, books; spending time with my friends; playing cards'
Extras: Sussex U14 Player of the Year 1994. Set record for highest score in Sussex Youth cricket, 189 v Middlesex 1998. Played two Development of Excellence games v Australia U19 1999. Sussex Young Cricketer of the Year 1999
Opinions on cricket: '1. 2nd XI cricket should mirror the first-class game. 2. All pitches should be prepared for what you would expect for a Test match. 3. All groundsmen should be employed by the ECB so home captains do not influence the kind of pitch being prepared. 4. You cannot produce quality Test match batsmen if they continue to play on sub-standard pitches. Batsmen should be able to express themselves rather than playing for survival.'

---

23. Which county did Essex bowl out for 14 at Chelmsford in the 1983 County Championship?

CLARKE, V. P.   Derbyshire

Name: Vincent Paul Clarke
Role: Right-hand bat, right-arm leg-break
and medium bowler
Born: 11 November 1971, Liverpool
Height: 6ft 3in **Weight:** 16st 7lbs
Nickname: FC, Fat Cat, Franky, Jelly,
Big Lad, Pommy, Aussie
County debut: 1994 (Somerset),
1995 (Leicestershire), 1997 (Derbyshire)
1st-Class 50s: 5
1st-Class catches: 15
Place in batting averages: (1998 278th
av. 9.57)
Strike rate: (career 101.54)
Parents: Sandra and Vinnie
Wife and date of marriage:
Natasha, 7 November 1998
Family links with cricket:

Father played representative schoolboy cricket. Sister played school cricket. Mum
played indoor cricket
Education: Craigie Primary School, Perth, Western Australia; Sacred Heart College,
Sorrento, Perth; Perth TAFE
Qualifications: Diploma in Social Training, Year 12 TEE Certificate
Career outside cricket: Social trainer
Overseas teams played for: Wanneroo Districts CC, Perth 1983-94; Hammersley
Carine CC, Perth 1995; Nollamara Turf CC, Perth 1996-99
Cricketers particularly admired: Shane Warne, Ian Botham
Other sports played: Indoor cricket (represented Western Australia in national
tournament – winners). Softball (represented Western Australia as pitcher)
Other sports followed: Football (Everton FC), Aussie Rules (West Coast Eagles)
Relaxations: Playing the guitar, music, windsurfing, 'spending lazy free weekends at
home with Natasha listening to music, doing some gardening, then having a BBQ'
Extras: Brought up in Australia but has English birth qualification. Was in Western
Australian Development Squads from U14 to U19. Represented Western Australia at
indoor cricket in 1991. Played for Bridgwater and Somerset 2nd XI in 1993. Joined
Leicestershire at the start of the 1995 season but was released at the end of the 1996
season. Joined Derbyshire for the 1997 season. Derby Cricket Lovers' Society Young
Cricketer of the Year 1997. Wombwell Cricket Lovers' Society Young Cricketer of the
Year 1997. Suburban Turf Player of the Year, Perth 1997 and 1998. Released by
Derbyshire in 1999. Played only in World Cup warm-up 1999
Opinions on cricket: 'I love it!!'

Best batting: 99 Derbyshire v Warwickshire, Edgbaston 1997
Best bowling: 3-47 Derbyshire v Cambridge University, Fenner's 1997

1999 Season (did not make any first-class or one-day competition appearances)

Career Performances

	M	Inns	NO	Runs	HS	Avge	100s	50s	Ct	St	Balls	Runs	Wkts	Avge	Best	5wl	10wM
Test																	
All First	30	50	7	1058	99	24.60	-	5	15	-	2234	1449	22	65.86	3-47	-	-
1-day Int																	
NatWest	8	4	2	58	24 *	29.00	-	-	5	-	424	221	5	44.20	2-29	-	
B & H	10	10	1	167	52	18.55	-	1	3	-	372	299	12	24.91	4-49	-	
1-day Lge	35	33	7	422	77 *	16.23	-	2	10	-	883	800	22	36.36	3-47	-	

CLINTON, R. S. Kent

Name: Richard Selvey Clinton
Role: Left-hand opening bat, right-arm medium bowler
Born: 1 September 1981, Sidcup, Kent
Height: 6ft 3in **Weight:** 12st 5lbs
Nickname: Clint, Bill
County debut: No first-team appearance
Parents: Catherine and Grahame
Marital status: Single
Family links with cricket: Father played professional cricket for Kent and Surrey
Education: Harenc Primary School; Colfes School
Qualifications: 10 GCSEs
Career outside cricket: At school
Off-season: Preparing for A-levels; training
Cricketers particularly admired: Graham Thorpe, Mark Butcher, 'my father'

Other sports played: Football, rugby (both for school 1st teams)
Other sports followed: Football (Chelsea FC)
Extras: Kent Premier League Young Cricketer of the Year 1998. Won AON Trophy with Kent 1999

COLLINGWOOD, P. D.   Durham

Name: Paul David Collingwood
Role: Right-hand bat, right-arm
medium bowler
Born: 26 May 1976, Shotley Bridge,
Tyneside
Height: 5ft 11in **Weight:** 11st 8lbs
Nickname: Colly
County debut: 1995 (one-day),
1996 (first-class)
County cap: 1998
1st-Class 50s: 12
1st-Class 100s: 3
1st-Class catches: 58
Place in batting averages: 156th av. 24.71
(1998 98th av. 30.85)
Place in bowling averages: (1998 135th
av. 44.76)
Strike rate: 68.37 (career 78.93)
Parents: David and Janet
Marital status: Single
Family links with cricket: Father and brother play in the Tyneside Senior League for Shotley Bridge CC
Education: Benfieldside Junior School; Blackfyne Comprehensive School; Derwentside College
Qualifications: 9 GCSEs and 2 A-levels
Career outside cricket: 'Whatever job I can find'
Off-season: 'Relaxing in Australia until the New Year, playing as many golf courses as possible and working exceptionally hard to try and draw the ball!'
Overseas tours: Durham Cricket Academy to Sri Lanka 1996 (captain)
Overseas teams played for: Bulleen CC, Melbourne 1995-96, 1997 ('won flag on both occasions'); Cornwall CC, Auckland 1997-98; Alberton CC, Johannesburg 1998-99
Cricketers particularly admired: David Boon, Allan Donald, Jacques Kallis, Waugh brothers
Young players to look out for: Darren Stevens
Other sports played: Golf – 'off 11, but hopefully in single figures by now'
Other sports followed: Football ('The Red and Whites – Sunderland – 25 August was a great occasion; a night to remember – 2-1')
Injuries: Out for one day with side strain
Relaxations: 'Watching Sunderland when I'm not away. Reading the *Sports Echo* (SAFC paper) when I am away. Sampling many fine lagers from around the world'
Extras: Took wicket with first ball on first-class debut against Northants, then scored

91. 'A hole-in-one on Durham's golf day'. 'Avoided Steve Harmison's (NUFC) bouncers in the nets on 26 August!'
Opinions on cricket: 'Floodlit cricket is a big success – let's play more. We have to play on better wickets for the benefit of both batsmen and bowlers.'
Best batting: 107 Durham v Oxford University, The Parks 1997
Best bowling: 3-7 Durham v Glamorgan, Cardiff 1999

1999 Season

	M	Inns	NO	Runs	HS	Avge	100s	50s	Ct	St	O	M	Runs	Wkts	Avge	Best	5wI	10wM
Test																		
All First	17	28	0	692	106	24.71	1	4	25	-	91.1	25	238	8	29.75	3-7	-	-
1-day Int																		
NatWest	1	1	0	7	7	7.00	-	-	1	-	4	0	15	0	-		-	-
B & H																		
1-day Lge	15	14	1	316	86	24.30	-	1	8	-	23	1	131	2	65.50	1-2	-	

Career Performances

	M	Inns	NO	Runs	HS	Avge	100s	50s	Ct	St	Balls	Runs	Wkts	Avge	Best	5wI	10wM
Test																	
All First	55	94	7	2305	107	26.49	3	12	58	-	2368	1204	30	40.13	3-7	-	-
1-day Int																	
NatWest	6	5	0	99	28	19.80	-	-	1	-	126	71	1	71.00	1-25	-	
B & H	12	11	2	250	49	27.77	-	-	2	-	307	275	7	39.28	3-28	-	
1-day Lge	52	49	4	1010	86	22.44	-	6	24	-	636	546	17	32.11	3-20	-	

24. What remarkable bowling feat did R.L. Johnson perform for Middlesex v Derbyshire in the Championship at Derby in 1994?

COOK, J. W.　　　　　　　　Northamptonshire

Name: Jeffrey William Cook
Role: Left-hand bat, right-arm medium
bowler, slip fielder
Born: 2 February 1972, Sydney
Height: 6ft 3in **Weight:** 14st
County debut: No first-team appearance
Parents: Roma and Les
Wife and date of marriage: Fiona,
October 1998
Family links with cricket: Mother played
for New South Wales
Education: Rockdale Public School, Sydney;
James Cook High School, Sydney
Qualifications: NCA Level 1 and senior
coaching awards, ACB Level 1 coaching
award
Off-season: Playing in Australia
Overseas teams played for: St George CC,
Sydney 1987-93; Eastern Suburbs, Sydney
1999-2000
Cricketers particularly admired: Steve Waugh, David Gower
Young players to look out for: David Sales, Richard Logan
Other sports played: Indoor cricket (represented New South Wales and Australia),
football
Other sports followed: Football (Liverpool)
Injuries: Out for two games with a fractured right wrist
Relaxations: Reading, music
Extras: Represented New South Wales at U17, U19 and U21 levels. Played for
Northants Board XI in 1999 NatWest
Opinions on cricket: 'More day/night games.'

1999 Season (did not make any first-class or one-day appearances)

Career Performances

	M	Inns	NO	Runs	HS	Avge	100s	50s	Ct	St	Balls	Runs	Wkts	Avge	Best	5wI	10wM
Test																	
All First																		
1-day Int																		
NatWest	1	1	0	130	130	130.00	1	-	-	-	48	50	0	-		-	-
B & H																		
1-day Lge																		

Name: Simon James Cook
Role: Right-hand bat, right-arm
medium-fast bowler
Born: 15 January 1977, Oxford
Height: 6ft 4in   **Weight:** 13st
Nickname: Cookie
County debut: 1997 (one-day),
1999 (first-class)
1st-Class 50s: 1
1st-Class catches: 3
Place in batting averages: 221st av. 18.23
Place in bowling averages: 120th av. 35.33
Strike rate: 61.48 (career 61.48)
Parents: Phil and Sue
Marital status: Single
Education: Botley Primary School;
Matthew Arnold School
Qualifications: GCSEs, NVQ Business
Administration II
Career outside cricket: Sales and marketing within the computer industry
Off-season: Working and training
Cricketers particularly admired: Angus Fraser, Allan Donald, Mark Waugh
Young players to look out for: Ed Joyce, John Maunders, Mike Brown
Other sports followed: Football (Liverpool), 'any other ball sport'
Relaxations: Sleeping, playing any sport, watching television and videos
Opinions on cricket: 'Cut down the number of games that we play and have more
short, sharp quality training sessions.'
Best batting: 51 Middlesex v Hampshire, Lord's 1999
Best bowling: 4-83 Middlesex v Yorkshire, Headingley 1999

1999 Season

	M	Inns	NO	Runs	HS	Avge	100s	50s	Ct	St	O	M	Runs	Wkts	Avge	Best	5wI	10wM
Test																		
All First	10	16	3	237	51	18.23	-	1	3	-	276.4	60	954	27	35.33	4-83	-	-
1-day Int																		
NatWest	1	1	0	5	5	5.00	-	-	-	-	8	0	40	1	40.00	1-40	-	
B & H																		
1-day Lge	16	12	2	100	20	10.00	-	-	2	-	124.2	11	576	24	24.00	3-16	-	

Career Performances

	M	Inns	NO	Runs	HS	Avge	100s	50s	Ct	St	Balls	Runs	Wkts	Avge	Best	5wl	10wM
Test																	
All First	10	16	3	237	51	18.23	-	1	3	-	1660	954	27	35.33	4-83	-	-
1-day Int																	
NatWest	1	1	0	5	5	5.00	-	-	-	-	48	40	1	40.00	1-40	-	
B & H	1	1	0	6	6	6.00	-	-	-	-	54	71	0	-	-	-	-
1-day Lge	16	12	2	100	20	10.00	-	-	2	-	746	576	24	24.00	3-16	-	

CORK, D. G. Derbyshire

Name: Dominic Gerald Cork
Role: Right-hand bat, right-arm,
fast-medium bowler, county captain
Born: 7 August 1971,
Newcastle-under-Lyme, Staffordshire
Height: 6ft 3in **Weight:** 13st 4lbs
Nickname: Corky
County debut: 1990
County cap: 1993
Test debut: 1995
Tests: 27
One-Day Internationals: 25
50 wickets in a season: 5
1st-Class 50s: 32
1st-Class 100s: 3
1st-Class 5 w. in innings: 19
1st-Class 10 w. in match: 2
1st-Class catches: 117
One-Day 5 w. in innings: 4
Place in batting averages: 132nd av. 26.75 (1998 171st av. 22.00)
Place in bowling averages: 35th av. 22.34 (1998 77th av. 28.89)
Strike rate: 46.63 (career 53.95)
Parents: Gerald and Mary
Children: Gregory Theodore Gerald, 29 September 1994
Family links with cricket: 'Father and brothers played for Betley CC in local North
Staffs & South Cheshire League with myself'
Education: St Joseph's College, Trent Vale, Stoke-on-Trent; Newcastle College of FE
Qualifications: 3 O-levels, leisure and recreation, qualified coach
Career outside cricket: 'None, but hopefully into commentary'
Off-season: 'Working for Sky Sports and praying for a call to join them in South
Africa'

Overseas tours: England YC to Australia 1989-90; England A to Bermuda and West Indies 1991-92, to Australia 1992-93, to South Africa 1993-94, to India 1994-95; England to South Africa 1995-96, to India and Pakistan (World Cup) 1995-96, to New Zealand 1996-97, to Australia 1998-99

Overseas teams played for: East Shirley, Christchurch, New Zealand 1990-91

Cricketers particularly admired: Ian Botham, Malcolm Marshall, Imran Khan

Young players to look out for: Trevor Smith, Darren Stevens

Other sports played: Football (Mickleover Sports), volleyball, golf

Other sports followed: Football (Stoke City)

Injuries: Out for four weeks with wrist injury; for two weeks with back injury

Relaxations: 'Relaxing with my partner and our children'

Extras: First played cricket for Betley CC in the North Staffs & South Cheshire League. In 1990 he took a wicket in his first over in first-class cricket v New Zealand at Derby and scored a century as nightwatchman for England U19 v Pakistan at Taunton. Played Minor Counties cricket for Staffordshire in 1989 and 1990. Selected for England A in 1991 – his first full season of first-class cricket. The Professional Cricketers' Association (PCA) Young Player of 1991. Took eight wickets for 53 runs on 20th birthday. Achieved first-class hat-trick against Kent 1994. Took seven wickets for 43 runs on Test debut against West Indies at Lord's. Achieved hat-trick against the West Indies at Old Trafford in the fourth Test – the first by an Englishman in Test cricket for 30 years. Won two Man of the Match awards in three Test matches. Voted Player of the Year by the PCA for 1995. Finished at the top of the Whyte and Mackay ratings for bowling in 1995. One of *Wisden*'s Five Cricketers of the Year 1996. Withdrew from the Zimbabwe leg of England's 1996-97 winter tour for personal reasons, but joined up with the team in New Zealand. Derbyshire captain since 1998

Opinions on cricket: 'Too many games, too many players, too many counties. We must play our cricket like Test matches – five days, new ball at 80 overs, wicket like a Test pitch.'

Best batting: 104 Derbyshire v Gloucestershire, Cheltenham 1993

Best bowling: 9-43 Derbyshire v Northamptonshire, Derby 1995

1999 Season

	M	Inns	NO	Runs	HS	Avge	100s	50s	Ct	St	O	M	Runs	Wkts	Avge	Best	5wl	10wM
Test																		
All First	14	22	2	535	82	26.75	-	4	18	-	427.3	95	1229	55	22.34	6-113	4	-
1-day Int																		
NatWest																		
B & H																		
1-day Lge	9	9	1	145	61 *	18.12	-	1	3	-	55.4	2	294	6	49.00	2-33	-	

Career Performances

	M	Inns	NO	Runs	HS	Avge	100s	50s	Ct	St	Balls	Runs	Wkts	Avge	Best	5wl	10wM
Test	27	42	6	634	59	17.61	-	2	13	-	5963	3118	98	31.81	7-43	5	-
All First	173	260	37	5421	104	24.30	3	32	117	-	29782	14790	552	26.79	9-43	19	2
1-day Int	25	15	2	132	31 *	10.15	-	-	6	-	1440	1071	35	30.60	3-27	-	
NatWest	17	15	4	394	62	35.81	-	4	5	-	1107	658	35	18.80	5-18	2	
B & H	22	18	5	360	92 *	27.69	-	2	11	-	1298	870	23	37.82	5-49	1	
1-day Lge	87	72	8	1109	66	17.32	-	3	33	-	3598	2855	96	29.73	6-21	1	

COSKER, D. A. Glamorgan

Name: Dean Andrew Cosker
Role: Right-hand bat, slow left-arm bowler
Born: 7 January 1978, Weymouth, Dorset
Height: 5ft 10in **Weight:** 12st 2lbs
Nickname: The Lurker, Lurks
County debut: 1996
1st-Class 5 w. in innings: 2
1st-Class catches: 36
Place in batting averages: 244th av. 15.14
(1998 288th av. 6.83)
Place in bowling averages: 140th av. 44.42
(1998 120th av. 35.13)
Strike rate: 101.36 (career 73.91)
Parents: Des and Carol
Marital status: 'Confused'
Family links with cricket: 'Brother Gareth
plays, Dad commentates, Mum watches, and
Grandfather is a fan'
Education: '"The Greenwood", North Sydney'; Millfield School
Qualifications: 10 GCSEs, 4 A-levels, Class 3 soccer referee, 10m swimming award
Career outside cricket: Camp site proprietor in North Wales
Off-season: 'Iron man trials in Manly, Sydney. Weights. Trying to get Steve James in
the gym. Hopefully playing soccer in the "tough" but widely respected league of Wales'
Overseas tours: West of England U15 to West Indies 1993-94; Millfield School to Sri
Lanka 1994-95; England U17 to Holland 1995; England U19 to Pakistan 1996-97;
England A to Kenya and Sri Lanka 1997-98, to Zimbabwe and South Africa 1998-99;
Glamorgan CCC to Jersey 1998
Overseas teams played for: Gordon, Sydney 1996-97
Cricketers particularly admired: Steve James, Al Jones
Young players to look out for: 'Damyn Sven Strang, Wayne Law, Daz Tom and
"Bubbaloo"'

Other sports played: Lawn bowls, football. 'Cardiff Rally Car Championships champion at 16 horsepower and 20 horsepower 1996-97'
Other sports followed: Soccer (Tottenham Hotspur FC)
Injuries: Out for two weeks with cracked thumb; numerous back spasms
Relaxations: 'Texting, aqua aerobics; a practising palaeontologist'
Extras: *Daily Telegraph* Regional Bowling Award, England U15 and U17. Played for U19 TCCB Development of Excellence XI against South Africa U19 in 1995. Played for England U19 against Zimbabwe in 1997. Leading wicket-taker on England A tour of Zimbabwe and South Africa 1998-99
Opinions on cricket: 'Hard to grip a cricket ball when it is wet, producing an unfair contest between batsman and bowler.'
Best batting: 49 Glamorgan v Sussex, Cardiff 1999
Best bowling: 6-140 Glamorgan v Lancashire, Colwyn Bay 1998

1999 Season

	M	Inns	NO	Runs	HS	Avge	100s	50s	Ct	St	O	M	Runs	Wkts	Avge	Best	5wl	10wM
Test																		
All First	13	18	4	212	49	15.14	-	-	14	-	321	81	844	19	44.42	3-100	-	-
1-day Int																		
NatWest	3	2	1	9	5	9.00	-	-	-	-	26	2	106	4	26.50	2-30	-	
B & H																		
1-day Lge	14	9	3	76	27 *	12.66	-	-	4	-	106	3	492	12	41.00	2-37	-	

Career Performances

	M	Inns	NO	Runs	HS	Avge	100s	50s	Ct	St	Balls	Runs	Wkts	Avge	Best	5wl	10wM
Test																	
All First	60	66	19	489	49	10.40	-	-	36	-	10422	4857	141	34.44	6-140	2	-
1-day Int																	
NatWest	5	4	3	16	5	16.00	-	-	-	-	260	152	7	21.71	3-26	-	
B & H	5	4	2	2	1 *	1.00	-	-	1	-	174	128	4	32.00	2-26	-	
1-day Lge	35	18	6	124	27 *	10.33	-	-	10	-	1476	1243	37	33.59	3-18	-	

25. Who holds the world record for the number of sixes in an innings, scored in a County Championship match at Abergavenny in 1995?

COTTERELL, T. P.   Gloucestershire

Name: Thomas Paul Cotterell
Role: Left-hand bat, left-arm spinner
Born: 9 March 1977, Isleworth, Middlesex
Height: 6ft 2in **Weight:** 10st
County debut: 1999
Strike rate: 64.00 (career 64.00)
Parents: Christopher and Jenny
Marital status: Single
Family links with cricket: Brother Joe has
played U19 and 2nd XI for Gloucestershire
Education: Birdlip CP; Kings School,
Gloucester; Kent University
Qualifications: BA in History
Cricketers particularly admired:
Phil Tufnell, Courtney Walsh, Dennis Lillee
Other sports played: Golf, rugby
Other sports followed: Rugby
(Gloucester RFC)

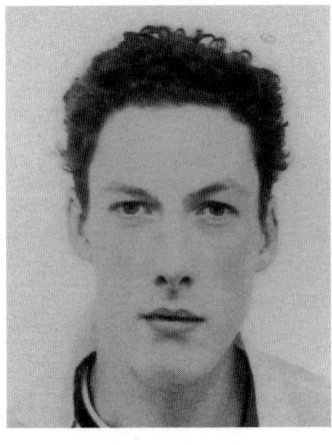

Relaxations: Reading, music
Extras: League bowling prize with Birdlip CC 1993. Kent University Player of the
Year 1998
Best bowling: 3-69 Gloucestershire v Northamptonshire, Northampton 1999

1999 Season

	M	Inns	NO	Runs	HS	Avge	100s	50s	Ct	St	O	M	Runs	Wkts	Avge	Best	5wI	10wM
Test																		
All First	1	1	0	0	0	0.00	-	-	-	-	32	8	81	3	27.00	3-69	-	-
1-day Int																		
NatWest																		
B & H																		
1-day Lge																		

Career Performances

	M	Inns	NO	Runs	HS	Avge	100s	50s	Ct	St	Balls	Runs	Wkts	Avge	Best	5wI	10wM
Test																	
All First	1	1	0	0	0	0.00	-	-	-	-	192	81	3	27.00	3-69	-	-
1-day Int																	
NatWest																	
B & H																	
1-day Lge																	

COTTEY, P. A.   Sussex

Name: Phillip Anthony Cottey
Role: Right-hand bat, right-arm off-spin
bowler, occasional wicket-keeper
('Eastbourne 1997')
Born: 2 June 1966, Swansea
Height: 5ft 5in **Weight:** 10st 7lbs
Nickname: Cotts, TC, Rudy, Tattoo, Seven
County debut: 1986 (Glamorgan),
1999 (Sussex)
County cap: 1992 (Glamorgan)
1000 runs in a season: 7
1st-Class 50s: 63
1st-Class 100s: 21
1st-Class 200s: 1
1st-Class catches: 153
Place in batting averages: 121st av. 27.85
(1998 63rd av. 34.89)
Strike rate: (career 84.50)
Parents: Bernard John and Ruth
Wife and date of marriage: Gail, 5 October 1992
Children: Lowri Rhiannon, 16 October 1993; Seren Nia, 6 August 1997
Family links with cricket: Father played club cricket for Swansea CC
Education: Bishopston Comprehensive School, Swansea
Qualifications: 9 O-levels, advanced coach
Career outside cricket: 'Undecided'
Off-season: 'Back in Wales coaching; enrolling on computer course; planning to run a marathon'
Overseas tours: Glamorgan to La Manga, Barbados, Trinidad, Zimbabwe and Cape Town 1987-96; Glamorgan CCC to Jersey 1998
Overseas teams played for: Penrith, Sydney 1986-88; Benoni, Johannesburg 1990-93; Eastern Transvaal 1991-92
Cricketers particularly admired: Sachin Tendulkar, Ian Botham, Shane Warne, Matthew Maynard
Young players to look out for: Nick Wilton, Robin Martin-Jenkins, Jamie Carpenter, Mike Powell, Simon Jones
Other sports played/followed: Golf, soccer (Swansea City AFC), rugby union (Dunvant RFC) and marathon running
Injuries: Back spasm, groin strain, tendonitis in hand – no time off required
Relaxations: Gym and road running; football for Ammanford FC (Welsh League); spending time with family; golf
Extras: Left school at 16 to play for Swansea City FC for three years as a

professional. Three Welsh Youth caps (one as captain). Glamorgan Player of the Year in 1994. Ran the New York Marathon in 1995 and the Athens Marathon in 1996. Left Glamorgan at the end of the 1998 season and joined Sussex on a five-year contract. In his first match against his old county, at Cardiff in 1999, he was out twice to Robert Croft, at whose wedding he was best man. Sussex Clubman of the Year 1999

Opinions on cricket: 'I can't believe the amount of criticism county cricket gets from ex-players now turned broadcasters. When they played there were far more first-class games and they seem to conveniently forget it provided them with a decent living'

Best batting: 203 Glamorgan v Leicestershire, Swansea 1996

Best bowling: 4-49 Glamorgan v Leicestershire, Swansea 1996

1999 Season

	M	Inns	NO	Runs	HS	Avge	100s	50s	Ct	St	O	M	Runs	Wkts	Avge	Best	5wI	10wM
Test																		
All First	17	29	1	780	126	27.85	1	4	11	-	2	1	3	0	-		-	-	-
1-day Int																		
NatWest	2	2	0	22	22	11.00	-	-	-	-								
B & H	2	2	0	8	8	4.00	-	-	3	-								
1-day Lge	15	12	6	289	62 *	48.16	-	2	3	-								

Career Performances

	M	Inns	NO	Runs	HS	Avge	100s	50s	Ct	St	Balls	Runs	Wkts	Avge	Best	5wI	10wM
Test																	
All First	220	358	50	11399	203	37.00	22	63	153	-	1352	862	16	53.87	4-49	-	-
1-day Int																	
NatWest	27	26	6	537	68	26.85	-	4	8	-	150	96	3	32.00	1-9	-	
B & H	35	33	5	632	96	22.57	-	3	14	-	78	53	1	53.00	1-49	-	
1-day Lge	147	124	26	2656	92 *	27.10	-	16	50	-	509	523	15	34.86	4-56	-	

COUSINS, D. M.   Northamptonshire

Name: Darren Mark Cousins
Role: Right-hand bat, right-arm fast-medium bowler, outfielder
Born: 24 September 1971, Cambridge
Height: 6ft 1in **Weight:** 13st 7lbs
Nickname: Mad Dog, Cuz, Cuzzi, Skuz
County debut: 1993 (Essex), 1999 (one-day, Surrey)
1st-Class 5 w. in innings: 1
1st-Class catches: 5
Strike rate: (career 73.33)
Parents: Dennis Charles and Deanna Maureen (deceased)

Marital status: Single
Family links with cricket: Father opened the bowling and was capped for Cambridgeshire
Education: Milton Primary School; Impington Village College
Qualifications: 7 GCSEs
Career outside cricket: Coaching and teaching PE in local secondary school
Overseas teams played for: Gold Coast Dolphins, Queensland 1994-95; Maritzburg Old Boys, Pietermaritzburg, South Africa 1995-96
Cricketers particularly admired: Neil Foster, Geoff Arnold, Alan Butcher, Keith Fletcher and 'anyone else who has given me help, advice and guidance during my career'
Young players to look out for: Ashley Cowan, Stephen Peters, Darren Robinson

Other sports played: 'I used to be a county swimmer and a county footballer but had to give up all other sports due to glass back syndrome'
Other sports followed: Football (Liverpool, Cambridge United)
Relaxations: 'Socialising. Listening to all types of music from Indie to soul to swing'
Extras: Represented Cambridgeshire at football and swimming and every level at cricket. Played for a Bull Development Squad against Australia in 1991, taking four wickets in each innings. Played 2nd XI cricket for Northants and Worcs. Set record for both number of wickets in any single Colts festival (21) and number of wickets taken in the Hilda Overy Festival overall (74). Awarded 2nd XI cap and Essex Young Player of the Year 1994. Essex Cricket Society 2nd XI Player of the Year 1994. Leading Essex wicket-taker in Sunday League and top of the bowling averages in 1994. Underwent three back operations in 22 months and missed three seasons of cricket. Released by Essex at end of 1998 season. Played some one-day matches for Surrey 1999. Has joined Northants for 2000
Best batting: 18* Essex v Durham, Chelmsford 1995
Best bowling: 6-35 Essex v Cambridge University, Fenner's 1994

1999 Season

	M	Inns	NO	Runs	HS	Avge	100s	50s	Ct	St	O	M	Runs	Wkts	Avge	Best	5wI	10wM
Test																		
All First																		
1-day Int																		
NatWest	1	1	0	12	12	12.00	-	-	-	-	10	0	47	0	-		-	-
B & H																		
1-day Lge	3	2	1	2	1*	2.00	-	-	1	-	27	0	125	4	31.25	2-38	-

Career Performances

	M	Inns	NO	Runs	HS	Avge	100s	50s	Ct	St	Balls	Runs	Wkts	Avge	Best	5wI	10wM
Test																	
All First	15	25	5	159	18 *	7.95	-	-	5	-	1980	1138	27	42.14	6-35	1	-
1-day Int																	
NatWest	5	3	1	13	12	6.50	-	-	-	-	210	192	1	192.00	1-33	-	
B & H	6	2	1	22	12 *	22.00	-	-	1	-	239	171	2	85.50	1-33	-	
1-day Lge	38	14	5	21	6	2.33	-	-	4	-	1611	1233	52	23.71	3-18	-	

COWAN, A. P.   Essex

Name: Ashley Preston Cowan
Role: Right-hand bat, right-hand fast-medium bowler
Born: 7 May 1975, Hitchin, Hertfordshire
Height: 6ft 5in **Weight:** 14st
Nickname: Victor, Dic Dic
County debut: 1995
50 w. in a season: 1
1st-Class 50s: 4
1st-Class 5 w. in innings: 5
1st-Class catches: 30
One-Day 5 w. in innings: 1
Place in batting averages: 237th av. 15.80 (1998 218th av. 17.53)
Place in bowling averages: 71st av. 27.54 (1998 136th av. 45.21)
Strike rate: 51.28 (career 58.75)
Parents: Jeff and Pam
Marital status: Single
Family links with cricket: 'Father tried to play in local village team'
Education: Kingshott Prep; Framlingham College
Qualifications: 5 GCSEs, 1 A-level, Business Vocation Degree
Career outside cricket: Family business
Overseas tours: England to West Indies 1997-98
Overseas teams played for: Zingan CC, Pietermaritzburg, South Africa 1995-97
Cricketers particularly admired: Ian Botham, Graham Dilley, Curtly Ambrose
Other sports followed: Rugby, hockey, golf, football (Newcastle United)
Relaxations: Socialising, playing golf, 'having fun'
Extras: Played rugby and hockey for East of England U18. Was the youngest person to play for Cambridgeshire. First-class hat-trick at Colchester in 1996. Was the joint leading scorer in the 1996 NatWest final

Opinions on cricket: 'Looking for a younger and more dedicated cricket crowd who will inspire the players through their enthusiasm.'
Best batting: 94 Essex v Leicestershire, Leicester 1998
Best bowling: 6-47 Essex v Glamorgan, Cardiff 1999

1999 Season

	M	Inns	NO	Runs	HS	Avge	100s	50s	Ct	St	O	M	Runs	Wkts	Avge	Best	5wI	10wM
Test																		
All First	17	24	3	332	52 *	15.80	-	1	10	-	393.1	66	1267	46	27.54	6-47	1	-
1-day Int																		
NatWest	1	1	1	0	0 *	-	-	-	-	-	10	0	46	2	23.00	2-46	-	
B & H																		
1-day Lge	14	12	2	97	27	9.70	-	-	7	-	108.2	13	469	13	36.07	3-17	-	

Career Performances

	M	Inns	NO	Runs	HS	Avge	100s	50s	Ct	St	Balls	Runs	Wkts	Avge	Best	5wI	10wM
Test																	
All First	61	90	17	1268	94	17.36	-	4	30	-	9342	5237	159	32.93	6-47	5	-
1-day Int																	
NatWest	10	6	3	42	17 *	14.00	-	-	4	-	601	403	15	26.86	3-29	-	
B & H	13	7	4	48	15 *	16.00	-	-	1	-	714	502	15	33.46	5-28	1	
1-day Lge	50	36	13	309	40 *	13.43	-	-	24	-	2035	1589	51	31.15	4-31	-	

26. Against which county and at which ground did B.C. Lara score his world record 501* for Warwickshire in the 1994 Championship?

COX, J.   Somerset

Name: Jamie Cox
Role: Right-hand bat, off-spin bowler, county captain
Born: 15 October 1969, Burnie, Tasmania
Height: 6ft **Weight:** 12st 7lbs
Nickname: Buzz
County debut: 1999
1000 runs in a season: 1
1st-Class 50s: 42
1st-Class 100s: 26
1st-Class 200s: 2
1st-Class catches: 55
One-Day 100s: 2
Place in batting averages: 4th av. 57.75
Strike rate: 74.25 (career 99.75)
Parents: David and Kaye
Marital status: Single
Family links with cricket: Father played
State colts and is life member of local club
Education: Wynyard Primary; Wynyard High; Deakin University (current)
Qualifications: School Certificate, Diploma of Management; currently studying for
Bachelor of Business degree
Career outside cricket: Banking analyst
Off-season: 'Playing for my home state Tasmania'
Overseas tours: Australia U19 to West Indies 1988; Australia A to Zimbabwe 1989, to
Malaysia 1997 (Super 8s); Australia XI to Zimbabwe 1991-92; Tasmania to Zimbabwe
1995-96
Overseas teams played for: Tasmania 1987 –
Cricketers particularly admired: David Boon, Steve Waugh, Ian Botham,
Andrew Caddick
Young players to look out for: Matt Bulbeck, Marcus Trescothick
Other sports played: Australian Rules football ('AFL retired')
Other sports followed: Australian Rules football (Western Bulldogs)
Relaxations: Music, sleeping
Extras: Scored 1349 runs in the 1996-97 Australian season, with five 100s, including
two in one match v New South Wales. Players' Player of the Year 1996-97. Tasmanian
Cricket Player of the Year 1996-97. Scored an unbeaten 115 in the first innings of the
1997-98 Sheffield Shield final v Western Australia, becoming the first player to carry
his bat in a Shield final. Represented Australia A in Super 8s (Malaysia) 1997. Joined
Somerset in 1999 as overseas player and captain. Took first first-class wicket of his
career in 1999 v Sussex at Taunton, dismissing fellow Tasmanian Michael DiVenuto;

took his second v Middlesex at Taunton, his victim this time being Justin Langer. Became the first Somerset player to score a 200 (216) and a 100 (129*) in a match, v Hampshire at Southampton 1999. Has taken over captaincy of Tasmania in succession to David Boon

Opinions on cricket: 'Cricket needs a mercy rule – if captains decide that a result is improbable then game should be called off to avoid farcical ends whilst filling in time. Amount of cricket played needs to be reduced to allow for rest, preparation and practice.'

Best batting: 216 Somerset v Hampshire, Southampton 1999
Best bowling: 3-46 Somerset v Middlesex, Taunton 1999

1999 Season

	M	Inns	NO	Runs	HS	Avge	100s	50s	Ct	St	O	M	Runs	Wkts	Avge	Best	5wI	10wM
Test																		
All First	18	30	2	1617	216	57.75	6	6	7	-	49.3	7	188	4	47.00	3-46	-	-
1-day Int																		
NatWest	5	5	0	234	114	46.80	1	1	-	-								
B & H																		
1-day Lge	14	14	0	593	101	42.35	1	3	6	-	7	0	28	3	9.33	3-28	-	

Career Performances

	M	Inns	NO	Runs	HS	Avge	100s	50s	Ct	St	Balls	Runs	Wkts	Avge	Best	5wI	10wM
Test																	
All First	131	235	15	9526	216	43.30	28	42	55	-	399	277	4	69.25	3-46	-	-
1-day Int																	
NatWest	5	5	0	234	114	46.80	1	1	-	-							
B & H																	
1-day Lge	14	14	0	593	101	42.35	1	3	6	-	42	28	3	9.33	3-28	-	

27. Who scored a 200 and a 100 in the same match on four occasions in the Championship for Gloucestershire (and was not out on each occasion)?

CRAVEN, V. J.   Yorkshire

Name: Victor John Craven
Role: Left-hand bat, right-arm medium bowler
Born: 31 July 1980, Harrogate
Height: 6ft **Weight:** 12st 13lbs
County debut: No first-team appearance
Parents: Victor and Susan
Marital status: Single
Family links with cricket: 'Father played for 30 years for local side. He introduced me to cricket'
Education: Beckwithshaw County Primary; Harrogate Grammar; Harrogate Grammar Sixth Form
Qualifications: GNVQ Advanced Business, first coaching award
Off-season: Fitness; part-time work
Overseas teams played for: Tatura CC, Victoria, Australia
Cricketers particularly admired: Graham Thorpe, Michael Atherton, Glenn McGrath
Young players to look out for: Richard Dawson, Michael Gough
Other sports played: Golf, football
Other sports followed: Football (Leeds United), rugby league (Leeds Rhinos)
Relaxations: Cinema, films, football, gym
Opinions on cricket: 'The game's getting faster and more exciting with the introduction of day-night cricket.'

CRAWLEY, J. P.   Lancashire

Name: John Paul Crawley
Role: Right-hand bat, occasional wicket-keeper, county captain
Born: 21 September 1971, Maldon, Essex
Height: 6ft 2in **Weight:** 13st 2lbs
Nickname: Creeps, Jonty, JC
County debut: 1990
Test debut: 1994
Tests: 29
One-Day Internationals: 13
1000 runs in a season: 7

1st-Class 50s: 83
1st-Class 100s: 28
1st-Class 200s: 4
1st-Class catches: 149
One-Day 100s: 3
Place in batting averages: 49th av. 37.82
(1998 1st av. 74.04)
Strike rate: (career 120.00)
Parents: Frank and Jean
Marital status: Single
Family links with cricket: Father played in
Manchester Association; brother Mark played
for Lancashire before moving to
Nottinghamshire; other brother Peter plays
for Warrington CC and has played for
Scottish Universities and Cambridge
University; uncle was excellent fast bowler;
godfather umpires in Manchester Association
Education: Manchester Grammar School; Trinity College, Cambridge
Qualifications: 10 O-levels, 2 AO-Levels, 3 A-levels, 2 S-levels, BA in History
Overseas tours: England YC to Australia 1989-90, to New Zealand 1990-91; England
A to South Africa 1993-94; England to Australia 1994-95, to South Africa 1995-96,
to Zimbabwe and New Zealand 1996-97, to West Indies 1997-98, to Australia 1998-99
Overseas teams played for: Midland Guildford, Perth 1990
Cricketers particularly admired: Michael Atherton, Neil Fairbrother, Graham
Gooch, Alec Stewart, David Gower, Allan Donald, Ian Salisbury
Other sports followed: Football (Manchester United), golf
Relaxations: 'Playing or trying to play the guitar'
Extras: Captained England YC (U19) to New Zealand 1990-91 and played for
England YC in three home series v New Zealand 1989, Pakistan 1990 and Australia
(as captain) 1991. Made his maiden first-class century for Cambridge University on
the same day that brother Mark made his for Notts. First to score 1000 runs in U19
Tests. Scored 286 for England A against Eastern Province at Port Elizabeth in 1994,
the highest score by an Englishman on an England or England A tour for almost 30
years. Finished top of the first-class batting averages on England's tour to South Africa
in 1995-96 with 336 runs at 67.20, but had to fly home after suffering a hamstring
injury whilst fielding in the third Test at Durban. Scored his maiden Test match
hundred (106) in the third Test against Pakistan at The Oval in 1996, followed by 112
in England's next Test against Zimbabwe in Bulawayo in 1996-97. Lancashire vice-
captain for the 1998 season. Scored century in each innings v Glamorgan 1998.
Topped first-class batting averages for 1998 season. Appointed Lancashire captain for
the 1999 season
Best batting: 286 England A v Eastern Province, Port Elizabeth 1993-94
Best bowling: 1-90 Lancashire v Sussex, Hove 1992

1999 Season

	M	Inns	NO	Runs	HS	Avge	100s	50s	Ct	St	O	M	Runs	Wkts	Avge	Best	5wI	10wM
Test																		
All First	15	25	2	870	158	37.82	2	6	10	-	6	0	51	0	-	-	-	-
1-day Int																		
NatWest	3	3	0	123	85	41.00	-	1	2	-								
B & H	1	1	0	5	5	5.00	-	-	-	-								
1-day Lge	14	13	2	483	85 *	43.90	-	3	2	3								

Career Performances

	M	Inns	NO	Runs	HS	Avge	100s	50s	Ct	St	Balls		Runs	Wkts	Avge	Best	5wI	10wM
Test	29	47	5	1329	156 *	31.64	3	7	26	-								
All First	200	327	31	14308	286	48.33	32	83	149	-	120		180	1	180.00	1-90	-	-
1-day Int	13	12	1	235	73	21.36	-	2	1	1								
NatWest	19	19	2	679	113 *	39.94	1	5	8	-	6		4	0	-		-	-
B & H	37	36	1	1267	114	36.20	1	7	11	-								
1-day Lge	85	82	4	2201	100	28.21	1	14	22	3								

CREESE, M. L. Middlesex

Name: Matthew Leonard Creese
Role: Left-hand bat, slow left-arm bowler
Born: 13 February 1982, Enfield
Height: 6ft 2in **Weight:** 14st
Nickname: Creesey
County debut: 1999
Strike rate: 153.00 (career 153.00)
Parents: John and Christine
Marital status: Single
Family links with cricket: 'Dad played for Calthorpe CC and Edmonton CC'
Education: Millbrook JMI; Goffs GM School
Qualifications: 10 GCSEs
Career outside cricket: School
Off-season: 'Hopefully I am going to take a year out before going to university and play in Australia or New Zealand'
Cricketers particularly admired: Phil Tufnell, Ian Botham
Young players to look out for: Michael Brown, Mark Wright, John Maunders
Other sports played: Rugby, football, 'anything I find time for'

Other sports followed: Rugby (Saracens)
Relaxations: 'Going out with friends – clubbing'
Extras: Middlesex Seaxe Young Player of the Year 1997. Played for England U15.
Played for ECB U19 XI v Australia 1999
Opinions on cricket: 'More floodlit day/night games to attract crowds back to cricket.
Further efforts and initiatives to spread cricket in state schools.'
Best batting: 4 Middlesex v Cambridge University, Fenner's 1999
Best bowling: 1-37 Middlesex v Cambridge University, Fenner's 1999

1999 Season

	M	Inns	NO	Runs	HS	Avge	100s	50s	Ct	St	O	M	Runs	Wkts	Avge	Best	5wI	10wM
Test																		
All First	1	1	0	4	4	4.00	-	-	-	-	25.3	7	98	1	98.00	1-37	-	-
1-day Int																		
NatWest																		
B & H																		
1-day Lge																		

Career Performances

	M	Inns	NO	Runs	HS	Avge	100s	50s	Ct	St	Balls	Runs	Wkts	Avge	Best	5wI	10wM
Test																	
All First	1	1	0	4	4	4.00	-	-	-	-	153	98	1	98.00	1-37	-	-
1-day Int																	
NatWest																	
B & H																	
1-day Lge																	

> 28. Warwickshire boasted no fewer than four West Indies Test cricketers
> when they won the 1972 Championship. Name them.

CROFT, R. D. B. — Glamorgan

Name: Robert Damien Bale Croft
Role: Right-hand bat, off-spin bowler
Born: 25 May 1970, Morriston, Swansea
Height: 5ft 11in **Weight:** 13st 10lbs
Nickname: Crofty
County debut: 1989
County cap: 1992
Test debut: 1996
Tests: 15
One-Day Internationals: 44
50 wickets in a season: 5
1st-Class 50s: 27
1st-Class 100s: 2
1st-Class 5 w. in innings: 26
1st-Class 10 w. in match: 4
1st-Class catches: 112
One-Day 5 w. in innings: 1
Place in batting averages: 212th av. 18.94
(1998 166th av. 22.86)
Place in bowling averages: 102nd av. 31.37 (1998 142nd av. 57.20)
Strike rate: 69.55 (career 79.06)
Parents: Malcolm and Susan
Wife: Marie
Children: Callum James Bale Croft
Family links with cricket: Father and grandfather played local league cricket
Education: Hendy CP School; St John Lloyd Catholic School, Llanelli; Neath Tertiary
College; West Glamorgan Institute of Higher Education
Qualifications: 6 O-levels; OND Business Studies; HND Business Studies; NCA
senior coaching certificate
Career outside cricket: 'Who knows?'
Off-season: 'Watching some rugby, organising my benefit year (2000) and getting
ready for the year 2000 cricket-wise'
Overseas tours: England A to Bermuda and West Indies 1991-92, to South Africa
1993-94; England to Zimbabwe and New Zealand 1996-97, to West Indies 1997-98, to
Australia 1998-99, to Sharjah (Coca-Cola Cup) 1998-99
Overseas teams played for: 'England'
Cricketers particularly admired: Alan Jones, Tom Cartwright, Don Shepherd,
John Steele, John Emburey
Young players to look out for: 'Too many Welsh youngsters to mention'
Other sports played: Golf, squash
Other sports followed: Rugby (Hendy and Wales)

Relaxations: Fishing and shooting
Extras: Captained England South to victory in International Youth Tournament 1989 and was voted Player of the Tournament. Glamorgan Young Player of the Year 1992. Represented England in the 1999 World Cup. Granted a benefit for 2000
Opinions on cricket: 'The cricket ball we use combined with the poor pitches we play on in this country does not provide a fair contest between batsman and bowler – i.e. pitches have got to improve! The ball must be looked at as well.'
Best batting: 143 Glamorgan v Somerset, Taunton 1995
Best bowling: 8-66 Glamorgan v Warwickshire, Swansea 1992

1999 Season

	M	Inns	NO	Runs	HS	Avge	100s	50s	Ct	St	O	M	Runs	Wkts	Avge	Best	5wI	10wM
Test																		
All First	15	21	4	322	58 *	18.94	-	2	5	-	521.4	135	1412	45	31.37	7-70	4	1
1-day Int	2	1	0	12	12	12.00	-	-	-	-	12	1	45	1	45.00	1-32	-	
NatWest	3	3	0	17	14	5.66	-	-	-	-	30	1	125	9	13.88	4-47	-	
B & H																		
1-day Lge	14	14	1	278	53	21.38	-	1	7	-	115.1	7	474	24	19.75	4-31	-	

Career Performances

	M	Inns	NO	Runs	HS	Avge	100s	50s	Ct	St	Balls	Runs	Wkts	Avge	Best	5wI	10wM
Test	15	24	6	295	37 *	16.38	-	-	8	-	3479	1380	36	38.33	5-95	1	-
All First	220	322	63	6422	143	24.79	2	27	112	-	47043	21570	595	36.25	8-66	26	4
1-day Int	44	31	11	299	32	14.95	-	-	9	-	2244	1567	41	38.21	3-51	-	
NatWest	27	23	5	375	64	20.83	-	3	4	-	1660	951	32	29.71	4-47	-	
B & H	27	23	7	580	77	36.25	-	5	8	-	1517	945	32	29.53	4-30	-	
1-day Lge	123	98	25	1577	68	21.60	-	5	34	-	5087	3783	120	31.52	6-20	1	

29. Two non-wicketkeeping fielders have taken seven catches in a County Championship innings; one for Surrey in 1957, the other for Gloucestershire in 1966. Name them.

CROWE, C. D.   Leicestershire

Name: Carl Daniel Crowe
Role: Right-hand bat, off-spin bowler
Born: 25 November 1975, Leicester
Height: 6ft **Weight:** 12st 7lbs
Nickname: Scooby
County debut: 1995
1st-Class catches: 6
Place in bowling averages: 104th av. 31.63
Strike rate: 50.18 (career 55.29)
Parents: Edward Patrick and Jeannette
Marital status: Engaged
Family links with cricket: Brother Craig has
played for Leicestershire 2nd XI
Education: Lutterworth High School;
Lutterworth Grammar School
Qualifications: 11 GCSEs, 2 A-levels,
NCA Senior Coach
Off-season: 'In the gym and indoor nets'
Overseas tours: Leicestershire U19 to South Africa 1993-94; Leicestershire to
Holland 1996, 1998, to Barbados 1998, to Sri Lanka 1999
Overseas teams played for: Old Mentonians, Melbourne 1997-99
Cricketers particularly admired: Mark and Steve Waugh, Saqlain Mushtaq
Young players to look out for: Jimmy Ormond, Kevin Dean, Craig Crowe
Other sports played: 'Try all sports.' 'Had a hole in one'
Other sports followed: 'Support Leicester at everything and follow Spurs'
Relaxations: 'Taking my girlfriend out. Going out for meals with friends'
Extras: Played for Leicestershire U12-U19 and Midlands Schools U14-U19. One of
the Cricketers of the Festival at Cambridge U19 Festival 1994. Won Leics 2nd XI
batting award 1998
Opinions on cricket: 'We must give the changes we make to the game (i.e. two
divisions) a chance to work before we then make more changes for change's sake.'
Best batting: 44* Leicestershire v Northamptonshire, Northampton 1999
Best bowling: 3-49 Leicestershire v Durham, Darlington 1998

---

30. Who took five Sussex wickets in six balls for Surrey in a
Championship match at Eastbourne in 1972?

1999 Season

	M	Inns	NO	Runs	HS	Avge	100s	50s	Ct	St	O	M	Runs	Wkts	Avge	Best	5wI	10wM
Test																		
All First	4	7	2	135	44 *	27.00	-	-	2	-	92	14	348	11	31.63	3-63	-	-
1-day Int																		
NatWest																			
B & H																			
1-day Lge																			

Career Performances

	M	Inns	NO	Runs	HS	Avge	100s	50s	Ct	St	Balls	Runs	Wkts	Avge	Best	5wI	10wM
Test																	
All First	11	15	3	233	44 *	19.41	-	-	6	-	940	553	17	32.52	3-49	-	-
1-day Int																	
NatWest																		
B & H																		
1-day Lge	2	1	1	4	4 *	-	-	-	-	-							

CUNLIFFE, R. J.　　　　　Gloucestershire

Name: Robert John Cunliffe
Role: Right-hand bat, cover fielder
Born: 8 November 1973, Oxford
Height: 5ft 10in **Weight:** 12st 8lbs
Nickname: 'Forrest Gump for some reason'
County debut: 1993 (one-day),
1994 (first-class)
1st-Class 50s: 9
1st-Class 100s: 3
1st-Class catches: 37
One-Day 100s: 3
Place in batting averages: 86th av. 32.38
(1998 239th av. 15.40)
Parents: Barry and Janet
Marital status: Engaged to Claire
Family links with cricket: 'Dad played in
his younger days for his wife's village team
and was groundsman for nine years at
Banbury Twenty CC'
Education: Grimsbury Primary; Banbury School; Banbury Technical College
Qualifications: Carpentry course, coaching award

Career outside cricket: Coaching
Overseas tours: England U19 to India 1992-93
Overseas teams played for: Richmond City CC, Melbourne 1995-97
Cricketers particularly admired: Robin Smith
Young players to look out for: Darren Maddy
Other sports played: Football
Relaxations: Walking the dog, watching TV
Extras: Played in England U19 home series against West Indies in 1993. Scored maiden Championship century v Northamptonshire at Northampton 1999
Best batting: 190* Gloucestershire v Oxford University, The Parks 1995

1999 Season

	M	Inns	NO	Runs	HS	Avge	100s	50s	Ct	St	O	M	Runs	Wkts	Avge	Best	5wl	10wM
Test																		
All First	7	13	0	421	108	32.38	1	2	8	-								
1-day Int																		
NatWest	5	4	0	55	38	13.75	-	-	1	-								
B & H	3	2	0	66	61	33.00	-	1	2	-								
1-day Lge	9	8	0	159	66	19.87	-	2	1	-								

Career Performances

	M	Inns	NO	Runs	HS	Avge	100s	50s	Ct	St	Balls	Runs	Wkts	Avge	Best	5wl	10wM
Test																	
All First	48	81	5	2051	190 *	26.98	3	9	37	-							
1-day Int																	
NatWest	10	8	0	165	40	20.62	-	-	2	-							
B & H	18	17	3	715	137 *	51.07	3	3	9	-							
1-day Lge	28	27	4	542	66	23.56	-	5	4	-							

CURRAN, K. M.   Northamptonshire

Name: Kevin Malcolm Curran
Role: Right-hand bat, right-arm fast-medium bowler
Born: 7 September 1959, Rusape, Zimbabwe
Height: 6ft 2in **Weight:** 14st
Nickname: KC
County debut: 1985 (Gloucestershire), 1991 (Northamptonshire)
County cap: 1985 (Gloucestershire), 1992 (Northamptonshire)
Benefit: 1999 (Northamptonshire)
One-Day Internationals: 11
1000 runs in a season: 7

50 wickets in a season: 5
1st-Class 50s: 83
1st-Class 100s: 25
1st-Class 5 w. in innings: 15
1st-Class 10 w. in match: 4
1st-Class catches: 209
One-Day 100s: 1
One-Day 5 w. in innings: 1
Place in batting averages: (1998 78th
av. 32.22)
Strike rate: 30.00 (career 52.88)
Parent: Kevin
Wife and date of marriage: Sarah,
5 May 1992
Children: Thomas Kevin, 12 March 1995;
Benjamin Jack, 7 June 1996;
Sam, 3 June 1998
Family links with cricket: Father played for
Rhodesia 1947-54. Cousin Patrick Curran played for Rhodesia 1975
Education: Marandellas High School, Zimbabwe
Qualifications: 6 O-levels, 2 M-levels
Career outside cricket: Tobacco buyer/farmer
Overseas tours: Zimbabwe to Sri Lanka 1982, 1983-84, to England 1982, 1983
(World Cup), to Pakistan and India 1987 (World Cup)
Overseas teams played for: Zimbabwe and Natal 1988-92; Boland 1994-95, 1997
Other sports followed: Rugby union
Relaxations: 'Game fishing, especially along the North Natal coast, the Mozambique
coast, and Magaruque Island'
Extras: First player to take a Sunday League hat-trick and score 50 in the same match,
Gloucestershire v Warwickshire, Edgbaston 1989. Released by Gloucestershire at end
of 1990 after he had completed the season's double of 1000 runs and 50 wickets. Chose
to join Northamptonshire for the 1991 season after he had been approached by several
counties. Northants captain 1998. Retired from county cricket at end of 1999 season
Best batting: 159 Northamptonshire v Glamorgan, Abergavenny 1997
Best bowling: 7-47 Northamptonshire v Yorkshire, Harrogate 1993

1999 Season

	M	Inns	NO	Runs	HS	Avge	100s	50s	Ct	St	O	M	Runs	Wkts	Avge	Best	5wI	10wM
Test																		
All First	1	2	0	1	1	0.50	-	-	-	-	5	1	21	1	21.00	1-21	-	-
1-day Int																		
NatWest	3	3	2	17	8	17.00	-	-	-	-	27	2	104	6	17.33	4-29	-	
B & H																			
1-day Lge	14	14	5	165	36	18.33	-	-	6	-	97	14	380	11	34.54	3-12	-	

Career Performances

	M	Inns	NO	Runs	HS	Avge	100s	50s	Ct	St	Balls	Runs	Wkts	Avge	Best	5wI	10wM
Test																	
All First	324	510	83	15740	159	36.86	25	83	209	-	31994	16730	605	27.65	7-47	15	4
1-day Int	11	11	0	287	73	26.09	-	2	1	-	506	398	9	44.22	3-65	-	
NatWest	45	39	9	879	78 *	29.30	-	4	13	-	2315	1335	47	28.40	4-29	-	
B & H	57	52	8	1142	71	25.95	-	7	13	-	2550	1768	53	33.35	4-38	-	
1-day Lge	214	204	43	5171	119 *	32.11	1	29	51	-	6540	5345	188	28.43	5-15	1	

DAGNALL, C. E. Warwickshire

Name: Charles Edward Dagnall
Role: Right-hand bat, right-arm
fast-medium bowler
Born: 10 July 1976, Bury, Lancashire
Height: 6ft 3in **Weight:** 14st 13lbs
Nickname: Baggo, Dog-face, Elvis, Slagnall,
Daggers, Dr Evil
County debut: 1999
Strike rate: 26.83 (career 26.83)
Parents: Mike and Jackie
Marital status: 'Very single'
Family links with cricket: Parents both
umpires; 'Dad ran town team U13'
Education: Bolton School; Bridgwater
School, Worsley; UMIST
Qualifications: 9 GCSEs, 3 A-levels,
BSc (Hons) Chemistry
Off-season: Working with coaches on
technique
Overseas teams played for: Newtown, Geelong, Australia 1994-95; St Josephs,
Geelong 1998-99
Cricketers particularly admired: Ian Botham, Paul Killey, Andy Cumberbatch,
Gladstone Small, Allan Donald
Young players to look out for: Ian Bell, Darren Altree, 'all of Cumberland CCC',
Scott Henderson, 'Dr Evil'
Other sports played: Volleyball
Other sports followed: Football (Burnley FC), golf, tennis
Injuries: Out for two weeks with calf strain
Relaxations: Meeting new people, golf, listening to music from the '70s; 'cooking for
A. Richardson'
Extras: Played for Cumberland. Man of the Match, Board XI final 1999

(Warwickshire v Essex). Topped 2nd XI batting averages 1998 and was second in bowling averages. Awarded 2nd XI cap 1999. Took a wicket with his fourth ball in first-class cricket v Oxford University at The Parks 1999

Opinions on cricket: 'Two division competition has made normally mundane end of season fixtures into potentially very competitive and exciting games. However, too much cricket is still being played, and injuries take their toll on players because of this.'

Best bowling: 4-20 Warwickshire v Oxford University, The Parks 1999

1999 Season

	M	Inns	NO	Runs	HS	Avge	100s	50s	Ct	St	O	M	Runs	Wkts	Avge	Best	5wI	10wM
Test																		
All First	1	1	0	0	0	0.00	-	-	-	-	26.5	7	88	6	14.66	4-20	-	-
1-day Int																		
NatWest																		
B & H																		
1-day Lge																		

Career Performances

	M	Inns	NO	Runs	HS	Avge	100s	50s	Ct	St	Balls	Runs	Wkts	Avge	Best	5wI	10wM
Test																	
All First	1	1	0	0	0	0.00	-	-	-	-	161	88	6	14.66	4-20	-	-
1-day Int																	
NatWest	1	1	0	4	4	4.00	-	-	-	-	54	37	1	37.00	1-37	-	
B & H																	
1-day Lge																	

31. Who led Hampshire to their first County Championship in 1961?

DAKIN, J. M.   Leicestershire

Name: Jonathan Michael Dakin
Role: Left-hand bat, right-arm
medium-fast bowler, 'benefit wicketkeeper'
Born: 28 February 1973, Hitchin, Herts
Height: 6ft 4in **Weight:** 16st
Nickname: JD, Butterbean
County debut: 1993
1st-Class 50s: 6
1st-Class 100s: 4
1st-Class catches: 13
One-Day 100s: 1
One-Day 5 w. in innings: 1
Place in batting averages: 118th av. 28.37
(1998 178th av. 21.33)
Place in bowling averages: 98th av. 30.26
Strike rate: 69.21 (career 78.15)
Parents: Fred John and Gloria May
Marital status: Single
Family links with cricket: Brother plays local cricket
Education: King Edward VII School, Johannesburg, South Africa
Qualifications: Matriculation
Off-season: Resting; training
Overseas tours: Rutland Tourists to Jersey 1992; Leicestershire CCC to South Africa 1996, 1997
Overseas teams played for: Wanderers, South Africa 1986-92; Alberts, South Africa 1993; Kaponga CC, New Zealand 1995-96
Cricketers particularly admired: Darren Maddy, Victor Patrick
Young players to look out for: Ashley Wright
Other sports followed: Football (Qwa Qwa Stars FC), rugby union (Leicester Tigers)
Relaxations: Cinema, television, golf, having *a* drink in a pub
Extras: Won three Bain Hogg trophies in four years. Scored 193 against Middlesex in the Bain Hogg in 1996. Won the Gold Award against Durham in the 1996 B&H
Opinions on cricket: 'Tea should be 30 minutes. Four-day games should be played on better pitches and not be over in two days.'
Best batting: 190 Leicestershire v Northamptonshire, Northampton 1997
Best bowling: 4-27 Leicestershire v Worcestershire, Worcester 1999

1999 Season

	M	Inns	NO	Runs	HS	Avge	100s	50s	Ct	St	O	M	Runs	Wkts	Avge	Best	5wI	10wM
Test																		
All First	11	18	2	454	124	28.37	1	3	2	-	219.1	61	575	19	30.26	4-27	-	-
1-day Int																		
NatWest	1	1	0	0	0	0.00	-	-	-	-	3	0	19	0	-		-	-
B & H																		
1-day Lge	15	12	2	236	41	23.60	-	-	3	-	93.3	5	441	17	25.94	5-30	1	

Career Performances

	M	Inns	NO	Runs	HS	Avge	100s	50s	Ct	St	Balls	Runs	Wkts	Avge	Best	5wI	10wM
Test																	
All First	33	48	5	1288	190	29.95	4	6	13	-	3439	1682	44	38.22	4-27	-	-
1-day Int																	
NatWest	5	5	0	63	26	12.60	-	-	-	-	162	119	1	119.00	1-63	-	
B & H	12	9	3	295	108*	49.16	1	-	5	-	327	317	10	31.70	3-68	-	
1-day Lge	81	71	8	932	45	14.79	-	-	17	-	1959	1743	69	25.26	5-30	1	

DALE, A.　　　　　　Glamorgan

Name: Adrian Dale
Role: Right-hand bat, right-arm medium bowler
Born: 24 October 1968, Johannesburg
Height: 5ft 11in **Weight:** 11st 10lbs
Nickname: Arthur
County debut: 1989
County cap: 1992
1000 runs in a season: 3
1st-Class 50s: 44
1st-Class 100s: 16
1st-Class 200s: 1
1st-Class 5 w. in innings: 2
1st-Class catches: 68
One-Day 100s: 2
One-Day 5 w. in innings: 2
Place in batting averages: 99th av. 31.11
(1998 79th av. 32.12)
Place in bowling averages: 67th av. 27.13 (1998 52nd av. 25.61)
Strike rate: 54.73 (career 68.62)
Parents: John and Maureen

Wife and date of marriage: Ruth, 9 January 1999
Family links with cricket: 'Father played for Chepstow CC and had the odd game for Glamorgan 2nd XI'
Education: Pembroke Primary; Chepstow Comprehensive; Swansea University
Qualifications: 9 O-levels, 3 A-levels, BA (Hons) Economics
Career outside cricket: 'Tried estate agency and marketing'
Off-season: Working for Glamorgan CCC in the marketing department
Overseas tours: Welsh Schools U16 to Australia 1986-87; Combined Universities to Barbados 1988-89; Glamorgan to Trinidad 1989-90, to Zimbabwe 1990-91, to Trinidad 1991-92, to Cape Town 1992-93, 1999; England A to South Africa 1993-94
Overseas teams played for: Bionics, Zimbabwe 1990-91; Cornwall, New Zealand 1991-93, 1995-97
Cricketers particularly admired: Ian Botham, Michael Holding, Mike Gatting
Young players to look out for: Mike Powell, Wayne Law
Other sports followed: Football (Arsenal), rugby union (Wales)
Injuries: Out for one week with back injury ('helping Owen Parkin to move house!')
Relaxations: Eating out, following other sports, travelling
Extras: Played in successful Combined Universities sides of 1989 and 1990. Only batsman to score two half-centuries against the West Indies tourists in the same match in 1991. Took a wicket with his first delivery at Lord's. Recorded Glamorgan's then best one-day bowling figures, 6-22, against Durham 1993. Recorded Glamorgan's highest ever partnership, 425*, with Viv Richards against Middlesex, 1993. Scored two centuries in Championship match v Gloucestershire at Cardiff 1999
Opinions on cricket: 'I think two divisions in the County Championship will not necessarily improve the standard. It may, however, improve the viability for sponsors. A transfer system is sure to follow now two divisions are in place. No one can say with any confidence the financial effect on the game, and it could lead to the shambles that we now see in rugby.'
Best batting: 214* Glamorgan v Middlesex, Cardiff 1993
Best bowling: 6-18 Glamorgan v Warwickshire, Cardiff 1993

1999 Season

	M	Inns	NO	Runs	HS	Avge	100s	50s	Ct	St	O	M	Runs	Wkts	Avge	Best	5wI	10wM
Test																		
All First	16	26	0	809	113	31.11	3	1	4	-	136.5	46	407	15	27.13	3-29	-	-
1-day Int																		
NatWest	3	3	0	102	43	34.00	-	-	-	-	12.4	0	72	3	24.00	2-38	-	
B & H																		
1-day Lge	15	14	3	365	74 *	33.18	-	3	3	-	83.3	5	339	9	37.66	3-19	-	

Career Performances

	M	Inns	NO	Runs	HS	Avge	100s	50s	Ct	St	Balls	Runs	Wkts	Avge	Best	5wI	10wM
Test																	
All First	181	299	24	8966	214 *	32.60	17	44	68	-	12215	6559	178	36.84	6-18	2	-
1-day Int																	
NatWest	29	26	2	782	110	32.58	1	3	6	-	1142	825	24	34.37	3-54	-	
B & H	33	32	4	758	100	27.07	1	1	10	-	1268	902	39	23.12	5-41	1	
1-day Lge	144	128	16	3200	82	28.57	-	19	33	-	4437	3909	119	32.84	6-22	1	

DALEY, J. A.   Durham

Name: James Arthur Daley
Role: Right-hand bat
Born: 24 September 1973, Sunderland
Height: 5ft 11in **Weight:** 12st
Nickname: Bebs, Jonty
County debut: 1992
County cap: 1999
1st-Class 50s: 17
1st-Class 100s: 3
1st-Class catches: 38
Place in batting averages: 136th av. 26.47
(1998 86th av. 31.70)
Strike rate: (career 84.00)
Parents: William and Christine
Marital status: Single
Family links with cricket: Brother played
representative cricket for Durham
Education: Hetton Comprehensive
Qualifications: 5 GCSEs
Career outside cricket: Travel agent
Overseas tours: Durham to Zimbabwe 1991-92; England U19 to India 1992-93;
England XI to Holland 1993
Cricketers particularly admired: David Graveney, Wayne Larkins, Jimmy Adams
Other sports followed: Most sports
Relaxations: Socialising, listening to all types of music
Extras: Scored three centuries in 1991 for MCC Young Cricketers at Lord's. Northern
Electric Foundation for Sport award winner 1992. Awarded Durham cap 1999
Best batting: 159* Durham v Hampshire, Portsmouth 1994
Best bowling: 1-12 Durham v Cambridge University, Fenner's 1998

1999 Season

	M	Inns	NO	Runs	HS	Avge	100s	50s	Ct	St	O	M	Runs	Wkts	Avge	Best	5wl	10wM
Test																		
All First	14	24	1	609	105	26.47	1	3	7	-	11	2	40	0	-	-	-	-
1-day Int																		
NatWest																		
B & H																		
1-day Lge	12	11	0	294	90	26.72	-	1	3	-								

Career Performances

	M	Inns	NO	Runs	HS	Avge	100s	50s	Ct	St	Balls	Runs	Wkts	Avge	Best	5wl	10wM
Test																	
All First	72	125	11	3467	159 *	30.41	3	17	38	-	84	61	1	61.00	1-12	-	-
1-day Int																	
NatWest																	
B & H	7	6	0	79	33	13.16	-	-	-	-	12	19	0	-	-	-
1-day Lge	38	34	8	875	98 *	33.65	-	5	10	-	1	4	0	-	-	-

DALRYMPLE, J. W. M. Middlesex

Name: James William Murray Dalrymple
Role: Right-hand bat, off-spin bowler
Born: 21 January 1981, Nairobi, Kenya
Height: 6ft **Weight:** 13st 3lbs
County debut: No first-team appearance
Parents: Dougie and Patricia
Marital status: Single
Family links with cricket: 'Dad played lots of club cricket'
Education: Ashfold School, Dorton; Radley College, Abingdon; St Peter's College, Oxford University ('October 2000')
Qualifications: 10 GCSEs, 5 A-levels
Career outside cricket: Student
Off-season: Studying/training
Cricketers particularly admired: Ian Botham, Mark Waugh, Mike Atherton, Courtney Walsh, Viv Richards
Other sports played: Rugby, hockey (county), golf, tennis
Other sports followed: Rugby (Northampton RUFC), football (Tottenham Hotspur)
Relaxations: Golf, tennis, flying, reading, music

DAVIES, A. P. — Glamorgan

Name: Andrew Philip Davies
Role: Left-hand bat, right-arm medium-fast bowler
Born: 7 November 1976, Neath
Height: 6ft **Weight:** 13st
Nickname: Diver
County debut: 1995
1st-Class catches: 1
Place in bowling averages: (1998 69th av. 27.85)
Strike rate: 126.00 (career 69.68)
Parents: Phil and Anne
Marital status: Girlfriend Sam
Family links with cricket: 'Dad and brother play for local side'
Education: Coedffranc; Dwr-y-Felin Comprehensive School; Christ College, Brecon
Qualifications: 6 GCSEs, 1 A-level; two coaching awards
Career outside cricket: 'Learning from the multi-talented, vastly experienced Glamorgan wicket-keeper, A. D. Shaw!'
Off-season: Rehabilitation after shoulder surgery
Overseas tours: Wales MC to Barbados; Glamorgan to Pretoria, to Cape Town
Overseas teams played for: Marist CC, Whangarei, New Zealand 1995-96
Cricketers particularly admired: Graham Thorpe, Steve Watkin, Adrian Shaw
Young players to look out for: David Harrison, Mark Wallace
Other sports played: 'Lucky enough once to be on the same touch rugby side as Adrian Shaw, that great Neath winger!!!'
Other sports followed: Football (Swansea City)
Injuries: Out for the last three weeks of the season with a second dislocation of the left shoulder
Relaxations: 'Interests include watching Adrian Shaw stretch before a game!!!'
Extras: Trials at Birmingham City FC. Rugby trials for Wales U17. Welsh U19 Player of the Year 1995. 'Special achievements in cricket would be receiving a pass from Alun Evans in the warm-up games of rugby or football.'
Opinions on cricket: 'Combine Minor Counties cricket with 2nd team cricket (and without doubt knight A. D. Shaw!).'
Best batting: 34 Glamorgan v Essex, Chelmsford 1998
Best bowling: 2-22 Glamorgan v Sussex, Hove 1998

1999 Season

	M	Inns	NO	Runs	HS	Avge	100s	50s	Ct	St	O	M	Runs	Wkts	Avge	Best	5wI	10wM
Test																		
All First	1	1	0	5	5	5.00	-	-	-	-	21	4	78	1	78.00	1-48	-	-
1-day Int																		
NatWest																		
B & H																		
1-day Lge	3	2	0	1	1	0.50	-	-	-	-	15	0	91	2	45.50	1-41	-	

Career Performances

	M	Inns	NO	Runs	HS	Avge	100s	50s	Ct	St	Balls	Runs	Wkts	Avge	Best	5wI	10wM
Test																	
All First	9	9	2	79	34	11.28	-	-	1	-	1115	603	16	37.68	2-22	-	-
1-day Int																	
NatWest																	
B & H																	
1-day Lge	10	7	3	27	18	6.75	-	-	1	-	370	281	12	23.41	2-17	-	

DAVIES, M. K.   Northamptonshire

Name: Michael Kenton Davies
Role: Right-hand bat, slow left-arm bowler
Born: 17 July 1976, Ashby-de-la-Zouch
Height: 6ft **Weight:** 12st
Nickname: Dicky
County debut: 1997
1st-Class 5 w. in innings: 5
1st-Class catches: 5
Place in batting averages: 283rd av. 7.85
Place in bowling averages:
27th av. 21.42
Strike rate: 63.52 (career 63.41)
Parents: Lyndon and Ann
Marital status: Single
Education: Fairfield Primary School,
Loughborough; Loughborough Grammar
School; Loughborough University
Qualifications: 8 GCSEs, 4 A-levels,
BSc PE, Sports Science and Recreation Management
Off-season: England A tour to Bangladesh and New Zealand
Overseas tours: England A to Bangladesh and New Zealand 1999-2000

Overseas teams played for: Techs CC, Cape Town 1999
Cricketers particularly admired: Nick Cook, Steve Waugh
Young players to look out for: Mark Powell, Monty Panesar
Other sports played: Golf
Other sports followed: 'Wales at anything, especially rugby'
Injuries: Shin splints – no time off required
Relaxations: Music, cinema, socialising
Extras: Leicestershire U19 Player of the Year. Represented British Universities; was a member of BUSA's cricket squad in the 1997 Benson and Hedges Cup
Opinions on cricket: 'Two divisions is a good idea. Tea should be longer.'
Best batting: 32* Northamptonshire v Durham, Northampton 1999
Best bowling: 6-49 Northamptonshire v Hampshire, Northampton 1999

1999 Season

	M	Inns	NO	Runs	HS	Avge	100s	50s	Ct	St	O	M	Runs	Wkts	Avge	Best	5wl	10wM
Test																		
All First	13	18	4	110	32 *	7.85	-	-	3	-	423.3	137	857	40	21.42	6-49	3	-
1-day Int																		
NatWest																		
B & H																		
1-day Lge																		

Career Performances

	M	Inns	NO	Runs	HS	Avge	100s	50s	Ct	St	Balls	Runs	Wkts	Avge	Best	5wl	10wM
Test																	
All First	21	30	9	182	32 *	8.66	-	-	5	-	4439	1723	70	24.61	6-49	5	-
1-day Int																	
NatWest																	
B & H	6	3	2	4	2 *	4.00	-	-	-	-	272	238	5	47.60	3-11	-	
1-day Lge																	

32. Which Test fast bowler topped the Surrey bowling averages in 1991
with 113 wickets at 14.36 each?

DAWOOD, I.   Glamorgan

Name: Ismail Dawood
Role: Right-hand bat, wicket-keeper
Born: 23 July 1976, Dewsbury
Height: 5ft 8in
Nickname: Hectic
County debut: 1994 (Northamptonshire),
1996 (Worcestershire), 1998 (Glamorgan)
1st-Class 50s: 1
1st-Class 100s: 1
1st-Class catches: 43
1st-Class stumpings: 3
Place in batting averages: 182nd av. 21.83
(1998 216th av. 17.63)
Parents: Saleem and Rashida
Marital status: Single
Family links with cricket: Grandfather and
father played local league cricket
Education: Batley Grammar School
Qualifications: 8 GCSEs, NCA Coaching Award
Overseas tours: England U19 to Sri Lanka 1993-94, to West Indies 1994-95
Overseas teams played for: Grafton, Auckland 1992-93
Cricketers particularly admired: Mohammed Azharuddin, Allan Border, Ian Healy
'and many others'
Other sports followed: Local soccer team
Relaxations: 'Spending time with family and friends'
Extras: Left Northamptonshire at the end of the 1995 season and joined
Worcestershire in 1996. Joined Glamorgan for the 1998 season. Scored maiden first-
class century v Gloucestershire at Cardiff 1999; took five catches at short leg in the
same match. Released by Glamorgan at the end of the 1999 season
Opinions on cricket: 'The game should be played in good spirit and enjoyed at all
levels from junior to Test cricket.'
Best batting: 102 Glamorgan v Gloucestershire, Cardiff 1999

1999 Season

	M	Inns	NO	Runs	HS	Avge	100s	50s	Ct	St	O	M	Runs	Wkts	Avge	Best	5wI	10wM
Test																		
All First	7	12	0	262	102	21.83	1	1	20	-								
1-day Int																		
NatWest	3	2	0	36	22	18.00	-	-	-	1								
B & H																		
1-day Lge	5	4	0	27	13	6.75	-	-	7	-								

Career Performances

	M	Inns	NO	Runs	HS	Avge	100s	50s	Ct	St	Balls	Runs	Wkts	Avge	Best	5wl	10wM
Test																	
All First	17	28	3	469	102	18.76	1	1	43	3							
1-day Int																	
NatWest	3	2	0	36	22	18.00	-	-	-	1							
B & H																	
1-day Lge	14	13	3	142	57	14.20	-	1	13	3							

DAWSON, R. I.   Gloucestershire

Name: Robert Ian Dawson
Role: Right-hand bat, right-arm
leg-spin bowler
Born: 29 March 1970, Exmouth, Devon
Height: 5ft 11in **Weight:** 14st
Nickname: Daws, Giggsy
County debut: 1991 (one-day),
1992 (first-class)
1000 runs in a season: 1
1st-Class 50s: 12
1st-Class 100s: 3
1st-Class catches: 31
Place in batting averages: (1998 255th
av. 13.61)
Strike rate: (career 49.37)
Parents: Barry and Shirley
Marital status: Single
Family links with cricket: Father and
brother both played club cricket
Education: Beacon School, Exmouth; Millfield School; Newcastle Polytechnic
Qualifications: 8 O-levels, 3 A-levels
Overseas tours: Exeter University to Barbados 1989; Gloucestershire Gypsies to
Zimbabwe 1995, to South Africa 1996, 1998; Gloucestershire CCC to Zimbabwe
1996, 1997
Overseas teams played for: Amamzimtoti, South Africa, 1993-94; Strathfield CC,
Sydney 1996-97; Vaal Tech Uni, Johannesburg 1997-98
Cricketers particularly admired: Ian Botham, David Gower, Sachin Tendulkar
Young players to look out for: Steve Harmison, Matthew Church, James Averis
Other sports played: Golf
Other sports followed: Football (Man Utd), 'most sports bar motor racing'
Relaxations: 'Watching sport and spending time with my mates'

Extras: Played in NatWest for Devon (from 1988), before joining Gloucestershire. Released by Gloucestershire at end of 1999 season
Best batting: 127* Gloucestershire v Cambridge University, Bristol 1994
Best bowling: 3-15 Gloucestershire v Lancashire, Old Trafford 1998

1999 Season

	M	Inns	NO	Runs	HS	Avge	100s	50s	Ct	St	O	M	Runs	Wkts	Avge	Best	5wI	10wM
Test																		
All First	1	2	0	46	36	23.00	-	-	1	-								
1-day Int																		
NatWest																		
B & H																		
1-day Lge	7	7	1	112	39	18.66	-	-	1	-								

Career Performances

	M	Inns	NO	Runs	HS	Avge	100s	50s	Ct	St	Balls	Runs	Wkts	Avge	Best	5wI	10wM
Test																	
All First	64	115	9	2598	127 *	24.50	3	12	31	-	395	199	8	24.87	3-15	-	-
1-day Int																	
NatWest	7	6	0	108	60	18.00	-	1	-	-	24	37	1	37.00	1-37	-	
B & H	18	17	0	345	38	20.29	-	-	1	-	18	12	0	-	-	-	
1-day Lge	89	81	9	1805	85	25.06	-	8	19	-	38	59	1	59.00	1-19	-	

DAWSON, R. K. J. Yorkshire

Name: Richard Kevin James Dawson
Role: Right-hand bat, right-arm off-spin bowler
Born: 4 August 1980, Doncaster
Height: 6ft 4in **Weight:** 11st 4lbs
Nickname: Billy Dog
County debut: No first-team appearance
Parents: Kevin and Pat
Marital status: Single
Family links with cricket: Brother Gareth plays for Doncaster Town CC
Education: Hill House Preparatory School; Batley Grammar School; Exeter University
Qualifications: 10 GCSEs, 4 A-levels
Career outside cricket: Student
Off-season: University studies
Overseas tours: England U18 to Bermuda 1997; England U19 to New Zealand 1998-99
Cricketers particularly admired: Steve Waugh, Graeme Swann

Young players to look out for: Graeme Bridge, Ian Bell
Other sports played: Football
Other sports followed: Football (Doncaster Rovers FC)
Relaxations: Sleeping, listening to music
Extras: Sir John Hobbs Jubilee Memorial Prize 1995. Captained England U15. Played for Devon 1999. Represented England U19 in one-day and 'Test' series v Australia U19 in 1999
Opinions on cricket: 'The wickets should be better. Tea should be made longer.'

1999 Season (did not make any first-class or one-day appearances)

Career Performances

	M	Inns	NO	Runs	HS	Avge	100s	50s	Ct	St	Balls	Runs	Wkts	Avge	Best	5wI	10wM
Test																	
All First																		
1-day Int																		
NatWest	2	2	0	9	7	4.50	-	-	1	-	108	83	3	27.66	2-32	-	
B & H																		
1-day Lge																		

33. Which all-rounder scored 962 Championship runs and took 121 Championship wickets for Nottinghamshire in 1988?

DEAN, K. J.   Derbyshire

Name: Kevin James Dean
Role: Left-hand bat, left-arm
medium-fast bowler
Born: 16 October 1975, Derby
Height: 6ft 4in **Weight:** 14st 7lbs
Nickname: Deany, Red Face, The Wall
County debut: 1996
County cap: 1998
50 wickets in a season: 1
1st-Class 5 w. in innings: 5
1st-Class 10 w. in match: 1
1st-Class catches: 5
One-Day 5 w. in innings: 1
Place in batting averages: (1998 200th
av. 19.25)
Place in bowling averages: 6th av. 16.50
(1998 23rd av. 21.24)
Strike rate: 33.33 (career 42.02)
Parents: Ken and Dorothy
Marital status: Single
Education: Waterhouses Primary School; Leek High School; Leek College of Further
Education
Qualifications: 8 GCSEs, 3 A-levels, 1 AS-level
Career outside cricket: Working for Ladbrokes
Off-season: Working for Ladbrokes and 'swimming, swimming, swimming, and – oh,
yes – a bit more swimming!!'
Overseas teams played for: Sturt CC, Adelaide 1996-97
Cricketers particularly admired: Wasim Akram, Courtney Walsh, Dominic Cork,
'also any member of the "Left Arm Union": Mullally, Ilott, Smith, Lewry, Sheriyar,
Taylor, Brown, Bulbeck, Hutchison, Sidebottom etc'
Young players to look out for: Dimitri Mascarenhas, Matt Bulbeck
Other sports played: Football (Blue Circle), golf, tennis, squash ('I will beat you, Cas')
Other sports followed: Football (Derby County), tennis ('Anna Kournikova!')
Injuries: Out for 'far too long' with a bad back
Relaxations: 'Trying to tip Krikk the winner of the most difficult horse race of the
day!! Going to the races. Playing golf'
Extras: A member of the Staffordshire U16 Texaco winning team. Achieved first-class
hat-trick against Kent at Derby 1998
Opinions on cricket: 'Day/night cricket is the best change in cricket for years. It feels
more of an event for players and spectators alike. There should be more matches under
lights and children should be admitted free.'

Best batting: 27* Derbyshire v South Africa, Derby 1998
Best bowling: 6-63 Derbyshire v Somerset, Taunton 1998

1999 Season

	M	Inns	NO	Runs	HS	Avge	100s	50s	Ct	St	O	M	Runs	Wkts	Avge	Best	5wI	10wM
Test																		
All First	3	2	1	15	10 *	15.00	-	-	1	-	66.4	14	198	12	16.50	4-34	-	-
1-day Int																		
NatWest	1	1	0	8	8	8.00	-	-	1	-	7	2	17	1	17.00	1-17	-	
B & H																		
1-day Lge	4	1	0	10	10	10.00	-	-	-	-	29	2	129	5	25.80	4-35	-	

Career Performances

	M	Inns	NO	Runs	HS	Avge	100s	50s	Ct	St	Balls	Runs	Wkts	Avge	Best	5wI	10wM
Test																	
All First	36	43	20	281	27 *	12.21	-	-	5	-	5466	3052	130	23.47	6-63	5	1
1-day Int																	
NatWest	10	3	2	8	8	8.00	-	-	4	-	570	407	17	23.94	3-13	-	
B & H	6	2	1	20	14 *	20.00	-	-	-	-	240	211	5	42.20	2-62	-	
1-day Lge	37	11	7	55	16 *	13.75	-	-	8	-	1521	1157	41	28.21	5-32	1	

DEANE, M. J.   Derbyshire

Name: Michael John Deane
Role: Right-hand bat, right-arm
fast-medium bowler
Born: 9 March 1977, Chesterfield
Height: 6ft 2in **Weight:** 11st 11lbs
Nickname: Deano, Deanie
County debut: 1999
1st-Class catches: 1
Strike rate: 95.00 (career 95.00)
Parents: John Anthony and Betty
Marital status: Single
Family links with cricket: Father played for
Trinidad plus cricket clubs in Leicestershire
and Derbyshire. Grandmother played cricket
for her school
Education: Christ the King, Alfreton; St
Joseph's RC School, Staveley; St Mary's
High School, Chesterfield; Abbotsholme

School, Rocester; Coventry University ('one year; wished to continue with cricket')
Qualifications: 8 GCSEs, 2 A-levels
Career outside cricket: Works for Beechdale Saab when not abroad
Overseas teams played for: Alma Marist, Cape Town 1997-98; Queen's Park CC, West Indies (temporary membership) 1998-99
Cricketers particularly admired: Stephen Waugh, Michael Holding
Other sports played: Soccer and other ball games
Other sports followed: Football (Derby County), 'interested in all sports'
Relaxations: Cinema, travel, music
Extras: Cricket bat signed by living England captains for 112 in 56 deliveries v MCC at Abbotsholme. Represented Derbyshire at every level from age of eight to U21 and 2nd XI. Represented North of England team. Set World Independent Schools 100-metre record of 10.90 seconds at age 17. Released by Derbyshire at end of 1999 season
Opinions on cricket: 'I am formulating ideas and learning about the game as I go along. I like being actively involved at all times. I just love the sport.'
Best batting: 10 Derbyshire v Somerset, Derby 1999
Best bowling: 2-42 Derbyshire v Yorkshire, Derby 1999

1999 Season

	M	Inns	NO	Runs	HS	Avge	100s	50s	Ct	St	O	M	Runs	Wkts	Avge	Best	5wI	10wM
Test																		
All First	2	3	0	11	10	3.66	-	-	1	-	31.4	8	112	2	56.00	2-42	-	-
1-day Int																		
NatWest	1	1	1	1	1 *	-	-	-	-	-	3	0	17	0	-		-	-
B & H																		
1-day Lge	1	0	0	0	0	-	-	-	-	-	9	0	42	3	14.00	3-42	-	

Career Performances

	M	Inns	NO	Runs	HS	Avge	100s	50s	Ct	St	Balls	Runs	Wkts	Avge	Best	5wI	10wM
Test																	
All First	2	3	0	11	10	3.66	-	-	1	-	190	112	2	56.00	2-42	-	-
1-day Int																	
NatWest	1	1	1	1	1 *	-	-	-	-	-	18	17	0	-		-	-
B & H																	
1-day Lge	1	0	0	0	0	-	-	-	-	-	54	42	3	14.00	3-42	-	

DEFREITAS, P. A. J.   Leicestershire

Name: Phillip Anthony Jason DeFreitas
Role: Right-hand bat, right-arm
fast-medium bowler
Born: 18 February 1966, Scotts Head,
Dominica
Height: 6ft **Weight:** 13st 7lbs
Nickname: Daffy, Lunchy
County debut: 1985 (Leics),
1989 (Lancs), 1994 (Derbys)
County cap: 1986 (Leics),
1989 (Lancs), 1994 (Derbys)
Test debut: 1986-87
Tests: 44
One-Day Internationals: 103
50 wickets in a season: 12
1st-Class 50s: 42
1st-Class 100s: 7
1st-Class 5 w. in innings: 54
1st-Class 10 w. in match: 5
1st-Class catches: 109
One-Day 5 w. in innings: 6
Place in batting averages: 141st av. 25.94 (1998 174th av. 21.75)
Place in bowling averages: 29th av. 21.76 (1998 56th av. 26.21)
Strike rate: 48.54 (career 56.59)
Parents: Sybil and Martin
Wife and date of marriage: Nicola, 10 December 1990
Children: Alexandra Elizabeth Jane, 5 August 1991
Family links with cricket: Father played in Windward Islands. All six brothers play
Education: Willesden High School
Qualifications: 2 O-levels
Overseas tours: England YC to West Indies 1984-85; England to Australia 1986-87,
to Pakistan, Australia and New Zealand 1987-88, to India (Nehru Cup) and West
Indies 1989-90, to Australia 1990-91, to New Zealand 1991-92, to India and Sri Lanka
1992-93, to Australia 1994-95, to South Africa 1995-96, to India and Pakistan (World
Cup) 1995-96
Overseas teams played for: Port Adelaide, South Australia 1985; Mosman, Sydney
1988; Boland, South Africa 1993-94, 1995-96
Cricketers particularly admired: Ian Botham, Graham Gooch, Geoff Boycott, Mike
Gatting
Other sports followed: Football (Manchester City) and rugby league (Warrington)
Relaxations: 'Golf, gardening, visiting stately homes, spending spare time with wife
and daughter Alexandra'

Extras: Left Leicestershire and joined Lancashire at end of 1988 season. Originally agreed to join unofficial English tour of South Africa 1989-90, but withdrew under pressure. Man of the Match in 1990 NatWest Trophy final. One of *Wisden*'s Five Cricketers of the Year 1992. Man of the Tournament in the Hong Kong Sixes 1993. Left Lancashire at the end of the 1993 season. Player of the Series against New Zealand 1994. Was called up to the England one-day squad in South Africa 1995-96 after spending the winter with Boland and went on to play in the World Cup. Captained Derbyshire for part of 1997 season after the departure of Dean Jones. Played for an England XI in the Cricket Max tournament in New Zealand in 1997. Is the only playing English cricketer to have appeared in two World Cup finals. Took 1000th first-class wicket (Usman Afzaal caught by Karl Krikken) v Notts at Trent Bridge 1999. Left Derbyshire at end of 1999 season and has rejoined Leicestershire for 2000
Best batting: 113 Leicestershire v Nottinghamshire, Worksop 1988
Best bowling: 7-21 Lancashire v Middlesex, Lord's 1989

1999 Season

	M	Inns	NO	Runs	HS	Avge	100s	50s	Ct	St	O	M	Runs	Wkts	Avge	Best	5wl	10wM
Test																		
All First	13	18	1	441	105	25.94	1	2	7	-	477.2	123	1284	59	21.76	6-41	4	-
1-day Int																		
NatWest	1	0	0	0	0	-	-	-	-	-	5	0	30	0	-		-	-
B & H																		
1-day Lge	10	10	0	223	61	22.30	-	1	3	-	81	9	283	7	40.42	2-19	-	

Career Performances

	M	Inns	NO	Runs	HS	Avge	100s	50s	Ct	St	Balls	Runs	Wkts	Avge	Best	5wl	10wM
Test	44	68	5	934	88	14.82	-	4	14	-	9838	4700	140	33.57	7-70	4	-
All First	300	426	39	8500	113	21.96	7	42	109	-	58118	28263	1027	27.52	7-21	54	5
1-day Int	103	66	23	690	67	16.04	-	1	26	-	5712	3775	115	32.82	4-35	-	
NatWest	37	24	4	363	69	18.15	-	1	6	-	2307	1182	51	23.17	5-13	4	
B & H	59	40	9	712	75 *	22.96	-	3	15	-	3307	1882	84	22.40	5-16	1	
1-day Lge	175	133	23	2168	72 *	19.70	-	6	33	-	7074	5218	191	27.31	5-26	1	

DE LA PENA, J. M.   Worcestershire

Name: Jason Michael de la Pena
Role: Right-hand bat, right-arm
fast-medium bowler
Born: 16 September 1972, Middlesex
Height: 6ft 6in **Weight:** 14st 7lbs

Nickname: Greasy Wop, Gin, Flying Spaniard
County debut: 1991 (Gloucestershire), 1994 (one-day, Surrey), 1995 (first-class, Surrey), 1998 (Kent), 1999 (Worcestershire)
1st-Class 5 w. in innings: 1
1st-Class 10 w. in match: 1
1st-Class catches: 1
Place in bowling averages: 11th av. 18.46
Strike rate: 29.46 (career 43.20)
Parents: Michael and Jacqueline, Mikki and Loy
Marital status: Single
Education: Lambrook Prep School, Ascot; Stowe School; Bournside Sixth Form College, Cheltenham
Qualifications: 8 GCSEs, 3 A-levels
Overseas tours: Gloucestershire to Namibia 1990, to Kenya 1991, to Sri Lanka 1992-93
Overseas teams played for: North Hobart, Tasmania 1991-93; Mossman, Sydney 1994-95
Cricketers particularly admired: David 'Syd' Lawrence, Dennis Lillee, Graham Dilley, Michael Holding, Allan Donald, Richard Hadlee
Other sports followed: Golf, tennis, surfing, windsurfing, rugby union
Relaxations: Cinema, music
Extras: Represented England U19 v Young Australia. Selected for England U19 tour to Pakistan 1991-92 but had to pull out two hours before leaving owing to severe illness and underwent an operation one day later. Joined Surrey from Gloucestershire in 1994; left Surrey at end of 1996 season. Attached to Kent 1998. Joined Worcs for 1999. Took 6-18 (10-52 in match) v Oxford University at The Parks 1999 on first-class debut for Worcs. Released by Worcs at end of 1999 season. Has also been registered for Hertfordshire
Best batting: 7* Gloucestershire v Yorkshire, Sheffield 1993
Best bowling: 6-18 Worcestershire v Oxford University, The Parks 1999

1999 Season

	M	Inns	NO	Runs	HS	Avge	100s	50s	Ct	St	O	M	Runs	Wkts	Avge	Best	5wI	10wM
Test																		
All First	3	3	0	0	0	0.00	-	-	1	-	63.5	19	240	13	18.46	6-18	1	1
1-day Int																		
NatWest																		
B & H																		
1-day Lge																		

Career Performances

	M	Inns	NO	Runs	HS	Avge	100s	50s	Ct	St	Balls	Runs	Wkts	Avge	Best	5wI	10wM
Test																	
All First	11	11	6	10	7 *	2.00	-	-	1	-	1253	896	29	30.89	6-18	1	1
1-day Int																	
NatWest																		
B & H																		
1-day Lge	2	2	2	2	2 *	-	-	-	-	-	42	61	0	-		-	-

DIVENUTO, M. J.   Derbyshire

Name: Michael James DiVenuto
Role: Left-hand (No. 3) bat, right-arm medium/leg-break bowler
Born: 12 December 1973, Hobart, Tasmania
Height: 5ft 11in **Weight:** 12st 12lbs
Nickname: Diva
County debut: 1999 (Sussex)
One-Day Internationals: 9
1000 runs in a season: 1
1st-Class 50s: 34
1st-Class 100s: 12
1st-Class catches: 68
Place in batting averages: 29th av. 41.03
Strike rate: 78.00 (career 330.00)
Parents: Enrico and Elizabeth
Marital status: Single
Family links with cricket: 'Dad and older brother Peter both played grade cricket in Tasmania'
Education: St Peter's School, Hobart; St Virgil's College, Hobart
Qualifications: HSC (5 x Level III subjects), Level III cricket coach
Career outside cricket: Part-time sports journalist with Southern Cross TV, Hobart
Off-season: Playing first-class cricket for Tasmania
Overseas tours: Australian Cricket Academy to India and Sri Lanka 1993, to South Africa 1996; Australia A to Malaysia 1997 (Super 8s; captain), to Scotland and Ireland 1998 (captain), to Los Angeles 1999; Australia to South Africa (one-day series) 1996-97, to Hong Kong 1998 (Super 6s), to Malaysia 1998 (Super 8s); Tasmania to Zimbabwe 1995-96
Overseas teams played for: North Hobart CC, Tasmania; Kingborough, Tasmania; Tasmania 1991-92 –
Cricketers particularly admired: David Boon, Dean Jones, Kepler Wessels, Mark and Steve Waugh

Young players to look out for: Simon Katich, Nathan Webb (young Tasmanian player), 'and Tony Cottey'
Other sports played: Australian Rules (Tasmanian U15, U16 and Sandy Bay FC)
Other sports followed: Australian Rules football (Geelong Cats)
Relaxations: Golf, sleeping
Extras: Represented Australia in Hong Kong 6s 1997 and Super 8s (Malaysia) 1998; captained Australia A in Super 8s (Malaysia) 1997. Scored career-best 189 v Western Australia in 1997-98 Sheffield Shield final, contributing more than 50 per cent of Tasmania's total in their second innings. Joined Sussex as overseas player for 1999, replacing Michael Bevan. Has joined Derbyshire as overseas player for 2000
Opinions on cricket: 'Playing cricket (first-class) on sub-standard wickets does nothing for the development of batsmen and bowlers striving to play at the highest level.'
Best batting: 189 Tasmania v Western Australia, Perth 1997-98
Best bowling: 1-3 Sussex v Somerset, Taunton 1999

1999 Season

	M	Inns	NO	Runs	HS	Avge	100s	50s	Ct	St	O	M	Runs	Wkts	Avge	Best	5wl	10wM
Test																		
All First	16	28	2	1067	162	41.03	3	5	20	-	13	2	40	1	40.00	1-3	-	-
1-day Int																		
NatWest	2	2	0	73	72	36.50	-	1	1	-								
B & H	2	2	0	103	62	51.50	-	1	-	-								
1-day Lge	14	14	4	596	94 *	59.60	-	6	6	-								

Career Performances

	M	Inns	NO	Runs	HS	Avge	100s	50s	Ct	St	Balls	Runs	Wkts	Avge	Best	5wl	10wM
Test																	
All First	83	145	6	5689	189	40.92	12	34	68	-	330	201	1	201.00	1-3	-	-
1-day Int	9	9	0	241	89	26.77	-	2	1	-							
NatWest	2	2	0	73	72	36.50	-	1	1	-							
B & H	2	2	0	103	62	51.50	-	1	-	-							
1-day Lge	14	14	4	596	94 *	59.60	-	6	6	-							

34. Which current international all-rounder made his
County Championship debut (for Nottinghamshire) in 1988?

DOBSON, M. C.   Northamptonshire

Name: Martyn Colin Dobson
Role: Right-hand bat, off-spin bowler
Born: 28 May 1982, Scunthorpe,
N. Lincolnshire
Height: 6ft **Weight:** 13st 12lbs
Nickname: Bonz
County debut: No first-team appearance
Parents: David and Susan
Marital status: Single
Family links with cricket: 'Dad played 2nd
XI cricket and was a league pro for many
years. Brother Michael was with Northants up
until last season'
Education: Bottesford Junior School;
Frederick Gough Comp; Oundle School
('Upper Sixth')
Qualifications: 9 GCSEs
Off-season: Studying for A-levels
Cricketers particularly admired: Carl Hooper, Viv Richards
Young players to look out for: Michael Dobson, John Sadler
Other sports played: Rugby (Oundle 1st XV, Lincs County Schools U15 and U16)
Other sports followed: Football (Liverpool FC, Scunthorpe Utd – 'somebody has to'),
rugby union (Scunthorpe RFC), rugby league (Bradford Bulls)
Relaxations: 'Music, socialising, any sport'
Extras: Captain of ESCA U14 and U15. Sir John Hobbs U16 prize from the Cricket
Society 1997. Top of both batting and bowling averages for Yorkshire U19 1998
Opinions on cricket: 'Too young and inexperienced to have any opinions. I look
forward to each and every game with great enthusiasm. I want to play for as long as
possible.'

DONALD, A. A.   Warwickshire

Name: Allan Anthony Donald
Role: Right-hand bat, right-arm fast bowler
Born: 20 October 1966, Bloemfontein, South Africa
Height: 6ft 3in **Weight:** 14st
County debut: 1987
County cap: 1989
Benefit: 1999

Test debut: 1991-92
Tests: 54
One-Day Internationals: 121
50 wickets in a season: 5
1st-Class 50s: 1
1st-Class 5 w. in innings: 61
1st-Class 10 w. in match: 8
1st-Class catches: 102
One-Day 5 w. in innings: 10
Place in bowling averages: (1998 17th
av. 20.12)
Strike rate: (career 47.25)
Parents: Stuart and Francine
Wife and date of marriage: Tina,
21 September 1991
Family links with cricket: Father and uncle
played club cricket
Education: Grey College High School;
Technical High School, Bloemfontein
Qualifications: Matriculation
Off-season: Playing for South Africa
Overseas tours: South Africa to India 1991-92, to Australia and New Zealand (World
Cup) 1991-92, to West Indies 1991-92, to Sri Lanka 1992-93, to Australia 1992-93, to
England 1994, to New Zealand 1994-95, to Zimbabwe 1995-96, to India and Pakistan
(World Cup) 1995-96, to India 1996-97, to Kenya 1996-97, to Pakistan 1997-98, to
Australia 1997-98, to England 1998, to New Zealand 1998-99, to UK, Ireland and
Holland (World Cup) 1999, to Zimbabwe 1999-2000
Overseas teams played for: Free State, South Africa 1985 –
Cricketers particularly admired: Richard Hadlee, Malcolm Marshall, Gladstone
Small, Andy Lloyd, Eddie Barlow
Other sports followed: Rugby, golf, tennis
Relaxations: 'Listening to music, having a barbecue, playing golf and having a few
beers with my friends'
Injuries: Ankle problems limited his appearances for Warwicks after World Cup to a
handful of games
Extras: Played for South African XI v Australian XI in 1986-87 and v English XI in
1989-90. Retained by Warwickshire for 1991 season ahead of Tom Moody. Toured
with South Africa on first-ever visit to India and to West Indies in 1991-92. One of
Wisden's Five Cricketers of the Year 1992. Took his 100th Test wicket against England
in Johannesburg 1995-96. Voted Man of the Series against England finishing with 19
wickets at an average of 26.15. Returned as overseas player for Warwickshire in 1997
after spending a year as the county's fitness coach. Took his 500th wicket for
Warwickshire during the 1997 season. Was awarded his country's highest sporting
honour when he was presented with a Gold Medal by Nelson Mandela at an awards
ceremony in Pretoria on 15 August 1997. Took his 200th Test wicket (Sanath

Jayasuriya) v Sri Lanka in 1998 in his 42nd Test, becoming the first South African to reach this landmark. Was South Africa's Man of the Series v England 1998. Took his 200th One-Day International wicket v Zimbabwe at Chelmsford in the 1999 World Cup. Featured in the Vodafone World Cup XI, a 'dream team' selected by journalists after the 1999 tournament. Returned to Warwickshire as overseas player for 1999
Best batting: 55* South Africa v Tasmania, Devonport 1997-98
Best bowling: 8-37 Orange Free State v Transvaal, Johannesburg 1986-87
Stop press: Selected for South Africa's tour of India 1999-2000

1999 Season

	M	Inns	NO	Runs	HS	Avge	100s	50s	Ct	St	O	M	Runs	Wkts	Avge	Best	5wl	10wM
Test																		
All First	2	4	2	14	10	7.00	-	-	1	-	50	15	136	0	-	-	-	-
1-day Int	9	3	1	10	7	5.00	-	-	2	-	82	7	325	16	20.31	4-17	-	
NatWest	1	1	0	7	7	7.00	-	-	-	-	10	0	53	2	26.50	2-53	-	
B & H	1	0	0	0	0	-	-	-	-	-	8.4	0	40	1	40.00	1-40	-	
1-day Lge	4	0	0	0	0	-	-	-	2	-	25	1	132	6	22.00	3-45	-	

Career Performances

	M	Inns	NO	Runs	HS	Avge	100s	50s	Ct	St	Balls	Runs	Wkts	Avge	Best	5wl	10wM
Test	54	70	26	504	34	11.45	-	-	14	-	12032	5742	265	21.66	8-71	17	2
All First	271	315	120	2386	55 *	12.23	-	1	102	-	50709	23970	1073	22.33	8-37	61	8
1-day Int	121	30	13	84	13	4.94	-	-	16	-	6438	4337	206	21.05	6-23	2	
NatWest	30	11	6	39	14 *	7.80	-	-	4	-	1889	1076	75	14.34	5-12	5	
B & H	27	15	8	87	23 *	12.42	-	-	4	-	1541	1036	39	26.56	5-25	1	
1-day Lge	75	24	12	139	18 *	11.58	-	-	18	-	3259	2206	108	20.42	6-15	2	

DOWMAN, M. P.   Derbyshire

Name: Mathew Peter Dowman
Role: Left-hand bat, right-arm medium bowler
Born: 10 May 1974, Grantham, Lincs
Height: 5ft 11in **Weight:** 12st
Nickname: Doomer, Rid Rod
County debut: 1993 (one-day, Nottinghamshire), 1994 (first-class, Nottinghamshire)
County cap: 1998 (Nottinghamshire)
1000 runs in a season: 1
1st-Class 50s: 12
1st-Class 100s: 6
1st-Class catches: 35
Place in batting averages: 74th av. 34.33 (1998 196th av. 19.60)

Place in bowling averages: (1998 106th av. 33.08)

Strike rate: 210.00 (career 88.00)

Parents: Clive and Jackie

Marital status: Single

Family links with cricket: Dad played for Grantham Town. Three brothers also play for Grantham, two of them representing Lincolnshire Schools and Lincolnshire U19

Education: Earl of Dysart Primary; St Hugh's Comprehensive; Grantham College

Qualifications: Senior coach

Career outside cricket: Undecided

Overseas tours: England U19 to India 1992-93; Lincolnshire U16 to Zimbabwe 1988-89; Nottinghamshire to Cape Town 1992-93, to Johannesburg 1996-97; also to Guernsey for Tim Robinson's benefit 1992

Overseas teams played for: South Burwon, Geelong, Melbourne 1995-96; East Shirley, Christchurch, New Zealand 1997-98

Cricketers particularly admired: Robin Smith, Mike Gatting, Malcolm Marshall, Jimmy Adams

Young players to look out for: Owais Shah, James Ormond, Andy Oram

Other sports followed: Golf, football ('follow Notts Forest and County and Lincoln City')

Relaxations: Watching films, playing golf, listening to music

Extras: Played in winning Midlands team at ESCA Festival 1989. Set record for most runs in a season for Lincolnshire Schools and record for most runs in Lincolnshire Schools career. Played for England U19 in home series against West Indies in 1993, scoring 267 in second 'Test'. Winner of the 1997 Uncapped Whyte and Mackay Batting Award. Released by Nottinghamshire at end of 1999 season and has joined Derbyshire for 2000 on a two-year contract

Opinions on cricket: 'None of any value.'

Best batting: 149 Nottinghamshire v Leicestershire, Leicester 1997

Best bowling: 3-10 Nottinghamshire v Pakistan A, Trent Bridge 1997

1999 Season

	M	Inns	NO	Runs	HS	Avge	100s	50s	Ct	St	O	M	Runs	Wkts	Avge	Best	5wI	10wM
Test																		
All First	9	15	3	412	67*	34.33	-	3	6	-	35	8	109	1	109.00	1-25	-	-
1-day Int																		
NatWest	2	2	0	23	15	11.50	-	-	-	-								
B & H																		
1-day Lge	8	8	1	134	52	19.14	-	1	1	-	16	0	92	2	46.00	1-26	-	

Career Performances

	M	Inns	NO	Runs	HS	Avge	100s	50s	Ct	St	Balls	Runs	Wkts	Avge	Best	5wI	10wM
Test																	
All First	62	109	7	2950	149	28.92	6	12	35	-	1848	963	21	45.85	3-10	-	-
1-day Int																	
NatWest	6	6	0	127	47	21.16	-	-	2	-	108	63	2	31.50	1-23	-	
B & H	14	10	2	329	92	41.12	-	2	5	-	332	248	11	22.54	3-21	-	
1-day Lge	61	61	3	1120	74 *	19.31	-	5	15	-	815	784	15	52.26	2-31	-	

DRAKES, V. C.   Nottinghamshire

Name: Vasbert Conniel Drakes
Role: Right-hand bat, right-arm fast bowler
Born: 5 August 1969, St Michael's, Barbados
Height: 6ft 2in **Weight:** 12st
County debut: 1996 (Sussex),
1999 (Nottinghamshire)
County cap: 1996 (Sussex),
1999 (Nottinghamshire)
One-day Internationals: 5
50 wickets in a season: 1
1st-Class 50s: 12
1st-Class 100s: 4
1st-Class 5 w. innings: 18
1st-Class 10 w. in match: 3
1st-Class catches: 30
One-Day 5 w. in innings: 2
Place in batting averages: 236th av. 15.81
Place in bowling averages: 38th av. 22.42
Strike rate: 43.97 (career 48.45)
Parents: Leon and Caroline
Marital status: Engaged
Family links with cricket: 'Sir Francis Drake is the famous bowler in the family – the only bowler to receive a knighthood. Introduced cricket to Barbados on an away day'
Education: St Lucy Secondary and College School, Barbados
Qualifications: NCA coach
Career outside cricket: Electrician
Overseas tours: Barbados U19 to UK 1987; Barbados U21 to UK 1990; Barbados to South Africa 1992; West Indies to England 1995
Overseas teams played for: Barbados 1991-92 –, Border, South Africa 1996-97 –
Cricketers particularly admired: Desmond Haynes, Malcolm Marshall, 'and all successful fast bowlers throughout the world'

Other sports followed: Tennis, golf, basketball, football (Arsenal) and volleyball
Relaxations: Listening to music
Extras: Was called up to the West Indies squad as a replacement for Winston Benjamin on the 1995 tour to England. Played for West Indies in One-Day International series against Australia in 1994-95. Once took 9-2 for Lamhey CC. Was Sussex overseas player in 1996 and 1997. Took 56 wickets for Border 1998-99, two short of the South African record shared by Peter Pollock and Sylvester Clarke. Joined Nottinghamshire as overseas player for 1999 on one-year contract. Took nine wickets on Championship debut for the county, v Worcestershire at Trent Bridge 1999. Took four wickets in four balls for Nottinghamshire in the final over of their National League victory v Derbyshire at Trent Bridge 1999; Derbyshire started the over needing ten runs with five wickets in hand. Awarded Nottinghamshire cap 1999; released by Nottinghamshire at end of 1999 season
Best batting: 180* Barbados v Leeward Islands, Anguilla 1994-95
Best bowling: 8-59 Border v KwaZulu-Natal, Durban 1996-97

1999 Season

	M	Inns	NO	Runs	HS	Avge	100s	50s	Ct	St	O	M	Runs	Wkts	Avge	Best	5wI	10wM
Test																		
All First	17	30	3	427	80	15.81	-	2	5	-	586.2	131	1794	80	22.42	6-39	5	2
1-day Int																		
NatWest	1	1	0	7	7	7.00	-	-	-	-	10	1	47	3	15.66	3-47	-	
B & H																		
1-day Lge	15	12	2	181	40	18.10	-	-	4	-	112.4	13	511	24	21.29	5-31	1	

Career Performances

	M	Inns	NO	Runs	HS	Avge	100s	50s	Ct	St	Balls	Runs	Wkts	Avge	Best	5wI	10wM
Test																	
All First	98	161	19	3138	180 *	22.09	4	12	30	-	17687	9357	365	25.63	8-59	18	3
1-day Int	5	2	0	25	16	12.50	-	-	1	-	239	204	3	68.00	1-36	-	
NatWest	8	5	1	111	35	27.75	-	-	-	-	501	297	18	16.50	4-62	-	
B & H	8	6	1	130	58	26.00	-	1	-	-	396	289	11	26.27	5-19	1	
1-day Lge	38	32	6	394	40	15.15	-	-	6	-	1638	1373	48	28.60	5-31	1	

DRAVID, R. Kent

Name: Rahul Dravid
Role: Right-hand bat, off-spin bowler
Born: 11 January 1973, Indore
Height: 5ft 11in
County debut: No first-team appearance
Test debut: 1996
Tests: 29
One-Day Internationals: 88
1st-Class 50s: 47
1st-Class 100s: 20
1st-Class 200s: 3
1st-Class catches: 111
1st-Class stumpings: 1
One-Day 100s: 5
Education: St Joseph's High School;
Bangalore University
Overseas tours: India to England 1996, to
South Africa 1996-97, to West Indies 1996-97,
to Sri Lanka 1997-98, to Zimbabwe 1998-99, to New Zealand 1998-99, to UK, Ireland
and Holland (World Cup) 1999, to Sri Lanka (Aiwa Cup) 1999, to Singapore (Coca-
Cola Challenge) 1999, to Toronto (DMC Toronto Festival) 1999, to Kenya (LG Cup)
1999, to Australia 1999-2000
Overseas teams played for: Karnataka, India 1990-91 –
Extras: Captained India U19 v New Zealand U19. Became the third Indian to score
100s in each innings of a Test with his 190 and 103* v New Zealand at Hamilton in
January 1999. Shared in a stand of 318 for the second wicket with Saurav Ganguly for
India v Sri Lanka at Taunton in the 1999 World Cup, a record for any wicket in One-
Day International cricket. Was leading run-scorer and topped the batting averages in
the 1999 World Cup with 461 runs at 65.85. Was named CEAT International Cricketer
of the World Cup 1999. Featured in the Vodafone World Cup XI, a 'dream team'
selected by journalists after the 1999 tournament. Has joined Kent as overseas player
for 2000 on a one-year contract
Best batting: 215 Karnataka v Uttar Pradesh, Bangalore 1997-98

1999 Season

	M	Inns	NO	Runs	HS	Avge	100s	50s	Ct	St	O	M	Runs	Wkts	Avge	Best	5wI	10wM
Test																		
All First																		
1-day Int	8	8	1	461	145	65.85	2	3	2	-								
NatWest																		
B & H																		
1-day Lge																		

Career Performances

	M	Inns	NO	Runs	HS	Avge	100s	50s	Ct	St	Balls	Runs	Wkts	Avge	Best	5wI	10wM
Test	29	48	4	2395	190	54.43	5	16	34	-	18	6	0	-	-	-	-
All First	107	170	26	8361	215	58.06	23	47	111	1	192	112	0	-	-	-	-
1-day Int	88	81	6	2828	145	37.70	5	19	38	1	108	92	1	92.00	1-21	-	
NatWest																	
B & H																	
1-day Lge																	

DRIVER, R. C. Worcestershire

Name: Ryan Craig Driver
Role: Left-hand bat, right-arm medium
bowler
Born: 30 April 1979, Truro
Height: 6ft 3in **Weight:** 14st 7lbs
Nickname: Bambi
County debut: 1998
1st-Class catches: 1
Parents: Les and Jan
Marital status: Single
Family links with cricket: Grandfather and
uncle played club cricket. Father was captain
of Truro CC for six years and still plays.
Mother keen supporter as is girlfriend
Education: St Gluvias and Trewirgie CP,
Redruth; Redruth Community School;
Durham University
Qualifications: 9 GCSEs, 3 A-levels, NCA
Level 2 coaching award
Career outside cricket: Student
Overseas tours: ESCA West U14 to West Indies 1993-94; Cornwall Colts to South
Africa 1996-97
Cricketers particularly admired: Graeme Hick, Allan Donald
Young players to look out for: Kadeer Ali, Depesh Patel
Other sports played: Basketball
Other sports followed: Football (Derby County)
Injuries: Torn infraspiatus; operation in October 1999
Relaxations: Socialising
Extras: CSCA Batting Award 1993-96. Played for ESCA U19 and MCC Schools in
1997. Played for Cornwall CCC from 1995. West Region *Daily Telegraph* Batsman of
the Year 1995. England Schoolboy Cricketer of the Year 1997. Opening bat for Truro

CC (Cornwall champions in 1996 and 1997). 2nd XI Player of the Month August/September 1998. 'I owe a lot to Malcolm Broad, Peter Bolland and the CSCA.' Played in Durham University's BUSA Championship winning side 1999

Opinions on cricket: 'Too much played in domestic season, and should play on better wickets to develop good techniques.'

Best batting: 42 Worcestershire v Essex, Chelmsford 1999

1999 Season

	M	Inns	NO	Runs	HS	Avge	100s	50s	Ct	St	O	M	Runs	Wkts	Avge	Best	5wl	10wM
Test																		
All First	3	5	0	103	42	20.60	-	-	1	-								
1-day Int																		
NatWest																		
B & H																		
1-day Lge	1	1	0	3	3	3.00	-	-	-	-								

Career Performances

	M	Inns	NO	Runs	HS	Avge	100s	50s	Ct	St	Balls	Runs	Wkts	Avge	Best	5wl	10wM
Test																	
All First	4	7	0	108	42	15.42	-	-	1	-							
1-day Int																	
NatWest	1	1	0	0	0	0.00	-	-	-	-							
B & H																	
1-day Lge	1	1	0	3	3	3.00	-	-									

DUTCH, K. P.   Middlesex

Name: Keith Philip Dutch
Role: Right-hand bat, off-spin bowler
Born: 21 March 1973, Harrow, Middlesex
Height: 5ft 9in **Weight:** 11st 4lbs
Nickname: Dutchy, Oik
County debut: 1993
1st-Class 50s: 1
1st-Class catches: 13
One-Day 5 w. in innings: 1
Place in batting averages: 262nd av. 11.90
Strike rate: 74.57 (career 76.04)
Parents: Alan and Ann
Marital status: Single
Children: Lauren Beth-Amy, 15 January 1999

Family links with cricket: Father coached
Education: Nower Hill High School, Pinner;
Weald College, Harrow
Qualifications: 5 GCSEs, 1 AS-level,
staff tutor coach
Off-season: Coaching
Overseas tours: MCC to Central and East
Africa 1997
Overseas teams played for: Worcester
United, South Africa 1992-93; Geelong City,
Australia, 1994; Rygersdal CC, Cape Town
1997-98
Cricketers particularly admired:
Mark Ramprakash, John Emburey
Young players to look out for: Owais Shah,
David Nash, Stephen Peters, Ed Joyce
Other sports followed: Football
(Arsenal FC)

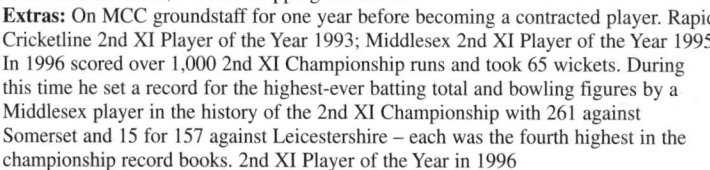

Relaxations: Music, TV and shopping for clothes
Extras: On MCC groundstaff for one year before becoming a contracted player. Rapid
Cricketline 2nd XI Player of the Year 1993; Middlesex 2nd XI Player of the Year 1995.
In 1996 scored over 1,000 2nd XI Championship runs and took 65 wickets. During
this time he set a record for the highest-ever batting total and bowling figures by a
Middlesex player in the history of the 2nd XI Championship with 261 against
Somerset and 15 for 157 against Leicestershire – each was the fourth highest in the
championship record books. 2nd XI Player of the Year in 1996
Best batting: 79 Middlesex v Gloucestershire, Bristol 1997
Best bowling: 3-25 Middlesex v Somerset, Uxbridge 1996

1999 Season

	M	Inns	NO	Runs	HS	Avge	100s	50s	Ct	St	O	M	Runs	Wkts	Avge	Best	5wI	10wM
Test																		
All First	6	10	0	119	23	11.90	-	-	2	-	87	17	278	7	39.71	3-69	-	-
1-day Int																		
NatWest	1	1	0	0	0	0.00	-	-	1	-	7	0	31	1	31.00	1-31	-	
B & H																		
1-day Lge	15	14	3	290	57	26.36	-	1	5	-	76.1	2	342	23	14.86	5-35	1	

Career Performances

	M	Inns	NO	Runs	HS	Avge	100s	50s	Ct	St	Balls	Runs	Wkts	Avge	Best	5wl	10wM
Test																	
All First	22	28	2	337	79	12.96	-	1	13	-	1597	825	21	39.28	3-25	-	-
1-day Int																	
NatWest	6	5	2	93	49 *	31.00	-	-	4	-	378	244	6	40.66	2-30	-	
B & H	6	6	1	48	20	9.60	-	-	2	-	186	152	7	21.71	4-42	-	
1-day Lge	55	47	13	663	58	19.50	-	2	15	-	1723	1370	62	22.09	5-35	1	

EAGLESON, R. L.   Derbyshire

Name: Ryan Logan Eagleson
Role: Right-hand bat, right-arm
fast-medium bowler
Born: 17 December 1974, Carrickfergus,
Co Antrim, Northern Ireland
Height: 6ft 3in **Weight:** 14st
Nickname: Eagey, Bomber
County debut: 1999
1st-Class 50s: 1
1st-Class catches: 3
Strike rate: 65.00 (career 63.00)
Parents: Trevor and Eleanor
Marital status: Single
Education: Central PS; Carrickfergus
College; Newtownabbey College of FE
Qualifications: 8 GCSEs, Grade 2 coach
Career outside cricket: Coaching
Off-season: Club cricket in New Zealand
Overseas tours: Ireland to Malaysia (ICC Trophy) 1997, to Malaysia (Commonwealth Games) 1998
Overseas teams played for: Birkenhead, Auckland 1994-95; Wonderboom, Pretoria 1998
Cricketers particularly admired: Viv Richards, Paul McCrum, Michael McIlroy, Ian Botham, Reggie Stinson
Young players to look out for: Ed Joyce, Ian Blackwell
Other sports played: Golf, football
Other sports followed: Football (Liverpool, Carrick Rangers), rugby (Ulster RFC)
Injuries: Out for ten weeks with finger injury in right hand
Relaxations: 'A quiet pint in Belfast; taking money off Michael McIlroy at golf'
Extras: Made first-class debut for Ireland v Scotland at Linlithgow 1996. Has been capped 50 times overall by Ireland

Opinions on cricket: 'To see Ireland in the next World Cup.'
Best batting: 50* Ireland v Scotland, Linlithgow 1996
Best bowling: 2-50 Ireland v Scotland, Linlithgow 1996

1999 Season

	M	Inns	NO	Runs	HS	Avge	100s	50s	Ct	St	O	M	Runs	Wkts	Avge	Best	5wI	10wM
Test																		
All First	1	1	0	0	0	0.00	-	-	1	-	10.5	2	34	1	34.00	1-34	-	-
1-day Int																		
NatWest	3	2	0	12	11	6.00	-	-	2	-	30	4	126	6	21.00	4-59	-	
B & H																		
1-day Lge	1	0	0	0	0	-	-	-	-	-	-	5	0	23	1	23.00	1-23	-

Career Performances

	M	Inns	NO	Runs	HS	Avge	100s	50s	Ct	St	Balls	Runs	Wkts	Avge	Best	5wI	10wM
Test																	
All First	2	3	2	91	50 *	91.00	-	1	3	-	252	183	4	45.75	2-50	-	-
1-day Int																	
NatWest	7	6	2	38	15 *	9.50	-	-	3	-	450	358	11	32.54	4-59	-	
B & H	7	7	1	58	15 *	9.66	-	-	2	-	293	311	3	103.66	1-36	-	
1-day Lge	1	0	0	0	0	-	-	-	-	-	30	23	1	23.00	1-23	-	

35. Which international fast bowler made his
County Championship debut (for Warwickshire) in 1987?

EALHAM, M. A. Kent

Name: Mark Alan Ealham
Role: Right-hand bat, right-arm
medium bowler
Born: 27 August 1969, Ashford, Kent
Height: 5ft 10in **Weight:** 14st
Nickname: Ealy, Boarder, Skater, Ealberg,
Fudge
County debut: 1989
County cap: 1992
Test debut: 1996
Tests: 8
One-Day Internationals: 39
1000 runs in a season: 1
1st-Class 50s: 40
1st-Class 100s: 5
1st-Class 5 w. in innings: 13
1st-Class 10 w. in match: 1
1st-Class catches: 53
One-Day 100s: 1

One-Day 5 w. in innings: 3
Place in batting averages: 101st av. 30.78 (1998 151st av. 24.26)
Place in bowling averages: 52nd av. 23.92 (1998 53rd av. 25.78)
Strike rate: 49.65 (career 59.28)
Parents: Alan and Sue
Wife and date of marriage: Kirsty, 24 February 1996
Family links with cricket: Father played for Kent
Education: Chartham; Stour Valley Secondary School
Qualifications: 9 CSEs
Off-season: England one-day squad to South Africa and Zimbabwe
Overseas tours: England A to Australia 1996-97, to Kenya and Sri Lanka 1997-98;
England VI to Hong Kong 1997; England to Sharjah (Champions Trophy) 1997-98, to
Bangladesh (Wills International Cup) 1998, to Australia (CUB Series) 1998-99, to
Sharjah (Coca-Cola Cup) 1998-99, to South Africa and Zimbabwe 1999-2000
(one-day series)
Overseas teams played for: South Perth, Australia 1992-93; University, Perth
1993-94
Cricketers particularly admired: Ian Botham, Viv Richards, Robin Smith,
Steve Waugh, Paul Blackmore and Albert 'for his F and G'
Young players to look out for: 'Angus Fraser, Neil Fairbrother (Rug Rat)'
Other sports followed: Football (Manchester United) and most other sports
Relaxations: Playing golf and snooker, watching films

Extras: Set record for fastest Sunday League century (44 balls), v Derbyshire at Maidstone 1995. Represented England in the 1997 Hong Kong Sixes tournament in which England finished as runners-up to Pakistan. Represented England in the 1999 World Cup

Opinions on cricket: 'In the one-day competitions where fixtures are "drawn", give the visiting side the choice of the toss to ensure the best possible surfaces are prepared.'

Best batting: 139 Kent v Leicestershire, Canterbury 1997

Best bowling: 8-36 Kent v Warwickshire, Edgbaston 1996

Stop press: Returned a new England best One-Day International bowling analysis with his 5-15 v Zimbabwe at Kimberley in January 2000; all five were lbw

1999 Season

	M	Inns	NO	Runs	HS	Avge	100s	50s	Ct	St	O	M	Runs	Wkts	Avge	Best	5wI	10wM
Test																		
All First	13	22	3	585	88 *	30.78	-	5	3	-	339.2	73	981	41	23.92	6-35	2	-
1-day Int	5	2	0	5	5	2.50	-	-	1	-	50	5	191	10	19.10	2-28	-	
NatWest	3	3	1	90	46 *	45.00	-	-	-	-	22	0	89	3	29.66	2-45	-	
B & H																		
1-day Lge	13	12	2	267	43 *	26.70	-	-	4	-	87.1	9	309	13	23.76	3-26	-	

Career Performances

	M	Inns	NO	Runs	HS	Avge	100s	50s	Ct	St	Balls	Runs	Wkts	Avge	Best	5wI	10wM
Test	8	13	3	210	53 *	21.00	-	2	4	-	1060	488	17	28.70	4-21	-	-
All First	137	225	37	6018	139	32.01	5	40	53	-	18200	8834	307	28.77	8-36	13	1
1-day Int	39	28	1	446	45	16.51	-	-	4	-	1994	1397	46	30.36	5-32	1	
NatWest	19	18	5	394	58 *	30.30	-	2	6	-	1025	532	21	25.33	4-10	-	
B & H	39	36	9	781	75	28.92	-	6	14	-	1976	1309	57	22.96	4-29	-	
1-day Lge	129	106	30	1982	112	26.07	1	9	33	-	4939	3776	121	31.20	6-53	2	

36. Which Yorkshire wicket-keeper did not miss a Championship game between his debut in 1955 and his retirement in 1969?

EDMOND, M. D.   Warwickshire

Name: Michael Dennis Edmond
Role: Right-hand bat, right-arm
medium-fast bowler
Born: 30 July 1969, Barrow-in-Furness
Height: 6ft 1in **Weight:** 14st 7lbs
Nickname: Eddo, Aus
County debut: 1996
1st-Class catches: 2
Strike rate: (career 99.28)
Parents: Tom and Carol
Marital status: Single
Children: Ryen
Family links with cricket: 'My brother
plays'
Education: Briar Road Public School,
Campbelltown, NSW; Airds High School,
Campbelltown, NSW
Qualifications: Level O coach in Australia
Career outside cricket: Barman
Overseas teams played for: Campbelltown, Sydney 1988-93; Fairfield, Sydney 1994
Cricketers particularly admired: Ian Botham, Viv Richards, Len Pascoe
Young players to look out for: 'All with an ambition to play for England'
Other sports played/followed: Indoor cricket (played for Australia 1993-96), football
(Manchester United), rugby league (Manly-Warringah)
Relaxations: Spending time with friends, going out and listening to music
Extras: Released by Warwickshire at end of 1999 season
Best batting: 32 Warwickshire v Durham, Edgbaston 1998
Best bowling: 2-26 Warwickshire v Oxford University, The Parks 1997

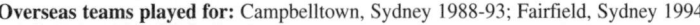

1999 Season

	M	Inns	NO	Runs	HS	Avge	100s	50s	Ct	St	O	M	Runs	Wkts	Avge	Best	5wl	10wM
Test																		
All First	1	1	0	31	31	31.00	-	-	1	-	8	3	24	0	-		-	-
1-day Int																		
NatWest																		
B & H																		
1-day Lge	2	2	2	15	15*	-	-	-	-	-	2	0	17	1	17.00	1-17	-	

Career Performances

	M	Inns	NO	Runs	HS	Avge	100s	50s	Ct	St	Balls	Runs	Wkts	Avge	Best	5wl	10wM
Test																	
All First	8	10	3	138	32	19.71	-	-	2	-	695	372	7	53.14	2-26	-	-
1-day Int																	
NatWest	1	1	0	0	0	0.00	-	-	-	-	48	24	1	24.00	1-24	-	
B & H																		
1-day Lge	10	7	4	58	19	19.33	-	-	2	-	323	250	13	19.23	2-4	-	

EDWARDS, A. D.   Middlesex

Name: Alexander David Edwards
Role: Right-hand bat, right-arm
fast-medium bowler
Born: 2 August 1975, Cuckfield, Sussex
Height: 6ft **Weight:** 12st 9lbs
Nickname: Al, Steads, Elvis
County debut: 1994 (one-day, Sussex),
1995 (first-class, Sussex)
1st-Class 5 w. in innings: 1
1st-Class catches: 11
Place in batting averages: (1998 293rd
av. 4.28)
Strike rate: 96.00 (career 62.38)
Parents: Richard John and Angela Janet
Marital status: Single
Family links with cricket: 'Parents drove me
everywhere to play or practise cricket and
have been absolutely wonderful'
Education: Felbridge Primary; Imberhorne Comprehensive; Loughborough University
Qualifications: 10 GCSEs, 4 A-levels
Overseas tours: Sussex U18 to India 1990-91; England U18 to South Africa 1992-93,
to Denmark 1993
Cricketers particularly admired: Dennis Lillee, Michael Holding, Viv Richards,
Stan Berry and Pat Cale 'for their tremendous support, belief and encouragement'
Other sports followed: Football (Liverpool FC)
Relaxations: Snooker, swimming, training, listening to a variety of music, watching
sport on television
Extras: Lord's Taverners U15 Young Cricketer of the Year 1991 and a *Cricketer*
magazine Young Cricketer of the Month in the same year. Played for England U19
against India U19 in 1994. Released by Sussex at end of 1999 season and has joined
Middlesex for 2000

Opinions on cricket: 'Second XI cricket should mirror the first-class game, e.g. same grounds, practice facilities and duration of matches in the championship (four days). This would help young players to make the transition from 2nd XI to first-class cricket. Young players should be given ample opportunity to prove themselves in first-class cricket. They shouldn't be afraid of initial failure.'

Best batting: 22 Sussex v Young Australia, Hove 1995
22 Sussex v Middlesex, Lord's 1999

Best bowling: 5-34 Sussex v Pakistan A, Hove 1997

1999 Season

	M	Inns	NO	Runs	HS	Avge	100s	50s	Ct	St	O	M	Runs	Wkts	Avge	Best	5wI	10wM
Test																		
All First	2	3	0	22	22	7.33	-	-	1	-	48	12	157	3	52.33	2-67	-	-
1-day Int																		
NatWest																		
B & H																		
1-day Lge	2	0	0	0	0	-	-	-	2	-	13	0	69	0	-		-	-

Career Performances

	M	Inns	NO	Runs	HS	Avge	100s	50s	Ct	St	Balls	Runs	Wkts	Avge	Best	5wI	10wM
Test																	
All First	15	23	2	156	22	7.42	-	-	11	-	1622	1069	26	41.11	5-34	1	-
1-day Int																	
NatWest																	
B & H	10	9	2	101	43	14.42	-	-	5	-	585	511	8	63.87	2-51	-	
1-day Lge	20	12	1	67	20	6.09	-	-	4	-	641	495	15	33.00	3-34	-	

ELLIOTT, M. T. G.   Glamorgan

Name: Matthew Thomas Gray Elliott
Role: Left-hand bat, 'pseudo left-arm orthodox' bowler
Born: 28 September 1971, Chelsea, Victoria
Height: 6ft 3in **Weight:** 12st 7lbs
Nickname: Herb
County debut: No first-team appearance
Test debut: 1996-97
Tests: 20
One-Day Internationals: 1
1st-Class 50s: 32
1st-Class 100s: 23
1st-Class 200s: 2

1st-Class catches: 103
Strike rate: (career 84.66)
Parents: John and Glenda
Wife and date of marriage: Megan,
11 December 1994
Children: Zachary, 22 December 1997
Family links with cricket: Father played
district cricket with Northcote (Melbourne)
Education: Lancaster Primary School;
Kyabram Secondary College
Qualifications: VCE certificate
Off-season: Playing for Victoria in
Australia's domestic season
Overseas tours: Australia to South Africa
1996-97, to England 1997, to West Indies
1998-99
Cricketers particularly admired:
Steve Waugh
Young players to look out for: Matthew Inness, Michael Klinger (Victoria)
Other sports followed: Australian Rules football (Collingwood FC)
Injuries: Out for six weeks with broken finger
Relaxations: Reading biographies/true stories; fishing
Extras: One of *Wisden*'s Five Cricketers of the Year 1998. Sheffield Shield Player of
the Year 1995-96 and 1998-99
Opinions on cricket: 'Generally in pretty good shape.'
Best batting: 203 Victoria v Tasmania, Melbourne 1995-96
Best bowling: 1-3 Victoria v Tasmania, Melbourne 1998-99

1999 Season (did not make any first-class or one-day appearances)

Career Performances

	M	Inns	NO	Runs	HS	Avge	100s	50s	Ct	St	Balls	Runs	Wkts	Avge	Best	5wl	10wM
Test	20	34	1	1171	199	35.48	3	4	13	-	12	4	0	-	-	-	-
All First	91	168	12	7608	203	48.76	25	32	103	-	762	463	9	51.44	1-3	-	-
1-day Int	1	1	0	1	1	1.00	-	-	-	-							
NatWest																	
B & H																	
1-day Lge																	

ELLISON, C. J. Yorkshire

Name: Christopher John Ellison
Role: Right-hand bat, slow left-arm orthodox bowler
Born: 12 April 1979, Sheffield, South Yorkshire
Height: 5ft 11in **Weight:** 11st 5lbs
Nickname: Elly
County debut: No first-team appearance
Parents: Graham and Sheila
Marital status: Single
Family links with cricket: 'Two brothers play cricket with me, as does Dad. Mother performs never-ending things such as cleaning grass-stained whites, making teas and supporting us when we are all playing'
Education: St Mewan County Primary School; Penrice School; St Austell College, Exeter University
Qualifications: 10 GCSEs, 3 A-levels, 2 NCF awards in coaching
Career outside cricket: Student
Off-season: Studying for Sports Science degree at Exeter University
Overseas tours: Cornwall U17 to South Africa 1996
Overseas teams played for: Sutherland District CC, Sydney 1997-98
Cricketers particularly admired: Anthony McGrath, Darren Gough, Steve Waugh
Young players to look out for: Richard Dawson, Gary Ramsden, John Sadler
Other sports played: Football, golf (8 handicap)
Other sports followed: Football (Sheffield Wednesday); rugby league (Leeds Rhinos)
Injuries: Out for two weeks with a virus
Relaxations: Keeping fit, reading, meeting friends and relatives
Extras: On debut for Cornwall in the Minor Counties Championship against Cheshire took 9-80, including a hat-trick, in the second innings. Overall match figures 14-154. St Austell CC Player of the Year 1997
Opinions on cricket: 'Too much one-day cricket is played. Too much cricket in general is played. Not enough time to rest, recover and prepare before the next game. Should be fewer four-day games and only two one-day competitions, leaving more time to recuperate. That way, games will become more intense, which will filter through to developing a more successful Test side.'

1999 Season (did not make any first-class or one-day appearances)

Career Performances

	M	Inns	NO	Runs	HS	Avge	100s	50s	Ct	St	Balls	Runs	Wkts	Avge	Best	5wI	10wM
Test																	
All First																	
1-day Int																	
NatWest	1	1	0	5	5	5.00	-	-	1	-	60	64	3	21.33	3-64	-	
B & H																	
1-day Lge																	

EVANS, A. W. Glamorgan

Name: Alun Wyn Evans
Role: Right-hand bat, right-arm medium bowler
Born: 20 August 1975, Glanamman, Dyfed
Height: 5ft 8in **Weight:** 12st 2lbs
Nickname: Troll
County debut: 1996
1st-Class 50s: 5
1st-Class 100s: 1
1st-Class catches: 23
One-Day 100s: 1
Place in batting averages: 159th av. 24.38 (1998 102nd av. 29.69)
Parents: Gareth and Lynfa
Marital status: Single
Family links with cricket: Brother played for Welsh Schools at all age groups and also Glamorgan. Father played for Ammanford CC
Education: Glanamman Primary School, Fishguard Primary School; Fishguard County High School; Neath Tertiary College
Qualifications: 11 GCSEs, BTEC National Diploma in Sports Science, Senior Cricket Coaching Award
Career outside cricket: 'Haven't thought about it yet'
Overseas tours: Welsh Schools U17 to Sydney, Australia 1992-93
Overseas teams played for: Marist CC, Whangarei, New Zealand 1995-96, 1997
Cricketers particularly admired: Brian Lara, Mark Ramprakash, Wasim Akram
Young players to look out for: Daniel Cherry, Graeme Swann
Other sports played: Rugby, golf, pool
Other sports followed: Rugby (Cardiff), football (Tottenham Hotspur FC), tennis

Relaxations: 'Getting the odd tip off my mate Ross'; playing for Fishguard RFC in the winter
Extras: Welsh Schools Player of the Year 1994, MCC Young Cricketer 1995. Balconiers 2nd XI Player of the Year 1996. ASW Young Player of the Year
Opinions on cricket: 'Too many overs in a day. Tea intervals should be longer. 2nd teams should play four-dayers every game.'
Best batting: 125 Glamorgan v Cambridge University, Fenner's 1998

1999 Season

	M	Inns	NO	Runs	HS	Avge	100s	50s	Ct	St	O	M	Runs	Wkts	Avge	Best	5wI	10wM
Test																		
All First	15	24	3	512	88 *	24.38	-	2	10	-	1	0	3	0	-	-	-	-
1-day Int																		
NatWest	3	3	0	93	52	31.00	-	1	-	-								
B & H																		
1-day Lge	13	10	0	299	108	29.90	1	1	7	-								

Career Performances

	M	Inns	NO	Runs	HS	Avge	100s	50s	Ct	St	Balls	Runs	Wkts	Avge	Best	5wI	10wM
Test																	
All First	32	54	7	1335	125	28.40	1	5	23	-	6	3	0	-	-	-	-
1-day Int																	
NatWest	3	3	0	93	52	31.00	-	1	-	-							
B & H	2	2	0	24	14	12.00	-	-	-	-							
1-day Lge	33	28	5	530	108	23.04	1	2	11	-							

EVANS, K. P.   Nottinghamshire

Name: Kevin Paul Evans
Role: Right-hand bat, right-arm medium bowler
Born: 10 September 1963, Calverton, Nottingham
Height: 6ft 2in **Weight:** 14st
Nickname: Ghost, Tex
County debut: 1984
County cap: 1990
Benefit: 1998
1st-Class 50s: 21
1st-Class 100s: 3
1st-Class 5 w. in innings: 10
1st-Class catches: 111
One-Day 5 w. in innings: 2

Place in batting averages: (1998 274th av. 9.92)
Place in bowling averages: (1998 64th av. 27.22)
Strike rate: 42.00 (career 68.17)
Parents: Eric and Eileen
Wife and date of marriage: Sandra, 19 March 1988
Children: Ryan Matthew, 24 January 1997
Family links with cricket: Brother Russell played for Nottinghamshire and still plays for Minor Counties and Lincolnshire. Father played local cricket
Education: William Lee Primary; Colonel Frank Seely Comprehensive, Calverton
Qualifications: 10 O-levels, 3 A-levels, qualified coach
Overseas teams played for: Wanuiomata, New Zealand 1989-91
Cricketers particularly admired: Richard Hadlee, Clive Rice
Young players to look out for: Guy Welton
Other sports followed: Football (Leeds United), tennis, squash
Relaxations: Listening to music, reading, DIY, gardening
Extras: With brother, Russell, first brothers to bat together for Nottinghamshire in first-class cricket for 50 years. Kept wicket for the first time in the Championship match against Essex at Colchester in 1992. Second Nottinghamshire cricketer to bowl Sunday League hat-trick v Glamorgan at Trent Bridge; Mark Saxelby was the other. Released by Nottinghamshire at end of 1999 season
Best batting: 104 Nottinghamshire v Surrey, Trent Bridge 1992
104 Nottinghamshire v Sussex, Trent Bridge 1994
Best bowling: 6-40 Nottinghamshire v Lancashire, Old Trafford 1997

1999 Season

	M	Inns	NO	Runs	HS	Avge	100s	50s	Ct	St	O	M	Runs	Wkts	Avge	Best	5wI	10wM
Test																		
All First	1	0	0	0	0	-	-	-	-	-	21	5	70	3	23.33	3-70	-	-
1-day Int																		
NatWest																		
B & H																		
1-day Lge																		

Career Performances

	M	Inns	NO	Runs	HS	Avge	100s	50s	Ct	St	Balls	Runs	Wkts	Avge	Best	5wI	10wM
Test																	
All First	161	220	44	4198	104	23.85	3	21	111	-	24817	12097	364	33.23	6-40	10	-
1-day Int																	
NatWest	25	17	3	143	21	10.21	-	-	7	-	1532	834	35	23.82	6-10	1	
B & H	34	22	6	245	47	15.31	-	-	10	-	1898	1288	49	26.28	4-19	-	
1-day Lge	148	91	38	856	30	16.15	-	-	27	-	6044	5051	159	31.76	5-29	1	

FAIRBROTHER, N. H. Lancashire

Name: Neil Harvey Fairbrother
Role: Left-hand bat, left-arm medium bowler
Born: 9 September 1963, Warrington, Cheshire
Height: 5ft 8in **Weight:** 11st 4lbs
Nickname: Harvey
County debut: 1982
County cap: 1985
Benefit: 1995
Test debut: 1987
Tests: 10
One-Day Internationals: 75
1000 runs in a season: 10
1st-Class 50s: 100
1st-Class 100s: 36
1st-Class 200s: 3
1st-Class 300s: 1
1st-Class catches: 248
One-Day 100s: 6
Place in batting averages: 137th av. 26.47 (1998 13th av. 50.60)
Strike rate: (career 137.00)
Parents: Les and Barbara
Wife and date of marriage: Audrey, 23 September 1988
Children: Rachael Elizabeth, 4 April 1991; Sam, 3 April 1994
Family links with cricket: Father and two uncles played local league cricket
Education: St Margaret's Church of England School, Oxford; Lymm Grammar School
Qualifications: 5 O-levels
Overseas tours: England A to Pakistan 1990-91; England to Sharjah 1986-87, to India and Pakistan (World Cup) 1987-88, to Australia and New Zealand 1987-88, to New Zealand 1991-92, to India 1992-93, to Australia 1994-95, to South Africa 1995-96, to India and Pakistan (World Cup) 1995-96, to Bangladesh (Wills International Cup) 1998-99, to Australia (CUB Series) 1998-99, to Sharjah (Coca-Cola Cup) 1998-99

Cricketers particularly admired: Clive Lloyd, Allan Border, David Gower
Other sports followed: Football, rugby union, rugby league
Relaxations: Music and playing sport
Extras: 'I was named after the Australian cricketer Neil Harvey, who was my mum's favourite cricketer.' Played for England YC v Australia 1983. His innings of 366 in 1990 was the third highest score ever made in the County Championship, the second highest first-class score by a Lancashire batsman and the best at The Oval. Appointed Lancashire captain for 1992 but resigned in 1993. Called up to join England tour party as a replacement in Australia 1994-95 but was immediately injured in a collision with Steven Rhodes while fielding and forced to return home. Played in the one-day series between England and South Africa and represented England in the World Cup in 1995-96. Represented England in the 1999 World Cup
Opinions on cricket: 'There is too much cricket. The game has to be made more entertaining.'
Best batting: 366 Lancashire v Surrey, The Oval 1990
Best bowling: 2-91 Lancashire v Nottinghamshire, Old Trafford 1987

1999 Season

	M	Inns	NO	Runs	HS	Avge	100s	50s	Ct	St	O	M	Runs	Wkts	Avge	Best	5wI	10wM
Test																		
All First	12	19	0	503	83	26.47	-	4	17	-	2	0	2	0	-	-	-	-
1-day Int	5	3	1	57	29	28.50	-	-	-	-								
NatWest	3	3	1	121	54	60.50	-	1	2	-								
B & H	1	1	0	18	18	18.00	-	-	-	-								
1-day Lge	12	11	5	278	66 *	46.33	-	3	2	-								

Career Performances

	M	Inns	NO	Runs	HS	Avge	100s	50s	Ct	St	Balls	Runs	Wkts	Avge	Best	5wI	10wM
Test	10	15	1	219	83	15.64	-	1	4	-	12	9	0	-	-	-	-
All First	327	519	70	18444	366	41.07	40	100	248	-	685	442	5	88.40	2-91	-	-
1-day Int	75	71	18	2092	113	39.47	1	16	33	-	6	9	0	-	-	-	-
NatWest	41	40	8	1554	93 *	48.56	-	12	21	-	48	44	1	44.00	1-28	-	
B & H	75	72	21	2598	116 *	50.94	1	21	34	-	54	67	1	67.00	1-17	-	
1-day Lge	222	206	53	6217	116 *	40.63	4	43	65	-	48	48	1	48.00	1-33	-	

FELLOWS, G. M. Yorkshire

Name: Gary Matthew Fellows
Role: Right-hand bat, right-arm medium bowler
Born: 30 July 1978, Halifax, West Yorkshire
Height: 5ft 9in **Weight:** 11st
Nickname: Mousey, Mick
County debut: 1998
1st-Class 50s: 1
1st-Class catches: 1
Strike rate: 42.00 (career 66.00)
Parents: Eric and Tina
Marital status: Single
Family links with cricket: Dad and two brothers play league cricket
Education: Whitehill Primary School, Illingworth, Halifax; North Halifax Grammar School, Illingworth, Halifax
Qualifications: 10 GCSEs, 1 A-level, coaching award
Overseas teams played for: Bulawayo Athletic Club, Bulawayo, Matabeleland, Zimbabwe 1996-97
Cricketers particularly admired: Craig White, Mark Waugh
Young players to look out for: Matt Thewlis
Other sports played: Football ('on Bradford City one season')
Other sports followed: Football (Halifax Town)
Relaxations: Most sports 'and a laugh with the lads after the game'. Golf
Extras: Set record for most catches by a fielder in a season (11) for Yorkshire Schools U15 1993. Awarded Yorkshire 2nd XI cap 1998
Opinions on cricket: 'General four-day cricket does not provide enough entertainment to bring in new spectators.'
Best batting: 50 Matabeleland v Mashonaland, Bulawayo 1996-97
Best bowling: 1-38 Yorkshire v Glamorgan, Headingley 1999

1999 Season

	M	Inns	NO	Runs	HS	Avge	100s	50s	Ct	St	O	M	Runs	Wkts	Avge	Best	5wI	10wM
Test																		
All First	3	6	1	74	34 *	14.80	-	-	1	-	7	0	38	1	38.00	1-38	-	-
1-day Int																		
NatWest	2	1	0	27	27	27.00	-	-	-	-	3	0	20	0	-		-	-
B & H	1	1	0	34	34	34.00	-	-	-	-								
1-day Lge	14	10	2	147	36	18.37	-	-	2	-	6	0	43	0	-		-	-

	M	Inns	NO	Runs	HS	Avge	100s	50s	Ct	St	Balls	Runs	Wkts	Avge	Best	5wl	10wM
Test																	
All First	6	11	1	161	50	16.10	-	1	1	-	66	64	1	64.00	1-38	-	-
1-day Int																	
NatWest	2	1	0	27	27	27.00	-	-	-	-	18	20	0	-		-	-
B & H	1	1	0	34	34	34.00	-	-	-	-							
1-day Lge	15	11	2	148	36	16.44	-	-	2	-	69	79	0	-		-	-

FISHER, I. D. Yorkshire

Name: Ian Douglas Fisher
Role: Left-hand bat, slow left-arm bowler
Born: 31 March 1976, Bradford
Height: 5ft 11in **Weight:** 14st
Nickname: Fish, Yoda, Flick
County debut: 1996
1st-Class 50s: 1
1st-Class 5 w. in innings: 2
Place in batting averages: 166th av. 23.72
Place in bowling averages: 115th av. 34.00
Strike rate: 69.42 (career 62.07)
Parents: Geoff and Linda
Marital status: Single
Family links with cricket: Father played club cricket
Education: Denholme First School; Parkside Middle School; Beckfoot Grammar School
Qualifications: 9 GCSEs, NCA coaching award, Sports Leaders Award, Lifesaver (bronze)
Off-season: 'Training, resting, doing a college course'
Overseas tours: Yorkshire to Zimbabwe 1996, to South Africa 1998, 1999
Overseas teams played for: Somerset West, Cape Town 1994-95; Petone Riverside, Wellington, New Zealand 1997-98
Cricketers particularly admired: Sachin Tendulkar, Steve Waugh, Shane Warne
Young players to look out for: Gary Fellows, Matthew Hoggard
Other sports played: Five-a-side football, squash
Other sports followed: Football (Leeds United), rugby league (Leeds Rhinos)
Relaxations: Watching movies, eating out, socialising with friends, shopping
Extras: Played England U17 and Yorkshire Schools U15, U16 and Yorkshire U19
Opinions on cricket: 'I think our game is now going in the right direction with two-division cricket. However, there were far too many bad pitches in 1999. We need to

have better pitches if we want to produce the type of cricket that is required at Test level.'

Best batting: 51 Yorkshire v Surrey, The Oval 1999
Best bowling: 5-35 Yorkshire v Lancashire, Old Trafford 1996

1999 Season

	M	Inns	NO	Runs	HS	Avge	100s	50s	Ct	St	O	M	Runs	Wkts	Avge	Best	5wI	10wM
Test																		
All First	11	16	5	261	51	23.72	-	1	-	-	162	42	476	14	34.00	5-73	1	-
1-day Int																		
NatWest	3	1	0	5	5	5.00	-	-	2	-	25	1	87	3	29.00	1-21	-	
B & H																		
1-day Lge	7	3	1	25	11 *	12.50	-	-	2	-	36	1	173	3	57.66	2-40	-	

Career Performances

	M	Inns	NO	Runs	HS	Avge	100s	50s	Ct	St	Balls	Runs	Wkts	Avge	Best	5wI	10wM
Test																	
All First	17	21	6	336	51	22.40	-	1	-	-	1614	764	26	29.38	5-35	2	-
1-day Int																	
NatWest	3	1	0	5	5	5.00	-	-	2	-	150	87	3	29.00	1-21	-	
B & H	1	0	0	0	0	-	-	-	1	-	48	26	1	26.00	1-26	-	
1-day Lge	15	6	3	34	11 *	11.33	-	-	3	-	486	338	14	24.14	3-25	-	

FLANAGAN, I. N.   Essex

Name: Ian Nicholas Flanagan
Role: Left-hand bat, right-arm medium bowler
Born: 5 June 1980, Colchester
Height: 6ft **Weight:** 13st
Nickname: Bud
County debut: 1997
1st-Class 50s: 3
1st-Class catches: 12
Place in batting averages: 233rd av. 16.50 (1998 162nd av. 23.09)
Strike rate: 87.00 (career 93.00)
Parents: Roy and Anita
Marital status: Single
Family links with cricket: Father played league cricket for Colchester and Carlisle. Mother makes teas
Education: Millfield County Primary School; The Colne Community School; The Sixth Form College, Colchester

Qualifications: 10 GCSEs, Level 2 coach
Off-season: Playing cricket in Perth
Overseas tours: England U19 to Pakistan
1996-97, to South Africa (including Youth
World Cup) 1997-98, to New Zealand
1998-99
Overseas teams played for: North Perth,
Western Australia 1999-2000
Cricketers particularly admired:
Geoff Arnold, Carl Hooper, David Gower
Young players to look out for: Ian Bell,
'Mad' Jim Crafford
Other sports played: Squash, football, rugby
Other sports followed: Rugby, football
(Tottenham Hotspur and Colchester United)
Relaxations: Sleeping, watching films,
spending time with friends 'and playing on
my PlayStation'

Extras: Represented England U19 in one-day and 'Test' series v Australia U19 1999.
Also played for England U17 and U18
Opinions on cricket: 'There is a need to improve the wickets we play on. The
authorities have to be stricter on sub-standard pitches. Two division cricket improved
the competition in 1999.'
Best batting: 61 Essex v Warwickshire, Edgbaston 1998
Best bowling: 1-50 Essex v Sri Lanka A, Chelmsford 1999

1999 Season

	M	Inns	NO	Runs	HS	Avge	100s	50s	Ct	St	O	M	Runs	Wkts	Avge	Best	5wl	10wM
Test																		
All First	6	10	0	165	52	16.50	-	1	3	-	14.3	4	50	1	50.00	1-50	-	-
1-day Int																		
NatWest																			
B & H																			
1-day Lge																			

Career Performances

	M	Inns	NO	Runs	HS	Avge	100s	50s	Ct	St	Balls	Runs	Wkts	Avge	Best	5wl	10wM
Test																	
All First	14	24	1	491	61	21.34	-	3	12	-	93	51	1	51.00	1-50	-	-
1-day Int																	
NatWest																		
B & H																		
1-day Lge																		

FLEMING, M. V.   Kent

Name: Matthew Valentine Fleming
Role: Right-hand bat, right-arm
medium bowler, county captain
Born: 12 December 1964, Macclesfield
Height: 5ft 11ins **Weight:** 13st
Nickname: Jazzer
County debut: 1988
County cap: 1990
One-Day Internationals: 11
1st-Class 50s: 41
1st-Class 100s: 10
1st-Class 5 w. in innings: 2
1st-Class catches: 73
One-Day 100s: 3
One-Day 5 w. in innings: 2
Place in batting averages: 41st av. 39.52

(1998 158th av. 23.53)
Place in bowling averages: 103rd av. 31.56
(1998 59th av. 26.52)
Strike rate: 69.52 (career 77.76)
Parents: Valentine and Elizabeth
Wife and date of marriage: Caroline, 23 September 1989
Children: Hannah, 9 October 1992; Victoria, 16 June 1994;
Matilda, 13 February 1997
Family links with cricket: Great-grandfather C.F.H. Leslie played for England
1882-83 – hit an all-run seven at Lord's; father played for Eton 2nd XI; mother opened
the bowling for Heathfield School
Education: St Aubyns School, Rottingdean; Eton College
Qualifications: 8 O-levels, 3 A-levels, granted short-service commission in Royal
Green Jackets 1985
Career outside cricket: 'Unemployable'
Off-season: 'Recovering'
Overseas tours: England VI to Hong Kong 1997; England to Sharjah 1997-98, to
West Indies 1997-98 (one-day series), to Bangladesh (Wills International Cup) 1998
Overseas teams played for: Avendale, Cape Town 1983-84
Cricketers particularly admired: Ian Botham, James Whitaker, Phil Simmons
Young players to look out for: Richard Clinton, Rob Key, Ed Smith
Other sports played: 'None with any distinction'
Other sports followed: Football (Arsenal), rugby union (London Wasps)
Injuries: Out for one match with 'tweaked hamstring'
Relaxations: Field sports

Extras: Ex-army officer in the Royal Green Jackets. First two scoring shots in Championship cricket were sixes. Chairman of the Professional Cricketers' Association. Out twice before lunch batting at number three for Kent against West Indies in 1995. Played for England in the 1997 Hong Kong Sixes tournament in which England finished runners-up to Pakistan and was named Player of the Tournament. Called up to the England squad for the one-day competition in Sharjah 1997 after the withdrawal of Darren Gough. Appointed captain of Kent 1999. Director of *The Cricketer* magazine. Shared in a new NatWest record sixth-wicket stand of 226 with Nigel Llong v Cheshire at Bowdon 1999, recording his first one-day 100 (117*) for Kent in the process; the second 50 of his 100 came off 13 balls

Opinions on cricket: 'Periods of transition are always painful – we mustn't shirk the pain. Turkeys may have to vote for Christmas.'

Best batting: 138 Kent v Essex, Canterbury 1997
138 Kent v Worcestershire, Worcester 1999

Best bowling: 5-51 Kent v Nottinghamshire, Trent Bridge 1997

1999 Season

	M	Inns	NO	Runs	HS	Avge	100s	50s	Ct	St	O	M	Runs	Wkts	Avge	Best	5wI	10wM
Test																		
All First	17	25	4	830	138	39.52	1	4	4	-	266.3	64	726	23	31.56	3-59	-	-
1-day Int																		
NatWest	2	2	1	128	117 *	128.00	1	-	1	-	10	1	34	3	11.33	3-34	-	
B & H																		
1-day Lge	15	13	3	221	39	22.10	-	-	2	-	80.2	1	386	12	32.16	3-15	-	

Career Performances

	M	Inns	NO	Runs	HS	Avge	100s	50s	Ct	St	Balls	Runs	Wkts	Avge	Best	5wI	10wM
Test																	
All First	183	299	35	8131	138	30.79	10	41	73	-	18196	8460	234	36.15	5-51	2	-
1-day Int	11	10	1	139	33	15.44	-	-	1	-	523	434	17	25.52	4-45	-	
NatWest	22	21	2	459	117 *	24.15	1	1	11	-	855	538	23	23.39	3-28	-	
B & H	47	44	3	1063	105 *	25.92	1	5	14	-	2230	1584	65	24.36	5-27	2	
1-day Lge	171	149	19	3030	112	23.30	1	12	39	-	6111	5371	207	25.94	4-13	-	

37. Who tops the list for the most County Championship matches umpired?

FLINTOFF, A.   Lancashire

Name: Andrew Flintoff
Role: Right-hand bat, right-arm medium bowler
Born: 6 December 1977, Preston
Height: 6ft 4in **Weight:** 13st 10lb
County debut: 1995
County cap: 1998
Test debut: 1998
Tests: 2
One-Day Internationals: 9
1st-Class 50s: 12
1st-Class 100s: 5
1st-Class 5 w. in innings: 1
1st-Class catches: 64
One-Day 100s: 1
Place in batting averages: 45th av. 38.26 (1998 150th av. 24.32)
Place in bowling averages: 74th av. 27.93
Strike rate: 58.26 (career 97.60)
Parents: Colin and Susan
Family links with cricket: Brother Chris and father both play local league cricket
Education: Greenlands County Primary; Ribbleton Hall High School
Qualifications: 9 GCSEs
Off-season: Touring South Africa and Zimbabwe with England
Overseas tours: England Schools U15 to South Africa 1993; England U19 to West Indies 1994-95, to Zimbabwe 1995-96, to Pakistan 1996-97; England A to Kenya and Sri Lanka 1997-98, to Zimbabwe and South Africa 1998-99; England to Sharjah (Coca-Cola Cup) 1998-99, to South Africa and Zimbabwe 1999-2000
Cricketers particularly admired: Jason Gallian, John Crawley, Stephen Titchard, Warren Hegg
Other sports followed: Football (Preston North End and Liverpool FC)
Relaxations: Listening to music and sleeping
Extras: Won a *Daily Telegraph* regional award for batting. Represented England U14 to U19 and played for U17 against India in 1994. Captained the England U19 tour to Pakistan in 1996-97 and was again captain in the series against Zimbabwe in 1997. Scored 61 off 24 balls in Championship match v Surrey at Old Trafford in June 1998, including 34 from one over by Alex Tudor. Became the 50th recipient of the Cricket Writers' Club Young Player of the Year award in September 1998. Professional Cricketers' Association's Young Player of the Year 1998. Was selected to represent England in the cancelled World Super Max 8s originally scheduled to take place in Perth in October 1998. Topped England A batting averages for tour to Zimbabwe and

South Africa 1998-99 with 542 runs at an average of 77.42. Scored 112 off 67 balls playing for Lahore Gymkhana v England in warm-up match for Coca-Cola Cup 1998-99. Struck 50 (including four sixes) on One-Day International debut, v Pakistan, Sharjah 1998-99. Scored 143 off 66 balls, including nine sixes in National League v Essex at Chelmsford 1999. His 160 v Yorkshire at Old Trafford 1999 included 111 runs before lunch, the first century before lunch by a Lancashire batsman in a Roses match. Won the EDS Walter Lawrence Trophy 1999 (for the fastest first-class century of the season) for his 100 off 61 balls for Lancashire v Gloucestershire at Bristol. Represented England in the 1999 World Cup

Opinions on cricket: 'Cricket should be promoted more in state schools.'

Best batting: 160 Lancashire v Yorkshire, Old Trafford 1999

Best bowling: 5-24 Lancashire v Hampshire, Southampton 1999

Stop press: Forced to return home early from England tour of South Africa and Zimbabwe after breaking a foot in the fourth Test at Cape Town. Awarded England contract (Band C) for 2000

1999 Season

	M	Inns	NO	Runs	HS	Avge	100s	50s	Ct	St	O	M	Runs	Wkts	Avge	Best	5wl	10wM
Test																		
All First	13	21	2	727	160	38.26	2	2	25	-	145.4	30	419	15	27.93	5-24	1	-
1-day Int	5	2	0	15	15	7.50	-	-	-	-	18	0	96	2	48.00	1-28	-	
NatWest	3	3	1	101	57 *	50.50	-	1	4	-	9	1	42	0	-	-	-	
B & H	1	1	0	5	5	5.00	-	-	-	-	2	0	3	0	-	-	-	
1-day Lge	11	10	1	338	143	37.55	1	1	7	-	67	5	287	17	16.88	4-24	-	

Career Performances

	M	Inns	NO	Runs	HS	Avge	100s	50s	Ct	St	Balls	Runs	Wkts	Avge	Best	5wl	10wM
Test	2	3	0	17	17	5.66	-	-	1	-	210	112	1	112.00	1-52	-	-
All First	45	70	6	2228	160	34.81	5	12	64	-	2440	1101	25	44.04	5-24	1	-
1-day Int	9	6	0	100	50	16.66	-	1	-	-	242	228	7	32.57	2-3	-	
NatWest	9	8	1	185	57 *	26.42	-	1	7	-	179	105	2	52.50	1-4	-	
B & H	9	8	0	178	92	22.25	-	1	3	-	102	61	2	30.50	1-10	-	
1-day Lge	32	31	2	822	143	28.34	1	4	11	-	552	411	21	19.57	4-24	-	

FOLLETT, D.   Northamptonshire

Name: David Follett
Role: Right-hand bat, right-arm
fast bowler
Born: 14 October 1968, Hanley,
Stoke-on-Trent
Height: 6ft 2in **Weight:** 12st 10lbs
Nickname: Foll
County debut: 1995 (Middlesex),
1997 (Northamptonshire)
1st-Class 5 w. in innings: 3
1st-Class 10 w. in match: 1
1st-Class catches: 5
Place in batting averages: (1998 299th
av. 2.16)
Place in bowling averages: (1998 100th
av. 32.50)

Strike rate: 90.00 (career 57.93)
Parents: Gordon and Sandra
Marital status: 'Engaged to Jo'
Family links with cricket: 'Dad played for Burslem CC in Stoke-on-Trent in the
NSSC League'
Education: Clarence Street Middle School, Hanley, Stoke-on-Trent; Moorland Road
High School, Burslem, Vale-on-Trent; Stoke-on-Trent Technical College
Qualifications: 2 O-levels
Career outside cricket: Engineer
Overseas teams played for: Australian Capital Territory 1994-95; Queenbeyan,
Canberra, 1994-95
Cricketers particularly admired: Imran Khan, Allan Donald, Derek Randall
Young players to look out for: Tony Naylor, Gareth Ainsworthy
Other sports followed: Football (Port Vale)
Relaxations: Watching football
Extras: Played for Staffordshire in the Minor Counties before joining Middlesex.
Was first team Player of the Month for April and May in 1996. Took 8 for 22 in the
Championship game against Durham at Chester-le-Street 1996. Moved to
Northamptonshire for the 1996 season. Retired at end of 1999 season
Best batting: 19 Northamptonshire v Surrey, Northampton 1999
Best bowling: 8-22 Middlesex v Durham, Chester-le-Street 1996

1999 Season

	M	Inns	NO	Runs	HS	Avge	100s	50s	Ct	St	O	M	Runs	Wkts	Avge	Best	5wI	10wM
Test																		
All First	5	5	1	44	19	11.00	-	-	-	-	120	23	377	8	47.12	3-64	-	-
1-day Int																		
NatWest																			
B & H																			
1-day Lge																			

Career Performances

	M	Inns	NO	Runs	HS	Avge	100s	50s	Ct	St	Balls	Runs	Wkts	Avge	Best	5wI	10wM
Test																	
All First	18	22	8	87	19	6.21	-	-	5	-	2549	1509	44	34.29	8-22	3	1
1-day Int																	
NatWest																	
B & H	9	3	0	8	4	2.66	-	-	-	-	408	302	12	25.16	4-39	-
1-day Lge	15	4	3	5	3*	5.00	-	-	6	-	651	526	22	23.90	3-26	-

FORDER, D. J.   Gloucestershire

Name: Damian Joseph Forder
Role: Right-hand bat, left-arm seam bowler
Born: Southmead, Bristol
Height: 6ft 4in **Weight:** 14st
Nickname: Damo
County debut: No first-team appearance
Parents: Helen and Stephen
Marital status: Single
Family links with cricket: Brothers played for local club
Education: Olveston School; Marlwood School; City of Bristol College
Qualifications: 1 GCSE, BTEC Sports Science, GNVQ Leisure and Tourism, Level 1 coaching award
Off-season: 'Fitness (weights and running); working on my batting'
Cricketers particularly admired: Allan Donald, Mike Smith, Courtney Walsh
Young players to look out for: Tom Cotterell, Chris Taylor, Stephen Pope
Other sports played: Golf, tennis
Other sports followed: Football (Man Utd), rugby (Bristol)

Injuries: Out for one month with torn hip fibre
Relaxations: Music, films, shopping, golf, tennis
Extras: Two-week trip to Dennis Lillee Pace Foundation in India, courtesy of *Daily Telegraph* Fast Bowler 1997. Played for the Gloucestershire Board XI in the 1999 NatWest Trophy
Opinions on cricket: 'Young bowlers must also work on their batting, so teams can bat all the way down the order.'

1999 Season (did not make any first-class or one-day appearances)

Career Performances

	M	Inns	NO	Runs	HS	Avge	100s	50s	Ct	St	Balls	Runs	Wkts	Avge	Best	5wI	10wM
Test																	
All First																	
1-day Int																	
NatWest	1	1	1	3	3 *	-	-	-	-	-	48	34	0	-		-	-
B & H																	
1-day Lge																	

FOSTER, J. S.   Essex

Name: James Savin Foster
Role: Right-hand bat, wicket-keeper
Born: 15 April 1980, Whipps Cross, London
Height: 6ft **Weight:** 12st
Nickname: Fozzy, Fozbe
County debut: No first-team appearance
Parents: Martin and Diana
Marital status: Single
Family links with cricket: 'Dad played for Essex Amateurs'
Education: Forest School; Durham University
Qualifications: 10 GCSEs, 3 A-levels
Off-season: Studying Sport in the Community at Durham University
Overseas tours: BUSA to South Africa 1999
Cricketers particularly admired:
Nasser Hussain, Stuart Law, Robert Rollins, Ian Healy, Ridley Jacobs, Steve Waugh
Young players to look out for: Matt Banes, Michael Brown, Charlie van der Gucht, Ryan Driver, Elliot Wilson, Ricky Anderson, Tim Phillips, Justin Bishop, Ian Bell, Richard Dawson

Other sports played: Hockey (Essex U21), tennis (played for GB U14 v Sweden U14; national training squad)
Other sports followed: Football (Wimbledon FC)
Injuries: Out from time to time during season with semi-dislocation of finger joint
Relaxations: Socialising, 'Klute and Rixy's'
Extras: Essex U17 Player of the Year 1997. Represented ECB U19 v Pakistan U19 1998. Represented England U19 v Australia U19 in 'Test' series 1999. Represented BUSA v South Africa Universities 1999
Opinions on cricket: 'County cricket needs to be more competitive.'

FOSTER, M. J. Durham

Name: Michael James Foster
Role: Right-hand bat, right arm medium-fast bowler
Born: 17 September 1972, Leeds
Height: 6ft 2in **Weight:** 15st
Nickname: Foz, Bear
County debut: 1993 (Yorkshire), 1995 (one-day, Northamptonshire), 1996 (Durham)
1st-Class 50s: 6
1st-Class 100s: 1
1st-Class catches: 10
One-Day 100s: 1
Place in batting averages: (1998 125th av. 26.75)
Place in bowling averages: (1998 21st av. 20.64)
Strike rate: (career 52.81)
Parents: Paul and Margaret
Wife and date of marriage: Lynne, 7 March 1998
Family links with cricket: 'Sister played for Yorkshire. Grandfather played in the Forces and for Great Preston. Father played for Great Preston'
Education: 'Las Vegas College'
Qualifications: 7 GCSEs, 2 A-levels
Overseas tours: England U19 to Pakistan 1991-92; Yorkshire to West Indies
Overseas teams played for: Fremantle, Perth, Western Australia; Queenstown, New Zealand; Ringwood, Melbourne, Australia
Cricketers particularly admired: Jeff Thomson, Ian Botham, Steve Waugh, Richie Richardson
Other sports followed: Rugby league (Castleford Tigers), football (Huddersfield Town), squash, 'various drinking games'
Relaxations: Socialising, sleeping, eating and keeping fit

Extras: 'Captained all the junior sides I played in up to and including Yorkshire Academy.' Off mark with a six in first first-class game. Retired at end of 1999 season
Opinions on cricket: 'One-day cricket is a pain in the arse.'
Best batting: 129 Durham v Glamorgan, Cardiff 1997
Best bowling: 4-21 Durham v Middlesex, Lord's 1996

1999 Season

	M	Inns	NO	Runs	HS	Avge	100s	50s	Ct	St	O	M	Runs	Wkts	Avge	Best	5wI	10wM
Test																		
All First																		
1-day Int																		
NatWest	1	1	0	3	3	3.00	-	-	-	-	6	0	26	0	-		-	-
B & H																		
1-day Lge	1	1	0	2	2	2.00	-	-	-	-	4	0	33	2	16.50	2-33	-	

Career Performances

	M	Inns	NO	Runs	HS	Avge	100s	50s	Ct	St	Balls	Runs	Wkts	Avge	Best	5wI	10wM
Test																	
All First	30	50	2	1128	129	23.50	1	6	10	-	3222	1839	61	30.14	4-21	-	-
1-day Int																	
NatWest	2	2	1	59	56 *	59.00	-	1	-	-	84	63	2	31.50	2-37	-	
B & H	12	12	3	297	73 *	33.00	-	3	-	-	578	434	9	48.22	3-26	-	
1-day Lge	49	40	4	606	118	16.83	1	2	9	-	1386	1321	31	42.61	3-34	-	

FRANCIS, S. R. G.   Hampshire

Name: Simon Richard George Francis
Role: Right-hand lower-order bat, right-arm fast-medium bowler
Born: 15 August 1978, Bromley
Height: 6ft 2in   **Weight:** 14st
Nickname: Frankie
County debut: 1997
Strike rate: 118.00 (career 108.00)
Parents: Daniel and Linda
Marital status: Single
Family links with cricket: 'Brother was the leading run-scorer in the 1996 U15 World Cup for England U15. Also played England U17, Hampshire Academy and Hampshire 2nd XI. Grandfather played club cricket and for the Navy. Father plays club cricket'
Education: Yardley Court, Tonbridge; King Edward VI, Southampton; Durham University
Qualifications: 10 GCSEs, 3 A-levels, BA (Hons) Sport, Level 1 coaching in cricket and hockey

Career outside cricket: Studying fitness training and sports therapy; coaching
Off-season: Diploma in Sports Therapy and Fitness Training; BUSA tour to South Africa ('hopefully'); coaching cricket
Overseas tours: England U17 to Holland for International Youth Tournament 1995; England U19 to Pakistan 1996-97; Durham University to Zimbabwe 1997-98
Cricketers particularly admired: Malcolm Marshall, Allan Donald
Young players to look out for: Lawrence Prittipaul
Other sports played: Squash, golf
Other sports followed: Football ('follow Southampton FC's demise')
Injuries: Out for one month with peroneal tendonitis
Relaxations: 'Reading fast bowlers' autobiographies'
Extras: *Daily Telegraph* West Region Bowling Award U15. Played hockey for England U18 1995. Played in Durham University's BUSA Championship winning side 1999
Opinions on cricket: 'Confused as to why the number of games is apparently being reduced, yet the B&H is reintroduced and 25-over slog-outs are being introduced!'
Best batting: 11 Hampshire v Somerset, Southampton 1999
Best bowling: 2-21 Hampshire v Sri Lanka, Southampton 1998

1999 Season

	M	Inns	NO	Runs	HS	Avge	100s	50s	Ct	St	O	M	Runs	Wkts	Avge	Best	5wI	10wM
Test																		
All First	4	6	2	13	11	3.25	-	-	-	-	118	25	392	6	65.33	2-94	-	-
1-day Int																		
NatWest																			
B & H																			
1-day Lge	4	1	0	1	1	1.00	-	-	-	-	23	3	93	3	31.00	2-28	-	

Career Performances

	M	Inns	NO	Runs	HS	Avge	100s	50s	Ct	St	Balls	Runs	Wkts	Avge	Best	5wI	10wM
Test																	
All First	7	9	3	27	11	4.50	-	-	-	-	1080	630	10	63.00	2-21	-	-
1-day Int																	
NatWest																	
B & H																	
1-day Lge	5	1	0	1	1	1.00	-	-	-	-	186	124	5	24.80	2-28	-	

FRANKLIN, G. D.　　　　Warwickshire

Name: Gavin David Franklin
Role: Right-hand bat, off-spin bowler
Born: 9 January 1978, Wolverhampton
Height: 6ft **Weight:** 12st 12lbs
Nickname: Franko
County debut: No first-team appearance
Parents: David and Helen
Marital status: Single
Family links with cricket: Father played for
Wolverhampton CC and is a qualified coach
Education: Birchfield Preparatory School;
Malvern College; Durham University
Qualifications: 3 A-levels, NCA coaching
Levels 1 and 2
Off-season: At university (reading Sport in
the Community) plus some coaching
Overseas tours: British Universities to South
Africa 1999-2000; Durham University to
South Africa 2000
Overseas teams played for: Newtown and Chilwell CC, Geelong, Australia 1996-97
Cricketers particularly admired: David Nash, David Gower
Other sports played: Golf, football
Other sports followed: Football (Aston Villa)
Relaxations: Playing golf and listening to Stone Roses
Extras: Was captain of the most successful post-war 1st XI at Malvern College

FRANKS, P. J.　　　　Nottinghamshire

Name: Paul John Franks
Role: Left-hand bat, right-arm fast-medium bowler
Born: 3 February 1979, Sutton-in-Ashfield
Height: 6ft 1in **Weight:** 13st
Nickname: Franksie, Pike, Franno
County debut: 1996
County cap: 1999
50 wickets in a season: 2
1st-Class 50s: 4
1st-Class 5 w. in innings: 5
1st-Class catches: 15

One-Day 5 w. in innings: 1
Place in batting averages: 246th av. 14.50
(1998 175th av. 21.66)
Place in bowling averages: 49th av. 23.63
(1998 58th av. 26.44)
Strike rate: 48.85 (career 55.47)
Parents: John and Patricia
Marital status: Single
Family links with cricket: Father played
league cricket for 30 years
Education: Walter D'Ayncourt Primary
School; Minster School, Southwell;
West Notts College
Qualifications: 9 GCSEs, Advanced GNVQ
Leisure and Tourism, NCA coaching award
Off-season: England A tour to Bangladesh
and New Zealand
Overseas tours: England U19 to Pakistan
1996-97, to South Africa (including Youth World Cup) 1997-98; England A to
Zimbabwe and South Africa 1998-99, to Bangladesh and New Zealand 1999-2000;
Notts CCC to South Africa 1998, 1999; Benefit tours to Guernsey 1998, 1999
Cricketers particularly admired: Shoaib Akhtar, Allan Donald, Dennis Lillee
Young players to look out for: Mark Wallace, Stephen Randall, Matthew Whiley,
Chris Schofield, Matt Bulbeck
Other sports played: Golf ('when not in "The Stingers"')
Other sports followed: Football, 'Oz aerobics'
Injuries: Out for one game with a 'dodgy shoulder'
Relaxations: Socialising, cinema
Extras: Became youngest ever Notts player (and third-youngest player ever, aged 18
years 163 days) to take a hat-trick, v Warwickshire in July 1997. Won Youth World
Cup winner's medal in Johannesburg 1998. Attended Dennis Lillee coaching school,
Madras, March 1997, February 1998 and March 1999. Was selected to represent
England in the cancelled World Super Max 8s originally scheduled to take place in
Perth in October 1998. Called up for 1998-99 England A tour of Zimbabwe and South
Africa as injury cover in the pace-bowling department. Awarded Notts cap 1999
Opinions on cricket: 'Too many overs in a day still!!'
Best batting: 66* Nottinghamshire v Kent, Canterbury 1998
Best bowling: 6-63 Nottinghamshire v Worcestershire, Kidderminster 1998

1999 Season

	M	Inns	NO	Runs	HS	Avge	100s	50s	Ct	St	O	M	Runs	Wkts	Avge	Best	5wI	10wM
Test																		
All First	16	27	3	348	61	14.50	-	1	2	-	513	124	1489	63	23.63	5-52	1	-
1-day Int																		
NatWest	2	2	2	41	26 *	-	-	-	1	-	18	4	56	5	11.20	3-7	-	
B & H																		
1-day Lge	15	13	3	131	40	13.10	-	-	-	-	107.5	4	512	16	32.00	5-27	1	

Career Performances

	M	Inns	NO	Runs	HS	Avge	100s	50s	Ct	St	Balls	Runs	Wkts	Avge	Best	5wI	10wM
Test																	
All First	44	67	11	1026	66 *	18.32	-	4	15	-	8210	4170	148	28.17	6-63	5	-
1-day Int																	
NatWest	8	6	3	103	26 *	34.33	-	-	3	-	420	282	13	21.69	3-7	-	
B & H																	
1-day Lge	31	24	5	218	40	11.47	-	-	2	-	1311	1032	42	24.57	5-27	1	

FRASER, A. R. C.   Middlesex

Name: Angus Robert Charles Fraser
Role: Right-hand late-order bat, right-arm fast-medium bowler, outfielder 'specialist', county vice-captain
Born: 8 August 1965, Billinge, Lancashire
Height: 6ft 6in **Weight:** 'Should be under 16st'
Nickname: Gus, Lard, Wiggy, Recall
County debut: 1984
County cap: 1988
Benefit: 1997
Test debut: 1989
Tests: 46
One-Day Internationals: 42
50 wickets in a season: 7
1st-Class 50s: 2
1st-Class 5 w. in innings: 32
1st-Class 10 w. in match: 4
1st-Class catches: 46
One-Day 5 w. in innings: 1
Place in batting averages: 258th av. 12.90 (1998 277th av. 9.57)

Place in bowling averages: 81st av. 28.76 (1998 16th av. 20.06)
Strike rate: 68.71 (career 62.80)
Parents: Don and Irene
Wife and date of marriage: Denise, March 1996
Children: Alexander Charles Mitchell, May 1993; Bethan Louise, July 1995
Family links with cricket: 'Mum and dad keen followers. Brother Alastair played for Middlesex, Essex, then Middlesex again'
Education: Weald First School; Gayton High School, Harrow; Orange Hill Senior High School, Edgware
Qualifications: 7 O-levels, qualified cricket coach
Off-season: 'Working for Middlesex CCC, *Sunday Telegraph*, plus any TV or radio channel that wants an opinion. Also spending time with family, catching up with mates, watching Liverpool FC and generally enjoying myself'
Overseas tours: Thames Valley Gentlemen to Barbados 1985; Middlesex to La Manga 1985, 1986, to Portugal 1991-93; England to India (Nehru Cup) 1989-90, to West Indies 1989-90, to Australia 1990-91, to West Indies 1993-94, to Australia 1994-95, to South Africa 1995-96, to West Indies 1997-98, to Australia 1998-99, to Sharjah (Coca-Cola Cup) 1998-99
Overseas teams played for: Plimmerton, Wellington 1985-86 and 1987-88; Western Suburbs, Sydney 1988-89 and 1994-95
Cricketers particularly admired: Graham Gooch, Allan Border, Curtly Ambrose, Courtney Walsh
Young players to look out for: Michael Powell (Glamorgan)
Other sports played: 'Golf with a sombrero on'
Other sports followed: 'Follow Liverpool FC keenly. Enjoy watching rugby internationals at my local rugby club, Harrow'
Injuries: Broken finger – no time off required
Relaxations: Spending time with family, golf, Liverpool FC, drinking good red wine
Extras: Middlesex Player of the Year 1988 and 1989. Took a hat-trick in the Benson and Hedges Cup in 1989. Selected for England tour to New Zealand 1991-92 but ruled out by injury. Originally left out of England tour party to Australia 1994-95 but called up when Martin McCague was injured. Took his 100th Test wicket (Brian Lara) against West Indies in 1995. Finished 2nd in the Whyte and Mackay bowling ratings for 1995. One of *Wisden*'s Five Cricketers of the Year 1996. His 8-53 v West Indies at Trinidad in 1998 is the best return by an English bowler in the West Indies. Peter Smith Award 1998. Winner of the KUMALA Cape Wines 'Century of Bottles' award for the best individual performance against the 1998 South Africans. Awarded MBE in New Year honours list 1999. Represented England in 1999 World Cup. Appointed vice-captain of Middlesex for 2000
Opinions on cricket: 'Let's give the changes we have made to the game a chance. Don't change them before we find out or it will be pointless. You can make as many changes as you like but to improve the standard of cricket in this country, everyone in the game needs to work harder, and that's not just the players.'
Best batting: 92 Middlesex v Surrey, The Oval 1990
Best bowling: 8-53 England v West Indies, Port of Spain 1997-98

1999 Season

	M	Inns	NO	Runs	HS	Avge	100s	50s	Ct	St	O	M	Runs	Wkts	Avge	Best	5wI	10wM
Test																		
All First	12	16	5	142	56 *	12.90	-	1	-	-	435.1	113	1093	38	28.76	5-63	1	-
1-day Int	3	2	1	18	15 *	18.00	-	-	3	-	30	2	111	1	111.00	1-27	-	
NatWest	1	1	0	4	4	4.00	-	-	1	-	10	1	40	0	-	-	-	-
B & H																		
1-day Lge	15	7	4	66	31	22.00	-	-	6	-	123.5	21	424	21	20.19	4-35	-	

Career Performances

	M	Inns	NO	Runs	HS	Avge	100s	50s	Ct	St	Balls	Runs	Wkts	Avge	Best	5wI	10wM
Test	46	67	15	388	32	7.46	-	-	9	-	10876	4836	177	27.32	8-53	11	1
All First	260	308	76	2522	92	10.87	-	2	46	-	50178	21772	799	27.24	8-53	32	4
1-day Int	42	20	9	141	38 *	12.81	-	-	5	-	2392	1412	47	30.04	4-22	-	
NatWest	32	12	9	72	19	24.00	-	-	6	-	2097	1056	45	23.46	4-34	-	
B & H	44	23	12	114	30 *	10.36	-	-	9	-	2595	1534	54	28.40	4-49	-	
1-day Lge	168	67	30	432	33	11.67	-	-	27	-	7495	4916	180	27.31	5-32	1	

FROST, T.   Warwickshire

Name: Tony Frost
Role: Right-hand bat, wicket-keeper
Born: 17 November 1975, Stoke-on-Trent
Height: 5ft 10in **Weight:** 10st 6lbs
County debut: 1997
County cap: 1999
1st-Class 50s: 3
1st-Class 100s: 1
1st-Class catches: 71
1st-Class stumpings: 3
Place in batting averages: 199th av. 20.47
(1998 76th av. 32.41)
Parents: Ivan and Christine
Marital status: Single
Family links with cricket: Father played for
Staffordshire
Education: James Brinkley High School;
Stoke-on-Trent College
Qualifications: 5 GCSEs
Overseas tours: Kidsgrove U18 to Australia 1990-91
Cricketers particularly admired: Ashley Giles 'could be described as a legend',

'Pop' Welch and George Burns 'in the JT bracket'
Other sports followed: Football, golf
Relaxations: Listening to music, watching films, reading aircraft magazines
Extras: Represented Staffordshire at all levels from U11 to U19. Won Texaco U16 competition with Staffordshire in 1992. Played for Development of Excellence XI U17 v South Africa and U18 v West Indies and U19 v India. Awarded Warwicks cap 1999
Opinions on cricket: 'A lot of people are too critical. If they spent more time building up the players' confidence instead of putting the player down then they may get better results.'
Best batting: 111* Warwickshire v Oxford University, The Parks 1998

1999 Season

	M	Inns	NO	Runs	HS	Avge	100s	50s	Ct	St	O	M	Runs	Wkts	Avge	Best	5wI	10wM
Test																		
All First	12	18	1	348	66	20.47	-	1	23	1								
1-day Int																		
NatWest	1	1	0	5	5	5.00	-	-	2	-								
B & H	1	0	0	0	0	-	-	-	2	-								
1-day Lge	11	5	1	67	22 *	16.75	-	-	6	2								

Career Performances

	M	Inns	NO	Runs	HS	Avge	100s	50s	Ct	St	Balls		Runs	Wkts	Avge	Best	5wI	10wM
Test																		
All First	29	43	5	895	111 *	23.55	1	3	71	3	6		6	0	-		-	-	-
1-day Int																		
NatWest	2	2	0	5	5	2.50	-	-	4	1								
B & H	3	2	1	11	10 *	11.00	-	-	3	-								
1-day Lge	21	8	3	70	22 *	14.00	-											

38. Who had match figures of 12-174 to add to his 137* in Middlesex's only innings in the Championship match v Surrey at The Oval in 1947?

FULTON, D. P.   Kent

Name: David Paul Fulton
Role: Right-hand opening/top-order bat,
occasional wicket-keeper
Born: 15 November 1971, Lewisham
Height: 6ft 2in **Weight:** 12st 7lbs
Nickname: Raver, Tav
County debut: 1992
County cap: 1998
1st-Class 50s: 26
1st-Class 100s: 5
1st-Class 200s: 1
1st-Class catches: 129
Place in batting averages: 133rd av. 26.74
(1998 84th av. 31.80)
Strike rate: (career 67.00)
Parents: John and Ann
Marital status: Single
Family links with cricket: Father used to

play for village side. 'When they blocked the mid-wicket area he was forced to retire'
Education: Otford County Primary; The Judd School, Tonbridge; University of Kent
at Canterbury
Qualifications: 10 GCSEs, 3 A-levels, BA (Hons) Politics and International Relations,
advanced cricket coach, rugby coach, gym instructor qualification
Career outside cricket: 'Part-time journalist/politician/entrepreneur'
Overseas tours: Kent Schools U17 to Singapore and New Zealand 1986-87; Kent to
France 1998
Overseas teams played for: Avendale CC, Cape Town 1993-94; Victoria CC,
Cape Town 1994-95, University of WA, Perth 1995-96; Petersham-Marrickville CC,
Sydney 1998-99
Cricketers particularly admired: Graham Gooch, Gordon Greenidge, Courtney Walsh
Young players to look out for: Rob Key, 'Me'
Other sports played: Chess (England junior), table tennis ('top 10 in UK as a junior';
played for South England juniors); rugby, football, tennis ('useful'); golf, swimming
('lousy')
Other sports followed: Rugby (Harlequins), football (Nottingham Forest and
Canterbury City)
Extras: Helped Dean Headley's hat-trick against Derbyshire by catching Kim Barnett
and Chris Adams. Was the last person to catch Viv Richards in a first-class match.
Opened the batting and the bowling against South Africa in their first county game
1994. Set record for the longest innings ever played by a Kent batsman in scoring his
207 against Yorkshire at Maidstone in 1998. 'Once scored 2000 runs without being
dismissed against my little sister in the back garden'

Opinions on cricket: 'It's important we keep pace with rugby, football etc. Marketing is the key. We need heroes in our game, which itself must be conducive to the watching public. Day/night cricket is a good start, but we must continue to embrace change. Groundsmen should be employed by ECB and be neutral.'

Best batting: 207 Kent v Yorkshire, Maidstone 1998
Best bowling: 1-37 Kent v Oxford University, Canterbury 1996

1999 Season

	M	Inns	NO	Runs	HS	Avge	100s	50s	Ct	St	O	M	Runs	Wkts	Avge	Best	5wl	10wM
Test																		
All First	17	29	2	722	126 *	26.74	1	3	18	-								
1-day Int																		
NatWest																		
B & H																		
1-day Lge																		

Career Performances

	M	Inns	NO	Runs	HS	Avge	100s	50s	Ct	St	Balls	Runs	Wkts	Avge	Best	5wl	10wM
Test																	
All First	93	166	11	4781	207	30.84	6	26	129	-	67	65	1	65.00	1-37	-	-
1-day Int																	
NatWest	6	6	0	65	19	10.83	-	-	-	-	6	9	0	-	-	-	
B & H	2	2	0	42	25	21.00	-	-	3	-							
1-day Lge	13	13	0	100	29	7.69	-	-	5	-							

39. Which county has won the title outright on the most occasions since the Championship was officially constituted in 1890?

GALLIAN, J. E. R.   Nottinghamshire

Name: Jason Edward Riche Gallian
Role: Right-hand bat, right-arm
medium bowler, county captain
Born: 25 June 1971, Manly, NSW, Australia
Height: 6ft **Weight:** 13st
Nickname: Gal
County debut: 1990 (Lancashire),
1998 (Nottinghamshire)
County cap: 1994 (Lancashire),
1998 (Nottinghamshire)
Test debut: 1995

Tests: 3
1000 runs in a season: 2
1st-Class 50s: 36
1st-Class 100s: 14
1st-Class 300s: 1
1st-Class 5 w. in innings: 1
1st-Class catches: 89
One-Day 100s: 7
One-Day 5 w. in innings: 1
Place in batting averages: 92nd av. 31.77 (1998 122nd av. 26.90)
Strike rate: 44.00 (career 69.21)
Parents: Ray and Marilyn
Marital status: Engaged
Family links with cricket: Father played for Stockport
Education: The Pittwater House Schools, Australia; Oxford University
Qualifications: Higher School Certificate, Diploma in Social Studies
(Keble College, Oxford)
Overseas tours: Australia U20 to West Indies 1989-90; England A to India 1994-95,
to Pakistan 1995-96, to Australia 1996-97; England to South Africa 1995-96
Overseas teams played for: NSW and Australia U19 1988-89; NSW Colts and NSW
2nd XI 1990-91; Manly 1993-94
Cricketers particularly admired: Desmond Haynes, Mike Gatting
Young players to look out for: Paul Franks
Other sports followed: Rugby league and union, football
Relaxations: Listening to music, playing golf
Extras: Captained Australia YC v England YC 1989-90. Represented Australia U20
and U21 1991-92. Took wicket of D. A. Hagan of Oxford University with his first ball
for Lancashire in first-class cricket. Played for Oxford University in 1992 and for
Combined Universities in the B&H Cup. Captained Oxford University 1993. Was
called up to the England squad in South Africa in 1995-96 as a replacement for the

injured John Crawley and played in the fourth Test at Port Elizabeth. He was dogged by finger injuries throughout the England A tour to Australia in 1996-97. Left Lancashire during the 1997-98 off-season and joined Nottinghamshire for 1998, being appointed captain after resignation of Paul Johnson

Best batting: 312 Lancashire v Derbyshire, Old Trafford 1996
Best bowling: 6-115 Lancashire v Surrey, Southport 1996

1999 Season

	M	Inns	NO	Runs	HS	Avge	100s	50s	Ct	St	O	M	Runs	Wkts	Avge	Best	5wI	10wM
Test																		
All First	19	34	3	985	120 *	31.77	2	5	19	-	36.4	11	112	5	22.40	2-28	-	-
1-day Int																		
NatWest	2	2	0	26	17	13.00	-	-	2	-	7	0	34	0	-		-	-
B & H																		
1-day Lge	15	15	1	490	130	35.00	2	1	5	-	7	0	52	0	-		-	-

Career Performances

	M	Inns	NO	Runs	HS	Avge	100s	50s	Ct	St	Balls	Runs	Wkts	Avge	Best	5wI	10wM
Test	3	6	0	74	28	12.33	-	-	1	-	84	62	0	-	-	-	-
All First	124	218	19	7305	312	36.70	15	36	89	-	6160	3547	89	39.85	6-115	1	-
1-day Int																	
NatWest	13	13	1	434	101 *	36.16	1	3	8	-	162	122	1	122.00	1-11	-	
B & H	30	29	2	910	134	33.70	2	6	5	-	665	548	15	36.53	5-15	1	
1-day Lge	74	73	9	2216	130	34.62	4	12	29	-	784	752	28	26.85	2-10	-	

40. Which Australian cricketer made his Championship debut
for Somerset in 1957 and went on to become a first-class umpire
in England after his retirement as a player?

GANGULY, S. C.   Lancashire

Name: Saurav Chandidas Ganguly
Role: Left-hand bat, right-arm
medium bowler
Born: 8 July 1973, Calcutta
Height: 5ft 11in
County debut: No first-team appearance
Test debut: 1996
Tests: 27
One-Day Internationals: 106
1st-Class 50s: 39
1st-Class 100s: 13
1st-Class 200s: 1
1st-Class catches: 65
1st-Class 5 w. in innings: 1
One-Day 100s: 7
One-Day 5 w. in innings: 1
Strike rate: (career 64.97)
Education: St Xavier's College

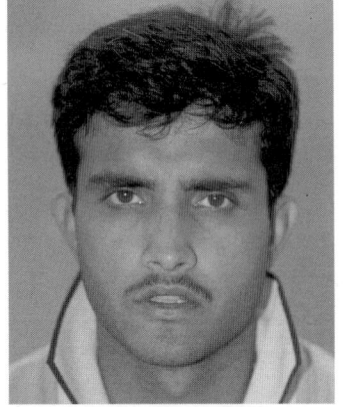

Overseas tours: India to England 1996, to South Africa 1996-97, to West Indies
1996-97, to Sri Lanka 1997-98, to Zimbabwe 1998-99, to New Zealand 1998-99,
to UK, Ireland and Holland (World Cup) 1999, to Sri Lanka (Aiwa Cup) 1999,
to Singapore (Coca-Cola Challenge) 1999, to Toronto (DMC Toronto Festival) 1999,
to Kenya (LG Cup) 1999, to Australia 1999-2000
Overseas teams played for: Bengal 1989-90 –
Extras: Scored century (131) on Test debut v England at Lord's 1996. Shared in a
stand of 318 for the second wicket with Rahul Dravid for India v Sri Lanka at Taunton
in the 1999 World Cup, a record for any wicket in One-Day International cricket; his
183 scored in that innings is the second-highest individual score in World Cup cricket
behind Gary Kirsten's 188
Best batting: 200* Bengal v Bihar, Calcutta 1994-95
Best bowling: 6-87 Bengal v Delhi, Delhi 1997-98
Stop press: Appointed captain of India February 2000

1999 Season

	M	Inns	NO	Runs	HS	Avge	100s	50s	Ct	St	O	M	Runs	Wkts	Avge	Best	5wI	10wM
Test																		
All First																		
1-day Int	7	7	0	379	183	54.14	1	1	-	-	38	0	195	6	32.50	3-27	-	
NatWest																		
B & H																		
1-day Lge																		

Career Performances

	M	Inns	NO	Runs	HS	Avge	100s	50s	Ct	St	Balls	Runs	Wkts	Avge	Best	5wl	10wM
Test	27	45	4	2037	173	49.68	6	9	10	-	1029	544	17	32.00	3-28	-	-
All First	97	153	24	6510	200*	50.46	14	39	65	-	5133	3018	79	38.20	6-87	1	-
1-day Int	106	101	8	3890	183	41.82	7	26	30	-	1687	1362	38	35.84	5-16	1	
NatWest																	
B & H																	
1-day Lge																	

GANNON, B. W.   Gloucestershire

Name: Benjamin Ward Gannon
Role: Right-hand bat, right-arm
medium bowler
Born: 5 September 1975, Oxford
Height: 6ft 3in **Weight:** 13st 7lbs
Nickname: Obi, Ganja
County debut: 1999
1st-Class 5 w. in innings: 2
1st-Class catches: 4
Place in batting averages: 278th av. 8.75
Place in bowling averages: 96th av. 30.06
Strike rate: 47.18 (career 47.18)
Parents: Martin and Jane
Marital status: Single
Education: Dragon School, Oxford;
Abingdon School; Cheltenham and
Gloucester College of Higher Education
Qualifications: 3 A-levels, BSc (Hons)
Geography and Sports Science
Career outside cricket: 'Self-unemployed'
Off-season: Playing for Old Grey CC, Jeffries Bay, South Africa
Overseas tours: Forest Nomads to Zimbabwe 1999
Overseas teams played for: Waverley, Sydney 1994-95
Cricketers particularly admired: Courtney Walsh, Curtly Ambrose, Glenn McGrath, Allan Donald, Shoaib Akhtar
Young players to look out for: Stephen Pope, Simon Jones, Steve Harmison
Other sports followed: Rugby, boxing, athletics, tennis
Injuries: Out for three weeks with a rib strain
Relaxations: Listening to music, keeping fit
Extras: Took seven wickets in his first-class debut match, v Glamorgan at Cardiff 1999

Best batting: 18 Gloucestershire v Glamorgan, Cardiff 1999
Best bowling: 6-80 Gloucestershire v Glamorgan, Cardiff 1999

1999 Season

	M	Inns	NO	Runs	HS	Avge	100s	50s	Ct	St	O	M	Runs	Wkts	Avge	Best	5wl	10wM
Test																		
All First	11	12	4	70	18	8.75	-	-	4	-	259.3	47	992	33	30.06	6-80	2	-
1-day Int																		
NatWest																		
B & H																		
1-day Lge																		

Career Performances

	M	Inns	NO	Runs	HS	Avge	100s	50s	Ct	St	Balls	Runs	Wkts	Avge	Best	5wl	10wM
Test																	
All First	11	12	4	70	18	8.75	-	-	4	-	1557	992	33	30.06	6-80	2	-
1-day Int																	
NatWest																	
B & H																	
1-day Lge																	

GARAWAY, M.   Hampshire

Name: Mark Garaway
Role: Right-hand bat, wicket-keeper
Born: 20 July 1973, Swindon, Wilts
Height: 5ft 7in **Weight:** 12st 7lbs
Nickname: Wolf, Garas, Phantom
County debut: 1996
1st-Class 50s: 1
1st-Class catches: 13
1st-Class stumpings: 2
Parents: Sam and Val
Marital status: Single
Family links with cricket: 'Sam still whacks it for Ventnor CC. Grandfather was a steady player'
Education: Carhampton Primary, Somerset; Ventnor Middle and Sandown High School, Isle of Wight; 'Ventnor CC; the Astoria (Hermanus, SA)'
Qualifications: 10 O-levels, 3 A-levels, coaching Levels I, II, III; presently Staff III (Level II) coach
Career outside cricket: Cricket coach

Off-season: Coaching for Hampshire; assisting in development of Hampshire's Cricket Academy; tutoring in ECB coach development

Overseas tours: Isle of Wight U14 and U17 to Jersey and Guernsey 1988-91; Ventnor to Winchester 1994; Hampshire to Vale do Lobo 1994

Overseas teams played for: Worcester, Boland, South Africa 1991-93; Hermanus, South Africa 1993, 1995-97; 'Ventnor, Isle of Wight 1982-94'

Cricketers particularly admired: Ian Botham, Robin Smith, Mark Brumer, Simon Rodney, Jeff Hose, Kevan James

Young players to look out for: Lawrie Prittipaul, Charlie van der Gucht

Other sports followed: Football (Swindon Town), squash

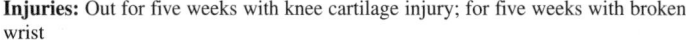

Injuries: Out for five weeks with knee cartilage injury; for five weeks with broken wrist

Relaxations: Music, art

Extras: Represented England at U15, U17 and U19 level. Played for Isle of Wight at U16, U17, U21 and senior level in the same season. Spent two years (1991 and 1992) as MCC Young Professional. Hampshire Schools Wicketkeepers Award 1988. Andrew Swallow Memorial Cup 1987. Wight Waters Sports Award 1989-91. 2nd XI Player of the Month June 1997. Retired at end of 1999 season

Opinions on cricket: 'A great game which shall become even greater thanks to the ban on all left-handed all-rounders (who throw with their wrong hand) which came in on 6 September 1999.'

Best batting: 55 Hampshire v New Zealand, Southampton 1999

1999 Season

	M	Inns	NO	Runs	HS	Avge	100s	50s	Ct	St	O	M	Runs	Wkts	Avge	Best	5wl	10wM
Test																		
All First	1	2	0	56	55	28.00	-	1	4	1								
1-day Int																		
NatWest																		
B & H																		
1-day Lge	1	1	0	4	4	4.00	-	-	1	-								

Career Performances

	M	Inns	NO	Runs	HS	Avge	100s	50s	Ct	St	Balls	Runs	Wkts	Avge	Best	5wI	10wM
Test																	
All First	4	5	0	124	55	24.80	-	1	13	2							
1-day Int																	
NatWest																	
B & H																	
1-day Lge	1	1	0	4	4	4.00	-	-	1	-							

GAZZARD, C. M. Somerset

Name: Carl Matthew Gazzard
Role: Right-hand bat, wicket-keeper
Born: 15 April 1982, Penzance
Height: 6ft **Weight:** 12st 4lbs
Nickname: Gazza
County debut: No first-team appearance
Parents: Paul and Alison
Marital status: Single
Family links with cricket: Father and
brother both played for Cornwall Schools
Education: St Mary's Roman Catholic,
Penzance; Mounts Bay Comprehensive;
Richard Huish College, Taunton
Qualifications: 10 GCSEs, Level 1 coaching
Career outside cricket: A-level student
Overseas tours: Cornwall Schools U13 to
Johannesburg; West of England U15 to West
Indies; Somerset Academy to Durban 1999
Cricketers particularly admired: Ian Allen, Shaquil Ahmed, Ian Healy
Young players to look out for: Jason Hall, Adam Barber
Other sports played: Football (played through age groups for Cornwall)
Other sports followed: Football (West Ham United)
Relaxations: Any sport, watching TV, socialising
Extras: Played for England U13, U14, U15. Won the Graham Kersey Award for Best
Wicket-keeper at Bunbury Festival. Played for Cornwall in Minor Counties aged 16
and in the NatWest Trophy 1999
Opinions on cricket: 'There is always something else to learn and somebody who
would willingly swap places, so you must take chances when they come and always
want to better yourself.'

Career Performances

	M	Inns	NO	Runs	HS	Avge	100s	50s	Ct	St	Balls	Runs	Wkts	Avge	Best	5wI	10wM
Test																	
All First																		
1-day Int																		
NatWest	1	1	0	16	16	16.00	-	-	2	-							
B & H																		
1-day Lge																		

GIDDINS, E. S. H.   Warwickshire

Name: Edward Simon Hunter Giddins
Role: Right-hand bat, right-arm
medium-fast bowler
Born: 20 July 1971, Eastbourne
Height: 6ft 4in **Weight:** 13st 7lbs
Nickname: Geezer
County debut: 1991 (Sussex),
1998 (Warwickshire)
County cap: 1994 (Sussex)
Test debut: 1999
Tests: 1
50 wickets in a season: 4
1st-Class 5 w. in innings: 20
1st-Class 10 w. in match: 2
1st-Class catches: 18
One-Day 5 w. in innings: 1
Place in batting averages: 280th av. 8.44
(1998 296th av. 3.35)
Place in bowling averages: 33rd av. 21.96 (1998 38th av. 23.88)
Strike rate: 44.01 (career 50.93)
Parents: Simon and Pauline
Marital status: Single
Family links with cricket: None
Education: St Bede's Prep School; Eastbourne College
Qualifications: 'Various O- and A-levels, national coaching certificate, recorder
(grade 2), shorthand and typing 100/60'
Career outside cricket: None
Overseas tours: England A to Pakistan 1995-96
Overseas teams played for: Mosman, Sydney 1994-95
Cricketers particularly admired: Derek Randall

Other sports followed: Football (Brighton & Hove Albion FC – 'fingers crossed')
Relaxations: Gym, fitness and mountain biking
Extras: Joined Warwickshire for the 1998 season. Made Test debut v New Zealand in the fourth Test at The Oval 1999
Best batting: 34 Sussex v Essex, Hove 1995
Best bowling: 6-47 Sussex v Yorkshire, Eastbourne 1996

1999 Season

	M	Inns	NO	Runs	HS	Avge	100s	50s	Ct	St	O	M	Runs	Wkts	Avge	Best	5wI	10wM
Test	1	2	1	0	0 *	0.00	-	-	-	-	26	7	79	4	19.75	3-38	-	-
All First	15	20	11	76	18	8.44	-	-	2	-	381.3	102	1142	52	21.96	6-90	2	-
1-day Int																		
NatWest	2	1	0	2	2	2.00	-	-	1	-	18	2	86	3	28.66	3-31	-	
B & H	2	1	0	1	1	1.00	-	-	-	-	19	3	61	6	10.16	5-21	1	
1-day Lge	11	3	1	6	4	3.00	-	-	1	-	87	7	366	11	33.27	2-36	-	

Career Performances

	M	Inns	NO	Runs	HS	Avge	100s	50s	Ct	St	Balls	Runs	Wkts	Avge	Best	5wI	10wM
Test	1	2	1	0	0 *	0.00	-	-	-	-	156	79	4	19.75	3-38	-	-
All First	113	139	58	440	34	5.43	-	-	18	-	19558	10575	384	27.53	6-47	20	2
1-day Int																	
NatWest	14	6	3	27	13	9.00	-	-	2	-	887	521	18	28.94	3-24	-	
B & H	19	6	4	6	4 *	3.00	-	-	5	-	1088	683	25	27.32	5-21	1	
1-day Lge	86	35	14	37	9 *	1.76	-	-	10	-	3644	2976	98	30.36	4-23	-	

GIE, N. A.   Nottinghamshire

Name: Noel Addison Gie
Role: Right-hand bat, right-arm medium bowler
Born: 12 April 1977, Pretoria, South Africa
Height: 6ft **Weight:** 12st 8lbs
County debut: 1995
1st-Class 50s: 3
1st-Class catches: 7
Place in batting averages: (1998 232nd av. 16.00)
Parents: Clive and Lindy
Marital status: Single
Family links with cricket: Father played first-class cricket in South Africa for Western Province, Northern Transvaal and Natal
Education: Fornwood School, Nottingham; Trent College, Nottingham; Nottingham Trent University

Qualifications: Studying for degree in Business Studies from October 1996, NCA coaching award
Overseas tours: Trent College to Australia 1993-94; England U19 to Zimbabwe 1995-96
Overseas teams played for: Berea Rovers, Durban, South Africa 1995
Cricketers particularly admired: Robin Smith
Other sports followed: Squash, tennis, rugby league
Relaxations: Reading and cycling
Extras: Scored 3153 runs for the 1st XI during his time at Trent College. Released by Notts at end of 1999 season
Best batting: 59* Nottinghamshire v Cambridge University, Nottingham 1999

1999 Season

	M	Inns	NO	Runs	HS	Avge	100s	50s	Ct	St	O	M	Runs	Wkts	Avge	Best	5wl	10wM
Test																		
All First	5	6	2	144	59 *	36.00	-	1	-	-	5	0	27	0	-	-	-	-
1-day Int																		
NatWest																		
B & H																		
1-day Lge	2	2	0	29	28	14.50	-	-	-	-								

Career Performances

	M	Inns	NO	Runs	HS	Avge	100s	50s	Ct	St	Balls	Runs	Wkts	Avge	Best	5wl	10wM
Test																	
All First	16	26	2	455	59 *	18.95	-	3	7	-	30	27	0	-	-	-	-
1-day Int																	
NatWest																	
B & H	4	4	0	131	70	32.75	-	1	-	-							
1-day Lge	17	15	2	282	75 *	21.69	-	2	5	-							

GILES, A. F. Warwickshire

Name: Ashley Fraser Giles
Role: Right-hand bat, slow left-arm bowler
Born: 19 March 1973, Chertsey, Surrey
Height: 6ft 4in **Weight:** 15st 7lbs
Nickname: Skinny, Splash, Melink
County debut: 1993
Test debut: 1998
Tests: 1
One-Day Internationals: 5
50 wickets in a season: 1
1st-Class 50s: 12
1st-Class 100s: 2
1st-Class 5 w. in innings: 8
1st-Class catches: 32
One-Day 5 w. in innings: 2
Place in batting averages: 195th av. 20.83
(1998 114th av. 28.52)
Place in bowling averages: 53rd av. 24.05
(1998 75th av. 28.47)

Strike rate: 68.87 (career 68.16)
Parents: Michael and Paula
Marital status: 'Girlfriend Stine'
Family links with cricket: 'Dad used to play. Brother Andrew still plays at Ripley, Surrey. Used to play with sisters Tracy and Carrie in the Colts at Ripley. Mum did the teas.'
Education: Kingfield Primary School, Old Woking; George Abbott County Secondary, Burpham, Guildford
Qualifications: 9 GCSEs, 2 A-levels, qualified cricket coach
Career outside cricket: 'Good question!'
Off-season: England one-day squad to South Africa and Zimbabwe
Overseas tours: Surrey U19 to Barbados 1990-91; Warwickshire to Cape Town 1996 and 1997, to Bloemfontein 1998; England A to Australia 1996-97, to Kenya and Sri Lanka 1997-98; England to Sharjah 1997-98 (Champions Trophy), to Bangladesh (Wills International Cup) 1998, to Australia (CUB Series) 1998-99, to South Africa and Zimbabwe 1999-2000 (one-day series)
Overseas teams played for: Vredenburg/Saldanha, Cape Town 1992-95; Avendale CC, Cape Town 1995-96
Cricketers particularly admired: Dougie Brown, Allan Donald, Mark Ealham, Tim Munton, Dermot Reeve
Young players to look out for: Mark Wagh, Ian Bell
Other sports played: Golf, football

Other sports followed: Football (QPR), golf, basketball
Relaxations: Music, cinema, *FHM* and *Maxim*, 'having a pint with the Bears down "The Swan"', 'spending time with girlfriend Stine'
Extras: Surrey Young Cricketer of the Year 1991, NBC Denis Compton Award for Warwickshire in 1996, Warwickshire Player of the Year in 1996, Warwickshire Most Improved Player 1996, Cricket Society Young Allrounder of the year 1996. Scored 100 (123*) and took five wickets (5-28) in an innings in same match (v Oxford University at The Parks) in 1999, the first time this feat had been performed by a Warwickshire player since Tom Cartwright achieved it v Lancashire at Edgbaston in 1961
Opinions on cricket: 'Play the game hard and always to win. Don't worry too much, enjoy it.'
Best batting: 123* Warwickshire v Oxford University, The Parks 1999
Best bowling: 6-45 Warwickshire v Durham, Edgbaston 1996

1999 Season

	M	Inns	NO	Runs	HS	Avge	100s	50s	Ct	St	O	M	Runs	Wkts	Avge	Best	5wl	10wM
Test																		
All First	16	23	5	375	123*	20.83	1	-	6	-	447.4	145	938	39	24.05	5-28	2	-
1-day Int																		
NatWest	1	1	1	28	28*	-	-	-	-	-	10	1	52	2	26.00	2-52	-	
B & H	1	1	1	12	12*	-	-	-	-	-	10	1	35	3	11.66	3-35	-	
1-day Lge	15	10	1	122	35	13.55	-	-	4	-	113	6	488	19	25.68	4-29	-	

Career Performances

	M	Inns	NO	Runs	HS	Avge	100s	50s	Ct	St	Balls	Runs	Wkts	Avge	Best	5wl	10wM
Test	1	2	1	17	16*	17.00	-	-	-	-	216	106	1	106.00	1-106	-	-
All First	80	110	25	2446	123*	28.77	2	12	32	-	15473	5954	227	26.22	6-45	8	-
1-day Int	5	3	2	17	10*	17.00	-	-	1	-	228	197	5	39.40	2-37	-	
NatWest	12	9	3	165	69	27.50	-	1	-	-	623	396	22	18.00	5-21	1	
B & H	16	13	3	173	37	17.30	-	-	9	-	694	529	22	24.04	3-22	-	
1-day Lge	63	37	8	518	57	17.86	-	1	18	-	2033	1508	77	19.58	5-36	1	

41. Which batsman and occasional wicket-keeper scored the winning run for Middlesex v Worcestershire to give them the County Championship in 1982, the year in which he officially retired from first-class cricket?

GOLDING, J. M.   Kent

Name: James Matthew Golding
Role: Right-hand bat, right-arm
medium-fast bowler
Born: 19 July 1977, Canterbury
Height: 6ft 4in **Weight:** 16st
Nickname: Jingo, Goldie
County debut: 1999
Strike rate: 132.00 (career 132.00)
Parents: Marilyn and Adrian
Marital status: Single
Family links with cricket: 'Father tore a
hamstring in his one and only game of
cricket'
Education: St Anne's, Sturry; Kent College,
Canterbury; University College, Worcester
Qualifications: 8 GCSEs, 3 A-levels,
BSc Geog with Sp Studies
Off-season: Coaching, fitness
training/technique work, hockey

Overseas teams played for: Kensington District CC, Adelaide
Cricketers particularly admired: Graeme Hick, Ian Botham, Allan Donald,
Jacques Kallis
Young players to look out for: Ian Gascoigne, Rupert Swetman, Robin Jackson,
Andrew Alford
Other sports played: Hockey, tennis, golf, squash
Other sports followed: Hockey (Canterbury HC)
Injuries: Out for three weeks with a groin strain
Relaxations: Golf, socialising with friends, all sports
Extras: Man of the Match playing for Kent Cricket Board v Hampshire in NatWest
third round 1999. Made first-class debut for Kent v New Zealand 1999 while still an
amateur; his first wicket was New Zealand captain Stephen Fleming
Opinions on cricket: 'Looking forward to first season.'
Best batting: 3 Kent v New Zealand, Canterbury 1999
Best bowling: 1-74 Kent v New Zealand, Canterbury 1999

1999 Season

	M	Inns	NO	Runs	HS	Avge	100s	50s	Ct	St	O	M	Runs	Wkts	Avge	Best	5wI	10wM
Test																		
All First	1	2	1	3	3	3.00	-	-	-	-	22	4	74	1	74.00	1-74	-	-
1-day Int																		
NatWest	3	2	0	52	47	26.00	-	-	2	-	25	0	141	0	-		-	-
B & H																		
1-day Lge																		

Career Performances

	M	Inns	NO	Runs	HS	Avge	100s	50s	Ct	St	Balls	Runs	Wkts	Avge	Best	5wI	10wM
Test																		
All First	1	2	1	3	3	3.00	-	-	-	-	132	74	1	74.00	1-74	-	-
1-day Int																		
NatWest	3	2	0	52	47	26.00	-	-	2	-	150	141	0	-		-	-
B & H																		
1-day Lge																		

GOODCHILD, D. J.   Middlesex

Name: David John Goodchild
Role: Right-hand opening bat, right-arm medium bowler
Born: 17 September 1976, Harrow
Height: 6ft 2in **Weight:** 15st
Nickname: G, Goody, Golden
County debut: 1996
1st-Class 50s: 2
1st-Class 100s: 1
1st-Class catches: 1
Place in batting averages: (1998 143rd av. 24.92)
Parents: John and Brenda
Marital status: Single
Family links with cricket:
'Dad played club cricket'
Education: Vaughan First and Middle School; Whitmore High School; Weald College; North London University
Qualifications: 9 GCSEs, 3 A-levels, degree in Business/Sports Management, senior coaching award

Career outside cricket: Coach
Off-season: Training, relaxing, coaching, practising
Cricketers particularly admired: Mark Ramprakash, Mike Gatting, Graham Gooch, Justin Langer
Young players to look out for: Steffan and Rhodri James, Omar Anwar
Other sports played: All sports – football, squash, basketball
Other sports followed: Football (Arsenal), golf
Injuries: Out for two and a half months after receiving a ball in the eye
Relaxations: Cinema, fishing, 'spending time with girlfriend Sarah'
Extras: Set record for highest score for Middlesex U11 side (153) and the top total aggregate for that age group (563); became youngest player to be awarded junior county cap (U11). Awarded 2nd XI county cap at the end of the 1996 season. First-ever game for Middlesex was for the 1st XI against Gloucestershire at Lord's in 1996. Scored maiden first-class century (105) v Sri Lanka at Lord's in 1998 and was Man of the Match
Opinions on cricket: 'More time required for better quality practice sessions. Promotion and relegation can only be good for the game. "Quality not quantity."'
Best batting: 105 Middlesex v Sri Lanka, Lord's 1998

1999 Season

	M	Inns	NO	Runs	HS	Avge	100s	50s	Ct	St	O	M	Runs	Wkts	Avge	Best	5wI	10wM
Test																		
All First	1	2	0	26	26	13.00	-	-	-	-								
1-day Int																		
NatWest																		
B & H																		
1-day Lge	2	1	0	7	7	7.00	-	-	1	-								

Career Performances

	M	Inns	NO	Runs	HS	Avge	100s	50s	Ct	St	Balls	Runs	Wkts	Avge	Best	5wI	10wM
Test																		
All First	9	18	1	354	105	20.82	1	2	1	-	131	88	0	-	-	-	-
1-day Int																		
NatWest																		
B & H																		
1-day Lge	8	6	2	91	38 *	22.75	-	-	6	-								

GOUGH, D. Yorkshire

Name: Darren Gough
Role: Right-hand bat, right-arm fast bowler
Born: 18 September 1970, Barnsley
Height: 5ft 11in **Weight:** 13st 4lbs
Nickname: Dazzler
County debut: 1989
County cap: 1993
Test debut: 1994
Tests: 31
One-Day Internationals: 65
50 wickets in a season: 3
1st-Class 50s: 11
1st-Class 100s: 1
1st-Class 5 w. in innings: 22
1st-Class 10 w. in innings: 3
1st-Class catches: 37
One-Day 5 w. in innings: 5
Place in batting averages:
(1998 202nd av. 19.21)

Place in bowling averages: 12th av. 18.76 (1998 50th av. 25.40)
Strike rate: 34.17 (career 51.07)
Parents: Trevor and Christine
Wife and date of marriage: Anna Marie, 16 October 1993
Children: Liam James, 24 November 1994; Brennan Kyle, 9 December 1997
Education: St Helens Junior; Priory Comprehensive; Airedale and Wharfdale College
(part-time)
Qualifications: 2 O-levels, 5 CSEs, BTEC Leisure, NCA coaching award
Off-season: England tour to South Africa and Zimbabwe
Overseas tours: England YC to Australia 1989-90; Yorkshire to Barbados 1989-90, to
South Africa 1991-92 and 1992-93; England A to South Africa 1993-94; England to
Australia 1994-95, to South Africa 1995-96, to India and Pakistan (World Cup) 1995-96,
to Zimbabwe and New Zealand 1996-97, to Australia 1998-99, to Sharjah (Coca-Cola
Cup) 1998-99, to South Africa and Zimbabwe 1999-2000
Overseas teams played for: East Shirley, Christchurch, New Zealand 1991-92
Cricketers particularly admired: Ian Botham, Steve Waugh, Shane Warne,
Michael Atherton ('mental strength')
Young players to look out for: Marcus Trescothick, Andrew Flintoff, Graeme Swann,
Paul Hutchison, Ryan Sidebottom, Rob Cunliffe, Darren Stevens
Other sports played: Golf
Other sports followed: Football (Tottenham Hotspur and Barnsley)
Injuries: Out for four months with calf injury

Relaxations: Golf, cinema, 'spending time with family'

Extras: Cornhill England Player of the Year 1994. Yorkshire Sports Personality of the Year 1994. Voted Man of the Match in England's third Test match against Australia at Sydney in 1994-95. Took a hat-trick against Kent in 1995. Named Player of the Year by Cornhill Insurance for 1995 season. Whyte and Mackay Bowler of the Year in 1996. Had to withdraw from the England tour to West Indies 1997-98 due to a persistent hamstring injury which required surgery. England Player of the Series in the Texaco one-day rubber v South Africa 1998. Took Test hat-trick v Australia at Sydney in January 1999, the first Ashes hat-trick by an England bowler since J. Hearne's at Leeds in 1899. Was third English cricketer to reach 100 One-Day International wickets. *Sheffield Star* Sports Personality of the Year. Cornhill England Player of the Year 1998-99. One of *Wisden*'s Five Cricketers of the Year 1999. Represented England in the 1999 World Cup

Opinions on cricket: 'Divisions improving the intensity of the matches, which in the long run will improve the standards. County cricket rewards mediocrity too well. Too many pros; four too many teams. Central contracts a must for at least 30 players – a target for everybody else to reach. "A" tours must be reserve Test team except for one or two young "could-bes".'

Best batting: 121 Yorkshire v Warwickshire, Headingley 1996
Best bowling: 7-28 Yorkshire v Lancashire, Headingley 1995
Stop press: Awarded England contract (Band A) for 2000

1999 Season

	M	Inns	NO	Runs	HS	Avge	100s	50s	Ct	St	O	M	Runs	Wkts	Avge	Best	5wI	10wM
Test																		
All First	3	5	1	66	33	16.50	-	-	-	-	96.5	20	319	17	18.76	4-27	-	-
1-day Int	5	2	0	29	19	14.50	-	-	1	-	48.4	4	192	11	17.45	4-34	-	
NatWest																		
B & H																			
1-day Lge	3	2	0	15	15	7.50	-	-	-	-	23.1	2	80	2	40.00	2-29	-	

Career Performances

	M	Inns	NO	Runs	HS	Avge	100s	50s	Ct	St	Balls	Runs	Wkts	Avge	Best	5wI	10wM
Test	31	47	6	468	65	11.41	-	2	9	-	6696	3578	125	28.62	6-42	5	-
All First	157	214	35	2871	121	16.03	1	11	37	-	28245	14884	553	26.91	7-28	22	3
1-day Int	65	43	14	329	45	11.34	-	-	10	-	3636	2580	108	23.88	5-44	2	
NatWest	22	12	0	225	46	18.75	-	-	3	-	1410	785	45	17.44	7-27	1	
B & H	29	16	5	160	48 *	14.54	-	-	11	-	1538	964	34	28.35	3-27	-	
1-day Lge	98	65	16	608	72 *	12.40	-	1	18	-	4185	3102	124	25.01	5-13	2	

GOUGH, M. A.   Durham

Name: Michael Andrew Gough
Role: Right-hand bat, off-spin bowler
Born: 18 December 1979, Hartlepool
Height: 6ft 5in   **Weight:** 13st 10lbs
Nickname: Goughy
County debut: 1998
1st-Class 50s: 6
1st-Class 100s: 1
1st-Class catches: 29
Place in batting averages: 191st av. 21.20
(1998 116th av. 28.22)
Strike rate: 116.50 (career 110.00)
Parents: Michael and Jean
Marital status: Single
Family links with cricket: Father has played
league cricket for over 30 years and has
represented Durham as an opening batsman
in the Minor Counties. Cousin Paul Gough

was a part of the Durham U17 team that won the 1998 Texaco U17 Trophy v Devon
Education: Sacred Heart RC Primary School, Hartlepool; English Martyrs School and
Sixth Form College, Hartlepool
Qualifications: 10 GCSEs, basic coaching award. 'Studied English, Sociology and
Business Studies at A-level but dropped out after first year because of selection to tour
South Africa with England U19'
Career outside cricket: 'Not decided'
Off-season: England A tour to Bangladesh and New Zealand. 'Plenty of cricket
practice and fitness work from January to April in year 2000. Can't wait for new-style
Division 1 league. Can't wait to face Warne, Kumble, Murali, Saqlain etc.'
Overseas tours: Durham U21 to Sri Lanka November 1996; England U17 to Bermuda
(International Youth Tournament) June 1997; England U19 to South Africa (inc Youth
World Cup) 1997-98, to New Zealand 1998-99 (captain); England A to Bangladesh
and New Zealand 1999-2000
Cricketers particularly admired: Steve Waugh, Mike Atherton, David Boon,
Nasser Hussain
Young players to look out for: Michael Carberry, Ian Bell, Graeme Bridge,
Mark Wallace
Other sports played: Football (had trials with Arsenal and Sheffield United and
attended Middlesbrough FC School of Excellence)
Other sports followed: Football (Hartlepool United season-ticket holder)
Relaxations: Music, eating out, socialising, cinema; spending time with friends and
family; watching TV, especially football and cricket

Extras: Captained North of England and England U15. Part of winning England U17 team at the International Youth Tournament in Bermuda 1997. Durham CCC Young Player of the Year 1997. Batted for more than four hours in scoring 32* for England U19 v South Africa U19 in first 'Test' 1997-98 to save match after England U19 had followed on. Scored 62 on first-class debut, against Essex 1998. Became youngest player to score a century for Durham, against Cambridge University 1998. Captained England U19 v Australia U19 in one-day and 'Test' series 1999

Opinions on cricket: 'Better standard of pitches should be provided for all forms of cricket if we are going to produce world-class cricketers to play for England. Should reduce the amount of cricket played to concentrate on technique and the specifics of cricket. Extend tea break by ten minutes.'

Best batting: 123 Durham v Cambridge University, Fenner's 1998
Best bowling: 4-49 Durham v Nottinghamshire, Chester-le-Street 1999

1999 Season

	M	Inns	NO	Runs	HS	Avge	100s	50s	Ct	St	O	M	Runs	Wkts	Avge	Best	5wl	10wM
Test																		
All First	12	20	0	424	67	21.20	-	4	17	-	77.4	14	259	4	64.75	4-49	-	-
1-day Int																		
NatWest																		
B & H																		
1-day Lge	3	2	0	16	16	8.00	-	-	1	-	7	0	45	0	-		-	-

Career Performances

	M	Inns	NO	Runs	HS	Avge	100s	50s	Ct	St	Balls	Runs	Wkts	Avge	Best	5wl	10wM
Test																	
All First	22	38	0	932	123	24.52	1	6	29	-	660	378	6	63.00	4-49	-	-
1-day Int																	
NatWest																	
B & H																	
1-day Lge	3	2	0	16	16	8.00	-	-	1	-	42	45	0	-		-	-

GRAYSON, A. P.   Essex

Name: Adrian Paul Grayson
Role: Right-hand bat, slow left-arm bowler
Born: 31 March 1971, Ripon
Height: 6ft 1in **Weight:** 12st
Nickname: Larry
County debut: 1990 (Yorkshire), 1996 (Essex)

County cap: 1996 (Essex)
1000 runs in a season: 3
1st-Class 50s: 31
1st-Class 100s: 7
1st-Class catches: 92
Place in batting averages: 60th av. 36.10
(1998 230th av. 16.41)
Place in bowling averages: 125th av. 38.59
(1998 125th av. 38.63)
Strike rate: 87.09 (career 91.65)
Parents: Adrian and Carol
Wife and date of marriage: Alison,
30 September 1994
Children: Oliver, 30 January 1997
Family links with cricket: 'Father played
good standard of league cricket and is an
excellent [NCA staff] coach; brother plays
when free from football commitments'
Education: Bedale Comprehensive School

Qualifications: 8 CSEs, BTEC in Leisure Studies, advanced cricket coach
Overseas tours: England YC to Australia 1989-90; Yorkshire to Barbados 1989-90,
to Cape Town 1991-92, 1992-93, 1994-95, to Leeward Islands 1993-94
Overseas teams played for: Petone, Wellington 1992-93 and 1995-96
Cricketers particularly admired: Martyn Moxon, Graham Gooch, Darren Gough
Young players to look out for: Dean Cosker, Graeme Swann
Other sports played: Golf (16 handicap), football ('was offered apprentice forms with
Middlesbrough FC at 16 but signed for Yorkshire')
Other sports followed: 'Follow any team my brother Simon is playing for'
Relaxations: Golf, 'spending time with the family and having the odd pint in my local
pub "The King William"'
Extras: Played for England YC v New Zealand 1989 and Pakistan 1990. Brother plays
professional football. Scored 1000 runs for first time in 1994. Yorkshire Player of the
Year 1994. Released by Yorkshire at end of 1995 and joined Essex for 1996 season.
Essex Player of the Year 1997
Opinions on cricket: 'Better pitches provided for four-day cricket. Too many games
finish on the second and third day. This will not produce top-class Test cricketers. For
example, if home teams produce a green and damp pitch, the opposing captain should
have the option of batting or fielding.'
Best batting: 159* Essex v Hampshire, Ilford 1999
Best bowling: 4-16 Essex v Middlesex, Southend 1999

1999 Season

	M	Inns	NO	Runs	HS	Avge	100s	50s	Ct	St	O	M	Runs	Wkts	Avge	Best	5wI	10wM
Test																		
All First	20	32	2	1083	159 *	36.10	3	6	8	-	319.2	98	849	22	38.59	4-16	-	-
1-day Int																		
NatWest	1	1	0	74	74	74.00	-	1	-	-	3	0	19	0	-		-	-
B & H																		
1-day Lge	15	14	2	276	66	23.00	-	1	1	-	98	0	525	11	47.72	3-48	-	

Career Performances

	M	Inns	NO	Runs	HS	Avge	100s	50s	Ct	St	Balls	Runs	Wkts	Avge	Best	5wI	10wM
Test																	
All First	125	201	18	5511	159 *	30.11	7	31	92	-	9165	4197	100	41.97	4-16	-	-
1-day Int																	
NatWest	20	16	1	388	82 *	25.86	-	3	7	-	827	648	20	32.40	3-24	-	
B & H	25	20	6	325	49 *	23.21	-	-	7	-	903	638	24	26.58	3-30	-	
1-day Lge	111	88	13	1292	69 *	17.22	-	4	28	-	3552	3225	93	34.67	4-25	-	

GREEN, R. J.   Lancashire

Name: Richard James Green
Role: Right-hand bat, right-arm medium-fast bowler
Born: 13 March 1976, Grappenhall, Warrington
Height: 6ft **Weight:** 12st 12lbs
Nickname: Slimey, Greendog, Spotty, Captain Darling
County debut: 1995
1st-Class 50s: 1
1st-Class 5 w. in innings: 1
1st-Class catches: 5
Place in bowling averages: 117th av. 34.60
Strike rate: 63.70 (career 69.72)
Parents: Jim and Christina
Marital status: Single
Family links with cricket: 'Father Manchester Association League legend'
Education: Bridgewater County High School, Warrington; Hartford College
Qualifications: 5 GCSEs, BTEC National Business and Finance
Career outside cricket: 'One day will own a wine bar'

Overseas tours: Lancashire to Jamaica 1996, to Cape Town 1997
Overseas teams played for: Waratah-Mayfield CC, Newcastle, NSW 1994-95;
Prahran CC, Melbourne, Australia 1996-97
Cricketers particularly admired: Warren Hegg
Young players to look out for: David Sales
Other sports followed: Football (Manchester United)
Relaxations: Music, fast Rover cars, the occasional night out
Extras: Was Cheshire County League's youngest century-maker. Played for England
U17 and England U19. Denis Compton Award winner in 1996
Opinions on cricket: 'Staffs of 16 players and pay them more money. Should be more
day/night cricket.'
Best batting: 51 Lancashire v Essex, Old Trafford 1997
Best bowling: 6-41 Lancashire v Yorkshire, Old Trafford 1996

1999 Season

	M	Inns	NO	Runs	HS	Avge	100s	50s	Ct	St	O	M	Runs	Wkts	Avge	Best	5wI	10wM
Test																		
All First	10	10	5	96	27	19.20	-	-	1	-	212.2	46	692	20	34.60	4-21	-	-
1-day Int																		
NatWest																		
B & H																		
1-day Lge	2	2	1	28	14 *	28.00	-	-	1	-	14	2	57	1	57.00	1-29	-	

Career Performances

	M	Inns	NO	Runs	HS	Avge	100s	50s	Ct	St	Balls	Runs	Wkts	Avge	Best	5wI	10wM
Test																	
All First	27	28	11	295	51	17.35	-	1	5	-	3765	2034	54	37.66	6-41	1	-
1-day Int																	
NatWest	1	1	0	0	0	0.00	-	-	-	-	66	35	1	35.00	1-35	-	
B & H	5	3	1	13	7	6.50	-	-	1	-	249	231	6	38.50	2-33	-	
1-day Lge	20	3	2	28	14 *	28.00	-	-	2	-	798	692	25	27.68	3-18	-	

42. Which current county coach hit four hundreds in successive
Championship innings in 1987, the final one against his former county, Yorkshire?

GREENFIELD, K.   Sussex

Name: Keith Greenfield
Role: Right-hand top-order bat, off-spin bowler, emergency wicket-keeper
Born: 6 December 1968, Brighton
Height: 6ft **Weight:** 13st 4lbs
Nickname: Grubby, G-Man
County debut: 1987
1st-Class 50s: 13
1st-Class 100s: 9
1st-Class catches: 65
One-Day 100s: 2
Strike rate: (career 162.80)
Parents: Leslie Ernest and Sheila
Wife and date of marriage:
Caroline Susannah, 22 February 1992
Children: Bethany Hannah,
18 December 1998
Family links with cricket: Father keen
spectator, as is father-in-law, who played club cricket for 20 years
Education: Coldean First and Middle Schools; Falmer High School
Qualifications: 3 O-levels, BTEC National Diploma in Leisure and Business, Levels 1, 2, and 3 coaching certificates, Level 1 and 2 tutor
Off-season: 'Coaching at Sussex through close season, except December, when taking U19 tour to South Africa'
Overseas tours: Sussex U16 to Guernsey 1985; Select XI to Malaga 1994, 1995; MCC to SE Asia and Far East 1994-95, to Bangladesh 1996, to New Zealand 1999 (captain); Sussex U19 to Barbados 1997 (as coach)
Overseas teams played for: Cornwall and Districts, Auckland 1988-90
Cricketers particularly admired: Ian Botham, Paul Parker, Derek Randall, Allan Border
Young players to look out for: Dominic Clapp, Michael Yardy, Matthew Prior, Grant Morrish, Glen Read, Chris Nash (all Sussex)
Other sports played: Golf
Other sports followed: Golf, football (Liverpool FC; Brighton & HA FC), 'any sport'
Relaxations: 'Spending time with family (Caz and Beth); concerts, eating out, having quiet drink with friends; golf'
Extras: First person taken on Youth Training Scheme to become a professional cricketer at Sussex. Only uncapped player to have captained Sussex in first-class match, at Hove (v Cambridge U); scored century in this game. Captained 2nd XI to Championship title in 1990. Sussex Young Player of the Year 1990. Sussex Team Man of the Year 1990, 1993. Joined Bill Athey on a trip to Belarus to take aid to the cancer hospital near Chernobyl. Is now a player/coach at Sussex

Opinions on cricket: 'Our Test team will only really start to improve when teams in the Championship start to prepare the best possible pitches, not ones to suit their bowlers, and certainly not ones that at the start of a four-day game are such that a draw will never happen. Otherwise our cricket will not go forward.'

Best batting: 154* Sussex v India, Hove 1996

Best bowling: 2-40 Sussex v Essex, Hove 1993

1999 Season

	M	Inns	NO	Runs	HS	Avge	100s	50s	Ct	St	O	M	Runs	Wkts	Avge	Best	5wI	10wM
Test																		
All First																		
1-day Int																		
NatWest																		
B & H																		
1-day Lge	1	1	1	16	16 *	-	-	-	-	-								

Career Performances

	M	Inns	NO	Runs	HS	Avge	100s	50s	Ct	St	Balls	Runs	Wkts	Avge	Best	5wI	10wM
Test																	
All First	78	135	15	3550	154 *	29.58	9	13	65	-	814	524	5	104.80	2-40	-	-
1-day Int																	
NatWest	15	14	3	431	129	39.18	1	2	7	-	402	303	3	101.00	2-35	-	
B & H	25	24	3	611	93 *	29.09	-	4	8	-	432	354	2	177.00	1-17	-	
1-day Lge	117	115	11	2751	102	26.45	1	16	34	-	994	978	22	44.45	3-34	-	

43. Who captained Leicestershire to their first County Championship in 1975?

GREENIDGE, C. G.   Surrey

Name: Carl Gary Greenidge
Role: Right-hand bat, right-arm
fast bowler
Born: 20 April 1978, Basingstoke
Height: 5ft 10in **Weight:** 12st 7lbs
Nickname: Carlos, Carlito, G
County debut: 1998 (one-day),
1999 (first-class)
1st-Class 5 w. in innings: 1
1st-Class catches: 3
Place in bowling averages: 24th av. 21.00
Strike rate: 41.81 (career 41.81)
Parents: Gordon and Anita
Marital status: Single
Family links with cricket: Father Gordon
played for Hampshire and West Indies, as did
cousin (on mother's side) Andy Roberts
Education: St Paul's, Barbados;

St Michael's, Barbados; Heathcote School, Chingford; City of Westminster College
Qualifications: GNVQ Leisure and Tourism, NCA senior coaching award
Career outside cricket: 'What?!'
Off-season: 'Going to Perth, getting fit and catching some rays'
Cricketers particularly admired: Malcolm Marshall, Dennis Lillee, Carl Hooper,
Mark Waugh, Graham Thorpe, Ricaldo Anderson, Muazam Ali, Gareth Batty,
Rupesh Amin, 'and many more'
Other sports followed: Football (Arsenal), basketball (LA Lakers)
Injuries: Out for several weeks with groin and knee injuries
Relaxations: 'Music, kung fu movies, PlayStation, and my bed'
Extras: Spent a year on Lord's groundstaff. Took eight wickets on his Championship
debut for Surrey, v Yorkshire at The Oval 1999
Opinions on cricket: 'There is just too much cricket being played. Cut down the
number of games played and have longer intervals (lunch and tea). This one bouncer
per batsman per over is just ridiculous. In Championship and Test cricket, batsmen
should learn to deal with it, or something. When is bowling going to get a little
easier??!!'
Best batting: 14 Surrey v Sri Lanka A, The Oval 1999
Best bowling: 5-60 Surrey v Yorkshire, The Oval 1999

1999 Season

	M	Inns	NO	Runs	HS	Avge	100s	50s	Ct	St	O	M	Runs	Wkts	Avge	Best	5wI	10wM
Test																		
All First	2	3	0	20	14	6.66	-	-	3	-	76.4	20	231	11	21.00	5-60	1	-
1-day Int																		
NatWest																		
B & H																		
1-day Lge	2	1	1	2	2 *	-	-	-	1	-	11	0	71	0	-	-	-	

Career Performances

	M	Inns	NO	Runs	HS	Avge	100s	50s	Ct	St	Balls	Runs	Wkts	Avge	Best	5wI	10wM
Test																	
All First	2	3	0	20	14	6.66	-	-	3	-	460	231	11	21.00	5-60	1	-
1-day Int																	
NatWest																	
B & H																	
1-day Lge	3	1	1	2	2 *	-	-	-	1	-	108	106	0	-	-	-	

GRIFFITH, F. A.　　　　　　　Derbyshire

Name: Frank Alexander Griffith
Role: Right-hand bat, right-arm medium bowler
Born: 15 August 1968, Leyton
Height: 6ft **Weight:** 12st
Nickname: Sir Learie
County debut: 1988
1st-Class 50s: 4
1st-Class catches: 28
Strike rate: (career 61.78)
Parents: Alex and Daisy
Marital status: Single
Education: William Morris High School, Walthamstow
Qualifications: Food and Nutrition and Art O-levels; NCA coaching certificate
Cricketers particularly admired: Collis King, Franklyn Stephenson
Other sports followed: Table tennis, basketball, football
Relaxations: Listening to music

Extras: Attended Haringey Cricket College. Released by Derbyshire at end of 1996 season. Re-registered by Derbyshire in 1999 because of injuries to current players
Best batting: 81 Derbyshire v Glamorgan, Chesterfield 1992
Best bowling: 4-33 Derbyshire v Leicestershire, Ilkeston 1992

1999 Season

	M	Inns	NO	Runs	HS	Avge	100s	50s	Ct	St	O	M	Runs	Wkts	Avge	Best	5wI	10wM
Test																		
All First																		
1-day Int																		
NatWest																		
B & H																		
1-day Lge	1	1	0	15	15	15.00	-	-	-	-	5	0	26	2	13.00	2-26	-	

Career Performances

	M	Inns	NO	Runs	HS	Avge	100s	50s	Ct	St	Balls	Runs	Wkts	Avge	Best	5wI	10wM
Test																	
All First	43	63	9	1087	81	20.12	-	4	28	-	4510	2571	73	35.21	4-33	-	-
1-day Int																	
NatWest	7	4	0	16	8	4.00	-	-	4	-	314	190	5	38.00	1-13	-	
B & H	10	8	1	68	24	9.71	-	-	3	-	380	355	11	32.27	3-63	-	
1-day Lge	48	34	6	282	31	10.07	-	-	8	-	1837	1623	52	31.21	4-48	-	

GRIFFITHS, S. P. Derbyshire

Name: Steven Paul Griffiths
Role: Right-hand bat, wicket-keeper
Born: 31 May 1973, Hereford
Height: 5ft 11in **Weight:** 12st
Nickname: 'Too many to name'
County debut: 1995
1st-Class catches: 37
1st-Class stumpings: 1
Place in batting averages: 224th av. 18.00
Parents: Paul Griffiths and Lesley Simmons
Marital status: 'Partner – Ceri Fenty'
Children: Joel Oliver Thomas Griffiths, 1 May 1998
Family links with cricket: 'Father has played a good standard of club cricket for many years'
Education: Bathford Junior School; Beechen Cliff School, Bath; Brunel College of Art and Design, Bristol

Qualifications: 7 GCSEs, City and Guilds in Furniture Restoration, basic coaching award
Career outside cricket: Antique furniture restorer
Overseas tours: Bath Schools to Zimbabwe and Kenya 1989
Overseas teams played for: CBC Old Boys, Bloemfontein, South Africa 1992-93
Cricketers particularly admired: Jack Russell, Carl Hooper, Gregg Brown, Dougie C. Storey
Young players to look out for: Ben Spendlove, Phil Smith
Other sports played: Rugby ('Not golf!!')
Other sports followed: Rugby (Bath RFC)
Relaxations: 'Spending time with Ceri and Joel. Socialising with friends in Bath. Listening to music, reading, and discussing

the imminent demise of Leek Town Football Club with Tim Tweats'
Extras: Took six catches on first-class debut against Worcestershire in 1995 (five of them in the first innings). Played for Somerset 2nd XI before joining Derbyshire. Member of Bath CC and Buccaneers CC. Captain of Derbyshire CCC 2nd XI 1998. Reached final of AON Risk Trophy. Released by Derbyshire at end of 1999 season
Opinions on cricket: '2nd XI cricket must be brought into line with the first-class game. Four-day matches nearly always produce a result in second-class cricket, rather than a manufactured conclusion. Better grounds and first-class and reserve umpires would enhance the quality of matches, which can sometimes suffer due to indifferent local umpires, poor grounds and bad practice facilities.'
Best batting: 35 Derbyshire v Warwickshire, Edgbaston 1999

1999 Season

	M	Inns	NO	Runs	HS	Avge	100s	50s	Ct	St	O	M	Runs	Wkts	Avge	Best	5wI	10wM
Test																		
All First	5	7	1	108	35	18.00	-	-	15	1								
1-day Int																		
NatWest	2	1	0	9	9	9.00	-	-	-	1								
B & H																		
1-day Lge	5	3	2	9	8 *	9.00	-	-	4	2								

Career Performances

	M	Inns	NO	Runs	HS	Avge	100s	50s	Ct	St	Balls	Runs	Wkts	Avge	Best	5wI	10wM
Test																	
All First	12	19	1	199	35	11.05	-	-	37	1							
1-day Int																	
NatWest	2	1	0	9	9	9.00	-	-	-	1							
B & H																	
1-day Lge	6	3	2	9	8*	9.00	-										

GROVE, J. O. Somerset

Name: Jamie Oliver Grove
Role: Right-hand bat, right-arm fast-medium bowler
Born: 3 July 1979, Bury St Edmunds
Height: 6ft 1in **Weight:** 12st 1lb
Nickname: Grover, Groover
County debut: 1998 (Essex)
Place in batting averages: (1998 246th av. 14.66)
Strike rate: 88.80 (career 63.50)
Parents: Christopher John and Patricia Susan
Marital status: Single
Family links with cricket: 'Dad played Minor Counties cricket. Brother plays club cricket. Mother's a keen fan'
Education: Whepstead Primary School; St James Middle School, Bury St Edmunds; County Upper School, Bury St Edmunds
Qualifications: 9 GCSEs, City and Guilds in Basic Engineering, Modern Apprenticeship in Mechanical Engineering
Career outside cricket: Car valeter
Off-season: Working as a car valeter
Overseas tours: England U19 to South Africa (inc Youth World Cup) 1997-98
Cricketers particularly admired: Shoaib Akhtar, Allan Donald
Young players to look out for: Ian Flanagan, Stephen Peters, Graeme Swann
Other sports played: 'All sports'
Other sports followed: Football (West Ham United)
Injuries: Out for seven weeks with periostitis of the shin
Relaxations: Going out with friends; listening to music
Extras: Played for England at U15, U17 and U19 level. Was part of the successful England U19 World Cup-winning squad in South Africa in 1997-98. Released by

Essex at end of 1999 season and has joined Somerset for 2000
Opinions on cricket: 'It's great!!'
Best batting: 33 Essex v Surrey, Chelmsford 1998
Best bowling: 3-74 Essex v Surrey, Chelmsford 1998

1999 Season

	M	Inns	NO	Runs	HS	Avge	100s	50s	Ct	St	O	M	Runs	Wkts	Avge	Best	5wI	10wM
Test																		
All First	4	5	1	17	7	4.25	-	-	-	-	74	14	304	5	60.80	1-52	-	-
1-day Int																		
NatWest																		
B & H																			
1-day Lge																			

Career Performances

	M	Inns	NO	Runs	HS	Avge	100s	50s	Ct	St	Balls	Runs	Wkts	Avge	Best	5wI	10wM
Test																	
All First	8	12	2	105	33	10.50	-	-	-	-	889	651	14	46.50	3-74	-	-
1-day Int																	
NatWest																	
B & H																	
1-day Lge																	

44. Which side scored 405-6 in their fourth innings to beat
Worcestershire at Worcester in 1994?

GUY, S. M.   Yorkshire

Name: Simon Mark Guy
Role: Right-hand bat, wicket-keeper
Born: 17 November 1978, Rotherham
Height: 5ft 7in **Weight:** 10st 6lbs
Nickname: Shy Guy, Fez, Roland Rat,
Mini Me
County debut: No first-team appearance
Parents: Darrell and Denise
Marital status: Single
Family links with cricket: 'Two brothers
and father play cricket. Elder brother played
Yorkshire Senior School U19 (when 17).
Father played for Notts and Worcs 2nd XI
and for Rotherham Town in Yorks League'
Education: Listerdale Junior; Wickersley
Comprehensive
Qualifications: Pass in GNVQ Leisure and
Recreation, qualified cricket coach, 'two
years at the Yorkshire Cricket School under Ralph Middlebrook'
Off-season: 'Orange, New South Wales, for six months as overseas pro'
Overseas teams played for: Orange, NSW 1999-2000
Cricketers particularly admired: Keith Piper, Karl Krikken, Richard Blakey
Young players to look out for: Richard Dawson, John Sadler
Other sports played: 'Interested in all sports', rugby (Rotherham RUFC,
South Yorkshire and Yorkshire)
Other sports followed: Rugby (Rotherham RUFC), football (Liverpool FC)
Relaxations: Playing all sports, socialising, having a good time, watching cartoons
Extras: Set fifth wicket record in Yorkshire League (199 unbroken). Topped Yorkshire
2nd XI batting averages 1998 (106.00). Scored first 50 for Yorkshire 2nd XI in 1998.
Followed up with 112 not out in next game
Opinions on cricket: 'I have not had any first-class experience as yet, so I have no
real opinions on the game. I'm just listening to people with more experience.'

HABIB, A.   Leicestershire

Name: Aftab Habib
Role: Right-hand bat, right-arm
slow-medium bowler
Born: 7 February 1972, Reading, Berks
Height: 5ft 11in **Weight:** 12st
Nickname: Afie, Tabby, Scabby, Habiby,
Alvin, Inzamam
County debut: 1992 (Middlesex),
1995 (Leicestershire)
County cap: 1998 (Leicestershire)
Test debut: 1999
Tests: 2
1000 runs in a season: 1
1st-Class 50s: 12
1st-Class 100s: 8
1st-Class 200s: 1
1st-Class catches: 28
One-Day 100s: 1
Place in batting averages: 32nd av. 40.57 (1998 9th av. 56.00)
Parents: Hussain and Tahira
Marital status: Single
Family links with cricket: Cousin of Zahid Sadiq (ex-Surrey and Derbyshire)
Education: Alfred Sutton Primary School; Millfield Junior School; Taunton School
Qualifications: 7 GCSEs, NCA coaching certificate
Off-season: England A tour to Bangladesh and New Zealand
Overseas tours: England YC to Australia 1989-90, to New Zealand 1990-91;
Berkshire CCC to South Africa 1996; England A to Bangladesh and New Zealand
1999-2000
Overseas teams played for: Globe Wakatu, Nelson, New Zealand, 1992-93 and
1996-97; Riccarton CC, Christchurch, New Zealand 1997-98
Cricketers particularly admired: Vince Wells, Mark Waugh, Steve Waugh, Saeed
Anwar, Paul Nixon, Darren Maddy, Graham Lloyd, Sachin Tendulkar, Phil Simmons
Young players to look out for: Darren Maddy, James Ormond, Chris Schofield
Other sports followed: Football ('follow Reading FC and enjoy watching Liverpool')
Relaxations: Music, cinema, reading, books, playing golf
Extras: Played for England U15-U19. Played football for Reading Schools. Middlesex
2nd XI Seaxe Player of the Year 1992. Released by Middlesex at end of 1994 season.
Played for Berkshire and had trials with Essex and Somerset. Leicestershire 2nd XI Player
of the Year in 1995. Championship medal with Leicestershire in 1996 and 1998. Gold
Award-winner in the Benson and Hedges Cup with 111 against Durham in 1997. With
James Whitaker, set then record partnership for Leicestershire for fifth wicket of 320,

v Worcestershire at Leicester in 1996. Made Test debut in first Test v New Zealand at Edgbaston 1999

Best batting: 215 Leicestershire v Worcestershire, Leicester 1996

1999 Season

	M	Inns	NO	Runs	HS	Avge	100s	50s	Ct	St	O	M	Runs	Wkts	Avge	Best	5wI	10wM
Test	2	3	0	26	19	8.66	-	-	-	-								
All First	18	29	3	1055	160 *	40.57	3	6	2	-								
1-day Int																		
NatWest	2	2	0	11	11	5.50	-	-	2	-	0.4	0	5	2	2.50	2-5	-	
B & H	1	1	0	25	25	25.00	-	-	1	-								
1-day Lge	13	13	3	238	42	23.80	-	-	4	-								

Career Performances

	M	Inns	NO	Runs	HS	Avge	100s	50s	Ct	St	Balls	Runs	Wkts	Avge	Best	5wI	10wM
Test	2	3	0.	26	19	8.66	-	-	-	-							
All First	66	96	17	3445	215	43.60	9	12	28	-	48	52	0	-		-	-	-
1-day Int																	
NatWest	8	7	0	173	67	24.71	-	2	2	-	4	5	2	2.50	2-5	-	
B & H	13	9	1	285	111	35.62	1	1	7	-							
1-day Lge	45	41	11	780	99 *	26.00	-	3	17	-	1	4	0	-		-	-

HAFEEZ, A.   Worcestershire

Name: Abdul Hafeez
Role: Right-hand bat, right-arm medium bowler
Born: 21 March 1977, Birmingham
Height: 6ft 3in **Weight:** 14st 7lbs
Nickname: King, Yogi
County debut: 1998
1st-Class 50s: 1
1st-Class catches: 8
Place in batting averages: 293rd av. 5.37 (1998 214th av. 17.82)
Parents: Abdul Ghafoor and Khushnooda Parveen
Marital status: Single
Family links with cricket: Younger brother plays for Warwickshire youth team (U12)
Education: Springfield Junior; Handsworth Grammar; Solihull College

Qualifications: GCSEs, A-levels, coaching award
Overseas tours: Birmingham Schools to India and Pakistan 1996
Overseas teams played for: Primrose CC, Cape Town 1996-97
Cricketers particularly admired: Graeme Hick, Alec Stewart, Sachin Tendulkar, Wasim Akram, Jacques Kallis
Young players to look out for: Maneer Mirza, Depesh Patel, Duncan Catterall
Other sports played: Football, table tennis
Other sports followed: Rugby
Relaxations: Spending time with friends, travelling
Extras: Part of Warwickshire side that won Oxbridge U19 Festival 1996. Coney Edmunds U19 Player of the Year award 1996 (Warwickshire). Released by Worcestershire at end of 1999 season
Opinions on cricket: 'Second-team cricket to be four days and also all 2nd XI Championship matches to be played on first-class grounds. Increase the number of day/night games.'
Best batting: 55 Worcestershire v Gloucestershire, Worcester 1998

1999 Season

	M	Inns	NO	Runs	HS	Avge	100s	50s	Ct	St	O	M	Runs	Wkts	Avge	Best	5wI	10wM
Test																		
All First	4	8	0	43	32	5.37	-	-	2	-								
1-day Int																		
NatWest																		
B & H																		
1-day Lge	1	1	1	8	8*	-	-	-	1	-	8	0	29	0	-		-	-

Career Performances

	M	Inns	NO	Runs	HS	Avge	100s	50s	Ct	St	Balls	Runs	Wkts	Avge	Best	5wI	10wM
Test																	
All First	14	26	1	346	55	13.84	-	1	8	-							
1-day Int																	
NatWest	1	1	0	33	33	33.00	-	-	-	-							
B & H																	
1-day Lge	7	4	1	17	8*	5.66	-	-	3	-	48	29	0	-		-	-

HAMBLIN, J. R. C.   Hampshire

Name: James Rupert Christopher Hamblin
Role: Right-hand bat, right-arm
medium-fast bowler
Born: 16 August 1978, Pembury, Kent
Height: 6ft **Weight:** 13st 7lbs
Nickname: Hambo, Hambles, Junior Jazzer
County debut: No first-team appearance
Parents: Bryan and Amanda
Marital status: Single
Family links with cricket: 'Father played for
Oxford University 1971-73 and Sussex 2nd
XI. Two brothers play good cricket. All
family are avid supporters'
Education: Vinehall Preparatory School;
Charterhouse School; University of the West
of England, Bristol
Qualifications: 9 GCSEs, 2 A/O-levels,
2 A-levels
Career outside cricket: Student
Off-season: University
Overseas teams played for: Harare Sports Club, Zimbabwe 1996-97
Cricketers particularly admired: James Kirtley, James Williams
Young players to look out for: James Kirtley, Lawrence Prittipaul, Matt Windows
Other sports played: Rackets, golf, tennis
Other sports followed: Golf
Relaxations: 'Any sport'
Extras: Voted 2nd XI ECB Player of August/September 1999
Opinions on cricket: 'Too much 2nd XI cricket played on poor grounds and wickets.'

HAMILTON, G. M.   Yorkshire

Name: Gavin Mark Hamilton
Role: Left-hand bat, right-arm medium-fast bowler
Born: 16 September 1974, Broxburn
Height: 6ft 3in **Weight:** 13st
Nickname: Hammy, Jock, Dits, 'anything Scottish'
County debut: 1994
County cap: 1998
One-Day Internationals: 5

50 wickets in a season: 1
1st-Class 50s: 11
1st-Class 5 w. in innings: 7
1st-Class 10 w. in match: 2
1st-Class catches: 16
One-Day 5 w. in innings: 1
Place in batting averages: 15th av. 47.25
(1998 80th av. 32.11)
Place in bowling averages: 14th av. 19.18
(1998 19th av. 20.54)
Strike rate: 38.67 (career 47.96)
Parents: Gavin and Wendy
Marital status: Single
Family links with cricket: Father 'long-term
fast bowler at club level' (Sidcup, Kent; West
Lothian, Scotland). Brother opening bat for
Sidcup CC and has opened batting for
Scotland
Education: Dulverton Primary School, New Eltham; Hurstmere School, Sidcup
Qualifications: 10 GCSEs and two coaching awards
Off-season: England tour to South Africa and Zimbabwe
Overseas tours: England to South Africa and Zimbabwe 1999-2000; Yorkshire
pre-season tours to South Africa, Zimbabwe and West Indies
Overseas teams played for: Welling, Municipals, and Stellenbosch University –
all South Africa; Spotswood, Melbourne
Cricketers particularly admired: Craig White, Mark Robinson, Chris Adams
Young players to look out for: Matthew Wood, Vikram Solanki, Gary Fellows
Other sports played: Golf ('a lot of it')
Other sports followed: Football (Falkirk FC)
Injuries: Out for 'a couple of weeks' with hamstring and back injuries
Relaxations: Listening to music and reading the paper
Extras: Took 10 wickets and scored 149 runs v Glamorgan at Cardiff in 1998, the
second best all-round contribution in Yorkshire history. Was selected to represent
England in the cancelled World Super Max 8s originally scheduled to take place in
Perth in October 1998. First-class All-rounder of the Year 1998; Yorkshire Players'
Player of the Year 1998; Yorkshire Supporters' Player of the Year 1998. Scored 76 for
Scotland v Pakistan at Chester-le-Street in the 1999 World Cup, the first 50 scored by
a Scotland player in World Cup cricket. Scored 217 runs (av. 54.25) in the 1999 World
Cup, more than any England batsman. Finished in top 15 of first-class batting and
bowling averages 1999. Has also played football (Arsenal YTS)
Opinions on cricket: 'Over-rates too hard and too expensive to keep up with –
especially nowadays when spinners don't bowl as much.'
Best batting: 94* Yorkshire v Worcestershire, Headingley 1999
Best bowling: 7-50 Yorkshire v Surrey, Headingley 1998
Stop press: Made Test debut v South Africa in the first Test, Johannesburg 1999

1999 Season

	M	Inns	NO	Runs	HS	Avge	100s	50s	Ct	St	O	M	Runs	Wkts	Avge	Best	5wI	10wM
Test																		
All First	11	20	8	567	94 *	47.25	-	4	3	-	277.1	64	825	43	19.18	5-30	1	-
1-day Int	5	5	1	217	76	54.25	-	2	1	-	35.4	3	149	3	49.66	2-36	-	
NatWest	3	3	1	46	24	23.00	-	-	1	-	26	3	103	5	20.60	3-37	-	
B & H	2	1	0	25	25	25.00	-	-	-	-	12	0	76	2	38.00	2-21	-	
1-day Lge	9	9	1	116	27 *	14.50	-	-	-	-	56.3	5	306	6	51.00	4-33	-	

Career Performances

	M	Inns	NO	Runs	HS	Avge	100s	50s	Ct	St	Balls	Runs	Wkts	Avge	Best	5wI	10wM
Test																	
All First	51	71	16	1621	94 *	29.47	-	11	16	-	7722	4070	161	25.27	7-50	7	2
1-day Int	5	5	1	217	76	54.25	-	2	1	-	214	149	3	49.66	2-36	-	
NatWest	7	5	1	87	39	21.75	-	-	3	-	360	230	12	19.16	3-27	-	
B & H	10	5	3	70	25	35.00	-	-	1	-	432	306	12	25.50	4-33	-	
1-day Lge	47	30	8	319	34 *	14.50	-	-	7	-	1692	1493	52	28.71	5-16	1	

HANCOCK, T. H. C.   Gloucestershire

Name: Timothy Harold Coulter Hancock
Role: Right-hand bat, right-arm medium
bowler, short-leg or cover fielder
Born: 20 April 1972, Reading
Height: 5ft 11in   **Weight:** 12st 7lbs
Nickname: Herbie
County debut: 1991
County cap: 1998
1000 runs in a season: 1
1st-Class 50s: 38
1st-Class 100s: 5
1st-Class 200s: 1
1st-Class catches: 81
One-Day 5 w. in innings: 1
Place in batting averages: 116th av. 28.60
(1998 51st av. 38.34)
Place in bowling averages: (1998 5th
av. 16.46)
Strike rate: 79.50 (career 63.17)
Parents: John and Jennifer
Wife: Rachael

Family links with cricket: 'Dad and brother play'
Education: St Piran's, Maidenhead; St Edward's, Oxford; Henley College
Qualifications: 8 GCSEs, senior coaching award
Overseas tours: Gloucestershire to Kenya 1991, to Sri Lanka 1992-93, to Zimbabwe (two visits)
Overseas teams played for: CBC Old Boys, Bloemfontein 1991-92; Wynnum Manley, Brisbane 1992-93; Durban Harlequins 1994-95
Cricketers particularly admired: 'Any successful Test player'
Other sports played: Hockey, golf
Other sports followed: 'Love watching rugby union and enjoy watching Bristol'
Relaxations: 'I like golf and generally winding down'
Extras: Played hockey for Oxfordshire U19
Best batting: 220* Gloucestershire v Glamorgan, Cardiff 1998
Best bowling: 3-5 Gloucestershire v Essex, Colchester 1998

1999 Season

	M	Inns	NO	Runs	HS	Avge	100s	50s	Ct	St	O	M	Runs	Wkts	Avge	Best	5wI	10wM
Test																		
All First	17	30	0	858	71	28.60	-	7	7	-	53	12	190	4	47.50	1-5	-	-
1-day Int																		
NatWest	5	5	0	318	90	63.60	-	4	-	-								
B & H	3	3	0	93	41	31.00	-	-	2	-								
1-day Lge	16	16	0	331	72	20.68	-	2	6	-	9.2	1	38	3	12.66	2-29	-	

Career Performances

	M	Inns	NO	Runs	HS	Avge	100s	50s	Ct	St	Balls	Runs	Wkts	Avge	Best	5wI	10wM
Test																	
All First	129	229	15	6100	220 *	28.50	6	38	81	-	2211	1349	35	38.54	3-5	-	-
1-day Int																	
NatWest	13	12	0	476	90	39.66	-	5	4	-	173	144	11	13.09	6-58	1	
B & H	29	26	3	553	71 *	24.04	-	2	5	-	319	243	10	24.30	3-13	-	
1-day Lge	99	90	2	1569	73	17.82	-	6	38	-	641	602	21	28.66	3-18	-	

HANSEN, T. M.   Hampshire

Name: Thomas Munkholt Hansen
Role: Right-hand bat, left-arm
fast-medium bowler
Born: 25 March 1976, Glostrup, Denmark
Height: 6ft 4in **Weight:** 14st 4lbs
Nickname: The Moose
County debut: 1997
Strike rate: 76.80 (career 108.00)
Parents: Lars and Birgitte
Marital status: Single
Family links with cricket: Father played
club cricket in Denmark and represented
Denmark four times
Education: Nørregaardsskolen;
Falkonérgaarden
Off-season: Working in Denmark
Overseas tours: Denmark to Cape Town
1996, to Malaysia 1997, to Namibia 1998, to
Zimbabwe 1999; Denmark U19 to Malaysia 1994
Overseas teams played for: Svanholm, Copenhagen 1985-97; Mount Waverley,
Melbourne 1997-98
Cricketers particularly admired: Ian Botham, Steve Waugh
Young players to look out for: Bobby Chawla
Other sports followed: Football (Brøndby and Tottenham)
Relaxations: Music, sleeping and eating
Extras: Played for Denmark at U17 and U19 level (as captain) and the national side in
the European Championships where they finished third behind Ireland and Holland.
Also played for Denmark in the ICC Trophy in Malaysia 1997 winning the Man of the
Match award against Canada and Holland. Released by Hampshire at end of 1999
season
Best batting: 24 Hampshire v Somerset, Southampton 1999
Best bowling: 3-59 Hampshire v Sussex, Southampton 1999

1999 Season

	M	Inns	NO	Runs	HS	Avge	100s	50s	Ct	St	O	M	Runs	Wkts	Avge	Best	5wl	10wM
Test																		
All First	3	4	0	33	24	8.25	-	-	-	-	64	17	196	5	39.20	3-59	-	-
1-day Int																		
NatWest																		
B & H																		
1-day Lge																		

Career Performances

	M	Inns	NO	Runs	HS	Avge	100s	50s	Ct	St	Balls	Runs	Wkts	Avge	Best	5wl	10wM
Test																	
All First	4	6	1	64	24	12.80	-	-	-	-	540	271	5	54.20	3-59	-	-
1-day Int																	
NatWest																		
B & H																		
1-day Lge																		

HARDEN, R. J. Yorkshire

Name: Richard John Harden
Role: Right-hand bat, left-arm medium bowler
Born: 16 August 1965, Bridgwater
Height: 5ft 11in **Weight:** 13st 7lbs
Nickname: Sumo, Curtis
County debut: 1985 (Somerset), 1999 (Yorkshire)
County cap: 1989 (Somerset)
1000 runs in a season: 6
1st-Class 50s: 70
1st-Class 100s: 28
1st-Class catches: 189
One-Day 100s: 4
Place in batting averages: 126th av. 27.37 (1998 234th av. 15.84)
Strike rate: (career 73.90)
Parents: Chris and Anne
Wife and date of marriage: Nicki Rae, 25 September 1992
Family links with cricket: Grandfather played club cricket for Bridgwater
Education: King's College, Taunton
Qualifications: 8 O-levels, 2 A-levels, coaching award
Overseas teams played for: Central Districts, New Zealand 1987-88
Cricketers particularly admired: Viv Richards, Jimmy Cook
Other sports followed: Squash, golf, rugby
Relaxations: 'Love my domestic duties (dusting, Hoovering, etc.) rather than golf. Good food and the odd drink.'
Extras: Joined Yorkshire for the 1999 season on a two-year contract after 13 years with Somerset
Best batting: 187 Somerset v Nottinghamshire, Taunton 1992
Best bowling: 2-7 Central Districts v Canterbury, Blenheim 1987-88

1999 Season

	M	Inns	NO	Runs	HS	Avge	100s	50s	Ct	St	O	M	Runs	Wkts	Avge	Best	5wI	10wM
Test																		
All First	10	19	3	438	69	27.37	-	3	2	-								
1-day Int																		
NatWest	4	4	0	54	37	13.50	-	-	-	-								
B & H	3	2	0	43	35	21.50	-	-	-	-								
1-day Lge	11	9	1	131	42	16.37	-	-	1	-								

Career Performances

	M	Inns	NO	Runs	HS	Avge	100s	50s	Ct	St	Balls	Runs	Wkts	Avge	Best	5wI	10wM
Test																	
All First	251	414	63	13335	187	37.99	28	70	189	-	1478	1023	20	51.15	2-7	-	-
1-day Int																	
NatWest	27	24	2	848	108 *	38.54	3	3	14	-	18	23	0	-		-	-
B & H	59	56	4	1126	76	21.65	-	6	15	-							
1-day Lge	179	171	31	4383	100 *	31.30	1	27	52	-	1	0	0	-		-	-

HARDINGES, M. A.   Gloucestershire

Name: Mark Andrew Hardinges
Role: Right-hand bat, right-arm medium bowler
Born: 5 February 1978, Gloucester
Height: 6ft 1in **Weight:** 13st
Nickname: Dinges
County debut: 1999
Strike rate: 138.00 (career 138.00)
Parents: David and Jean
Marital status: Single
Family links with cricket: 'Uncle played for Glamorgan 2nd XI; Dad played club cricket; brother played for Loughborough Uni first team'
Education: Hillstone; Malvern College; Bath University
Qualifications: 10 GCSEs, 3 A-levels
Career outside cricket: Student
Off-season: At university
Overseas tours: Malvern College to South Africa 1995
Overseas teams played for: Newtown and Chilwell, Geelong, Australia

Cricketers particularly admired: Steve Waugh, Mark Alleyne
Young players to look out for: Gavin Franklin, David Nash, Ben Knowles
Other sports played: Tennis (Gloucester U14), football (University first team)
Other sports followed: Football (Tottenham), golf, 'most sports really'
Relaxations: 'Golf, going out with my friends'
Opinions on cricket: 'Not been in the game long enough, although I do believe that two divisions is the way forward because it keeps interest going throughout the season.'
Best batting: 1 Gloucestershire v Northamptonshire, Northampton 1999
Best bowling: 1-9 Gloucestershire v Northamptonshire, Northampton 1999

1999 Season

	M	Inns	NO	Runs	HS	Avge	100s	50s	Ct	St	O	M	Runs	Wkts	Avge	Best	5wI	10wM
Test																		
All First	1	1	0	1	1	1.00	-	-	-	-	23	6	60	1	60.00	1-9	-	-
1-day Int																		
NatWest																		
B & H																		
1-day Lge																		

Career Performances

	M	Inns	NO	Runs	HS	Avge	100s	50s	Ct	St	Balls	Runs	Wkts	Avge	Best	5wI	10wM
Test																	
All First	1	1	0	1	1	1.00	-	-	-	-	138	60	1	60.00	1-9	-	-
1-day Int																	
NatWest																	
B & H																	
1-day Lge																	

45. Which current ECB official scored three 100s in successive Championship innings in 1994, the first of them at his home ground, Lord's?

HARMISON, S. J.   Durham

Name: Stephen James Harmison
Role: Right-hand bat, right-arm
fast-medium bowler
Born: 23 October 1978, Ashington,
Northumberland
Height: 6ft 4in **Weight:** 14st
Nickname: Harmy
County debut: 1996
County cap: 1999
50 wickets in a season: 2
1st-Class 5 w. in innings: 2
1st-Class catches: 7
Place in batting averages: 294th av. 5.26
(1998 261st av. 12.38)
Place in bowling averages: 73rd av. 27.73
(1998 88th av. 30.29)
Strike rate: 53.03 (career 56.24)
Parents: Margaret and James

Wife and date of marriage: Hayley, 8 October 1999
Children: Emily Alice, 1 June 1999
Family links with cricket: Brothers (James and Ben) play for Northumberland and,
with father, for Ashington
Education: Ashington High School
Overseas tours: England U19 to Pakistan 1996-97; England A to Zimbabwe and
South Africa 1998-99
Sportsmen particularly admired: Alan Shearer, David Boon, Courtney Walsh
Young players to look out for: Neil Killeen
Other sports played: Football, snooker, golf
Other sports followed: Football (Newcastle United season ticket holder)
Relaxations: Socialising and spending time with family
Extras: Represented Northumberland U17. Described as 'seriously fast' by Justin
Langer. Played football for Ashington in the Northern League. Awarded Durham cap
1999. Was selected for England A tour of Bangladesh and New Zealand 1999-2000
but was forced to withdraw with a knee injury
Best batting: 36 Durham v Worcestershire, Worcester 1998
Best bowling: 5-70 Durham v Gloucestershire, Riverside 1998

1999 Season

	M	Inns	NO	Runs	HS	Avge	100s	50s	Ct	St	O	M	Runs	Wkts	Avge	Best	5wl	10wM
Test																		
All First	17	24	9	79	14*	5.26	-	-	4	-	565.5	120	1775	64	27.73	5-76	1	-
1-day Int																		
NatWest	1	1	1	2	2*	-	-	-	1	-	9	0	42	1	42.00	1-42	-	
B & H																		
1-day Lge	5	3	3	5	4*	-	-	-	1	-	35	2	176	3	58.66	2-40	-	

Career Performances

	M	Inns	NO	Runs	HS	Avge	100s	50s	Ct	St	Balls	Runs	Wkts	Avge	Best	5wl	10wM
Test																	
All First	35	52	15	339	36	9.16	-	-	7	-	6862	3669	122	30.07	5-70	2	-
1-day Int																	
NatWest	1	1	1	2	2*	-	-	-	1	-	54	42	1	42.00	1-42	-	
B & H	1	0	0	0	0	-	-	-	-	-	36	36	0	-	-	-	
1-day Lge	8	4	4	6	4*	-	-	-	2	-	330	280	3	93.33	2-40	-	

HARRIS, A. J. — Nottinghamshire

Name: Andrew James Harris
Role: Right-hand bat, right-arm fast bowler
Born: 26 June 1973, Ashton-under-Lyne, Lancashire
Height: 6ft **Weight:** 11st 7lbs
Nickname: AJ
County debut: 1994 (Derbyshire)
County cap: 1996 (Derbyshire)
1st-Class 5 w. in innings: 4
1st-Class 10 w. in match: 1
1st-Class catches: 16
Place in bowling averages:
84th av. 28.92
Strike rate: 52.96 (career 54.96)
Parent: Joyce
Marital status: Engaged to Kate
Education: Tintwistle Primary School; Hadfield Comprehensive School; Glossopdale Community College
Qualifications: 6 GCSEs, 1 A-level
Off-season: 'At home'

Overseas tours: England A to Australia 1996-97
Overseas teams played for: Ginninderra, West Belconnen, Australia 1992-93; Victoria University of Wellington CC, New Zealand 1997-98
Cricketers particularly admired: Kim Barnett, Merv Hughes 'for his effort and determination'
Other sports followed: Football (Man City)
Injuries: Out for five weeks with a broken right thumb
Relaxations: 'Playing any sport, golf in particular. As relaxing goes, watching television, playing on my Sega, and how could I forget having quite a few beers, although I have never been to the "Pink Coconut"'
Extras: Left Derbyshire at end of 1999 season and has joined Notts for 2000
Best batting: 36 Derbyshire v Worcestershire, Worcester 1997
Best bowling: 6-40 Derbyshire v Middlesex, Derby 1996

1999 Season

	M	Inns	NO	Runs	HS	Avge	100s	50s	Ct	St	O	M	Runs	Wkts	Avge	Best	5wI	10wM
Test																		
All First	7	11	7	48	8 *	12.00	-	-	4	-	229.3	44	752	26	28.92	5-63	2	-
1-day Int																		
NatWest	2	1	0	2	2	2.00	-	-	-	-	17.1	3	42	3	14.00	3-10	-	
B & H																		
1-day Lge	4	3	2	14	8 *	14.00	-	-	-	-	27	2	135	2	67.50	1-19	-	

Career Performances

	M	Inns	NO	Runs	HS	Avge	100s	50s	Ct	St	Balls	Runs	Wkts	Avge	Best	5wI	10wM
Test																	
All First	46	65	18	392	36	8.34	-	-	16	-	7530	4535	137	33.10	6-40	4	1
1-day Int																	
NatWest	6	3	2	18	11 *	18.00	-	-	1	-	337	198	9	22.00	3-10	-	
B & H	10	3	1	11	5	5.50	-	-	4	-	549	435	16	27.18	3-41	-	
1-day Lge	42	15	8	45	10 *	6.42	-	-	9	-	1692	1442	58	24.86	4-22	-	

HARRISON, D. S.   Glamorgan

Name: David Stuart Harrison
Role: Right-hand bat, right-arm fast-medium bowler
Born: 31 July 1981, Newport
Height: 6ft 4in **Weight:** 13st 6lbs
Nickname: Rodney, Mensa, Moses, Harry, Radical Parting
County debut: 1999
Strike rate: 132.00 (career 132.00)

Parents: Stuart and Susan
Marital status: Single
Family links with cricket: Father played for Glamorgan during 1970s
Education: Greenlawn Junior, New Inn, Pontypool; West Mon Comprehensive, Pontypool; Pontypool College
Qualifications: BTEC National Diploma Sports Studies
Off-season: England U19 tour to Malaysia and Sri Lanka
Overseas tours: Gwent Schools to South Africa (Cape Town) 1996; England U19 to Malaysia and (Youth World Cup) Sri Lanka 1999-2000
Cricketers particularly admired: Steve Waugh, Steve James, Chris Brown
Young players to look out for: Mark Wallace, Ian Bell, Mike Powell
Other sports played: Squash (represented Wales as junior), rugby union (represented Pontypool Schools XV in Welsh Cup final)
Other sports followed: Rugby union (Pontypool), football (Manchester United)
Injuries: Back injury forced withdrawal from England U19 team to play Australia
Relaxations: Golf, music, 'socialising with friends I rarely see in summer'
Opinions on cricket: 'More day/night cricket. Provide more entertainment during Test matches and One-Day Internationals. Market the game more.'
Best batting: 16 Glamorgan v Oxford University, The Parks 1999
Best bowling: 1-15 Glamorgan v Oxford University, The Parks 1999

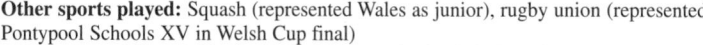

1999 Season

	M	Inns	NO	Runs	HS	Avge	100s	50s	Ct	St	O	M	Runs	Wkts	Avge	Best	5wl	10wM
Test																		
All First	2	2	0	29	16	14.50	-	-	-	-	22	3	64	1	64.00	1-15	-	-
1-day Int																		
NatWest																		
B & H																		
1-day Lge																		

Career Performances

	M	Inns	NO	Runs	HS	Avge	100s	50s	Ct	St	Balls	Runs	Wkts	Avge	Best	5wI	10wM
Test																	
All First	2	2	0	29	16	14.50	-	-	-	-	132	64	1	64.00	1-15	-	-
1-day Int																	
NatWest																	
B & H																	
1-day Lge																	

HARTLEY, P. J.   Hampshire

Name: Peter John Hartley
Role: Right-hand bat, right-arm
fast-medium bowler
Born: 18 April 1960, Keighley
Height: 6ft **Weight:** 14st 3lb
Nickname: Jack, PJ
County debut: 1982 (Warwickshire),
1985 (Yorkshire), 1998 (Hampshire)
County cap: 1987 (Yorkshire),
1998 (Hampshire)
Benefit: 1996 (Yorkshire)
50 wickets in a season: 7
1st-Class 50s: 14
1st-Class 100s: 2
1st-Class 5 w. in innings: 23
1st-Class 10 w. in match: 3
1st-Class catches: 68
One-Day 5 w. in innings: 4
Place in batting averages: 200th av. 20.33 (1998 262nd av. 12.30)
Place in bowling averages: 30th av. 21.77 (1998 110th av. 33.60)
Strike rate: 43.66 (career 53.71)
Parents: Thomas and Molly
Wife and date of marriage: Sharon Louise, 12 March 1988
Children: Megan Grace, 25 April 1992; Courtney, 25 July 1995
Family links with cricket: Father played local league cricket
Education: Haworth; Hartington Middle/Greenhead Grammar School;
Bradford College
Qualifications: City & Guilds in Textile Design and Management, NCA coaching award
Career outside cricket: Sales consultant
Off-season: 'Playing golf and above job'
Overseas tours: Yorkshire pre-season tours to Barbados 1986-87, to South Africa
1991-92, 1992-93; to Zimbabwe

Overseas teams played for: Melville, New Zealand 1983-84; Adelaide, Australia 1985-86; Harmony and Orange Free State, South Africa 1988-89
Cricketers particularly admired: Malcolm Marshall, Richard Hadlee
Young sportsmen to look out for: Sergio Garcia, Lee Westwood
Other sports played: Golf (4 handicap)
Other sports followed: Football (Chelsea FC)
Injuries: Various
Relaxations: Gardening, walking
Opinions on cricket: 'Poor pitches. Grounds should be under the control of the ECB (pitches doctored too much). Reduce the amount of cricket played.'
Extras: Returned 8-65, his best figures for Hampshire, against Yorkshire, his former county, at Basingstoke 1999
Best batting: 127* Yorkshire v Lancashire, Old Trafford 1988
Best bowling: 9-41 Yorkshire v Derbyshire, Chesterfield 1995

1999 Season

	M	Inns	NO	Runs	HS	Avge	100s	50s	Ct	St	O	M	Runs	Wkts	Avge	Best	5wI	10wM
Test																		
All First	12	15	6	183	58	20.33	-	1	3	-	393	93	1176	54	21.77	8-65	2	1
1-day Int																		
NatWest	2	0	0	0	0	-	-	-	-	-	16	0	62	3	20.66	2-21	-	
B & H	1	1	1	6	6 *	-	-	-	-	-	6	1	26	0	-	-	-	
1-day Lge	13	5	4	15	12 *	15.00	-	-	3	-	95.2	5	484	17	28.47	4-29	-	

Career Performances

	M	Inns	NO	Runs	HS	Avge	100s	50s	Ct	St	Balls	Runs	Wkts	Avge	Best	5wI	10wM
Test																	
All First	223	272	61	4218	127 *	19.99	2	14	68	-	35882	19938	668	29.84	9-41	23	3
1-day Int																	
NatWest	33	18	8	250	83	25.00	-	2	2	-	1965	1256	53	23.69	5-46	1	
B & H	49	31	11	236	29 *	11.80	-	-	12	-	2661	1736	68	25.52	5-43	1	
1-day Lge	173	116	40	1228	52	16.15	-	2	31	-	7332	5670	209	27.12	5-36	2	

46. Who scored Durham's first double century, in the Championship match v Warwickshire at Edgbaston in 1994?

HARVEY, I. J.   Gloucestershire

Name: Ian Joseph Harvey
Role: Right-hand bat, right-arm fast-medium
bowler
Born: 10 April 1972, Wonthaggi, Victoria
Nickname: Freak
County debut: 1999
County cap: 1999
One-Day Internationals: 11
1st-Class 50s: 13
1st-Class 100s: 3
1st-Class 5w. in innings: 4
1st-Class catches: 38
One-Day 5 w. in innings: 1
Place in batting averages: 176th av. 22.57
Place in bowling averages: 76th av. 28.25
Strike rate: 57.32 (career 69.60)
Overseas tours: Australian Academy to New
Zealand 1994-95; Australia to Sharjah
1997-98

Overseas teams played for: Dandenong, Victoria; Victoria 1993-94 –
Extras: Took a wicket (Jonty Rhodes) with his second ball in One-Day International
cricket. Top scorer (57) for Victoria in their Mercantile Mutual Cup final victory over
New South Wales 1998-99. Joined Gloucestershire in 1999 as overseas player. Won
NatWest Man of the Match award v Durham Cricket Board XI at Chester-le-Street
1999. Awarded Gloucestershire cap 1999
Best batting: 136 Victoria v South Australia, Melbourne 1995-96
Best bowling: 7-44 Victoria v South Australia, Melbourne 1996-97
Stop press: Named in Australia squad for one-day series in New Zealand 1999-2000

1999 Season

	M	Inns	NO	Runs	HS	Avge	100s	50s	Ct	St	O	M	Runs	Wkts	Avge	Best	5wI	10wM
Test																		
All First	12	19	0	429	123	22.57	1	-	6	-	296.1	77	876	31	28.25	5-76	1	-
1-day Int																		
NatWest	5	4	0	49	32	12.25	-	-	2	-	41.1	5	125	10	12.50	4-29	-	
B & H	3	2	0	48	35	24.00	-	-	-	-	24	2	105	7	15.00	4-42	-	
1-day Lge	14	14	1	297	47	22.84	-	-	1	-	107.5	10	474	30	15.80	5-41	1	

Career Performances

	M	Inns	NO	Runs	HS	Avge	100s	50s	Ct	St	Balls	Runs	Wkts	Avge	Best	5wI	10wM
Test																	
All First	55	96	4	2421	136	26.31	3	13	38	-	8005	4077	115	35.45	7-44	4	-
1-day Int	11	9	2	101	43	14.42	-	-	6	-	417	325	7	46.42	3-17	-	
NatWest	5	4	0	49	32	12.25	-	-	2	-	247	125	10	12.50	4-29	-	
B & H	3	2	0	48	35	24.00	-	-	-	-	144	105	7	15.00	4-42	-	
1-day Lge	14	14	1	297	47	22.84	-	-	1	-	647	474	30	15.80	5-41	1	

HARVEY, M. E. Lancashire

Name: Mark Edward Harvey
Role: Right-hand bat, right-arm medium/off-spin bowler
Born: 26 June 1974, Burnley, Lancs
Height: 5ft 9in **Weight:** 12st
Nickname: Harv, Becks, Baz
County debut: 1994
1st-Class catches: 3
Parents: David and Wendy
Marital status: Single
Family links with cricket: Brother Jonathan spent four years as MCC young player and was professional for Greenmount CC in the Bolton League; is now professional for Earby CC in the Ribblesdale League. 'Father, David, is still playing local club cricket'
Education: Worsthorne County Primary; Habergham High School, Burnley; Loughborough University
Qualifications: 8 GCSEs, 3 A-levels, BSc (Hons) PE Sports Management and Recreational Management
Career outside cricket: 'None yet!'
Off-season: 'Barbados and relaxing'
Overseas tours: England U19 to India 1992-93
Overseas teams played for: Queanbeyan CC, Canberra, Australia 1996-97
Cricketers particularly admired: 'David Gower (someone who makes it all look so easy), Dean Jones (exciting both batting and fielding), Mudassar Nazar (an admired professional for many years at Burnley), Les "The Whirlwind" Seal'
Young players to look out for: Chris Schofield
Other sports played: Football ('Burnley Town team!'), golf, squash 'and almost anything'
Other sports followed: Football (Manchester United, Burnley and Oxford United)

Injuries: Out for four weeks pre-season with lower back problems

Relaxations: 'I'd love to say that watching Burnley FC was a relaxation, but unfortunately it's very frustrating; drinking at the "Crooked Billet", Workthorne, with father and brother'

Extras: Captained England U17, represented England at U17, U18 and U19 levels, represented Lancashire from U13 to U19. In an attempt to produce a result in a rain-affected 2nd XI match v Yorkshire at Todmorden, he bowled an over costing 108 runs from 18 no-balls, all of which went for four without hitting the bat. 'This allowed both teams to contrive a game in five rather than 50 minutes. A claim to fame which earns me never-ending stick at the local pub!' Played for Combined Universities in 1995 and 1996. Retained Vaux Ribblesdale League Championship with Padiham CC

Opinions on cricket: 'The introduction of two divisions should benefit the progression of the game, ensuring hard competition until the last day of the season. Day/night cricket is fresh and fun for all and should be encouraged throughout the game to attract a younger and wider-ranging audience.'

Best batting: 39 Lancashire v Cambridge University, Fenner's 1999

1999 Season

	M	Inns	NO	Runs	HS	Avge	100s	50s	Ct	St	0	M	Runs	Wkts	Avge	Best	5wl	10wM
Test																		
All First	1	1	0	39	39	39.00	-	-	1	-								
1-day Int																		
NatWest																		
B & H																		
1-day Lge	1	1	0	15	15	15.00	-	-	4	-								

Career Performances

	M	Inns	NO	Runs	HS	Avge	100s	50s	Ct	St	Balls	Runs	Wkts	Avge	Best	5wl	10wM
Test																	
All First	7	11	1	155	39	15.50	-	-	3	-	30	48	0	-	-	-	-
1-day Int																	
NatWest	1	1	0	86	86	86.00	-	1	1	-							
B & H	4	4	0	9	5	2.25	-	-	3	-							
1-day Lge	4	3	0	62	39	20.66	-	-	4	-							

47. Which of the 1999 England World Cup squad won the Walter Lawrence Trophy in 1991 for his 61-ball 100 v Yorkshire at Scarborough?

HAVELL, P. M. R. Sussex

Name: Paul Matthew Roger Havell
Role: Left-hand bat, right-arm fast bowler
Born: 4 July 1980, Melbourne, Australia
Height: 6ft 3in
Nickname: Trigger, Dave
County debut: No first-team appearance
Parents: Roger and Cheryl
Marital status: Single
Family links with cricket: Brother Mark
played for Sussex U19
Education: Great Walstead School; Warden
Park School; Haywards Heath College
Qualifications: 9 GCSEs, Level 1 coaching
award
Career outside cricket: 'A crafty salesman'
Off-season: 'Working hard on fitness and
coaching cricket!'
Overseas tours: Sussex U19 to Barbados
1997

Overseas teams played for: East Doncaster CC, Australia 1998-99
Cricketers particularly admired: Darren Gough, Glenn McGrath, 'and all cricketers
at Sussex CCC'
Young players to look out for: James Kirtley, Billy Taylor, Justin Bates, Robin
Martin-Jenkins
Other sports played: Golf, tennis and squash
Other sports followed: Football (Brighton & Hove Albion)
Injuries: Out for three weeks with a side strain
Relaxations: 'Having a nice long bath and going out!'
Extras: Sussex Young Cricketer of the Year 1995
Opinions on cricket: 'The game today seems to be getting a lot tougher and harder to
succeed in! If you want to do well, then you have to listen and work hard. If England
are to succeed in the future, they must blood young players with talent at a young age
and give them a real go in the team, instead of playing them, then dropping them a few
games later – it takes time to succeed!'

HAYDEN, M. L.   Northamptonshire

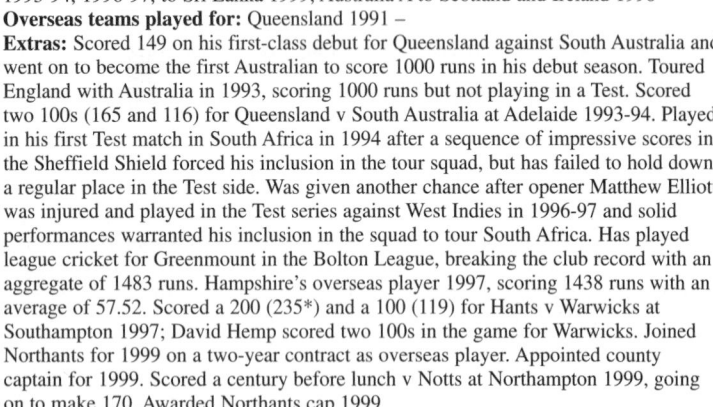

Name: Matthew Lawrence Hayden
Role: Left-hand bat, right-arm medium bowler, county captain
Born: 29 October 1971, Kingaroy, Australia
County debut: 1997 (Hampshire), 1999 (Northamptonshire)
County cap: 1997 (Hampshire), 1999 (Northamptonshire)
Test debut: 1993-94
Tests: 7
One-Day Internationals: 13
1000 runs in a season: 1
1st-Class 50s: 51
1st-Class 100s: 34
1st-Class 200s: 4
1st-Class catches: 117
One-Day 100s: 4
Place in batting averages: 5th av. 57.30
Strike rate: 45.00 (career 68.87)
Overseas tours: Australia to England 1993, to Sharjah 1993-94, to South Africa 1993-94, 1996-97, to Sri Lanka 1999; Australia A to Scotland and Ireland 1998
Overseas teams played for: Queensland 1991 –
Extras: Scored 149 on his first-class debut for Queensland against South Australia and went on to become the first Australian to score 1000 runs in his debut season. Toured England with Australia in 1993, scoring 1000 runs but not playing in a Test. Scored two 100s (165 and 116) for Queensland v South Australia at Adelaide 1993-94. Played in his first Test match in South Africa in 1994 after a sequence of impressive scores in the Sheffield Shield forced his inclusion in the tour squad, but has failed to hold down a regular place in the Test side. Was given another chance after opener Matthew Elliott was injured and played in the Test series against West Indies in 1996-97 and solid performances warranted his inclusion in the squad to tour South Africa. Has played league cricket for Greenmount in the Bolton League, breaking the club record with an aggregate of 1483 runs. Hampshire's overseas player 1997, scoring 1438 runs with an average of 57.52. Scored a 200 (235*) and a 100 (119) for Hants v Warwicks at Southampton 1997; David Hemp scored two 100s in the game for Warwicks. Joined Northants for 1999 on a two-year contract as overseas player. Appointed county captain for 1999. Scored a century before lunch v Notts at Northampton 1999, going on to make 170. Awarded Northants cap 1999
Best batting: 235* Hampshire v Warwickshire, Southampton 1997
Best bowling: 3-10 Northamptonshire v Worcestershire, Northampton 1999
Stop press: Selected for Australia's tour of New Zealand 1999-2000

1999 Season

	M	Inns	NO	Runs	HS	Avge	100s	50s	Ct	St	O	M	Runs	Wkts	Avge	Best	5wI	10wM
Test																		
All First	9	15	2	745	170	57.30	4	1	6	-	30	7	92	4	23.00	3-10	-	-
1-day Int																		
NatWest	3	3	0	163	107	54.33	1	-	1	-								
B & H																		
1-day Lge	8	8	0	228	86	28.50	-	1	3	-								

Career Performances

	M	Inns	NO	Runs	HS	Avge	100s	50s	Ct	St	Balls	Runs	Wkts	Avge	Best	5wI	10wM
Test	7	12	0	261	125	21.75	1	-	8	-								
All First	142	249	26	11886	235 *	53.30	38	51	117	-	551	374	8	46.75	3-10	-	-
1-day Int	13	12	1	286	67	26.00	-	2	4	-								
NatWest	5	5	0	273	107	54.60	1	1	2	-								
B & H	5	5	1	216	120 *	54.00	1	-	3	-	54	45	2	22.50	2-45	-	
1-day Lge	24	23	0	882	118	38.34	2	4	10	-	81	78	2	39.00	2-38	-	

HAYNES, G. R. Worcestershire

Name: Gavin Richard Haynes
Role: Right-hand bat, right-arm
medium bowler
Born: 29 September 1969, Wordsley,
Stourbridge
Height: 5ft 10in **Weight:** 12st
Nickname: Splash
County debut: 1991
County cap: 1994
1000 runs in a season: 1
1st-Class 50s: 24
1st-Class 100s: 3
1st-Class 5 w. in innings: 2
1st-Class catches: 39
One-Day 100s: 1
Place in batting averages: 227th av. 17.70
(1998 72nd av. 33.25)
Place in bowling averages: (1998 63rd
av. 27.11)
Strike rate: 198.33 (career 73.64)
Parents: Nicholas and Dorothy

Wife and date of marriage: Joanne, 25 October 1997

Children: Joshua, 13 February 1999

Family links with cricket: Father played club cricket and manages Worcester U14 side. Cousin Peter Haynes played very good club cricket

Education: Gigmill Junior School; High Park Comprehensive; King Edward VI College, Stourbridge

Qualifications: 5 O-levels, 1 A-level, NCA advanced coaching award

Off-season: 'Playing with Joshua's toys'

Overseas tours: Worcestershire to Zimbabwe, to South Africa, to Barbados – all 1996, to Guernsey 1997

Overseas teams played for: Sunrise Sports Club, Zimbabwe 1989-90

Cricketers particularly admired: Ian Botham, Graham Dilley, Graham Gooch, Malcolm Marshall, Viv Richards, Graeme Hick

Young players to look out for: 'The good ones'

Other sports followed: Football (Aston Villa), golf

Injuries: Out for two weeks with back injury; for one week with knee injury

Relaxations: Playing golf, watching television

Extras: Represented England Schools U15. Worcestershire Uncapped Player of the Year 1993

Opinions on cricket: 'Pitches are absolutely diabolical. Ridiculous year to split into two divisions with the World Cup taking place. Everyone says we play too much cricket, yet next year we could play more!'

Best batting: 158 Worcestershire v Kent, Worcester 1993

Best bowling: 6-50 Worcestershire v Hampshire, Worcester 1998

1999 Season

	M	Inns	NO	Runs	HS	Avge	100s	50s	Ct	St	O	M	Runs	Wkts	Avge	Best	5wI	10wM
Test																		
All First	8	12	2	177	60 *	17.70	-	1	-	-	99.1	22	278	3	92.66	2-35	-	-
1-day Int																		
NatWest	2	2	0	30	21	15.00	-	-	1	-	19	3	58	3	19.33	2-31	-	
B & H																		
1-day Lge	14	11	1	158	66	15.80	-	1	8	-	92	9	383	20	19.15	4-28	-	

Career Performances

	M	Inns	NO	Runs	HS	Avge	100s	50s	Ct	St	Balls	Runs	Wkts	Avge	Best	5wI	10wM
Test																	
All First	100	155	16	4173	158	30.02	3	24	39	-	7070	3541	96	36.88	6-50	2	-
1-day Int																	
NatWest	12	10	1	413	116 *	45.88	1	2	4	-	480	272	8	34.00	2-31	-	
B & H	21	19	3	372	65	23.25	-	1	6	-	815	486	18	27.00	3-17	-	
1-day Lge	87	71	8	1452	83	23.04	-	4	26	-	2626	1828	69	26.49	4-13	-	

HAYNES, J. J. Lancashire

Name: Jamie Jonathan Haynes
Role: Right-hand bat, wicket-keeper
Born: 5 July 1974, Bristol
Height: 5ft 10in **Weight:** 12st 7lbs
Nickname: JJ, Champ, The Mole
County debut: 1996
1st-Class 50s: 1
1st-Class catches: 20
1st-Class stumpings: 2
Parents: Steve Haynes and Moiya Ford
Marital status: Single
Family links with cricket: Father and uncle
both played for Gloucestershire CCC
Education: Garran Primary, Canberra,
Australia; Padua High School, Canberra;
St Edmunds College, Canberra; University of
Canberra

Qualifications: Year 12 Certificate, coaching
certificate, part-way through BA Sports Media
Career outside cricket: 12-month contract at Lancashire
Off-season: Holiday to Australia to see family; start training as part of Lancs 12-month contract
Overseas tours: Lancashire CCC, Cape Town 1999
Overseas teams played for: Tuggeranong Valley CC, Australia 1995-96; South Canberra CC, Australia 1996-97
Cricketers particularly admired: Mike Watkinson, Gary Yates, Mike Atherton, Warren Hegg
Young players to look out for: Chris Schofield, James Anderson
Other sports played: Australian Rules football
Other sports followed: Football (Manchester United, Burnley)
Relaxations: Golf, shopping, eating (Thai food), 'going to the movies'
Extras: Top scorer with 80 as nightwatchman in Lancashire's first innings v Sri Lanka A at Old Trafford 1999
Opinions on cricket: 'Day/night cricket is the way forward. National League should be exclusively day/night cricket. Coloured clothing should be worn for all limited over competitions.'
Best batting: 80 Lancashire v Sri Lanka A, Old Trafford 1999

1999 Season

	M	Inns	NO	Runs	HS	Avge	100s	50s	Ct	St	O	M	Runs	Wkts	Avge	Best	5wl	10wM
Test																		
All First	2	2	1	114	80	114.00	-	1	8	1								
1-day Int																		
NatWest																		
B & H																		
1-day Lge																		

Career Performances

	M	Inns	NO	Runs	HS	Avge	100s	50s	Ct	St	Balls	Runs	Wkts	Avge	Best	5wl	10wM
Test																		
All First	5	7	1	181	80	30.16	-	1	20	2							
1-day Int																		
NatWest																		
B & H																		
1-day Lge	1	0	0	0	0	-		-	-	-							

HAYWOOD, G. R.   Nottinghamshire

Name: Giles Ronald Haywood
Role: Left-hand bat, right-arm
medium bowler
Born: 8 September 1979, Chichester
Height: 6ft 1in **Weight:** 12st
Nickname: Porno, Chopper, Lord Lucan
County debut: 1996 (one-day, Sussex),
1999 (first-class, Sussex)
Parents: Ron and Shirley
Marital status: Single
Family links with cricket: Father and
brother both play club cricket
Education: The Prebendal, Chichester;
Lancing College; Sussex University
Qualifications: 11 GCSEs, 3 A-levels
Career outside cricket: Student
Off-season: Reading Geography at university
Overseas tours: Sussex U19 to Sri Lanka
1995; England U17 to Bermuda (International Youth Tournament) 1997; England U19
to South Africa (including Youth World Cup) 1997-98, to New Zealand 1998-99
Cricketers particularly admired: Chris Broad, Desmond Haynes, Sachin Tendulkar

Young players to look out for: Paul Havell, Paul Robbins
Other sports played: Golf, squash
Other sports followed: Football (Brighton & Hove Albion FC)
Relaxations: Eating out, watching sport on TV, sleeping, 'VH-1'
Extras: Played for ESCA U15, England U16. Made Sunday League debut at age 17. Represented England U19 in one-day series v Australia U19 1999. Released by Sussex at end of 1999 season and has joined Nottinghamshire for 2000
Opinions on cricket: 'People react to England's inconsistent results over the last few years by trying to copy what is being done in domestic cricket in Australia (i.e. two-tier systems etc) which may not necessarily work for English cricket. More emphasis is required on the development of young cricketers than following the Australian system.'
Best batting: 14 Sussex v Leicestershire, Arundel 1999

1999 Season

	M	Inns	NO	Runs	HS	Avge	100s	50s	Ct	St	O	M	Runs	Wkts	Avge	Best	5wI	10wM
Test																		
All First	1	2	0	15	14	7.50	-	-	-	-	13.2	1	66	0	-	-	-	-
1-day Int																		
NatWest	2	2	1	20	18 *	20.00	-	-	-	-	10	2	37	1	37.00	1-18	-	
B & H	2	2	0	0	0	0.00	-	-	-	-	18	1	63	2	31.50	1-24	-	
1-day Lge	7	5	0	50	24	10.00	-	-	4	-	42.1	0	208	4	52.00	1-19	-	

Career Performances

	M	Inns	NO	Runs	HS	Avge	100s	50s	Ct	St	Balls	Runs	Wkts	Avge	Best	5wI	10wM
Test																	
All First	1	2	0	15	14	7.50	-	-	-	-	80	66	0	-	-	-	-
1-day Int																	
NatWest	2	2	1	20	18 *	20.00	-	-	-	-	60	37	1	37.00	1-18	-	
B & H	2	2	0	0	0	0.00	-	-	-	-	108	63	2	31.50	1-24	-	
1-day Lge	9	7	0	68	24	9.71	-	-	4	-	271	224	4	56.00	1-19	-	

HEADLEY, D. W.   Kent

Name: Dean Warren Headley
Role: Right-hand bat, right-arm medium-fast bowler
Born: 27 January 1970, Stourbridge
Height: 6ft 4in   **Weight:** 14st 3lbs
Nickname: Froggy
County debut: 1991 (Middlesex), 1993 (Kent)
County cap: 1993 (Kent)
Test debut: 1997
Tests: 15
One-Day Internationals: 13
50 wickets in a season: 2
1st-Class 50s: 6
1st-Class 5 w. in innings: 25
1st-Class 10 w. in match: 2
1st-Class catches: 60
One-Day 5 w. in innings: 3

Place in batting averages: 216th av. 18.56 (1998 228th av. 16.56)
Place in bowling averages: 129th av. 38.97 (1998 27th av. 21.75)
Strike rate: 74.24 (career 55.37)
Parents: Ron and Gail
Marital status: Single
Family links with cricket: Grandfather (George) and father (Ron) both played for West Indies
Education: Gigmill Junior School, Stourbridge; Oldswinford Hospital School; Royal Grammar School, Worcester
Qualifications: 7 O-levels
Career outside cricket: 'Various'
Off-season: 'Expected to play against South Africa, but that has changed to relaxing' (see **Stop press**)
Overseas tours: RGS Worcester to Zimbabwe 1988; Christians in Sport to India 1989-90; England A to Pakistan 1995-96, to Australia 1996-97; England to Sharjah (Champions Trophy) 1997-98, to West Indies 1997-98, to Australia 1998-99, to South Africa 1999-2000
Overseas teams played for: Melbourne, Jamaica 1991-92; Primrose CC, South Africa 1993-95
Cricketers particularly admired: Malcolm Marshall, 'my dad', Ian Botham, Gavin O'Hanlon, Adam Patrick, Min Patel
Young players to look out for: Matthew Walker, Owais Shah, Andrew Harris
Other sports played: 'Have a go at anything'

Other sports followed: Football (WBA)

Relaxations: Socialising, watching films, playing golf and eating out

Extras: Played for Staffordshire. Took five wickets on debut including a wicket with his first ball in Championship cricket. Played for Worcestershire 2nd XI 1988-89. Left Middlesex at the end of 1992 season and signed for Kent. Called up as a replacement for the England A tour to Pakistan 1995-96. Took a record-breaking three hat-tricks during the summer of 1996. The third generation of his family to play Test cricket, both his father and grandfather played Test cricket for West Indies. Received Man of the Match award for his 6-60 in Australia's second innings in the fourth Test at Melbourne 1998-99, which included a burst of 5-9

Opinions on cricket: 'Time for a change (revolution).'

Best batting: 91 Middlesex v Leicestershire, Leicester 1992

Best bowling: 8-98 Kent v Derbyshire, Derby 1996

Stop press: Forced to return home early from England tour to South Africa with stress fracture of back. Awarded England contract (Band C) for 2000

1999 Season

	M	Inns	NO	Runs	HS	Avge	100s	50s	Ct	St	O	M	Runs	Wkts	Avge	Best	5wl	10wM
Test	2	3	0	34	18	11.33	-	-	-	-	58	11	189	4	47.25	3-74	-	-
All First	14	19	3	297	72	18.56	-	1	9	-	457.5	93	1442	37	38.97	4-74	-	-
1-day Int																		
NatWest	2	1	0	0	0	0.00	-	-	-	-	13.5	3	44	4	11.00	3-16	-	
B & H																		
1-day Lge	11	5	3	24	14 *	12.00	-	-	1	-	81	10	320	14	22.85	5-43	1	

Career Performances

	M	Inns	NO	Runs	HS	Avge	100s	50s	Ct	St	Balls	Runs	Wkts	Avge	Best	5wl	10wM
Test	15	26	4	186	31	8.45	-	-	7	-	3026	1671	60	27.85	6-60	1	-
All First	139	187	44	2373	91	16.59	-	6	60	-	25803	13293	466	28.52	8-98	25	2
1-day Int	13	6	4	22	10 *	11.00	-	-	3	-	594	520	11	47.27	2-38	-	
NatWest	16	8	4	46	24 *	11.50	-	-	2	-	960	569	28	20.32	5-20	1	
B & H	27	10	3	62	26	8.85	-	-	6	-	1505	1007	30	33.56	4-19	-	
1-day Lge	100	33	19	160	29 *	11.42	-	-	17	-	4216	3173	128	24.78	6-42	2	

HEGG, W. K.   Lancashire

Name: Warren Kevin Hegg
Role: Right-hand bat, wicket-keeper
Born: 23 February 1968, Manchester
Height: 5ft 9in **Weight:** 12st 10lbs
Nickname: Chucky, Bertie
County debut: 1986
Benefit: 1999
Test debut: 1998-99
Tests: 2
1st-Class 50s: 40
1st-Class 100s: 4
1st-Class catches: 624
1st-Class stumpings: 70
Place in batting averages: 90th av. 31.90
(1998 55th av. 36.94)
Parents: Glenda and Kevin (deceased)
Wife and date of marriage:
Joanne, 29 October 1994
Children: Chloe 1998
Family links with cricket: Brother Martin plays in local leagues
Education: Unsworth High School; Stand College, Whitefield
Qualifications: 5 O-levels, 7 CSEs, qualified coach
Overseas tours: NCA North U19 to Bermuda 1985; England YC to Sri Lanka 1986-87, to Australia (Youth World Cup) 1987-88; England A to Pakistan and Sri Lanka 1990-91, to Australia 1996-97; England to Australia 1998-99
Overseas teams played for: Sheffield, Tasmania 1988-90, 1992-93
Cricketers particularly admired: Ian Botham, Alan Knott, Bob Taylor, Gehan Mendis, Ian Healy
Young players to look out for: Mark Chilton, Chris Schofield, Gordon Howarth
Other sports played: Football (Old Standians)
Other sports followed: Football (Manchester United), rugby league (Salford Reds)
Relaxations: 'Golf, golf, golf'
Extras: Became youngest player for 30 years to score a century for Lancashire with his 130 v Northamptonshire in his fourth first-class game. Took 11 catches in match v Derbyshire, equalling world first-class record. Wombwell Cricket Lovers' Society joint Wicket-keeper of the Year 1993. Vice-captain of Lancashire in 1999
Opinions on cricket: 'Enjoy it as long as you can. It doesn't last forever!'
Best batting: 134 Lancashire v Leicestershire, Old Trafford 1996

1999 Season

	M	Inns	NO	Runs	HS	Avge	100s	50s	Ct	St	O	M	Runs	Wkts	Avge	Best	5wI	10wM
Test																		
All First	16	24	3	670	94	31.90	-	3	45	4								
1-day Int																		
NatWest	3	2	0	17	10	8.50	-	-	3	1								
B & H	1	1	0	8	8	8.00	-	-	1	1								
1-day Lge	14	8	3	101	30 *	20.20	-	-	14	3								

Career Performances

	M	Inns	NO	Runs	HS	Avge	100s	50s	Ct	St	Balls	Runs	Wkts	Avge	Best	5wI	10wM
Test	2	4	0	30	15	7.50	-	-	8	-							
All First	258	378	72	8103	134	26.48	4	40	624	70	6	7	0	-	-	-	-
1-day Int																	
NatWest	34	20	1	348	37	18.31	-	-	45	3							
B & H	61	30	13	492	81	28.94	-	2	82	6							
1-day Lge	187	109	47	1340	52	21.61	-	1									

HEMP, D. L.   Warwickshire

Name: David Lloyd Hemp
Role: Left-hand bat, right-arm
medium bowler
Born: 15 November 1970,
Hamilton, Bermuda
Height: 6ft 1in **Weight:** 13st
Nickname: Hempy, Jonesy
County debut: 1991 (Glamorgan),
1997 (Warwickshire)
County cap: 1994 (Glamorgan),
1997 (Warwickshire)
1000 runs in a season: 3
1st-Class 50s: 37
1st-Class 100s: 12
1st-Class catches: 86
One-Day 100s: 4
Place in batting averages: 70th av. 34.96
(1998 136th av. 25.84)
Strike rate: 126.00 (career 55.20)
Parents: Clive and Elisabeth
Wife and date of marriage: Angie, 16 March 1996

Family links with cricket: Father plays for Ffynone CC; brother Tim captains Swansea and plays for Wales Minor Counties; sister Charlotte played for Parklands Junior School

Education: Parklands Junior; Olchfa Comprehensive School; Millfield School; West Glamorgan Institute of Higher Education; Birmingham University

Qualifications: 5 O-levels, 2 A-levels, NCA coaching awards

Off-season: Continuing MBA Business Administration at Birmingham University

Overseas tours: Welsh Cricket Association U18 to Barbados 1986; Welsh Schools U19 to Australia 1987-88; Glamorgan to Trinidad 1990; South Wales Cricket Association to New Zealand and Australia 1991-92; England A to India 1994-95

Overseas teams played for: Hirsh Crusaders, Durban 1992-98

Cricketers particularly admired: David Gower, Viv Richards

Young players to look out for: Ian Bell

Other sports followed: Football (West Ham United, Swansea City), golf

Injuries: Out for three weeks with a hamstring injury

Relaxations: Playing golf

Extras: Scored 258* for Wales v MCC 1991. In 1989 scored 104* and 101* for Welsh Schools U19 v Scottish Schools U19 and 120 and 102* v Irish Schools U19. Left Glamorgan at the end of the 1996 season and joined Warwickshire. Scored two 100s (138 and 114*) for Warwicks v Hants at Southampton 1997; Matthew Hayden scored a 200 and a 100 for Hants in the same match

Opinions on cricket: 'Reduce amount of cricket played, which would allow for more quality practice in between games. Bowlers would remain fairly fresh all season. Batters should become more disciplined because of less innings, which would hopefully raise standard and competitiveness of cricket played. Away captain should have choice of whether to bat or bowl. Cricketers are only as good as the surface they play on. Improve the wickets, which will improve the standard of players.'

Best batting: 157 Glamorgan v Gloucestershire, Abergavenny 1995

Best bowling: 3-23 Glamorgan v South Africa A, Cardiff 1996

1999 Season

	M	Inns	NO	Runs	HS	Avge	100s	50s	Ct	St	O	M	Runs	Wkts	Avge	Best	5wI	10wM
Test																		
All First	18	29	0	1014	144	34.96	2	6	11	-	21	5	71	1	71.00	1-18	-	-
1-day Int																		
NatWest	2	2	1	165	110 *	165.00	1	1	1	-								
B & H	1	1	0	56	56	56.00	-	1	-	-								
1-day Lge	13	13	2	336	83 *	30.54	-	2	6	-								

Career Performances

	M	Inns	NO	Runs	HS	Avge	100s	50s	Ct	St	Balls	Runs	Wkts	Avge	Best	5wI	10wM
Test																	
All First	127	219	17	6644	157	32.89	12	37	86	-	828	661	15	44.06	3-23	-	-
1-day Int																	
NatWest	16	15	2	704	112	54.15	3	3	4	-	48	43	1	43.00	1-40	-	
B & H	19	18	0	536	121	29.77	1	4	2	-	49	32	4	8.00	4-32	-	
1-day Lge	89	78	10	1437	83 *	21.13	-	7	42	-	74	86	3	28.66	2-43	-	

HEWITT, J. P.   Middlesex

Name: James Peter Hewitt
Role: Left-hand bat, right-arm
medium-fast bowler
Born: 26 February 1976, Southwark, London
Height: 6ft 3in **Weight:** 12st 8lbs
Nickname: Shoes, Hewey, Danny,
Bambi, Dumbo
County debut: 1995 (one-day),
1996 (first-class)
County cap: 1998
50 wickets in a season: 1
1st-Class 50s: 3
1st-Class 5 w. in innings: 5
1st-Class catches: 22
Place in batting averages: 230th av. 17.50
(1998 236th av. 15.76)
Place in bowling averages: 87th av. 29.20
(1998 111th av. 33.60)
Strike rate: 53.34 (career 48.94)
Parents: Gillian Underhay and Terry Hewitt
Marital status: Single
Family links with cricket: Father played club cricket and had trials with Surrey.
Grandfather 'played a bit'
Education: Buckingham Primary School, Hampton; Teddington Secondary School,
Middlesex; Richmond College; Kingston College; City of Westminster College
Qualifications: GCSEs; City and Guilds Part I, II and III in Recreation and Leisure;
GNVQ Leisure and Tourism; coaching awards in cricket (intermediate and advanced),
squash, basketball, hockey, gymnastics, badminton, football, volleyball, plus referee
qualifications; Community Sports Leadership Award
Overseas teams played for: Western Australia University 1997-98
Cricketers particularly admired: Richard Hadlee, David Gower, Curtly Ambrose,

Dominic Cork, Richard Johnson, Philip Hudson
Young players to look out for: Stephen Peters, Owais Shah, Paul Franks, Graeme Swann, Matthew Wood, 'and Angus Fraser'
Other sports played/followed: Athletics ('represented South of England at cross-country'), football ('played for Chelsea Youth'), badminton, volleyball, rugby (Harlequins)
Relaxations: Watching and playing a number of sports and sports quiz programmes
Extras: 'I was invited back to my old school, Teddington, to present the sports awards to the pupils – I consider this to be an honour'
Opinions on cricket: 'Teatime should be longer.'
Best batting: 75 Middlesex v Essex, Chelmsford 1997
Best bowling: 6-14 Middlesex v Glamorgan, Cardiff 1997

1999 Season

	M	Inns	NO	Runs	HS	Avge	100s	50s	Ct	St	O	M	Runs	Wkts	Avge	Best	5wl	10wM
Test																		
All First	13	21	1	350	49 *	17.50	-	-	6	-	311.1	69	1022	35	29.20	5-50	1	-
1-day Int																		
NatWest	1	1	0	5	5	5.00	-	-	1	-	6	0	26	1	26.00	1-26	-	
B & H																		
1-day Lge	9	5	2	40	13	13.33	-	-	3	-	51	1	250	9	27.77	2-23	-	

Career Performances

	M	Inns	NO	Runs	HS	Avge	100s	50s	Ct	St	Balls	Runs	Wkts	Avge	Best	5wl	10wM
Test																	
All First	56	76	11	1194	75	18.36	-	3	22	-	7831	4470	160	27.93	6-14	5	-
1-day Int																	
NatWest	5	3	2	23	14 *	23.00	-	-	2	-	234	174	3	58.00	1-26	-	
B & H	8	4	0	22	14	5.50	-	-	2	-	396	344	5	68.80	2-49	-	
1-day Lge	49	27	11	227	32 *	14.18	-	-	16	-	1779	1303	51	25.54	4-24	-	

HEWSON, D. R.   Gloucestershire

Name: Dominic Robert Hewson
Role: Right-hand bat, right-arm medium bowler
Born: 3 October 1974, Cheltenham
Height: 5ft 10in **Weight:** 13st
Nickname: Chopper
County debut: 1996
1st-Class 50s: 6

1st-Class catches: 12
Place in batting averages: 248th av. 14.40
(1998 159th av. 23.52)
Strike rate: (career 24.00)
Parents: Robert and Julie
Marital status: Single
Education: Cheltenham College; University
of West of England
Qualifications: 10 GCSEs, 3 A-levels
Cricketers particularly admired:
Jon Lewis, Jack Russell, Courtney Walsh,
Mark Snape
Young players to look out for: Jon Lewis,
Dom Hewson, Matt Windows,
Rob Cunliffe, Andrew Symonds
Other sports followed: Rugby, ice hockey,
Aussie Rules, football
Relaxations: Seeing friends

Extras: Made debut for Gloucestershire 2nd XI in July 1993
Best batting: 87 Gloucestershire v Hampshire, Southampton 1996
Best bowling: 1-7 Gloucestershire v Kent, Bristol 1998

1999 Season

	M	Inns	NO	Runs	HS	Avge	100s	50s	Ct	St	O	M	Runs	Wkts	Avge	Best	5wl	10wM
Test																		
All First	5	10	0	144	40	14.40	-	-	3	-	1	1	0	0	-	-	-	-
1-day Int																		
NatWest																		
B & H																		
1-day Lge	2	2	0	1	1	0.50	-	-	-	-								

Career Performances

	M	Inns	NO	Runs	HS	Avge	100s	50s	Ct	St	Balls	Runs	Wkts	Avge	Best	5wl	10wM
Test																	
All First	26	48	4	908	87	20.63	-	6	12	-	24	7	1	7.00	1-7	-	-
1-day Int																	
NatWest	2	2	0	57	45	28.50	-	-	1	-							
B & H																	
1-day Lge	7	4	0	29	25	7.25	-	-									

HICK, G. A.   Worcestershire

Name: Graeme Ashley Hick
Role: Right-hand bat, off-spin bowler, county captain
Born: 23 May 1966, Harare, Zimbabwe
Height: 6ft 3in **Weight:** 14st 7lbs
Nickname: Hicky, Ash
County debut: 1984
County cap: 1986
Benefit: 1999
Test debut: 1991
Tests: 54
One-Day Internationals: 96
1000 runs in a season: 15
1st-Class 50s: 118
1st-Class 100s: 97
1st-Class 200s: 9
1st-Class 300s: 1
1st-Class 400s: 1

1st-Class 5 w. in innings: 5
1st-Class 10 w. in match: 1
1st-Class catches: 474
One-Day 100s: 26
Place in batting averages: 12th av. 48.31 (1998 25th av. 43.46)
Strike rate: 73.20 (career 88.21)
Parents: John and Eve
Wife and date of marriage: Jackie, 5 October 1991
Children: Lauren Amy, 12 September 1992
Family links with cricket: Father has served on Zimbabwe Cricket Union Board of Control since 1984 and played representative cricket in Zimbabwe
Education: Banket Primary; Prince Edward Boys' High School, Zimbabwe
Qualifications: 4 O-levels, NCA coaching award
Off-season: England one-day squad to South Africa and Zimbabwe
Overseas tours: Zimbabwe to England (World Cup) 1983, to Sri Lanka 1983-84, to England 1985; England to New Zealand and Australia (World Cup) 1991-92, to India and Sri Lanka 1992-93, to West Indies 1993-94, to Australia 1994-95, to South Africa 1995-96, to India and Pakistan (World Cup) 1995-96, to Sharjah 1997-98, to West Indies 1997-98 (one-day series), to Bangladesh (Wills International Cup) 1998-99, to Australia 1998-99, to Sharjah (Coca-Cola Cup) 1998-99, to South Africa and Zimbabwe 1999-2000 (one-day series)
Overseas teams played for: Old Hararians, Zimbabwe 1982-90; Northern Districts, New Zealand 1987-89; Queensland, Australia 1990-91; Auckland 1997-98

Cricketers particularly admired: Duncan Fletcher (former Zimbabwe captain; now England coach) for approach and understanding of the game, David Houghton, Basil D'Oliveira

Other sports followed: Football (Liverpool FC), golf, tennis, squash, hockey

Relaxations: 'Leaning against Steve Rhodes at first slip'

Extras: Made first century aged six for school team. Youngest player participating in 1983 Prudential World Cup (aged 17); youngest player to represent Zimbabwe. Scored 1234 runs in Birmingham League and played for Worcestershire 2nd XI in 1984 – hitting six successive centuries. In 1986, at age 20, he became the youngest player to score 2000 runs in an English season. One of *Wisden*'s Five Cricketers of the Year 1987. In 1988 he made 405* v Somerset at Taunton, the highest individual score in England since 1895, and scored 1000 first-class runs by end of May, hitting a record 410 runs in April. In 1990 became youngest batsman ever to make 50 first-class centuries and scored 645 runs without being dismissed – a record for English cricket. Also in 1990 became the fastest to 10,000 runs in county cricket (179 innings). Qualified as an English player in 1991. Scored first Test century v India in Bombay 1992-93 and was England's leading batsman, bowler and fielder. Published *Hick 'n' Dilley Circus* and *A Champion's Diary*. Also played hockey for Zimbabwe. Finished third in the Whyte and Mackay batting ratings in 1995 and top of the first-class batting averages in 1997. Scored hundredth first-class 100 v Sussex at Worcester in 1998 with his second 100 of the match; at the age of 32, he became the second youngest player after Wally Hammond to score one hundred 100s; received an Individual Performance Award from the PCA in recognition of his achievement. Added late to the 1998-99 Ashes tour party as cover for Michael Atherton, remaining for the rest of the tour. Represented England in the 1999 World Cup. Scored two centuries in a match for the fourth time, v Essex at Chelmsford 1999; the second 100, his 108th, put him level with Zaheer Abbas at 15th in the all-time century-scoring list. Appointed captain of Worcestershire for 2000

Opinions on cricket: 'What a great game.'

Best batting: 405* Worcestershire v Somerset, Taunton 1988

Best bowling: 5-18 Worcestershire v Leicestershire, Worcester 1995

Stop press: Won One-Day International Man of the Match awards v Zimbabwe, the country of his birth, for his match-winning 87* at Bulawayo and his 80 and 5-33 at Harare, February 2000. Awarded England contract (Band B) for 2000

1999 Season

	M	Inns	NO	Runs	HS	Avge	100s	50s	Ct	St	O	M	Runs	Wkts	Avge	Best	5wI	10wM
Test	1	1	0	12	12	12.00	-	-	-	-	1	0	8	0	-	-	-	-
All First	13	22	0	1063	150	48.31	4	6	18	-	61	18	163	5	32.60	2-8	-	-
1-day Int	5	5	2	159	73 *	53.00	-	2	6	-	3	0	19	0	-	-	-	
NatWest	2	2	0	95	66	47.50	-	1	-	-	3	0	32	1	32.00	1-32	-	
B & H																		
1-day Lge	11	10	2	480	110 *	60.00	1	3	8	-	11.1	1	55	1	55.00	1-26	-	

Career Performances

	M	Inns	NO	Runs	HS	Avge	100s	50s	Ct	St	Balls	Runs	Wkts	Avge	Best	5wl	10wM
Test	54	94	6	3005	178	34.14	5	17	76	-	2985	1256	22	57.09	4-126	-	-
All First	382	628	60	31252	405 *	55.02	108	118	474	-	19583	9649	222	43.46	5-18	5	1
1-day Int	96	95	11	3271	126 *	38.94	5	22	51	-	973	804	21	38.28	3-41	-	
NatWest	38	38	6	1656	172 *	51.75	4	9	19	-	1211	748	23	32.52	4-54	-	
B & H	62	61	12	2717	127 *	55.44	7	18	38	-	732	562	12	46.83	3-36	-	
1-day Lge	193	185	33	7035	130	46.28	10	51	57	-	2536	2169	79	27.45	4-21	-	

HOCKLEY, J. B. Kent

Name: James Bernard Hockley
Role: Right-hand bat, off-spin bowler
Born: 16 April 1979, Stone Park, Beckenham
Height: 6ft 2in **Weight:** 13st
Nickname: Hockers, Ice, Casper, Ghost
County debut: 1998
Strike rate: 72.00 (career 72.00)
Parents: Bernard and Joan
Marital status: Single
Education: Churchfield Primary School, Beckenham; Kelsey Park School, Beckenham
Qualifications: 7 GCSEs, NCA coaching award
Career outside cricket: Working for Legal Aid Board
Off-season: Playing in Australia for Wests in Brisbane
Overseas tours: Kent to Jamaica
Overseas teams played for: Wests, Brisbane 1999-2000
Cricketers particularly admired: Ian Botham, Aravinda De Silva
Young players to look out for: Robert Key
Other sports played: Football, golf, tennis, rugby, snooker
Other sports followed: Football (Arsenal)
Relaxations: Watching TV; music, driving
Extras: AKCL Player of the Year Award in 1995. Equalled Trevor Ward's Kent U15 batting record with a total of 1,000 runs in the season. Kent Schools Player of the Year in 1996
Opinions on cricket: 'The 2nd XI Championship should be played over four days, to give the younger players the experience of playing the longer game.'
Best batting: 34 Kent v Gloucestershire, Canterbury 1999
Best bowling: 1-57 Kent v Gloucestershire, Canterbury 1999

1999 Season

	M	Inns	NO	Runs	HS	Avge	100s	50s	Ct	St	O	M	Runs	Wkts	Avge	Best	5wI	10wM
Test																		
All First	1	1	0	34	34	34.00	-	-	-	-	12	1	57	1	57.00	1-57	-	-
1-day Int																		
NatWest																			
B & H																			
1-day Lge	2	2	0	27	19	13.50	-	-	2	-								

Career Performances

	M	Inns	NO	Runs	HS	Avge	100s	50s	Ct	St	Balls	Runs	Wkts	Avge	Best	5wI	10wM
Test																	
All First	2	3	0	64	34	21.33	-	-	-	-	72	57	1	57.00	1-57	-	-
1-day Int																	
NatWest																		
B & H																			
1-day Lge	2	2	0	27	19	13.50	-	-	2	-							

HODGSON, T. P.   Essex

Name: Timothy Philip Hodgson
Role: Left-hand bat
Born: 27 March 1975, Guildford
Height: 5ft 10in **Weight:** 12st
Nickname: Jimmy Widges
County debut: 1996 (one-day),
1997 (first-class)
1st-Class 50s: 1
1st-Class catches: 4
One-Day 100s: 1
Place in batting averages: (1998 212th
av. 18.15)
Strike rate: 54.00 (career 54.00)
Parents: Simon and Vicky
Marital status: Single
Family links with cricket: 'Dad bowls leg-spin off 24 yards. Brother Jamie played for Cambridge University, Mark for Surrey 2nds and Charlie for England Schools U19'
Education: Milbourne Lodge, Esher; Wellington College, Berkshire; Durham University

Qualifications: GCSEs, A-levels, 2:2 in Sociology
Career outside cricket: 'Working for Sporting Index – spread betting'
Off-season: As above
Overseas tours: Wellington College to South Africa; Durham University to Vienna for European Indoor Cricket Championships
Overseas teams played for: Balmain DCC 1997-99
Cricketers particularly admired: Graham Gooch, Stuart Law, Peter Such
Young players to look out for: Graham Napier, Tim Phillips
Other sports played: 'Football in warm-ups – my finishing needs some work'
Other sports followed: Football (Southampton FC and Woking FC) and golf
Relaxations: 'Watching or playing most sports, spending time at home'
Extras: Shared in record first wicket partnership in second team (366). Played Surrey U12 to U19 and several second team games. Member of Wellington Cricketer Cup winning side in 1995. Member of Durham University's UAU winning side in 1995 and 1997. Set record for highest score on 'The Turf'(Wellington school ground) with 205 not out. Played for British Universities XI in 1997. Essex 2nd XI Player of the Year 1998. Released by Essex at end of 1999 season
Opinions on cricket: 'It would be nice to be able to have a drink with Aussie mates without constantly being reminded how bad we are. So, for me, the sooner we wake up to the idea of reducing the number of teams in England and concentrating the talent into regions the better. Unfortunately, there was more chance of me getting in the Essex 1st XI last year than that ever happening!'
Best batting: 54 Essex v Yorkshire, Scarborough 1998
Best bowling: 1-34 Essex v Oxford University, Chelmsford 1999

1999 Season

	M	Inns	NO	Runs	HS	Avge	100s	50s	Ct	St	O	M	Runs	Wkts	Avge	Best	5wI	10wM
Test																		
All First	1	1	0	24	24	24.00	-	-	-	-	9	2	34	1	34.00	1-34	-	-
1-day Int																		
NatWest																		
B & H																		
1-day Lge																		

Career Performances

	M	Inns	NO	Runs	HS	Avge	100s	50s	Ct	St	Balls	Runs	Wkts	Avge	Best	5wI	10wM
Test																	
All First	11	20	0	361	54	18.05	-	1	4	-	54	34	1	34.00	1-34	-	-
1-day Int																	
NatWest	1	1	0	2	2	2.00	-	-	-	-							
B & H	5	5	0	237	113	47.40	1	1	2	-							
1-day Lge	6	5	0	47	21	9.40	-	-									

HOGGARD, M. J. — Yorkshire

Name: Matthew James Hoggard
Role: Right-hand bat, right-arm
fast-medium bowler
Born: 31 December 1976, Leeds
Height: 6ft 2in **Weight:** 14st
Nickname: Hoggie, Mingh
County debut: 1996
1st-Class 5 w. in innings: 3
1st-Class catches: 6
Place in batting averages: 288th av. 6.62
(1998 292nd av. 5.00)
Place in bowling averages: 34th av. 22.10
(1998 28th av. 21.82)
Strike rate: 46.10 (career 45.52)
Parents: Margaret and John
('Mum and Dad')
Marital status: Single
Education: Lowtown Junior and Infants;

Pudsey Grangefield; Pudsey Grangefield Sixth Form
Qualifications: GCSEs and A-levels
Career outside cricket: 'Beer taster'
Off-season: In South Africa playing for Free State as the overseas professional
Overseas tours: England U19 to Zimbabwe 1995-96; Yorkshire CCC to South Africa
Overseas teams played for: Pirates, Johannesburg 1994-96; Free State 1998-2000
Cricketers particularly admired: Viv Richards, Ian Botham, Allan Donald
Young players to look out for: Matthew Wood
Other sports played: Rugby
Other sports followed: Rugby league (Leeds Rhinos)
Injuries: Out for three months with torn cartilage in the right knee
Relaxations: 'Walking my dog'
Extras: Joined England U19 tour to Zimbabwe as a replacement in 1995-96
Opinions on cricket: 'No comment.'
Best batting: 21 Yorkshire v Somerset, Taunton 1999
Best bowling: 5-47 Yorkshire v Derbyshire, Derby 1999

1999 Season

	M	Inns	NO	Runs	HS	Avge	100s	50s	Ct	St	O	M	Runs	Wkts	Avge	Best	5wI	10wM
Test																		
All First	8	11	3	53	21	6.62	-	-	2	-	215.1	58	619	28	22.10	5-47	1	-
1-day Int																		
NatWest	1	0	0	0	0	-	-	-	-	-	5	1	6	0	-		-	-
B & H	2	0	0	0	0	-	-	-	-	-	14.1	2	52	3	17.33	2-31	-	
1-day Lge	3	2	2	3	2*	-	-	-	-	-	23	2	117	4	29.25	2-45	-	

Career Performances

	M	Inns	NO	Runs	HS	Avge	100s	50s	Ct	St	Balls	Runs	Wkts	Avge	Best	5wI	10wM
Test																	
All First	23	30	9	126	21	6.00	-	-	6	-	4052	2021	89	22.70	5-47	3	-
1-day Int																	
NatWest	1	0	0	0	0	-	-	-	-	-	30	6	0	-		-	-
B & H	2	0	0	0	0	-	-	-	-	-	85	52	3	17.33	2-31	-	
1-day Lge	5	4	2	4	2*	2.00	-	-	-	-	192	150	6	25.00	2-12	-	

HOLLIOAKE, A. J.   Surrey

Name: Adam John Hollioake
Role: Right-hand bat, right-arm
medium-fast bowler, county captain
Born: 5 September 1971,
Melbourne, Australia
Height: 5ft 11in **Weight:** 13st 4lbs
Nickname: Smokey, Smokin' Joe, Wolf,
Rock, Rambo, Holly, Strong Dance,
Millionaire, Oaky, The Oak, Hokey Cokey,
Abo, Bong, Stumpy, Raj Maru, Gatt, Judgy
County debut: 1992 (one-day),
1993 (first-class)
County cap: 1995
Test debut: 1997
Tests: 4
One-Day Internationals: 35
1000 runs in a season: 2
1st-Class 50s: 35
1st-Class 100s: 13
1st-Class 5 w. in innings: 1
1st-Class catches: 88

One-Day 5 w. in innings: 3
Place in batting averages: 79th av. 33.37 (1998 68th av. 34.20)
Strike rate: 58.16 (career 72.73)
Parents: John and Daria
Marital status: Single
Family links with cricket: 'Brother Ben tries to play but is far too skinny to really progress any further'
Education: St Joseph's College, Sydney; St Patrick's College, Ballarat, Australia; St George's School, Weybridge; Surrey Tutorial College, Guildford
Qualifications: 'Some GCSEs and A-levels'
Overseas tours: School trip to Zimbabwe; Surrey YC to Australia; England YC to New Zealand 1990-91; England A to Australia 1996-97; England to Sharjah (Champions Trophy) 1997-98, to West Indies 1997-98, to Bangladesh (Wills International Cup) 1998-99, to Australia (CUB Series) 1998-99, to Sharjah (Coca-Cola Cup) 1998-99
Overseas teams played for: Fremantle, Western Australia 1990-91; North Shore, Sydney 1992-93; Geelong, Victoria; North Perth, Western Australia 1995-97
Cricketers particularly admired: Steve Waugh, 'anyone who gives 100 per cent'
Young players to look out for: Alex Tudor
Other sports followed: Rugby, boxing, Aussie Rules football, American football, 'chess and mind games'
Extras: Played rugby for London Counties, Middlesex and South of England as well as having a trial for England U18. Scored a century on first-class debut against Derbyshire. Surrey Young Player of the Year 1993. Scored fastest ever one-day 50 – in 15 balls v Yorkshire. Surrey Supporters' Player of the Year 1996 and Surrey Players' Player of the Year 1996. Captained the England A side on their 1996-97 tour to Australia. His 39 wickets in the Sunday league in 1996 was a record for the competition. Man of the Match in the first One-Day International against Australia at Headingley in 1997. Along with brother Ben became the first brothers to make their England Test debut together this century in the fifth Test against Australia at Trent Bridge 1997. Captained England in the 1997 Hong Kong Sixes tournament in which England finished runners-up to Pakistan. Captained England in Champions Trophy in Sharjah in 1997, in one-day series v West Indies 1997-98, in the Texaco Trophy one-day series v South Africa 1998 and in the Wills International Cup in Bangladesh 1998-99. Represented England in the 1999 World Cup. Is contracted to Surrey until 2003
Opinions on cricket: 'Boundaries are too small and outfields are too short – it is too easy to score runs. How come everyone in England knows we are playing too much quantity and not enough quality cricket, but no one has the balls to do anything about it?'
Best batting: 182 Surrey v Middlesex, Lord's 1997
Best bowling: 5-62 Surrey v Glamorgan, Swansea 1998

1999 Season

	M	Inns	NO	Runs	HS	Avge	100s	50s	Ct	St	O	M	Runs	Wkts	Avge	Best	5wI	10wM
Test																		
All First	13	18	2	534	116	33.37	1	3	8	-	58.1	10	220	6	36.66	1-7	-	-
1-day Int	3	1	0	6	6	6.00	-	-	-	-	18	0	90	1	90.00	1-21	-	
NatWest	4	2	0	5	5	2.50	-	-	1	-	8	0	54	3	18.00	2-2	-	
B & H	1	1	0	32	32	32.00	-	-	-	-	6	0	43	0	-	-	-	
1-day Lge	12	12	0	226	45	18.83	-	-	1	-	53.2	5	300	11	27.27	3-47	-	

Career Performances

	M	Inns	NO	Runs	HS	Avge	100s	50s	Ct	St	Balls	Runs	Wkts	Avge	Best	5wI	10wM
Test	4	6	0	65	45	10.83	-	-	4	-	144	67	2	33.50	2-31	-	-
All First	110	169	16	6091	182	39.81	13	35	88	-	7055	3875	97	39.94	5-62	1	-
1-day Int	35	30	6	606	83 *	25.25	-	3	13	-	1208	1019	32	31.84	4-23	-	
NatWest	19	15	2	438	88	33.69	-	3	9	-	650	500	17	29.41	4-53	-	
B & H	29	23	3	622	85	31.10	-	4	10	-	1028	921	28	32.89	4-34	-	
1-day Lge	98	88	10	1956	93	25.07	-	9	20	-	3334	3207	139	23.07	5-38	3	

HOLLIOAKE, B. C.   Surrey

Name: Ben Caine Hollioake
Role: Right-hand bat, right-arm
fast-medium bowler, 'a new generation of
gully fielder'
Born: 11 November 1977,
Melbourne, Australia
Height: 6ft 2in **Weight:** 14st
Nickname: Pely, Big Dog, Bedroom Bully
County debut: 1996
County cap: 1999
Test debut: 1997
Tests: 2
One-Day Internationals: 7
1st-Class 50s: 10
1st-Class 100s: 2
1st-Class 5 w. in innings: 1
1st-Class catches: 41
One-Day 5 w. in innings: 1
Place in batting averages: 131st av. 26.90 (1998 185th av. 20.39)
Place in bowling averages: 119th av. 34.82 (1998 48th av. 25.22)
Strike rate: 65.17 (career 54.58)

Parents: John and Daria

Marital status: Single

Family links with cricket: 'Dad played for Victoria; brother plays for Surrey and England'

Education: Edgarley Hall; Millfield School; Wesley College, Perth, Western Australia; 'Joey Benjamin's house'

Qualifications: 'A couple of GCSEs and NCA coaching award'

Off-season: In Perth, Australia

Overseas tours: Millfield to Zimbabwe 1992; West of England to West Indies 1992; England U19 to Pakistan 1996-97; England A to Kenya and Sri Lanka 1997-98; England VI to Hong Kong 1997; England to Sharjah (Champions Trophy) 1997-98, to West Indies 1997-98 (one-day series), to Australia 1998-99

Overseas teams played for: Melville, Perth 1992-95; North Perth 1996-97; South Perth 1999-2000

Cricketers particularly admired: 'Waqar, Wasim, Saqlain, Waugh Bros, Graham Dilley'

Young players to look out for: Ian Bishop, Carl Greenidge ('for more than one reason')

Other sports played: Golf ('First of three holes-in-one at the Belfry 10th 1996'), 'goat racing'

Other sports followed: Football (Chelsea), Aussie Rules (West Coast Eagles)

Injuries: Out for last month of season with torn calf

Relaxations: Listening to music and 'spending time with the "Praying Mantis"'

Extras: Played England U14 and U15. Played Western Australia U17 and U19. Became the youngest player to take five wickets in a Sunday League game when he took 5-10 v Derbyshire at The Oval in 1996. His first two appearances at Lord's both resulted in him winning Man of the Match awards – his 63 off 48 balls in the third One-Day International against Australia in 1997 (his England one-day debut) and his 98 off 113 balls for Surrey against Kent in the Benson and Hedges Cup final in 1997. Became the youngest player (aged 19) to make his Test debut for England since Brian Close in 1949 and he and brother Adam became the first brothers to make their Test debuts together for England this century. Played for England during the 1997 Hong Kong Sixes tournament in which they finished runners-up to Pakistan. Was voted the Young Cricketer of the Year by both the Cricket Writers' Club and the PCA in 1997. Scored 100s (103 and 163) for England A in the second and third 'Tests' v Sri Lanka A 1997-98. Awarded Surrey cap 1999. Is contracted to Surrey until 2001

Opinions on cricket: 'England is approaching a golden era.'

Best batting: 163 England A v Sri Lanka A, Moratuwa 1997-98

Best bowling: 5-51 Surrey v Glamorgan, The Oval 1999

1999 Season

	M	Inns	NO	Runs	HS	Avge	100s	50s	Ct	St	O	M	Runs	Wkts	Avge	Best	5wI	10wM
Test																		
All First	13	20	0	538	71	26.90	-	4	12	-	249.5	49	801	23	34.82	5-51	1	-
1-day Int																		
NatWest	4	3	0	37	26	12.33	-	-	3	-	26	2	130	2	65.00	1-35	-	
B & H	1	1	0	33	33	33.00	-	-	-	-	2	0	17	0	-	-	-	
1-day Lge	11	11	0	244	48	22.18	-	-	3	-	66	4	293	12	24.41	3-31	-	

Career Performances

	M	Inns	NO	Runs	HS	Avge	100s	50s	Ct	St	Balls	Runs	Wkts	Avge	Best	5wI	10wM
Test	2	4	0	44	28	11.00	-	-	2	-	252	199	4	49.75	2-105	-	-
All First	53	81	5	2066	163	27.18	2	10	41	-	5786	3277	106	30.91	5-51	1	-
1-day Int	7	6	0	122	63	20.33	-	1	1	-	150	122	2	61.00	2-43	-	
NatWest	10	7	0	95	33	13.57	-	-	6	-	432	324	8	40.50	2-28	-	
B & H	17	15	1	507	98	36.21	-	4	2	-	693	629	20	31.45	3-23	-	
1-day Lge	45	40	3	660	61	17.83	-	1	13	-	1566	1348	52	25.92	5-10	1	

HOLLOWAY, P. C. L.   Somerset

Name: Piran Christopher Laity Holloway
Role: Left-hand bat, off-spin bowler, wicket-keeper
Born: 1 October 1970, Helston, Cornwall
Height: 5ft 8in **Weight:** 11st 5lbs
Nickname: Oggy, Leg, Piras
County debut: 1988 (Warwickshire), 1994 (Somerset)
County cap: 1997 (Somerset)
1st-Class 50s: 23
1st-Class 100s: 8
1st-Class catches: 70
1st-Class stumpings: 1
One-Day 100s: 2
Place in batting averages: 87th av. 32.18 (1998 142nd av. 24.96)
Parents: Chris and Mary
Marital status: 'Engaged to the lovely Nikki'
Family links with cricket: 'Mum and Dad are keen'
Education: Nansloe CP School, Helston; Millfield School; Taunton School; Loughborough University

Qualifications: 7 O-levels, 2 A-levels, BSc (Hons) Sports Science
Career outside cricket: Coaching
Off-season: 'Setting up cricket coaching schemes in schools; also coaching for other clubs, counties etc'
Overseas tours: Millfield School to Barbados 1986; England YC to Australia 1989-90; Warwickshire CCC to Cape Town 1992 and 1993; Somerset CCC to Holland 1994
Overseas teams played for: North Perth, 1993-94; Nedlands, Perth 1994-96; Claremont Nedlands 1996-98
Cricketers particularly admired: Ian Botham, David Gower
Young players to look out for: Matt Bulbeck, Steve Harmison
Other sports followed: Squash, football, rugby, tennis, surfing
Relaxations: Music, surfing, travel
Extras: Won the Jack Hobbs Trophy in 1990. Played Young England for three years. Was fourth in the county averages in 1991. Somerset Young Player of the Year 1995. Scored the most runs in A-grade cricket in Perth in 1997-98 season in which Claremont Nedlands won the Bank West Cup
Opinions on cricket: 'Too many (Championship) games in a season, especially when you still have to play the tourists etc. This limits the standard of competition, due to tiredness etc. There should also be a mercy law allowing the game to be called off at tea on the last day, to prevent the hour of joke bowling before the game is abandoned as a draw. The pitch inspection system is not working in my opinion. I think there should be points deducted more frequently, not only if a pitch is too dangerous but also if sides prepare feather beds to ensure draws. I also think that there should be a salary cap on county contracts well below that of the Test side to encourage young talent to improve and make the step up to Test cricket. I also believe a core of centrally contracted players will be a benefit to the Test side.'
Best batting: 168 Somerset v Middlesex, Uxbridge 1996

1999 Season

	M	Inns	NO	Runs	HS	Avge	100s	50s	Ct	St	O	M	Runs	Wkts	Avge	Best	5wl	10wM
Test																		
All First	19	32	5	869	114 *	32.18	2	5	9	-								
1-day Int																		
NatWest	5	5	1	258	79	64.50	-	2	3	-								
B & H																		
1-day Lge	15	15	4	645	101 *	58.63	1	6	4	-								

Career Performances

	M	Inns	NO	Runs	HS	Avge	100s	50s	Ct	St	Balls	Runs	Wkts	Avge	Best	5wl	10wM
Test																	
All First	94	159	26	4414	168	33.18	8	23	70	1	40	46	0	-	-	-	-
1-day Int																	
NatWest	13	12	3	504	90	56.00	-	4	7	1							
B & H	7	7	1	67	27	11.16	-	-	7	-							
1-day Lge	79	70	15	1665	117	30.27	2	10	33	7							

HOUSE, W. J. Sussex

Name: William John House
Role: Left-hand bat, right-arm
medium bowler (all-rounder)
Born: 16 March 1976, Sheffield
Height: 5ft 11in **Weight:** 13st
Nickname: Wendy, Curry, Housey
County debut: 1997 (Kent)
1st-Class 50s: 7
1st-Class 100s: 2
1st-Class catches: 16
One-Day 5 w. in innings: 1
Place in batting averages: (1998 108th
av. 29.27)
Strike rate: (career 415.66)
Parents: Bill and Anna
Marital status: Single
Family links with cricket: 'Dad played
Yorkshire League'
Education: British School in the Netherlands, The Hague; Sevenoaks School;
University of Cambridge (Gonville and Caius College)
Qualifications: 11 GCSEs, International Baccalaureate, NCA coaching award
Career outside cricket: Teaching/business
Overseas tours: MCC to Bangladesh 1999-2000
Overseas teams played for: Royal Hague CC 1985-89; University CC, Adelaide
1994-95
Cricketers particularly admired: Ian Botham, David Gower
Young players to look out for: Robert Key, Anurag Singh
Other sports played: Rugby (Cambridge University U21 XV 1996-97), football
(Cambridge Blue 1998)
Other sports followed: Rugby, football (Sheffield Wednesday), golf
Relaxations: Music, history

Extras: Cricket Society's leading all-rounder in schools cricket in 1993. Kent CCC's Most Improved Player 1996. Cambridge University's Player of the Year 1996 and 1998. Benson and Hedges Gold Awards for British Universities v Surrey 1997 (93 runs), v Gloucestershire 1998 (5-34). Left Kent at end of 1999 season and has joined Sussex for 2000 on a two-year contract

Best batting: 136 Cambridge University v Derbyshire, Fenner's 1996
Best bowling: 1-34 Cambridge University v Oxford University, Lord's 1998

1999 Season

	M	Inns	NO	Runs	HS	Avge	100s	50s	Ct	St	O	M	Runs	Wkts	Avge	Best	5wI	10wM
Test																		
All First	1	1	1	22	22*	-	-	-	-	-	6	0	12	0	-	-	-	-
1-day Int																		
NatWest	1	1	0	15	15	15.00	-	-	-	-	4	0	23	0	-	-	-	
B & H																		
1-day Lge	10	10	0	230	49	23.00	-	-	1	-	1	0	12	0	-	-	-	

Career Performances

	M	Inns	NO	Runs	HS	Avge	100s	50s	Ct	St	Balls	Runs	Wkts	Avge	Best	5wI	10wM
Test																	
All First	27	41	7	1201	136	35.32	2	7	16	-	1247	843	3	281.00	1-34	-	-
1-day Int																	
NatWest	1	1	0	15	15	15.00	-	-	-	-	24	23	0	-	-	-	
B & H	11	11	0	314	93	28.54	-	2	3	-	89	96	5	19.20	5-58	1	
1-day Lge	21	17	1	321	49	20.06	-	-	2	-	51	54	1	54.00	1-4	-	

48. Which international all-rounder took 8-53 v Essex before lunch on his 20th birthday in 1991?

HUMPHRIES, S.   Sussex

Name: Shaun Humphries
Role: Right-hand bat, right-arm 'filth'
bowler, wicket-keeper
Born: 11 January 1973, Horsham,
West Sussex
Height: 5ft 11in **Weight:** 10st 7lbs
Nickname: Stan, Gooner
County debut: 1993
1st-Class 50s: 2
1st-Class catches: 52
1st-Class stumpings: 2
Place in batting averages: 266th av. 11.00
(1998 254th av. 13.61)
Parents: Peter John and Marilyn Christine
Marital status: Engaged
Family links with cricket: Parents avid
watchers

Education: The Weald School, Billingshurst;
Kingston College of Further Education
Qualifications: 5 GCSEs, BTEC National Diploma in Leisure Studies
Career outside cricket: 'Looking for one; any offers, please write to Sussex CCC'
Off-season: 'Following the Arsenal, looking after the "missus", travelling to Vegas'
Overseas tours: Sussex U13 to Barbados 1987; Sussex U18 to India 1990-91; Keith
Greenfield Malaga Tour 1994-95
Overseas teams played for: Sutherland CC, Sydney 1994-95
Cricketers particularly admired: Peter Moores, Alec Stewart, John Berry,
Geoff Kirkham, Ian Healy, Nick 'the Ledge', Mark Hamilton
Young players to look out for: 'Any one of Dr Dew's production line'
Other sports played: 9-ball pool, golf ('v. poorly')
Other sports followed: 'Watching the Arsenal', cycling, rugby league
(Cronulla Sharks)
Injuries: 'Usual wicket-keepers' niggles'
Relaxations: 'Music, Kate, PlayStation'
Opinions on cricket: 'The mercenary godfathers are changing cricket forever. Beware
the wolf in sheep's clothing!'
Best batting: 66 Sussex v Kent, Tunbridge Wells 1998

1999 Season

	M	Inns	NO	Runs	HS	Avge	100s	50s	Ct	St	O	M	Runs	Wkts	Avge	Best	5wI	10wM
Test																		
All First	11	18	2	176	57	11.00	-	1	18	2								
1-day Int																		
NatWest	2	1	0	1	1	1.00	-	-	2	1								
B & H	2	1	0	0	0	0.00	-	-	1	1								
1-day Lge	13	4	0	18	8	4.50	-	-	8	6								

Career Performances

	M	Inns	NO	Runs	HS	Avge	100s	50s	Ct	St	Balls	Runs	Wkts	Avge	Best	5wI	10wM
Test																	
All First	29	43	4	514	66	13.17	-	2	52	2							
1-day Int																	
NatWest	3	2	0	11	10	5.50	-	-	4	1							
B & H	3	2	0	16	16	8.00	-	-	2	1							
1-day Lge	25	11	3	58	13	7.25	-	-	15	11							

HUNT, T. A.   Middlesex

Name: Thomas Aaron Hunt
Role: Right-hand bat, right-arm
medium-fast bowler
Born: 19 January 1982, Melbourne, Australia
Height: 6ft 3in **Weight:** 13st
Nickname: Thos
County debut: No first-team appearance
Parents: Jennifer Hunt and Tim Woodbridge
Marital status: Single
Education: Brackenberry, Hammersmith;
Acton High; St Clement Danes
Qualifications: 7 GCSEs, 1 A-level, 1st level
coaching award
Off-season: 'Hope to play a club season in
Australia, New Zealand or South Africa.
Other than that, relax and stay fit'
Cricketers particularly admired:
Curtly Ambrose, Sachin Tendulkar,
Michael Holding, Allan Donald, Brian Lara
Other sports played: Football (Pitshanger FC and school), golf, basketball
Other sports followed: Football (Man Utd), basketball (LA Lakers)

Injuries: Out for two years with a knee injury
Relaxations: 'Relaxing with friends; music (House and Garage, EZ)'

HUNTER, I. D. Durham

Name: Ian David Hunter
Role: Right-hand bat, right-arm medium-fast bowler
Born: 11 September 1979, Dryburn Hospital, Durham
Height: 6ft 2in **Weight:** 11st 10lbs
Nickname: Hunts, Sticks
County debut: 1999 (one-day)
Parents: Ken and Linda
Marital status: Single
Family links with cricket: Brother plays for local village side
Education: Sacriston Junior School; Fyndoune Community College, Sacriston; New College, Durham
Qualifications: 9 GCSEs, 1 A-level (PE), BTEC National Diploma in Sports Science
Overseas tours: Durham U21 to Sri Lanka 1996
Cricketers particularly admired: Glenn McGrath, Jacques Kallis
Young players to look out for: Ian Bell, John Sadler
Other sports followed: Football (Newcastle United FC), athletics
Relaxations: Snooker, socialising with friends
Extras: Set a new Durham best analysis for the 2nd XI Championship with his 11-155 v Lancashire 2nd XI 1999. Represented England U19 in 'Test' series v Australia U19 1999
Opinions on cricket: 'Too much one-day cricket played and not enough three- and four-day cricket. Good idea to split County Championship into two divisions (make it more competitive!).'

1999 Season

	M	Inns	NO	Runs	HS	Avge	100s	50s	Ct	St	O	M	Runs	Wkts	Avge	Best	5wI	10wM
Test																		
All First																			
1-day Int																			
NatWest																			
B & H																			
1-day Lge	4	2	0	7	4	3.50	-	-	-	-	32.1	1	132	4	33.00	2-34	-	

Career Performances

	M	Inns	NO	Runs	HS	Avge	100s	50s	Ct	St	Balls	Runs	Wkts	Avge	Best	5wI	10wM
Test																	
All First																	
1-day Int																	
NatWest																	
B & H																	
1-day Lge	4	2	0	7	4	3.50	-	-	-	-	193	132	4	33.00	2-34	-	

HUSSAIN, N.   Essex

Name: Nasser Hussain
Role: Right-hand bat, county captain
Born: 28 March 1968, Madras, India
Height: 6ft **Weight:** 12st 7lbs
Nickname: Nashwan
County debut: 1987
County cap: 1989
Benefit: 1999
Test debut: 1989-90
Tests: 42
One-Day Internationals: 33
1000 runs in a season: 5
1st-Class 50s: 79
1st-Class 100s: 40
1st-Class 200s: 1
1st-Class catches: 296
One-Day 100s: 5
Place in batting averages: 7th av. 52.00
(1998 94th av. 31.10)
Strike rate: (career 138.00)
Parents: Joe and Shireen
Wife and date of marriage: Karen, 24 September 1993
Family links with cricket: Father played zonal cricket in India. Played for Madras in Ranji Trophy 1966-67. Brother Mel played for Hampshire. Brother Abbas played for Essex 2nd XI
Education: Forest School, Snaresbrook; Durham University
Qualifications: 10 O-levels, 3 A-levels; BSc (Hons) in Natural Sciences; NCA cricket coaching award
Off-season: Touring South Africa and Zimbabwe with England
Overseas tours: England YC to Sri Lanka 1986-87, to Australia (Youth World Cup) 1987-88; England A to Pakistan and Sri Lanka 1990-91, to Bermuda and West Indies

1991-92, to Pakistan 1995-96 (captain); England to India (Nehru Cup) 1989-90, to West Indies 1989-90, to West Indies 1993-94, to Zimbabwe and New Zealand 1996-97, to West Indies 1997-98, to Australia 1998-99, to South Africa and Zimbabwe 1999-2000 (captain)

Overseas teams played for: Madras 1986-87; Petersham, Sydney 1992-93; Adelaide University 1990; Stellenbosch University, South Africa 1994-95; Primrose, Cape Town; Petersham, Sydney

Cricketers particularly admired: Mark Waugh, Graham Gooch, Sachin Tendulkar

Young players to look out for: Stephen Peters, Ian Flanagan

Other sports played: Golf (10 handicap), football

Other sports followed: Football (Leeds United)

Relaxations: Listening to music. Listening to Mark Ilott. Watching television

Extras: Played for England Schools U15 for two years (one as captain). Became youngest player to play for Essex Schools U11 at the age of eight and U15 at the age of 12. At 15, was considered the best young leg-break bowler in the country. Cricket Writers' Club Young Cricketer of the Year, 1989. Set records for third (347* v Lancashire at Ilford 1992), fourth (314 v Surrey at The Oval 1991) and fifth (316 v Leicestershire at Leicester 1991) wicket partnerships for Essex (with Mark Waugh, Salim Malik and Mike Garnham respectively). Essex Player of the Year 1993. Appointed Essex's vice-captain 1996. Captained the England A tour to Pakistan in 1995-96. Finished 2nd in the Whyte and Mackay batting ratings in 1995. Appointed England's vice-captain in 1996-97. Appointed Essex's captain for 1999. Represented England in the 1999 World Cup, having been drafted into the squad as replacement for the injured Michael Atherton. Appointed England captain after 1999 World Cup

Opinions on cricket: 'Too much soft cricket. Quality not quantity. Better one-day wickets, especially in September at Lord's.'

Best batting: 207 England v Australia, Edgbaston 1997

Best bowling: 1-38 Essex v Worcestershire, Kidderminster 1992

Stop press: Topped England batting averages in the Test series v South Africa with 370 runs at 61.66. Awarded England contract (Band A) for 2000

1999 Season

	M	Inns	NO	Runs	HS	Avge	100s	50s	Ct	St	O	M	Runs	Wkts	Avge	Best	5wl	10wM
Test	3	5	0	164	61	32.80	-	1	3	-								
All First	12	20	1	988	143	52.00	2	8	13	-								
1-day Int	5	5	2	194	88 *	64.66	-	2	2	-								
NatWest	1	1	0	38	38	38.00	-	-	1	-								
B & H																		
1-day Lge	8	8	0	375	114	46.87	1	3	7	-								

Career Performances

	M	Inns	NO	Runs	HS	Avge	100s	50s	Ct	St	Balls	Runs	Wkts	Avge	Best	5wI	10wM
Test	42	76	6	2604	207	37.20	7	11	34	-							
All First	251	405	39	15939	207	43.54	41	79	296	-	276	307	2	153.50	1-38	-	-
1-day Int	33	33	7	743	93	28.57	-	4	16	-							
NatWest	26	24	3	895	108	42.61	2	4	18	-							
B & H	47	42	8	1654	118	48.64	2	15	21	-							
1-day Lge	137	126	18	3408	114	31.55	1	22	60	-							

HUTCHISON, P. M. Yorkshire

Name: Paul Michael Hutchison
Role: Left-hand 'stonewall' bat, left-arm
fast-medium swing bowler
Born: 9 June 1977, Leeds
Height: 6ft 3in **Weight:** 12st 2lbs
Nickname: Hutch
County debut: 1996
County cap: 1998
50 wickets in a season: 1
1st-Class 5 w. in innings: 7
1st-Class 10 w. in match: 1
1st-Class catches: 6
Place in batting averages: (1998 233rd
av. 15.87)
Place in bowling averages: 17th av. 20.23
(1998 41st av. 24.27)
Strike rate: 30.38 (career 41.38)
Parents: David Hutchison and Rita Laycock
Marital status: Engaged to Emma
Family links with cricket: 'Brother Richard played a bit for Pudsey St Lawrence in
the Bradford League'
Education: Pudsey Greenside; Pudsey Crawshaw High; Yorkshire Cricket School
Qualifications: 8 GCSEs, sports leadership coaching award, GNVQ Leisure and
Tourism, qualified cricket coach
Career outside cricket: 'No thanks!!'
Off-season: 'Couple of holidays, train hard and play on my PlayStation'
Overseas tours: England U19 to Zimbabwe 1995-96; England A to Kenya and Sri
Lanka 1997-98, to Zimbabwe and South Africa 1998-99; Yorkshire CCC to Zimbabwe
and Botswana 1996, to South Africa 1998, 1999, to Australia 2000
Cricketers particularly admired: Neil Fairbrother, Matt Maynard
Young players to look out for: Gary Fellows, Ry Robinson

Other sports played: Golf, football
Other sports followed: Football (Leeds United), rugby league (Leeds Rhinos)
Injuries: Out for five months with a bad back
Relaxations: 'My PlayStation, cinema, eating out, socialising with friends'
Extras: Represented England at U17, U18 and U19 levels. Played for Pudsey St Lawrence in the Bradford League. Had a place at the Yorkshire Academy. Took 7 for 50 on county debut against Hampshire at Portsmouth, only bettered by Wilfred Rhodes 99 years previously. Took 7 for 38 on first first-class appearance of 1997, against Pakistan A. Voted Wombwell Cricket Lovers' Young Player of the Year for 1997. Returned early from England A tour of Zimbabwe and South Africa with a back injury. Took 6-35 v Worcestershire at Headingley on his return to Championship cricket in August 1999
Opinions on cricket: 'The standard of Championship wickets needs to improve a lot to help both batters and bowlers when they take the step up to Test match cricket. Two divisions and floodlit cricket is a good step in the right direction.'
Best batting: 30 Yorkshire v Essex, Scarborough 1998
Best bowling: 7-31 Yorkshire v Sussex, Hove 1998

1999 Season

	M	Inns	NO	Runs	HS	Avge	100s	50s	Ct	St	O	M	Runs	Wkts	Avge	Best	5wI	10wM
Test																		
All First	3	4	3	6	4 *	6.00	-	-	-	-	65.5	16	263	13	20.23	6-35	1	-
1-day Int																		
NatWest	1	0	0	0	0	-	-	-	-	-	8	1	38	2	19.00	2-38	-	
B & H	1	1	1	2	2 *	-	-	-	-	-	5	0	30	3	10.00	3-30	-	
1-day Lge	3	1	1	2	2 *	-	-	-	-	-	25.3	3	96	5	19.20	3-30	-	

Career Performances

	M	Inns	NO	Runs	HS	Avge	100s	50s	Ct	St	Balls	Runs	Wkts	Avge	Best	5wI	10wM
Test																	
All First	34	34	20	175	30	12.50	-	-	6	-	5463	2918	132	22.10	7-31	7	1
1-day Int																	
NatWest	3	1	1	4	4 *	-	-	-	-	-	132	62	5	12.40	3-18	-	
B & H	6	2	2	6	4 *	-	-	-	-	-	191	112	10	11.20	3-14	-	
1-day Lge	15	6	3	7	2 *	2.33	-	-	1	-	593	427	16	26.68	4-34	-	

HUTTON, B. L.   Middlesex

Name: Benjamin Leonard Hutton
Role: Left-hand opening bat, right-arm
medium bowler; all-rounder
Born: 29 January 1977,
Johannesburg, South Africa
Height: 6ft 2in **Weight:** 12st
Nickname: Gibbs, Gibbo
County debut: 1999
1st-Class 50s: 2
1st-Class catches: 5
Place in batting averages: 180th av. 22.06
Strike rate: 108.00 (career 128.00)
Parents: Richard and Charmaine
Marital status: Single

Family links with cricket: Son of Richard
(Yorkshire and England) and grandson of Sir
Leonard (Yorkshire and England)
Education: Holmwood House Prep School;
Radley College; Durham University
Qualifications: 10 GCSEs, 3 A-levels, BA (Hons) Social Sciences, NCA
coaching award
Off-season: 'Worked in a health club 1999-2000 winter'
Overseas tours: Durham University to Zimbabwe 1997-98; Middlesex to Portugal
1997
Overseas teams played for: Wanderers CC, Johannesburg 1995-96; Pirates CC,
Johannesburg 1995-96
Cricketers particularly admired: Sir Leonard Hutton, Michael Atherton,
Justin Langer, Angus Fraser
Young players to look out for: Ed Joyce
Other sports played: Golf (12 handicap), rackets
Other sports followed: Football (Chelsea)
Relaxations: 'Running, reading and betting (spread)'
Extras: BUSA Halifax medal 1997. Palatinate at Durham University. 'Deposited into
mobile lavatory by Chris Adams at Arundel following no ball fiasco.' Opened for
Middlesex v Essex at Southend 1999 with Andrew Strauss, his former opening partner
at Radley. Played in Durham University's BUSA Championship winning side 1999
Opinions on cricket: 'Follow the example of any Australian Test cricketer for their
dedication, will to succeed and extraordinary self-belief.'
Best batting: 59 Middlesex v Nottinghamshire, Southgate 1999
Best bowling: 2-100 British Universities v New Zealand, The Parks 1999

1999 Season

	M	Inns	NO	Runs	HS	Avge	100s	50s	Ct	St	O	M	Runs	Wkts	Avge	Best	5wI	10wM
Test																		
All First	8	15	0	331	59	22.06	-	2	5	-	54	9	226	3	75.33	2-100	-	-
1-day Int																		
NatWest																		
B & H																		
1-day Lge	8	6	1	75	24	15.00	-	-	7	-	6	0	62	1	62.00	1-31	-	

Career Performances

	M	Inns	NO	Runs	HS	Avge	100s	50s	Ct	St	Balls	Runs	Wkts	Avge	Best	5wI	10wM
Test																	
All First	9	16	0	341	59	21.31	-	2	5	-	384	268	3	89.33	2-100	-	-
1-day Int																	
NatWest																	
B & H	4	2	0	4	4	2.00	-	-	1	-	127	101	4	25.25	2-43	-	
1-day Lge	8	6	1	75	24	15.00	-	-	7	-	36	62	1	62.00	1-31	-	

HYAM, B. J.　　　　　　　　　　Essex

Name: Barry James Hyam
Role: Right-hand bat, wicket-keeper
Born: 9 September 1975, Romford, Essex
Height: 5ft 11in　**Weight:** 11st 7lbs
Nickname: Bazza
County debut: 1993
County cap: 1999
1st-Class 50s: 1
1st-Class catches: 98
1st-Class stumpings: 4
Place in batting averages: 170th av. 23.36
(1998 203rd av. 19.18)
Parents: Peter and Gloria
Marital status: 'Engaged to Villene; getting married in March 2001'
Family links with cricket: 'Mum and Dad are keen fans; brother Matthew is captain of Harold Wood CC; brother Richard plays for Harold Wood U17'
Education: Marshalls Park; Havering Sixth Form College; Westminster College
Qualifications: 9 GCSEs, 1 A-level, NCA coaching award

Career outside cricket: Coaching
Off-season: 'Coaching, and decorating our new house with Villene'
Overseas tours: MCC to Bangladesh 1999-2000
Cricketers particularly admired: Jack Russell, Stuart Law, Nasser Hussain
Young players to look out for: Tim Phillips, Justin Bishop
Other sports played: Golf, football
Other sports followed: Football (West Ham United)
Relaxations: Playing any sport and socialising with friends
Extras: Made first-class debut on his 18th birthday. Awarded Essex cap 1999
Opinions on cricket: 'National League should be 40 overs because 45 overs is too long.'
Best batting: 51 Essex v Surrey, The Oval 1999

1999 Season

	M	Inns	NO	Runs	HS	Avge	100s	50s	Ct	St	O	M	Runs	Wkts	Avge	Best	5wI	10wM
Test																		
All First	18	26	4	514	51	23.36	-	1	46	1	2	0	8	0	-	-	-	-
1-day Int																		
NatWest	1	0	0	0	0	-	-	-	-	-								
B & H																		
1-day Lge	11	8	2	128	37	21.33	-	-	12	1								

Career Performances

	M	Inns	NO	Runs	HS	Avge	100s	50s	Ct	St	Balls	Runs	Wkts	Avge	Best	5wI	10wM
Test																	
All First	38	61	9	974	51	18.73	-	1	98	4	12	8	0	-	-	-	-
1-day Int																	
NatWest	1	0	0	0	0	-	-	-	-	-							
B & H																	
1-day Lge	21	14	3	150	37	13.63	-	-	20	1							

49. Which batsman, since moved on, was vice-captain of Glamorgan when they won the 1997 County Championship?

ILLINGWORTH, R. K.   Worcestershire

Name: Richard Keith Illingworth
Role: Right-hand bat, slow left-arm bowler
Born: 23 August 1963, Bradford
Height: 6ft **Weight:** 13st
Nickname: Lucy, Harry
County debut: 1982
County cap: 1986
Benefit: 1997 (£271,275)
Test debut: 1991
Tests: 9
One-Day Internationals: 25
50 wickets in a season: 5
1st-Class 50s: 20
1st-Class 100s: 4
1st-Class 5 w. in innings: 27
1st-Class 10 w. in match: 6
1st-Class catches: 156
One-Day 5 w. in innings: 2
Place in batting averages: 184th av. 21.76 (1998 88th av. 31.53)
Place in bowling averages: 145th av. 51.13 (1998 144th av. 65.61)
Strike rate: 134.66 (career 78.93)
Parents: Keith and Margaret
Wife and date of marriage: Anne, 20 September 1985
Children: Miles, 28 August 1987; Thomas, 20 April 1989
Family links with cricket: Father played Bradford League cricket
Education: Wrose Brow Middle; Salts Grammar School ('same school as the late Jim Laker')
Qualifications: 6 O-levels, advanced coaching award
Career outside cricket: 'None as yet'
Overseas tours: England A to Zimbabwe and Kenya 1989-90, to Pakistan and Sri Lanka 1990-91; England to New Zealand and Australia (World Cup) 1991-92, to South Africa 1995-96, to India and Pakistan (World Cup) 1995-96
Overseas teams played for: Natal 1988-89
Cricketers particularly admired: Ian Botham, Wasim Akram, Derek Underwood
Young players to look out for: Reuben Spiring, Alamgir Sheriyar
Other sports played: Golf
Other sports followed: Football (Leeds United), rugby league (Bradford Bulls), rugby union (Worcester), golf (European PGA)
Relaxations: 'Watching Miles and Thomas play rugby, football and cricket. DIY'
Extras: Took 11 for 108 on South African first-class debut for Natal B v Boland 1988. In 1991, v West Indies, became 11th person in history to take a wicket with first ball in

Test cricket. Took a hat-trick in Sunday League v Sussex in 1993, the first Worcestershire player to take hat-trick in one-day cricket. Won 1993 Dick Lygon award for contribution to Worcestershire CCC. Has made three centuries as a nightwatchman

Opinions on cricket: 'I've been very fortunate to play this game for 16 years and enjoyed most of it. I hope everyone gets the same enjoyment as myself.'

Best batting: 120* Worcestershire v Warwickshire, Worcester 1987

Best bowling: 7-50 Worcestershire v Oxford University, The Parks 1985

1999 Season

	M	Inns	NO	Runs	HS	Avge	100s	50s	Ct	St	O	M	Runs	Wkts	Avge	Best	5wI	10wM
Test																		
All First	16	26	5	457	91 *	21.76	-	1	5	-	336.4	92	767	15	51.13	3-58	-	-
1-day Int																		
NatWest	2	2	1	23	18 *	23.00	-	-	-	-	13	0	52	1	52.00	1-38	-	
B & H																		
1-day Lge	15	5	3	38	15 *	19.00	-	-	5	-	102.1	6	402	22	18.27	4-49	-	

Career Performances

	M	Inns	NO	Runs	HS	Avge	100s	50s	Ct	St	Balls	Runs	Wkts	Avge	Best	5wI	10wM
Test	9	14	7	128	28	18.28	-	-	5	-	1485	615	19	32.36	4-96	-	-
All First	361	415	119	6748	120 *	22.79	4	20	156	-	63777	25414	808	31.45	7-50	27	6
1-day Int	25	11	5	68	14	11.33	-	-	8	-	1501	1059	30	35.30	3-33	-	
NatWest	36	19	8	162	29 *	14.72	-	-	10	-	2119	1114	29	38.41	4-20	-	
B & H	58	29	16	260	36 *	20.00	-	-	13	-	2915	1670	54	30.92	4-27	-	
1-day Lge	211	94	48	633	31	13.76	-	-	49	-	8104	5816	250	23.26	5-24	2	

50. In which season was the 25-point penalty for a sub-standard pitch introduced, and which was the first county to be penalised?

ILOTT, M. C.   Essex

Name: Mark Christopher Ilott
Role: Left-hand bat, left-arm fast-medium bowler
Born: 27 August 1970, Watford
Height: 6ft **Weight:** 13st 8lbs
Nickname: Ramble, Choock
County debut: 1988
County cap: 1993
Test debut: 1993
Tests: 5
50 wickets in a season: 5
1st-Class 50s: 4
1st-Class 5 w. in innings: 26
1st-Class 10 w. in match: 3
1st-Class catches: 40
One-Day 5 w. in innings: 1
Place in batting averages: 222nd av. 18.12 (1998 267th av. 11.80)
Place in bowling averages: 50th av. 23.68 (1998 36th av. 23.18)
Strike rate: 49.05 (career 54.56)
Parents: John and Glenys
Wife and date of marriage: Sandra Jane, 14 October 1994
Children: James Christopher Mark, 6 October 1996; Madeleine Rose, 3 March 1999
Family links with cricket: 'Dad now umpires Minor Counties and continues to test me about my knowledge of the rules – sorry, Dad – laws. Brother plays in Hertfordshire premier league and has played for Hertfordshire. Mum's still watching.'
Education: Kingsway Junior; Francis Combe Secondary Modern; '*The Simpsons* and Linguaphone'
Qualifications: 6 O-levels, 2 AO-levels, 2 A-levels, senior coach, diploma in Fitness and Nutrition, Securities and Futures Authority (SFA) registered
Career outside cricket: 'Corporate hospitality business, Hole-in-One Worldwide Insurance, GNI bond options dealer's assistant'
Off-season: 'Running the Essex County Cricketers' Benefit Association, working for GNI futures and options brokers, and building up hospitality business'
Overseas tours: England A to Sri Lanka 1990-91, to Australia 1992-93, to South Africa 1993-94, to India 1994-95; England to South Africa 1995-96
Overseas teams played for: East Torrens District, Adelaide 1989-91
Cricketers particularly admired: Stuart Law, Malcolm Marshall, Nasser Hussain, 'and Mark Butcher (on guitar)'
Other sports played: Golf ('badly')
Other sports followed: Football (Watford FC – 'Come on you Hornets')

Injuries: Out for seven weeks with total lateral meniscectomy

Relaxations: 'Guitar playing, gardening – especially my veg – and of course spending time with my family'

Extras: Took his 450th wicket for Essex (Nick Knight) v Warwickshire at Chelmsford 1999

Opinions on cricket: 'We've got to get children playing the game. Parents, don't be lazy; don't buy your kids a PlayStation and leave them for two hours so you can read a magazine. Take them in the garden and play with them; let them enjoy your company, and introduce sport into their lives.'

Best batting: 60 England A v Warwickshire, Edgbaston 1995

Best bowling: 9-19 Essex v Northamptonshire, Luton 1995

1999 Season

	M	Inns	NO	Runs	HS	Avge	100s	50s	Ct	St	O	M	Runs	Wkts	Avge	Best	5wI	10wM
Test																		
All First	12	17	1	290	44	18.12	-	-	5	-	310.4	85	900	38	23.68	6-38	1	-
1-day Int																		
NatWest	1	0	0	0	0	-	-	-	-	-	9	0	40	0	-		-	-
B & H																		
1-day Lge	9	7	2	67	17	13.40	-	-	-	-	60.5	3	279	13	21.46	3-36	-	

Career Performances

	M	Inns	NO	Runs	HS	Avge	100s	50s	Ct	St	Balls	Runs	Wkts	Avge	Best	5wI	10wM
Test	5	6	2	28	15	7.00	-	-	-	-	1042	542	12	45.16	3-48	-	-
All First	166	215	44	2480	60	14.50	-	4	40	-	30774	15253	564	27.04	9-19	26	3
1-day Int																	
NatWest	21	11	5	119	54 *	19.83	-	1	5	-	1332	811	21	38.61	2-23	-	
B & H	33	11	1	81	21	8.10	-	-	3	-	1776	1045	52	20.09	5-21	1	
1-day Lge	111	69	23	505	56 *	10.97	-	1	17	-	4682	3506	133	26.36	4-15	-	

51. Who was Yorkshire's first overseas player, and in which season did he make his Championship debut for the county?

INGLIS, J. W. Yorkshire

Name: John William Inglis
Role: Right-hand opening bat
Born: 19 October 1979, Ripon,
North Yorkshire
Height: 6ft 2in **Weight:** 12st 7lbs
Nickname: Jingles
County debut: No first-team appearance
Parents: William and June
Marital status: Single
Family links with cricket: Father played
local amateur cricket, Markington/Ripon
Education: St Wilfrid's RC, Ripon;
Holy Trinity Juniors, Ripon; Ripon Grammar
School; St Aidan's Sixth Form, Harrogate
Qualifications: 10 GCSEs
Off-season: 'Trying to repair the torn
hamstring received whilst playing in U19
"One-Day International" v Australia'
Overseas teams played for: Marist Newman Old Boys, Perth 1997-98
Cricketers particularly admired: Hasan Raza
Young players to look out for: John Sadler, Chris Taylor, Michael Lumb
Other sports played: Rugby (captain of Ripon GS; captain of Harrogate U13)
Other sports followed: Rugby league (Hull FC Sharks)
Injuries: Out for a total of eight weeks with two broken fingers and a torn hamstring
Relaxations: Watching rugby league, relaxing with friends, playing on the computer
Extras: Wombwell Neil Lloyd Cricket Association winner (Bunbury Festival) 1995.
Daily Telegraph Batsman of the Year 1995. Yorkshire League Batsman Senior and
Junior winner (youngest ever) 1997. Played for England U15, U17, U18 and U19.
Played for England U19 v Pakistan U19 1998 and in first two 'One-Day
Internationals' v Australia U19 1999
Opinions on cricket: 'Not enough money in the game today for the grass-roots players.'

---

52. Who scored an eight-minute 50 for Leicestershire
v Nottinghamshire at Trent Bridge in 1965?

INNES, K. J.   Northamptonshire

Name: Kevin John Innes
Role: Right-hand bat, right-arm
medium bowler
Born: 24 September 1975, Wellingborough
Height: 5ft 10in   **Weight:** 11st 5lbs
Nickname: KJ, Squirrel, Ernie
County debut: 1994
1st-Class 50s: 1
1st-Class catches: 9
Place in batting averages: 128th av. 27.12
Place in bowling averages: 80th av. 28.60
Strike rate: 54.80 (career 58.95)
Parents: Peter and Jane
Marital status: Engaged to Caroline Pinnock
Education: Boothville Middle School;
Weston Favell Upper School, Northampton
Qualifications: 6 GCSEs, 4 O-levels,
NCA coaching award

Off-season: Coaching cricket and getting fit for the coming season
Overseas tours: England U18 to South Africa 1992-93, to Denmark 1993;
England U19 to Sri Lanka 1993-94
Overseas teams played for: Karori, New Zealand 1995-97
Cricketers particularly admired: Glenn McGrath, Steve Waugh
Young players to look out for: Mark Powell
Other sports played: 'Particularly enjoy playing golf and snooker'
Injuries: Out for five weeks with a side strain
Relaxations: 'Spending time with my girlfriend, sleeping and eating out; music,
reading books/magazines'
Extras: Played for England U19 in home series against India in 1994. Won the MCC
Lord's Taverners Award U13 and U15. Northants 2nd XI Player of the Year 1998.
Became youngest player to play for Northants 2nd XI, aged 14 years 9 months
Opinions on cricket: 'There are too many games/fixtures throughout the season, and
players are therefore not able to get in as much quality practice.'
Best batting: 63 Northamptonshire v Lancashire, Northampton 1996
Best bowling: 4-61 Northamptonshire v Lancashire, Northampton 1996

1999 Season

	M	Inns	NO	Runs	HS	Avge	100s	50s	Ct	St	O	M	Runs	Wkts	Avge	Best	5wI	10wM
Test																		
All First	8	11	3	217	47 *	27.12	-	-	4	-	137	37	429	15	28.60	4-85	-	-
1-day Int																		
NatWest	3	2	2	8	8 *	-	-	-	1	-	20.3	0	114	5	22.80	3-26	-	
B & H																		
1-day Lge	10	8	3	104	27	20.80	-	-	4	-	52.2	1	286	14	20.42	4-37	-	

Career Performances

	M	Inns	NO	Runs	HS	Avge	100s	50s	Ct	St	Balls	Runs	Wkts	Avge	Best	5wI	10wM
Test																	
All First	15	21	4	370	63	21.76	-	1	9	-	1356	704	23	30.60	4-61	-	-
1-day Int																	
NatWest	4	3	2	33	25	33.00	-	-	1	-	123	114	5	22.80	3-26	-	
B & H	2	1	0	1	1	1.00	-	-	-	-	60	56	1	56.00	1-25	-	
1-day Lge	22	13	6	138	27	19.71	-	-	8	-	570	595	17	35.00	4-37	-	

IRANI, R. C. Essex

Name: Ronald Charles Irani
Role: Right-hand bat, right-arm
medium bowler, county vice-captain
Born: 26 October 1971, Leigh, Lancashire
Height: 6ft 4in **Weight:** 13st 10lbs
Nickname: Reggie, Ledge
County debut: 1990 (Lancashire),
1994 (Essex)
County cap: 1994 (Essex)
Test debut: 1996
Tests: 3
One-Day Internationals: 10
1000 runs in a season: 4
50 wickets in a season: 1
1st-Class 50s: 34
1st-Class 100s: 13
1st-Class 5 w. in innings: 4
1st-Class catches: 55
One-Day 100s: 2
One-Day 5 w. in innings: 1
Place in batting averages: 42nd av. 38.65 (1998 77th av. 32.29)

Place in bowling averages: 25th av. 21.25 (1998 115th av. 33.95)
Strike rate: 46.50 (career 59.96)
Parents: Jimmy and Anne
Marital status: Single
Family links with cricket: 'Father played local league cricket in Bolton for 30 years; mother did teas for many years!'
Education: Church Road Primary School; Smithills Comprehensive School
Qualifications: 9 GCSEs
Off-season: England A tour of Bangladesh and New Zealand
Overseas tours: England YC to Australia 1989-90; England A to Pakistan 1995-96, to Bangladesh and New Zealand 1999-2000; England to Zimbabwe and New Zealand 1996-97
Overseas teams played for: Technicol Natal, Durban 1992-93; Eden-Roskill, Auckland 1993-94
Cricketers particularly admired: Mark Waugh, Javed Miandad, Wasim Akram, John Crawley, Graham Gooch
Other sports followed: 'Most sports especially football'
Relaxations: Sleeping and watching football
Extras: Played for England U19 in home series v Australia 1991, scoring a century and three 50s in six innings and being named Bull Man of the Series. Made his Test debut in the first Test against India at Edgbaston in 1996. Was selected to represent England in the cancelled World Super Max 8s originally scheduled to take place in Perth in October 1998. Appointed vice-captain of Essex in 1999. Recalled to the Test side for fourth Test v New Zealand at The Oval 1999. Achieved double of 1000 first-class runs and 50 first-class wickets in 1999
Opinions on cricket: 'Too much cricket played by English county cricket professionals.'
Best batting: 153 Essex v Sri Lanka A, Chelmsford 1999
Best bowling: 5-19 England A v Board XI, Karachi 1995-96

1999 Season

	M	Inns	NO	Runs	HS	Avge	100s	50s	Ct	St	O	M	Runs	Wkts	Avge	Best	5wI	10wM
Test	1	2	0	10	9	5.00	-	-	2	-	11	3	38	1	38.00	1-38	-	-
All First	21	34	5	1121	153	38.65	4	3	12	-	395.2	101	1084	51	21.25	4-29	-	-
1-day Int																		
NatWest	1	1	0	88	88	88.00	-	1	-	-	10	1	62	2	31.00	2-62	-	
B & H																		
1-day Lge	14	14	1	223	64	17.15	-	2	2	-	102.2	13	470	24	19.58	5-33	1	

Career Performances

	M	Inns	NO	Runs	HS	Avge	100s	50s	Ct	St	Balls	Runs	Wkts	Avge	Best	5wI	10wM
Test	3	5	0	86	41	17.20	-	-	2	-	192	112	3	37.33	1-22	-	-
All First	125	206	23	6456	153	35.27	13	34	55	-	13613	7023	227	30.93	5-19	4	-
1-day Int	10	10	2	78	45 *	9.75	-	-	2	-	329	246	4	61.50	1-23	-	
NatWest	17	15	2	554	124	42.61	1	5	4	-	1046	694	23	30.17	4-41	-	
B & H	23	17	2	605	82 *	40.33	-	3	3	-	1080	836	29	28.82	4-30	-	
1-day Lge	98	92	14	2057	101 *	26.37	1	12	21	-	3295	2626	114	23.03	5-33	1	

JAMES, K. D. Hampshire

Name: Kevan David James
Role: Left-hand bat, left-arm medium bowler
Born: 18 March 1961, Lambeth, South London
Height: 6ft 0¹/₂in **Weight:** 13st 8lbs
Nickname: Jambo, Jaimo, Jockey
County debut: 1980 (Middlesex), 1985 (Hampshire)
County cap: 1989 (Hampshire)
Benefit: 1999 (Hampshire)
1000 runs in a season: 2
1st-Class 50s: 42
1st-Class 100s: 10
1st-Class 5 w. in innings: 11
1st-Class 10 w. in match: 1
1st-Class catches: 78
One-Day 5 w. in innings: 2
Place in batting averages: (1998 69th av. 33.52)
Place in bowling averages: (1998 114th av. 33.84)
Strike rate: 54.16 (career 62.48)
Parents: David (deceased) and Helen
Wife and date of marriage: Debbie, October 1987
Children: Natalie Ann, 8 October 1992; Naomi Claire, 25 October 1995
Family links with cricket: Late father played club cricket in North London; brother Martin plays for Hertfordshire
Education: Edmonton County High School
Qualifications: 5 O-levels, qualified coach, City and Guilds in Electric Theories
Career outside cricket: 'Yes, please'
Overseas tours: England YC to Australia 1978-79, to West Indies 1979-80; England to Hong Kong Sixes 1996

Overseas teams played for: Wellington, New Zealand 1982-84
Cricketers particularly admired: Chris Smith
Young players to look out for: Simon Francis
Other sports followed: 'Football but never achieved anything – about the same as cricket'
Relaxations: 'Enjoy my work with local radio. Find it a welcome relaxation during the summer when I am writing my scripts'
Extras: Left Middlesex at end of 1984 season and joined Hampshire. Achieved a world record in 1996 when he became the first player in a first-class match to score a century and take four wickets in four balls in Hampshire's game against India at Southampton. Retired at end of 1999 season
Best batting: 162 Hampshire v Glamorgan, Cardiff 1989
Best bowling: 8-49 Hampshire v Somerset, Basingstoke 1997

1999 Season

	M	Inns	NO	Runs	HS	Avge	100s	50s	Ct	St	O	M	Runs	Wkts	Avge	Best	5wl	10wM
Test																		
All First	2	4	0	28	18	7.00	-	-	2	-	54.1	13	201	6	33.50	3-38	-	-
1-day Int																		
NatWest																		
B & H	1	1	0	0	0	0.00	-	-	-	-	6	0	33	0	-		-	-
1-day Lge	2	1	1	4	4*	-	-	-	-	-	11	0	71	2	35.50	2-43	-	

Career Performances

	M	Inns	NO	Runs	HS	Avge	100s	50s	Ct	St	Balls	Runs	Wkts	Avge	Best	5wl	10wM
Test																	
All First	225	337	57	8526	162	30.45	10	42	78	-	24681	12607	395	31.91	8-49	11	1
1-day Int																	
NatWest	27	16	3	235	52	18.07	-	1	6	-	1540	958	35	27.37	4-42	-	
B & H	47	34	7	511	56	18.92	-	1	12	-	2251	1530	38	40.26	3-31	-	
1-day Lge	169	114	34	1661	66	20.76	-	5	46	-	6658	4905	163	30.09	6-35	2	

JAMES, S. P.   Glamorgan

Name: Stephen Peter James
Role: Right-hand opening bat, county vice-captain
Born: 7 September 1967, Lydney
Height: 6ft **Weight:** 13st
Nickname: Sid, Jamo
County debut: 1985
County cap: 1992
Test debut: 1998
Tests: 2
1000 runs in a season: 7
1st-Class 50s: 49
1st-Class 100s: 35
1st-Class 200s: 4
1st-Class catches: 155
One-Day 100s: 7
Place in batting averages: 24th av. 42.37
(1998 14th av. 49.59)

Parents: Peter and Margaret
Wife and date of marriage: Jane Louise, 26 September 1997
Children: Bethan Amy, 28 August 1998 ('during Test match!')
Family links with cricket: Father played for Gloucestershire 2nd XI. Distant relative of Dominic Ostler
Education: Monmouth School; University College, Swansea; Cambridge University
Qualifications: BA (Hons) Wales – Classics; BA (Hons) Cantab – Land Economy
Off-season: 'Writing, coaching, training, watching rugby'
Overseas tours: Welsh Schools to Barbados 1984; Monmouth Schools to Sri Lanka 1985; Combined Universities to Barbados 1989; Glamorgan to Trinidad 1989-90, to Zimbabwe 1990-91, to Cape Town 1993-94, to Pretoria 1995-96; England A to Kenya and Sri Lanka 1997-98
Overseas teams played for: Bionics, Zimbabwe 1990-92; Universals Sports Club, Zimbabwe 1992-96
Cricketers particularly admired: Michael Atherton, Graham Burgess
Young players to look out for: Mike Powell
Other sports played/followed: Rugby union (Cardiff RFC and Lydney RFC; 'played for Lydney, Gloucestershire and Cambridge University and was on bench for Varsity Match'), football (West Ham United)
Injuries: Out for three weeks with a broken thumb
Relaxations: Reading, *Telegraph* crosswords, videos, weight-training
Extras: Scored maiden century in only second first-class game. Broke Matthew Maynard's club record for number of one-day runs in a season in 1995. Also broke

Hugh Morris's club record for number of Sunday League runs in a season. First player to reach 1000 runs in 1997 and was voted the Cricketer of the Year by both the Wombwell Cricket Lovers' Society and the PCA. Appointed vice-captain for the England A tour to Kenya and Sri Lanka 1997-98. Appointed vice-captain of Glamorgan in 1999. Broke record for highest post-war score by Glamorgan batsman, with 259* v Notts at Colwyn Bay 1999 (his fifth successive century v Notts), beating Matthew Maynard's 243 in 1991

Opinions on cricket: 'The pitches this year have been dreadful.'

Best batting: 259* Glamorgan v Nottinghamshire, Colwyn Bay 1999

1999 Season

	M	Inns	NO	Runs	HS	Avge	100s	50s	Ct	St	O	M	Runs	Wkts	Avge	Best	5wI	10wM
Test																		
All First	16	25	1	1017	259 *	42.37	4	3	9	-								
1-day Int																		
NatWest	3	3	1	208	118 *	104.00	1	1	-	-								
B & H																			
1-day Lge	15	15	2	257	49	19.76	-	-	3	-	7	0	39	1	39.00	1-39	-	

Career Performances

	M	Inns	NO	Runs	HS	Avge	100s	50s	Ct	St	Balls	Runs	Wkts	Avge	Best	5wI	10wM
Test	2	4	0	71	36	17.75	-	-	-	-							
All First	204	357	27	13127	259 *	39.77	39	49	155	-	2	3	0	-	-	-	-
1-day Int																	
NatWest	24	23	2	995	123	47.38	3	6	5	-							
B & H	33	33	2	1118	135	36.06	2	9	10	-							
1-day Lge	114	111	13	3243	107	33.09	2	21	26	-	42	39	1	39.00	1-39	-	

53. Which batsman scored 424 for Lancashire v Somerset at Taunton in 1895, a record in English first-class cricket until B.C. Lara's intervention in 1994?

JARVIS, P. W. Somerset

Name: Paul William Jarvis
Role: Right-hand bat, right-arm
fast-medium bowler
Born: 29 June 1965, Redcar, North Yorkshire
Height: 5ft 11in **Weight:** 12st 7lbs
Nickname: Gnash, Jarv, Krusty
County debut: 1981 (Yorkshire),
1994 (Sussex), 1999 (Somerset)
County cap: 1986 (Yorkshire), 1994
(Sussex)
Test debut: 1987-88

Tests: 9
One-Day Internationals: 16
50 wickets in a season: 4
1st-Class 50s: 10
1st-Class 5 w. in innings: 22
1st-Class 10 w. in match: 3
1st-Class catches: 64
One-Day 5 w. in innings: 6
Place in batting averages: 276th av. 9.12 (1998 211th av. 18.33)
Place in bowling averages: 107th av. 32.57
Strike rate: 63.57 (career 54.55)
Parents: Malcolm and Marjorie
Marital status: Divorced
Children: Alexander Michael, 13 June 1989; Isabella Grace, 21 March 1993
Family links with cricket: Father still plays league cricket for Sudbrooke CC in
Gwent. Brother plays in Yorkshire (Selby Londesborough)
Education: Bydales Comprehensive School, Marske, Cleveland; 'studying Sports
Science degree'
Qualifications: 4 O-levels, advanced cricket coach
Off-season: Studying
Overseas tours: Yorkshire to St Lucia and Barbados 1987, to South Africa 1991;
England to India and Pakistan (World Cup) and Pakistan 1987-88, to Australia and
New Zealand 1987-88, to India and Sri Lanka 1992-93; unofficial England XI to
South Africa 1989-90
Overseas teams played for: Mossman Middle Harbour, Sydney 1984-85; Avendale,
Cape Town 1985-86; Manly Warringah, Sydney 1987; Onslow, Wellington 1994-95
Cricketers particularly admired: Ian Botham, Malcolm Marshall
Young players to look out for: Matt Bulbeck
Other sports followed: Football
Injuries: Out for a total of about six weeks with various leg strains

Relaxations: 'Walking my dogs, eating out, drinking real ale and good wine'
Extras: In 1981 became youngest player ever to play for Yorkshire in County Championship (16 years, 2 months, 13 days). Became youngest player to take hat-trick in Sunday League, in 1982, and Championship, in 1985. Played for England YC v West Indies 1982 and Australia 1983. Banned from Test cricket for joining 1989-90 tour of South Africa; suspension remitted in 1992. Released by Sussex at end of 1998 season and joined Somerset for 1999
Opinions on cricket: 'Two divisions in one-day game has created an immense interest and gives all clubs more incentives. This should have the same effect in the four-day game, creating a higher standard of cricket throughout the whole season.'
Best batting: 80 Yorkshire v Northamptonshire, Scarborough 1992
Best bowling: 7-55 Yorkshire v Surrey, Headingley 1986

1999 Season

	M	Inns	NO	Runs	HS	Avge	100s	50s	Ct	St	O	M	Runs	Wkts	Avge	Best	5wI	10wM
Test																		
All First	7	8	0	73	20	9.12	-	-	2	-	201.2	43	619	19	32.57	4-76	-	-
1-day Int																		
NatWest	5	1	1	3	3 *	-	-	-	2	-	44.3	5	223	10	22.30	5-55	1	
B & H																		
1-day Lge	11	4	3	34	20 *	34.00	-	-	4	-	84	0	475	16	29.68	4-28	-	

Career Performances

	M	Inns	NO	Runs	HS	Avge	100s	50s	Ct	St	Balls	Runs	Wkts	Avge	Best	5wI	10wM
Test	9	15	2	132	29 *	10.15	-	-	2	-	1912	965	21	45.95	4-107	-	-
All First	213	267	67	3372	80	16.86	-	10	64	-	35300	18773	647	29.01	7-55	22	3
1-day Int	16	8	2	31	16 *	5.16	-	-	1	-	879	672	24	28.00	5-35	1	
NatWest	27	15	4	175	34 *	15.90	-	-	7	-	1652	1163	34	34.20	5-55	1	
B & H	47	26	9	352	63	20.70	-	1	4	-	2702	1667	76	21.93	4-34	-	
1-day Lge	152	89	31	660	43	11.37	-	-	34	-	6404	4874	217	22.46	6-27	4	

54. What was unusual about G.B. Stevenson's century for
Yorkshire v Warwickshire at Edgbaston in 1982?

JEFFERSON, W. I. Essex

Name: William Ingleby Jefferson
Role: Right-hand bat, right-arm medium bowler
Born: 25 October 1979, Derby
Height: 6ft 9in **Weight:** 14st 7lbs
Nickname: Jeffers, Ingles, Wilbur
County debut: No first-team appearance
Parents: Richard and Pauline
Marital status: Single
Family links with cricket: Grandfather Jefferson played for the Army and Combined Services in the 1920s. Father, R. I. Jefferson, played for Cambridge University 1961 and Surrey 1961-66

Education: Beeston Hall School, Norfolk; Oundle School, Northants; 'Durham University, reading Sport in the Community from October 1999'
Qualifications: 9 GCSEs, 3 A-levels, Level 1 cricket coaching award 1998
Career outside cricket: Student
Off-season: At Durham University
Overseas tours: Oundle School to South Africa 1995
Overseas teams played for: Young People's Club, Paarl, South Africa 1998-99
Cricketers particularly admired: Shaun Pollock, Jacques Kallis, Graeme Hick, Stuart Law, Ricky Ponting, Nasser Hussain
Young players to look out for: Tim Phillips, Justin Ontong (South African)
Other sports played: Golf, tennis, Rugby fives, table tennis
Other sports followed: Rugby
Injuries: Out for three months with disc bulge pressing on the sciatic nerve
Relaxations: Listening to music, reading cricket biographies, playing cards, watching sport on television
Extras: Holmwoods School Cricketer of the Year 1998
Opinions on cricket: 'Until less cricket is played on the county circuit, English players will struggle to compete at international level. Batsmen's techniques are lost through the amount of one-day cricket played. Not enough good facilities at the grounds, and not enough time to use them anyway. It has got to be changed to quality not quantity.'

JOHNSON, P.   Nottinghamshire

Name: Paul Johnson
Role: Right-hand bat, right-arm
'occasional' bowler
Born: 24 April 1965, Newark, Notts
Height: 'Below average' **Weight:** 'Above
average'
Nickname: Johno, Midge
County debut: 1982
County cap: 1986
Benefit: 1995
1000 runs in a season: 8
1st-Class 50s: 112
1st-Class 100s: 37
1st-Class catches: 213
1st-Class stumpings: 1
One-Day 100s: 13
Place in batting averages: 23rd av. 42.46
(1998 48th av. 39.04)

Strike rate: (career 106.66)
Parents: Donald Edward and Joyce
Wife and date of marriage: Jackie, 24 December 1993
Children: Ruth, 28 September 1994; Eve, 9 September 1996
Family links with cricket: Father played local cricket and is a qualified coach
Education: Grove Comprehensive School, Newark
Qualifications: 9 CSEs, NCA advanced coach
Career outside cricket: Coaching
Off-season: Coaching; 'getting/trying to stay fit!'
Overseas tours: England A to Bermuda and West Indies 1991-92; Christians in Sport
to Zimbabwe 1997
Overseas teams played for: RAU Johannesburg 1985-86; Hutt District, Wellington,
New Zealand 1988-89
Cricketers particularly admired: Clive Rice and Mike Gatting
Young players to look out for: Stephen Randall, Bilal Shafayat; 'there's lots of
exceptional young talent around'
Other sports played: '"Royal Oak" pool team'
Other sports followed: Ice hockey (Nottingham Panthers), football
(Nottingham Forest and Notts County)
Injuries: Out for last four games of season with disc protrusion in neck
Relaxations: Listening to music, crosswords and reading autobiographies
Extras: Played for English Schools in 1980-81 and England YC 1982 and 1983.
Youngest player to join the Nottinghamshire staff. Made 235 for Nottinghamshire 2nd

XI, July 1982, aged 17. Won Man of the Match award in his first NatWest game (101*
v Staffordshire) in 1985, but missed the final owing to appendicitis. Sunday morning
soccer referee in Nottingham. Took over the Nottinghamshire captaincy from Tim
Robinson at the start of the 1996 season. Relinquished captaincy during 1998 season
Opinions on cricket: 'Who would take any notice?'
Best batting: 187 Nottinghamshire v Lancashire, Old Trafford 1993
Best bowling: 1-9 Nottinghamshire v Oxford University, Trent Bridge 1984

1999 Season

	M	Inns	NO	Runs	HS	Avge	100s	50s	Ct	St	O	M	Runs	Wkts	Avge	Best	5wI	10wM
Test																		
All First	16	29	3	1104	126	42.46	1	10	11	-	1	0	10	0	-	-	-	-
1-day Int																		
NatWest	2	2	0	101	51	50.50	-	2	-	-								
B & H																			
1-day Lge	13	13	0	291	68	22.38	-	2	1	-								

Career Performances

	M	Inns	NO	Runs	HS	Avge	100s	50s	Ct	St	Balls	Runs	Wkts	Avge	Best	5wI	10wM
Test																	
All First	332	556	53	18835	187	37.44	37	112	213	1	640	605	6	100.83	1-9	-	-
1-day Int																	
NatWest	36	36	2	1048	146	30.82	3	3	12	-	18	20	0	-	-	-
B & H	58	54	11	1455	104 *	33.83	2	10	15	-							
1-day Lge	231	220	27	6466	167 *	33.50	8	38	75	-	1	1	0	-	-	-

JOHNSON, R. L. Middlesex

Name: Richard Leonard Johnson
Role: Right-hand bat, right-arm fast-medium bowler, outfielder
Born: 29 December 1974, Chertsey, Surrey
Height: 6ft 2in **Weight:** 13st 6lbs
Nickname: Jono, Lenny
County debut: 1992
50 wickets in a season: 2
1st-Class 50s: 1
1st-Class 5 w. in innings: 5
1st-Class 10 w. in match: 2
1st-Class catches: 29
One-Day 5 w. in innings: 1
Place in batting averages: 268th av. 10.75 (1998 257th av. 13.44)

Place in bowling averages: 77th av. 28.31
(1998 67th av. 27.38)
Strike rate: 50.06 (career 51.04)
Parents: Roger and Mary Ann
Marital status: Single
Family links with cricket: Father and
grandfather played club cricket
Education: Sunbury Manor School;
Spelthorne College
Qualifications: 9 GCSEs, A-level in Physical
Education, NCA senior coaching award
Overseas tours: England U18 to South
Africa 1992-93; England U19 to Sri Lanka
1993-94; England A to India 1994-95; MCC
to Bangladesh 1999-2000
Cricketers particularly admired: Ian
Botham, Richard Hadlee and Angus Fraser
'for his quality bowling and his dedication to
moaning'
Young players to look out for: David Nash, Owais Shah
Other sports followed: Basketball, soccer, snooker and most other sports
Relaxations: Sport and music
Extras: Plays for Sunbury CC. Has represented Middlesex at all levels since U11.
Took 10 for 45 v Derbyshire in July 1994, becoming first person to take ten wickets in
an innings since Ian Thomson (Sussex) in 1964; also most economical ten-wicket haul
since Hedley Verity's 10 for 10 in 1932. Had to pull out of England's 1995-96 tour to
South Africa due to a persistent back injury
Best batting: 50* Middlesex v Cambridge University, Fenner's 1994
Best bowling: 10-45 Middlesex v Derbyshire, Derby 1994

1999 Season

	M	Inns	NO	Runs	HS	Avge	100s	50s	Ct	St	O	M	Runs	Wkts	Avge	Best	5wI	10wM
Test																		
All First	6	8	0	86	39	10.75	-	-	1	-	133.3	30	453	16	28.31	4-50	-	-
1-day Int																		
NatWest																		
B & H																		
1-day Lge	5	4	1	18	10	6.00	-	-	-	-	36.2	0	177	1	177.00	1-53	-	

Career Performances

	M	Inns	NO	Runs	HS	Avge	100s	50s	Ct	St	Balls	Runs	Wkts	Avge	Best	5wI	10wM
Test																	
All First	76	106	11	1333	50 *	14.03	-	1	29	-	11435	6239	224	27.85	10-45	5	2
1-day Int																	
NatWest	14	11	3	155	45 *	19.37	-	-	1	-	780	535	21	25.47	5-50	1	
B & H	14	11	0	117	26	10.63	-	-	2	-	756	609	18	33.83	3-33	-	
1-day Lge	69	47	14	395	29	11.96	-	-	8	-	2775	2449	63	38.87	4-45	-	

JONES, I. Somerset

Name: Ian Jones
Role: Right-hand bat, right-arm fast-medium bowler
Born: 11 March 1977, London
Height: 6ft 4in **Weight:** 16st
Nickname: Bubba, Jonah
County debut: 1999
Strike rate: 79.33 (career 79.33)
Parents: Dianne and Ronnie
Marital status: Single
Family links with cricket: Brother plays league cricket in Durham for Shotley Bridge
Education: Fyndoune Community College, Sacriston, Durham
Qualifications: 9 GCSEs, City and Guilds Diploma in Engineering, Level 1 coaching award
Career outside cricket: 'Washing Bulbeck's socks'
Off-season: 'Training with Kevin Shine and Darren Veness in Taunton'
Overseas tours: Durham Academy to Sri Lanka 1996
Cricketers particularly admired: Andrew Caddick, Allan Donald, Glenn McGrath
Young players to look out for: Matt Bulbeck
Other sports followed: Football (Sunderland AFC)
Injuries: Out for last three weeks of season with ankle inversion
Relaxations: Playing football, watching television, listening to music
Extras: First player to sign on at Durham Cricket Academy
Opinions on cricket: 'Not enough experience to comment.'
Best batting: 35 Somerset v Durham, Chester-le-Street 1999
Best bowling: 3-81 Somerset v New Zealand, Taunton 1999

1999 Season

	M	Inns	NO	Runs	HS	Avge	100s	50s	Ct	St	O	M	Runs	Wkts	Avge	Best	5wI	10wM
Test																		
All First	3	4	1	78	35	26.00	-	-	-	-	79.2	13	341	6	56.83	3-81	-	-
1-day Int																		
NatWest																		
B & H																		
1-day Lge	1	1	1	5	5*	-	-	-	-	-	7.1	0	53	1	53.00	1-53	-	

Career Performances

	M	Inns	NO	Runs	HS	Avge	100s	50s	Ct	St	Balls	Runs	Wkts	Avge	Best	5wI	10wM
Test																	
All First	3	4	1	78	35	26.00	-	-	-	-	476	341	6	56.83	3-81	-	-
1-day Int																	
NatWest																	
B & H																	
1-day Lge	1	1	1	5	5*	-	-	-	-	-	43	53	1	53.00	1-53	-	

JONES, P. S.　　　　　　　　　Somerset

Name: Philip Steffan Jones
Role: Right-hand bat, right-arm fast-medium bowler
Born: 9 February 1974, Llanelli
Height: 6ft 1in **Weight:** 14st 6lbs
Nickname: Jona, Jonesy, Myfanwy, Elvis, Show Pony
County debut: 1997
1st-Class 100s: 1
1st-Class 5 w. in innings: 1
1st-Class catches: 7
One-Day 5 w. in innings: 1
Place in batting averages:
145th av. 25.54
Place in bowling averages:
135th av. 40.23
Strike rate: 72.95 (career 67.25)
Parents: Lyndon and Ann
Marital status: Single; girlfriend Michelle
Family links with cricket: Father played cricket for Glamorgan 2nd XI and first-class rugby

Education: Llangennech Primary School; Strade Comprehensive, Llanelli; Loughborough University; Neath College; Cambridge University
Qualifications: BSc Sports Science, PGCE in Physical Education
Career outside cricket: Professional rugby player; teaching and coaching
Off-season: 'Playing rugby for Bridgwater RFC. Last season of playing rugby. I intend concentrating solely on cricket (and I'm absolutely exhausted!!)'
Overseas tours: Wales Minor Counties to Barbados 1994; Somerset CCC to South Africa 1999
Cricketers particularly admired: Dermot Reeve ('for continually pushing me'), Andy Caddick ('phenomenal bowler who runs in all day'), Ian Botham ('for wanting to entertain the masses'), Graham Henry ('if only he was a cricketer')
Young players to look out for: Luke Sutton, Matt Bulbeck
Other sports played: Rugby union (Welsh Schools, Youth, U20, U21; Loughborough University, Cambridge University, Swansea, Bristol, Exeter; professional player for three years)
Other sports followed: Rugby union (New Zealand All Blacks)
Injuries: Out for four weeks with an Achilles tendon strain
Relaxations: 'Working out in the gym; spending time with family and Michelle'
Extras: Schoolboy international from U13 to U19. Represented Wales Minor Counties. Took nine wickets in the Varsity match at Lord's in 1997. Man of the Match (5-23) in Sunday League game against Warwickshire 1998. For two years was only dual professional rugby player and cricketer in the country. Scored maiden first-class century (105) v New Zealand at Taunton 1999
Opinions on cricket: 'I'm very fortunate to be given the opportunity and ability to play this great game. The game, in my opinion, is a healthy game. However, the politics that surrounds it is not!!'
Best batting: 105 Somerset v New Zealand, Taunton 1999
Best bowling: 6-67 Cambridge University v Oxford University, Lord's 1997

1999 Season

	M	Inns	NO	Runs	HS	Avge	100s	50s	Ct	St	O	M	Runs	Wkts	Avge	Best	5wI	10wM
Test																		
All First	9	14	3	281	105	25.54	1	-	3	-	255.2	50	845	21	40.23	4-126	-	-
1-day Int																		
NatWest	4	1	1	6	6 *	-	-	-	2	-	33	2	152	6	25.33	4-25	-	
B & H																		
1-day Lge	15	8	2	28	12	4.66	-	-	4	-	113.5	6	653	26	25.11	4-49	-	

Career Performances

	M	Inns	NO	Runs	HS	Avge	100s	50s	Ct	St	Balls	Runs	Wkts	Avge	Best	5wI	10wM
Test																	
All First	23	32	9	454	105	19.73	1	-	7	-	3228	1829	48	38.10	6-67	1	-
1-day Int																	
NatWest	6	2	2	32	26 *	-	-	-	2	-	264	218	8	27.25	4-25	-	
B & H	5	3	2	26	12	26.00	-	-	2	-	258	188	5	37.60	2-51	-	
1-day Lge	29	13	5	35	12	4.37	-	-	8	-	1162	1027	44	23.34	5-23	1	

JONES, S. P. Glamorgan

Name: Simon Philip Jones
Role: Left-hand bat, right-arm fast bowler
Born: 25 December 1978, Morriston
Hospital, Swansea
Height: 6ft 3in **Weight:** 13st 9lbs
Nickname: Racehorse, Ray, Raymond,
Ray Sauce
County debut: 1998
1st-Class 5 w. in innings: 1
1st-Class catches: 3
Place in batting averages: 284th av. 7.70
Place in bowling averages: 136th av. 40.84
Strike rate: 65.68 (career 67.84)
Parents: Jeff and Irene
Marital status: Single
Family links with cricket: 'My dad, Jeff,
played for Glamorgan and England as a left-
arm fast bowler'
Education: Halfway CP School; Coedcae Comprehensive School; Millfield School,
Street, Somerset
Qualifications: 12 GCSEs, 1 A-level, Level 1 coach
Career outside cricket: 'Have not thought about it'
Off-season: 'Relax, have a few beers; go on holiday; train hard'
Overseas tours: Dyfed U15 to Zimbabwe 1994; Glamorgan to South Africa 1999
Cricketers particularly admired: Allan Donald, Michael Holding
Young players to look out for: Mike Powell, Wayne Law, David Harrison,
Mark Wallace
Other sports followed: Football (Manchester United)
Injuries: Out for last five games of season with shin splints
Relaxations: Going out, relaxing with friends
Opinions on cricket: 'Too much cricket in the season. More rest in between games.'

Best batting: 19* Glamorgan v Oxford University, The Parks 1999
Best bowling: 5-31 Glamorgan v Sussex, Cardiff 1999

1999 Season

	M	Inns	NO	Runs	HS	Avge	100s	50s	Ct	St	O	M	Runs	Wkts	Avge	Best	5wI	10wM
Test																		
All First	10	13	3	77	19*	7.70	-	-	2	-	208	31	776	19	40.84	5-31	1	-
1-day Int																		
NatWest	1	0	0	0	0	-	-	-	-	-	5	0	30	0	-		-	-
B & H																			
1-day Lge	2	2	0	107	91	53.50	-	1	-	-								

Career Performances

	M	Inns	NO	Runs	HS	Avge	100s	50s	Ct	St	Balls	Runs	Wkts	Avge	Best	5wI	10wM
Test																	
All First	13	16	6	79	19*	7.90	-	-	3	-	1764	1121	26	43.11	5-31	1	-
1-day Int																	
NatWest	1	0	0	0	0	-	-	-	-	-	30	30	0	-		-	-
B & H																	
1-day Lge	2	2	0	107	91	53.50	-	1	-	-							

JOYCE, E. C.   Middlesex

Name: Edmund Christopher Joyce
Role: Left-hand bat, right-arm medium
bowler, gully fielder, occasional
wicket-keeper
Born: 22 September 1978, Dublin
Height: 5ft 10in
County debut: 1999
1st-Class catches: 2
Parents: Maureen and Jimmy
Marital status: Single
Family links with cricket: Father was an
occasional player; elder brother captains
Merrion CC and has played for Ireland age
group sides; younger brother represented
Ireland U19 in Youth World Cup in Sri Lanka
1999-2000; two sisters (twins) are in Irish
Ladies squad
Education: Presentation College, Bray,

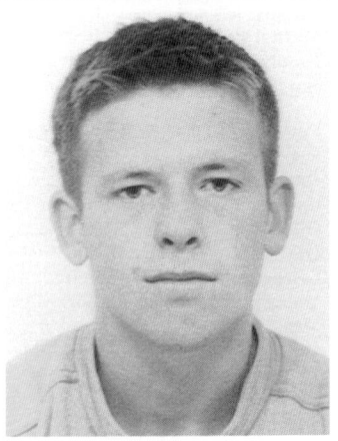

County Wicklow; Trinity College, Dublin (currently in year three of Economics and Geography degree)
Qualifications: Irish Leaving Cert
Career outside cricket: Student
Overseas tours: Ireland U19 to Bermuda (International Youth Tournament) 1997, to South Africa (Youth World Cup) 1997-98
Overseas teams played for: Coburg CC, Melbourne 1996-97
Cricketers particularly admired: Larry Gomes, Steve Waugh
Young players to look out for: Dominic Joyce (younger brother)
Other sports played: Rugby, soccer, golf
Relaxations: Music
Extras: Leinster U19 to Oxford Festival. Was only player to score a century at the International Youth Tournament, Bermuda 1997. Has represented Ireland senior side since 1997, including appearances in the Triple Crown tournament
Opinions on cricket: 'One competition less.'
Best batting: 43 Ireland v Scotland, Dublin 1997

1999 Season

	M	Inns	NO	Runs	HS	Avge	100s	50s	Ct	St	O	M	Runs	Wkts	Avge	Best	5wl	10wM
Test																		
All First	1	1	0	9	9	9.00	-	-	1	-								
1-day Int																		
NatWest	3	3	2	94	39*	94.00	-	-	1	-								
B & H																		
1-day Lge	1	1	0	20	20	20.00	-	-	-	-								

Career Performances

	M	Inns	NO	Runs	HS	Avge	100s	50s	Ct	St	Balls	Runs	Wkts	Avge	Best	5wl	10wM
Test																	
All First	3	5	0	91	43	18.20	-	-	2	-	84	78	0	-	-	-	-
1-day Int																	
NatWest	4	4	2	167	73	83.50	-	1	1	-							
B & H	3	3	0	76	42	25.33	-	-	1	-							
1-day Lge	1	1	0	20	20	20.00	-	-	-	-							

55. Which batsman scored 100s for Sussex in each innings of the same match on the same day in 1896?

KABIR ALI   Worcestershire

Name: Kabir Ali
Role: Right-hand bat, right-arm fast bowler
Born: 24 November 1980, Birmingham
Height: 6ft **Weight:** 11st 7lbs
Nickname: Taxi
County debut: 1999
Parents: Shabir Ali and Maqbool Begum
Marital status: Single
Family links with cricket: Father a club
cricketer. Cousin Kadeer Ali also plays for
Worcestershire
Education: Moseley School; Moseley Sixth
Form College
Qualifications: GNVQ
Career outside cricket: Studying – Leisure
and Tourism
Off-season: Fitness training
Overseas tours: Warwickshire U19
Development Squad to South Africa 1998
Cricketers particularly admired: Ian Botham, Wasim Akram
Young players to look out for: Moeen Munir
Other sports played: Football
Other sports followed: Football (Birmingham City)
Relaxations: Listening to music and going out with friends
Extras: Warwickshire Youth Young Player of the Year award
Opinions on cricket: 'More bouncers to be allowed in one-day games. Neutral
umpiring for international games.'
Best batting: 11 Worcestershire v Middlesex, Worcester 1999
Best bowling: 2-36 Worcestershire v Middlesex, Worcester 1999

1999 Season

	M	Inns	NO	Runs	HS	Avge	100s	50s	Ct	St	O	M	Runs	Wkts	Avge	Best	5wI	10wM
Test																		
All First	1	1	0	11	11	11.00	-	-	-	-	20	8	58	3	19.33	2-36	-	-
1-day Int																		
NatWest																		
B & H																		
1-day Lge																		

Career Performances

	M	Inns	NO	Runs	HS	Avge	100s	50s	Ct	St	Balls	Runs	Wkts	Avge	Best	5wI	10wM
Test																	
All First	1	1	0	11	11	11.00	-	-	-	-	120	58	3	19.33	2-36	-	-
1-day Int																	
NatWest																	
B & H																	
1-day Lge																	

KADEER ALI   Worcestershire

Name: Kadeer Ali
Role: Right-hand bat
Born: 7 March 1983, Birmingham
Height: 6ft 2in **Weight:** 10st 7lbs
Nickname: Kaddy
County debut: No first-team appearance
Parents: Munir Ali and Maqsood Begum
Marital status: Single
Family links with cricket: Father a cricket
coach and club cricketer. Cousin Kabir Ali
also plays for Worcestershire
Education: Handsworth Grammar; Moseley
Sixth Form College
Qualifications: 5 GCSEs
Career outside cricket: Studying
Off-season: Concentrating on fitness work
Cricketers particularly admired:
Sachin Tendulkar, Vikram Solanki
Young players to look out for: Kabir Ali,
Depesh Patel
Other sports played: Football
Other sports followed: Football (Liverpool FC)
Relaxations: Listening to music, going out with friends
Extras: Young Player awards at Warwickshire CCC. Played for the Worcestershire
Board XI in the NatWest Trophy in 1999
Opinions on cricket: 'Need to play longer version of game more than limited over
game.'

1999 Season (did not make any first-class or one-day appearances)

Career Performances

	M	Inns	NO	Runs	HS	Avge	100s	50s	Ct	St	Balls	Runs	Wkts	Avge	Best	5wl	10wM
Test																	
All First																	
1-day Int																	
NatWest	1	1	0	24	24	24.00	-	-	-	-							
B & H																	
1-day Lge																	

KALLIS, J. H. Glamorgan

Name: Jacques Henry Kallis
Role: Right-hand bat, right-arm
medium-fast bowler
Born: 16 October 1975, Pinelands,
South Africa
County debut: 1997 (Middlesex),
1999 (Glamorgan)
County cap: 1997 (Middlesex),
1999 (Glamorgan)
Test debut: 1995-96
Tests: 27
One-Day Internationals: 73
1st-Class 50s: 35
1st-Class 100s: 16
1st-Class 5 w. in innings: 3
1st-Class catches: 70
One-Day 100s: 8
One-Day 5 w. in innings: 1
Place in batting averages: 36th av. 40.22

(1998 10th av. 55.63)
Place in bowling averages: 101st av. 31.36 (1998 104th av. 33.06)
Strike rate: 51.81 (career 65.91)
Overseas tours: Western Province to Queensland 1995-96; South Africa U24 to
Sri Lanka 1995-96; South Africa A to England 1996; South Africa to India and
Pakistan (World Cup) 1995-96, to Sharjah 1995-96, to Pakistan 1997-98, to Australia
1997-98, to England 1998, to New Zealand 1998-99, to UK, Ireland and Holland
(World Cup) 1999, to Kenya (one-day series) 1999, to Zimbabwe 1999-2000
Overseas teams played for: Western Province 1993-94 –
Injuries: Stomach muscle injury delayed his debut for Glamorgan after the World Cup
Extras: Made first-class debut in 1993-94. Signed as overseas player for Middlesex
after Greg Blewett, the county's original choice, was selected for the 1997 Ashes

series. He was struck down with appendicitis during South Africa's 1997-98 tour of Pakistan. Hit both his maiden Test and One-Day International centuries during South Africa's 1997-98 winter tour of Australia. Scored 113* v Sri Lanka in South Africa's semi-final victory in the Wills International Cup 1998, then followed up with 5-30 as South Africa beat West Indies in the final. Man of the Match in fourth Test v West Indies at Cape Town 1998-99, scoring 110 and 88* and taking 7-124 in the match. Man of the Series, South Africa v West Indies 1998-99 with 485 runs, 16 wickets and seven catches. Shared in record second-wicket stand for South Africa of 315* with Herschelle Gibbs in the second Test v New Zealand at Christchurch in March 1999. Represented South Africa in the 1999 World Cup. Featured in the Vodafone World Cup XI, a 'dream team' selected by journalists after the 1999 tournament. Joined Glamorgan in 1999 as overseas player. Scored 155* in National League match v Surrey at Pontypridd 1999 on his one-day debut for Glamorgan, sharing a new Glamorgan record one-day third-wicket stand of 204 with Matthew Maynard and beating Maynard's individual Glamorgan record for the Sunday/National League (132 v Surrey 1997). Awarded Glamorgan cap 1999. One of South Africa's Five Cricketers of the Year 1999. CEAT International Cricketer of the Year Award 1998-99. Pricewaterhouse-Cooper/FICA International Young Player of the Year 1998-99. Left Glamorgan at end of 1999 season because of South Africa commitments but has agreed to return for 2001

Best batting: 186* Western Province v Queensland, Brisbane 1995-96
Best bowling: 5-54 Middlesex v Kent, Lord's 1997
Stop press: Selected for South Africa's tour of India 1999-2000

1999 Season

	M	Inns	NO	Runs	HS	Avge	100s	50s	Ct	St	O	M	Runs	Wkts	Avge	Best	5wI	10wM
Test																		
All First	6	9	0	362	101	40.22	1	2	3	-	95	12	345	11	31.36	3-52	-	-
1-day Int	8	8	2	312	96	52.00	-	4	1	-	66	5	260	8	32.50	3-26	-	
NatWest	1	1	0	12	12	12.00	-	-	1	-								
B & H																		
1-day Lge	7	7	2	484	155 *	96.80	2	2	2	-	39.3	3	151	6	25.16	2-27	-	

Career Performances

	M	Inns	NO	Runs	HS	Avge	100s	50s	Ct	St	Balls	Runs	Wkts	Avge	Best	5wI	10wM
Test	27	44	5	1503	148 *	38.53	4	7	23	-	3390	1336	44	30.36	5-90	1	-
All First	97	151	18	6108	186 *	45.92	16	35	70	-	9822	4398	149	29.51	5-54	3	-
1-day Int	73	71	12	2439	113 *	41.33	5	16	28	-	2072	1599	52	30.75	5-30	1	
NatWest	4	4	0	128	100	32.00	1	-	2	-	138	107	5	21.40	4-47	-	
B & H	2	2	0	82	72	41.00	-	1	-	-	90	79	2	39.50	2-49	-	
1-day Lge	18	17	2	624	155 *	41.60	2	2	6	-	443	275	11	25.00	2-19	-	

KASIR SHAH   Derbyshire

Name: Kasir Shah
Role: Left-hand bat, left-arm fast bowler
Born: 15 June 1978, Jhelum, Punjab,
Pakistan
Height: 6ft **Weight:** 12st
Nickname: The Cap
County debut: 1999 (one-day)
Parents: Zamir Shah and Zabeda Bibi
Marital status: Single
Education: Anderton Park School; Wheelers
Lane Secondary School, Birmingham;
Cadbury College, King's Norton,
Birmingham; University of Manchester
Qualifications: 11 GCSEs, 3 A-levels,
BSc Pharmacy (2:1)
Career outside cricket: Trainee pharmacist
Cricketers particularly admired: Wasim
Akram ('played with him at Smethwick CC
in Birmingham Premier League'), Shoaib Akhtar, Graham Thorpe
Young players to look out for: 'My little brother Qasim'
Other sports played: Football (Acock Green FC, Central Warwickshire League; also
won college football championship with 1st XI)
Other sports followed: Football (Manchester United – 'winning team')
Injuries: Out for 'a couple of games' with knee injury
Relaxations: 'Spending time with my friends'
Extras: Played for Warwickshire U19 and 2nd XI. Took hat-trick v Notts in U19
competition. Was in Warwickshire's U19 Festival winning side at Fenner's. 'Scored
42* for Smethwick CC v Pakistan in 1999 World Cup warm-up match ("most
enjoyable innings")'
Opinions on cricket: 'Not enough natural talent; too many average players.'

1999 Season

	M	Inns	NO	Runs	HS	Avge	100s	50s	Ct	St	O	M	Runs	Wkts	Avge	Best	5wI	10wM
Test																		
All First																		
1-day Int																		
NatWest																		
B & H																		
1-day Lge	3	1	1	0	0*	-	-	-	1	-	18	0	113	3	37.66	2-36	-	

Career Performances

	M	Inns	NO	Runs	HS	Avge	100s	50s	Ct	St	Balls	Runs	Wkts	Avge	Best	5wI	10wM
Test																	
All First																	
1-day Int																	
NatWest																	
B & H																	
1-day Lge	3	1	1	0	0*	-	-	-	-	1	-	108	113	3	37.66	2-36	-

KASPROWICZ, M. S. Leicestershire

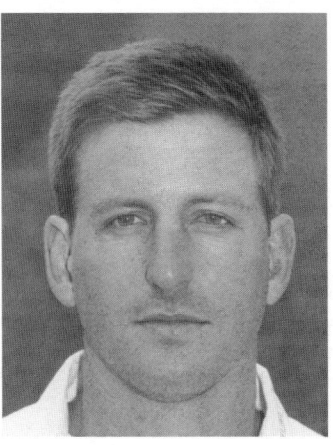

Name: Michael Scott Kasprowicz
Role: Right-hand bat, right-arm fast bowler
Born: 10 February 1972, Brisbane
Height: 6ft 3in
County debut: 1994 (Essex), 1999 (Leicestershire)
County cap: 1994 (Essex)
Test debut: 1996-97
Tests: 14
One-Day Internationals: 16
50 wickets in a season: 2
1st-Class 50s: 6
1st-Class 5 w. in innings: 26
1st-Class 10 w. in match: 2
1st-Class catches: 49
One-Day 5 w. in innings: 1
Place in batting averages: 134th av. 26.68
Place in bowling averages: 69th av. 27.50
Strike rate: 55.00 (career 54.34)
Marital status: Single
Education: Brisbane State High School
Overseas tours: Australia YC to England 1991; Australia to England 1997, to India 1997-98
Overseas teams played for: Queensland 1989-90 –
Extras: Was captain of cricket for four years at Brisbane State High School and played for Queensland U17 and U19. Played for Australia U17 and made his Queensland debut aged 17. Took nine wickets in first 'Test' at Grace Road, Leicester, on Australia YC tour to England 1991. Was second leading wicket-taker in the Sheffield Shield 1992-93 with 51 wickets (av. 24.13). Toured New Zealand with Australian Schoolboys rugby team in 1989. Left Essex at end of 1994 season. Joined Leicestershire in 1999 as overseas player on one-year contract; released by Leicestershire at end of 1999 season

Best batting: 73 Leicestershire v Hampshire, Southampton 1999
Best bowling: 7-36 Australia v England, The Oval 1997

1999 Season

	M	Inns	NO	Runs	HS	Avge	100s	50s	Ct	St	O	M	Runs	Wkts	Avge	Best	5wI	10wM
Test																		
All First	16	23	4	507	73	26.68	-	5	3	-	485.5	112	1458	53	27.50	5-42	2	-
1-day Int																		
NatWest	1	1	0	15	15	15.00	-	-	-	-	10	1	27	1	27.00	1-27	-	
B & H	1	1	0	40	40	40.00	-	-	-	-	10	0	36	2	18.00	2-36	-	
1-day Lge	13	9	2	133	38	19.00	-	-	-	-	100.1	10	435	18	24.16	4-30	-	

Career Performances

	M	Inns	NO	Runs	HS	Avge	100s	50s	Ct	St	Balls	Runs	Wkts	Avge	Best	5wI	10wM
Test	14	18	2	180	25	11.25	-	-	5	-	2780	1345	38	35.39	7-36	2	-
All First	131	171	33	2292	73	16.60	-	6	49	-	26251	13498	483	27.94	7-36	26	2
1-day Int	16	10	8	105	28 *	52.50	-	-	3	-	817	709	22	32.22	3-50	-	
NatWest	2	2	0	28	15	14.00	-	-	-	-	132	87	6	14.50	5-60	1	
B & H	3	1	0	40	40	40.00	-	-	1	-	150	112	4	28.00	2-36	-	
1-day Lge	28	21	2	194	38	10.21	-	-	2	-	1169	893	29	30.79	4-30	-	

KATICH, S. M. Durham

Name: Simon Mathew Katich
Role: Left-hand bat, left-arm spin bowler
Born: 21 August 1975, Middle Swan, Western Australia
County debut: No first-team appearance
1st-Class 50s: 8
1st-Class 100s: 5
1st-Class catches: 19
Strike rate: (career 134.00)
Marital status: Single
Off-season: Contracted to Australia
Overseas tours: Australia to Sri Lanka and Zimbabwe 1999-2000
Overseas teams played for: Midland-Guildford, Western Australia; Western Australia 1996-97 –
Extras: Scored century (106) for Western Australia v England at Perth 1998-99; this was middle 100 of three centuries in successive first-class matches for Western

Australia. Captained ACB Chairman's XI v England 1998-99. Scored 115 in Western Australia's first innings in their 1998-99 Sheffield Shield final victory. Second in Sheffield Shield averages 1998-99 with 909 runs at 56.81. Has joined Durham for 2000 as overseas player, replacing David Boon
Best batting: 154* Western Australia v Tasmania, Hobart 1998-99
Best bowling: 1-4 Western Australia v Victoria, Perth 1998-99

1999 Season (did not make any first-class or one-day appearances)

Career Performances

	M	Inns	NO	Runs	HS	Avge	100s	50s	Ct	St	Balls	Runs	Wkts	Avge	Best	5wl	10wM
Test																	
All First	21	39	8	1632	154*	52.64	5	8	19	-	402	244	3	81.33	1-4	-	-
1-day Int																	
NatWest																	
B & H																	
1-day Lge																	

KEECH, M.   Hampshire

Name: Matthew Keech
Role: Right-hand bat, right-arm 'military medium' bowler
Born: 21 October 1970, Hampstead
Height: 6ft   **Weight:** 13st 4lbs
County debut: 1991 (Middlesex), 1994 (Hampshire)
1st-Class 50s: 15
1st-Class 100s: 3
1st-Class catches: 56
Place in batting averages: 111th av. 29.41 (1998 153rd av. 23.92)
Strike rate: (career 101.25)
Parents: Ron and Brenda
Marital status: Single
Family links with cricket: 'Mother and father like to watch a good game'
Education: Northumberland Park School, Tottenham; 'Middlesex and Hampshire dressing-rooms'
Qualifications: 5 O-levels, NCA coaching certificate
Career outside cricket: Coaching

Overseas tours: England YC to Australia 1989-90
Overseas teams played for: Mosman, Sydney 1988-89; Lancaster Park, Christchurch, New Zealand 1990-91
Cricketers particularly admired: Mike Gatting, Robin Smith and Tony Middleton
Young players to look out for: Jason Laney, Owais Shah
Other sports followed: Football, golf, squash
Relaxations: 'Caffrey's, avoiding jobs to be done around the house'
Extras: Released by Hampshire at end of 1999 season
Best batting: 127 Hampshire v Oxford University, The Parks 1997
Best bowling: 2-28 Middlesex v Gloucestershire, Bristol 1993

1999 Season

	M	Inns	NO	Runs	HS	Avge	100s	50s	Ct	St	O	M	Runs	Wkts	Avge	Best	5wI	10wM
Test																		
All First	8	13	1	353	50	29.41	-	1	8	-	9	1	37	0	-	-	-	-
1-day Int																		
NatWest	2	2	1	18	17 *	18.00	-	-	-	-	5	0	16	2	8.00	2-16	-	
B & H																		
1-day Lge	4	3	0	36	27	12.00	-	-	1	-								

Career Performances

	M	Inns	NO	Runs	HS	Avge	100s	50s	Ct	St	Balls	Runs	Wkts	Avge	Best	5wI	10wM
Test																	
All First	69	111	12	2824	127	28.52	3	15	56	-	810	420	8	52.50	2-28	-	-
1-day Int																	
NatWest	7	5	1	80	34	20.00	-	-	3	-	96	63	2	31.50	2-16	-	
B & H	14	13	0	313	74	24.07	-	1	8	-	66	47	1	47.00	1-37	-	
1-day Lge	80	74	10	1421	98	22.20	-	4	16	-	492	393	9	43.66	2-22	-	

KEEDY, G.   Lancashire

Name: Gary Keedy
Role: Left-hand bat, slow left-arm 'with a few revs on it'
Born: 27 November 1974, Wakefield
Height: 6ft **Weight:** 11st 7lbs
Nickname: Bod, Seedy, Linus, Binbag
County debut: 1994 (Yorkshire), 1995 (Lancashire)
1st-Class 5 w. in innings: 3
1st-Class 10 w. in match: 1
1st-Class catches: 13
Place in bowling averages: 68th av. 27.34 (1998 96th av. 31.27)

Strike rate: 61.30 (career 78.90)
Parents: Roy and Pat
Marital status: Single
Family links with cricket: Twin brother
plays for Castleford in the Yorkshire League
Education: Garforth Comprehensive
Qualifications: 4 GCSEs, junior coaching
award
Overseas tours: England U18 to South
Africa 1992-93, to Denmark 1994;
England U19 to Sri Lanka 1993-94
Overseas teams played for: Frankston,
Melbourne 1995-96
Cricketers particularly admired:
Shane Warne, Graham Gooch
Other sports followed: Rugby league
(Leeds), football (Leeds United)
Extras: Player of the Series for England U19
v West Indies U19 in 1993. Graduate of the Yorkshire Cricket Academy. Played for
England U19 in the home series against India in 1994
Best batting: 26 Lancashire v Essex, Chelmsford 1996
Best bowling: 6-79 Lancashire v Surrey, The Oval 1997

1999 Season

	M	Inns	NO	Runs	HS	Avge	100s	50s	Ct	St	O	M	Runs	Wkts	Avge	Best	5wI	10wM
Test																		
All First	7	9	6	17	9 *	5.66	-	-	1	-	265.4	73	711	26	27.34	5-67	1	-
1-day Int																		
NatWest																		
B & H																		
1-day Lge																		

Career Performances

	M	Inns	NO	Runs	HS	Avge	100s	50s	Ct	St	Balls	Runs	Wkts	Avge	Best	5wI	10wM
Test																	
All First	52	59	38	219	26	10.42	-	-	13	-	10494	4977	133	37.42	6-79	3	1
1-day Int																	
NatWest																	
B & H																	
1-day Lge	5	0	0	0	0	-	-	-	-	-	175	175	1	175.00	1-40	-	

KENDALL, W. S.   Hampshire

Name: William Salwey Kendall
Role: Right-hand bat, right-arm medium
bowler, occasional wicket-keeper
Born: 18 December 1973, Wimbledon
Height: 5ft 10in **Weight:** 12st 7lbs
Nickname: Villy, Lemon, Baldy, Wiggy
County debut: 1996
1000 runs in a season: 2
1st-Class 50s: 19
1st-Class 100s: 5
1st-Class 200s: 1
1st-Class catches: 65
Place in batting averages: 40th av. 39.53
(1998 30th av. 42.50)
Strike rate: (career 68.30)
Parents: Tom and Sue
Marital status: Single
Family links with cricket: Father played
club cricket with East Horsley, Hampshire Hogs and MCC. Older brother James
played for Durham University
Education: Bradfield College, Berkshire; Keble College, Oxford University
Qualifications: 10 GCSEs, 3 A-levels, 1 AS-level, BA (Hons) Modern History
Career outside cricket: Journalism – weekly column in *Hampshire Chronicle*
Off-season: Working for sports marketing company in London
Overseas tours: Bradfield College to Barbados 1991; Troubadours to Argentina 1997;
Hampshire CCC to Anguilla 1997
Overseas teams played for: Frankston Peninsular CC, Melbourne 1997-98
Cricketers particularly admired: Robin Smith, Graham Thorpe, Mark Ramprakash,
'and anyone playing over 36'
Young players to look out for: Derek Kenway, Charlie van der Gucht, Lawrence
Prittipaul, James Adams
Other sports played/followed: Hockey (for Oxford University), football (offered
terms by Reading) and golf
Relaxations: Playing or watching sport, socialising with friends, relaxing at home;
'hacking up golf courses, travelling and quiet days with girlfriend, Emily'
Extras: Surrey Young Cricketer of the Year 1992. Awarded Gray-Nicolls Trophy for
Schoolboy Cricketer of the Year in memory of Len Newbery 1992. Made first-class
debut for Oxford University in 1994. Played football for Independent Schools 1992.
Offered one-year contract with Reading FC. Hampshire Exiles Player of the Year for
1996. Awarded county cap 1999
Opinions on cricket: 'The key must be to find a balance between giving county

members enough cricket to watch and keeping players fresh enough to produce quality. The Championship, a one-day league (50 overs) and one knockout trophy is enough. Consistency and patience are required by all. Good food at all grounds is vital.'

Best batting: 201 Hampshire v Sussex, Southampton 1999
Best bowling: 3-37 Oxford University v Derbyshire, The Parks 1995

1999 Season

	M	Inns	NO	Runs	HS	Avge	100s	50s	Ct	St	O	M	Runs	Wkts	Avge	Best	5wI	10wM
Test																		
All First	19	32	2	1186	201	39.53	2	7	25	-	4.5	0	17	0	-	-	-	-
1-day Int																		
NatWest	2	2	0	43	39	21.50	-	-	2	-								
B & H	1	1	0	28	28	28.00	-	-	-	-								
1-day Lge	11	10	2	136	31	17.00	-	-	4	-								

Career Performances

	M	Inns	NO	Runs	HS	Avge	100s	50s	Ct	St	Balls	Runs	Wkts	Avge	Best	5wI	10wM
Test																	
All First	71	111	16	3694	201	38.88	6	19	65	-	683	416	10	41.60	3-37	-	-
1-day Int																	
NatWest	4	4	1	59	39	19.66	-	-	2	-							
B & H	10	10	0	157	28	15.70	-	-	-	-							
1-day Lge	40	35	3	574	55	17.93	-	1	22	-	12	22	0	-	-	-	

56. Who captained Middlesex to their first County Championship in 1903?

KENNIS, G. J.   Somerset

Name: Gregor John Kennis
Role: Right-hand bat, right-arm
off-spin bowler
Born: 9 March 1974, Yokohama, Japan
Height: 6ft 2in **Weight:** 13st
Nickname: G
County debut: 1994 (Surrey),
1998 (Somerset)
1st-Class 100s: 1
1st-Class catches: 13
Place in batting averages: 52nd av. 37.50
(1998 266th av. 11.83)
Parents: Michael and Sally
Marital status: Single
Family links with cricket: 'Dad played for his
company side and is now a qualified coach'
Education: Tiffin Boys' School; Stewart
Cricket Academy

Qualifications: 9 GCSEs, 1 A-level, senior cricket coach
Career outside cricket: Hospitality
Off-season: 'Training. Touring around the racecourses of England'
Overseas tours: Surrey U19 to Barbados 1991
Overseas teams played for: Claremont Nedlands, Perth 1995-96; Marist Newman
Old Boys CC, Perth 1996-99
Cricketers particularly admired: Steve Waugh, Andrew Howes
Young players to look out for: Ben Hollioake
Other sports played: Golf
Other sports followed: Horse racing
Injuries: Out for a total of six weeks with disc trouble in lower back and broken hand
Relaxations: Going racing, playing golf
Extras: Set a record for Surrey 2nd XI with his 258 against Leicestershire in 1995.
Surrey 2nd XI Batsman of the Year 1995. Joined Somerset for 1998 and was released
at end of 1998 season. Re-engaged for 1999 on summer contract after injury to Mark
Lathwell and scored maiden first-class century (175) v New Zealand at Taunton
Opinions on cricket: 'Twelve-month contracts should be brought in to make the sport
in general more professional. How many other sportsmen at the top of their game have
a six-month "close season"?'
Best batting: 175 Somerset v New Zealand, Taunton 1999

1999 Season

	M	Inns	NO	Runs	HS	Avge	100s	50s	Ct	St	O	M	Runs	Wkts	Avge	Best	5wI	10wM
Test																		
All First	3	6	0	225	175	37.50	1	-	2	-								
1-day Int																		
NatWest																		
B & H																		
1-day Lge	1	0	0	0	0	-	-	-	-	-								

Career Performances

	M	Inns	NO	Runs	HS	Avge	100s	50s	Ct	St	Balls	Runs	Wkts	Avge	Best	5wI	10wM
Test																	
All First	12	23	1	436	175	19.81	1	-	13	-	24	4	0	-	-	-	-
1-day Int																	
NatWest																	
B & H																	
1-day Lge	2	1	0	5	5	5.00	-	-	-								

KENWAY, D. A.   Hampshire

Name: Derek Anthony Kenway
Role: Right-hand bat, occasional
wicket-keeper
Born: 12 June 1978, Fareham
Height: 5ft 10in **Weight:** 14st
Nickname: Kenners
County debut: 1997
1000 runs in a season: 1
1st-Class 50s: 8
1st-Class 100s: 1
1st-Class catches: 15
Place in batting averages: 26th av. 42.20
Strike rate: (career 36.00)
Parents: Keith and Geraldine
Marital status: Single
Family links with cricket: Brother plays in
the Southern League
Education: Botley Primary School;
St George's, Southampton; Barton Peveril College
Qualifications: 6 GCSEs, NCA coaching award, qualified snowboard instructor,
'Cypriot dancing'

Career outside cricket: 'Holidays'
Off-season: 'Holidays'
Overseas tours: West of England U15 to West Indies 1993
Overseas teams played for: Beaumaris CC, Melbourne 1997-98
Cricketers particularly admired: Steve Soper, Robin Smith, Mark Waugh
Young players to look out for: Ricky Fox, Rich Kenway, Dave Adams
Other sports played: Football, kickboxing, boxing, golf
Other sports followed: Football (Southampton FC)
Relaxations: Socialising, music
Extras: *Daily Telegraph* Batting Award (West) 1994. Southern League Young Player of the Year in 1996. Scored maiden first-class century (102) v Warwickshire at Southampton 1999. Made 1000 runs in a season for the first time in 1999
Opinions on cricket: 'Longer lunch and tea breaks.'
Best batting: 102 Hampshire v Warwickshire, Southampton 1999
Best bowling: 1-5 Hampshire v Warwickshire, Southampton 1997

1999 Season

	M	Inns	NO	Runs	HS	Avge	100s	50s	Ct	St	O	M	Runs	Wkts	Avge	Best	5wI	10wM
Test																		
All First	19	31	6	1055	102	42.20	1	7	13	-	1	0	1	0	-	-	-	-
1-day Int																		
NatWest	2	2	0	100	53	50.00	-	1	1	-								
B & H	1	1	0	9	9	9.00	-	-	-	-								
1-day Lge	16	14	0	341	58	24.35	-	2	5	-								

Career Performances

	M	Inns	NO	Runs	HS	Avge	100s	50s	Ct	St	Balls	Runs	Wkts	Avge	Best	5wI	10wM
Test																	
All First	23	38	7	1195	102	38.54	1	8	15	-	72	76	2	38.00	1-5	-	-
1-day Int																	
NatWest	2	2	0	100	53	50.00	-	1	1	-							
B & H	1	1	0	9	9	9.00	-	-	-	-							
1-day Lge	19	15	0	346	58	23.06	-	2	5	-							

KERR, J. I. D.   Somerset

Name: Jason Ian Douglas Kerr
Role: Right-hand bat, right-arm
fast-medium bowler, (wicket-keeper 'if
required')
Born: 7 April 1974, Bolton, Lancashire
Height: 6ft 3in **Weight:** 12st 6lbs
Nickname: Junior B
County debut: 1993
1st-Class 50s: 5
1st-Class 5 w. in innings: 2
1st-Class catches: 15
Place in batting averages: 192nd av. 21.16
Place in bowling averages: 118th av. 34.67
Strike rate: 59.09 (career 59.97)
Parents: Len and Janet
Marital status: Single
Family links with cricket: 'Brother Andy is
becoming a young legend'
Education: Withins High School; Bolton Met College
Qualifications: 5 GCSEs, BTEC National Diploma in Business Studies, cricket coach
Overseas tours: England U19 to India 1992-93; Lancashire U19 to Isle of Man
Overseas teams played for: Gordon Districts CC, Sydney, Australia 1994-95; Taita
CC, Wellington, New Zealand 1996-97; Subiaco Floriat, Perth
Cricketers particularly admired: A.R. Caddick ('bowling machine')
Young players to look out for: Andy Kerr
Other sports followed: Bolton 'The Great' Wanderers
Relaxations: 'Playing golf, socialising, squash, television, swimming, sleeping,
listening to music, spending time with friends and girlfriend Emma'
Extras: His 7-23 v Leics at Taunton 1999 included a spell of 5-6 from 3.1 overs
Opinions on cricket: 'Still the best.'
Best batting: 80 Somerset v West Indies, Taunton 1995
Best bowling: 7-23 Somerset v Leicestershire, Taunton 1999

1999 Season

	M	Inns	NO	Runs	HS	Avge	100s	50s	Ct	St	O	M	Runs	Wkts	Avge	Best	5wI	10wM
Test																		
All First	14	19	1	381	64	21.16	-	2	5	-	305.2	68	1075	31	34.67	7-23	1	-
1-day Int																		
NatWest	5	4	2	29	21	14.50	-	-	2	-	31	0	150	1	150.00	1-29	-	
B & H																		
1-day Lge	15	10	1	151	56	16.77	-	1	4	-	86	1	434	17	25.52	2-22	-	

Career Performances

	M	Inns	NO	Runs	HS	Avge	100s	50s	Ct	St	Balls	Runs	Wkts	Avge	Best	5wI	10wM
Test																	
All First	46	66	10	1111	80	19.83	-	5	15	-	5698	3665	95	38.57	7-23	2	-
1-day Int																	
NatWest	9	7	2	32	21	6.40	-	-	2	-	342	297	8	37.12	3-32	-	
B & H	6	3	0	31	17	10.33	-	-	-	-	234	173	7	24.71	3-34	-	
1-day Lge	58	36	9	372	56	13.77	-	1	9	-	2113	1911	67	28.52	4-28	-	

KETTLEBOROUGH, R. A.　　　Middlesex

Name: Richard Allan Kettleborough
Role: Left-hand bat, right-arm
medium bowler
Born: 15 March 1973, Sheffield
Height: 5ft 10in **Weight:** 12st
Nickname: Ketts
County debut: 1994 (Yorkshire),
1998 (Middlesex)
1st-Class 50s: 7
1st-Class 100s: 1
1st-Class catches: 20
Place in batting averages: 202nd av. 20.00
(1998 115th av. 28.44)
Strike rate: (career 126.00)
Parents: Allan and Pat
Marital status: Single
Family links with cricket: Father played for
Yorkshire and is now coach at Worksop
College
Education: Laughton All Saints Junior School; Worksop College; Airedale and
Wharfdale College, Leeds
Qualifications: 5 GCSEs, BTEC in Recreational Management, senior coaching award
Career outside cricket: 'Would like to own my own pub'
Overseas tours: Worksop College to Australia 1988-89; England U18 to Canada 1991;
Yorkshire CCC to South Africa 1995
Overseas teams played for: Somerset West, Cape Town 1993-94
Cricketers particularly admired: David Gower
Other sports followed: Football (Sheffield Wednesday FC)
Extras: Won the Lord's Taverners U15 award for the Most Promising Young Cricketer
in 1988. 2nd XI cap at Yorkshire. Joined Middlesex for 1998. Released by Middlesex
at end of 1999 season

Opinions on cricket: 'Not enough time to practise during the season.'
Best batting: 108 Yorkshire v Essex, Headingley 1996
Best bowling: 2-26 Yorkshire v Nottinghamshire, Scarborough 1996

1999 Season

	M	Inns	NO	Runs	HS	Avge	100s	50s	Ct	St	O	M	Runs	Wkts	Avge	Best	5wl	10wM
Test																		
All First| 8	15	0	300	93	20.00	-	2	4	-	7	6	1	0	-		-	-	-
1-day Int																		
NatWest																		
B & H																		
1-day Lge	4	3	0	62	58	20.66	-	1	-	-	4	0	28	0	-		-	-

Career Performances

	M	Inns	NO	Runs	HS	Avge	100s	50s	Ct	St	Balls	Runs	Wkts	Avge	Best	5wl	10wM
Test																	
All First	33	56	6	1258	108	25.16	1	7	20	-	378	243	3	81.00	2-26	-	-
1-day Int																	
NatWest																	
B & H																	
1-day Lge	18	13	4	206	58	22.88	-	1	5	-	126	129	3	43.00	2-43	-	

57. On the third morning of Worcestershire's match v Warwickshire at Worcester in 1979, two Worcestershire batsmen scored 100s before lunch. One was G.M. Turner (107). Who was the other?

KEY, R. W. T.   Kent

Name: Robert William Trevor Key
Role: Right-hand bat
Born: 12 May 1979, Dulwich
Height: 6ft 1in **Weight:** 12st 7lbs
Nickname: Keysy
County debut: 1998
1st-Class 50s: 6
1st-Class 100s: 3
1st-Class catches: 33
Place in batting averages: 130th av. 26.96
(1998 126th av. 26.60)
Parents: Trevor and Lynn
Marital status: Single
Family links with cricket: Mother played
for Kent Ladies. Father played club cricket in
Derby. Sister Elizabeth played for her junior
school side
Education: Worsley Bridge Primary School;
Langley Park Boys' School
Qualifications: 10 GCSEs, NCA coaching award, GNVQ Business
Career outside cricket: 'Work in the futures market'
Overseas tours: Kent U13 to Holland; England U17 to Bermuda 1997; England U19
to South Africa (including Youth World Cup) 1997-98; England A to Zimbabwe and
South Africa 1998-99
Overseas teams played for: Green Point CC, Cape Town 1996-97
Cricketers particularly admired: Alan Wells, Steve Marsh, Graham Cowdrey,
'and all the Kent staff'
Young players to look out for: Andrew Pickering, Matthew Walker, Darren Thomas,
Graeme Swann, Nev Wharton
Other sports played: Hockey, football, snooker
Other sports followed: Football (Chelsea), basketball (Chicago Bulls)
Relaxations: Snooker, socialising with friends
Extras: Played for England U17 and England U19 Development XI. Also played for
South England U14 and U19. County tennis player. Played for England U19 against
Zimbabwe in 1997 and captained the England U17 side to victory in the International
Youth Tournament in Bermuda in July; played for the victorious England side in the
U19 World Cup in South Africa. Shared England U19 Man of the Series award with
Graeme Swann v Pakistan U19 1998
Opinions on cricket: 'The game needs to be marketed a lot better by highly qualified
marketing people.'
Best batting: 125 Kent v Somerset, Taunton 1999

1999 Season

	M	Inns	NO	Runs	HS	Avge	100s	50s	Ct	St	O	M	Runs	Wkts	Avge	Best	5wI	10wM
Test																		
All First	19	33	2	836	125	26.96	1	5	18	-								
1-day Int																		
NatWest	2	2	0	133	67	66.50	-	2	1	-								
B & H																		
1-day Lge	10	10	3	329	76 *	47.00	-	2	1	-								

Career Performances

	M	Inns	NO	Runs	HS	Avge	100s	50s	Ct	St	Balls	Runs	Wkts	Avge	Best	5wI	10wM
Test																	
All First	35	61	2	1500	125	25.42	3	6	33	-	6	1	0	-	-	-	-
1-day Int																	
NatWest	4	4	0	157	67	39.25	-	2	1	-							
B & H	1	1	0	4	4	4.00	-	-	-	-							
1-day Lge	21	18	3	555	76 *	37.00	-	5	1	-							

KHAN, A.   Kent

Name: Amjad Khan
Role: Right-hand bat, right-arm fast bowler
Born: 14 October 1980, Copenhagen, Denmark
Height: 6ft **Weight:** 11st 7lbs
County debut: No first-team appearance
Parents: Aslam and Raisa
Marital status: Single
Education: Skolen på Duevej, Denmark; Falkonĕrgårdens Gymnasium
Overseas tours: Denmark U19 to Canada 1996, to Bermuda 1997, to South Africa and Wales 1998, to Ireland 1999; Denmark to Holland 1998, to Zimbabwe 1999
Overseas teams played for: Kjøbenhavns Boldklub, Denmark
Cricketers particularly admired: Wasim Akram, Sachin Tendulkar, Allan Donald
Young players to look out for: Baljit Singh, Andy Lambert
Other sports followed: Football (Denmark)
Injuries: Out for three months with back injury

Relaxations: Working out, listening to music, sleeping
Extras: The youngest Danish international ever at age of 17. Played for Denmark in the NatWest Trophy 1999
Opinions on cricket: 'Action should be taken to make the game more attractive and thereby remove all prejudices related to cricket. Coloured clothing and floodlights are a good start.'

1999 Season (did not make any first-class or one-day appearances)

Career Performances

	M	Inns	NO	Runs	HS	Avge	100s	50s	Ct	St	Balls	Runs	Wkts	Avge	Best	5wI	10wM
Test																	
All First																	
1-day Int																	
NatWest	1	1	0	0	0	0.00	-	-	-	-	60	38	2	19.00	2-38	-	
B & H																	
1-day Lge																	

KHAN, A. A. Leicestershire

Name: Amer Ali Khan
Role: Right-hand bat, leg-break bowler
Born: 5 November 1969, Lahore, Pakistan
Height: 5ft 9in **Weight:** 12st 7lbs
Nickname: Aga
County debut: 1995 (Middlesex), 1997 (Sussex), 1999 (Leics)
1st-Class 50s: 1
1st-Class 5 w. in innings: 1
1st-Class catches: 9
One-Day 5 w. in innings: 1
Strike rate: 146.00 (career 82.60)
Parents: M. Hanif Khan and Shireen Hanif
Marital status: Single
Family links with cricket: 'Dad used to play club cricket; my cousin Sajid Hussain used to play for RDCA and PIA (first-class cricket); my cousin Amir Raza used to play for Islamabad (first-class cricket)'

Education: 25F Model Town; Muslim Model High School; MAO College (all Lahore)
Qualifications: Coaching
Off-season: Going overseas to play cricket

Overseas teams played for: Wakatu CC, Nelson, New Zealand 1995-96; Motueka CA, New Zealand 1997-98; Kuils River CC and Coronation CC, Cape Town 1998-99
Cricketers particularly admired: 'All of them who go out on the park and do the business'
Young players to look out for: Ashley Wright, Atul Sachdeva, Cliff Eaton
Other sports played: Two-touch football, touch rugby
Other sports followed: Basketball (Chicago Bulls)
Injuries: One week off with 'whiplash given to me by Mr Darren Maddy; if you see him keep away from him'
Relaxations: 'Going to the gym and cinema; chilling out; listening to music'
Extras: Released by Sussex at end of 1998 season and joined Leics for 1999
Best batting: 52 Sussex v Hampshire, Southampton 1997
Best bowling: 5-137 Sussex v Middlesex, Lord's 1997

1999 Season

	M	Inns	NO	Runs	HS	Avge	100s	50s	Ct	St	O	M	Runs	Wkts	Avge	Best	5wI	10wM
Test																		
All First	1	1	0	5	5	5.00	-	-	-	-	24.2	9	63	1	63.00	1-11	-	-
1-day Int																		
NatWest																		
B & H																		
1-day Lge																		

Career Performances

	M	Inns	NO	Runs	HS	Avge	100s	50s	Ct	St	Balls	Runs	Wkts	Avge	Best	5wI	10wM
Test																	
All First	23	29	5	337	52	14.04	-	1	9	-	3965	1991	48	41.47	5-137	1	-
1-day Int																	
NatWest	4	1	0	4	4	4.00	-	-	1	-	240	196	2	98.00	1-13	-	
B & H	5	3	0	15	8	5.00	-	-	2	-	294	217	8	27.12	3-31	-	
1-day Lge	13	9	3	48	22*	8.00	-	-	2	-	545	474	15	31.60	5-40	1	

KHAN, R. M.　　　　　　　　　　Derbyshire

Name: Rawait M. Khan
Role: Right-hand bat
Born: 5 March 1982, Birmingham
Height: 5ft 9in **Weight:** 9st 7lbs
Nickname: Ray
County debut: No first-team appearance
Parents: Hashim Khan and Barish Begum
Marital status: Single
Family links with cricket: Father played for
Warwickshire 2nd XI. Brother Zubair also
plays for Derbyshire
Education: Parkhill School; Moseley School;
Solihull College
Career outside cricket: Studying
Cricketers particularly admired: Steve
Waugh
Other sports played: Football, badminton
Relaxations: 'Socialising with friends'

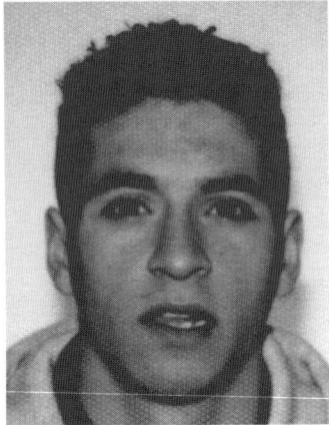

Opinions on cricket: 'I feel the game is getting more and more exciting because of
more one-day games and floodlit games.'

KHAN, W. G.　　　　　　　　　　　Sussex

Name: Wasim Gulzar Khan
Role: Left-hand bat, leg-break bowler
Born: 26 February 1971, Birmingham
Height: 6ft 1in **Weight:** 11st 11lbs
Nickname: Mowgli, Jai ('son of Tarzan')
County debut: 1992 (one-day, Warwicks),
1995 (first-class, Warwicks), 1998 (Sussex)
1st-Class 50s: 16
1st-Class 100s: 5
1st-Class catches: 36
Place in batting averages: 217th av. 18.55 (1998 110th av. 28.86)
Parents: Gulzar Ahmed (deceased) and Zarina Begum
Marital status: Single
Education: Somerville; Small Heath Comprehensive; Josiah Mason Sixth Form
College (all Birmingham)
Qualifications: 6 O-levels, 1 A-level, coaching qualifications

Career outside cricket: Personal fitness training
Off-season: 'Second year of Sports Science degree'
Overseas tours: Warwickshire to Cape Town 1993, 1995
Overseas teams played for: Western Suburbs, Sydney 1990-91; North Perth 1991-93; Albion, Melbourne 1993-95; Petone Riverside, Wellington, New Zealand 1996-97
Cricketers particularly admired: Dermot Reeve, Saeed Anwar, Graham Thorpe, Michael DiVenuto
Young players to look out for: Paul Havell, Nick Wilton
Other sports played: Squash, football
Other sports followed: Football (Birmingham City FC)
Relaxations: Reading, listening to music, 'spending time on Brighton sea front!'
Extras: Most Promising Young Cricketer 1990. Scored four centuries in a row for Warwickshire U19. Scored 171* v Northants in second trial game for Warwickshire 2nd XI. England Schools U19. Won Oxford/Cambridge U19 Festival 1989, 1990. Left Warwickshire at the end of the 1997 season to join Sussex
Best batting: 181 Warwickshire v Hampshire, Southampton 1995

1999 Season

	M	Inns	NO	Runs	HS	Avge	100s	50s	Ct	St	O	M	Runs	Wkts	Avge	Best	5wl	10wM
Test																		
All First	5	9	0	167	88	18.55	-	2	1	-								
1-day Int																		
NatWest																		
B & H																		
1-day Lge																		

Career Performances

	M	Inns	NO	Runs	HS	Avge	100s	50s	Ct	St	Balls	Runs	Wkts	Avge	Best	5wl	10wM
Test																	
All First	54	95	8	2691	181	30.93	5	16	36	-	72	31	0	-	-	-	-
1-day Int																	
NatWest	1	1	0	2	2	2.00	-	-	1	-							
B & H	2	2	1	33	33	33.00	-	-	1	-							
1-day Lge	17	15	0	143	33	9.53	-	-	3	-							

KHAN, Z. M.   Derbyshire

Name: Zubair Mahmood Khan
Role: Left-hand bat, right-arm fast bowler
Born: 7 February 1983, Birmingham
Height: 6ft 1in **Weight:** 11st
Nickname: Zubs
County debut: No first-team appearance
Parents: Hashim Khan
Marital status: Single
Family links with cricket: Father played
cricket and coached cricket for a number of
years. Brother Rawait also plays for
Derbyshire
Education: Parkhill School; Moseley School;
Solihull Sixth Form College
Cricketers particularly admired:
Shaun Pollock
Young players to look out for: Zubair Khan,
Rawait Khan

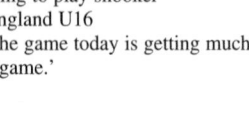

Other sports played: Football, snooker
Other sports followed: Football (Manchester United)
Relaxations: 'Socialising with mates or going to play snooker'
Extras: Represented West Midlands and England U16
Opinions on cricket: 'My opinion is that the game today is getting much better
because people are investing money in the game.'

KILLEEN, N.   Durham

Name: Neil Killeen
Role: Right-hand bat, right-arm fast-medium bowler
Born: 17 October 1975, Shotley Bridge
Height: 6ft 2in **Weight:** 14st 12lbs
Nickname: Killer, Squeaky, Quinny
County debut: 1995
County cap: 1999
50 wickets in a season: 1
1st-Class 5 w. in innings: 6
1st-Class catches: 11
One-Day 5 w. in innings: 1
Place in batting averages: 239th av. 15.68

Place in bowling averages: 10th av. 18.44
(1998 79th av. 29.08)
Strike rate: 42.56 (career 50.21)
Parents: Glen and Thora
Marital status: Single
Education: Greencroft Comprehensive
School; Derwentside College, University of
Teesside
Qualifications: 8 GCSEs, 2 A-levels,
advanced coaching award
Overseas tours: Durham CCC to Zimbabwe
1992; England U19 to West Indies 1994-95;
MCC to Bangladesh 1999-2000
Cricketers particularly admired:
Ian Botham, Curtly Ambrose
Young players to look out for: Melvyn Betts
Other sports played/followed: Athletics
(English Schools javelin) and football
Relaxations: 'Spending time with friends and going out. Listening to music and
watching television'
Extras: Was first Durham bowler to take five wickets in a Sunday League game (5-26
against Northamptonshire in 1995). Awarded Durham cap 1999
Opinions on cricket: 'Too many overs in a day in the first-class game.'
Best batting: 48 Durham v Somerset, Chester-le-Street 1995
Best bowling: 7-85 Durham v Leicestershire, Leicester 1999

1999 Season

	M	Inns	NO	Runs	HS	Avge	100s	50s	Ct	St	O	M	Runs	Wkts	Avge	Best	5wI	10wM
Test																		
All First	12	19	3	251	46	15.68	-	-	1	-	411.3	114	1070	58	18.44	7-85	4	-
1-day Int																		
NatWest	1	1	0	0	0	0.00	-	-	-	-	8	0	37	1	37.00	1-37	-	
B & H																		
1-day Lge	13	8	2	36	11	6.00	-	-	2	-	99.4	14	405	11	36.81	3-38	-	

Career Performances

	M	Inns	NO	Runs	HS	Avge	100s	50s	Ct	St	Balls	Runs	Wkts	Avge	Best	5wI	10wM
Test																	
All First	30	45	10	479	48	13.68	-	-	11	-	5323	2825	106	26.65	7-85	6	-
1-day Int																	
NatWest	4	2	1	1	1 *	1.00	-	-	1	-	264	192	5	38.40	2-46	-	
B & H	16	10	3	46	24 *	6.57	-	-	2	-	880	653	13	50.23	2-28	-	
1-day Lge	55	37	11	216	32	8.30	-	-	9	-	2330	1907	63	30.26	5-26	1	

KIRTLEY, R. J. Sussex

Name: Robert James Kirtley
Role: Right-hand bat, right-arm
fast-medium bowler
Born: 10 January 1975, Eastbourne
Height: 6ft **Weight:** 12st
Nickname: Ambi, Hurtler, Springer
County debut: 1995
County cap: 1998
50 wickets in a season: 2
1st-Class 50s: 1
1st-Class 5 w. in innings: 10
1st-Class 10 w. in match: 1
1st-Class catches: 15
One-Day 5 w. in innings: 1
Place in batting averages: 267th av. 10.77
(1998 190th av. 20.00)
Place in bowling averages: 43rd av. 23.13
(1998 73rd av. 28.37)
Strike rate: 47.49 (career 49.25)
Parents: Bob and Pip
Marital status: Single
Family links with cricket: Brother plays league cricket
Education: St Andrews School, Eastbourne; Clifton College, Bristol
Qualifications: 9 GCSEs, 2 A-levels, NCA coaching first level
Career outside cricket: Coaching
Off-season: England A tour to Bangladesh and New Zealand; coaching Namibia
Overseas tours: Sussex YC to Barbados 1993, to Sri Lanka 1995; England A to
Bangladesh and New Zealand 1999-2000
Overseas teams played for: Mashonaland, Zimbabwe 1996-97; Namibian Cricket
Board, Wanderers, Windhoek, Namibia 1998-99
Cricketers particularly admired: Curtly Ambrose, Jim Andrew, Darren Gough
Other sports followed: Hockey, golf, football (Brighton & Hove Albion)
Relaxations: Sleeping
Extras: Played in the Mashonaland side which defeated England on their 1996-97 tour
of Zimbabwe, taking seven wickets in the match. Winner of an NBC Denis Compton
Award for promising cricketers. Called into England A tour party to Bangladesh and
New Zealand 1999-2000 following withdrawal through injury of Steve Harmison
Opinions on cricket: 'There should be a guaranteed two weeks off during the middle
of the season in order to recharge, if we continue to play in the current set-up.'
Best batting: 59 Sussex v Durham, Eastbourne 1998
Best bowling: 7-21 Sussex v Hampshire, Southampton 1999

1999 Season

	M	Inns	NO	Runs	HS	Avge	100s	50s	Ct	St	O	M	Runs	Wkts	Avge	Best	5wI	10wM
Test																		
All First	15	23	5	194	32	10.77	-	-	2	-	514.3	133	1504	65	23.13	7-21	3	-
1-day Int																		
NatWest	2	0	0	0	0	-	-	-	-	-	20	2	95	4	23.75	2-47	-	
B & H	2	1	0	1	1	1.00	-	-	-	-	19.5	2	93	5	18.60	3-42	-	
1-day Lge	13	4	4	25	17 *	-	-	-	-	7	-	91.2	7	379	26	14.57	4-31	-

Career Performances

	M	Inns	NO	Runs	HS	Avge	100s	50s	Ct	St	Balls	Runs	Wkts	Avge	Best	5wI	10wM
Test																	
All First	56	80	28	591	59	11.36	-	1	15	-	9507	5161	193	26.74	7-21	10	1
1-day Int																	
NatWest	5	1	0	6	6	6.00	-	-	-	-	318	233	13	17.92	5-39	1	
B & H	3	2	0	3	2	1.50	-	-	-	-	179	150	7	21.42	3-42	-	
1-day Lge	45	19	12	92	17 *	13.14	-	-	15	-	1761	1427	63	22.65	4-21	-	

KNIGHT, N. V. Warwickshire

Name: Nicholas Verity Knight
Role: Left-hand bat, right-arm medium-fast
bowler, close fielder
Born: 28 November 1969, Watford
Height: 6ft 1in **Weight:** 13st
Nickname: Stitch, Fungus
County debut: 1991 (Essex),
1995 (Warwickshire)
County cap: 1994 (Essex),
1995 (Warwickshire)
Test debut: 1995
Tests: 12
One-Day Internationals: 44
1000 runs in a season: 2
1st-Class 50s: 44
1st-Class 100s: 20
1st-Class catches: 207
One-Day 100s: 10
Place in batting averages: 75th av. 34.23 (1998 22nd av. 44.54)
Strike rate: (career 159.00)
Parents: John and Rosemary

Wife and date of marriage: Trudie, 3 October 1998
Family links with cricket: Father played for Cambridgeshire. Brother Andy plays club cricket in local Cambridge leagues
Education: St John's School, Cambridge; Felsted Prep; Felsted School; Loughborough University
Qualifications: 9 O-levels, 3 A-levels, BSc (Hons) Sociology, coaching qualification
Off-season: England one-day squad to South Africa and Zimbabwe
Overseas tours: Felsted School to Australia 1986-87; England A to India 1994-95, to Pakistan 1995-96, to Kenya and Sri Lanka 1997-98; England to Zimbabwe and New Zealand 1996-97, to Sharjah 1997-98 (one-day tournament), to West Indies 1997-98 (one-day series), to Bangladesh (Wills International Cup) 1998, to Australia (CUB Series) 1998-99, to Sharjah (Coca-Cola Cup) 1998-99, to South Africa and Zimbabwe 1999-2000 (one-day series)
Overseas teams played for: Northern Districts, Sydney 1991-92; East Torrens, Adelaide 1992-94
Cricketers particularly admired: David Gower, Graham Gooch
Young players to look out for: Mark Wagh, Anurag Singh
Other sports played: Rugby, hockey
Relaxations: Eating good food, painting
Extras: Captained English Schools 1987 and 1988, England YC v New Zealand 1989 and Combined Universities 1991. Played hockey for Essex and Young England. Played rugby for Eastern Counties. Won *Daily Telegraph* award 1988; voted Gray-Nicolls Cricketer of the Year 1988, Cricket Society Cricketer of the Year 1989, Essex Young Player of the Year 1991 and Essex U19 Player of the Year. Left Essex at the end of 1994 season to join Warwickshire. Scored successive centuries in the Texaco Trophy against Pakistan in 1996. Man of the Match after striking 96 off 117 balls in first Test v Zimbabwe at Bulawayo 1996-97 as England chased 205 for victory; he was run out off the last ball of the match while attempting the winning run and the match was drawn with the scores level (the first such Test result). Won successive one-day Man of the Match awards v West Indies 1997-98. Warwickshire vice-captain 1999. Member of England's 1999 World Cup squad
Opinions on cricket: 'Tea break not long enough and too many overs in a day.'
Best batting: 192 Warwickshire v Lancashire, Edgbaston 1998
Best bowling: 1-61 Essex v Middlesex, Uxbridge 1994

1999 Season

	M	Inns	NO	Runs	HS	Avge	100s	50s	Ct	St	O	M	Runs	Wkts	Avge	Best	5wI	10wM
Test																		
All First	14	23	2	719	94	34.23	-	6	30	-								
1-day Int																		
NatWest	2	2	0	69	36	34.50	-	-	1	-								
B & H	2	2	0	141	96	70.50	-	1	1	-								
1-day Lge	14	14	2	412	106 *	34.33	2	2	14	-								

Career Performances

	M	Inns	NO	Runs	HS	Avge	100s	50s	Ct	St	Balls	Runs	Wkts	Avge	Best	5wI	10wM
Test	12	21	0	585	113	27.85	1	4	21	-							
All First	142	239	25	8561	192	40.00	20	44	207	-	159	191	1	191.00	1-61	-	-
1-day Int	44	44	3	1620	125 *	39.51	3	9	15	-							
NatWest	17	17	2	644	151	42.93	2	3	7	-							
B & H	32	29	3	839	104	32.26	1	4	10	-	6	4	0	-	-	-	-
1-day Lge	103	93	13	2457	134	30.71	4	8	46	-	84	85	2	42.50	1-14	-	

KRIKKEN, K. M. Derbyshire

Name: Karl Matthew Krikken
Role: Right-hand bat, wicket-keeper, off-spin bowler, county vice-captain
Born: 9 April 1969, Bolton
Height: 5ft 10in **Weight:** 13st 2lbs
Nickname: Krikk
County debut: 1987 (one-day), 1989 (first-class)
County cap: 1992
1st-Class 50s: 21
1st-Class 100s: 1
1st-Class catches: 448
1st-Class stumpings: 28
Place in batting averages: 160th av. 24.31 (1998 192nd av. 19.95)
Strike rate: 56.00 (career 92.00)
Parents: Brian and Irene
Wife and date of marriage:
Leesha, 3 October 1998
Children: Harry Evan, 20 December 1996; Chester, 19 December 1998
Family links with cricket: Father played for Lancashire and Worcestershire
Education: Horwich Parish Church School; Rivington and Blackrod High School and Sixth Form College
Qualifications: 6 O-levels, 3 A-levels, staff cricket coach
Career outside cricket: 'Dad'
Off-season: Coaching
Overseas tours: Derbyshire to Bermuda 1993, to Torremolinos 1995
Overseas teams played for: CBC Old Boys, Kimberley, South Africa 1988-89; Green Island, Dunedin, New Zealand 1990-91; United, Cape Town 1992-93; Rivertonians, Cape Town 1993-94
Cricketers particularly admired: Derek Randall, Bob Taylor, Alan Knott, Alan Hill, Kim Barnett

Young players to look out for: 'Most of Derbyshire CCC'
Other sports followed: Football (Bolton Wanderers FC, Wigan Athletic FC)
Injuries: Ten weeks out with torn hamstrings (both)
Relaxations: 'Family'
Extras: Derbyshire Supporters' Player of the Year 1991 and 1996; Derbyshire Clubman of the Year 1993. Derbyshire vice-captain since 1998 season
Best batting: 104 Derbyshire v Lancashire, Old Trafford 1996
Best bowling: 1-54 Derbyshire v Hampshire, Derby 1999

1999 Season

	M	Inns	NO	Runs	HS	Avge	100s	50s	Ct	St	O	M	Runs	Wkts	Avge	Best	5wl	10wM
Test																		
All First	12	19	3	389	88	24.31	-	3	30	1	9.2	2	54	1	54.00	1-54	-	-
1-day Int																		
NatWest																		
B & H																		
1-day Lge	10	10	4	90	25 *	15.00	-	-	8	2								

Career Performances

	M	Inns	NO	Runs	HS	Avge	100s	50s	Ct	St	Balls	Runs	Wkts	Avge	Best	5wl	10wM
Test																	
All First	180	267	54	4885	104	22.93	1	21	448	28	92	94	1	94.00	1-54	-	-
1-day Int																	
NatWest	18	11	5	166	55	27.66	-	1	14	1							
B & H	27	19	8	275	42 *	25.00	-	-	26	3							
1-day Lge	113	78	28	858	44 *	17.16	-	-	122	20							

KUMBLE, A.   Leicestershire

Name: Anil Kumble
Role: Right-hand bat, leg-spin bowler
Born: 17 December 1969, Bangalore
Height: 6ft 1in **Weight:** 12st 8lbs
Nickname: Apple, Kumbles
County debut: 1995 (Northants)
County cap: 1995 (Northants)
Test debut: 1990
Tests: 53
One-Day Internationals: 181
100 wickets in a season: 1
1st-Class 50s: 14

1st-Class 100s: 6
1st-Class 5 w. in innings: 44
1st-Class 10 w. in match: 11
1st-Class catches: 69
One-Day 5 w. in innings: 2
Strike rate: (career 56.24)
Parents: K.N. Krishnaswani and
Sarola Swami
Marital status: Single
Education: Holy Saint English School,
Bangalore; National High School, Bangalore;
National College and RV College of
Engineering, Bangalore
Overseas tours: India to England 1990, to
Australia 1991-92, to South Africa 1992-93,
to Zimbabwe 1992-93, to Sri Lanka 1993-94,
to New Zealand 1993-94, to Pakistan and Sri
Lanka (World Cup) 1995-96, to England

1996, to South Africa 1996-97, to West Indies 1996-97, to Sri Lanka 1997-98, to
Zimbabwe 1998-99, to New Zealand 1998-99, to UK, Ireland and Holland (World
Cup) 1999, to Australia 1999-2000
Overseas teams played for: Karnataka, India 1989-90 –
Other sports followed: Tennis, football
Relaxations: Listening to music, watching television
Extras: Took 10-74 (14-159 in the match) v Pakistan in the second Test at Delhi,
February 1999, the first ten-wicket haul by a bowler in Tests since Jim Laker's 10-53 v
Australia at Old Trafford 1956. Represented India in the 1999 World Cup. Man of the
Series, India v New Zealand 1999. Played for Northants 1995. Has joined
Leicestershire for 2000 as overseas player
Best batting: 154* Karnataka v Kerala, Bijapur 1991-92
Best bowling: 10-74 India v Pakistan, Delhi 1998-99
Stop press: Second in list of leading Test wicket-takers of 1999 with 54 (av. 27.06)

1999 Season

	M	Inns	NO	Runs	HS	Avge	100s	50s	Ct	St	O	M	Runs	Wkts	Avge	Best	5wl	10wM
Test																		
All First																		
1-day Int	7	3	2	10	6 *	10.00	-	-	5	-	67.2	1	282	8	35.25	2-30	-	
NatWest																		
B & H																		
1-day Lge																		

Career Performances

	M	Inns	NO	Runs	HS	Avge	100s	50s	Ct	St	Balls	Runs	Wkts	Avge	Best	5wI	10wM
Test	53	68	11	979	88	17.17	-	3	27	-	16345	6658	239	27.85	10-74	13	2
All First	130	166	35	3534	154 *	26.97	6	14	69	-	34700	14221	617	23.04	10-74	44	11
1-day Int	181	85	30	551	24	10.01	-	-	72	-	9429	6453	232	27.81	6-12	2	
NatWest	5	2	1	8	6 *	8.00	-	-	1	-	357	203	11	18.45	4-50	-	
B & H	4	3	0	5	3	1.66	-	-	1	-	226	135	3	45.00	2-40	-	
1-day Lge	10	3	1	11	8	5.50	-	-	3	-	414	347	16	21.68	3-25	-	

LACEY, S. J.   Derbyshire

Name: Simon James Lacey
Role: Right-hand bat, off-spin bowler
Born: 9 March 1975, Nottingham
Height: 5ft 11in **Weight:** 12st 11lbs
Nickname: Lace, Bone, Boneface, Spaceace, Junior Champ
County debut: 1997
1st-Class 50s: 1
1st-Class catches: 7
1st-Class stumpings: 1
Place in batting averages: 144th av. 25.66
Strike rate: 162.00 (career 112.71)
Parents: Phil and Anne
Wife and date of marriage: Keleigh, 26 October 1999
Family links with cricket: Brother plays league cricket for Langley Mill CC in Derbyshire County League
Education: Mundy Street School, Heanor; Aldercar Comprehensive School, Langley Mill; Mill Hill Sixth Form, Ripley
Qualifications: 6 GCSEs, senior coaching award
Career outside cricket: Police force or PE teacher
Cricketers particularly admired: Robin Smith, Phil Tufnell
Young players to look out for: Sam Patel, Ian Blackwell
Other sports played: Golf, volleyball (Nottingham Rockets)
Other sports followed: Football (Derby County, Ilkeston Town)
Relaxations: Golf, gardening, DIY
Extras: Was a member of the England Junior Volleyball squad in 1991. Captained the NAYC at U19 level against ESCA at Lord's in 1994
Opinions on cricket: 'All groundsmen should be contracted to the ECB to prevent clubs preparing sub-standard pitches to suit their own means. Points for a draw should be scrapped to try and provide more positive cricket.'

Best batting: 50 Derbyshire v Somerset, Derby 1997
Best bowling: 3-97 Derbyshire v Essex, Southend 1997

1999 Season

	M	Inns	NO	Runs	HS	Avge	100s	50s	Ct	St	O	M	Runs	Wkts	Avge	Best	5wI	10wM
Test																		
All First	6	8	2	154	42	25.66	-	-	5	1	81	15	238	3	79.33	1-16	-	-
1-day Int																		
NatWest																		
B & H																		
1-day Lge	3	3	0	19	15	6.33	-	-	1	-	27	1	121	3	40.33	3-38	-	

Career Performances

	M	Inns	NO	Runs	HS	Avge	100s	50s	Ct	St	Balls	Runs	Wkts	Avge	Best	5wI	10wM
Test																	
All First	15	19	6	311	50	23.92	-	1	7	1	1578	803	14	57.35	3-97	-	-
1-day Int																	
NatWest																	
B & H																	
1-day Lge	7	4	0	28	15	7.00	-	-	1	-	276	233	5	46.60	3-38	-	

LAMPITT, S. R. Worcestershire

Name: Stuart Richard Lampitt
Role: Right-hand bat, right-arm
medium-fast bowler
Born: 29 July 1966, Wolverhampton
Height: 5ft 11in **Weight:** 13st 7lbs
Nickname: Jed
County debut: 1985
County cap: 1989
50 wickets in a season: 6
1st-Class 50s: 19
1st-Class 100s: 1
1st-Class 5 w. in innings: 17
1st-Class catches: 132
One-Day 5 w. in innings: 3
Place in batting averages: 110th av. 29.50
(1998 165th av. 22.90)
Place in bowling averages: 40th av. 22.76
(1998 60th av. 26.60)

Strike rate: 44.17 (career 54.41)
Parents: Joseph Charles and Muriel Ann
Marital status: Engaged to Clare
Family links with cricket: 'Dad watches the scores on Teletext'
Education: Kingswinford Secondary School; Dudley College of Technology
Qualifications: 7 O-levels, Diploma in Business Studies, NCA advanced coach
Career outside cricket: Youth development coach at Worcestershire CCC
Off-season: Coaching 'and the benefit year'
Overseas tours: NCA U19 to Bermuda; Worcestershire to Bahamas 1990, to
Zimbabwe 1990-91, to South Africa 1991-92, to Barbados 1996
Overseas teams played for: Mangere, Auckland 1986-88; University CC, Perth 1991-93
Cricketers particularly admired: Ian Botham, Malcolm Marshall
Young players to look out for: 'The good ones'
Other sports played: Golf, fishing
Other sports followed: Football (Wolves FC)
Relaxations: 'Spending time with our Clare'
Extras: Took five wickets and made 42 for Stourbridge in final of the William
Younger Cup at Lord's in 1986. One of the Whittingdale Young Players of the Year
1990. 'Must be the only bowler to be hit for six first ball by Adrian Jones and Phil
Tufnell (two master batsmen).' Granted a benefit for 2000
Opinions on cricket: 'Good game, good game!!'
Best batting: 122 Worcestershire v Middlesex, Lord's 1994
Best bowling: 5-32 Worcestershire v Kent, Worcester 1989

1999 Season

	M	Inns	NO	Runs	HS	Avge	100s	50s	Ct	St	O	M	Runs	Wkts	Avge	Best	5wI	10wM
Test																		
All First	14	19	5	413	66 *	29.50	-	2	7	-	287.1	70	888	39	22.76	4-28	-	-
1-day Int																		
NatWest	2	2	0	3	2	1.50	-	-	-	-	19	1	68	3	22.66	2-36	-	
B & H																		
1-day Lge	11	6	5	58	30 *	58.00	-	-	3	-	72.4	6	286	17	16.82	4-18	-	

Career Performances

	M	Inns	NO	Runs	HS	Avge	100s	50s	Ct	St	Balls	Runs	Wkts	Avge	Best	5wI	10wM
Test																	
All First	208	271	61	5113	122	24.34	1	19	132	-	28352	15382	521	29.52	5-32	17	-
1-day Int																	
NatWest	25	18	4	220	54	15.71	-	1	7	-	1337	953	38	25.07	5-22	1	
B & H	39	22	7	277	41	18.46	-	-	11	-	2056	1363	63	21.63	6-26	1	
1-day Lge	164	96	35	1221	41 *	20.01	-	-	49	-	5744	4558	185	24.63	5-67	1	

LANEY, J. S.   Hampshire

Name: Jason Scott Laney
Role: Right-hand bat, off-spin bowler
Born: 27 April 1973, Winchester
Height: 5ft 10in **Weight:** 12st 7lbs
Nickname: Chucky, The Rimmer, Wasp
County debut: 1993 (one-day),
1995 (first-class)
County cap: 1996
1000 runs in a season: 1
1st-Class 50s: 21
1st-Class 100s: 5
1st-Class catches: 45
One-Day 100s: 2
Place in batting averages: 44th av. 38.38
(1998 222nd av. 17.23)
Strike rate: 117.00 (career 192.00)
Parents: Geoff and Pam
Marital status: Single
Family links with cricket: Grandfather played good club cricket.
Education: Pewsey Vale Comprehensive; St John's, Marlborough;
Leeds Metropolitan University
Qualifications: 8 GCSEs, 2 A-levels, BA (Hons) in Human Movement Studies
Overseas tours: England U18 to Canada 1991
Overseas teams played for: Waikato, New Zealand 1994-95; Matabeleland and Old
Miltonians, Zimbabwe 1995-96; DHS Old Boys, South Africa 1996-97
Cricketers particularly admired: Michael Slater, Courtney Walsh, Robin Smith,
Malcolm Marshall, Ian Botham, Paul Baker, Gary Sobers
Young players to look out for: Alex Morris and Dimitri Mascarenhas ('for their
cricket and spit-roasting abilities'), Graham Napier, John Rickard Jnr
Other sports played: Golf (10 handicap)
Other sports followed: Football
Relaxations: 'Playing golf with Ferret whilst ignoring the constant drivel he comes
out with. Socialising, drinking, laughing, "Jackpot Cafe", music'
Extras: Hampshire Young Cricketer of the Year 1995. Became first Hampshire
cricketer to score a century before lunch on debut in the NatWest trophy 1996
Best batting: 112 Hampshire v Oxford University, The Parks 1996
Best bowling: 1-24 Hampshire v Northamptonshire, Northampton 1999

1999 Season

	M	Inns	NO	Runs	HS	Avge	100s	50s	Ct	St	O	M	Runs	Wkts	Avge	Best	5wI	10wM
Test																		
All First	11	19	1	691	99	38.38	-	6	7	-	39	5	126	2	63.00	1-24	-	-
1-day Int																		
NatWest	2	2	0	148	95	74.00	-	2	2	-								
B & H	1	1	0	41	41	41.00	-	-	-	-								
1-day Lge	12	12	1	304	106 *	27.63	1	1	5	-	0.3	0	9	0	-		-	-

Career Performances

	M	Inns	NO	Runs	HS	Avge	100s	50s	Ct	St	Balls	Runs	Wkts	Avge	Best	5wI	10wM
Test																	
All First	62	110	3	3499	112	32.70	5	21	45	-	384	224	2	112.00	1-24	-	-
1-day Int																	
NatWest	10	10	0	560	153	56.00	1	3	5	-							
B & H	13	13	0	221	41	17.00	-	-	3	-							
1-day Lge	49	49	1	1174	106 *	24.45	1	5	16	-	3	9	0	-		-	-

LANGER, J. L.   Middlesex

Name: Justin Lee Langer
Role: Left-hand bat, right-arm medium bowler, county captain
Born: 21 November 1970, Subiaco, Western Australia
Height: 5ft 8in **Weight:** 12st 4lbs
Nickname: JL
County debut: 1998
County cap: 1998
Test debut: 1992-93
Tests: 20
One-Day Internationals: 8
1000 runs in a season: 2
1st-Class 50s: 43
1st-Class 100s: 26
1st-Class 200s: 7
1st-Class catches: 115
One-Day 100s: 1

Place in batting averages: 3rd av. 58.22 (1998 5th av. 62.95)
Strike rate: (career 100.00)
Parents: Colin and Joy-Anne

Wife and date of marriage: Sue, 13 April 1996
Children: Jessica, 28 March 1997; Ali Rose 1998
Family links with cricket: Uncle, Robbie Langer, played Sheffield Shield cricket for Western Australia and World Series for Australia
Education: Liwara Catholic School; Aquinas College, Perth; University of Western Australia
Career outside cricket: Writing, stockbroking
Off-season: Playing in Australia
Overseas tours: Young Australia to England 1995; Australia to New Zealand 1992-93, to South Africa 1996-97, to England 1997, to Pakistan 1998-99, to West Indies 1998-99, to Sri Lanka 1999, to Zimbabwe 1999
Overseas teams played for: Western Australia 1990 –
Cricketers particularly admired: Graham Gooch, Mike Gatting, Graeme Hick, Allan Border, David Boon, Dennis Lillee
Young players to look out for: 'Ace' Shah, Jamie Hewitt
Other sports played: Tennis, golf, Aussie Rules, martial arts (has black belts in judo and taekwondo)
Other sports followed: Football (Man Utd), Aussie Rules (West Coast Eagles)
Relaxations: Family, writing
Extras: A prolific run-scorer for Western Australia in recent years, Justin Langer was drafted into the Australia 1992-93 side after Damien Martyn suffered an injury during the practice session for the match against the West Indies. He scored an heroic 54 in the face of some aggressive bowling by the West Indies but played in only another five Tests over the next three years until he forced his way back into the Test side in 1996-97 – ironically against the West Indies. Scored 233* on first-class debut for Middlesex at Lord's v Somerset 1998. With Mike Gatting, took part in an opening stand of 372 v Essex at Southgate in 1998, setting a new county record for the first wicket; during his innings of 166 he became the first batsman to reach 1000 first-class runs for the 1998 season. Scored maiden Test century (116) v Pakistan at Peshawar in 1998. Has contributed articles to the Australian Cricket Board website. His 241* for Middlesex v Kent at Lord's on 16 April 1999 was the earliest Championship double-century in an English first-class season and the highest score ever at Lord's in April. Appointed Middlesex vice-captain for 1999. Scored 179* and 52 in the third Test v England at Adelaide 1998-99, receiving Man of the Match award. Appointed Middlesex captain for 2000
Best batting: 274* Western Australia v South Australia, Perth 1996-97
Best bowling: 2-17 Australia A v South Africa, Brisbane 1997-98
Stop press: Put on 238 for the sixth wicket with Adam Gilchrist in the fourth innings of Australia's victory v Pakistan at Hobart in November 1999; his 127 and 59 in the first innings won him the Man of the Match award. His 223 at Sydney in the third Test v India, January 2000, was the highest Test score by an Australian v India. Selected for Australia's tour of New Zealand 1999-2000

1999 Season

	M	Inns	NO	Runs	HS	Avge	100s	50s	Ct	St	O	M	Runs	Wkts	Avge	Best	5wI	10wM
Test																		
All First	12	22	4	1048	241 *	58.22	4	2	12	-	2	1	3	0	-	-	-	-
1-day Int																		
NatWest	1	1	0	6	6	6.00	-	-	-	-								
B & H																		
1-day Lge	11	10	0	301	84	30.10	-	3	1	-	10.5	0	74	2	37.00	1-24	-	

Career Performances

	M	Inns	NO	Runs	HS	Avge	100s	50s	Ct	St	Balls	Runs	Wkts	Avge	Best	5wI	10wM
Test	20	35	1	1210	179 *	35.58	3	8	12	-							
All First	139	248	31	11183	274 *	51.53	33	43	115	-	300	136	3	45.33	2-17	-	-
1-day Int	8	7	2	160	36	32.00	-	-	2	1							
NatWest	4	4	1	224	114 *	74.66	1	1	-	-	30	45	1	45.00	1-45	-	
B & H	5	5	0	136	71	27.20	-	1	3	-							
1-day Lge	23	22	1	728	87 *	34.66	-	6	7	-	163	170	6	28.33	3-51	-	

LARAMAN, A. W.   Middlesex

Name: Aaron William Laraman
Role: Right-hand bat, right-arm fast bowler
Born: 10 January 1979, Enfield
Height: 6ft 5in **Weight:** 13st 5lbs
Nickname: Lazza
County debut: 1998 (one-day)
Parents: William and Lynda
Marital status: Single
Education: St Paul's C of E School;
Enfield Grammar School
Qualifications: 8 GCSEs
Overseas tours: England U17 to Holland
1995; England U19 to South Africa 1997-98
Cricketers particularly admired:
Viv Richards, Ian Botham
Young players to look out for: Robert Key,
Stephen Peters
Other sports followed: Football (Arsenal)
Injuries: Missed 1999 season through injury
Relaxations: Working out at the gym, football, golf
Extras: Enfield Grammar School cap at the age of 13. Middlesex Colts county cap.
Seaxe 2nd XI Player of the Year 1997

Opinions on cricket: 'In the game today, I feel that a high level of fitness is required. The game is becoming much more exciting and much more of a spectator sport.'

1999 Season (did not make any first-class or one-day appearances)

Career Performances

	M	Inns	NO	Runs	HS	Avge	100s	50s	Ct	St	Balls	Runs	Wkts	Avge	Best	5wI	10wM
Test																	
All First	1	0	0	0	0	-	-	-	-	-							
1-day Int																	
NatWest																	
B & H																	
1-day Lge	2	1	0	3	3	3.00	-	-	2	-	21	24	0	-		-	-

LATHWELL, M. N. Somerset

Name: Mark Nicholas Lathwell
Role: Right-hand bat, right-arm
off-spin bowler
Born: 26 December 1971, Bletchley, Bucks
Height: 5ft 8in **Weight:** 12st
Nickname: Trough, Lathers
County debut: 1991
County cap: 1992
Test debut: 1993
Tests: 2
1000 runs in a season: 4
1st-Class 50s: 48
1st-Class 100s: 11
1st-Class 200s: 1
1st-Class catches: 92
One-Day 100s: 4
Place in batting averages: (1998 100th
av. 30.21)

Strike rate: (career 84.76)
Parents: Derek Peter and Valerie
Wife and date of marriage: Lisa, October 1996
Children: Jason, 16 January 1995; Sam, 27 October 1997
Family links with cricket: Father and brother both club cricketers; father qualified coach
Education: Overstone Primary, Wing, Bucks; Southmead School, Braunton, North Devon; Braunton School and Community College

Qualifications: 5 GCSEs, cricket coaching certificate
Career outside cricket: Coaching
Off-season: Coaching in North Devon
Overseas tours: England A to Australia 1992-93, to South Africa 1993-94
Cricketers particularly admired: Ian Botham, Graham Gooch
Other sports played: Darts
Other sports followed: Snooker
Injuries: Out for entire 1999 season with snapped anterior cruciate ligament in right knee
Relaxations: Cooking, eating, sleeping
Extras: Played for Devon. Spent one season on Lord's groundstaff. Played for England U19 v Australia U19 1991. PCA Young Player of the Year and Somerset Player of the Year 1992. Cricket Writers' Club Young Cricketer of the Year 1993
Opinions on cricket: 'Day/night cricket has brought another dimension to the one-day game, but to keep these occasions special they must not be overplayed.'
Best batting: 206 Somerset v Surrey, Bath 1994
Best bowling: 2-21 Somerset v Sussex, Hove 1994

1999 Season (did not make any first-class or one-day appearances)

Career Performances

	M	Inns	NO	Runs	HS	Avge	100s	50s	Ct	St	Balls	Runs	Wkts	Avge	Best	5wI	10wM
Test	2	4	0	78	33	19.50	-	-	-	-							
All First	134	237	9	7768	206	34.07	12	48	92	-	1102	684	13	52.61	2-21	-	-
1-day Int																	
NatWest	18	17	0	465	103	27.35	1	2	7	-	66	23	1	23.00	1-23	-	
B & H	21	21	0	821	121	39.09	2	6	7	-	25	50	0	-	-	-	
1-day Lge	104	102	5	2645	117	27.26	1	16	25	-	102	85	0	-	-	-	

LAW, D. R.   Essex

Name: Danny Richard Law
Role: Right-hand bat, right-arm fast bowler
Born: 15 July 1975, Lambeth, London
Height: 6ft 5in **Weight:** 15st
Nickname: Decas
County debut: 1993 (Sussex), 1997 (Essex)
County cap: 1996 (Sussex)
1st-Class 50s: 9
1st-Class 100s: 1
1st-Class 5 w. in innings: 4
1st-Class catches: 36

Place in batting averages: (1998 209th av. 18.64)
Place in bowling averages: (1998 121st av. 36.03)
Strike rate: 70.00 (career 52.97)
Parents: Richard (deceased) and Claudette
Wife: Carly-Anne
Children: Sade-Victoria
Education: Steyning Grammar School; Wolverstone Hall
Qualifications: Cricket coach
Career outside cricket: Coach
Off-season: Playing in Australia
Overseas tours: Sussex Schools U16 to Jersey 1991; England U18 to South Africa 1992-93, to Denmark 1993; England U19 to Sri Lanka 1993-94
Overseas teams played for: Ashburton CC, Melbourne 1992-94; Essendon, Melbourne 1995-96
Cricketers particularly admired: Stuart Law, Graham Gooch, Nasser Hussain, Franklyn Stephenson, Vasbert Drakes
Young players to look out for: Tim Phillips, Justin Bishop
Other sports played: Football ('team hacker'), golf
Other sports followed: Football (West Ham United)
Injuries: Out for five weeks with torn ligament in knee
Relaxations: Cinema, golf
Extras: Winner of Denis Compton award 1996. Left Sussex during the 1996 off-season and joined Essex for the 1997 season on a three-year contract. Took Championship hat-trick v Durham at Riverside 1998
Opinions on cricket: '2nd XI pitches should be of a higher standard. Split the 2nd XI Championship into two divisions in same way as 1st XI Championship.'
Best batting: 115 Sussex v Young Australia, Hove 1995
Best bowling: 5-33 Sussex v Durham, Hove 1996

1999 Season

	M	Inns	NO	Runs	HS	Avge	100s	50s	Ct	St	O	M	Runs	Wkts	Avge	Best	5wI	10wM
Test																		
All First	4	4	2	136	63 *	68.00	-	1	2	-	105	17	418	9	46.44	4-32	-	-
1-day Int																		
NatWest	1	1	1	23	23 *	-	-	-	-	-								
B & H																			
1-day Lge	13	12	0	193	48	16.08	-	-	2	-	21.5	0	129	5	25.80	3-26	-	

Career Performances

	M	Inns	NO	Runs	HS	Avge	100s	50s	Ct	St	Balls	Runs	Wkts	Avge	Best	5wI	10wM
Test																	
All First	65	101	2	1972	115	19.91	1	9	36	-	6463	4172	122	34.19	5-33	4	-
1-day Int																	
NatWest	12	8	1	135	47	19.28	-	-	3	-	99	95	1	95.00	1-2	-	
B & H	9	8	1	95	36 *	13.57	-	-	1	-	96	76	1	76.00	1-44	-	
1-day Lge	71	60	10	1222	82	24.44	-	5	15	-	988	951	30	31.70	3-26	-	

LAW, S. G. Essex

Name: Stuart Grant Law
Role: Right-hand bat, right-arm occasional bowler
Born: 18 October 1968, Herston, Brisbane, Australia
Height: 6ft 1in **Weight:** 13st 7lbs
Nickname: Judge, LA
County debut: 1996
County cap: 1996
Test debut: 1995-96
Tests: 1
One-Day Internationals: 54
1000 runs in a season: 4
1st-Class 50s: 61
1st-Class 100s: 39
1st-Class 200s: 2
1st-Class 5 w. in innings: 1
1st-Class catches: 201
One-Day 100s: 10
Place in batting averages: 1st av. 73.32 (1998 38th av. 40.91)
Strike rate: 71.33 (career 97.57)
Parents: Grant and Pam
Wife and date of marriage: Debbie Lee, 31 December 1998
Family links with cricket: Grandfather and father played club cricket
Education: Stafford State School; Craiglsea State High School
Off-season: Playing for Queensland in Sheffield Shield competition
Overseas tours: Young Australia to England 1995; Australia to India and Pakistan (World Cup) 1995-96, to Sri Lanka (Singer World Series), India and South Africa 1996-97, to New Zealand (one-day series) 1997-98
Overseas teams played for: Queensland 1988 –
Cricketers particularly admired: Greg Chappell, Martin Crowe, Viv Richards

Young players to look out for: Ricky Anderson, Matt Windows
Other sports played: Golf ('very social'), 'try anything once', tennis
Other sports followed: Rugby league (Brisbane Broncos)
Relaxations: 'Spending days at the beach with my wife. Sports cars.'
Extras: Made his first-class debut for Queensland as a 19-year-old, scoring 179 in only his second appearance. Captained Queensland to their first Sheffield Shield title 1994-95. Made his Test debut for Australia against Sri Lanka at Perth in 1995-96 and scored an unbeaten 54. Played in all 17 One-Day Internationals for Australia in 1995-96. Man of the Match in the 1997 NatWest final at Lord's. One of *Wisden*'s Five Cricketers of the Year 1998. Scored centuries (159 and 113*) in each innings v Yorkshire at Chelmsford 1999; Michael Vaughan scored two 100s for Yorks in the same match. Became the first player to pass 1000 runs in 1999 season (v Middlesex at Southend) and topped the first-class batting averages for 1999. Professional Cricketers' Association Player of the Year 1999
Opinions on cricket: 'Play too much.'
Best batting: 263 Essex v Somerset, Chelmsford 1999
Best bowling: 5-39 Queensland v Tasmania, Brisbane 1995-96

1999 Season

	M	Inns	NO	Runs	HS	Avge	100s	50s	Ct	St	O	M	Runs	Wkts	Avge	Best	5wI	10wM
Test																		
All First	17	29	4	1833	263	73.32	8	6	29	-	35.4	6	133	3	44.33	1-3	-	-
1-day Int																		
NatWest	1	1	0	25	25	25.00	-	-	2	-	9	0	64	1	64.00	1-64	-	
B & H																		
1-day Lge	14	14	1	396	55	30.46	-	1	4	-	21	0	99	2	49.50	2-56	-	

Career Performances

	M	Inns	NO	Runs	HS	Avge	100s	50s	Ct	St	Balls	Runs	Wkts	Avge	Best	5wI	10wM
Test	1	1	1	54	54 *	-	-	1	1	-	18	9	0	-	-	-	-
All First	181	305	32	13367	263	48.96	41	61	201	-	7416	3565	76	46.90	5-39	1	-
1-day Int	54	51	5	1237	110	26.89	1	7	12	-	807	635	12	52.91	2-22	-	
NatWest	12	11	1	651	107	65.10	3	3	10	-	439	366	8	45.75	2-36	-	
B & H	16	15	0	545	116	36.33	1	2	10	-	354	320	9	35.55	2-13	-	
1-day Lge	58	57	3	1958	126	36.25	5	6	28	-	886	781	22	35.50	4-37	-	

LAW, W. L.   Glamorgan

Name: Wayne Lincoln Law
Role: Right-hand bat
Born: 4 September 1978, Swansea
Height: 5ft 10in **Weight:** 11st 5lbs
Nickname: Sods
County debut: 1997
1st-Class 50s: 4
1st-Class 100s: 1
1st-Class catches: 7
Place in batting averages: 135th av. 26.66
(1998 54th av. 37.00)
Strike rate: (career 46.33)
Parents: Lincoln and Barbara
Marital status: Single
Education: Pentip; Graig School, Llanelli
Qualifications: 1 GCSE, NCA senior and
advanced coaching awards
Career outside cricket: Coaching
Off-season: Playing in New Zealand
Overseas tours: Dyfed U15 to Zimbabwe 1994; Glamorgan to Cape Town 1998
Cricketers particularly admired: Robert Croft 'the hard man of county cricket'
Young players to look out for: David Harrison, Owen Parkin
Other sports played: Squash, running
Other sports followed: Rugby (Llanelli, Felinfoel)
Injuries: Out for three weeks with hamstring and back injuries
Relaxations: Reading
Extras: Scored first-class century (131) v Lancashire at Colwyn Bay in 1998 in only
his second Championship match
Best batting: 131 Glamorgan v Lancashire, Colwyn Bay 1998
Best bowling: 2-29 Glamorgan v Cambridge University, Fenner's 1998

1999 Season

	M	Inns	NO	Runs	HS	Avge	100s	50s	Ct	St	O	M	Runs	Wkts	Avge	Best	5wI	10wM
Test																		
All First	5	9	0	240	64	26.66	-	2	3	-	0.1	0	4	0	-		-	-
1-day Int																		
NatWest	1	1	1	2	2 *	-	-	-	-	-								
B & H																		
1-day Lge	3	3	0	38	21	12.66	-	-	-	-	1	0	6	0	-		-	-

384

Career Performances

	M	Inns	NO	Runs	HS	Avge	100s	50s	Ct	St	Balls	Runs	Wkts	Avge	Best	5wI	10wM
Test																	
All First	15	24	3	722	131	34.38	1	4	7	-	139	89	3	29.66	2-29	-	-
1-day Int																	
NatWest	1	1	1	2	2*	-	-	-	-	-							
B & H																	
1-day Lge	9	9	1	102	24	12.75	-	-	3	-	6	6	0	-		-	-

LEATHERDALE, D. A. Worcestershire

Name: David Anthony Leatherdale
Role: Right-hand bat, right-arm medium
bowler, cover fielder
Born: 26 November 1967, Bradford
Height: 5ft 10in **Weight:** 11st
Nickname: Lugsy, Spock
County debut: 1988
County cap: 1994
1000 runs in a season: 1
1st-Class 50s: 39
1st-Class 100s: 10
1st-Class 5 w. in innings: 2
1st-Class catches: 129
Place in batting averages: 178th av. 22.35
(1998 70th av. 33.36)
Place in bowling averages: (1998 13th
av. 19.80)
Strike rate: 62.75 (career 53.44)
Parents: Paul and Rosalyn
Wife: Vanessa
Children: Callum Edward, 6 July 1990; Christian Ellis, 4 years old
Family links with cricket: Father played local cricket; brother plays for East Bierley
in Bradford League; brother-in-law played for England YC in 1979
Education: Bolton Royd Primary School; Pudsey Grangefield Secondary School
Qualifications: 8 O-levels, 2 A-levels; NCA coaching award (stage 1)
Off-season: Working as trainee accountant
Overseas tours: England Indoor to Australia and New Zealand 1994-95
Overseas teams played for: Pretoria Police, South Africa 1987-88
Cricketers particularly admired: Mark Scott, George Batty, Peter Kippax
Other sports followed: Football, American football
Injuries: Out for three days with a broken nose
Relaxations: Golf

Opinions on cricket: 'Changing the structure of cricket to make it more competitive is fine, but the amount of cricket played is still detrimental to the quality produced, due to the lack of time to rest, causing many players to play with injury and therefore not competing at their best.'

Best batting: 157 Worcestershire v Somerset, Worcester 1991

Best bowling: 5-20 Worcestershire v Gloucestershire, Worcester 1998

1999 Season

	M	Inns	NO	Runs	HS	Avge	100s	50s	Ct	St	O	M	Runs	Wkts	Avge	Best	5wI	10wM
Test																		
All First	19	34	3	693	85	22.35	-	3	9	-	83.4	17	283	8	35.37	2-14	-	-
1-day Int																		
NatWest	2	2	0	63	37	31.50	-	-	1	-	2	0	17	0	-		-	-
B & H																		
1-day Lge	14	12	3	260	70 *	28.88	-	2	7	-	36.3	1	176	10	17.60	4-23	-	

Career Performances

	M	Inns	NO	Runs	HS	Avge	100s	50s	Ct	St	Balls	Runs	Wkts	Avge	Best	5wI	10wM
Test																	
All First	162	259	29	7471	157	32.48	10	39	129	-	4062	2346	76	30.86	5-20	2	-
1-day Int																	
NatWest	22	19	1	363	43	20.16	-	-	8	-	178	152	3	50.66	3-14	-	
B & H	28	23	5	298	66	16.55	-	1	6	-	380	256	11	23.27	4-13	-	
1-day Lge	141	116	21	1831	70 *	19.27	-	8	68	-	1136	1007	53	19.00	4-19	-	

LEHMANN, D. S.   Yorkshire

Name: Darren Scott Lehmann

Role: Left-hand bat, slow left-arm bowler

Born: 5 February 1970, Gawler, Australia

County debut: 1997

County cap: 1997

Test debut: 1997-98

Tests: 5

One-Day Internationals: 54

1000 runs in a season: 1

1st-Class 50s: 59

1st-Class 100s: 32

1st-Class 200s: 5

1st-Class catches: 83

One-Day 100s: 5

Place in batting averages: (1998 7th av. 60.56)

Strike rate: (career 105.27)

Off-season: Playing for South Australia

Overseas tours: Australia to Sri Lanka 1996-97, to New Zealand 1997-98, to Sharjah 1997-98, to India 1997-98, to Pakistan 1998-99, to Bangladesh 1998-99, to West Indies 1998-99 (one-day series), to UK, Ireland and Holland (World Cup) 1999, to Sri Lanka 1999 (one-day series), to Zimbabwe 1999 (one-day series)

Overseas teams played for: Salisbury District CC (now Northern Districts), Adelaide; South Australia 1987-1990; Victoria 1990-93; South Australia 1993 –

Extras: Represented South Australia at all age groups. Scored 1128 runs (av. 57.50) in

his first full Sheffield Shield season. Played for Australia in their Carlton and United One-Day International series win 1997-98. Man of the Match in CUB second final v England at Melbourne 1998-99. Took over captaincy of South Australia from the injured Jamie Siddons in 1998-99. Played in Australia's 1999 World Cup winning side, striking the winning runs in the final v Pakistan. Released by Yorkshire at end of 1998 season; has returned to Yorkshire as overseas player for 2000

Best batting: 255 South Australia v Queensland, Adelaide 1996-97

Best bowling: 4-42 Yorkshire v Kent, Maidstone 1998

1999 Season

	M	Inns	NO	Runs	HS	Avge	100s	50s	Ct	St	O	M	Runs	Wkts	Avge	Best	5wI	10wM
Test																		
All First																			
1-day Int	9	8	2	136	76	22.66	-	1	-	-	2	0	17	0	-		-	-
NatWest																			
B & H																				
1-day Lge																				

Career Performances

	M	Inns	NO	Runs	HS	Avge	100s	50s	Ct	St	Balls	Runs	Wkts	Avge	Best	5wI	10wM
Test	5	8	0	228	98	28.50	-	2	3	-	102	45	2	22.50	1-6	-	-
All First	143	245	15	12210	255	53.08	37	59	83	-	2316	1195	22	54.31	4-42	-	-
1-day Int	54	51	8	1447	110 *	33.65	2	8	7	-	414	376	8	47.00	2-11	-	
NatWest	5	4	0	133	105	33.25	1	-	1	-	48	19	1	19.00	1-14	-	
B & H	11	11	2	546	119	60.66	2	2	3	-	96	77	4	19.25	2-17	-	
1-day Lge	27	27	3	1098	99	45.75	-	10	7	-	226	210	7	30.00	3-43	-	

LEWIS, C. C.   Leicestershire

Name: Christopher Clairmonte Lewis
Role: Right-hand bat, right-arm
fast-medium bowler
Born: 14 February 1968,
Georgetown, Guyana
Height: 6ft 2in **Weight:** 13st
Nickname: Carl
County debut: 1987 (Leics), 1992 (Notts),
1996 (Surrey)
County cap: 1990 (Leics), 1994 (Notts),
1996 (Surrey)
Test debut: 1990
Tests: 32
One-Day Internationals: 53
50 wickets in a season: 2
1st-Class 50s: 34
1st-Class 100s: 7
1st-Class 200s: 2
1st-Class 5w. in innings: 20
1st-Class 10 w. in match: 3
1st-Class catches: 148
One-Day 100s: 1
One-Day 5 w. in innings: 2
Place in batting averages: 14th av. 47.27 (1998 71st av. 33.36)
Place in bowling averages: 122nd av. 36.56 (1998 47th av. 24.92)
Strike rate: 71.68 (career 58.60)
Parents: Philip and Patricia
Marital status: Single
Education: Willesden High School
Qualifications: 2 O-levels
Overseas tours: England YC to Australia (Youth World Cup) 1987-88; England A to
Kenya and Zimbabwe 1989-90; England to West Indies 1989-90, to Australia 1990-91,
to New Zealand 1991-92, to India and Sri Lanka 1992-93, to West Indies 1993-94,
to Australia 1994-95
Cricketers particularly admired: Graham Gooch, Robin Smith
Other sports followed: Snooker, football, darts, American football, basketball
Relaxations: Music, sleeping
Extras: Joined England's tour of West Indies in 1989-90 as a replacement for Ricky
Ellcock. Suffers from Raynaud's disease, a problem of blood circulation, and has to
spend one night in hospital every two months to have the disease treated. Left
Leicestershire at the end of 1991 season and signed for Nottinghamshire. Hit first Test

century v India at Madras on 1992-93 tour to India and Sri Lanka. Joined England tour party in Australia 1994-95 following injury to Darren Gough. Suffered a compressed fracture in the ball of his hip joint which prevented him from playing any Championship cricket in 1995. Left Nottinghamshire and joined Surrey for the 1996 season. Played for an England XI in the Cricket Max tournament in 1997. Rejoined Leicestershire as vice-captain for the 1998 season and captained the club for much of the season in the absence through injury of James Whitaker. Scored 71* in 33 balls as Leicestershire made 204 in 19 overs and one ball to beat Northamptonshire at Grace Road in 1998

Best batting: 247 Nottinghamshire v Durham, Chester-le-Street 1993
Best bowling: 6-22 Leicestershire v Oxford University, The Parks 1988

1999 Season

	M	Inns	NO	Runs	HS	Avge	100s	50s	Ct	St	O	M	Runs	Wkts	Avge	Best	5wI	10wM
Test																		
All First	10	13	2	520	139	47.27	2	2	7	-	191.1	51	585	16	36.56	3-18	-	-
1-day Int																		
NatWest	1	1	0	22	22	22.00	-	-	-	-	9	1	54	0	-	-	-	-
B & H																		
1-day Lge	9	9	1	214	116 *	26.75	1	-	3	-	50.5	5	215	6	35.83	2-22	-	

Career Performances

	M	Inns	NO	Runs	HS	Avge	100s	50s	Ct	St	Balls	Runs	Wkts	Avge	Best	5wI	10wM
Test	32	51	3	1105	117	23.02	1	4	25	-	6852	3490	93	37.52	6-111	3	-
All First	184	268	34	7326	247	31.30	9	34	148	-	31414	15923	536	29.70	6-22	20	3
1-day Int	53	40	14	374	33	14.38	-	-	20	-	2625	1942	66	29.42	4-30	-	
NatWest	24	19	2	392	89	23.05	-	2	14	-	1270	743	32	23.21	5-19	1	
B & H	43	30	12	549	55 *	30.50	-	1	18	-	2271	1534	65	23.60	5-46	1	
1-day Lge	120	105	24	2257	116 *	27.86	1	9	40	-	4510	3259	123	26.49	4-13	-	

58. Which Surrey spinner took ten wickets in an innings
v Kent at Blackheath in 1956?

LEWIS, J.   Gloucestershire

Name: Jonathan Lewis
Role: Right-hand bat,
right-arm medium-fast bowler
Born: 26 August 1975, Aylesbury
Height: 6ft 2in **Weight:** 13st
Nickname: JJ, Nugget, Stupid
County debut: 1995
County cap: 1998
50 wickets in a season: 2
1st-Class 50s: 2
1st-Class 5 w. in innings: 8
1st-Class 10 w. in match: 1
1st-Class catches: 13
Place in batting averages: 255th av. 13.30
(1998 256th av. 13.44)
Place in bowling averages: 90th av. 29.46
(1998 42nd av. 24.52)
Strike rate: 60.28 (career 53.65)
Parents: John and Jane
Marital status: Single

Education: Lawn Junior School; Churchfields Comprehensive School;
Swindon College
Qualifications: 9 GCSEs, BTEC in Leisure and Hospitality
Overseas tours: Bath Schools to New South Wales, Australia 1993
Overseas teams played for: Marist, Christchurch, New Zealand 1994-95;
Richmond City, Melbourne 1995-96
Cricketers particularly admired: Dom Hewson, Jack Russell, Courtney Walsh,
Jon Summer, Alan Biggins, Paul Rignall
Other sports followed: 'Gurning'
Extras: Was on Northamptonshire staff in 1994 but made no first-team appearance.
Best batting: 62 Gloucestershire v Leicestershire, Cheltenham 1999
Best bowling: 7-56 Gloucestershire v Nottinghamshire, Bristol 1999

1999 Season

	M	Inns	NO	Runs	HS	Avge	100s	50s	Ct	St	O	M	Runs	Wkts	Avge	Best	5wI	10wM
Test																		
All First	14	23	3	266	62	13.30	-	1	2	-	492.2	134	1444	49	29.46	7-56	2	1
1-day Int																		
NatWest	1	0	0	0	0	-	-	-	1	-	10	2	23	2	11.50	2-23	-	
B & H	3	2	0	2	2	1.00	-	-	-	-	24	2	117	7	16.71	3-32	-	
1-day Lge	8	8	1	54	12	7.71	-	-	2	-	50.1	4	225	6	37.50	2-42	-	

Career Performances

	M	Inns	NO	Runs	HS	Avge	100s	50s	Ct	St	Balls	Runs	Wkts	Avge	Best	5wl	10wM
Test																	
All First	60	92	15	971	62	12.61	-	2	13	-	10302	5347	192	27.84	7-56	8	1
1-day Int																	
NatWest	6	4	2	10	6 *	5.00	-	-	3	-	326	192	8	24.00	3-27	-	
B & H	10	6	2	49	33 *	12.25	-	-	-	-	528	469	16	29.31	3-31	-	
1-day Lge	51	32	13	191	26 *	10.05	-	-	9	-	2014	1674	51	32.82	3-27	-	

LEWIS, J. J. B. Durham

Name: Jonathan James Benjamin Lewis
Role: Right-hand bat, right-arm
slow-medium net bowler
Born: 21 May 1970, Isleworth, Middlesex
Height: 5ft 9in **Weight:** 12st
Nickname: Judge, JJ, Miny-Me
County debut: 1990 (Essex), 1997 (Durham)
County cap: 1994 (Essex), 1998 (Durham)
1000 runs in a season: 2
1st-Class 50s: 37
1st-Class 100s: 8
1st-Class 200s: 1
1st-Class catches: 76
One-Day 100s: 1
Place in batting averages: 30th av. 40.92
(1998 164th av. 23.03)
Strike rate: (career 120.00)
Parents: Ted and Nina
Wife and date of marriage: Fiona, 6 July 1999
Family links with cricket: Father played county schools. Uncle is a lifelong Somerset supporter. Sister is right-arm medium-fast bowler for NorTel
Education: King Edward VI School, Chelmsford; Roehampton Institute of Higher Education
Qualifications: 5 O-levels, 3 A-levels, BSc (Hons) Sports Science, NCA Senior Coach
Career outside cricket: Precision engineer with Tees Precision
Off-season: Playing and coaching in South Africa
Overseas teams played for: Old Hararians, Zimbabwe 1991-92; Taita District, New Zealand 1992-93; Eshowe and Zululand 1994-95; Richards Bay 1996-97; Empangeni, Natal 1997-98
Cricketers particularly admired: John Childs, Greg Matthews, Alan Walker
Young players to look out for: Steve Harmison

Other sports followed: Soccer (West Ham United), rugby, basketball, 'most sports really'

Injuries: Missed last Championship game with a hip injury

Relaxations: Sleep

Extras: Hit century on first-class debut in Essex's final Championship match of the 1990 season. Joined Durham for the 1997 season – 'I am slowly learning the local dialect'. Scored a double century on his debut for Durham (210* v Oxford University), placing him in a small club, alongside Peter Bowler and Neil Taylor, of players who have scored centuries on debut for two different counties

Opinions on cricket: 'Standard of cricket journalism (with some exceptions) is falling to a level that some pitches are.'

Best batting: 210* Durham v Oxford University, The Parks 1997

Best bowling: 1-73 Durham v Surrey, Riverside 1998

1999 Season

	M	Inns	NO	Runs	HS	Avge	100s	50s	Ct	St	O	M	Runs	Wkts	Avge	Best	5wI	10wM
Test																		
All First	16	28	0	1146	132	40.92	2	8	7	-								
1-day Int																		
NatWest	1	1	0	24	24	24.00	-	-	-	-								
B & H																		
1-day Lge	16	15	3	455	85	37.91	-	1	-	-								

Career Performances

	M	Inns	NO	Runs	HS	Avge	100s	50s	Ct	St	Balls	Runs	Wkts	Avge	Best	5wI	10wM
Test																	
All First	107	189	19	5979	210 *	35.17	9	37	76	-	120	121	1	121.00	1-73	-	-
1-day Int																	
NatWest	10	10	1	133	24 *	14.77	-	-	1	-							
B & H	14	14	1	339	67	26.07	-	1	3	-							
1-day Lge	87	74	16	1617	102	27.87	1	9	14	-	8	35	0	-	-	-	

LEWRY, J. D.   Sussex

Name: Jason David Lewry

Role: Left-hand bat, left-arm fast-medium bowler

Born: 2 April 1971, Worthing, West Sussex

Height: 6ft 3in **Weight:** 14st 6lbs

Nickname: Looey, Urco

County debut: 1994

County cap: 1996

50 wickets in a season: 2
1st-Class 5 w. in innings: 14
1st-Class 10 w. in match: 2
1st-Class catches: 5
Place in batting averages: 254th av. 13.58
(1998 291st av. 5.73)
Place in bowling averages: 51st av. 23.75
(1998 34th av. 22.72)
Strike rate: 40.89 (career 45.09)
Parents: David and Veronica
Wife and date of marriage:
Naomi Madeleine, 18 August 1997
Children: William Jason Joseph,
14 February 1998
Family links with cricket: Father coaches
Education: Thomas à Becket, Worthing;
Durrington High School, Worthing; Worthing
Sixth Form College
Qualifications: 6 O-levels, 3 GCSEs, City & Guilds, NCA Award Course
Career outside cricket: 'Still looking'
Overseas tours: 'Goring CC to Isle of Wight 1992, 1993'; England A to Zimbabwe
and South Africa 1998-99
Cricketers particularly admired: The Sussex staff, David Gower, Wasim Akram,
Martin Andrews
Young players to look out for: 'Swing bowlers'
Other sports followed: Football (West Ham United), golf, squash, 'kicking on … zzz'
Relaxations: Golf, eating out, 'kicking on with Stan and annoying the wife'
Opinions on cricket: 'Play each game as if it is your last.'
Best batting: 34 Sussex v Kent, Hove 1995
Best bowling: 7-38 Sussex v Derbyshire, Derby 1999

1999 Season

	M	Inns	NO	Runs	HS	Avge	100s	50s	Ct	St	O	M	Runs	Wkts	Avge	Best	5wl	10wM
Test																		
All First	12	19	7	163	30 *	13.58	-	-	2	-	381.4	84	1330	56	23.75	7-38	4	1
1-day Int																		
NatWest																		
B & H	1	1	0	3	3	3.00	-	-	-	-	10	0	57	2	28.50	2-57	-	
1-day Lge	1	1	0	0	0	0.00	-	-	-	-	7	0	55	1	55.00	1-55	-	

Career Performances

	M	Inns	NO	Runs	HS	Avge	100s	50s	Ct	St	Balls	Runs	Wkts	Avge	Best	5wI	10wM
Test																	
All First	57	84	18	614	34	9.30	-	-	5	-	9830	5372	218	24.64	7-38	14	2
1-day Int																	
NatWest	5	4	3	19	9	19.00	-	-	-	-	324	224	11	20.36	4-42	-	
B & H	8	5	2	41	14 *	13.66	-	-	-	-	426	373	6	62.16	2-51	-	
1-day Lge	30	16	6	43	10 *	4.30	-	-	5	-	1222	994	42	23.66	4-29	-	

LIPTROT, C. G.   Worcestershire

Name: Christopher George Liptrot
Role: Left-hand bat, right-arm
fast-medium bowler
Born: 13 December 1980, Wigan
Height: 6ft 2in **Weight:** 12st 6lbs
Nickname: Lippy
County debut: 1999
1st-Class 50s: 1
1st-Class 5 w. in innings: 1
Place in batting averages: 250th av. 14.20
Place in bowling averages: 112th av. 33.25
Strike rate: 58.25 (career 58.25)
Parents: Brian and Susan
Marital status: Single
Family links with cricket: 'My father and
brother play local cricket'
Education: St Matthews, Highfield, Wigan;
The Deanery High School, Wigan
Qualifications: 9 GCSEs
Career outside cricket: 'I was formerly an electrician'
Off-season: 'I will be going to the Sunshine Coast, Brisbane, to play cricket
this winter'
Overseas tours: Lancashire Leagues U19 Select XI to South Africa 1998
Overseas teams played for: Sunshine Coast, Brisbane 1999-2000
Cricketers particularly admired: Glenn McGrath, Darren Gough, Allan Donald,
Graeme Hick
Young players to look out for: Vikram Solanki
Other sports played: Football, rugby
Other sports followed: Football (Everton FC), rugby league (Wigan Warriors)
Relaxations: Watching all sports; music
Extras: Represented England U19 in one-day and 'Test' series v Australia U19 1999

Best batting: 61 Worcestershire v Warwickshire, Edgbaston 1999
Best bowling: 5-51 Worcestershire v Surrey, Worcester 1999

1999 Season

	M	Inns	NO	Runs	HS	Avge	100s	50s	Ct	St	O	M	Runs	Wkts	Avge	Best	5wI	10wM
Test																		
All First	11	16	6	142	61	14.20	-	1	-	-	194.1	49	665	20	33.25	5-51	1	-
1-day Int																		
NatWest																		
B & H																		
1-day Lge																		

Career Performances

	M	Inns	NO	Runs	HS	Avge	100s	50s	Ct	St	Balls	Runs	Wkts	Avge	Best	5wI	10wM
Test																	
All First	11	16	6	142	61	14.20	-	1	-	-	1165	665	20	33.25	5-51	1	-
1-day Int																	
NatWest																	
B & H																	
1-day Lge																	

LLONG, N. J.   Kent

Name: Nigel James Llong
Role: Left-hand bat, off-spin bowler
Born: 11 February 1969, Ashford, Kent
Height: 6ft **Weight:** 11st 3lbs
Nickname: Nidge, Lloydie
County debut: 1991
County cap: 1993
1st-Class 50s: 16
1st-Class 100s: 6
1st-Class 5 w. in innings: 2
1st-Class catches: 59
One-Day 100s: 2
Strike rate: (career 64.94)
Parents: Peggy (deceased) and Richard
Wife and date of marriage:
Melissa, 20 February 1999
Family links with cricket: Father and
brother played club cricket

Education: Newtown County Primary; North School for Boys
Qualifications: 6 CSEs, Level 1 coaching award
Career outside cricket: Snooker table technician and groundsman
Overseas tours: Kent to Zimbabwe 1992-93, to France 1998
Overseas teams played for: Ashburton, Melbourne 1988-89, 1996-97; Greenpoint CC, Cape Town 1990-94, 1997-98
Cricketers particularly admired: David Gower
Other sports played: 'Very bad golf'
Other sports followed: Football (Arsenal)
Relaxations: 'Watching most sport; fishing'
Extras: Kent Uncapped Young Player of the Year 1992. Kent Supporters Club Young Player of the Year Award 1993. Shared in NatWest record sixth-wicket stand of 226 with Matthew Fleming v Cheshire at Bowdon 1999. Was Man of the Match in the 1999 AON Trophy final, scoring 37 and taking 5-32. Released by Kent at end of 1999 season
Opinions on cricket: 'Pitches should be prepared to last four days. Why not play five-day games on good, flat pitches, 90 overs a day to simulate Test cricket? Take the power away from counties. ECB should dictate what developments for the game should take place.'
Best batting: 130 Kent v Hampshire, Canterbury 1996
Best bowling: 5-21 Kent v Middlesex, Canterbury 1996

1999 Season

	M	Inns	NO	Runs	HS	Avge	100s	50s	Ct	St	O	M	Runs	Wkts	Avge	Best	5wI	10wM
Test																		
All First																		
1-day Int																		
NatWest	3	3	1	133	123	66.50	1	-	1	-	7	0	35	3	11.66	3-35	-	
B & H																		
1-day Lge	12	12	3	273	42 *	30.33	-	-	6	-	22	0	104	2	52.00	1-18	-	

Career Performances

	M	Inns	NO	Runs	HS	Avge	100s	50s	Ct	St	Balls	Runs	Wkts	Avge	Best	5wI	10wM
Test																	
All First	68	108	11	3024	130	31.17	6	16	59	-	2273	1259	35	35.97	5-21	2	-
1-day Int																	
NatWest	9	9	4	394	123	78.80	2	1	4	-	176	131	9	14.55	3-35	-	
B & H	17	14	1	320	75	24.61	-	2	4	-	204	175	3	58.33	2-38	-	
1-day Lge	106	88	19	1495	70	21.66	-	5	33	-	835	806	27	29.85	4-24	-	

LLOYD, G. D.   Lancashire

Name: Graham David Lloyd
Role: Right-hand bat, right-arm
medium bowler
Born: 1 July 1969, Accrington
Height: 5ft 9in **Weight:** 12st 10lbs
Nickname: Bumble
County debut: 1988
County cap: 1992
One-Day Internationals: 6
1000 runs in a season: 5
1st-Class 50s: 57
1st-Class 100s: 20
1st-Class 200s: 3
1st-Class catches: 113
One-Day 100s: 3
Place in batting averages: 22nd av. 42.64
(1998 45th av. 39.57)
Strike rate: (career 169.50)
Parents: David and Susan

Wife and date of marriage: Sharron, 11 October 1997
Children: Joseph, 20 December 1998
Family links with cricket: Father played for Lancashire and England
Education: Peel Park Primary; Hollins County High School, Accrington
Qualifications: 3 O-levels, NCA coaching certificate
Career outside cricket: Bookmaker
Off-season: Training with Lancashire from 1 January
Overseas tours: England A to Australia 1992-93; Lancashire CCC to Guernsey 1995;
England VI to Hong Kong (Hong Kong Sixes) 1997; England to Bangladesh (Wills
International Cup) 1998
Overseas teams played for: Maroochydore CC, Queensland 1988-89 and 1991-95
Cricketers particularly admired: Steve Waugh
Young players to look out for: Andrew Flintoff, Chris Schofield
Other sports played: Football
Other sports followed: Football (Manchester United)
Relaxations: Horse racing
Extras: His school did not play cricket, so he learnt at Accrington, playing in the same
team as his father. Won the EDS Walter Lawrence Trophy (for the fastest century of
the year) two years running 1996, 1997. Played for England in the 1997 Hong Kong
Sixes tournament in which England were runners-up to Pakistan
Opinions on cricket: 'Day/night games have been a success this season.'
Best batting: 241 Lancashire v Essex, Chelmsford 1996
Best bowling: 1-4 Lancashire v Warwickshire, Edgbaston 1996

1999 Season

	M	Inns	NO	Runs	HS	Avge	100s	50s	Ct	St	O	M	Runs	Wkts	Avge	Best	5wI	10wM
Test																		
All First	17	26	1	1066	144	42.64	3	6	7	-	10	0	100	0	-	-	-	-
1-day Int																		
NatWest	3	2	0	53	42	26.50	-	-	2	-								
B & H	1	1	1	45	45 *	-	-	-	-	-								
1-day Lge	14	11	5	183	55 *	30.50	-	1	3	-								

Career Performances

	M	Inns	NO	Runs	HS	Avge	100s	50s	Ct	St	Balls	Runs	Wkts	Avge	Best	5wI	10wM
Test																	
All First	177	284	26	10203	241	39.54	23	57	113	-	339	440	2	220.00	1-4	-	-
1-day Int	6	5	1	39	22	9.75	-	-	2	-							
NatWest	24	21	2	589	96	31.00	-	3	5	-	30	35	1	35.00	1-23	-	
B & H	42	36	11	752	81 *	30.08	-	3	6	-	30	50	0	-	-	-	
1-day Lge	155	142	24	3697	134	31.33	3	20	37	-	12	18	0	-	-	-	

LOGAN, R. J.   Northamptonshire

Name: Richard James Logan
Role: Right-hand bat, right-arm fast bowler
Born: 28 January 1980, Stone, Staffs
Height: 6ft 1in **Weight:** 13st 7lbs
Nickname: Gus, Logie, Loges
County debut: 1999
1st-Class catches: 1
Strike rate: 43.50 (career 43.50)
Parents: Margaret and Robert
Marital status: Girlfriend Sarah
Family links with cricket: Father played for local club Cannock as batsman/wicket-keeper
Education: Walhouse C of E School, Cannock; Wolverhampton Grammar School
Qualifications: 10 GCSEs
Overseas tours: England U17 to Bermuda 1997 (International Youth Tournament); England U19 to South Africa 1997-98, to New Zealand 1998-99
Cricketers particularly admired: Curtly Ambrose, Allan Donald
Young players to look out for: Graeme Swann, Paul Franks, John Blain, Stephen Peters

Other sports played: Hockey (Cannock – 'also played for Staffordshire from age 9. Played for Midlands U14 but had to decline Midlands training due to commitment to cricket')

Other sports followed: Football (Wolverhampton Wanderers)

Relaxations: Spending time with girlfriend. Cinema, keeping fit, socialising

Extras: Played for Staffordshire at every level from U11 to U19, and as captain from U13 to U17. Played for Midlands U14 and U15 (both as captain), HMC Schools U15. 1995 *Daily Telegraph*/Lombard U15 Midlands Bowler and Batsman of the Year. Played for Northamptonshire U17 and U19 national champions in 1997. Has played for England U15, U17 and U19, including one-day and 'Test' series v Australia U19 1999

Opinions on cricket: 'I feel that now that two divisions have been introduced to the Championship, the gap between the two divisions will grow and we will end up with all the best players in the country in the top division getting paid the best money, and the bottom division will have the weaker players, earning less money.'

Best batting: 1 Northamptonshire v Sri Lanka A, Northampton 1999

Best bowling: 3-42 Northamptonshire v Cambridge University, Fenner's 1999

1999 Season

	M	Inns	NO	Runs	HS	Avge	100s	50s	Ct	St	O	M	Runs	Wkts	Avge	Best	5wI	10wM
Test																		
All First	2	2	0	1	1	0.50	-	-	1	-	58	18	178	8	22.25	3-42	-	-
1-day Int																		
NatWest																		
B & H																		
1-day Lge	4	1	0	8	8	8.00	-	-	2	-	17	0	101	3	33.66	2-31	-	

Career Performances

	M	Inns	NO	Runs	HS	Avge	100s	50s	Ct	St	Balls	Runs	Wkts	Avge	Best	5wI	10wM
Test																	
All First	2	2	0	1	1	0.50	-	-	1	-	348	178	8	22.25	3-42	-	-
1-day Int																	
NatWest																	
B & H																	
1-day Lge	4	1	0	8	8	8.00	-	-	2	-	102	101	3	33.66	2-31	-	

LOYE, M. B.   Northamptonshire

Name: Malachy Bernard Loye
Role: Right-hand bat, off-spin bowler
Born: 27 September 1972, Northampton
Height: 6ft 2in **Weight:** 13st 7lbs
Nickname: Mal, Chairman
County debut: 1991
County cap: 1994
1000 runs in a season: 1
1st-Class 50s: 27
1st-Class 100s: 12
1st-Class 200s: 1
1st-Class 300s: 1
1st-Class catches: 63
One-Day 100s: 2
Place in batting averages: 172nd av. 22.78
(1998 8th av. 59.90)
Parents: Patrick and Anne
Marital status: Single

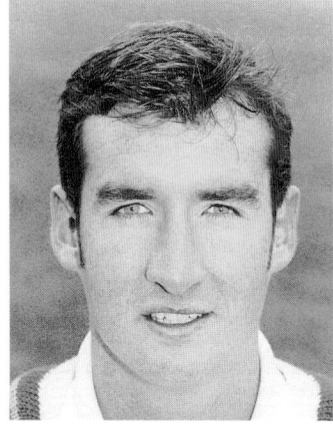

Family links with cricket: Father and brother both played for Cogenhoe CC in
Northampton
Education: Brixworth Primary School; Moulton Comprehensive School
Qualifications: GCSEs and senior coaching certificate
Off-season: Playing and training in Perth
Overseas tours: England U18 to Canada 1991; England U19 to Pakistan 1991-92;
England A to South Africa 1993-94, to Zimbabwe and South Africa 1998-99;
Northamptonshire to Cape Town 1993, to Zimbabwe 1995, 1998, to Johannesburg 1996
Overseas teams played for: Riccarton, Christchurch, New Zealand 1992-95; Onslow,
Wellington, New Zealand 1995-96; North Perth, Australia 1997-98
Cricketers particularly admired: Wayne Larkins ('talent'), Gordon Greenidge
('power'), Curtly Ambrose ('ultimate cricketer')
Young players to look out for: Jason Brown, Monty Panesar
Other sports played: Swimming, boxing
Other sports followed: Football (Northampton Town and Liverpool FC), rugby union
(Ireland), boxing
Injuries: Out for one month with back and finger injuries
Relaxations: 'Playing the guitar, going out to bars, swimming and sleeping'
Extras: Played for England U19 in the home series against Australia U19 in 1991 and
against Sri Lanka U19 1992. Voted Professional Cricketers' Association's Young
Player of the Year 1993 and Whittingdale Young Player of the Year 1993. Shared a
county record opening stand of 372 with Richard Montgomerie versus Yorkshire in
1996. His 322* v Glamorgan in 1998 is the highest individual first-class score for the

county; the highest to that point was Raman Subba Row's 300. During his innings, Loye put on 401 for the fifth wicket with David Ripley, setting a new fifth wicket record for first-class cricket in England. Voted the PCA's Player of the Year in 1998. Signed a new four-year contract with Northamptonshire in November 1998
Opinions on cricket: 'Great game; just not enough "great" people running it.'
Best batting: 322* Northamptonshire v Glamorgan, Northampton 1998

1999 Season

	M	Inns	NO	Runs	HS	Avge	100s	50s	Ct	St	O	M	Runs	Wkts	Avge	Best	5wI	10wM
Test																		
All First	13	20	1	433	102 *	22.78	2	-	4	-								
1-day Int																		
NatWest	1	1	0	9	9	9.00	-	-	-	-								
B & H																		
1-day Lge	9	9	0	164	55	18.22	-	1	3	-								

Career Performances

	M	Inns	NO	Runs	HS	Avge	100s	50s	Ct	St	Balls	Runs	Wkts	Avge	Best	5wI	10wM
Test																		
All First	114	182	18	6074	322 *	37.03	14	27	63	-	13	43	0	-	-	-	-
1-day Int																		
NatWest	14	13	3	267	65	26.70	-	1	4	-								
B & H	21	21	5	475	68 *	29.68	-	2	7	-								
1-day Lge	85	81	7	2314	122	31.27	2	13	18	-								

59. In 1911, at Brighton, E.B. Alletson arrived at the crease with his side seven wickets down in their second innings v Sussex and only nine runs ahead. He proceeded to score 189. For which county did Alletson play?

LUCAS, D. S.   Nottinghamshire

Name: David Scott Lucas
Role: Right-hand bat, left-arm medium
swing bowler
Born: 19 August 1978, Nottingham
Height: 6ft 2in **Weight:** 13st
Nickname: Muc, Gary, Mucus, Carcinogen,
Conquistador
County debut: 1999
1st-Class 5 w. in innings: 1
Place in bowling averages: 65th av. 26.26
Strike rate: 41.53 (career 41.53)
Parents: Mary and Terry
Marital status: Single
Family links with cricket: 'Dad played
local cricket'
Qualifications: 6 GCSEs, pass in
Computer-Aided Design
Overseas teams played for: Bankstown

Canterbury Bulldogs, Sydney 1996-97
Cricketers particularly admired: Steve and Mark Waugh, Wasim Akram, Allan
Donald, Chris Murden, Rick Smith ('particularly for his catching'), Joe Thorpe
Young players to look out for: 'The Pikelets and Galas!', Stephen Randall, Matt
Whiley, Chris Read, Noel Gie, Rick Smith
Other sports played: 'I have played a good standard of local football', indoor cricket,
'indoor golf'
Other sports followed: Football (Arsenal), rugby league (Wigan)
Relaxations: Eating, going out, films, sleeping, going to the gym
Extras: Was selected to represent England at Indoor Cricket World Cup in Australia in
October 1998. Won Yorkshire League with Rotherham in 1996
Opinions on cricket: 'There should be more day/night games, and also cheerleaders.'
Best batting: 24* Nottinghamshire v Essex, Nottingham 1999
Best bowling: 5-104 Nottinghamshire v Essex, Nottingham 1999

1999 Season

	M	Inns	NO	Runs	HS	Avge	100s	50s	Ct	St	O	M	Runs	Wkts	Avge	Best	5wl	10wM
Test																		
All First	6	7	3	58	24*	14.50	-	-	-	-	103.5	21	394	15	26.26	5-104	1	-
1-day Int																		
NatWest	1	1	1	14	14*	-	-	-	-	-	6	0	40	0	-	-	-	
B & H																		
1-day Lge	4	1	1	19	19*	-	-	-	1	-	19	0	117	4	29.25	3-49	-	

Career Performances

	M	Inns	NO	Runs	HS	Avge	100s	50s	Ct	St	Balls	Runs	Wkts	Avge	Best	5wI	10wM
Test																	
All First	6	7	3	58	24 *	14.50	-	-	-	-	623	394	15	26.26	5-104	1	-
1-day Int																	
NatWest	1	1	1	14	14 *	-	-	-	-	-	36	40	0	-	-	-	-
B & H																	
1-day Lge	4	1	1	19	19 *	-	-	-	1	-	114	117	4	29.25	3-49	-	

LUGSDEN, S. Hampshire

Name: Steven Lugsden
Role: Right-hand bat, right-arm fast bowler
Born: 10 July 1976, Gateshead
Height: 6ft 3in **Weight:** 13st
Nickname: 8-ball, Lugsy, Dime Bar, Bluntest-tool-in-the-box
County debut: 1993 (Durham), 1999 (Hampshire)
1st-Class catches: 2
Strike rate: 76.50 (career 70.96)
Parents: William and Nora
Wife and date of marriage: Janette, 19 December 1997
Children: John James, 21 December 1997
Education: St Edmund Campion RC School, Wrekenton, Gateshead
Qualifications: 7 GCSEs, BTEC Business and Finance
Career outside cricket: Landscape gardener and model ('clothed')
Overseas tours: England U19 to West Indies 1994-95
Cricketers particularly admired: Geoff Cook, Allan Donald
Young players to look out for: Myself and Jason Searle
Other sports played/followed: 'Boxed to amateur county level' and snooker
Extras: In 1993 became youngest player (17 years 27 days) to make first-class debut for Durham. Played against India for England U19 in home series 1994. 'Daftest cricketer in the north east.' Released by Durham at end of 1998 season. Joined Hampshire for 1999 on a one-year contract; released by Hampshire at end of 1999 season
Best batting: 16 Hampshire v Oxford University, The Parks 1999
Best bowling: 3-45 Durham v Lancashire, Chester-le-Street 1996

1999 Season

	M	Inns	NO	Runs	HS	Avge	100s	50s	Ct	St	O	M	Runs	Wkts	Avge	Best	5wI	10wM
Test																		
All First	2	3	1	25	16	12.50	-	-	-	-	51	12	161	4	40.25	3-105	-	-
1-day Int																		
NatWest																		
B & H																		
1-day Lge																		

Career Performances

	M	Inns	NO	Runs	HS	Avge	100s	50s	Ct	St	Balls	Runs	Wkts	Avge	Best	5wI	10wM
Test																		
All First	15	21	8	70	16	5.38	-	-	2	-	2058	1333	29	45.96	3-45	-	-
1-day Int																		
NatWest																		
B & H																		
1-day Lge	1	0	0	0	0	-	-	-	-	-	48	55	1	55.00	1-55	-	

MADDY, D. L.   Leicestershire

Name: Darren Lee Maddy
Role: Right-hand opening bat, right-arm medium bowler
Born: 23 May 1974, Leicester
Height: 5ft 9in ('One inch taller than Dominic Williamson, two inches taller than Tim Mason') **Weight:** 11st
Nickname: Roaster, Dazza, Fire Starter
County debut: 1993 (one-day), 1994 (first-class)
County cap: 1996
Test debut: 1999
Tests: 1
One-Day Internationals: 2
1000 runs in a season: 2
1st-Class 50s: 21
1st-Class 100s: 11
1st-Class 200s: 1
1st-Class catches: 96
One-Day 100s: 5
Place in batting averages: 47th av. 37.85 (1998 155th av. 23.70)

Place in bowling averages: 28th av. 21.66
Strike rate: 42.83 (career 70.20)
Parents: William Arthur and Hilary Jean
Marital status: Engaged to Justine
Family links with cricket: Father and younger brother, Greg, play club cricket
Education: Herrick Junior School, Leicester; Roundhills, Thurmaston;
Wreake Valley, Syston
Qualifications: 8 GCSEs
Career outside cricket: 'Undecided'
Off-season: England tour to South Africa and Zimbabwe
Overseas tours: Leicestershire to Bloemfontein 1995, to Western Transvaal 1996, to
Durban 1997, to Barbados 1998; England A to Kenya and Sri Lanka 1997-98, to
Zimbabwe and South Africa 1998-99; England to South Africa and Zimbabwe
1999-2000
Overseas teams played for: Wanderers, Johannesburg 1992-93; Northern Free State,
Orange Free State 1993-95; Rhodes University, South Africa 1995-97
Cricketers particularly admired: Brian Lara, Michael Atherton, Richard Hadlee,
Viv Richards, 'Babe Ruth' Dakin
Young players to look out for: Atul Sachdeva
Other sports played: 5-a-side football, golf, squash
Other sports followed: Rugby (Leicester Tigers), football (Leicester City), baseball,
golf, boxing – 'most sports really except for horse racing and motor racing'
Relaxations: 'Going to the gym, playing sport, spending time with my girlfriend,
Justine; listening to music, watching TV, going on holiday, scuba diving, bungee
jumping'
Extras: 'Voted having the biggest thighs in Leicester by team-mates.' Set a new 2nd
XI Championship run aggregate record (1498) beating the previous one which had
stood since 1961. Rapid Cricketline 2nd XI Player of the Year 1994. Scored his
maiden first-class 200 against Kenya at Nairobi on England A's 1997-98 tour and was
leading run-scorer on the tour with 687 runs at 68.7. Set a new record for the number
of runs scored in the B&H competition in one season, previously held by Graham
Gooch. Also set a record for the most B&H Gold Awards won in one season (five in
1998). Carried his bat (158*) for Leicestershire v Yorkshire at Leicester 1999. Won
Vodafone Man of the Match award for his 110 for First Class Counties Select XI v Sri
Lanka A in one-day match at Chester-le-Street 1999. Made Test debut v New Zealand
in the fourth Test at The Oval 1999
Opinions on cricket: 'Counties should employ players on a nine-month contract.
National League should be played over 40 overs and not 45. The over-rate fine system
is still too severe. The third umpire should be used in all one-day competitions. Two
divisions is a good idea as it will make our cricket more competitive; we saw this at
the end of the 1999 season.'
Best batting: 202 England A v Kenya, Nairobi 1997-98
Best bowling: 3-5 Leicestershire v Gloucestershire, Leicester 1999

1999 Season

	M	Inns	NO	Runs	HS	Avge	100s	50s	Ct	St	O	M	Runs	Wkts	Avge	Best	5wI	10wM
Test	1	2	0	19	14	9.50	-	-	1	-								
All First	18	30	2	1060	158 *	37.85	2	4	18	-	85.4	22	260	12	21.66	3-5	-	-
1-day Int																		
NatWest	2	2	0	90	89	45.00	-	1	2	-	9.3	1	39	2	19.50	1-12	-	
B & H	1	1	0	84	84	84.00	-	1	-	-	6	0	29	0	-		-	-
1-day Lge	14	14	1	349	89 *	26.84	-	2	5	-	22.2	0	113	3	37.66	3-27	-	

Career Performances

	M	Inns	NO	Runs	HS	Avge	100s	50s	Ct	St	Balls	Runs	Wkts	Avge	Best	5wI	10wM
Test	1	2	0	19	14	9.50	-	-	1	-							
All First	98	158	9	5046	202	33.86	12	21	96	-	1404	725	20	36.25	3-5	-	-
1-day Int	2	1	0	1	1	1.00	-	-	-	-							
NatWest	11	10	0	188	89	18.80	-	1	6	-	201	166	7	23.71	2-38	-	
B & H	23	23	4	1210	151	63.68	4	6	7	-	186	172	6	28.66	3-32	-	
1-day Lge	87	78	6	1896	106 *	26.33	1	14	33	-	956	934	31	30.12	3-11	-	

MAHMOOD, S. Somerset

Name: Saqib Mahmood
Role: Right-hand middle-order bat,
leg-spin bowler
Born: 24 August 1977, Kettering
Height: 5ft 10in **Weight:** 11st
Nickname: Saqqi, Empty, Mushy, Spaddy
County debut: 1999
1st-Class catches: 1
Parents: Rashad and Azra
Marital status: Single
Family links with cricket: Brother played
county cricket for Essex CCC. Father played
local club cricket
Education: Hartley School, East Ham,
London; Langdon Comprehensive School;
Havering College, Essex; King's College,
University of London
Qualifications: 9 GCSEs, 3 A-levels ('top 20
per cent in Europe'), BSc/MSc Computer Science
Career outside cricket: 'Hoping to work as a consultant or as a lecturer'
Off-season: 'In either one of the professions above, or travelling to either Lahore or
Melbourne to play grade cricket'

Overseas teams played for: Gul CC, Rawalpindi, Pakistan 1993-94; P&T Gymkhana 1997, 1998, 1999

Cricketers particularly admired: Steve Waugh, Nasser Hussain, Sachin Tendulkar, Yousuf Youhana, Saqlain Mushtaq, Shane Warne, Mushtaq Ahmed, Darren Gough, Peter Bowler

Young players to look out for: Qasim Hafeez, Jamal Mehdi

Other sports played: Table tennis, pool, badminton, football, golf

Other sports followed: Football (Tottenham Hotspur FC), boxing (Prince Naseem), golf (Tiger Woods)

Injuries: Out from July to end of season with nerve and muscle injuries in bowling hand

Relaxations: 'Music, IT, watching films, clean living, worshipping'

Extras: Set London record by taking 8-1. Hit six sixes in an over in club match. Released by Somerset at end of 1999 season

Opinions on cricket: 'Counties should combine to form regional cricket. There are too many professional and especially idle cricketers on the circuit. Number of first-class matches should be reduced to nine, and the wickets and practice facilities should be close to Test cricket. More emphasis should be placed on preparation, both physical and mental approach. By playing less, cricketers may recover from injuries, spend more time with family and above all be more hungry for success. ECB and counties should also direct their attention to inner city schools to extract natural talent and not continue to produce manufactured cricketers.'

Best batting: 7* Somerset v New Zealand, Taunton 1999

1999 Season

	M	Inns	NO	Runs	HS	Avge	100s	50s	Ct	St	O	M	Runs	Wkts	Avge	Best	5wI	10wM
Test																		
All First	1	2	1	7	7*	7.00	-	-	1	-	3	0	43	0	-		-	-	-
1-day Int																		
NatWest																		
B & H																		
1-day Lge																		

Career Performances

	M	Inns	NO	Runs	HS	Avge	100s	50s	Ct	St	Balls	Runs	Wkts	Avge	Best	5wI	10wM
Test																		
All First	1	2	1	7	7*	7.00	-	-	1	-	18	43	0	-		-	-	-
1-day Int																		
NatWest																		
B & H																		
1-day Lge																		

MALCOLM, D. E.   Northamptonshire

Name: Devon Eugene Malcolm
Role: Right-hand bat, right-arm fast bowler
Born: 22 February 1963, Kingston, Jamaica
Height: 6ft 2in **Weight:** 15st
Nickname: Dude
County debut: 1984 (Derbyshire),
1998 (Northamptonshire)
County cap: 1989 (Derbyshire),
1999 (Northamptonshire)
Benefit: 1997 (Derbyshire)
Test debut: 1989
Tests: 40
One-Day Internationals: 10
50 wickets in a season: 7
1st-Class 50s: 1
1st-Class 5 w. in innings: 36
1st-Class 10 w. in match: 7
1st-Class catches: 40
One-Day 5 w. in innings: 2
Place in batting averages: 300th av. 3.20 (1998 271st av. 10.36)
Place in bowling averages: 82nd av. 28.76 (1998 107th av. 33.27)
Strike rate: 48.51 (career 50.92)
Parents: Albert and Brendalee (deceased)
Wife and date of marriage: Jennifer, October 1989
Children: Erica Cian, 11 June 1991; Natile Jade, 25 June 1993
Education: St Elizabeth Technical High School; Richmond College;
Derby College of Higher Education
Qualifications: College certificates, O-levels, coaching certificate
Overseas tours: England to West Indies 1989-90, to Australia 1990-91, to India and
Sri Lanka 1992-93, to West Indies 1993-94, to Australia 1994-95, to South Africa
1995-96; England A to Bermuda and West Indies 1991-92
Overseas teams played for: Ellerslie, Auckland 1985-87
Cricketers particularly admired: Michael Holding, Richard Hadlee, Malcolm
Marshall, Alan Warner, Viv Richards
Other sports followed: Football, boxing
Relaxations: Music and movies, eating
Extras: Played league cricket for Sheffield Works and Sheffield United. Became
eligible to play for England in 1987. Took 10 for 137 v West Indies in Port-of-Spain
Test, 1989-90. Took 9-57 v South Africa at The Oval in 1994; received the 'Century of
Bottles' Award for this best performance against the touring South Africans. Was one
of *Wisden's* Five Cricketers of the Year 1995. Struck down with chickenpox early in

the England tour to Australia 1994-95. Joined Northamptonshire for 1998. Awarded
Northants cap 1999
Best batting: 51 Derbyshire v Surrey, Derby 1989
Best bowling: 9-57 England v South Africa, The Oval 1994

1999 Season

	M	Inns	NO	Runs	HS	Avge	100s	50s	Ct	St	O	M	Runs	Wkts	Avge	Best	5wl	10wM
Test																		
All First	15	16	6	32	10 *	3.20	-	-	4	-	485.1	90	1726	60	28.76	6-39	3	-
1-day Int																		
NatWest	3	1	0	1	1	1.00	-	-	-	-	19	1	77	1	77.00	1-40	-	
B & H																		
1-day Lge	13	5	1	3	2	0.75	-	-	2	-	86	6	385	20	19.25	3-16	-	

Career Performances

	M	Inns	NO	Runs	HS	Avge	100s	50s	Ct	St	Balls	Runs	Wkts	Avge	Best	5wl	10wM
Test	40	58	19	236	29	6.05	-	-	7	-	8480	4748	128	37.09	9-57	5	2
All First	261	309	97	1670	51	7.87	-	1	40	-	45476	27304	893	30.57	9-57	36	7
1-day Int	10	5	2	9	4	3.00	-	-	1	-	526	404	16	25.25	3-40	-	
NatWest	25	12	1	31	10 *	2.81	-	-	1	-	1493	979	36	27.19	7-35	1	
B & H	36	20	6	104	16	7.42	-	-	4	-	2039	1469	54	27.20	5-27	1	
1-day Lge	78	30	11	137	42	7.21	-	-	9	-	3391	2853	107	26.66	4-21	-	

60. Which Kent and England batsman (and later, Test umpire) scored a 200
in each innings v Essex at Colchester in 1938?

MARSH, S. A.   Kent

Name: Steven Andrew Marsh
Role: Right-hand bat, wicket-keeper
Born: 27 January 1961, Westminster
Height: 5ft 11in **Weight:** 13st 7lbs
Nickname: Marshy
County debut: 1982
County cap: 1986
Benefit: 1995
1st-Class 50s: 55
1st-Class 100s: 9
1st-Class catches: 688
1st-Class stumpings: 61
Place in batting averages: 171st av. 23.30
(1998 137th av. 29.83)
Strike rate: (career 101.00)
Parents: Melvyn Graham and Valerie Ann
Wife and date of marriage:
Julie, 27 September 1986
Children: Hayley Ann, 15 May 1987; Christian James Robert, 20 November 1990
Family links with cricket: Father played local cricket for Lordswood. Father-in-law, Bob Wilson, played for Kent 1954-66
Education: Walderslade Secondary School for Boys; Mid-Kent College of Higher and Further Education
Qualifications: 6 O-levels, 2 A-levels, OND in Business Studies, 'Cycling proficiency'
Career outside cricket: Partner in Box Royale, a corporate hospitality company
Off-season: Working for Box Royale, 'and taking money off Steve Juster on the golf course!'
Overseas tours: Fred Rumsey XI to Barbados 1986-87
Overseas teams played for: Avendale CC, Cape Town 1985-86
Cricketers particularly admired: Robin Smith, Graham Cowdrey, Ian Botham, Colin Johns, Mark Bradley
Young players to look out for: Robert Key, Ben Phillips
Other sports followed: Golf, football (Chelsea FC)
Injuries: Out for one week with back spasm
Extras: Appointed Kent vice-captain in 1991. In the match v Middlesex at Lord's in 1991 he equalled the world record of eight catches in an innings and scored 108*. Took over as Kent captain during 1996 season after injury to Mark Benson and held post until end of 1998 season
Opinions on cricket: 'Much better now we have two divisions in both one- and four-day cricket.'
Best batting: 142 Kent v Sussex, Horsham 1997
Best bowling: 2-20 Kent v Warwickshire, Edgbaston 1990

	M	Inns	NO	Runs	HS	Avge	100s	50s	Ct	St	O	M	Runs	Wkts	Avge	Best	5wl	10wM
Test																		
All First	15	22	2	466	73 *	23.30	-	2	28	7								
1-day Int																		
NatWest	3	2	0	5	4	2.50	-	-	2	1	1	0	11	0	-		-	-
B & H																		
1-day Lge	14	11	3	119	21	14.87	-	-	14	1								

Career Performances

	M	Inns	NO	Runs	HS	Avge	100s	50s	Ct	St	Balls	Runs	Wkts	Avge	Best	5wl	10wM
Test																	
All First	291	429	69	10098	142	28.05	9	55	688	61	202	240	2	120.00	2-20	-	-
1-day Int																	
NatWest	26	18	3	214	55	14.26	-	1	35	5	9	14	1	14.00	1-3	-	
B & H	64	48	14	641	71	18.85	-	1	78	6							
1-day Lge	209	147	45	1939	59	19.00	-	4	197	23							

MARTIN, P. J.   Lancashire

Name: Peter James Martin
Role: Right-hand bat, right-arm
fast-medium bowler
Born: 15 November 1968, Accrington
Height: 6ft 5in **Weight:** 15st 4lbs
Nickname: Digger, Long John
County debut: 1989
County cap: 1994
Test debut: 1995
Tests: 8
One-Day Internationals: 20
50 wickets in a season: 2
1st-Class 50s: 5
1st-Class 100s: 1
1st-Class 5 w. in innings: 11
1st-Class 10 w. in match: 1
1st-Class catches: 38
One-Day 5 w. in innings: 5

Place in batting averages: 238th av. 15.71 (1998 240th av. 15.40)
Place in bowling averages: 21st av. 20.56 (1998 32nd av. 22.12)
Strike rate: 53.60 (career 62.29)

Parents: Keith and Catherine Lina
Marital status: Single
Education: Danum School, Doncaster
Qualifications: 6 O-levels, 2 A-levels
Overseas tours: England YC to Australia (Youth World Cup) 1987-88; 'and various other tours with English Schools and NAYC'; England to South Africa 1995-96, to India and Pakistan (World Cup) 1995-96, to Sharjah 1997-98 (Champions Trophy), to Bangladesh (Wills International Cup) 1998-99
Overseas teams played for: Southern Districts, Queensland 1988-89; South Launceston, Tasmania 1989-90; South Canberra, ACT 1990-92
Cricketers particularly admired: 'Too many to mention'
Other sports followed: Football (Manchester United), rugby league (St Helens), golf
Relaxations: Music, painting, golf, cooking, walking, rugby league
Extras: Plays district football and basketball for Doncaster. Played for England A v Sri Lankans 1991. Was originally selected for the England A tour to Pakistan in 1995-96, but was drafted on to the senior tour after the withdrawal of Richard Johnson
Opinions on cricket: 'Should only be six-hour days with 100 overs a day.'
Best batting: 133 Lancashire v Durham, Gateshead Fell 1992
Best bowling: 8-32 Lancashire v Middlesex, Uxbridge 1997

1999 Season

	M	Inns	NO	Runs	HS		Avge	100s	50s	Ct	St	O	M	Runs	Wkts	Avge	Best	5wI	10wM
Test																			
All First	14	19	5	220	30	*	15.71	-	-	2	-	446.4	134	1028	50	20.56	5-43	4	-
1-day Int																			
NatWest	3	2	2	32	31	*	-	-	-	-	-	27	4	126	2	63.00	1-29	-	
B & H	1	1	1	11	11	*	-	-	-	-	-	10	1	36	3	12.00	3-36	-	
1-day Lge	14	4	0	22	12		5.50	-	-	5	-	110.4	9	403	18	22.38	5-28	1	

Career Performances

	M	Inns	NO	Runs	HS		Avge	100s	50s	Ct	St	Balls	Runs	Wkts	Avge	Best	5wI	10wM
Test	8	13	0	115	29		8.84	-	-	6	-	1452	580	17	34.11	4-60	-	-
All First	162	188	48	2690	133		19.21	1	5	38	-	27347	12504	439	28.48	8-32	11	1
1-day Int	20	13	7	38	6		6.33	-	-	1	-	1048	806	27	29.85	4-44	-	
NatWest	22	8	6	76	31	*	38.00	-	-	1	-	1316	761	40	19.02	5-30	1	
B & H	26	9	7	43	11	*	21.50	-	-	8	-	1449	1022	36	28.38	3-31	-	
1-day Lge	109	32	17	177	35	*	11.80	-	-	22	-	4292	3078	140	21.98	5-21	4	

MARTIN-JENKINS, R. S. C. Sussex

Name: Robin Simon Christopher
Martin-Jenkins
Role: Right-hand bat, right-arm
medium-fast bowler
Born: 28 October 1975, Guildford
Height: 6ft 5in **Weight:** 14st
Nickname: Tucker
County debut: 1995
1st-Class 50s: 5
1st-Class 5 w. in innings: 1
1st-Class catches: 7
Place in batting averages: 213th av. 18.77
(1998 107th av. 29.41)
Place in bowling averages: 62nd av. 25.57
(1998 15th av. 19.86)
Strike rate: 52.90 (career 54.01)
Parents: Christopher and Judy
Marital status: Single
Family links with cricket: Father is *The Times* chief cricket correspondent and *TMS* commentator. Brother captains the Radley Rangers
Education: Cranleigh Prep School, Surrey; Radley College, Oxon; Durham University
Qualifications: 10 GCSEs, 3 A-levels, 1 AS-level, Grade 3 bassoon, BA (Hons) Social Sciences
Career outside cricket: Coach
Off-season: Rehabilitation after knee surgery
Overseas tours: Radley College to Barbados 1992; Sussex U19 to Sri Lanka 1995; Durham University to Vienna 1995; MCC to Kenya 1998-99
Overseas teams played for: Lima CC, Peru 1994
Cricketers particularly admired: Angus Fraser, Robin Smith
Young players to look out for: Jon Bond, Nick Hoyle
Other sports played: Hockey, fives
Other sports followed: Tennis, skiing, football (Liverpool FC)
Injuries: Out for five weeks with a broken finger
Relaxations: Food, drink, television
Extras: European Player of the Year, Vienna 1995. Played for ESCA from U15 to U19. *Daily Telegraph* Bowling Award 1994. Best Performance Award for Sussex 1998
Opinions on cricket: 'I thought Notts bowled a bit full, but we batted well nonetheless.'
Best batting: 78 Sussex v Glamorgan, Hove 1998
Best bowling: 7-54 Sussex v Glamorgan, Hove 1998

1999 Season

	M	Inns	NO	Runs	HS	Avge	100s	50s	Ct	St	O	M	Runs	Wkts	Avge	Best	5wI	10wM
Test																		
All First	14	24	2	413	70	18.77	-	2	2	-	370.2	99	1074	42	25.57	4-50	-	-
1-day Int																		
NatWest	1	0	0	0	0	-	-	-	-	-	10	2	24	2	12.00	2-24	-	
B & H	1	1	0	13	13	13.00	-	-	-	-	10	2	24	0	-	-	-	-
1-day Lge	12	4	0	35	26	8.75	-	-	5	-	95	16	297	10	29.70	3-27	-	

Career Performances

	M	Inns	NO	Runs	HS	Avge	100s	50s	Ct	St	Balls	Runs	Wkts	Avge	Best	5wI	10wM
Test																	
All First	29	46	5	913	78	22.26	-	5	7	-	3781	1864	70	26.62	7-54	1	-
1-day Int																	
NatWest	1	0	0	0	0	-	-	-	-	-	60	24	2	12.00	2-24	-	
B & H	12	10	0	102	39	10.20	-	-	-	-	609	499	17	29.35	4-57	-	
1-day Lge	33	21	1	207	44	10.35	-	-	8	-	1332	894	23	38.86	3-27	-	

MASCARENHAS, A. D.   Hampshire

Name: Adrian Dimitri Mascarenhas
Role: Right-hand bat, right-arm medium bowler
Born: 30 October 1977, Chiswick, London
Height: 6ft 2in **Weight:** 11st 7lbs
Nickname: Dimmie, Genii, Gibson
County debut: 1996
County cap: 1998
1st-Class 50s: 8
1st-Class 5 w. in innings: 2
1st-Class catches: 15
Place in batting averages: 142nd av. 25.83 (1998 118th av. 28.04)
Place in bowling averages: 144th av. 51.05 (1998 108th av. 33.33)
Strike rate: 108.70 (career 68.23)
Parents: Malik and Pauline
Marital status: Single
Family links with cricket: Uncle played in Sri Lanka and brothers both play for Melville CC in Perth, WA
Education: Our Lady's Primary, Melbourne; Trinity College, Perth

Overseas teams played for: Melville CC, Perth 1991-97
Cricketers particularly admired: Viv Richards, Malcolm Marshall, the Waugh twins
Young players to look out for: Ben Hollioake
Other sports followed: Aussie Rules (Collingwood)
Relaxations: Aussie Rules, tennis, golf, 'occasional scenario'
Extras: Played for Western Australia at U17 and U19 level as captain. Man of the Match award (3-28 and 73) in NatWest semi-final v Lancashire 1998
Opinions on cricket: 'Great game'
Best batting: 89 Hampshire v Nottinghamshire, Portsmouth 1998
Best bowling: 6-88 Hampshire v Glamorgan, Southampton 1996

1999 Season

	M	Inns	NO	Runs	HS	Avge	100s	50s	Ct	St	O	M	Runs	Wkts	Avge	Best	5wI	10wM
Test																		
All First	14	20	2	465	62	25.83	-	2	4	-	308	98	868	17	51.05	2-2	-	-
1-day Int																		
NatWest	2	2	0	25	25	12.50	-	-	1	-	19	3	84	4	21.00	3-51	-	
B & H	1	1	0	9	9	9.00	-	-	-	-	8	0	25	0	-		-	-
1-day Lge	15	13	1	285	79	23.75	-	3	5	-	99.4	7	446	17	26.23	3-23	-	

Career Performances

	M	Inns	NO	Runs	HS	Avge	100s	50s	Ct	St	Balls	Runs	Wkts	Avge	Best	5wI	10wM
Test																	
All First	39	55	5	1184	89	23.68	-	8	15	-	4845	2582	71	36.36	6-88	2	-
1-day Int																	
NatWest	6	6	2	170	73	42.50	-	1	2	-	258	170	8	21.25	3-28	-	
B & H	8	8	1	169	53	24.14	-	2	-	-	288	214	4	53.50	4-28	-	
1-day Lge	38	33	4	588	79	20.27	-	5	13	-	1109	920	36	25.55	3-9	-	

61. Who scored 322 in 133 scoring strokes off 258 deliveries for Somerset v Warwickshire at Taunton in 1985?

MASON, T. J.

Essex

Name: Timothy James Mason
Role: Right-hand middle order bat, off-spin bowler
Born: 12 April 1975, Leicester
Height: 5ft 9in **Weight:** 10st 8lbs
Nickname: Biffa, Perry, Stone
County debut: 1994 (Leicestershire)
1st-Class catches: 4
Strike rate: 78.00 (career 104.40)
Parents: Phillip John and Anthea Jane
Marital status: Single
Family links with cricket: Father plays club cricket and is manager of Leicestershire Schools U11
Education: Brookvale High School, Leicester; Denstone College
Qualifications: 9 GCSEs, 3 A-levels
Off-season: Coaching, training and practising
Overseas tours: Denstone College to South Africa 1993; England U19 to Sri Lanka 1993-94; Westgold CC to Northern Transvaal 1996; Leicestershire to Sri Lanka 1999
Overseas teams played for: Eastern Freestate, South Africa 1994-95; Westgold CC, Western Transvaal 1995-97
Cricketers particularly admired: Allan Lamb, Malcolm Marshall, Jon Dakin, Darren 'Roasting' Maddy
Young players to look out for: Ashley Wright, Tom Kemp, Pete Handford, Duncan Naylor
Other sports followed: Rugby union (Leicester Tigers), football (Leicester City)
Relaxations: 'Going out with girlfriend Nicole and friends; listening to most types of music; watching virtually all sports'
Extras: Captained Leicestershire Schools at all age levels. 1992 *Daily Telegraph* U19 Midlands Bowler of the Year; 1993 *Daily Telegraph* U19 National Bowler of the Year; 1993 Gray-Nicolls Outstanding Schoolboy Player of the Year. Dislocated shoulder prevented him from going on England U18 tour to South Africa 1992-93. Played in the winning Bain Hogg team in 1996. Left Leicestershire at end of 1999 season and has joined Essex for 2000
Opinions on cricket: 'Two divisions will be good for the game to make us collectively stronger and harder players. More entertainment at grounds would appeal to younger audiences and therefore get a buzz back into the game.'
Best batting: 36 Leicestershire v Worcestershire, Worcester 1999
Best bowling: 3-32 Leicestershire v Worcestershire, Worcester 1999

1999 Season

	M	Inns	NO	Runs	HS	Avge	100s	50s	Ct	St	O	M	Runs	Wkts	Avge	Best	5wI	10wM
Test																		
All First	2	4	1	79	36	26.33	-	-	-	-	91	28	182	7	26.00	3-32	-	-
1-day Int																		
NatWest																		
B & H																		
1-day Lge	10	6	2	30	21 *	7.50	-	-	1	-	51	0	265	6	44.16	2-37	-	

Career Performances

	M	Inns	NO	Runs	HS	Avge	100s	50s	Ct	St	Balls	Runs	Wkts	Avge	Best	5wI	10wM
Test																	
All First	7	6	1	86	36	17.20	-	-	4	-	1044	444	10	44.40	3-32	-	-
1-day Int																	
NatWest	5	3	0	71	36	23.66	-	-	3	-	288	164	3	54.66	3-29	-	
B & H	8	4	2	61	30	30.50	-	-	2	-	378	271	10	27.10	3-41	-	
1-day Lge	41	26	10	137	21 *	8.56	-	-	7	-	1235	1101	27	40.77	4-12	-	

MASTERS, D. D.   Kent

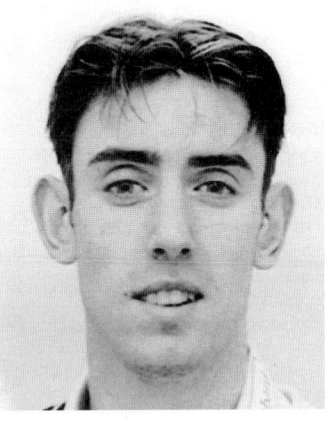

Name: David Daniel Masters
Role: Right-hand bat, right-arm
medium-fast bowler
Born: 22 April 1978, Chatham
Height: 6ft 3ins **Weight:** 12st 9lbs
Nickname: Hod, Hodlit
County debut: No first-team appearance
Parents: Kevin and Tracey
Marital status: Single
Family links with cricket:
Father played for Kent and Surrey
Education: Luton Junior School; Fort Luton
High School; Mid-Kent College
Qualifications: 8 GCSEs, GNVQ in Leisure
and Tourism, qualified football coach,
bricklayer and plasterer
Career outside cricket: Builder
Cricketers particularly admired: 'My
father', Ian Botham
Young players to look out for: 'My brother Daniel Masters', Buster Gibbons,
Peter Stock

Other sports played: Football ('Tonbridge Angels in semi-pro'), 'and all other sports'
Other sports followed: Football (Manchester United)
Relaxations: Playing football, 'going out with my mates'
Opinions on cricket: 'Great game. Can only get better.'

MAUNDERS, J. K.   Middlesex

Name: John Kenneth Maunders
Role: Left-hand bat, part-time wicket-keeper
Born: 4 April 1981, Ashford, Middlesex
Height: 5ft 10in **Weight:** 11st 7lbs
Nickname: Chop
County debut: 1999
1st-Class catches: 1
Parents: Kenny and Lynn
Marital status: Single
Family links with cricket: 'Grandad and two uncles play club cricket'
Education: Ashford Park Primary School; Ashford High School; Spelthorne College of Further Education
Qualifications: 10 GCSEs, Duke of Edinburgh Awards (Bronze and Silver)
Career outside cricket: Student
Off-season: England U19 tour to Sri Lanka for Youth World Cup

Overseas tours: England U19 to New Zealand 1998-99, to Malaysia and (Youth World Cup) Sri Lanka 1999-2000
Cricketers particularly admired: Justin Langer, Angus Fraser
Young players to look out for: Mark Wallace, Ian Bell
Other sports played: Hockey
Other sports followed: Football (Liverpool)
Relaxations: Socialising with friends, playing sports, listening to music, sleeping
Extras: Awarded junior county cap at the age of 12. Seaxe Player of Year. Represented England U17 and U19
Opinions on cricket: 'Tea should be extended so that players have more time to recoup and get ready for the last session's play.'
Best batting: 9 Middlesex v Cambridge University, Fenner's 1999

1999 Season

	M	Inns	NO	Runs	HS	Avge	100s	50s	Ct	St	O	M	Runs	Wkts	Avge	Best	5wI	10wM
Test																		
All First	1	2	0	13	9	6.50	-	-	1	-								
1-day Int																		
NatWest																		
B & H																		
1-day Lge																		

Career Performances

	M	Inns	NO	Runs	HS	Avge	100s	50s	Ct	St	Balls	Runs	Wkts	Avge	Best	5wI	10wM
Test																	
All First	1	2	0	13	9	6.50	-	-	1	-							
1-day Int																	
NatWest																	
B & H																	
1-day Lge																	

MAY, M. R. Derbyshire

Name: Michael Robert May
Role: Right-hand bat, off-spin bowler
Born: 22 July 1971, Chesterfield, Derbyshire
Height: 5ft 9in **Weight:** 14st 3lbs
Nickname: Maggie, Boonie, Maggo, Mazzey
County debut: 1996
1st-Class 50s: 5
1st-Class 100s: 3
1st-Class catches: 7
Place in batting averages: (1998 194th av. 19.70)
Parents: Michael and Christine
Wife and date of marriage:
Sasha, 14 January 1996
Children: Benjamin Michael, 6 May 1998
Family links with cricket: Brother Paul has played 2nd XI cricket for Derbyshire
Education: Duckmanton Primary School; The Bolsover School; North East Derbyshire College
Qualifications: 4 O-levels, City and Guilds in Recreation and Leisure, NCA cricket coach

Overseas teams played for: Marist, New Zealand 1987-88; Johannesburg Municipals 1991-93; Sandringham CC, Melbourne 1994-96; St Kilda CC, Australia 1996-97; Donvale, Australia 1997-99
Cricketers particularly admired: Steve Waugh, Ian Botham
Young players to look out for: Kevin Dean, Ben Spendlove
Other sports played: Football, tennis, golf
Other sports followed: Football (Chesterfield), Australian Rules (Essendon), rugby league (Melbourne Storm)
Relaxations: 'Spending time with my family. Listening to music and reading'
Extras: Played only in World Cup warm-up match 1999. Released by Derbyshire at end of 1999 season
Opinions on cricket: 'Should be more coaching provided for the younger age groups in schools (create more interest).'
Best batting: 116 Derbyshire v Glamorgan, Chesterfield 1997

1999 Season (did not make any first-class or one-day competition appearances)

Career Performances

	M	Inns	NO	Runs	HS	Avge	100s	50s	Ct	St	Balls	Runs	Wkts	Avge	Best	5wI	10wM
Test																	
All First	25	45	4	1221	116	29.78	3	5	7	-	61	120	0	-	-	-	-
1-day Int																	
NatWest	1	1	0	5	5	5.00	-	-	-	-							
B & H																	
1-day Lge																	

MAYNARD, M. P.   Glamorgan

Name: Matthew Peter Maynard
Role: Right-hand bat, right-arm medium bowler, occasional wicket-keeper, county captain
Born: 21 March 1966, Oldham, Lancashire
Height: 5ft 11in **Weight:** 13st
Nickname: Ollie
County debut: 1985
County cap: 1987
Benefit: 1996
Test debut: 1988
Tests: 4
One-Day Internationals: 10
1000 runs in a season: 10
1st-Class 50s: 109

1st-Class 100s: 42
1st-Class 200s: 3
1st-Class catches: 309
1st-Class stumpings: 5
One-Day 100s: 10
Place in batting averages: 35th av. 40.29
(1998 111th av. 28.74)
Strike rate: (career 168.66)
Parents: Ken (deceased) and Pat
Wife and date of marriage: Susan,
27 September 1986
Children: Tom, 25 March 1989;
Ceri Lloyd, 5 August 1993
Family links with cricket: Father played for
many years for Duckinfield. Brother Charles
plays for St Fagans. Son Tom plays for
Cardiff County and the Vale U11 and Wales
U12
Education: Ysgol David Hughes, Menai Bridge, Anglesey
Qualifications: Cricket coach
Career outside cricket: 'Ice cream taster'
Off-season: Working for Sporting Ideas on the Rugby World Cup
Overseas tours: North Wales XI to Barbados 1982; Glamorgan to Barbados 1982, to
South Africa 1993; unofficial England XI to South Africa 1989-90; HKCC (Australia)
to Bangkok and Hong Kong 1990; England VI to Hong Kong Sixes 1992 and 1994;
England to West Indies 1993-94
Overseas teams played for: St Joseph's, Whakatane, New Zealand 1986-88; Gosnells,
Perth, Western Australia 1988-89; Papakura and Northern Districts, New Zealand
1990-92; Morrinsville College and Northern Districts 1991-92; Otago, New Zealand
1996-97
Cricketers particularly admired: Ian Botham, Viv Richards, David Gower
Young players to look out for: Tom Maynard
Other sports played: Golf
Other sports followed: Football (Manchester City), golf and squash
Injuries: Out for seven weeks with fracture/dislocation of right little finger
Relaxations: 'Spending time with my wife and family and relaxing'
Extras: Scored century on first-class debut v Yorkshire at Swansea in 1985, becoming
the youngest centurion for Glamorgan, and scored 1000 runs in first full season. In
1987 set record for fastest 50 for Glamorgan (14 mins) v Yorkshire and became
youngest player to be awarded Glamorgan cap. Voted Young Cricketer of the Year
1988 by the Cricket Writers' Club. Banned from Test cricket for five years for joining
1989-90 tour of South Africa; ban remitted 1992. Scored 987 runs in July 1991,
including a century in each innings v Gloucestershire at Cheltenham. Captained
Glamorgan for most of 1992 in Alan Butcher's absence. Second child was born on the
morning of the fifth Test against Australia at Edgbaston 1993 – he had a daughter and

a duck on the same day. Voted Wombwell Cricket Lovers' Society captain of the year for 1997. He captained an England XI in the Cricket Max tournament in New Zealand in 1997-98. Has been Glamorgan's captain since the 1996 season. Was one of *Wisden*'s Five Cricketers of the Year 1998. Appointed honorary fellow of University of Wales, Bangor. Set new Glamorgan one-day record stand for third wicket (204) with Jacques Kallis in National League match v Surrey at Pontypridd 1999. Passed 20,000 first-class runs during his 186 in Glamorgan's first innings v Yorkshire at Headingley 1999
Opinions on cricket: 'Bad wickets will produce bad techniques.'
Best batting: 243 Glamorgan v Hampshire, Southampton 1991
Best bowling: 3-21 Glamorgan v Oxford University, The Parks 1987

1999 Season

	M	Inns	NO	Runs	HS	Avge	100s	50s	Ct	St	O	M	Runs	Wkts	Avge	Best	5wl	10wM
Test																		
All First	13	18	1	685	186	40.29	2	2	9	-	2	2	0	0	-	-	-	-
1-day Int																		
NatWest	3	3	0	51	39	17.00	-	-	3	-								
B & H																		
1-day Lge	11	11	1	346	79	34.60	-	3	4	1	3	0	13	1	13.00	1-13	-	

Career Performances

	M	Inns	NO	Runs	HS	Avge	100s	50s	Ct	St	Balls	Runs	Wkts	Avge	Best	5wl	10wM
Test	4	8	0	87	35	10.87	-	-	3	-							
All First	322	527	55	20181	243	42.75	45	109	309	5	1012	829	6	138.16	3-21	-	-
1-day Int	10	10	1	153	41	17.00	-	-	2	-							
NatWest	39	38	3	1523	151 *	43.51	2	12	18	-	18	8	0	-	-	-	
B & H	48	48	6	1802	151 *	42.90	4	9	17	-	30	38	0	-	-	-	
1-day Lge	197	189	14	5440	132	31.08	4	35	78	1	64	64	1	64.00	1-13	-	

McCAGUE, M. J.   Kent

Name: Martin John McCague
Role: Right-hand bat, right-arm fast bowler
Born: 24 May 1969, Larne, Northern Ireland
Height: 6ft 5in **Weight:** 17st
Nickname: Macca, Pigsy
County debut: 1991
County cap: 1992
Test debut: 1993
Tests: 3
50 wickets in a season: 4

1st-Class 50s: 5
1st-Class 5 w. in innings: 24
1st-Class 10 w. in match: 2
1st-Class catches: 73
One-Day 5 w. in innings: 3
Place in batting averages: 155th av. 24.72
(1998 182nd av. 20.75)
Place in bowling averages: 121st av. 35.90
(1998 70th av. 28.07)
Strike rate: 67.14 (career 49.96)
Parents: Mal and Mary
Wife and date of marriage: Leigh-Anne,
8 February 1997
Children: Monte Frederick, 15 September
1998
Education: Hedland Senior High School
Qualifications: Electrician
Overseas tours: England A to South Africa

1993-94; England to Australia 1994-95; Kent Cricket Board XI to West Indies 1998-99
Overseas teams played for: Western Australia 1990-91
Cricketers particularly admired: Paul Strang, Courtney Walsh
Young players to look out for: Paul Franks, Steve Harmison, James Hockley
Other sports followed: Football (Crystal Palace FC), golf and snooker
Relaxations: Playing golf
Extras: Kent Player of the Year in 1996
Best batting: 63* Kent v Surrey, The Oval 1996
Best bowling: 9-86 Kent v Derbyshire, Derby 1994

1999 Season

	M	Inns	NO	Runs	HS	Avge	100s	50s	Ct	St	O	M	Runs	Wkts	Avge	Best	5wI	10wM
Test																		
All First	10	13	2	272	53	24.72	-	1	7	-	235	44	754	21	35.90	4-36	-	-
1-day Int																		
NatWest	2	1	1	7	7*	-	-	-	1	-	16	1	82	0	-		-	-
B & H																		
1-day Lge	7	5	1	21	7	5.25	-	-	1	-	46	2	224	7	32.00	3-29	-	

Career Performances

	M	Inns	NO	Runs	HS	Avge	100s	50s	Ct	St	Balls	Runs	Wkts	Avge	Best	5wl	10wM
Test	3	5	0	21	11	4.20	-	-	1	-	593	390	6	65.00	4-121	-	-
All First	126	174	45	2129	63 *	16.50	-	5	73	-	21984	11881	440	27.00	9-86	24	2
1-day Int																	
NatWest	16	12	7	126	31 *	25.20	-	-	4	-	882	592	22	26.90	5-26	1	
B & H	30	19	8	169	30	15.36	-	-	7	-	1532	1186	39	30.41	5-43	1	
1-day Lge	95	51	15	307	22 *	8.52	-	-	16	-	3595	3125	123	25.40	5-40	1	

McGARRY, A. C. Essex

Name: Andrew Charles McGarry
Role: Right-hand lower order bat,
right-arm fast bowler
Born: 8 November 1981, Basildon, Essex
Height: 6ft 6in **Weight:** 12st 7lbs
Nickname: Lurch
County debut: 1999
Strike rate: 60.00 (career 60.00)
Parents: George (deceased) and Christine
Marital status: Single
Family links with cricket: Father played,
and eldest brother plays recreational cricket
Education: Widford Lodge Preparatory
School, Chelmsford; King Edward VI GS,
Chelmsford; South-East Essex College,
Southend-on-Sea
Qualifications: 9 GCSEs, Level 1 and 2 ECB
coaching awards
Career outside cricket: Student (studying BTEC National Diploma in Sports Science)
Cricketers particularly admired: Ian Botham, Allan Donald
Young players to look out for: Ian Bell
Other sports played: Basketball, volleyball, football
Other sports followed: Football (Aston Villa)
Relaxations: Listening to music, reading
Extras: First Brian Johnston Scholarship winner 1996
Opinions on cricket: 'I haven't played enough to form any opinions.'
Best bowling: 2-72 Essex v Sri Lanka A, Chelmsford 1999

1999 Season

	M	Inns	NO	Runs	HS	Avge	100s	50s	Ct	St	O	M	Runs	Wkts	Avge	Best	5wI	10wM
Test																		
All First	1	1	1	0	0*	-	-	-	-	-	40	5	149	4	37.25	2-72	-	-
1-day Int																		
NatWest																		
B & H																		
1-day Lge																		

Career Performances

	M	Inns	NO	Runs	HS	Avge	100s	50s	Ct	St	Balls	Runs	Wkts	Avge	Best	5wI	10wM
Test																	
All First	1	1	1	0	0*	-	-	-	-	-	240	149	4	37.25	2-72	-	-
1-day Int																	
NatWest																	
B & H																	
1-day Lge																	

McGRATH, A. *Yorkshire*

Name: Anthony McGrath
Role: Right-hand bat, right-arm medium bowler
Born: 6 October 1975, Bradford
Height: 6ft 1in **Weight:** 14st
Nickname: Gripper, Mags
County debut: 1995
County cap: 1999
1st-Class 50s: 18
1st-Class 100s: 6
1st-Class catches: 49
One-Day 100s: 1
Place in batting averages: 107th av. 29.67 (1998 146th av. 24.48)
Strike rate: 57.33 (career 69.35)
Parents: Terry and Kathleen
Marital status: Single
Family links with cricket: Brother Dermot

plays in the Bradford League. 'Sisters Anne and Catherine could have played for England Ladies. Nephews Aidan, Thomas and Niall are future stars'
Education: St Winefrides; St Blaize; Yorkshire Martyrs Collegiate School

Qualifications: 9 GCSEs, BTEC National Diploma in Leisure Studies, senior coaching award
Overseas tours: England U19 to West Indies 1994-95; England A to Pakistan 1995-96, to Australia 1996-97; MCC to Bangladesh 1999-2000
Overseas teams played for: Deep Dene, Melbourne 1998-99
Cricketers particularly admired: Darren Lehmann, Nasser Hussain, Ronnie Irani, Robin Smith
Young players to look out for: Matthew Wood, Ian Fisher, Alex Morris
Other sports played: Football (Green Man FC)
Other sports followed: Football (Manchester United)
Relaxations: Watching football. Music. Socialising with friends
Extras: Captained Yorkshire Schools U13, U14, U15 and U16; captained English Schools U17. Bradford League Young Cricketer of the Year 1992 and 1993. Played for England U17, and for England U19 in home series against India 1994. Appeared as 12th man for England in the first Test against West Indies at Headingley in 1995. Scored his maiden first-class century on the England A tour to Pakistan. Awarded Yorkshire cap 1999
Best batting: 142* Yorkshire v Middlesex, Headingley 1999
Best bowling: 3-18 Yorkshire v Surrey, The Oval 1999

1999 Season

	M	Inns	NO	Runs	HS	Avge	100s	50s	Ct	St	O	M	Runs	Wkts	Avge	Best	5wI	10wM
Test																		
All First	16	30	2	831	142 *	29.67	1	6	15	-	86	26	204	9	22.66	3-18	-	-
1-day Int																		
NatWest	4	4	0	216	84	54.00	-	3	1	-	3	0	14	0	-		-	-
B & H	3	2	0	29	20	14.50	-	-	1	-								
1-day Lge	15	14	2	450	75	37.50	-	3	5	-	27	3	105	3	35.00	1-16	-	

Career Performances

	M	Inns	NO	Runs	HS	Avge	100s	50s	Ct	St	Balls	Runs	Wkts	Avge	Best	5wI	10wM
Test																	
All First	82	142	9	3879	142 *	29.16	6	18	49	-	971	492	14	35.14	3-18	-	-
1-day Int																	
NatWest	13	12	1	356	84	32.36	-	3	5	-	18	14	0	-		-	-
B & H	22	20	1	511	109 *	26.89	1	1	8	-	12	10	2	5.00	2-10	-	
1-day Lge	60	54	9	1340	75	29.77	-	10	16	-	270	187	7	26.71	2-20	-	

McGRATH, G. D.   Worcestershire

Name: Glenn Donald McGrath
Role: Right-hand bat, right-arm fast bowler
Born: 9 February 1970, Dubbo,
New South Wales
Height: 6ft 6in **Weight:** 14st
Nickname: Pigeon
County debut: No first-team appearance
Test debut: 1993-94
Tests: 49
One-Day Internationals: 96
1st-Class 5 w. in innings: 20
1st-Class 10 w. in match: 2
1st-Class catches: 20
One-Day 5 w. in innings: 3
Strike rate: (career 52.81)
Parents: Kevin and Bev
Wife and date of marriage:
Jane, 17 July 1999
Children: James, 20 January 2000
Education: Narromine High School
Off-season: Playing cricket in Australia
Overseas tours: Australia to South Africa 1993-94, to Pakistan 1994-95, to West
Indies 1994-95, to India 1995-96, to India, Pakistan and Sri Lanka (World Cup) 1995-
96, to South Africa 1996-97, to England 1997, to Pakistan 1998-99, to West Indies
1998-99, to UK, Ireland and Holland (World Cup) 1999, to Sri Lanka and Zimbabwe
1999-2000
Overseas teams played for: New South Wales 1992-93 –
Cricketers particularly admired: Dennis Lillee, Rod Marsh
Young players to look out for: Don Nash
Other sports played: Golf
Other sports followed: Rugby league (Cronulla Sharks)
Relaxations: 'Going to my property in outback NSW'
Extras: One of *Wisden*'s Five Cricketers of the Year 1998. Became the tenth
Australian to take 200 Test wickets when he dismissed Alec Stewart in England's first
innings in the fifth Test at Sydney, January 1999. Broke John Snow's and Bruce
Taylor's record of 27 wickets by a visiting bowler in a Caribbean Test series, taking
30 wickets in Australia's 1998-99 tour. Played in Australia's 1999 World Cup winning
side. Has joined Worcestershire as overseas player for 2000
Opinions on cricket: 'As the game is becoming more and more professional, to
succeed you need to be as dedicated to fitness and developing a positive attitude as you
are to the skills of the game.'

Best batting: 39 Australia v West Indies, Port of Spain 1998-99
Best bowling: 8-38 Australia v England, Lord's 1997
Stop press: His dismissal of Ijaz Ahmed in the second Test v Pakistan at Hobart, November 1999, put him above Richie Benaud in the list of Australian Test wicket-takers with 249. Was leading Test wicket-taker of 1999 with 67 (av. 21.27). Selected for Australia's tour of New Zealand 1999-2000

1999 Season

	M	Inns	NO	Runs	HS	Avge	100s	50s	Ct	St	O	M	Runs	Wkts	Avge	Best	5wl	10wM
Test																		
All First																		
1-day Int	10	2	1	0	0*	0.00	-	-	-	-	95.4	9	367	18	20.38	5-14	1
NatWest																		
B & H																		
1-day Lge																		

Career Performances

	M	Inns	NO	Runs	HS	Avge	100s	50s	Ct	St	Balls	Runs	Wkts	Avge	Best	5wl	10wM
Test	49	62	20	246	39	5.85	-	-	13	-	11952	5244	232	22.60	8-38	15	1
All First	84	89	31	328	39	5.65	-	-	20	-	19010	8283	360	23.00	8-38	20	2
1-day Int	96	29	16	49	10	3.76	-	-	11	-	5187	3452	140	24.65	5-14	3	
NatWest																	
B & H																	
1-day Lge																	

McKEOWN, P. C.   Lancashire

Name: Patrick Christopher McKeown
Role: Right-hand bat
Born: 1 June 1976, Liverpool
Height: 6ft 3in **Weight:** 13st
Nickname: Paddy
County debut: 1996
1st-Class 50s: 3
1st-Class catches: 13
Place in batting averages: 100th av. 30.85 (1998 128th av. 26.57)
Parents: Paddy and Cathy
Marital status: Single
Education: St Mary's College, Crosby; Rossall School (Blackpool)
Qualifications: 7 GCSEs, 3 A-levels
Overseas tours: Rossall School to Australia 1994-95

Overseas teams played for: Subiaco-Floriat, Perth, Australia 1995-96
Cricketers particularly admired: Graeme Hick and Neil Fairbrother
Other sports followed: Football (Liverpool)
Relaxations: 'Playing most sports, especially football and rugby. I enjoy spending time on the golf course'
Extras: Represented England Schools U19, and U18 versus India. Played for Development of Excellence U19, National Cricket Association U19, Headmasters' Conference U19. Awarded 2nd XI cap in 1996. Scored 307 in less than a day for Lancashire 2nd XI v Gloucestershire 2nd XI at Bristol in 1998, setting a record for the highest individual score made for Lancashire 2nd XI
Best batting: 75 Lancashire v Cambridge University, Fenner's 1999

1999 Season

	M	Inns	NO	Runs	HS	Avge	100s	50s	Ct	St	O	M	Runs	Wkts	Avge	Best	5wl	10wM
Test																		
All First	5	8	1	216	75	30.85	-	2	4	-								
1-day Int																		
NatWest																		
B & H																		
1-day Lge	3	3	0	64	48	21.33	-	-	-	-								

Career Performances

	M	Inns	NO	Runs	HS	Avge	100s	50s	Ct	St	Balls	Runs	Wkts	Avge	Best	5wl	10wM
Test																	
All First	16	23	1	610	75	27.72	-	3	13	-							
1-day Int																	
NatWest	1	1	0	42	42	42.00	-	-	-	-	60	51	0	-	-	-	
B & H	1	1	0	10	10	10.00	-	-	-	-							
1-day Lge	17	17	0	263	69	15.47	-	1	5	-							

McLEAN, N. A. M.　　　　　　　　　Hampshire

Name: Nixon Alexei McNamara McLean
Role: Left-hand bat, right-arm fast bowler
Born: 28 July 1973, Stubbs, St Vincent
Height: 6ft 5in
Nickname: Nicko
County debut: 1998
County cap: 1998
Test debut: 1997-98
Tests: 8
One-Day Internationals: 16
50 wickets in a season: 1
1st-Class 50s: 2
1st-Class 5 w. in innings: 5
1st-Class catches: 19
Place in batting averages: 260th av. 12.87
(1998 247th av. 14.40)
Place in bowling averages: 106th av. 32.36
(1998 49th av. 25.40)

Strike rate: 61.43 (career 55.10)
Marital status: Single
Overseas tours: West Indies to Australia 1996-97, to Bangladesh 1998-99,
to South Africa 1998-99, to Singapore (Coca-Cola Challenge) 1999, to Bangladesh
(one-day series) 1999
Extras: Released by Hampshire at end of 1999 season
Best batting: 70 Hampshire v Surrey, Guildford 1999
Best bowling: 7-28 West Indies v Free State, Bloemfontein 1998-99

1999 Season

	M	Inns	NO	Runs	HS	Avge	100s	50s	Ct	St	O	M	Runs	Wkts	Avge	Best	5wI	10wM
Test																		
All First	14	19	3	206	70	12.87	-	1	6	-	471	105	1489	46	32.36	4-63	-	-
1-day Int																		
NatWest	2	2	1	23	20 *	23.00	-	-	-	-	15.3	2	36	3	12.00	3-27	-	
B & H	1	1	0	4	4	4.00	-	-	-	-	7.4	2	32	1	32.00	1-32	-	
1-day Lge	14	12	2	145	32	14.50	-	-	2	-	101	8	500	18	27.77	3-27	-	

Career Performances

	M	Inns	NO	Runs	HS	Avge	100s	50s	Ct	St	Balls	Runs	Wkts	Avge	Best	5wI	10wM
Test	8	12	1	187	39	17.00	-	-	3	-	1244	660	17	38.82	3-53	-	-
All First	66	101	17	1402	70	16.69	-	2	19	-	11242	5982	204	29.32	7-28	5	-
1-day Int	16	11	0	69	23	6.27	-	-	4	-	707	590	16	36.87	3-41	-	
NatWest	6	6	3	112	36	37.33	-	-	-	-	307	177	9	19.66	3-27	-	
B & H	5	4	1	35	28 *	11.66	-	-	2	-	271	230	2	115.00	1-32	-	
1-day Lge	31	24	3	280	32	13.33	-	-	3	-	1242	1016	40	25.40	3-27	-	

MIDDLEBROOK, J. D. — Yorkshire

Name: James Daniel Middlebrook
Role: Right-hand bat, off-spin bowler
Born: 13 May 1977, Leeds
Height: 6ft 1in **Weight:** 13st
Nickname: Midi, Midders, Midhouse
County debut: 1998
1st-Class catches: 7
Place in batting averages: (1998 251st av. 13.90)
Place in bowling averages: (1998 99th av. 32.46)
Strike rate: (career 75.76)
Parents: Ralph and Mavis
Marital status: Single
Family links with cricket: 'Dad is a senior staff coach/Cricket Development Officer for Leeds and Manager, Yorkshire Cricket School'
Education: Greenside, Pudsey ('same class as Paul Hutchison'); Crawshaw, Pudsey
Qualifications: NVQ Level 2 in Sport and Recreation, ECB senior coach
Off-season: 'Staying at home, going to the gym, and a little bit of work'
Overseas tours: Yorkshire CCC to Guernsey
Overseas teams played for: Stokes Valley CC, New Zealand; Gold Coast Dolphins, Brisbane; Surfers Paradise CC, Brisbane
Cricketers particularly admired: John Emburey, Ian Botham
Young players to look out for: Matthew Wood, Matthew Hoggard, 'Me!'
Other sports played: Golf, tennis, squash, badminton
Other sports followed: Football (Leeds United), athletics
Injuries: Out for three to four weeks with dislocated finger of left hand
Relaxations: 'Any music – MTV – sleeping, socialising, catching up with old friends'
Extras: Played for Pudsey Congs since age of seven. Played for Yorkshire at all age

levels U11 to 1st XI. Awarded Yorkshire 2nd XI cap 1998
Opinions on cricket: 'Great fun. More day/night cricket – four segments of 20 overs: bat/bowl/bat/bowl.'
Best batting: 41 Yorkshire v Lancashire, Headingley 1998
Best bowling: 3-20 Yorkshire v Worcestershire, Worcester 1998

1999 Season (did not make any first-class or one-day appearances)

Career Performances

	M	Inns	NO	Runs	HS	Avge	100s	50s	Ct	St	Balls	Runs	Wkts	Avge	Best	5wI	10wM
Test																	
All First	8	12	2	139	41	13.90	-	-	7	-	985	422	13	32.46	3-20	-	-
1-day Int																	
NatWest																	
B & H																	
1-day Lge	1	1	0	5	5	5.00	-	-	-	-	12	19	0	-		-	-

MILLNS, D. J.   Nottinghamshire

Name: David James Millns
Role: Left-hand bat, right-arm
fast-medium swing bowler
Born: 27 February 1965,
Mansfield, Nottinghamshire
Height: 6ft 3in **Weight:** 14st 7lbs
Nickname: Rocket Man
County debut: 1988 (Nottinghamshire),
1990 (Leicestershire)
County cap: 1991 (Leicestershire)
Benefit: 1999 (Leicestershire)
50 wickets in a season: 4
1st-Class 50s: 7
1st-Class 100s: 3
1st-Class 5 w. in innings: 22
1st-Class 10 w. in match: 4
1st-Class catches: 73
Place in batting averages: 174th av. 22.66
(1998 16th av. 48.16)
Place in bowling averages: 5th av. 16.17 (1998 40th av. 24.02)
Strike rate: 37.17 (career 48.01)
Parents: Bernard and Brenda
Wife and date of marriage: Wanda Marie, 25 September 1993

Children: Dylan, 17 April 1998

Family links with cricket: Andy Pick, former Notts CCC player, is brother-in-law. Brother Paul and his son Matthew play for Clipstone MWCC

Education: Samuel Barlow Junior; Garibaldi Comprehensive; North Notts College of Further Education; Nottingham Trent Polytechnic

Qualifications: Advanced coach

Career outside cricket: 'Undecided'

Off-season: 'Holiday'

Overseas tours: England A to Australia 1992-93; Leicestershire to South Africa 1994 and 1995, to Holland 1994 and 1996, to Barbados 1998

Overseas teams played for: Uitenhage, Port Elizabeth, South Africa 1988-89; Birkenhead, Auckland 1989-91; Tasmania, Australia 1994-95; Boland, South Africa 1996-97

Cricketers particularly admired: Vince Wells, Aftab Habib

Young players to look out for: Ben Smith, Carl Crowe, Paul Franks

Other sports followed: Football (Leicester City), rugby union (Leicester Tigers), golf ('taking money off J.J. Whitaker on the golf course gives me great pleasure')

Injuries: Out for six to seven weeks with strained tendon in left foot

Relaxations: Computers and property development

Extras: Harold Larwood Bowling Award 1984. Asked to be released by Nottinghamshire at the end of 1989 season and joined Leicestershire in 1990. Finished third in national bowling averages in 1990. Britannic Assurance Player of the Month in August 1991 after taking 9-37 v Derbyshire, the best Leicestershire figures since George Geary's 10-18 v Glamorgan in 1929. Was players' representative on Cricketers' Association Executive for Leicestershire. Leicestershire Cricketer of the Year 1992. Leicestershire Bowling Award 1990, 1991, 1992 and 1994. Left Leicestershire at end of 1999 season and has rejoined Nottinghamshire for 2000

Opinions on cricket: 'Some of our young players are put into Test cricket before they have sorted out the first-class game. This is not good for the future if you have already destroyed a player's confidence at 19.'

Best batting: 121 Leicestershire v Northamptonshire, Northampton 1997

Best bowling: 9-37 Leicestershire v Derbyshire, Derby 1991

1999 Season

	M	Inns	NO	Runs	HS	Avge	100s	50s	Ct	St	O	M	Runs	Wkts	Avge	Best	5wl	10wM
Test																		
All First	6	9	3	136	47	22.66	-	-	5	-	142.3	35	372	23	16.17	5-62	1	-
1-day Int																		
NatWest																		
B & H																		
1-day Lge	2	2	1	22	13	22.00	-	-	-	-	14	2	51	2	25.50	1-24	-	

Career Performances

	M	Inns	NO	Runs	HS	Avge	100s	50s	Ct	St	Balls	Runs	Wkts	Avge	Best	5wl	10wM
Test																	
All First	162	190	58	2880	121	21.81	3	7	73	-	25063	14162	522	27.13	9-37	22	4
1-day Int																	
NatWest	11	5	3	49	29 *	24.50	-	-	2	-	648	423	12	35.25	3-22	-	
B & H	27	14	8	103	39 *	17.16	-	-	5	-	1244	908	29	31.31	4-26	-	
1-day Lge	43	22	11	132	20 *	12.00	-	-	9	-	1614	1400	33	42.42	2-11	-	

MIRZA, M. M.   Worcestershire

Name: Maneer Mohammed Mirza
Role: Right-hand bat, right-arm fast bowler
Born: 1 April 1978, Birmingham
Height: 5ft 10in **Weight:** 11st 9lbs
Nickname: Mo
County debut: 1997
1st-Class catches: 1
Strike rate: (career 48.21)
Parents: Mirza Sherbaz (deceased) and
Zarda Bi
Marital status: Single
Family links with cricket: 'My brother
Parvaz played for Worcestershire CCC
1993-1995'
Education: Wyndcliffe Primary School;
Sheldon Heath Secondary School;
Bourneville College of Further Education
Qualifications: 5 GCSEs and 2 A-levels
Career outside cricket: Studying for a degree in Business Management and
Sports Studies
Overseas tours: England U15 to South Africa 1993; Birmingham Schools to India and
Pakistan 1996
Cricketers particularly admired: Parvaz (brother), Imran Khan, Wasim Akram,
Malcolm Marshall, Ian Botham
Other sports followed: Boxing and basketball
Relaxations: Sleeping and spending time with friends and family
Opinions on cricket: 'The standard of wickets could be improved to produce better
players. Contracts should be extended to nine months instead of six.'
Best batting: 10* Worcestershire v Warwickshire, Edgbaston 1997
Best bowling: 4-51 Worcestershire v Warwickshire, Edgbaston 1997

1999 Season (did not make any first-class or one-day appearances)

Career Performances

	M	Inns	NO	Runs	HS	Avge	100s	50s	Ct	St	Balls	Runs	Wkts	Avge	Best	5wl	10wM
Test																	
All First	6	7	4	17	10 *	5.66	-	-	1	-	916	620	19	32.63	4-51	-	-
1-day Int																	
NatWest																	
B & H																	
1-day Lge	4	0	0	0	0	-	-	-	1	-	96	113	1	113.00	1-31	-	

MOHAMMED, I. Gloucestershire

Name: Imraan Mohammed
Role: Right-hand opening bat,
right-arm off-spin bowler
Born: 31 December 1976, Solihull
Height: 5ft 9in **Weight:** 11st
Nickname: Immy
County debut: No first-team appearance
1st-Class 50s: 2
1st-Class 100s: 1
1st-Class catches: 1
Place in batting averages: 57th av. 37.14
Strike rate: 125.50 (career 107.66)
Parents: Sadiq and Nighat
Marital status: Single
Family links with cricket: Father Sadiq
played for Pakistan and Gloucestershire.
Uncles Hanif, Mushtaq and Wazir also played
for Pakistan
Education: Crossways School, Thornbury; St Patricks High School, Karachi; Karachi
Grammar School; Joseph Chamberlain College, Birmingham; Cambridge University
Qualifications: BA (Hons) Economics
Career outside cricket: 'Not quite sure but perhaps in the City'
Off-season: Playing first-class cricket in Pakistan
Overseas tours: Cambridge University CC to Pakistan 1999
Overseas teams played for: Pakistan Customs, Pakistan 1999-2000
Cricketers particularly admired: Sachin Tendulkar, Steve Waugh, Imran Khan,
Javed Miandad, Hanif Mohammed, Martin Crowe, Wasim Akram, Ricky Ponting
Young players to look out for: Anurag Singh, Ed Smith, Owais Shah
Other sports played: Table tennis, tennis, badminton, football (all recreational)

Other sports followed: Tennis, boxing and football
Relaxations: Reading fiction and autobiographies, going to the movies, 'my music'
Extras: A member of the Mohammed family that has produced five Test cricketers so far and holds the record for producing the most first-class cricketers from a single family. Achieved two Blues while at Cambridge. Played for Cambridge University and British Universities in 1999
Opinions on cricket: 'The game has become far more competitive, testing, aggressive, and demanding of endurance and fitness. The price of some of the above may have been that it has lost some of its old world charm and the spirit which cricket advocates, not to mention some of the old colourful "characters". It has certainly become more exciting and spectator-friendly, which is probably the most important thing.'
Best batting: 136 Cambridge University v Yorkshire, Headingley 1998
Best bowling: 1-13 Cambridge University v Yorkshire, Headingley 1998

1999 Season (did not make any first-class or one-day appearances)

Career Performances

	M	Inns	NO	Runs	HS	Avge	100s	50s	Ct	St	Balls	Runs	Wkts	Avge	Best	5wI	10wM
Test																	
All First	16	24	3	769	136	36.61	2	2	1	-	323	186	3	62.00	1-13	-	-
1-day Int																	
NatWest																	
B & H																	
1-day Lge																	

MONTGOMERIE, R. R.   Sussex

Name: Richard Robert Montgomerie
Role: Right-hand opening bat
Born: 3 July 1971, Rugby
Height: 5ft 10in **Weight:** 13st
Nickname: Monty, Fish
County debut: 1991 (Northamptonshire), 1999 (Sussex)
County cap: 1995 (Northamptonshire), 1999 (Sussex)
1000 runs in a season: 2
1st-Class 50s: 33
1st-Class 100s: 11
1st-Class catches: 103
One-Day 100s: 1
Place in batting averages: 58th av. 37.00 (1998 184th av. 20.61)
Parents: Robert and Gillian
Marital status: Single

Family links with cricket: Father captained Oxfordshire

Education: Bilton Grange; Rugby School; Worcester College, Oxford University

Qualifications: 12 O-levels, 4 A-levels, BA (Hons) Chemistry, Level II coaching

Off-season: 'Buying a flat; holiday to Venezuela; tour to South Africa with Christians in Sport; coaching; maybe find a job'

Overseas tours: Oxford University to Namibia 1991

Overseas teams played for: Sydney University CC 1995-96

Cricketers particularly admired: Many

Young players to look out for: Richard Logan

Other sports followed: Golf, rackets, real tennis and many others

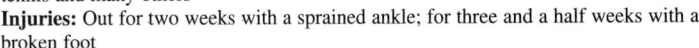

Injuries: Out for two weeks with a sprained ankle; for three and a half weeks with a broken foot

Relaxations: Any sport, good television, reading and 'occasionally testing my brain'

Extras: Scored unbeaten 50 in each innings of 1991 Varsity match and was Oxford captain in 1994. Oxford rackets Blue 1990. Captained Combined Universities 1994. Released by Northants at the end of the 1998 season and joined Sussex for 1999. Scored his first 100 for Sussex (113*) against Northants, his former county, at Hove 1999. Awarded Sussex cap 1999

Opinions on cricket: 'The new two-league system should keep the interest up right to the end of the season – it certainly did for us this year. However, I would still like every county to be able to win the Championship at the start of the season. English cricket has not been performing as it should. Players must shoulder the majority of the responsibility, but everyone (players, administrators, press) must start seeing the advantages in our system and not use it as an excuse.'

Best batting: 192 Northamptonshire v Kent, Canterbury 1995

1999 Season

	M	Inns	NO	Runs	HS	Avge	100s	50s	Ct	St	O	M	Runs	Wkts	Avge	Best	5wI	10wM
Test																		
All First	15	27	1	962	113 *	37.00	2	6	19	-	1	0	6	0	-	-	-	-
1-day Int																		
NatWest	1	1	1	56	56 *	-	-	1	-	-								
B & H																		
1-day Lge	13	13	2	393	80 *	35.72	-	3	3	-								

Career Performances

	M	Inns	NO	Runs	HS	Avge	100s	50s	Ct	St	Balls	Runs	Wkts	Avge	Best	5wl	10wM
Test																	
All First	113	197	20	5905	192	33.36	11	33	103	-	108	72	0	-	-	-	-
1-day Int																	
NatWest	8	8	2	356	109	59.33	1	3	3	-							
B & H	17	15	2	421	75	32.38	-	2	2	-	6	0	0	-	-	-	
1-day Lge	50	49	3	1451	86 *	31.54	-	13	13	-							

MOODY, T. M. Worcestershire

Name: Thomas Masson Moody
Role: Right-hand bat, right-arm medium bowler
Born: 2 October 1965, Adelaide
Height: 6ft 7in **Weight:** 16st
Nickname: Moods, Tex
County debut: 1990 (Warwickshire), 1991 (Worcestershire)
County cap: 1990 (Warwickshire), 1991 (Worcestershire)
Test debut: 1989-90
Tests: 8
One-Day Internationals: 70
1000 runs in a season: 5
1st-Class 50s: 92
1st-Class 100s: 60
1st-Class 200s: 4
1st-Class 5 w. in innings: 9
1st-Class 10 w. in match: 2
1st-Class catches: 289
One-Day 100s: 15
Place in batting averages: 62nd av. 35.75 (1998 31st av. 42.19)
Place in bowling averages: (1998 81st av. 29.25)
Strike rate: 89.83 (career 66.99)
Parents: John and Janet
Wife and date of marriage: Helen, 3 March 1993
Children: Jackson, 5 March 1995
Family links with cricket: Father played A Grade cricket in South Australia
Education: Guildford Grammar School, Western Australia
Qualifications: HSE
Career outside cricket: Sports shop owner

Overseas tours: Australia to India and Pakistan (World Cup) 1987-88, to England 1989, to India 1989-90, to Sri Lanka 1992-93, to New Zealand 1997-98, to Sharjah 1997-98, to India 1997-98, to UK, Ireland and Holland (World Cup) 1999, to Sri Lanka 1999 (one-day series), to Zimbabwe 1999 (one-day series)
Overseas teams played for: Midland Guildford, Perth, Western Australia; Western Australia 1985 –
Cricketers particularly admired: Dennis Lillee, Allan Border, Viv Richards, Rod Marsh
Other sports followed: Aussie Rules football (West Coast Eagles), football, golf, tennis
Relaxations: Golf, sleeping and films
Extras: Scored 150s in both innings of 1988-89 Sheffield Shield final for Western Australia v Queensland; has scored a total of four centuries in Sheffield Shield finals. Hit a century against Warwickshire during Australia's 1989 tour and signed a one-year contract with them for 1990. In 1990, hit centuries in first three first-class matches for Warwickshire, and seven in first eight matches – a unique achievement; scored the (then) fastest ever first-class century v Glamorgan in 26 minutes – taking advantage of declaration bowling; reached 1000 first-class runs in first season of county cricket in only 12 innings – another record. Released by Warwickshire at the end of the 1990 season after they had chosen Allan Donald as their one overseas player and was signed by Worcestershire for 1991 when Graeme Hick was no longer considered an overseas player. Not re-signed for 1993 season because he was expected to be touring with the Australian team, although in the event he was not selected. Returned for 1994 season. Scored 180* and shared record unbroken partnership with Tim Curtis in the semi-final of the NatWest Trophy 1994. Appointed Worcestershire's captain in 1996 after replacing Tim Curtis halfway through the 1995 season. Reclaimed a place in the Australian one-day side for the World Series against West Indies and Pakistan in 1996-97. Became the fastest player to score 4000 runs in the Sunday League, achieving the feat in only 100 innings. Represented Australia in the World Series against South Africa and New Zealand in 1997-98. Captained Western Australia to their Sheffield Shield final victory in 1998-99 – his fourth victory as captain and his fifth overall. Was in Australia's World Cup winning side in 1999. Retired from county cricket at end of 1999 season
Opinions on cricket: 'We need more quality not quantity.'
Best batting: 272 Western Australia v Tasmania, Hobart 1994-95
Best bowling: 7-38 Western Australia v Tasmania, Hobart 1995-96

1999 Season

	M	Inns	NO	Runs	HS	Avge	100s	50s	Ct	St	O	M	Runs	Wkts	Avge	Best	5wI	10wM
Test																		
All First	5	10	2	286	63 *	35.75	-	3	5	-	89.5	25	267	6	44.50	4-27	-	-
1-day Int	7	5	4	117	56 *	117.00	-	1	2	-	51	5	220	7	31.42	3-25	-	
NatWest	1	1	0	12	12	12.00	-	-	-	-	8	0	33	0	-		-	-
B & H																		
1-day Lge	6	5	0	188	56	37.60	-	2	-	-	39	6	124	4	31.00	2-25	-	

Career Performances

	M	Inns	NO	Runs	HS	Avge	100s	50s	Ct	St	Balls	Runs	Wkts	Avge	Best	5wI	10wM
Test	8	14	0	456	106	32.57	2	3	9	-	432	147	2	73.50	1-17	-	-
All First	291	487	45	20677	272	46.78	64	92	289	-	22846	10628	341	31.16	7-38	9	2
1-day Int	70	61	10	1188	89	23.29	-	10	19	-	2515	1851	45	41.13	3-25	-	
NatWest	17	17	3	872	180 *	62.28	3	3	10	-	679	396	11	36.00	2-33	-	
B & H	38	36	7	1555	110 *	53.62	2	14	17	-	972	587	23	25.52	4-24	-	
1-day Lge	124	121	10	4753	160	42.81	10	32	37	-	2949	2058	75	27.44	4-46	-	

MORRIS, A. C. Hampshire

Name: Alexander Corfield Morris
Role: Left-hand bat ('should be top four'),
right-arm medium-fast bowler ('whenever
needed, usually against the wind')
Born: 4 October 1976, Barnsley
Height: 6ft 6in ('when I've just got out of
bed') **Weight:** 'Off-season 18st; season
hopefully 14st 7lbs'
County debut: 1995 (Yorkshire),
1998 (Hampshire)
50 wickets in a season: 1
1st-Class 50s: 3
1st-Class 5 w. in innings: 3
1st-Class 10 w. in match: 1
1st-Class catches: 18
Place in batting averages:
(1998 172nd av. 21.90)
Place in bowling averages: 8th av. 17.75
(1998 18th av. 20.24)
Strike rate: 36.85 (career 43.24)
Parents: Chris and Janet
Marital status: Single
Family links with cricket: Brother Zac plays for Hampshire
Education: Wilthorpe Primary School; Holgate School, Barnsley; Barnsley College
Qualifications: 4 GCSEs, BTEC National Diploma in Sports Science, senior cricket
coach
Off-season: 'Hibernating like a big polar bear'
Overseas tours: England U19 to West Indies 1994-95, to Zimbabwe 1995-96;
England VI to Hong Kong 1996; Michael Vaughan XI to Tenerife 1996; Craig Dudley
XI to Cyprus 1997; Anthony McGrath XI to Gran Canaria 1998; Alex Morris XI to
Cyprus 1999

Cricketers particularly admired: 'Everyone I've ever been on an overseas tour with'
Young players to look out for: 'Mark Hirst and Craig Murtagh played extremely well this year in Cyprus'
Other sports followed: Football (Barnsley FC)
Injuries: Out for three months with stress fracture in shin
Relaxations: 'Feeding the horse; enjoying a quiet drink with the Judge'
Extras: Played for Yorkshire U11-U19; made debut for 2nd XI at age 16. Played for England U15 against Barbados and in 1994 for both England U17 and U19 against India. Played junior football with both Barnsley and Rotherham and had trials for Nottingham Forest and Leeds. Left Yorkshire and signed for Hampshire along with his brother Zac for the 1998 season
Best batting: 60 Yorkshire v Lancashire, Old Trafford 1996
Best bowling: 5-52 Hampshire v Worcestershire, Southampton 1999

1999 Season

	M	Inns	NO	Runs	HS	Avge	100s	50s	Ct	St	O	M	Runs	Wkts	Avge	Best	5wI	10wM
Test																		
All First	6	7	2	131	58 *	26.20	-	1	-	-	172	51	497	28	17.75	5-52	3	1
1-day Int																		
NatWest																		
B & H																			
1-day Lge	3	1	0	5	5	5.00	-	-	-	-	18	0	104	4	26.00	3-59	-	

Career Performances

	M	Inns	NO	Runs	HS	Avge	100s	50s	Ct	St	Balls	Runs	Wkts	Avge	Best	5wI	10wM
Test																	
All First	34	45	9	712	60	19.77	-	3	18	-	3762	2017	87	23.18	5-52	3	1
1-day Int																	
NatWest	1	1	1	1	1 *	-	-	-	-	-	48	43	1	43.00	1-43	-	
B & H	1	0	0	0	0	-	-	-	1	-	6	4	0	-	-	-	-
1-day Lge	27	17	4	216	48 *	16.61	-	-	5	-	540	485	19	25.52	4-49	-	

---

62. Which bowler took the most Championship wickets
from 1993, when the four-day Championship began, to the end of the
single-division era in 1999?

MORRIS, J. E.   Nottinghamshire

Name: John Edward Morris
Role: Right-hand bat, right-arm
medium bowler
Born: 1 April 1964, Crewe
Height: 5ft 10in **Weight:** 13st 6lbs
Nickname: Animal
County debut: 1982 (Derbyshire),
1994 (Durham)
County cap: 1986 (Derbyshire),
1998 (Durham)
Benefit: 1999 (Durham)
Test debut: 1990
Tests: 3
One-Day Internationals: 8
1000 runs in a season: 11
1st-Class 50s: 97
1st-Class 100s: 47
1st-Class 200s: 2
1st-Class catches: 146
One-Day 100s: 9

Place in batting averages: 94th av. 31.68 (1998 64th av. 34.86)
Strike rate: (career 142.57)
Parents: George (Eddie) and Jean
Wife and date of marriage: Sally, 30 September 1990
Children: Thomas Edward, 27 June 1991
Family links with cricket: Father played for Crewe for many years as an opening
bowler
Education: Shavington Comprehensive School; Dane Bank College of Further Education
Qualifications: O-levels
Overseas tours: England to Australia 1990-91; Romany to South Africa 1993;
MCC to Bahrain 1994-95
Overseas teams played for: Umbilo, Durban, South Africa 1982-84; Alex Old Boys,
Pietermaritzburg, South Africa 1984-85; Subiaco-Floriat, Western Australia 1986-87;
Griqualand West, South Africa 1988-89, 1993-94; Protea, Johannesburg, South Africa
1993
Other sports followed: Golf, football (Derby County)
Relaxations: The golf course and home life
Extras: In 1984 became youngest player to score a Sunday League century. Was the
first batsman to pass 5000 runs for Durham. Passed 20,000 first-class runs during
Durham's first innings v Derbyshire, his former county, at Chester-le-Street 1999. Left
Durham at end of 1999 season and has joined Nottinghamshire for 2000

Best batting: 229 Derbyshire v Gloucestershire, Cheltenham 1993
Best bowling: 1-6 Derbyshire v Cambridge University, Fenner's 1993

1999 Season

	M	Inns	NO	Runs	HS	Avge	100s	50s	Ct	St	O	M	Runs	Wkts	Avge	Best	5wl	10wM
Test																		
All First	15	25	0	792	119	31.68	2	4	7	-								
1-day Int																		
NatWest	1	1	0	10	10	10.00	-	-	-	-								
B & H																		
1-day Lge	9	9	0	175	41	19.44	-	-	-	-								

Career Performances

	M	Inns	NO	Runs	HS	Avge	100s	50s	Ct	St	Balls	Runs	Wkts	Avge	Best	5wl	10wM
Test	3	5	2	71	32	23.66	-	-	3	-								
All First	341	576	33	20298	229	37.38	49	97	146	-	998	913	7	130.42	1-6	-	-	
1-day Int	8	8	1	167	63 *	23.85	-	1	2	-								
NatWest	30	29	3	856	109	32.92	1	5	9	-								
B & H	58	54	6	1481	145	30.85	3	7	13	-	24	14	0	-		-	-	
1-day Lge	216	206	12	4965	134	25.59	5	21	48	-	9	8	0	-		-	-	

MORRIS, Z. C. Hampshire

Name: Zachary Clegg Morris
Role: Right-hand bat, slow left-arm bowler
Born: 4 September 1978, Barnsley
Height: 6ft 1in **Weight:** 14st
Nickname: Zaco, Badger
County debut: 1998
Parents: Lance and Janet
Marital status: Single
Family links with cricket: 'Brother plays in the Mr Blobby XI'
Education: Wilthorpe Primary School; Holgate Secondary School
Qualifications: NCA coaching award
Career outside cricket: 'Pass'
Overseas tours: England U19 to Pakistan 1996-97
Cricketers particularly admired: Peter Hartley

Young players to look out for: Derek Kenway, Lawrence Prittipaul
Other sports played: Football (Fareham Dynamos; OTs)
Other sports followed: Formula One, Superbikes
Relaxations: Travelling, foreign languages, reading (Wilbur Smith novels)
Extras: 'Pretty useful groundsman!' Moved to Hampshire in the 1997-98 close season along with his brother, Alex. Represented England U19 v Pakistan U19 1998
Opinions on cricket: 'All for two divisions but don't agree with the proposed contract set-up for England players. Still believe that topless cheerleaders would raise the standard of English cricket. Spin bowlers and the one bouncer per over rule should be thrown out of the game.'
Best batting: 10 Hampshire v Gloucestershire, Southampton 1998

1999 Season

	M	Inns	NO	Runs	HS	Avge	100s	50s	Ct	St	O	M	Runs	Wkts	Avge	Best	5wl	10wM
Test																		
All First	1	2	0	1	1	0.50	-	-	-	-	33.1	7	94	0	-	-	-	-
1-day Int																		
NatWest																		
B & H																		
1-day Lge																		

Career Performances

	M	Inns	NO	Runs	HS	Avge	100s	50s	Ct	St	Balls	Runs	Wkts	Avge	Best	5wl	10wM
Test																	
All First	2	4	0	11	10	2.75	-	-	-	-	205	99	0	-	-	-	-
1-day Int																	
NatWest																	
B & H																	
1-day Lge																	

MUAZAM ALI   Durham

Name: Muazam Ali
Role: Right-hand bat, occasional leg-spin bowler
Born: 23 October 1979, Whipps Cross, London
Height: 5ft 7in **Weight:** 10st 6lbs
Nickname: Muz, Geeze
County debut: 1999 (one-day)
Parents: Masroor and Elean
Marital status: Single
Family links with cricket: Father's brother played first-class cricket in Pakistan

Education: St Aubyn's; Chigwell School
Qualifications: 10 GCSEs, 3 A-levels
Off-season: 'Hopefully playing in Perth, Australia'
Overseas tours: Essex U14 to Hong Kong 1993; Essex U15 to Barbados 1994
Cricketers particularly admired: Graham Gooch, Steve Waugh
Young players to look out for: Marc Symington, Mike Carberry, Jit Bahl
Other sports followed: Football (Tottenham Hotspur)
Relaxations: Music, going out with friends and reading
Extras: MCC Young Cricketer of the Year 1993 (U13), 1995 (U15), 1997 (U19). Man of the Tour, Essex U15 to Barbados 1994

1999 Season

	M	Inns	NO	Runs	HS	Avge	100s	50s	Ct	St	O	M	Runs	Wkts	Avge	Best	5wI	10wM
Test																		
All First	-																	
1-day Int																		
NatWest																		
B & H																		
1-day Lge	2	2	0	18	17	8.50	-	-	-	-	-							

Career Performances

	M	Inns	NO	Runs	HS	Avge	100s	50s	Ct	St	Balls	Runs	Wkts	Avge	Best	5wI	10wM
Test																	
All First																	
1-day Int																	
NatWest																	
B & H																	
1-day Lge	2	2	0	18	17	8.50	-	-	-	-							

MULLALLY, A. D.   Hampshire

Name: Alan David Mullally
Role: Right-hand bat, left-arm fast bowler
Born: 12 July 1969, Southend
Height: 6ft 5in   **Weight:** 14st
Nickname: Bob, Bryan, Eric, Spider,
'too many to mention'
County debut: 1988 (Hampshire),
1990 (Leicestershire)
County cap: 1993 (Leicestershire)
Test debut: 1996
Tests: 16
One-Day Internationals: 29
50 wickets in a season: 4
1st-Class 50s: 2
1st-Class 5 w. in innings: 18
1st-Class 10 w. in match: 3
1st-Class catches: 35
One-Day 5 w. in innings: 2

Place in batting averages: 289th av. 6.25 (1998 245th av. 14.66)
Place in bowling averages: 70th av. 27.53 (1998 9th av. 18.80)
Strike rate: 66.57 (career 64.11)
Parents: Michael and Ann
Marital status: Single
Education: Cannington High School and Primary, Perth, Australia; Wembley and
Carlisle Technical College
Qualifications: 'This and that'
Career outside cricket: Musician
Off-season: England tour to South Africa and Zimbabwe
Overseas tours: Western Australia to India; Leicestershire to Jamaica 1992-93; England
to Zimbabwe and New Zealand 1996-97, to Australia 1998-99, to Sharjah (Coca-Cola
Cup) 1998-99, to South Africa and Zimbabwe 1999-2000
Overseas teams played for: Western Australia 1987-90; Victoria 1990-91
Cricketers particularly admired: Geoff Marsh, Dermot Reeve
Young players to look out for: Darren Maddy
Other sports followed: Australian Rules football, basketball, most sports
Relaxations: Music
Extras: English-qualified as he was born in Southend, he made his first-class debut for
Western Australia in the 1987-88 Sheffield Shield final, and played for Australian YC
1988-89. Played one match for Hampshire in 1988 before joining Leicestershire.
Represented England in the 1999 World Cup. Left Leicestershire at end of 1999 season
and has rejoined Hampshire for 2000
Opinions on cricket: 'Good fun.'

Best batting: 75 Leicestershire v Middlesex, Leicester 1996
Best bowling: 7-55 Leicestershire v Nottinghamshire, Worksop 1998

1999 Season

	M	Inns	NO	Runs	HS	Avge	100s	50s	Ct	St	O	M	Runs	Wkts	Avge	Best	5wI	10wM
Test	3	5	0	18	10	3.60	-	-	2	-	111.4	29	300	11	27.27	3-48	-	-
All First	9	12	4	50	13	6.25	-	-	2	-	310.4	93	771	28	27.53	5-106	1	-
1-day Int	5	2	1	1	1 *	1.00	-	-	-	-	50	6	176	10	17.60	4-37	-	
NatWest	2	2	0	16	15	8.00	-	-	-	-	17	3	38	6	6.33	4-23	-	
B & H	1	1	0	2	2	2.00	-	-	-	-	10	1	42	0	-	-	-	
1-day Lge	5	3	1	11	9	5.50	-	-	-	-	38.4	6	120	6	20.00	2-12	-	

Career Performances

	M	Inns	NO	Runs	HS	Avge	100s	50s	Ct	St	Balls	Runs	Wkts	Avge	Best	5wI	10wM
Test	16	24	4	117	24	5.85	-	-	5	-	3994	1591	51	31.19	5-105	1	-
All First	172	192	50	1284	75	9.04	-	2	35	-	31995	15016	499	30.09	7-55	18	3
1-day Int	29	13	5	46	20	5.75	-	-	5	-	1586	1044	38	27.47	4-18	-	
NatWest	20	10	5	58	19 *	11.60	-	-	2	-	1254	660	35	18.85	5-18	1	
B & H	41	16	5	36	11	3.27	-	-	1	-	2266	1428	41	34.82	3-33	-	
1-day Lge	94	41	19	198	38	9.00	-	-	17	-	4089	2959	99	29.88	5-15	1	

MUNTON, T. A.   Derbyshire

Name: Timothy Alan Munton
Role: Right-hand bat, right-arm
fast-medium bowler
Born: 30 July 1965, Melton Mowbray
Height: 6ft 6in **Weight:** 15st 7lbs
Nickname: Harry, Captain Sensible
County debut: 1985 (Warwicks)
County cap: 1990 (Warwicks)
Benefit: 1998 (Warwicks)
Test debut: 1991
Tests: 2
50 wickets in a season: 6
1st-Class 50s: 2
1st-Class 5 w. in innings: 32
1st-Class 10 w. in match: 6
1st-Class catches: 73
One-Day 5 w. in innings: 2
Place in batting averages: 295th av. 5.00

(1998 285th av. 7.20)
Place in bowling averages: 16th av. 19.76 (1998 11th av. 19.13)
Strike rate: 47.21 (career 58.24)
Parents: Alan and Brenda
Wife and date of marriage: Helen, 20 September 1986
Children: Camilla Dallas, 13 August 1988; Harrison George Samuel, 17 February 1992
Family links with cricket: Father played for Buckminster CC
Education: Sarson High School; King Edward VII Upper School, Melton Mowbray
Qualifications: CSE grade 1, 9 O-levels, 1 A-level
Overseas tours: England A to Pakistan 1990-91, to Bermuda and West Indies
1991-92, to Pakistan 1995-96
Overseas teams played for: Victoria University, Wellington, New Zealand 1985-86;
Witwatersrand University, Johannesburg, South Africa 1986-87
Cricketers particularly admired: Richard Hadlee, David Gower
Other sports followed: Basketball, soccer, golf
Relaxations: 'Playing golf, spending time with my family'
Extras: Appeared for Leicestershire 2nd XI 1982-84. Second highest wicket-taker in
1990 with 78. Called into England A squad to tour Bermuda and West Indies 1991-92
when Dermot Reeve replaced the injured Angus Fraser on the senior tour. Was voted
Warwickshire Player of the Season 1990, 1991 and 1994. Was one of *Wisden*'s Five
Cricketers of the Year 1995. Missed the first six months of the 1995 season recovering
from a back operation. He was flown out to Pakistan as a replacement for the injured
Mike Smith on the England A tour to Pakistan in 1995-96, and played in the second
'Test' less than a week after his arrival. Assumed the Warwickshire captaincy after the
retirement of Dermot Reeve in 1996 but replaced by Brian Lara for the 1998 season
after missing the whole of the 1997 season through injury. Made Championship
comeback v Glamorgan in 1998, taking 3-41 in the first innings. Took Championship
hat-trick v Kent at Maidstone 1999. Left Warwickshire in 1999-2000 off-season and
has joined Derbyshire for 2000 on a two-year contract
Best batting: 54* Warwickshire v Worcestershire, Worcester 1992
Best bowling: 8-89 Warwickshire v Middlesex, Edgbaston 1991

1999 Season

	M	Inns	NO	Runs	HS	Avge	100s	50s	Ct	St	O	M	Runs	Wkts	Avge	Best	5wI	10wM
Test																		
All First	13	19	3	80	24	5.00	-	-	5	-	409.1	107	1028	52	19.76	7-36	3	-
1-day Int																		
NatWest	2	1	0	17	17	17.00	-	-	1	-	16	2	56	1	56.00	1-5	-	
B & H	1	1	0	2	2	2.00	-	-	-	-	10	0	37	0	-	-	-	
1-day Lge	9	5	3	13	6 *	6.50	-	-	4	-	62	6	286	10	28.60	2-14	-	

Career Performances

	M	Inns	NO	Runs	HS	Avge	100s	50s	Ct	St	Balls	Runs	Wkts	Avge	Best	5wl	10wM
Test	2	2	1	25	25 *	25.00	-	-	-	-	405	200	4	50.00	2-22	-	-
All First	227	237	90	1491	54 *	10.14	-	2	73	-	39783	17313	683	25.34	8-89	32	6
1-day Int																	
NatWest	35	11	6	28	17	5.60	-	-	6	-	2140	1085	37	29.32	3-36	-	
B & H	33	15	9	60	13	10.00	-	-	6	-	2014	1180	36	32.77	4-35	-	
1-day Lge	155	41	28	142	15 *	10.92	-	-	32	-	6665	4387	154	28.48	5-23	2	

MURALITHARAN, M.   Lancashire

Name: Muttiah Muralitharan
Role: Right-hand bat, off-spin bowler
Born: 17 April 1972, Kandy, Sri Lanka
Height: 5ft 5in
Nickname: Murali
County debut: 1999
Test debut: 1992-93
Tests: 42
One-Day Internationals: 115
50 wickets in a season: 1
1st-Class 5 w. in innings: 44
1st-Class 10 w. in match: 11
1st-Class catches: 59
One-Day 5 w. in innings: 2
Place in batting averages: 298th av. 3.75
Place in bowling averages: 2nd av. 11.77
(1998 1st av. 13.61)
Strike rate: 35.12 (career 49.41)
Education: St Anthony's College, Kandy

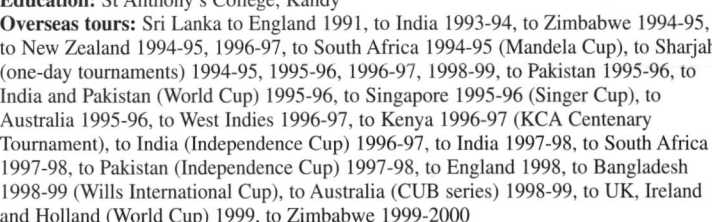

Overseas tours: Sri Lanka to England 1991, to India 1993-94, to Zimbabwe 1994-95, to New Zealand 1994-95, 1996-97, to South Africa 1994-95 (Mandela Cup), to Sharjah (one-day tournaments) 1994-95, 1995-96, 1996-97, 1998-99, to Pakistan 1995-96, to India and Pakistan (World Cup) 1995-96, to Singapore 1995-96 (Singer Cup), to Australia 1995-96, to West Indies 1996-97, to Kenya 1996-97 (KCA Centenary Tournament), to India (Independence Cup) 1996-97, to India 1997-98, to South Africa 1997-98, to Pakistan (Independence Cup) 1997-98, to England 1998, to Bangladesh 1998-99 (Wills International Cup), to Australia (CUB series) 1998-99, to UK, Ireland and Holland (World Cup) 1999, to Zimbabwe 1999-2000
Overseas teams played for: Tamil Union Cricket and Athletic Club
Extras: Took 16-220 from 113.5 overs v England at The Oval 1998, the fifth best bowling analysis in Test cricket; included 9-65 in England's second innings, in which he took his 200th Test victim (Dominic Cork) in 42 Tests. His bowling action has

attracted controversy – including calls for throwing – but was studied by the ICC in 1996 and cleared. One of *Wisden*'s Five Cricketers of the Year 1999. Like Saqlain Mushtaq, has also reportedly developed a leg-break delivered with little discernible change of action. Represented Sri Lanka in the 1999 World Cup. Was Lancashire's overseas player in 1999. Took an astonishing 66 wickets in the 12 Championship innings in which he bowled in 1999. His haul included eight returns of five or more wickets in an innings (including five returns of seven); he had five match returns of ten or more wickets. Commitments to Sri Lanka have prevented his return to county cricket for 2000

Best batting: 39 Sri Lanka v India, Colombo 1997-98
Best bowling: 9-65 Sri Lanka v England, The Oval 1998
Stop press: Selected for Sri Lanka's tour to Pakistan 1999-2000

1999 Season

	M	Inns	NO	Runs	HS	Avge	100s	50s	Ct	St	O	M	Runs	Wkts	Avge	Best	5wI	10wM
Test																		
All First	7	9	1	30	10	3.75	-	-	2	-	386.2	122	777	66	11.77	7-39	8	5
1-day Int	5	4	2	16	12	8.00	-	-	2	-	43	3	158	6	26.33	3-25	-	
NatWest	3	2	0	15	15	7.50	-	-	-	-	28	2	141	1	141.00	1-43	-	
B & H	1	0	0	0	0	-	-	-	-	-	10	4	14	1	14.00	1-14	-	
1-day Lge	7	1	1	13	13 *	-	-	-	4	-	56.2	12	188	10	18.80	3-12	-	

Career Performances

	M	Inns	NO	Runs	HS	Avge	100s	50s	Ct	St	Balls	Runs	Wkts	Avge	Best	5wI	10wM
Test	42	57	24	458	39	13.87	-	-	23	-	13041	5464	203	26.91	9-65	16	2
All First	101	122	40	912	39	11.12	-	-	59	-	25399	10233	514	19.90	9-65	44	11
1-day Int	115	53	25	167	18	5.96	-	-	55	-	6231	4379	157	27.89	5-23	2	
NatWest	3	2	0	15	15	7.50	-	-	-	-	168	141	1	141.00	1-43	-	
B & H	1	0	0	0	0	-	-	-	-	-	60	14	1	14.00	1-14	-	
1-day Lge	7	1	1	13	13 *	-	-	-	4	-	338	188	10	18.80	3-12	-	

MURTAGH, T. J.   Surrey

Name: Timothy James Murtagh
Role: Left-hand bat, right-arm
fast-medium bowler
Born: 2 August 1981, Lambeth, London
Height: 6ft **Weight:** 12st
Nickname: Murts
County debut: No first-team appearance
Parents: Dominic and Elizabeth

Marital status: Single
Family links with cricket: 'Chris, younger brother, plays in Surrey age-group cricket and is in their Development of Excellence Programme; Uncle Andy (A. J. Murtagh) played for Hampshire'
Education: Regina Coeli, Purley, Surrey; John Fisher, Purley, Surrey; St Mary's University, Twickenham
Qualifications: 10 GCSEs, 2 A-levels
Career outside cricket: Student (Sports Science and Media Studies)
Overseas tours: Surrey U17 to South Africa 1997; England U19 to Malaysia and (Youth World Cup) Sri Lanka 1999-2000
Cricketers particularly admired: Darren Gough, Glenn McGrath
Young players to look out for: Michael Carberry, Ian Bell
Other sports played: Rugby (was captain of John Fisher 2nd XV), skiing ('in the past')
Other sports followed: Football (Liverpool FC), rugby
Relaxations: Playing golf, watching sport, films, reading

NAPIER, G. R. Essex

Name: Graham Richard Napier
Role: Right-hand bat, right-arm medium bowler
Born: 6 January 1980, Colchester
Height: 5ft 10in **Weight:** 12st 7lbs
Nickname: Baldrick, Terry, Napes, Mensa
County debut: 1997
1st-Class catches: 2
Strike rate: (career 44.40)
Parents: Roger and Carol
Marital status: Single
Family links with cricket: Father played for Palmers Boys School 1st XI (1965-68), Essex Police divisional teams, and Harwich Immigration CC. 'Now makes guest appearances on Walton beach'
Education: Myland School, Colchester; Gilberd School, Colchester

Qualifications: NCA coaching award
Overseas tours: England U17 to Bermuda; England U19 to South Africa (including Youth World Cup) 1997-98
Cricketers particularly admired: Peter Such, Stuart Law, Barry Richards, Viv Richards
Young players to look out for: Michael Carberry, James Foster
Other sports followed: Football (Ipswich Town and Wimbledon FC)
Relaxations: 'Going out and having a good time with my mates. I enjoy a good sleep, too, just after eating during the day'
Extras: Represented England U19 in one-day and 'Test' series v Australia U19 1999
Opinions on cricket: 'I have only played in a small handful of games at first-class level and I feel that I don't have the experience to comment on the game in its current state. But I would love to play more games at this level and become successful.'
Best batting: 35* Essex v Nottinghamshire, Worksop 1997
Best bowling: 2-25 Essex v Cambridge University, Fenner's 1997

1999 Season

	M	Inns	NO	Runs	HS	Avge	100s	50s	Ct	St	O	M	Runs	Wkts	Avge	Best	5wl	10wM
Test																		
All First	1	1	0	27	27	27.00	-	-	2	-	3	0	20	0	-		-	-	-
1-day Int																		
NatWest																		
B & H																		
1-day Lge	4	3	0	38	19	12.66	-	-	-	-								

Career Performances

	M	Inns	NO	Runs	HS	Avge	100s	50s	Ct	St	Balls	Runs	Wkts	Avge	Best	5wl	10wM
Test																	
All First	5	6	2	81	35 *	20.25	-	-	2	-	222	157	5	31.40	2-25	-	-
1-day Int																	
NatWest																	
B & H	2	0	0	0	0	-	-	-	-	-	54	62	0	-		-	-
1-day Lge	13	8	0	88	19	11.00	-	-	2	-	138	128	6	21.33	3-22	-

NASH, D. C.   Middlesex

Name: David Charles Nash
Role: Right-hand bat, wicket-keeper
Born: 19 January 1978, Chertsey, Surrey
Height: 5ft 8in **Weight:** 11st 3lbs
Nickname: Nashy

County debut: 1995 (one-day), 1997 (first-class)
1st-Class 50s: 6
1st-Class 100s: 2
1st-Class catches: 64
1st-Class stumpings: 5
Place in batting averages: 59th av. 36.63
(1998 179th av. 21.26)
Strike rate: (career 19.00)
Parents: David and Christine
Marital status: Single
Family links with cricket: 'Father played club cricket, and brother Glen is a very talented left-hand bat and off-spinner. Mother is an avid watcher and tea lady'
Education: Chennestone County Middle; Sunbury Manor; Malvern College, Worcs
Qualifications: 10 GCSEs, 1 A-level, NCA coaching award, qualified football referee
Overseas tours: England U15 to South Africa 1993; British Airways Youth Team to West Indies 1993-94; England U19 to Zimbabwe 1995-96, to Pakistan 1996-97; England A to Kenya and Sri Lanka 1997-98
Cricketers particularly admired: George Simons and Gareth Rees 'for their big hearts', 'the whole victorious Sunbury CC squad', and Angus Fraser 'for always smiling and enjoying his cricket, however unlucky he is!'
Young players to look out for: Owais Shah, David Sales
Other sports played: Football ('played for Millwall U15s and my district side') rugby, snooker ('always getting beaten by Richard Johnson')
Other sports followed: Football (Brentford), rugby union (London Irish)
Relaxations: 'I enjoy playing golf, listening to music, going out with my mates, and visiting friends at uni in Leeds and Nottingham'
Extras: Represented Middlesex at all ages. Played for England U14, U15, U17 and U19. Once took six wickets in six balls when aged 11 – 'when I could bowl!'. *Daily Telegraph* Southern England Batting Award 1993. Seaxe Young Player of the Year 1993
Best batting: 114 Middlesex v Somerset, Lord's 1998
Best bowling: 1-8 Middlesex v Essex, Chelmsford 1997

1999 Season

	M	Inns	NO	Runs	HS	Avge	100s	50s	Ct	St	O	M	Runs	Wkts	Avge	Best	5wI	10wM
Test																		
All First	17	27	8	696	92	36.63	-	4	46	4								
1-day Int																		
NatWest	1	1	0	3	3	3.00	-	-	1	-								
B & H																		
1-day Lge	16	12	4	187	43	23.37	-	-	17	4								

Career Performances

	M	Inns	NO	Runs	HS	Avge	100s	50s	Ct	St	Balls	Runs	Wkts	Avge	Best	5wI	10wM
Test																	
All First	39	57	10	1453	114	30.91	2	6	64	5	19	19	1	19.00	1-8	-	-
1-day Int																	
NatWest	1	1	0	3	3	3.00	-	-	1	-
B & H	4	2	2	10	9*	-	-	-	2	-
1-day Lge	35	27	4	427	43	18.56	-	-	32	5

NEWELL, K.   Glamorgan

Name: Keith Newell
Role: Right-hand bat, occasional
right-arm medium bowler
Born: 25 March 1972, Crawley
Height: 6ft **Weight:** 12st 7lbs
Nickname: Nightstalker, Greavsie
County debut: 1993 (one-day, Sussex),
1995 (first-class, Sussex), 1999 (Glamorgan)
1st-Class 50s: 9
1st-Class 100s: 4
1st-Class catches: 15
One-Day 5 w. in innings: 1
Place in batting averages: 186th av. 21.72
(1998 83rd av. 31.84)
Strike rate: 39.00 (career 87.73)
Parents: Peter Charles and Julie Anne
Marital status: Single
Family links with cricket: Brother Mark

played for Sussex and Derbyshire. Brother Jonathan plays for Sussex U17 and U19
Education: Gossops Green Junior School; Ifield Community College
Qualifications: 'A few GCSEs', coaching certificate
Career outside cricket: Cricket coach
Off-season: Working in local hotel gym
Overseas teams played for: Zimbabwe Universals 1989-90; Bulawayo Athletic Club
1991-92, 1995-96; Riverside CC, Wellington 1992-93; Randwick CC, Sydney 1998-99
Cricketers particularly admired: Ian Botham
Young players to look out for: Mike Powell
Other sports played: Table tennis, golf, football (Henfield FC)
Other sports followed: Football (Spurs)
Injuries: Out for four weeks with broken bone in hand
Relaxations: Cinema and videos
Extras: Released by Sussex at end of 1998 season and joined Glamorgan

Opinions on cricket: 'Wickets need to improve. We are playing four-day cricket not two-and-a-half-day cricket, aren't we?'
Best batting: 135 Sussex v West Indies, Hove 1995
Best bowling: 4-61 Sussex v Kent, Horsham 1997

1999 Season

	M	Inns	NO	Runs	HS	Avge	100s	50s	Ct	St	O	M	Runs	Wkts	Avge	Best	5wI	10wM
Test																		
All First	8	11	0	239	46	21.72	-	-	2	-	13	1	38	2	19.00	2-15	-	-
1-day Int																		
NatWest																		
B & H																		
1-day Lge	8	8	0	138	41	17.25	-	-	3	-	2	0	12	0	-		-	-

Career Performances

	M	Inns	NO	Runs	HS	Avge	100s	50s	Ct	St	Balls	Runs	Wkts	Avge	Best	5wI	10wM
Test																	
All First	52	91	11	2278	135	28.47	4	9	15	-	1667	875	19	46.05	4-61	-	-
1-day Int																	
NatWest	6	4	1	152	52	50.66	-	1	1	-	210	148	2	74.00	1-61	-	
B & H	10	8	1	193	62*	27.57	-	1	1	-	205	182	2	91.00	1-25	-	
1-day Lge	54	47	4	844	97	19.62	-	2	12	-	840	702	18	39.00	5-33	1	

NEWELL, M.   Derbyshire

Name: Mark Newell
Role: Right-hand bat, right-arm fast-medium bowler
Born: 19 December 1973, Crawley
Height: 6ft 1in **Weight:** 12st
Nickname: Little Ede
County debut: 1996 (Sussex), 1999 (Derbys)
1st-Class 50s: 3
1st-Class 100s: 3
1st-Class catches: 17
Place in batting averages: (1998 103rd av. 29.69)
Parents: Peter Charles and Julie Anne
Marital status: Single
Family links with cricket: Brother Keith was on the Sussex staff and is now at Glamorgan, younger brother Jonathan plays for Sussex Young Cricketers

Education: Hazelwick Comprehensive; City of Westminster College
Qualifications: 9 GCSEs, GNVQ Advanced Leisure and Tourism, NCA senior coaching award
Overseas tours: Sussex U18 to India 1990-91; Sussex U19 to Barbados (as captain) 1993-94
Overseas teams played for: Bulawayo Athletic Club, Zimbabwe 1991-92; Marist CC, Whangerei, New Zealand 1996-97
Cricketers particularly admired: Curtly Ambrose, Allan Donald, Allan Border, Graham Gooch
Other sports followed: 'A bit of football every now and then (support West Ham)'
Relaxations: 'Building a nest in the changing-room and sleeping in it.' Films and the film industry
Extras: MCC Young Cricketer in 1994. Was on a sponsored scholarship at Arundel Castle which enabled him and two others to work, play and coach all over Sussex for two years. Played Sussex youth cricket from the age of nine. 'Bagged them, first-class debut versus Worcestershire – thanks "G"'. Released by Sussex at end of 1998 season. Joined Derbyshire for 1999; released by Derbyshire at end of 1999 season. Played for the Sussex Board XI in the NatWest Trophy in 1999
Opinions on cricket: 'Four-day cricket in 2nd XI.'
Best batting: 135* Sussex v Derbyshire, Horsham 1998

1999 Season

	M	Inns	NO	Runs	HS	Avge	100s	50s	Ct	St	O	M	Runs	Wkts	Avge	Best	5wI	10wM
Test																		
All First	1	2	0	32	25	16.00	-	-	1	-								
1-day Int																		
NatWest	1	1	0	92	92	92.00	-	1	1	-								
B & H																		
1-day Lge	3	3	0	9	7	3.00	-	-	1	-								

Career Performances

	M	Inns	NO	Runs	HS	Avge	100s	50s	Ct	St	Balls	Runs	Wkts	Avge	Best	5wI	10wM
Test																	
All First	24	40	2	889	135 *	23.39	3	3	17	-	12	15	0	-	-	-	-
1-day Int																	
NatWest	6	5	2	341	929	113.660	-	4	1	-							
B & H	2	2	0	147	87	73.50	-	2	-	-							
1-day Lge	33	32	3	636	77	21.93											

NEWELL, M.

Nottinghamshire

Name: Michael Newell
Role: Right-hand opening bat, leg-break
bowler, occasional wicket-keeper
Born: 25 February 1965, Blackburn
Height: 5ft 9in **Weight:** 11st 4lbs
Nickname: Mugly, Tricky, Animal
County debut: 1984
County cap: 1987
Benefit: 1999
1000 runs in a season: 1
1st-Class 50s: 24
1st-Class 100s: 5
1st-Class 200s: 1
1st-Class catches: 93
1st-Class stumpings: 1
One-Day 100s: 1
Strike rate: (career 51.86)
Parents: Barry and Janet

Wife and date of marriage: Jayne, 23 September 1989
Children: Elizabeth Rose, 1 September 1993
Family links with cricket: Father chairman of Notts Unity CC and brother, Paul, is
the captain
Education: West Bridgford Comprehensive
Qualifications: 8 O-levels, 3 A-levels, NCA advanced coach
Off-season: 'Talking about Shoaib Akhtar'
Cricketers particularly admired: Mathew Dowman, Dominic Cork, James Hindson
Young players to look out for: Paul Franks, Mathew Dowman
Other sports followed: Rugby union, football, darts
Relaxations: Football, studying, being at home
Opinions on cricket: 'Too many pros – maximum of 20 per club. Four-day cricket is a
must at 2nd XI. Bob Willis is a pain in the backside.'
Best batting: 203* Nottinghamshire v Derbyshire, Derby 1987
Best bowling: 2-38 Nottinghamshire v Sri Lankans, Trent Bridge 1988

1999 Season (did not make any first-class or one-day appearances)

Career Performances

	M	Inns	NO	Runs	HS	Avge	100s	50s	Ct	St	Balls	Runs	Wkts	Avge	Best	5wI	10wM
Test																	
All First	102	178	26	4636	203 *	30.50	6	24	93	1	363	282	7	40.28	2-38	-	-
1-day Int																	
NatWest	5	5	0	136	60	27.20	-	1	3	-	6	10	0	-		-	-
B & H	10	10	1	205	39	22.77	-	-	2	-							
1-day Lge	24	21	4	611	109 *	35.94	1	3	8	-							

NEWPORT, P. J.   Worcestershire

Name: Philip John Newport
Role: Right-hand bat, right-arm
fast-medium bowler, outfielder
Born: 11 October 1962, High Wycombe
Height: 6ft 2in **Weight:** 13st 7lbs
Nickname: Schnozz, Newps
County debut: 1982
County cap: 1986
Benefit: 1998
Test debut: 1988
Tests: 3
50 wickets in a season: 8
1st-Class 50s: 22
1st-Class 5 w. in innings: 35
1st-Class 10 w. in match: 3
1st-Class catches: 79
One-Day 5 w. in innings: 3
Place in batting averages: 219th av. 18.43
(1998 181st av. 20.76)
Place in bowling averages: 54th av. 24.09 (1998 46th av. 24.80)
Strike rate: 53.16 (career 52.67)
Parents: John and Sheila Diana (deceased)
Wife and date of marriage: Christine Anne, 26 October 1985
Children: Nathan Alexander, 10 May 1989
Family links with cricket: Brother Stewart is captain of Octopus CC in North London
Education: Royal Grammar School, High Wycombe; Portsmouth University
Qualifications: 8 O-levels, 3 A-levels, BA (Hons) Geography,
advanced coaching qualification
Overseas tours: NCA to Denmark 1981; England A to Pakistan 1990-91;
England to Australia 1990-91
Overseas teams played for: Vogeltown, New Plymouth, New Zealand 1986; Boland,

South Africa 1987-88; Ginnenderra and ACT, Australia 1991; Northern Transvaal, South Africa 1992-93
Other sports followed: American football, basketball, golf, football (QPR)
Extras: Had trial as schoolboy for Southampton FC. Played cricket for NAYC England Schoolboys 1981 and for Buckinghamshire in Minor Counties Championship in 1981 and 1982. Selected for cancelled England tour to India 1988-89 and selected as a replacement for England's tour to Australia in 1990-91. Winner of Worcestershire's Dick Lygon Award 1992 and voted Worcestershire Player of the Year 1992 and 1993. Finished 3rd in the Whyte and Mackay bowling ratings in 1995. Retired at end of 1999 season
Best batting: 98 Worcestershire v New Zealanders, Worcester 1990
Best bowling: 8-52 Worcestershire v Middlesex, Lord's 1988

1999 Season

	M	Inns	NO	Runs	HS	Avge	100s	50s	Ct	St	O	M	Runs	Wkts	Avge	Best	5wI	10wM
Test																		
All First	11	19	3	295	65 *	18.43	-	1	3	-	274.4	77	747	31	24.09	4-57	-	-
1-day Int																		
NatWest																			
B & H																			
1-day Lge	6	0	0	0	0	-	-	-	1	-	42	5	179	5	35.80	2-36	-	

Career Performances

	M	Inns	NO	Runs	HS	Avge	100s	50s	Ct	St	Balls	Runs	Wkts	Avge	Best	5wI	10wM
Test	3	5	1	110	40 *	27.50	-	-	1	-	669	417	10	41.70	4-87	-	-
All First	290	342	93	6010	98	24.13	-	22	79	-	46352	23737	880	26.97	8-52	35	3
1-day Int																	
NatWest	32	16	5	134	25	12.18	-	-	4	-	1731	1086	42	25.85	4-30	-	
B & H	56	29	8	239	28 *	11.38	-	-	10	-	3293	1770	87	20.34	5-22	2	
1-day Lge	175	72	29	457	26 *	10.62	-	-	34	-	6832	4823	182	26.50	5-32	1	

63. Which cricketer tops the list for the number of consecutive County Championship appearances?

NIXON, P. A. Kent

Name: Paul Andrew Nixon
Role: Left-hand bat, wicket-keeper
Born: 21 October 1970, Carlisle
Height: 5ft 11in **Weight:** 12st 12lbs
Nickname: Nico, Nobby, Merdoc
County debut: 1989 (Leicestershire)
County cap: 1984 (Leicestershire)
1000 runs in a season: 1
1st-Class 50s: 23
1st-Class 100s: 11
1st-Class catches: 469
1st-Class stumpings: 40
Place in batting averages: 102nd av. 30.66
(1998 52nd av. 37.52)
Parents: Brian and Sylvia
Wife and date of marriage: Jennifer,
9 October 1999
Family links with cricket: 'Grandad and

father played local league cricket. Mum made the teas for Edenhall CC, Penrith'
Education: Langwathby Primary; Ullswater High
Qualifications: 2 O-levels, 6 GCSEs, coaching certificates
Career outside cricket: 'Used to be farming. Father sold up'
Off-season: 'MCC tour to Bangladesh; get very fit; get married; move to Kent'
Overseas tours: Cumbria Schools U15 to Denmark 1985; Leicestershire to Barbados, Jamaica, Holland, Johannesburg, Bloemfontein; England A to India and Bangladesh 1994-95; MCC to Bangladesh 1999-2000
Overseas teams played for: Melville, Western Australia; North Fremantle, Western Australia; Mitchells Plain, Cape Town 1993; Primrose CC, Cape Town 1995-96
Cricketers particularly admired: David Gower, Ian Botham, Ian Healy, Viv Richards
Young players to look out for: Darren Stevens
Other sports played: Golf, training with Leicester Tigers rugby team
Other sports followed: Football (Leicester City, Carlisle United, Liverpool), rugby (Leicester Tigers)
Injuries: Broken right index finger; no time off
Relaxations: Team-building; winning books and tapes; health hydros
Extras: County captain of Cumbria at football, cricket and rugby. Youngest person to score a century against Yorkshire (at U15). Played for England U15. Played in Minor Counties Championship for Cumberland at 16. MCC Young Pro in 1988. Took eight catches in debut match v Warwickshire at Hinckley in 1989. Played for Carlisle United. 'Once got lost in South African township at 3.30am.' Leicester Young Player of the Year two years running. Only second Leicester wicket-keeper to score 1000 runs in

a season. Voted Cumbria Sports Personality of the Year 1994-95. Was part of Leicestershire's County Championship winning side in 1996 and 1998. Was selected to represent England in the cancelled World Super Max 8s originally scheduled to take place in Perth in October 1998. Left Leicestershire at end of 1999 season and has joined Kent for 2000

Opinions on cricket: 'Two overseas pros – one in second team. Every player should only be allowed to sign one-year contracts. Clubs should sign players on 12-month contracts. First division should be called "Premier". Players should have sponsorship on their backs for advertising. Cricket bats should have any name of any company on – to bring money into the game. Regional cricket also for tourists.'

Best batting: 131 Leicestershire v Hampshire, Leicester 1994

1999 Season

	M	Inns	NO	Runs	HS	Avge	100s	50s	Ct	St	O	M	Runs	Wkts	Avge	Best	5wl	10wM
Test																		
All First	18	29	2	828	121	30.66	1	3	46	4								
1-day Int																		
NatWest	2	2	0	63	51	31.50	-	1	1	-								
B & H	1	1	0	0	0	0.00	-	-	1	-								
1-day Lge	15	14	4	325	96 *	32.50	-	1	22	2								

Career Performances

	M	Inns	NO	Runs	HS	Avge	100s	50s	Ct	St	Balls	Runs	Wkts	Avge	Best	5wl	10wM
Test																		
All First	181	256	54	6269	131	31.03	11	23	469	40	12	4	0	-	-	-	-
1-day Int																		
NatWest	22	19	7	304	51	25.33	-	1	28	5							
B & H	27	21	5	320	53	20.00	-	1	30	6							
1-day Lge	140	120	22	2147	96 *	21.90	-	10	125	25							

64. In 1991, which county tied with Kent, having scored 436 in the fourth innings of the match?

NOON, W. M. Nottinghamshire

Name: Wayne Michael Noon
Role: Right-hand bat, wicket-keeper
Born: 5 February 1971, Grimsby
Height: 5ft 9in **Weight:** 11st 7lbs
Nickname: Noonie, Spain Boon
County debut: 1988 (one-day, Northants),
1989 (first-class, Northants),
1994 (Notts)
County cap: 1995 (Notts)
1st-Class 50s: 12
1st-Class catches: 186
1st-Class stumpings: 20
Parents: Trafford and Rosemary
Marital status: Engaged
Education: Caistor Grammar School
Qualifications: 5 O-levels
Career outside cricket:
Manager of G. Atkins (bookmakers)
Overseas tours: Lincolnshire U15 to Pakistan 1984; England YC to Australia
1989-90; Rutland tourists to South Africa 1988; Northamptonshire to Durban 1992, to
Cape Town 1993
Overseas teams played for: Burnside West, Christchurch, New Zealand 1989-90 and
1993-96; Rivertonians, Cape Town 1993-94; Canterbury, Christchurch 1994-95
Cricketers particularly admired: Ian Botham
Young players to look out for: Guy Welton
Other sports followed: Football (Lincoln City), horse racing (flat)
Relaxations: Having a bet. Eating out and having a pint
Extras: Played for England YC v New Zealand YC 1989; captain v Australian YC
1989-90 and Pakistan YC 1990. Was the 1000th player to appear in the Sunday League
competition. Broke the Northants record for most 2nd XI hundreds in one season in 1993.
Took seven catches in Kent's first innings at Trent Bridge 1999, breaking Bruce French's
county record of six (which he achieved on four occasions)
Best batting: 83 Nottinghamshire v Northamptonshire, Northampton 1997

---

65. Against which county did P. Holmes and H. Sutcliffe
put on 555 for the first wicket in 1932?

1999 Season

	M	Inns	NO	Runs	HS	Avge	100s	50s	Ct	St	O	M	Runs	Wkts	Avge	Best	5wI	10wM
Test																		
All First	3	5	0	22	8	4.40	-	-	9	-								
1-day Int																		
NatWest																		
B & H																		
1-day Lge	1	0	0	0	0	-	-	-	-	-								

Career Performances

	M	Inns	NO	Runs	HS	Avge	100s	50s	Ct	St	Balls	Runs	Wkts	Avge	Best	5wI	10wM
Test																	
All First	88	138	22	2467	83	21.26	-	12	186	20	30	34	0	-	-	-	-
1-day Int																	
NatWest	7	4	1	73	34	24.33	-	-	4	2							
B & H	18	11	3	152	46	19.00	-	-	9	4							
1-day Lge	80	51	14	460	38	12.43	-	-	60	14							

ORAM, A. R. Nottinghamshire

Name: Andrew Richard Oram
Role: Right-hand bat, right-arm medium-fast bowler
Born: 7 March 1975, Northampton
Height: 6ft 2in **Weight:** 12st 3lbs
Nickname: Ching Ching, Tonto, O-Myster
County debut: 1997
1st-Class catches: 6
Place in batting averages: (1998 295th av. 3.54)
Place in bowling averages: (1998 95th av. 31.25)
Strike rate: (career 56.05)
Parents: Richard and Anne
Marital status: Single
Family links with cricket: Father played club cricket in Northamptonshire leagues
Education: Hackleton Primary School; Roade Comprehensive
Qualifications: 10 GCSEs, 3 A-levels, 1 AS-level, NCA coaching award
Career outside cricket: Marketing and media projects
Off-season: 'A winter of rehabilitation is planned, based in the UK!'

463

Overseas teams played for: Wanneroo Districts CC, Perth 1993-94, 1997-98; Perth CC, Perth 1998-99
Cricketers particularly admired: Allan Donald, Darren Gough, Mark Bowen
Young players to look out for: Paul Franks, David Lucas
Other sports played: Golf, hockey, tennis, 'snowboarding!!'
Other sports followed: Football (Liverpool FC), golf
Injuries: Out for entire 1999 season with double stress fracture of the back
Relaxations: 'Spending money, eating out, socialising with friends and snowboarding!!'
Opinions on cricket: 'Until English cricket becomes an elitist game, it will never dramatically change!'
Best batting: 13 Nottinghamshire v Surrey, Trent Bridge 1998
Best bowling: 4-37 Nottinghamshire v Surrey, Trent Bridge 1998

1999 Season (did not make any first-class or one-day appearances)

Career Performances

	M	Inns	NO	Runs	HS	Avge	100s	50s	Ct	St	Balls	Runs	Wkts	Avge	Best	5wl	10wM
Test																	
All First	19	28	13	53	13	3.53	-	-	6	-	3195	1653	57	29.00	4-37	-	-
1-day Int																	
NatWest	1	0	0	0	0	-	-	-	-	-	66	51	1	51.00	1-51	-	
B & H	5	1	1	1	1 *	-	-	-	3	-	286	215	5	43.00	1-19	-	
1-day Lge	14	3	2	0	0 *	0.00	-	-	2	-	535	451	17	26.52	4-45	-	

ORMOND, J.   Leicestershire

Name: James Ormond
Role: Right-hand bat, right-arm fast bowler
Born: 20 August 1977, Walsgrave, Coventry
Height: 6ft 3in **Weight:** 14st 7lbs
Nickname: Stavros, Horse, Fred, Del, Bob
County debut: 1995
County cap: 1999
50 wickets in a season: 1
1st-Class 50s: 1
1st-Class 5 w. in innings: 8
1st-Class catches: 9
Place in batting averages: 257th av. 13.07
Place in bowling averages: 56th av. 24.67 (1998 4th av. 16.36)
Strike rate: 46.86 (career 45.82)
Parents: Richard and Margaret
Marital status: Single

Family links with cricket: 'Dad plays local club cricket'
Education: St Anthony's, Bedworth; St Thomas More, Nuneaton; North Warwickshire College of Further Education
Qualifications: 6 GCSEs
Overseas tours: England U19 to Zimbabwe 1995-96; England A to Kenya and Sri Lanka 1997-98
Overseas teams played for: Sydney University CC 1996-97
Cricketers particularly admired: Allan Donald, Ian Botham, Richard Hadlee
Young sportsmen to look out for: Darren Maddy, Lee Westwood
Other sports followed: Football (Coventry City)

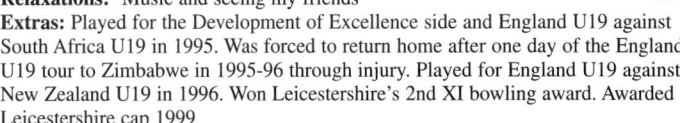

Relaxations: 'Music and seeing my friends'
Extras: Played for the Development of Excellence side and England U19 against South Africa U19 in 1995. Was forced to return home after one day of the England U19 tour to Zimbabwe in 1995-96 through injury. Played for England U19 against New Zealand U19 in 1996. Won Leicestershire's 2nd XI bowling award. Awarded Leicestershire cap 1999
Best batting: 50* Leicestershire v Warwickshire, Leicester 1999
Best bowling: 6-33 Leicestershire v Somerset, Leicester 1998

1999 Season

	M	Inns	NO	Runs	HS	Avge	100s	50s	Ct	St	O	M	Runs	Wkts	Avge	Best	5wI	10wM
Test																		
All First	13	17	3	183	50 *	13.07	-	1	2	-	406.1	88	1283	52	24.67	5-63	3	-
1-day Int																		
NatWest	1	1	0	10	10	10.00	-	-	1	-	10	1	34	1	34.00	1-34	-	
B & H	1	1	0	0	0	0.00	-	-	-	-	10	1	47	2	23.50	2-47	-	
1-day Lge	8	5	2	22	11 *	7.33	-	-	2	-	64	3	297	12	24.75	3-30	-	

Career Performances

	M	Inns	NO	Runs	HS	Avge	100s	50s	Ct	St	Balls	Runs	Wkts	Avge	Best	5wI	10wM
Test																	
All First	38	38	5	391	50 *	11.84	-	1	9	-	6049	3194	132	24.19	6-33	8	-
1-day Int																	
NatWest	2	1	0	10	10	10.00	-	-	1	-	120	92	2	46.00	1-34	-	
B & H	3	1	0	0	0	0.00	-	-	-	-	162	136	6	22.66	3-31	-	
1-day Lge	26	17	10	112	18	16.00	-	-	5	-	1002	707	38	18.60	4-12	-	

OSTLER, D. P.   Warwickshire

Name: Dominic Piers Ostler
Role: Right-hand bat, right-arm medium bowler
Born: 15 July 1970, Solihull
Height: 6ft 2in **Weight:** 13st 7lbs
Nickname: Ossie
County debut: 1990
County cap: 1991
1000 runs in a season: 4
1st-Class 50s: 52
1st-Class 100s: 9
1st-Class 200s: 1
1st-Class catches: 191
One-Day 100s: 1
Place in batting averages: 173rd av. 22.72 (1998 201st av. 19.22)
Parents: Mike and Ann
Marital status: Engaged to Karen
Family links with cricket: Brother used to play for Knowle and Dorridge CC
Education: Our Lady of the Wayside; Princethorpe College; Solihull College of Technology
Qualifications: 4 O-levels, A-levels, City and Guilds Recreation Course
Career outside cricket: 'In business'
Off-season: 'Working on benefit year'
Overseas tours: Gladstone Small's Benefit Tour to Barbados, 1991; England A to Pakistan 1995-96; England Cricket Max Tour to New Zealand 1997; Andy Moles' Benefit Tour to Barbados 1997
Overseas teams played for: Avendale CC, Cape Town 1991-92
Cricketers particularly admired: Jason Ratcliffe, Simon Millington, Graeme Welch
Young players to look out for: Ian Bell, Nick Warren
Other sports played: Golf, snooker
Other sports followed: Football (Birmingham City FC)
Injuries: Out for three months with a broken ankle
Relaxations: 'Spending time with fiancée, Karen; snooker and golf'
Extras: Played club cricket for Moseley in the Birmingham League. Made his Warwickshire 2nd XI debut in 1989 and was a member of Warwickshire U19 side that won Esso U19 County Festivals in 1988 and 1989. Has collected winner's medals for B&H Cup, County Championship, NatWest Trophy and Sunday League. Played for an England XI in the Cricket Max tournament in New Zealand in 1997. Granted a benefit for 2000
Opinions on cricket: 'Wickets need to improve dramatically.'
Best batting: 208 Warwickshire v Surrey, Edgbaston 1995

1999 Season

	M	Inns	NO	Runs	HS	Avge	100s	50s	Ct	St	O	M	Runs	Wkts	Avge	Best	5wI	10wM
Test																		
All First	7	11	0	250	87	22.72	-	2	5	-	1	0	2	0	-	-	-	-
1-day Int																		
NatWest	1	1	0	4	4	4.00	-	-	-	-								
B & H	1	1	0	0	0	0.00	-	-	-	-								
1-day Lge	9	9	1	232	53	29.00	-	2	2	-								

Career Performances

	M	Inns	NO	Runs	HS	Avge	100s	50s	Ct	St	Balls	Runs	Wkts	Avge	Best	5wI	10wM
Test																		
All First	160	267	21	8082	208	32.85	10	52	191	-	203	203	0	-	-	-	-	
1-day Int																		
NatWest	33	32	3	889	104	30.65	1	6	16	-	15	10	1	10.00	1-4	-		
B & H	31	30	4	1055	87	40.57	-	9	16	-								
1-day Lge	137	127	17	3395	91 *	30.86	-	25	35	-	6	4	0	-	-	-		

PANESAR, M. S.   Northamptonshire

Name: Mudhsuden Singh Panesar
Role: Left-hand bat, slow left-arm bowler
Born: 25 April 1982, Luton
Height: 5ft 11in **Weight:** 11st 7lbs
Nickname: Monty
County debut: No first-team appearance
Parents: Paramjit Singh Panesar and
Gurshran Kaur Panesar
Marital status: Single
Education: St Matthew's Junior School;
Stopsley High School; Bedford Modern
School
Qualifications: 10 GCSEs
Off-season: 'Studying A-levels'
Overseas tours: Bedford Modern School to
Barbados 1999
Cricketers particularly admired: Bishen
Bedi, David Gower, Sachin Tendulkar
Other sports played: Badminton, table tennis
Other sports followed: Football (Arsenal)
Relaxations: Reading, music
Opinions on cricket: 'Everything is fine.'

PARKER, B.   Yorkshire

Name: Bradley Parker
Role: Right-hand bat, right-arm medium bowler, cover point fielder
Born: 23 June 1970, Mirfield
Height: 5ft 10in **Weight:** 12st 7lbs
Nickname: Nesty, Ceefax, Floyd
County debut: 1992
1st-Class 50s: 9
1st-Class 100s: 2
1st-Class catches: 19
Place in batting averages: (1998 168th av. 22.50)
Parents: Diane and David
Marital status: Single
Family links with cricket: Father played club cricket and Lincolnshire U23
Education: Bingley Grammar School
Qualifications: 'None worth mentioning from school.' Cricket coaching awards
Overseas teams played for: Ellerslie, Auckland 1988-90
Cricketers particularly admired: Chris Spence, Alec Stewart, Graham Thorpe
Other sports followed: Rugby league, boxing
Relaxations: Films, eating out, drinking and socialising
Extras: Released by Yorkshire at end of 1999 season
Opinions on cricket: 'Far too much cricket played in too short a time.'
Best batting: 138* Yorkshire v Oxford University, The Parks 1997

1999 Season

	M	Inns	NO	Runs	HS	Avge	100s	50s	Ct	St	O	M	Runs	Wkts	Avge	Best	5wI	10wM
Test																		
All First																		
1-day Int																		
NatWest	1	1	0	16	16	16.00	-	-	-	-								
B & H																		
1-day Lge	2	2	0	8	5	4.00	-	-	1	-								

Career Performances

	M	Inns	NO	Runs	HS	Avge	100s	50s	Ct	St	Balls	Runs	Wkts	Avge	Best	5wl	10wM
Test																	
All First	44	71	10	1839	138 *	30.14	2	9	19	-	6	3	0	-	-	-	-
1-day Int																	
NatWest	6	4	0	87	69	21.75	-	1	-	-							
B & H	10	7	2	154	58	30.80	-	1	3	-							
1-day Lge	56	49	6	723	42	16.81	-	-	8	-	12	18	0	-	-	-

PARKIN, O. T. Glamorgan

Name: Owen Thomas Parkin
Role: Right-hand bat, right-arm
medium-fast swing bowler
Born: 24 August 1972, Coventry
Height: 6ft 3in **Weight:** 12st 7lbs
Nickname: Parky, Calamari, Longterm
County debut: 1994
1st-Class 5 w. in innings: 2
1st-Class catches: 9
One-Day 5 w. in innings: 1
Place in batting averages: 299th av. 3.50
(1998 280th av. 9.44)
Place in bowling averages: 44th av. 23.38
(1998 33rd av. 22.26)
Strike rate: 44.47 (career 58.39)
Parents: Vernon Cyrus and Sarah Patricia
Marital status: Single
Family links with cricket: Younger brother
Morgan plays for Glamorgan at U17 and U19 level
Education: Bournemouth Grammar School; Bath University
Qualifications: 9 GCSEs, 4 A-levels, 1 S-level, BSc (Hons) Mathematics
Career outside cricket: Maths teacher
Off-season: 'In Australia as a player/coach in Bunderberg, Queensland'
Overseas tours: Dorset Youth to Denmark
Overseas teams played for: Kew, Melbourne 1992-93; North Balwyn, Melbourne
1994-95; Balmain, Sydney 1997-99
Cricketers particularly admired: Malcolm Marshall, Richard Hadlee
Young players to look out for: Michael Powell, Wayne Law
Other sports played: 'Most sports socially'
Other sports followed: Rugby, football (Nottingham Forest), golf
Relaxations: '*Telegraph* crossword'

Extras: Played for Dorset in the NatWest Trophy 1992 and 1993. ASW Young Player of the Month July 1994. Took 5 for 28 on debut in Sunday League at Hove – a club record

Opinions on cricket: 'The reverse sweep should be banned – as bowlers you have to tell the batsman which hand you are going to use and which side of the wicket you are going to bowl, yet as a right-handed batsman you play this shot and become a left-handed player whenever you like – it would be a refreshing change to have a rule brought in that was not in favour of the batsman.'

Best batting: 24* Glamorgan v Essex, Chelmsford 1998
Best bowling: 5-24 Glamorgan v Somerset, Cardiff, 1998

1999 Season

	M	Inns	NO	Runs	HS	Avge	100s	50s	Ct	St	O	M	Runs	Wkts	Avge	Best	5wI	10wM
Test																		
All First	7	9	3	21	11	3.50	-	-	2	-	155.4	39	491	21	23.38	4-38	-	-
1-day Int																		
NatWest	2	1	1	0	0*	-	-	-	1	-	14	0	67	1	67.00	1-46	-	
B & H																		
1-day Lge	15	6	1	16	6	3.20	-	-	3	-	115	7	520	28	18.57	3-31	-	

Career Performances

	M	Inns	NO	Runs	HS	Avge	100s	50s	Ct	St	Balls	Runs	Wkts	Avge	Best	5wI	10wM
Test																	
All First	31	37	17	173	24*	8.65	-	-	9	-	4613	2278	79	28.83	5-24	2	-
1-day Int																	
NatWest	7	4	2	3	2	1.50	-	-	4	-	318	218	4	54.50	3-23	-	
B & H	4	2	0	15	8	7.50	-	-	1	-	192	149	5	29.80	3-42	-	
1-day Lge	39	14	5	21	6	2.33	-	-	5	-	1665	1219	58	21.01	5-28	1	

PARSONS, K. A. Somerset

Name: Keith Alan Parsons
Role: Right-hand bat, right-arm medium bowler
Born: 2 May 1973, Taunton
Height: 6ft 1in **Weight:** 13st 10lbs
Nickname: Pilot, Pars, Orv
County debut: 1992
County cap: 1999
1st-Class 50s: 18
1st-Class 100s: 2
1st-Class 5 w. in innings: 1

1st-Class catches: 60
Place in batting averages: 124th av. 27.72
(1998 227th av. 16.68)
Place in bowling averages: 89th av. 29.39
Strike rate: 61.14 (career 75.47)
Parents: Alan and Lynne
Marital status: Single
Family links with cricket: Identical twin
brother, Kevin, was on the Somerset staff
1992-94 and now captains the Somerset
Board XI. Father played six seasons for
Somerset 2nd XI and captained National
Civil Service XI
Education: Bishop Henderson Primary
School; The Castle School, Taunton; Richard
Huish Sixth Form College, Taunton
Qualifications: 8 GCSEs, 3 A-levels,
NCA senior coach

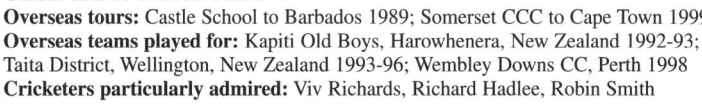

Career outside cricket: Unknown
Overseas tours: Castle School to Barbados 1989; Somerset CCC to Cape Town 1999
Overseas teams played for: Kapiti Old Boys, Harowhenera, New Zealand 1992-93;
Taita District, Wellington, New Zealand 1993-96; Wembley Downs CC, Perth 1998
Cricketers particularly admired: Viv Richards, Richard Hadlee, Robin Smith
Young players to look out for: Matt Bulbeck
Other sports followed: Rugby union (Bath RFC), football (Nottingham Forest FC),
golf, horse racing
Relaxations: Playing golf, watching movies, listening to music 'and the odd social
pint of beer'
Extras: Captained two National Cup winning sides – Taunton St Andrews in National
U15 Club Championship and Richard Huish College in National U17 School
Championship. Represented English Schools at U15 and U19 level. Somerset Young
Player of the Year 1993. Awarded Somerset cap 1999
Opinions on cricket: 'Looking forward to start of the two-division Championship as
the two-division National League seemed to prove popular with everyone. Thankfully
the proposed 25-over competition has been postponed – I can't see how that can be
good for cricketers' games in any way.'
Best batting: 105 Somerset v Young Australia, Taunton 1995
Best bowling: 5-57 Somerset v Durham, Chester-le-Street 1999

1999 Season

	M	Inns	NO	Runs	HS	Avge	100s	50s	Ct	St	O	M	Runs	Wkts	Avge	Best	5wI	10wM
Test																		
All First	15	21	3	499	80	27.72	-	3	12	-	285.2	80	823	28	29.39	5-57	1	-
1-day Int																		
NatWest	5	4	1	92	42	30.66	-	-	2	-	40.2	2	185	7	26.42	4-43	-	
B & H																		
1-day Lge	16	14	4	270	45 *	27.00	-	-	8	-	84	4	422	12	35.16	3-21	-	

Career Performances

	M	Inns	NO	Runs	HS	Avge	100s	50s	Ct	St	Balls	Runs	Wkts	Avge	Best	5wI	10wM
Test																	
All First	72	118	12	2705	105	25.51	2	18	60	-	3849	2086	51	40.90	5-57	1	-
1-day Int																	
NatWest	15	13	4	292	51	32.44	-	1	3	-	560	410	15	27.33	4-43	-	
B & H	10	9	4	119	33 *	23.80	-	-	5	-	168	215	3	71.66	2-60	-	
1-day Lge	75	59	12	1067	56	22.70	-	4	35	-	1824	1468	40	36.70	3-21	-	

PATEL, D.   Worcestershire

Name: Depesh Patel
Role: Right-hand bat, right-arm fast bowler
Born: 23 September 1981, Wolverhampton
Height: 6ft 4in **Weight:** 11st
Nickname: Dip, Dippy, Petal
County debut: No first-team appearance
Parents: Balvant and Mena
Marital status: Single
Family links with cricket: 'Dad played for Thompsons CC for 18 years. Brother Vijay has just started playing cricket for Wolverhampton CC'
Education: Wilkinson Park Primary School; Mosely Park GM School; Bilston Community College
Qualifications: GCSEs
Career outside cricket: Studying GNVQ (Advanced) Leisure and Tourism
Cricketers particularly admired: Allan Donald, Sachin Tendulkar, Glenn McGrath
Young players to look out for: Vikram Solanki
Other sports followed: Football (Wolverhampton Wanderers)

Relaxations: Keeping fit, playing snooker, watching television
Extras: Scored 120 aged 15 against Cheshire playing for Staffordshire. Has best bowling of 7 for 1 playing against Glamorgan U11 for Staffordshire U11. Played for Worcestershire Board XI in the 1999 NatWest
Opinions on cricket: 'One-day cricket is played at a faster pace than five years ago.'

1999 Season (did not make any first-class or one-day appearances)

Career Performances

	M	Inns	NO	Runs	HS	Avge	100s	50s	Ct	St	Balls	Runs	Wkts	Avge	Best	5wI	10wM
Test																	
All First																	
1-day Int																	
NatWest	1	1	1	19	19 *	-	-	-	-	-	42	36	1	36.00	1-36	-	
B & H																	
1-day Lge																	

PATEL, M. M.   Kent

Name: Minal Mahesh Patel
Role: Right-hand bat, slow left-arm bowler
Born: 7 July 1970, Bombay, India
Height: 5ft 8in **Weight:** 10st
Nickname: Min, Spin, Diamond, Ho-Chi, Geezer
County debut: 1989
County cap: 1994
Test debut: 1996
Tests: 2
50 wickets in a season: 3
1st-Class 50s: 5
1st-Class 5 w. in innings: 19
1st-Class 10 w. in match: 8
1st-Class catches: 56
Place in batting averages: 251st av. 13.80 (1998 188th av. 20.20)
Place in bowling averages: 58th av. 24.88 (1998 103rd av. 33.02)
Strike rate: 64.23 (career 71.32)
Parents: Mahesh and Aruna
Wife and date of marriage: Karuna, 8 October 1995
Family links with cricket: Father played good club cricket in Africa, India and England

Education: Maypole CP; Dartford Grammar School; Erith College of Technology; Manchester Polytechnic

Qualifications: 6 O-levels, 3 A-levels, BA (Hons) Economics

Career outside cricket: Writes for *Racing Post*

Off-season: MCC tour to Malta in November; captain of MCC tour to Bangladesh in January

Overseas tours: Dartford GS to Barbados 1988; England A to India and Bangladesh 1994-95; MCC to Malta 1997, 1999, to Fiji, Sydney and Hong Kong 1998, to East and Central Africa 1999, to Bangladesh 1999-2000 (captain)

Overseas teams played for: St Augustine's, Cape Town 1993-94; Alberton, Johannesburg 1997-98

Cricketers particularly admired: Derek Underwood, Aravinda De Silva

Young players to look out for: Bobby Key

Other sports followed: Football (Tottenham Hotspur), snooker 'and most American sports'

Relaxations: Spread betting, DJ-ing, golf

Extras: Played for English Schools 1988, 1989 and NCA England South 1989. Was voted Kent League Young Player of the Year 1987 while playing for Blackheath. First six overs in NatWest Trophy were all maidens. Whittingdale Young Player of the Year 1994

Opinions on cricket: 'Domestic cricket is in need of change – quality not quantity.'

Best batting: 67 Kent v Gloucestershire, Canterbury 1999

Best bowling: 8-96 Kent v Lancashire, Canterbury 1994

1999 Season

	M	Inns	NO	Runs	HS	Avge	100s	50s	Ct	St	O	M	Runs	Wkts	Avge	Best	5wI	10wM
Test																		
All First	18	24	3	290	67	13.80	-	1	6	-	674.3	209	1568	63	24.88	8-115	3	1
1-day Int																		
NatWest	3	1	0	2	2	2.00	-	-	-	-	27	3	108	2	54.00	1-39	-	
B & H																		
1-day Lge	10	6	3	27	11	9.00	-	-	2	-	76	3	292	12	24.33	3-22	-	

Career Performances

	M	Inns	NO	Runs	HS	Avge	100s	50s	Ct	St	Balls	Runs	Wkts	Avge	Best	5wI	10wM
Test	2	2	0	45	27	22.50	-	-	2	-	276	180	1	180.00	1-101	-	-
All First	112	158	33	1824	67	14.59	-	5	56	-	24749	10809	347	31.14	8-96	19	8
1-day Int																	
NatWest	9	3	1	11	5 *	5.50	-	-	5	-	548	308	9	34.22	2-29	-	
B & H	13	7	5	46	18 *	23.00	-	-	4	-	576	437	9	48.55	2-29	-	
1-day Lge	17	8	3	33	11	6.60	-	-	3	-	662	515	19	27.10	3-22	-	

PATTERSON, M. W. Surrey

Name: Mark William Patterson
Role: Right-hand bat, right-arm
fast-medium bowler
Born: 2 February 1974, Belfast
Height: 6ft 1in **Weight:** 13st 7lbs
Nickname: Patto, Irish, Patsy
County debut: 1996
1st-Class 5 w. in innings: 1
Strike rate: (career 23.57)
Parents: Billy and Phyllis
Marital status: Engaged to Shavarne – 'what
a lucky girl!'
Family links with cricket: Father played
club cricket. Younger brother has played for
Ireland as a wicket-keeper/batsman; 'played
for Surrey in 1998; in 1999 trialled with
Kent, hoping to be taken on'
Education: Carnmoney Primary School;
Belfast Royal Academy; University of Ulster
Qualifications: 9 GCSEs, 3 A-levels, BA (Hons) Sport and Leisure Studies. Qualified
coach in soccer, cricket, rugby, hockey, basketball, swimming and squash. 'Now also a
football referee for Surrey FA – hoping to pursue much further'
Off-season: Playing in Perth with the Marist Newman club, 'and being looked after in
the manner I'm accustomed to by Shavarne; she is working in radiography/ultrasound
in a Perth hospital'
Overseas tours: Ireland U19 to Denmark for International Youth Tournament 1993;
Ireland to Denmark for European Championships 1996; 'Surrey pre-season to Royal
Marines, Exmouth 1999'
Overseas teams played for: Mount Maunganui, Bay of Plenty, New Zealand 1994-95;
Marist Newman, Perth 1999-2000
Cricketers particularly admired: Malcolm Marshall, Glenn McGrath; John Solanky
and Raman Lamba, 'my club's first professionals in Ireland'
Young players to look out for: Ian Ward, Rupesh Amin, Ben Phillips
Other sports followed: Football (Linfield FC and Northern Ireland – 'the British
champions!')
Injuries: Out for four weeks with tendonitis of left knee
Relaxations: 'Anything to do with sport – playing and watching; spending time with
my girlfriend and mates; also trying to educate my young brother about life, with the
help of Nadeem Shahid and Jason Ratcliffe – it still isn't working, though'
Extras: 1993 Irish Young Cricketer of the Year. In 1996 took 6 for 80 against South
Africa A – the best ever figures by a Surrey bowler on debut. Represented Ireland in

the ICC Trophy in Kuala Lumpur in March 1997; Ireland finished fourth. Represented Northern Ireland at the 1998 Commonwealth Games, also in Kuala Lumpur

Opinions on cricket: 'Two divisions in both one-day and four-day cricket is excellent, but we still need better wickets. The national team will come good. Groundsmen – keep repairing those footholes well!'

Best batting: 4 Surrey v South Africa A, The Oval 1996

Best bowling: 6-80 Surrey v South Africa A, The Oval 1996

1999 Season

	M	Inns	NO	Runs	HS	Avge	100s	50s	Ct	St	O	M	Runs	Wkts	Avge	Best	5wI	10wM
Test																		
All First	1	1	0	0	0	0.00	-	-	-	-	13	2	39	3	13.00	3-25	--	
1-day Int																		
NatWest																		
B & H																		
1-day Lge																		

Career Performances

	M	Inns	NO	Runs	HS	Avge	100s	50s	Ct	St	Balls	Runs	Wkts	Avge	Best	5wI	10wM
Test																	
All First	2	3	0	6	4	2.00	-	-	-	-	243	163	10	16.30	6-80	1	-
1-day Int																	
NatWest	2	1	0	1	1	1.00	-	-	-	-	138	154	4	38.50	3-66	-	
B & H	7	5	1	23	9	5.75	-	-	-	-	342	330	10	33.00	3-48	-	
1-day Lge																	

PEIRCE, M. T. E.   Sussex

Name: Michael Toby Edward Peirce
Role: Left-hand bat, slow left-arm bowler
Born: 14 June 1973, Maidenhead
Height: 5ft 10in **Weight:** 12st
Nickname: Carrot, Juice
County debut: 1994 (one-day),
1995 (first-class)
1st-Class 50s: 15
1st-Class 100s: 2
1st-Class catches: 27
Place in batting averages: 108th av. 29.64 (1998 152nd av. 24.00)
Strike rate: 36.00 (career 234.50)
Parents: Mike and Kate
Marital status: Engaged to Natasha ('marry in Feb 2000 – hopefully!')

Education: Ardingly College; Durham University

Qualifications: 11 GCSEs, 3 A-levels, BA (Hons) Dunelm

Career outside cricket: 'Open to offers'

Off-season: 'In South Africa coaching, playing and relaxing'

Overseas tours: Ardingly College to India 1988-89; Sussex Schools U14 to Barbados 1986; Sussex Schools U19 to India 1990-91; MCC to New Zealand 1999

Overseas teams played for: Kilbirnie CC, Wellington, New Zealand 1991-92; Van der Stel CC, Stellenbosch, South Africa 1996-99; Somerset West, South Africa 1999-2000

Cricketers particularly admired: David Smith, David Gower

Young players to look out for:
Steve Harmison, Nick Wilton

Other sports played: Golf, touch rugby

Other sports followed: Football (Brighton & Hove Albion), 'most sports'

Relaxations: 'Golf, good food and drink; Natasha'

Opinions on cricket: 'Try not to get too excited when a dark cloud comes over – they don't all bring rain. Beware the cross-eyed tiger in sheep's clothing.'

Best batting: 123 Sussex v Glamorgan, Cardiff 1999

Best bowling: 1-16 Sussex v Warwickshire, Hove 1998
              1-16 Sussex v Northamptonshire, Hove 1999

1999 Season

	M	Inns	NO	Runs	HS	Avge	100s	50s	Ct	St	O	M	Runs	Wkts	Avge	Best	5wl	10wM
Test																		
All First	17	31	0	919	123	29.64	1	6	5	-	6	1	30	1	30.00	1-16	-	-
1-day Int																		
NatWest																		
B & H																		
1-day Lge																		

Career Performances

	M	Inns	NO	Runs	HS	Avge	100s	50s	Ct	St	Balls	Runs	Wkts	Avge	Best	5wI	10wM
Test																	
All First	55	98	1	2482	123	25.58	2	15	27	-	469	235	2	117.50	1-16	-	-
1-day Int																	
NatWest	1	1	0	1	1	1.00	-	-	-	-							
B & H	6	6	0	150	44	25.00	-	-	2	-							
1-day Lge	9	9	1	94	29	11.75	-	-	2	-							

PENBERTHY, A. L.   Northamptonshire

Name: Anthony Leonard Penberthy
Role: Left-hand bat, right-arm
medium bowler
Born: 1 September 1969, Troon, Cornwall
Height: 6ft 1in **Weight:** 12st
Nickname: Berth, Penbers, Sir Leonard,
Denzil
County debut: 1989
County cap: 1994
1st-Class 50s: 25
1st-Class 100s: 4
1st-Class 5 w. in innings: 3
1st-Class catches: 78
One-Day 5 w. in innings: 3
Place in batting averages: 97th av. 31.21
(1998 40th av. 39.73)
Place in bowling averages: 127th av. 38.68
Strike rate: 84.26 (career 72.35)
Parents: Gerald and Wendy
Wife and date of marriage: Rebecca, 9 November 1996
Children: Georgia Lily, 4 March 1998
Family links with cricket: Father played in local leagues in Cornwall and is now a
qualified umpire instructor
Education: Troon County Primary; Camborne Comprehensive
Qualifications: 3 O-levels, 3 CSEs, coaching certificate
Career outside cricket: Coaching
Off-season: Coaching
Overseas tours: Druids to Zimbabwe 1988; Northants to Durban 1992, to Cape Town
1993, to Zimbabwe 1995, 1998, to Johannesburg 1996
Cricketers particularly admired: Ian Botham, David Gower, Dennis Lillee,
Viv Richards, Eldine Baptiste

Young players to look out for: Graeme Swann, Michael Davies, David Sales
Other sports played: Football, golf
Other sports followed: Football (West Ham United), rugby (Northampton Saints)
Relaxations: Listening to music, watching films and comedy programmes, 'walking my Irish setter'
Extras: Had football trials for Plymouth Argyle but came to Northampton for cricket trials instead. Took wicket with first ball in first-class cricket – Mark Taylor caught behind, June 1989. Played for England YC v New Zealand YC 1989. Scored maiden Championship century (102*) v Middlesex at Northampton in June 1998. Took only the second Sunday/National League hat-trick in Northants history v Somerset at Northampton in 1999
Opinions on cricket: 'Two divisions in one-day cricket has meant more competitive cricket. Hopefully this will be the same with the two-divisional Championship system, but wickets must improve. What were they thinking of by way of a 25-overs league? Are they mad? Do we not play enough cricket as it is? Quality not quantity!'
Best batting: 128 Northamptonshire v Warwickshire, Northampton 1998
Best bowling: 5-37 Northamptonshire v Glamorgan, Swansea 1993

1999 Season

	M	Inns	NO	Runs	HS	Avge	100s	50s	Ct	St	O	M	Runs	Wkts	Avge	Best	5wl	10wM
Test																		
All First	18	25	2	718	123*	31.21	1	4	6	-	266.5	89	735	19	38.68	3-13	-	-
1-day Int																		
NatWest	3	3	1	38	24*	19.00	-	-	1	-	22	2	100	2	50.00	2-41	-	
B & H																		
1-day Lge	14	14	4	379	64*	37.90	-	2	6	-	108	3	504	27	18.66	5-41	1	

Career Performances

	M	Inns	NO	Runs	HS	Avge	100s	50s	Ct	St	Balls	Runs	Wkts	Avge	Best	5wl	10wM
Test																	
All First	133	197	23	4483	128	25.76	4	25	78	-	12518	6787	173	39.23	5-37	3	-
1-day Int																	
NatWest	23	16	2	358	79	25.57	-	3	8	-	997	716	19	37.68	5-56	1	
B & H	29	23	5	529	62	29.38	-	2	7	-	1250	890	25	35.60	3-22	-	
1-day Lge	124	101	21	1956	81*	24.45	-	10	29	-	4137	3542	124	28.56	5-36	2	

PENNEY, T. L. Warwickshire

Name: Trevor Lionel Penney
Role: Right-hand bat, leg-break bowler
Born: 12 June 1968, Harare, Zimbabwe
Height: 6ft **Weight:** 11st 2lbs
Nickname: TP, Blondie
County debut: 1992
County cap: 1994
1000 runs in a season: 2
1st-Class 50s: 34
1st-Class 100s: 14
1st-Class catches: 80
1st-Class stumpings: 2
Place in batting averages: 158th av. 24.61
(1998 160th av. 23.50)
Strike rate: (career 43.16)
Parents: George and Bets
Wife and date of marriage: Deborah-Anne,
19 December 1992

Children: Samantha Anne, 20 August 1995; Kevin, 7 June 1998
Family links with cricket: Father played club cricket. Brother Stephen captained
Zimbabwe Schools
Education: Blakiston Junior School; Prince Edward Boys High School, Zimbabwe
Qualifications: 3 O-levels
Career outside cricket: Tobacco buyer. Zimbabwe B cricket coach
Off-season: Coaching Zimbabwe B and playing club cricket. Getting fit
Overseas tours: Zimbabwe U24 to England 1984; Zimbabwe to Sri Lanka 1987;
ICC Associates team to Australia (Youth World Cup) 1987-88
Overseas teams played for: Old Hararians, Zimbabwe 1983-89 and 1992-98;
Scarborough, Perth 1989-90; Boland, South Africa 1991-92; Avendale, South Africa
1990-91
Cricketers particularly admired: Colin Bland, Ian Botham, Allan Donald,
Steve Waugh
Young players to look out for: Shaun Pollock
Other sports played: Hockey (Zimbabwe and Africa), squash, tennis, golf and white
water rafting
Other sports followed: Basketball (Chicago Bulls), American football (San Francisco
49ers), Formula 1 motor racing
Injuries: Out for four weeks with a groin injury
Relaxations: 'Playing golf and drinking cold Castles on Lake Kariba. Spending time
with my family'
Extras: Captained the ICC Associates team at the Youth World Cup in 1987-88.

Played for Zimbabwe against Sri Lanka in 1987. Played hockey for Zimbabwe from 1984-87 and also made the African team who played Asia in 1987. Qualified to play for England in 1992. Captained Old Hararians to victory in three Zimbabwe domestic trophies 1998-99

Opinions on cricket: 'The wickets played on generally in county cricket are not good enough. Most games finish in two or three days, which does not benefit anyone but the bowler. Two divisions will help tremendously.'

Best batting: 151 Warwickshire v Middlesex, Lord's 1992

Best bowling: 3-18 Mashonaland v Mashonaland U24, Harare 1993-94

1999 Season

	M	Inns	NO	Runs	HS	Avge	100s	50s	Ct	St	O	M	Runs	Wkts	Avge	Best	5wI	10wM
Test																		
All First	15	24	3	517	73	24.61	-	3	6	2	2	1	1	0	-	-	-	-
1-day Int																		
NatWest	2	2	0	27	21	13.50	-	-	1	-								
B & H	2	2	0	29	20	14.50	-	-	-	-								
1-day Lge	11	11	3	189	55	23.62	-	1	3	-								

Career Performances

	M	Inns	NO	Runs	HS	Avge	100s	50s	Ct	St	Balls	Runs	Wkts	Avge	Best	5wI	10wM
Test																	
All First	141	226	41	7383	151	39.90	14	34	80	2	259	184	6	30.66	3-18	-	-
1-day Int																	
NatWest	29	27	6	539	90	25.66	-	2	16	-	13	16	1	16.00	1-8	-	
B & H	30	27	6	610	57 *	29.04	-	3	11	1							
1-day Lge	116	101	34	1873	83 *	27.95	-	8	41	-	6	2	0	-	-	-	

---

66. What was significant about the first-wicket partnership between J.T. Brown and J. Tunnicliffe for Yorkshire v Derbyshire at Chesterfield in 1898?

PETERS, S. D. Essex

Name: Stephen David Peters
Role: Right-hand bat, leg-break bowler
Born: 10 December 1978, Harold Wood
Height: 5ft 11in **Weight:** 11st
Nickname: Geezer, Pedro
County debut: 1996
1st-Class 50s: 5
1st-Class 100s: 2
1st-Class catches: 28
Place in batting averages: 114th av. 28.76
(1998 163rd av. 23.04)
Strike rate: 23.00 (career 23.00)
Parents: Brian and Lesley
Marital status: Single
Family links with cricket: 'All family is
linked with Upminster CC. The best bar in
Upminster!!'
Education: Upminster Junior School;
Coopers Coborn and Company School

Qualifications: 9 GCSEs
Career outside cricket: 'Making sure all bars in Romford sell Budweiser!'
Off-season: 'Enjoying the time off before Xmas, then back into training'
Overseas tours: Essex U14 to Barbados; Essex U15 to Hong Kong; England U19 to
Pakistan 1996-97, to South Africa (including Youth World Cup) 1997-98
Cricketers particularly admired: 'Anyone who plays at the top level'
Young players to look out for: Tim Phillips, Barry Hyam, Michael Davies
Other sports played: Football, golf
Other sports followed: Football (West Ham United)
Injuries: Back injury, but no time off needed
Relaxations: Sky Digital, bars, sleep
Extras: The Sir John Hobbs Jubilee Memorial Prize 1994; a *Daily Telegraph* regional
batting award 1994. Represented England at U14, U15, U17 and U19. Scored 100
(110) on county debut v Cambridge University at Fenner's 1996. Essex Young Player
of the Year 1996. Scored a century (107) and was Man of the Match in the U19 World
Cup final in South Africa 1997-98
Opinions on cricket: 'Short leg fielders should be paid more, and day/night cricket is
the way forward.'
Best batting: 110 Essex v Cambridge University, Fenner's 1996
Best bowling: 1-19 Essex v Oxford University, Chelmsford 1999

1999 Season

	M	Inns	NO	Runs	HS	Avge	100s	50s	Ct	St	O	M	Runs	Wkts	Avge	Best	5wl	10wM
Test																		
All First	11	15	2	374	99	28.76	-	2	13	-	3.5	0	19	1	19.00	1-19	-	-
1-day Int																		
NatWest																		
B & H																		
1-day Lge	9	8	1	102	28 *	14.57	-	-	3	-								

Career Performances

	M	Inns	NO	Runs	HS	Avge	100s	50s	Ct	St	Balls	Runs	Wkts	Avge	Best	5wl	10wM
Test																	
All First	31	48	6	1135	110	27.02	2	5	28	-	23	19	1	19.00	1-19	-	-
1-day Int																	
NatWest	1	1	0	6	6	6.00	-	-	1	-							
B & H	7	5	1	86	58 *	21.50	-	1	2	-							
1-day Lge	28	22	1	214	54	10.19	-	1	8	-							

PETTINI, M. L. Essex

Name: Mark Lewis Pettini
Role: Right-hand bat, right-arm medium bowler
Born: 7 August 1983, Brighton, East Sussex
Height: 5ft 11in **Weight:** 10st 8lbs
County debut: No first-team appearance
Parents: Pauline and Max
Marital status: Single
Family links with cricket: 'Brother Tom currently captains Cambridgeshire U14 county side. Mum and Dad are very keen supporters while Grandad plays a demon game of beach cricket'
Education: Avalon Primary School, Sydney, Australia; Meridian Primary School; Comberton Village College and Hills Road Sixth Form College, Cambridge
Qualifications: 10 GCSEs, Level 1 cricket coaching award
Off-season: Studying for A-levels
Cricketers particularly admired: Brian Lara, Sachin Tendulkar, Steve Waugh

Young players to look out for: 'Brother Tom'
Other sports played: Tennis, swimming ('keeping fit'), table tennis
Other sports followed: Tennis, basketball
Relaxations: Fishing, watching sport, sleeping
Extras: Captained Cambridgeshire county sides from U11-U16. Took hat-trick against Bedfordshire U12. Highest score of 173* v Hampshire U16 1999
Opinions on cricket: 'The best game there is, the best game there was, and the best game there ever will be.'

PHILLIPS, B. J. Kent

Name: Ben James Phillips
Role: Right-hand bat, right-arm
fast-medium bowler
Born: 30 September 1975, Lewisham
Height: 6ft 6in **Weight:** 15st 2lbs
Nickname: Bus, Action, Barbie Doll,
Bomb, Golden Arm
County debut: 1996
1st-Class 50s: 2
1st-Class 100s: 1
1st-Class 5 w. in innings: 2
1st-Class catches: 8
Place in batting averages: (1998 265th
av. 11.94)
Place in bowling averages: 141st av. 54.58
(1997 9th av. 19.93)
Strike rate: (career 56.87)
Parents: Trevor and Glynis
Marital status: Single

Family links with cricket: Father and brother keen club cricketers
Education: St Joseph's Primary, Bromley; Langley Park School for Boys, Beckenham; Langley Park Sixth Form
Qualifications: 9 GCSEs and 3 A-levels
Career outside cricket: 'Keeping my options open, but hopefully something sports related. Almost joined Met Police before I was offered contract with Kent'
Overseas teams played for: University of Queensland, Australia 1993-94; Cape Technikon Greenpoint, Cape Town, South Africa 1994-95, 1996-98; University of Western Australia, Perth 1998-99
Cricketers particularly admired: Carl Hooper, Courtney Walsh, Dennis Lillee
Young players to look out for: Rob Key
Other sports followed: Football (West Ham United) and basketball (Chicago Bulls)
Injuries: Missed 1999 season with shoulder injury

Relaxations: 'Enjoy watching a decent film or listening to music. Slothing it on a beach somewhere sunny in the off-season'
Extras: Represented England U19 Schools in 1993-94. Set Langley Park School record for the fastest half century, off 11 balls
Opinions on cricket: 'The problem with English cricket is the lack of adequate off-season structure in place to improve playing standards. I would like to see 12-month contracts therefore allowing players to develop aspects of their game during the off-season.'
Best batting: 100* Kent v Lancashire, Old Trafford 1997
Best bowling: 5-47 Kent v Sussex, Horsham 1997

1999 Season (did not make any first-class or one-day appearances)

Career Performances

	M	Inns	NO	Runs	HS	Avge	100s	50s	Ct	St	Balls	Runs	Wkts	Avge	Best	5wI	10wM
Test																	
All First	27	39	4	584	100 *	16.68	1	2	8	-	3697	1914	65	29.44	5-47	2	-
1-day Int																	
NatWest	2	1	1	9	9 *	-	-	-	1	-	90	67	3	22.33	3-14	-	
B & H	4	2	1	1	1 *	1.00	-	-	1	-	152	103	6	17.16	3-13	-	
1-day Lge	17	8	2	49	29	8.16	-	-	7	-	520	418	16	26.12	3-31	-	

PHILLIPS, N. C.   Durham

Name: Nicholas Charles Phillips
Role: Right-hand bat, off-spin bowler
Born: 10 May 1974, Pembury, Kent
Height: 6ft **Weight:** 11st 4lbs
Nickname: Milky, Spoons, Beastie, Nicky P
County debut: 1994 (Sussex),
1998 (Durham)
1st-Class 50s: 3
1st-Class 5 w. in innings: 3
1st-Class 10 w. in match: 1
1st-Class catches: 22
Place in batting averages: 263rd av. 11.66
(1998 275th av. 9.86)
Place in bowling averages: 124th av. 37.61
(1998 134th av. 43.42)
Strike rate: 70.66 (career 92.17)
Parents: Robert and Joan
Marital status: Single

Family links with cricket: Father plays club cricket for Hastings. Represents Sussex Over 50s and has represented Kent 2nd XI, Kent League XI and has scored over 100 club 100s

Education: Hilden Grange School, Tonbridge; St Thomas's School, Winchelsea; William Parker School, Hastings

Qualifications: 8 GCSEs, NCA coaching award

Overseas tours: Sussex U18 to India 1990-91

Overseas teams played for: Maris CC, Auckland 1996-97

Cricketers particularly admired: Eddie Hemmings, Derek Randall

Other sports followed: Hockey, football

Relaxations: Spending time with friends and girlfriend. Listening to music. Eating out and socialising with fellow players

Extras: Represented England U19 in home series against West Indies U19 in 1993. Has played hockey for Sussex U14 and U16. Released by Sussex at the end of the 1997 season and joined Durham. Returned the best figures for a Durham spinner since the county attained first-class status with his 12-268 v Glamorgan at Cardiff 1999

Best batting: 53 Sussex v Young Australia, Hove 1995

Best bowling: 6-97 Durham v Glamorgan, Cardiff 1999

1999 Season

	M	Inns	NO	Runs	HS	Avge	100s	50s	Ct	St	O	M	Runs	Wkts	Avge	Best	5wI	10wM
Test																		
All First	6	9	0	105	42	11.66	-	-	5	-	212	41	677	18	37.61	6-97	2	1
1-day Int																		
NatWest	1	1	0	15	15	15.00	-	-	-	-	10	0	35	1	35.00	1-35	-	
B & H																		
1-day Lge	16	14	2	109	19 *	9.08	-	-	5	-	124.5	1	599	22	27.22	4-13	-	

Career Performances

	M	Inns	NO	Runs	HS	Avge	100s	50s	Ct	St	Balls	Runs	Wkts	Avge	Best	5wI	10wM
Test																	
All First	42	60	12	782	53	16.29	-	3	22	-	6729	3536	73	48.43	6-97	3	1
1-day Int																	
NatWest	4	3	0	37	21	12.33	-	-	-	-	198	94	3	31.33	2-16	-	
B & H	7	6	1	34	13	6.80	-	-	2	-	295	257	7	36.71	3-48	-	
1-day Lge	47	35	7	284	38 *	10.14	-	-	11	-	1684	1444	40	36.10	4-13	-	

PHILLIPS, T. J.   Essex

Name: Timothy James Phillips
Role: Left-hand bat, slow left-arm bowler
Born: 13 March 1981, Cambridge
Height: 6ft 1in **Weight:** 11st 5lb
Nickname: TP
County debut: 1999
1st-Class catches: 1
Strike rate: 57.00 (career 57.00)
Parents: Martin (deceased) and Carolyn
Marital status: Single
Family links with cricket: Father played in
Lancashire League. Brother Nick plays local
village cricket
Education: Felsted Preparatory School;
Felsted School; 'starting at Durham
University, September 2000'
Qualifications: 10 GCSEs, 3 A-levels
Career outside cricket: Gap year student
Off-season: England U19 tour to Malaysia and Sri Lanka
Overseas tours: Felsted School to Australia 1995-96; England U19 to Malaysia and
(Youth World Cup) Sri Lanka 1999-2000
Cricketers particularly admired: David Gower, Phil Tufnell
Young players to look out for: Mark Pettini
Other sports played: Hockey (Essex Schools U14, U15; East of England U21 trials),
squash, golf
Other sports followed: Football (Cambridge United FC)
Relaxations: 'Spending time with friends at the local pub; cinema, travelling'
Extras: Winner of *Daily Telegraph* U14 National Bowling Award 1995. Holmwoods
School Cricketer of the Year runner-up 1997 and 1998. Broke Felsted School record
for runs scored in a season
Opinions on cricket: 'More games should be played spanning the weekend. National
League should have more day/night games.'
Best batting: 16 Essex v Sri Lanka A, Chelmsford 1999
Best bowling: 4-42 Essex v Sri Lanka A, Chelmsford 1999

---

67. Which England Test wicket-keeper took
a hat-trick with the ball v Essex at Clacton in 1965?

1999 Season

	M	Inns	NO	Runs	HS	Avge	100s	50s	Ct	St	O	M	Runs	Wkts	Avge	Best	5wI	10wM
Test																		
All First	3	4	0	27	16	6.75	-	-	1	-	76	17	278	8	34.75	4-42	-	-
1-day Int																		
NatWest																		
B & H																		
1-day Lge	1	1	0	0	0	0.00	-	-	1	-	8	0	56	2	28.00	2-56	-	

Career Performances

	M	Inns	NO	Runs	HS	Avge	100s	50s	Ct	St	Balls	Runs	Wkts	Avge	Best	5wI	10wM
Test																	
All First	3	4	0	27	16	6.75	-	-	1	-	456	278	8	34.75	4-42	-	-
1-day Int																	
NatWest																	
B & H																	
1-day Lge	1	1	0	0	0	0.00	-	-	1	-	48	56	2	28.00	2-56	-	

PIERSON, A. R. K.   Somerset

Name: Adrian Roger Kirshaw Pierson
Role: Right-hand bat, off-spin bowler
Born: 21 July 1963, Enfield, Middlesex
Height: 6ft 4in **Weight:** 12st
Nickname: Skirlog, Stick, Bunny, Logga
County debut: 1985 (Warwickshire),
1993 (Leicestershire), 1998 (Somerset)
County cap: 1995 (Leicestershire)
50 wickets in a season: 1
1st-Class 50s: 5
1st-Class 100s: 1
1st-Class 5 w. in innings: 14
1st-Class catches: 83
One-Day 5 w. in innings: 1
Place in batting averages: 259th av. 12.90
(1998 138th av. 25.76)
Place in bowling averages: 147th av. 60.69
(1998 131st av. 40.09)
Strike rate: 125.23 (career 74.41)
Parents: Patrick and Patricia
Wife and date of marriage: Helen Majella, 28 September 1990

Children: Eleanor, 7 February 1997
Education: Lochinver House, Potters Bar, Herts; Kent College, Canterbury;
Hatfield Polytechnic
Qualifications: 8 O-levels, 2 A-levels, ECB advanced coach, private pilot's licence
Career outside cricket: 'Marketing account handler, picture framing, sub-editing, coaching, liaison officer for World Masters tournaments etc'
Off-season: 'Working towards an airline transport pilot's licence'
Overseas tours: Warwickshire to Barbados, St Lucia, Trinidad; Leicestershire to Jamaica, Bloemfontein, Durban
Overseas teams played for: Walmer CC, Port Elizabeth 1985-90; Manicaland, Zimbabwe 1990-91
Cricketers particularly admired: Tony Greig, Phil Edmonds, John Emburey
Young players to look out for: Marcus Trescothick, Darren Maddy, Matthew Brimson
Other sports played: Golf – 'won the County Cricketers' Golf Society Silver Salver with my mate Colin Metson and won the *Daily Mail* "Mijas" trophy with Chris Balderstone in 1996'
Other sports followed: 'Any sport except horse racing, but especially Formula 1 motor racing'
Injuries: Out for three weeks with a side strain
Relaxations: Flying, driving, reading, chess 'and playing with my daughter'
Extras: On Lord's groundstaff 1984-85 and on Warwickshire staff from 1985-91. First Championship wicket was Viv Richards. Won two Gold Awards in the Benson and Hedges. Released by Leicestershire at the end of the 1997 season and joined Somerset
Opinions on cricket: 'I believe counties will soon be playing one-day cricket only, with the longer game being played by regional sides picked from these teams in order to select a Test side. As time goes on there is more interest in one-day cricket publicly and so market forces will push the game this way. PS: Off-spinners (at least "orthodox" ones) are becoming an endangered species. Change the lbw rule – pads are for protecting the legs!!'
Best batting: 108* Somerset v Sussex, Hove 1998
Best bowling: 8-42 Leicestershire v Warwickshire, Edgbaston 1994

1999 Season

	M	Inns	NO	Runs	HS	Avge	100s	50s	Ct	St	O	M	Runs	Wkts	Avge	Best	5wI	10wM
Test																		
All First	13	13	3	129	66	12.90	-	1	5	-	271.2	52	789	13	60.69	4-131	-	-
1-day Int																		
NatWest	2	0	0	0	0	-	-	-	-	-	20	1	71	4	17.75	2-31	-	
B & H																		
1-day Lge	2	2	2	1	1*	-	-	-	1	-	15	0	77	2	38.50	1-35	-	

Career Performances

	M	Inns	NO	Runs	HS	Avge	100s	50s	Ct	St	Balls	Runs	Wkts	Avge	Best	5wI	10wM
Test																	
All First	173	213	66	2515	108 *	17.10	1	5	83	-	26490	13446	356	37.76	8-42	14	-
1-day Int																	
NatWest	14	7	2	42	20 *	8.40	-	-	2	-	854	448	13	34.46	3-20	-	
B & H	20	14	10	57	11	14.25	-	-	6	-	950	584	14	41.71	3-34	-	
1-day Lge	76	40	16	219	29 *	9.12	-	-	34	-	2703	2222	65	34.18	5-36	1	

PIPE, D. J.   Worcestershire

Name: David James Pipe
Role: Right-hand bat, wicket-keeper
Born: 16 December 1977, Bradford
Height: 5ft 10in **Weight:** 11st 7lbs
Nickname: Pipes, Pipey, Pip
County debut: 1998
1st-Class catches: 2
1st-Class stumpings: 1
Parents: David and Dorothy
Marital status: Single
Family links with cricket: 'My dad and
uncle played in the local league'
Education: Stocks Lane Primary School;
Hainsworth Moor Middle School;
Queensbury School; BICC
Qualifications: 8 GCSEs, BTEC National in
Business and Finance, HND Leisure Studies,
senior coaching award
Career outside cricket: Coaching and studying
Off-season: Playing and training in Manly, Australia
Overseas teams played for: Leeming Spartans CC and South Metropolitan Cricket
Association, Perth 1998-99; Manly CC, Australia 1999-2000
Cricketers particularly admired: 'Any player that consistently puts in 100 per cent
effort for both their preparation and participation in the game of cricket'
Young players to look out for: 'All the up-and-coming young players at
Worcestershire'
Other sports followed: Rugby league (Bradford Bulls), football (Bradford City), AFL
(West Coast Eagles), boxing ('all British fighters'), golf
Relaxations: Watching sport, watching films, playing golf, socialising with friends,
listening to music
Extras: MCC School of Merit Wilf Slack Memorial Trophy winner 1995. Awarded
2nd XI cap 1999

Opinions on cricket: 'Wickets must be improved and all 2nd XI Championship games should be played over four days.'
Best batting: 16 Worcestershire v Sri Lanka A, Worcester 1999

1999 Season

	M	Inns	NO	Runs	HS	Avge	100s	50s	Ct	St	O	M	Runs	Wkts	Avge	Best	5wI	10wM
Test																		
All First	1	2	0	21	16	10.50	-	-	-	-								
1-day Int																		
NatWest																		
B & H																		
1-day Lge																		

Career Performances

	M	Inns	NO	Runs	HS	Avge	100s	50s	Ct	St	Balls	Runs	Wkts	Avge	Best	5wI	10wM
Test																		
All First	2	2	0	21	16	10.50	-	-	2	1							
1-day Int																		
NatWest																		
B & H																		
1-day Lge																		

PIPER, K. J. Warwickshire

Name: Keith John Piper
Role: Right-hand bat, wicket-keeper
Born: 18 December 1969, Leicester
Height: 5ft 7in **Weight:** 10st 8lbs
Nickname: Tubbsy, Garden Boy
County debut: 1989
County cap: 1992
1st-Class 50s: 10
1st-Class 100s: 2
1st-Class catches: 409
1st-Class stumpings: 28
Place in batting averages: 187th av. 21.71
(1998 238th av. 15.72)
Strike rate: (career 28.00)
Parents: John and Charlotte
Marital status: Single
Family links with cricket: Father plays club
cricket in Leicester

Education: Seven Sisters Junior; Somerset Senior
Qualifications: Senior coaching award, basketball coaching award, volleyball coaching award
Overseas tours: Haringey Cricket College to Barbados 1986, to Trinidad 1987, to Jamaica 1988; Warwickshire to La Manga 1989, to St Lucia 1990; England A to India 1994-95, to Pakistan 1995-96
Overseas teams played for: Desmond Haynes's XI, Barbados v Haringey Cricket College
Cricketers particularly admired: Jack Russell, Alec Stewart, Dermot Reeve, Colin Metson
Other sports followed: Snooker, football, tennis
Relaxations: Music, eating
Extras: London Young Cricketer of the Year 1989 and in the last five 1992. Played for England YC 1989. Was batting partner (116*) to Brian Lara when he reached his 501*, v Durham, Edgbaston 1994
Best batting: 116* Warwickshire v Durham, Edgbaston 1994
Best bowling: 1-57 Warwickshire v Nottinghamshire, Edgbaston 1992

1999 Season

	M	Inns	NO	Runs	HS	Avge	100s	50s	Ct	St	O	M	Runs	Wkts	Avge	Best	5wl	10wM
Test																		
All First	5	7	0	152	66	21.71	-	1	8	1								
1-day Int																		
NatWest	1	1	0	15	15	15.00	-	-	1	-								
B & H	1	1	0	29	29	29.00	-	-	2	2								
1-day Lge	5	2	1	38	38 *	38.00	-	-	6	-								

Career Performances

	M	Inns	NO	Runs	HS	Avge	100s	50s	Ct	St	Balls	Runs	Wkts	Avge	Best	5wl	10wM
Test																	
All First	156	221	34	3632	116 *	19.42	2	10	409	28	28	57	1	57.00	1-57	-	-
1-day Int																	
NatWest	29	14	6	138	19	17.25	-	-	42	3							
B & H	25	17	6	128	29	11.63	-	-	35	5							
1-day Lge	94	50	25	401	38 *	16.04	-	-	91	21							

68. Who took ten wickets in the space of 52 deliveries
for Yorkshire v Nottinghamshire at Leeds in 1932?

POLLARD, P. R.   Worcestershire

Name: Paul Raymond Pollard
Role: Left-hand opening bat, right-arm
medium bowler
Born: 24 September 1968, Carlton,
Nottinghamshire
Height: 5ft 11in **Weight:** 12st
Nickname: Polly, Sugar Ray
County debut: 1987 (Nottinghamshire),
1999 (Worcestershire)
County cap: 1992 (Nottinghamshire)
1000 runs in a season: 3
1st-Class 50s: 43
1st-Class 100s: 13
1st-Class catches: 150
One-Day 100s: 5
Place in batting averages: 203rd av. 19.84
(1998 220th av. 17.28)
Strike rate: (career 68.50)
Parents: Eric (deceased) and Mary
Wife and date of marriage: Kate, 14 March 1992
Education: Gedling Comprehensive
Overseas teams played for: Southern Districts, Brisbane 1988; North Perth 1990
Cricketers particularly admired: David Gower, Derek Randall, Ian Botham,
Graham Gooch
Other sports followed: Football, golf, ice hockey
Relaxations: Watching videos, playing golf and music
Extras: Made debut for Nottinghamshire 2nd XI in 1985. Worked in Nottinghamshire
CCC office on a Youth Training Scheme. Shared stands of 222 and 282 with Tim
Robinson in the same game v Kent 1989. Was youngest player to reach 1000 runs for
Nottinghamshire. Released by Nottinghamshire at end of 1998 season and joined
Worcestershire for 1999
Opinions on cricket: 'The one bouncer rule should be abolished.'
Best batting: 180 Nottinghamshire v Derbyshire, Trent Bridge 1993
Best bowling: 2-79 Nottinghamshire v Gloucestershire, Bristol 1993

1999 Season

	M	Inns	NO	Runs	HS	Avge	100s	50s	Ct	St	O	M	Runs	Wkts	Avge	Best	5wI	10wM
Test																		
All First	11	21	2	377	60	19.84	-	3	2	-								
1-day Int																		
NatWest	2	2	0	62	47	31.00	-	-	-	-								
B & H																		
1-day Lge	7	7	1	266	70	44.33	-	3	2	-								

Career Performances

	M	Inns	NO	Runs	HS	Avge	100s	50s	Ct	St	Balls	Runs	Wkts	Avge	Best	5wI	10wM
Test																		
All First	168	296	22	8724	180	31.83	13	43	150	-	274	268	4	67.00	2-79	-	-	
1-day Int																		
NatWest	15	15	2	431	96	33.15	-	2	4	-	18	9	0	-		-	-	
B & H	32	31	2	863	104	29.75	1	7	11	-								
1-day Lge	107	97	10	2996	132 *	34.43	4	16	42	-								

PORTER, J. J.   Surrey

Name: Joseph James Porter
Role: Left-hand bat
Born: 5 May 1980
Height: 5ft 11in **Weight:** 12st 7lbs
Nickame: JP
County debut: No first-team appearance
Parents: Bob and Judy
Marital status: Single
Education: Rokeby; St John's, Leatherhead;
Oxford Brookes University
Qualifications: 7 GCSEs, 3 A-levels
Off-season: At university
Overseas tours: Surrey Cricket Board to
Barbados 1999
Overseas teams played for: Havelock North,
Hawkes Bay, New Zealand 1998-99
Cricketers particularly admired:
Alec Stewart, Jimmy Adams, Brian Lara
Young players to look out for: Andrew Hollingsworth, Tim Murtagh
Other sports played: Rugby (Sutton and Epsom Rugby Club)
Other sports followed: Rugby (London Wasps)

Relaxations: Watching films
Extras: The Cricket Society's Wetherell Award for the leading all-rounder in schools cricket 1998

POWELL, J. C. Essex

Name: Jonathan Christopher Powell
Role: Right-hand bat, off-spin bowler
Born: 13 June 1979, Harold Wood
Height: 5ft 11in **Weight:** 11st 2lbs
Nickname: Ralphy, Powelly
County debut: 1996 (one-day),
1997 (first-class)
1st-Class catches: 2
Strike rate: (career 264.00)
Parents: Geoff and Joan
Marital status: Single
Family links with cricket: Brother Mark was
on the Essex staff for two years and now
plays Minor Counties cricket for Norfolk.
Father plays local cricket
Education: St Peter's C of E Primary School,
Brentwood; Brentwood County High;
Chelmsford College

Qualifications: 9 GCSEs, NCA coaching award (level 2)
Overseas tours: Essex U14 to Barbados, to Hong Kong; England U19 to Pakistan 1996-97, to South Africa 1997-98; England A to Kenya and Sri Lanka 1997-98
Cricketers particularly admired: Ronnie Irani
Young players to look out for: Robert Key, Chris Read, Stephen Peters
Other sports played: Golf
Other sports followed: Football (Arsenal FC)
Relaxations: Music, TV and going out
Extras: Winner of the *Daily Telegraph* U15 Bowling Award in 1994. Was a member of the England U19 side that won the Youth World Cup 1997-98. Released by Essex at end of 1999 season
Opinions on cricket: '2nd XI games should be played on first-class grounds. Lunch and tea should be longer.'
Best batting: 6 England A v Sri Lanka A, Moratuwa 1997-98
Best bowling: 1-109 Essex v Leicestershire, Leicester 1997

1999 Season

	M	Inns	NO	Runs	HS	Avge	100s	50s	Ct	St	O	M	Runs	Wkts	Avge	Best	5wI	10wM
Test																		
All First	1	0	0	0	0	-	-	-	2	-								
1-day Int																		
NatWest																		
B & H																		
1-day Lge																		

Career Performances

	M	Inns	NO	Runs	HS	Avge	100s	50s	Ct	St	Balls	Runs	Wkts	Avge	Best	5wI	10wM
Test																	
All First	3	2	1	10	6	10.00	-	-	2	-	264	137	1	137.00	1-109	-	-
1-day Int																	
NatWest																	
B & H																	
1-day Lge	6	3	1	4	2	2.00	-	-	1	-	114	125	4	31.25	2-10	-

POWELL, M. J.   Northamptonshire

Name: Mark John Powell
Role: Right-hand bat, off-spin bowler
Born: 4 November 1980, Northampton
Height: 5ft 11in **Weight:** 11st
Nickname: Powelly, Perfect, Piggy, Cosy
County debut: No first-team appearance
Parents: David and Philippa
Marital status: Single
Education: Flore Primary, Northants;
Campion School, Bugbrooke, Northants;
Loughborough University
Qualifications: 10 GCSEs, 3 A-levels
Career outside cricket: Student
Off-season: University
Cricketers particularly admired:
Matthew Hayden, David Ripley, Mark and
Steve Waugh
Young players to look out for:
Graeme Swann, Michael Davies, Richard Logan, Monty Panesar
Other sports played: Football, golf, tennis
Other sports followed: Football (Tottenham Hotspur), rugby (Northampton Saints)
Relaxations: Listening to music, going to the cinema, 'going out with mates'

Extras: Played for England U15 in inaugural Youth World Cup 1996; knocked out in semi-finals by Pakistan at Headingley. Played for Midlands U19 v Australia U19 1999
Opinions on cricket: 'Pitches have to improve for first- and second-class games, and also practice facilities. Less matches so that there is more time to work on your game in between fixtures, injuries aren't carried through from match to match, and players are more hungry to perform.'

POWELL, M. J.   Warwickshire

Name: Michael James Powell
Role: Right-hand bat, right-arm medium bowler
Born: 5 April 1975, Bolton
Height: 5ft 11in **Weight:** 11st
Nickname: Arthur, Powelly
County debut: 1996
County cap: 1999
1st-Class 50s: 4
1st-Class 100s: 3
1st-Class catches: 22
Place in batting averages: 68th av. 35.28
(1998 148th av. 24.33)
Strike rate: (career 90.00)
Parents: Terry and Pat
Wife and date of marriage:
Sarah, 26 October 1996
Family links with cricket: 'Dad loves the
game.' Brother played for Warwickshire youth teams
Education: Horwich Parish C of E School; Rivington and Blackrod High School, Horwich; Lawrence Sheriff Grammar School, Rugby
Qualifications: 6 GCSEs, 2 A-levels, basic and senior coaching awards
Career outside cricket: Coaching cricket and teaching
Off-season: 'Coaching, teaching and playing golf'
Overseas tours: England U18 to South Africa 1992-93 (captain), to Denmark 1993 (captain); England U19 to Sri Lanka 1993-94
Overseas teams played for: Avendale CC, Cape Town 1994-95, 1997-98
Cricketers particularly admired: Ian Botham, David Gower, Dermot Reeve
Young players to look out for: Ian Bell
Other sports played: Rugby (Warwickshire and Midlands)
Other sports followed: Golf, football (Manchester United)
Injuries: Out for two weeks with a back injury
Relaxations: 'Spending time with my wife, Sarah. Also a little golf'
Extras: 2nd XI Player of the Month June 1996. Scored a career-best 210 against

Somerset 2nd XI in July 1996. Became first uncapped Warwickshire player for 49 years to carry his bat, against Nottinghamshire at Edgbaston, June 1998. Awarded Warwickshire cap 1999

Opinions on cricket: 'Too many uneven wickets. One-day games played on a variety of days, and spectators would prefer an organised fixture list, so they know what they are watching and when.'

Best batting: 136 Warwickshire v Glamorgan, Cardiff 1999

Best bowling: 2-16 Warwickshire v Oxford University, The Parks 1998

1999 Season

	M	Inns	NO	Runs	HS	Avge	100s	50s	Ct	St	O	M	Runs	Wkts	Avge	Best	5wl	10wM
Test																		
All First	9	14	0	494	136	35.28	2	1	5	-	25	6	56	0	-		-	-
1-day Int																		
NatWest																		
B & H																		
1-day Lge	7	5	2	157	51	52.33	-	1	1	-	3	0	23	0	-		-	-

Career Performances

	M	Inns	NO	Runs	HS	Avge	100s	50s	Ct	St	Balls	Runs	Wkts	Avge	Best	5wl	10wM
Test																	
All First	27	45	1	1207	136	27.43	3	4	22	-	270	120	3	40.00	2-16	-	-
1-day Int																	
NatWest																	
B & H																	
1-day Lge	7	5	2	157	51	52.33	-	1	1	-	18	23	0	-		-	-

POWELL, M. J.   Glamorgan

Name: Michael John Powell
Role: Right-hand bat
Born: 3 February 1977, Abergavenny, South Wales
Height: 6ft 1in **Weight:** 14st 4lbs
Nickname: Powelly, Ape Man
County debut: 1997
1000 runs in a season: 1
1st-Class 50s: 10
1st-Class 100s: 3
1st-Class 200s: 1
1st-Class catches: 16
Place in batting averages: 13th av. 48.18 (1998 62nd av. 35.00)
Strike rate: 60.00 (career 64.00)

Parents: John and Linda
Family links with cricket: 'My dad played for Abergavenny CC and my uncle played for Glamorgan 2nd XI'
Education: Crickhowell Primary School; Crickhowell Secondary School; Pontypool College
Qualifications: 5 GCSEs, BTEC National Sports Science, NCA coaching award
Off-season: Training; playing rugby
Overseas teams played for: Western Suburbs, Brisbane 1996-97, Cornwall, New Zealand 1998-99
Cricketers particularly admired: Stuart Law, Mark Waugh
Young players to look out for: Dean Cosker, Vikram Solanki
Other sports played: Rugby (Crickhowell)
Relaxations: 'Going out with my girlfriend Emma and my friends'
Extras: Scored 200 not out on his first-class debut. Scored 1210 runs at 75.63 in the 1997 2nd XI Championship, the second-highest ever total behind Alan Brazier's 1212 for Surrey 2nd XI in 1948
Opinions on cricket: 'Play more day/night cricket.'
Best batting: 200* Glamorgan v Oxford University, The Parks 1997
Best bowling: 2-39 Glamorgan v Oxford University, The Parks 1999

1999 Season

	M	Inns	NO	Runs	HS	Avge	100s	50s	Ct	St	O	M	Runs	Wkts	Avge	Best	5wI	10wM
Test																		
All First	16	26	4	1060	164	48.18	2	5	5	-	20	1	100	2	50.00	2-39	-	-
1-day Int																		
NatWest	1	1	0	1	1	1.00	-	-	-	-								
B & H																		
1-day Lge	13	11	2	145	44	16.11	-	-	4	-								

Career Performances

	M	Inns	NO	Runs	HS	Avge	100s	50s	Ct	St	Balls	Runs	Wkts	Avge	Best	5wI	10wM
Test																	
All First	37	61	10	2186	200 *	42.86	4	10	16	-	128	111	2	55.50	2-39	-	-
1-day Int																	
NatWest	3	3	0	16	11	5.33	-	-	-	-							
B & H																	
1-day Lge	31	29	3	535	55	20.57	-										

PRATT, A.   Durham

Name: Andrew Pratt
Role: Left-hand bat, wicket-keeper
Born: 4 March 1975, Bishop Auckland
Height: 6ft **Weight:** 11st 3lbs
County debut: 1997
1st-Class catches: 4
Parents: Gordon and Brenda
Marital status: Single
Family links with cricket: Brother was with
MCC Young Cricketers for four years.
Younger brother plays for Durham County
Schools and father played in local leagues
Education: Parkside Comprehensive School;
Durham New College
Qualifications: 9 GCSEs, Advanced Diploma
in Information Technology, cricket coaching
certificate
Cricketers particularly admired:
Alan Knott, Jack Russell
Young players to look out for: Jimmy Daley
Other sports followed: Golf and football (Middlesbrough FC)
Extras: Played for Durham County Schools at all levels and for the North of England
U15. Played for MCC Young Cricketers for three years
Opinions on cricket: 'I think that the English game is very demanding both
physically and mentally. England should take note of Australia and play less matches,
especially one-day games. I also think that the better young English players should be
given more of a chance to play for their country.'
Best batting: 34 Durham v Lancashire, Riverside 1998

1999 Season

	M	Inns	NO	Runs	HS	Avge	100s	50s	Ct	St	O	M	Runs	Wkts	Avge	Best	5wl	10wM
Test																		
All First																		
1-day Int																		
NatWest																		
B & H																		
1-day Lge	2	2	0	29	26	14.50	-	-	-	-								

Career Performances

	M	Inns	NO	Runs	HS	Avge	100s	50s	Ct	St	Balls	Runs	Wkts	Avge	Best	5wl	10wM
Test																	
All First	3	3	0	40	34	13.33	-	-	4	-							
1-day Int																		
NatWest																		
B & H																			
1-day Lge	3	3	1	34	26	17.00	-	-	3	-							

PRICHARD, P. J.   Essex

Name: Paul John Prichard
Role: Right-hand bat,
cover/mid-wicket fielder
Born: 7 January 1965, Brentwood, Essex
Height: 5ft 10in **Weight:** 12st 7lbs
Nickname: Pablo
County debut: 1984
County cap: 1986
Benefit: 1996
1000 runs in a season: 8
1st-Class 50s: 92
1st-Class 100s: 28
1st-Class 200s: 3
1st-Class catches: 191
One-Day 100s: 6
Place in batting averages: 83rd av. 32.76
(1998 258th av. 13.16)
Strike rate: (career 144.50)
Parents: John and Margaret
Marital status: Single
Children: Danielle Jade, 23 April 1993; Alexander James, 16 August 1995
Family links with cricket: Father played club cricket in Essex
Education: Warley Primary School; Brentwood County High School
Qualifications: NCA coaching certificate
Off-season: Resting
Overseas tours: England A to Australia 1992-93
Overseas teams played for: VOB Cavaliers, Cape Town 1981-82; Sutherland, Sydney
1984-87; Waverley, Sydney 1987-92
Cricketers particularly admired: Malcolm Marshall, Allan Border, David Gower,
Mark Waugh, Greg Matthews
Young players to look out for: Vikram Solanki, Paul Franks

Other sports played: Golf, soccer
Other sports followed: Football (West Ham United)
Injuries: Out for six weeks with a wrist injury
Relaxations: Golf, sleeping, good wine
Extras: Shared county record first-wicket partnership of 316 v Kent in 1994 and county record second-wicket partnership of 403 v Leicestershire in 1990, both with Graham Gooch at Chelmsford. Britannic Assurance Cricketer of the Year 1992. Essex joint Player of the Year 1993. Appointed Essex captain for 1995. Won the B&H Gold Award for his 92 from 113 balls v Leicestershire in the 1998 final at Lord's. Resigned as Essex captain at end of 1998 season
Opinions on cricket: 'Floodlit cricket with one or two minor alterations should become a regular spectacle in county cricket as well as international in this country.'
Best batting: 245 Essex v Leicestershire, Chelmsford 1990
Best bowling: 1-28 Essex v Hampshire, Chelmsford 1991

1999 Season

	M	Inns	NO	Runs	HS	Avge	100s	50s	Ct	St	O	M	Runs	Wkts	Avge	Best	5wl	10wM
Test																		
All First	16	26	0	852	110	32.76	2	6	6	-								
1-day Int																		
NatWest																		
B & H																		
1-day Lge	9	9	0	183	49	20.33	-	-	2	-								

Career Performances

	M	Inns	NO	Runs	HS	Avge	100s	50s	Ct	St	Balls	Runs	Wkts	Avge	Best	5wl	10wM
Test																	
All First	306	498	46	15858	245	35.08	31	92	191	-	289	497	2	248.50	1-28	-	-
1-day Int																	
NatWest	34	33	5	1112	94	39.71	-	9	14	-							
B & H	56	53	8	1480	114	32.88	2	8	14	-							
1-day Lge	187	168	10	4202	107	26.59	4	19	52	-							

PRITTIPAUL, L. R. Hampshire

Name: Lawrence Roland Prittipaul
Role: Right-hand bat, right-arm fast bowler
Born: 19 October 1979, Portsmouth
Height: 6ft **Weight:** 13st 7lbs
Nickname: Caz
County debut: 1999 (one-day)

Parents: Roland and Christine
Marital status: Single
Family links with cricket: Father plays Hampshire league cricket. Cousin Shivnarine Chanderpaul plays for West Indies
Education: Meon First and Middle School, Portsmouth; St John's College, Southsea; Portsmouth College
Qualifications: 7 GCSEs
Off-season: 'Going abroad to play cricket for Milnerton, Cape Town, for six months'
Overseas teams played for: Milnerton, Cape Town 1999-2000
Cricketers particularly admired: Carl Hooper, Viv Richards, 'my Dad'
Young players to look out for: John Francis
Other sports played: Tennis, golf, basketball
Other sports followed: Football (Portsmouth)
Relaxations: Cricket, music

Extras: Scored first century at age 13 for St John's College. Played for Hants Colts from age 11 to 18; took 29 wickets and broke bowling record aged 11. Scored 185 for Hants U19 in 1998. Won Player of the Year award in Southern League 1998. Has played for Hants 2nd XI since age 18; scored over 1000 runs for Hants 2nd XI in 1999
Opinions on cricket: 'Enjoy whatever you are doing, be it batting, fielding, bowling or watching the game. Life is too short for worrying.'

1999 Season

	M	Inns	NO	Runs	HS	Avge	100s	50s	Ct	St	O	M	Runs	Wkts	Avge	Best	5wI	10wM
Test																		
All First																		
1-day Int																		
NatWest	3	3	0	66	30	22.00	-	-	3	-	26	1	125	4	31.25	2-53	-	
B & H																		
1-day Lge	2	0	0	0	0	-	-	-	1	-								

Career Performances

	M	Inns	NO	Runs	HS	Avge	100s	50s	Ct	St	Balls	Runs	Wkts	Avge	Best	5wI	10wM
Test																	
All First																	
1-day Int																	
NatWest	3	3	0	66	30	22.00	-	-	3	-	156	125	4	31.25	2-53	-	
B & H																	
1-day Lge	2	0	0	0	0	-	-	-	1	-							

PYEMONT, J. P.   Derbyshire

Name: James Patrick Pyemont
Role: Right-hand top-order bat,
off-spin bowler
Born: 10 April 1978, Eastbourne
Height: 6ft **Weight:** 11st 7lbs
Nickname: Pumper, Cleggers, Pyeko, Pye,
Pyemo, Piggy
County debut: 1999
1st-Class 50s: 4
1st-Class catches: 11
Place in batting averages: 169th av. 23.41
Parents: Christopher and Christina
Marital status: Single
Family links with cricket: Father played for
Cambridge University and Sussex 2nd XI
Education: St Bede's School, Eastbourne;
Tonbridge School, Kent; Trinity Hall,
Cambridge University
Qualifications: 9 GCSEs, 3 A-levels, NCA qualified coach
Career outside cricket: Teaching/journalism
Off-season: Studying
Overseas tours: Sussex U19 to Barbados 1993; Cambridge University to Pakistan 1999
Cricketers particularly admired: David Gower, Ian Botham
Young players to look out for: Mike Yardy, Dom Clapp
Other sports played: 'Anything'
Other sports followed: 'Again, anything (unless it involves horses)'
Injuries: Out for two to three weeks with a bad back
Relaxations: 'Reading, films and the odd drink'
Extras: Joined Derbyshire in 1999 from Sussex. 'Bagged a king pair on
Championship debut on television.' Played in the Old Tonbridgians side that won *The
Cricketer* Cup 1999. Captain of Cambridge University CC for 2000 season
Opinions on cricket: 'Wickets should be prepared to ensure that the best possible
cricket should be on offer both for the players and the crowd.'
Best batting: 90* Cambridge University v Middlesex, Fenner's 1999

---

69. Which current national selector scored 105* out of 143
for Nottinghamshire v Hampshire at Bournemouth in 1981?

1999 Season

	M	Inns	NO	Runs	HS	Avge	100s	50s	Ct	St	O	M	Runs	Wkts	Avge	Best	5wI	10wM
Test																		
All First	11	19	2	398	90 *	23.41	-	3	6	-								
1-day Int																		
NatWest																		
B & H																		
1-day Lge	4	4	0	32	14	8.00	-	-	1	-								

Career Performances

	M	Inns	NO	Runs	HS	Avge	100s	50s	Ct	St	Balls	Runs	Wkts	Avge	Best	5wI	10wM
Test																	
All First	18	27	2	525	90 *	21.00	-	4	11	-	12	20	0	-	-	-	-
1-day Int																	
NatWest																	
B & H	5	5	0	74	25	14.80	-	-	3	-							
1-day Lge	8	8	1	55	18 *	7.85	-	-	2	-							

RAMPRAKASH, M. R.   Middlesex

Name: Mark Ravindra Ramprakash
Role: Right-hand bat, right-arm off-spin bowler
Born: 5 September 1969, Bushey, Herts
Height: 5ft 10in **Weight:** 12st 4lbs
Nickname: Ramps, Bloodaxe
County debut: 1987
County cap: 1990
Test debut: 1991
Tests: 38
One-Day Internationals: 13
1000 runs in a season: 9
1st-Class 50s: 90
1st-Class 100s: 42
1st-Class 200s: 5
1st-Class catches: 155
One-Day 100s: 7
One-Day 5 w. in innings: 1
Place in batting averages: 25th av. 42.24 (1998 29th av. 42.56)
Strike rate: (career 99.70)
Parents: Deonarine and Jennifer
Date of marriage: 24 September 1993

Family links with cricket: Father played club cricket in Guyana
Education: Gayton High School; Harrow Weald Sixth Form College
Qualifications: 6 O-levels, 2 A-levels
Career outside cricket: 'Any ideas welcome'
Overseas tours: England YC to Sri Lanka 1986-87, to Australia (Youth World Cup) 1987-88; England A to Pakistan 1990-91, to West Indies 1991-92, to India (vice-captain) 1994-95; Lion Cubs to Barbados 1993; England to New Zealand 1991-92, to West Indies 1993-94, to Australia 1994-95, to South Africa 1995-96, to West Indies 1997-98, to Australia 1998-99, to South Africa 1999-2000
Overseas teams played for: Nairobi Jafferys, Kenya 1988; North Melbourne 1989
Cricketers particularly admired: 'All the great all-rounders'
Other sports followed: Snooker, football
Relaxations: 'Being at home with the family, going to movies, eating out'
Extras: Did not begin to play cricket until he was nine years old; played for Bessborough CC at age 13, played for Middlesex 2nd XI aged 16 and made first-team debut for Middlesex aged 17. Scored 204* in NCA Guernsey Festival Tournament and in 1987 made 186* on his debut for Stanmore CC. Voted Best U15 Schoolboy of 1985 by Cricket Society, Best Young Cricketer of 1986 and Most Promising Player of the Year in 1988. Played for England YC v New Zealand YC in 1989. Man of the Match in Middlesex's NatWest Trophy final win in 1988, on his debut in the competition. While on tour with England A in India 1994-95 was called up as replacement for Graeme Hick on the senior tour to Australia. Finished top of the Whyte and Mackay batting ratings in 1995 and again in 1997. Appointed Middlesex captain during 1997 season after Mike Gatting stood down. Scored maiden Test 100 (154) v West Indies at Bridgetown 1997-98, sharing in a record England v West Indies sixth wicket Test partnership (205) with Graham Thorpe and receiving Man of the Match award; took first Test wicket (Roland Holder) in same game. Achieved feat of scoring a century against all other first-class counties with his 128* v Glamorgan in 1998. During 1998-99 Ashes tour, put on 377 for England with Graham Thorpe in an unbroken fifth wicket stand v South Australia in Adelaide. Became the first player to score three 200s v Surrey with his 209* at Lord's 1999. Stood down as Middlesex captain at end of 1999 season. Leading run-scorer in the single-division four-day era of the County Championship with 8392 runs (av. 56.32) 1993-99. Granted a benefit for 2000
Best batting: 235 Middlesex v Yorkshire, Headingley 1995
Best bowling: 3-32 Middlesex v Glamorgan, Lord's 1998
Stop press: Joined England tour party in South Africa but did not play. Awarded England contract (Band B) for 2000

1999 Season

	M	Inns	NO	Runs	HS	Avge	100s	50s	Ct	St	O	M	Runs	Wkts	Avge	Best	5wl	10wM
Test	4	6	1	127	69 *	25.40	-	1	3	-	1	0	1	0	-	-	-	-
All First	16	28	3	1056	209 *	42.24	2	7	11	-	10	0	36	0	-	-	-	-
1-day Int																		
NatWest	1	1	0	49	49	49.00	-	-	-	-	6	0	24	1	24.00	1-24	-	
B & H																		
1-day Lge	12	11	1	255	57	25.50	-	1	6	-	11	0	50	1	50.00	1-14	-	

Career Performances

	M	Inns	NO	Runs	HS	Avge	100s	50s	Ct	St	Balls	Runs	Wkts	Avge	Best	5wI	10wM
Test	38	67	6	1701	154	27.88	1	10	28	-	841	445	4	111.25	1-2	-	-
All First	270	445	58	17865	235	46.16	47	90	155	-	3091	1778	31	57.35	3-32	-	-
1-day Int	13	13	3	265	51	26.50	-	1	6	-	12	14	0	-	-	-	
NatWest	28	27	1	814	104	31.30	1	3	10	-	360	217	9	24.11	2-15	-	
B & H	40	39	8	1290	119 *	41.61	2	7	17	-	240	166	9	18.44	3-35	-	
1-day Lge	149	141	25	4712	147 *	40.62	4	33	46	-	379	369	15	24.60	5-38	1	

RANDALL, S. J.   Nottinghamshire

Name: Stephen John Randall
Role: Right-hand bat, right-arm
off-spin bowler
Born: 9 June 1980, Nottingham
Height: 5ft 10in **Weight:** 11st 7lbs
Nickname: Rags, Rago
County debut: 1999
1st-Class catches: 3
Parents: Rob and Glenda
Marital status: Single
Family links with cricket: 'Dad played club
cricket to a good standard'
Education: Heyman; The West Bridgford
School
Qualifications: 9 GCSEs
Career outside cricket: 'Working in
computers'
Off-season: 'Working for Pegasus UK'
Overseas tours: England U17 to Bermuda 1997; Nottinghamshire to
South Africa 1998
Cricketers particularly admired: Peter Such, Paul Franks, 'Notts Unity Casuals 1st
XI 1999, mainly Dave Pinder ?? and John Dawson'
Young players to look out for: Dave Lucas, Vickram Atri
Other sports played: Golf
Other sports followed: Football (Notts County FC), ice hockey (Nottingham
Panthers)
Relaxations: 'Spending time socialising with my girlfriend and friends in
Nottingham'
Opinions on cricket: 'Pitches should be good enough to make a four-day game last
four days.'
Best batting: 20 Nottinghamshire v Glamorgan, Colwyn Bay 1999

1999 Season

	M	Inns	NO	Runs	HS	Avge	100s	50s	Ct	St	O	M	Runs	Wkts	Avge	Best	5wI	10wM
Test																		
All First	3	5	1	30	20	7.50	-	-	3	-	77	18	237	0	-		-	-	-
1-day Int																		
NatWest	1	1	0	1	1	1.00	-	-	-	-	10	0	43	0	-		-	-
B & H																		
1-day Lge																		

Career Performances

	M	Inns	NO	Runs	HS	Avge	100s	50s	Ct	St	Balls	Runs	Wkts	Avge	Best	5wI	10wM
Test																	
All First	3	5	1	30	20	7.50	-	-	3	-	462	237	0	-		-	-	-
1-day Int																	
NatWest	1	1	0	1	1	1.00	-	-	-	-	60	43	0	-		-	-
B & H																	
1-day Lge																	

RAO, R. K.   Sussex

Name: Rajesh Krishnakant Rao
Role: Right-hand bat, right-arm
leg-spin bowler
Born: 9 December 1974, London
Height: 5ft 10in **Weight:** 12st 7lbs
Nickname: Harry, 2pac
County debut: 1996
1st-Class 50s: 6
1st-Class catches: 7
One-Day 100s: 1
Place in batting averages: (1998 186th
av. 20.31)
Strike rate: 89.00 (career 122.75)
Parents: Krishnakant and Meena
Marital status: Single
Family links with cricket: 'Dad played for
Ugandan national side and East Africa.
Brother Rishi represented Middlesex youth
regional sides. All my cousins play club cricket'
Education: Lyon Park Junior School; Alperton High School; City of Westminster
College; Manchester Metropolitan University

Qualifications: 7 GCSEs, GNVQ Advanced Leisure and Tourism, basic coaching award, currently studying for BSc in Sports Science
Career outside cricket: Coach, personal fitness adviser, 'anything related to sport'
Overseas tours: Sussex to Spain 1996
Cricketers particularly admired: 'My Dad, Sachin Tendulkar, Shane Warne'
Young players to look out for: 'Too many to mention'
Other sports played: Football (Bedfont Eagles), tennis, badminton
Other sports followed: Football (Liverpool), boxing
Relaxations: Music – soul, R&B, hip-hop; reading biographies of famous sportsmen – 'Dennis Rodman *Bad as I wanna be* highly recommended'
Extras: Played for England at all youth levels from U11 to U18. MCC Lord's Taverners' Player of the Year 1989 (at Under 14). Sussex 2nd XI Player of the Year 1998. Achieved then highest one-day score by Sussex player – 158 v Derbyshire in the NatWest competition 1997
Opinions on cricket: 'The introduction of day/night games can only better the promotion of cricket to a wider audience.'
Best batting: 89 Sussex v Essex, Hove 1997
Best bowling: 1-1 Sussex v Yorkshire, Hove 1998

1999 Season

	M	Inns	NO	Runs	HS	Avge	100s	50s	Ct	St	O	M	Runs	Wkts	Avge	Best	5wl	10wM
Test																		
All First	4	6	1	87	52 *	17.40	-	1	1	-	14.5	2	53	1	53.00	1-27	-	-
1-day Int																		
NatWest	1	1	0	67	67	67.00	-	1	-	-								
B & H	1	1	0	1	1	1.00	-	-	-	-								
1-day Lge	2	1	0	9	9	9.00	-	-	-	-								

Career Performances

	M	Inns	NO	Runs	HS	Avge	100s	50s	Ct	St	Balls	Runs	Wkts	Avge	Best	5wl	10wM
Test																	
All First	27	46	4	874	89	20.80	-	6	7	-	491	296	4	74.00	1-1	-	-
1-day Int																	
NatWest	3	3	0	225	158	75.00	1	1	2	-							
B & H	3	3	0	77	61	25.66	-	1	1	-							
1-day Lge	34	33	1	659	91	20.59	-	5	9	-	126	127	5	25.40	3-31	-	

RASHID, U. B. A. — Sussex

Name: Umer Bin Abdul Rashid
Role: Left-hand bat, slow left-arm bowler
Born: 6 February 1976, Southampton
Height: 6ft 3in **Weight:** 12st 7lbs
Nickname: Umie, Looney, Bin
County debut: 1995 (one-day, Middlesex),
1996 (first-class, Middlesex), 1999 (Sussex)
1st-Class 50s: 3
1st-Class catches: 5
One-Day 5 w. in innings: 1
Place in batting averages: 106th av. 30.26
Place in bowling averages: 139th av. 44.26
Strike rate: 87.40 (career 89.80)
Parents: Mirza and Sebea
Marital status: Single
Education: Southfield Combined First and
Middle School; Ealing Green High; Ealing
Tertiary College; South Bank University
Qualifications: 7 GCSEs, 2 A-levels, 'currently studying for BA (Hons) in
Business Studies'
Cricketers particularly admired: Carl Hooper, Aamir Sohail
Young players to look out for: Vikram Solanki, Owais Shah, David Nash,
David Sales, Anurag Singh
Other sports followed: Football (Southampton FC), Formula 1 motor racing
Relaxations: 'Chilling out with family and friends, playing Nintendo and computer
games. A keen reader of books by John Grisham'
Extras: Lord's Taverners' Cricketer of the Year 1994-95. Played England U19 against
South Africa in 1995. Played for the Combined Universities side in the B&H Cup.
Released by Middlesex at end of 1998 season and joined Sussex for the 1999 season
on a two-year contract
Best batting: 73 Sussex v Kent, Hove 1999
Best bowling: 4-41 Sussex v Yorkshire, Headingley 1999

1999 Season

	M	Inns	NO	Runs	HS	Avge	100s	50s	Ct	St	O	M	Runs	Wkts	Avge	Best	5wI	10wM
Test																		
All First	10	18	3	454	73	30.26	-	3	5	-	218.3	67	664	15	44.26	4-41	-	-
1-day Int																		
NatWest	2	1	1	24	24 *	-	-	-	-	-	17	0	87	1	87.00	1-44	-	
B & H	2	2	1	14	8 *	14.00	-	-	-	-	12	0	51	2	25.50	2-38	-	
1-day Lge	15	6	1	39	26	7.80	-	-	10	-	115.4	9	457	27	16.92	5-24	1	

Career Performances

	M	Inns	NO	Runs	HS	Avge	100s	50s	Ct	St	Balls	Runs	Wkts	Avge	Best	5wI	10wM
Test																	
All First	12	20	3	469	73	27.58	-	3	5	-	1347	681	15	45.40	4-41	-	-
1-day Int																	
NatWest	2	1	1	24	24 *	-	-	-	-	-	102	87	1	87.00	1-44	-	
B & H	14	13	3	260	82	26.00	-	1	3	-	735	594	11	54.00	2-38	-	
1-day Lge	23	10	1	53	26	5.88	-	-	11	-	976	727	35	20.77	5-24	1	

RATCLIFFE, J. D. Surrey

Name: Jason David Ratcliffe
Role: Right-hand opening bat, right-arm
medium/off-spin bowler, slip fielder
Born: 19 June 1969, Solihull
Height: 6ft 4in **Weight:** 14st 7lbs
Nickname: Ratters, Fridge
County debut: 1988 (Warwickshire),
1995 (Surrey)
1st-Class 50s: 38
1st-Class 100s: 5
1st-Class 5 w. in innings: 1
1st-Class catches: 66
One-Day 100s: 1
Place in batting averages: 193rd av. 21.15
(1998 81st av. 32.07)
Place in bowling averages: 9th av. 17.93
Strike rate: 39.60 (career 61.96)
Parents: David and Sheila
Wife and date of marriage: Andrea, 7 January 1995
Family links with cricket: Father (D.P. Ratcliffe) played for Warwickshire 1956-62
Education: Meadow Green Primary School; Sharmans Cross Secondary School;
Solihull Sixth Form College
Qualifications: 6 O-levels, 3 A-levels; NCA staff coach
Career outside cricket: Sports PR and marketing
Off-season: Working for PCA management in London
Overseas tours: NCA (South) to Ireland 1988; Warwickshire to South Africa 1991-92
Overseas teams played for: West End, Kimberley, South Africa 1987-88; Belmont,
Newcastle, NSW 1990-91; Penrith, Sydney 1992-94
Cricketers particularly admired: 'Too many to name'
Players to look out for: 'Martin Bicknell'
Other sports followed: Football (Birmingham City FC)

Relaxations: Music, reading, eating out
Extras: Has won two Championship winner's medals (Warwickshire and Surrey), a NatWest winner's medal (Warwicks), a Sunday League winner's medal (Surrey) and a B&H winner's medal (Surrey). Is treasurer of the Professional Cricketers' Association
Best batting: 135 Surrey v Worcestershire, Worcester 1997
Best bowling: 6-48 Surrey v Sri Lanka A, The Oval 1999

1999 Season

	M	Inns	NO	Runs	HS	Avge	100s	50s	Ct	St	O	M	Runs	Wkts	Avge	Best	5wI	10wM
Test																		
All First	13	20	1	402	91	21.15	-	2	6	-	99	27	269	15	17.93	6-48	1	-
1-day Int																		
NatWest	1	1	0	10	10	10.00	-	-	-	-	3	0	21	0	-		-	-
B & H																		
1-day Lge	9	9	1	159	59	19.87	-	1	2	-	40	0	169	3	56.33	1-17	-	

Career Performances

	M	Inns	NO	Runs	HS	Avge	100s	50s	Ct	St	Balls	Runs	Wkts	Avge	Best	5wI	10wM
Test																	
All First	133	238	13	6517	135	28.96	5	38	66	-	1549	851	25	34.04	6-48	1	-
1-day Int																	
NatWest	15	15	1	479	105	34.21	1	3	1	-	48	41	0	-		-	-
B & H	12	10	1	125	41	13.88	-	-	6	-	48	42	2	21.00	2-42	-	
1-day Lge	57	51	4	924	82	19.65	-	5	16	-	568	488	12	40.66	2-11	-	

RAWNSLEY, M. J.   Worcestershire

Name: Matthew James Rawnsley
Role: Right-hand bat, slow left-arm bowler
Born: 8 June 1976, Birmingham
Height: 6ft 3in **Weight:** 12st 8lbs
Nickname: Scrawny, Dog
County debut: 1996
1st-Class 5 w. in innings: 2
1st-Class 10 w. in match: 1
1st-Class catches: 9
One-Day 5 w. in innings: 1
Place in batting averages: (1998 287th av. 6.87)
Place in bowling averages: (1998 80th av. 29.23)
Strike rate: 82.50 (career 74.11)
Parents: Christopher (deceased) and June

Marital status: Single
Family links with cricket: 'Brother sometimes turns out for Old Griffinians RFC's cricket section's 3rd XI Sunday irregulars'
Education: Northfield Manor Primary School, Birmingham; Bourneville Secondary School, Birmingham; Brynteg Comprehensive, Bridgend
Qualifications: 9 GCSEs and 4 A-levels, NCA coaching award, qualified canoe instructor
Overseas tours: Worcestershire CCC to Zimbabwe 1997
Overseas teams played for: Kumeu, Auckland 1995-96; Sunrise Sports Club, Harare, Zimbabwe 1996-97
Cricketers particularly admired: Richard Illingworth, Dave Houghton

Young players to look out for: Vikram Solanki
Other sports played: Rugby (Old Griffinians RFC)
Other sports followed: Rugby
Relaxations: TV, eating
Extras: Set record for the most wickets at the Oxford Festival (27). Warwickshire U19 Player of the Year in 1995. Took ten wickets and scored 133 not out against Gloucestershire 2nd XI in 1997
Best batting: 26 Worcestershire v Essex, Chelmsford 1997
Best bowling: 6-44 Worcestershire v Oxford University, The Parks 1998

1999 Season

	M	Inns	NO	Runs	HS	Avge	100s	50s	Ct	St	O	M	Runs	Wkts	Avge	Best	5wI	10wM
Test																		
All First	4	6	1	67	21	13.40	-	-	1	-	110	28	291	8	36.37	3-84	-	-
1-day Int																		
NatWest	2	2	1	2	1 *	2.00	-	-	1	-	14	0	55	2	27.50	2-36	-	
B & H																		
1-day Lge	10	2	0	6	4	3.00	-	-	3	-	49.3	3	225	12	18.75	5-26	1	

Career Performances

	M	Inns	NO	Runs	HS	Avge	100s	50s	Ct	St	Balls	Runs	Wkts	Avge	Best	5wI	10wM
Test																	
All First	18	20	4	197	26	12.31	-	-	9	-	2668	1225	36	34.02	6-44	2	1
1-day Int																	
NatWest	3	2	1	2	1 *	2.00	-	-	1	-	150	105	4	26.25	2-36	-	
B & H																	
1-day Lge	21	10	1	25	7	2.77	-	-	6	-	650	510	17	30.00	5-26	1	

READ, C. M. W.   Nottinghamshire

Name: Christopher Mark Wells Read
Role: Right-hand bat, wicket-keeper
Born: 10 August 1978, Paignton, Devon
Height: 5ft 8in **Weight:** 11st
Nickname: Readie, Little Eddie, Lambchops, Wells Road, Bouch
County debut: 1997 (one-day, Glos), 1998 (Notts)
County cap: 1999 (Notts)
1st-Class 50s: 3
1st-Class 100s: 1
1st-Class catches: 116
1st-Class stumpings: 6
Place in batting averages: 183rd av. 21.76 (1998 141st av. 25.06)
Parents: Geoffrey and Carolyn
Marital status: Single
Family links with cricket: Father played local club cricket and is an avid fan
Education: Roselands Primary School; Torquay Boys' Grammar School; University of Bath
Qualifications: 9 GCSEs, 4 A-levels, senior coaching award
Career outside cricket: 'Unsure'
Off-season: England tour to South Africa and Zimbabwe
Overseas tours: West of England U13 to Holland 1991; West of England U15 to West Indies 1992-93; England U17 to Holland (ICC Youth tournament) 1995; England U19 to Pakistan 1996-97; England A to Kenya and Sri Lanka 1997-98, to Zimbabwe and South Africa 1998-99; England to South Africa and Zimbabwe 1999-2000
Cricketers particularly admired: Alan Knott, Jack Russell
Young players to look out for: Graeme Swann, Matt Whiley

Other sports played: Hockey, table tennis
Other sports followed: Football (Torquay United)
Relaxations: Reading, listening to music, keeping fit and going out with friends
Extras: Represented Devon in Minor Counties Championship and NatWest in 1995, 1996 and 1997, the county winning the Minor Counties Championship three years running. Played for England U18 against New Zealand U19 in 1996. Has also played hockey for Devon U18 and U21 and for West of England U17. Played for England U19 in the series against Zimbabwe U19. He was selected for the England A tour to Kenya and Sri Lanka aged 18 and without having played a first-class game. Asked to be released by Gloucestershire whilst still on tour with England A. Joined Nottinghamshire for 1998 season. Scored maiden first-class century v Warwickshire at Trent Bridge 1999; his 160 was the highest score by a Notts wicket-keeper for more than 30 years. Made Test debut in the first Test v New Zealand at Edgbaston 1999, making eight dismissals in the match. Awarded Notts cap 1999
Opinions on cricket: 'I believe there is a wealth of talent in this country, but I feel it is not being harnessed properly since we do not have enough time to work at our game. I feel that if we did not play as much county cricket, it would give us more time to prepare for each match and iron out any technical faults. In my opinion this would help to raise the standard of cricket in this country.'
Best batting: 160 Nottinghamshire v Warwickshire, Trent Bridge 1999
Stop press: Made One-Day International debut v South Africa at Bloemfontein, January 2000

1999 Season

	M	Inns	NO	Runs	HS	Avge	100s	50s	Ct	St	O	M	Runs	Wkts	Avge	Best	5wI	10wM
Test	3	4	0	38	37	9.50	-	-	10	1								
All First	19	31	1	653	160	21.76	1	1	59	2								
1-day Int																		
NatWest	2	2	0	42	30	21.00	-	-	6	-								
B & H																		
1-day Lge	14	13	0	374	62	28.76	-	1	18	1								

Career Performances

	M	Inns	NO	Runs	HS	Avge	100s	50s	Ct	St	Balls	Runs	Wkts	Avge	Best	5wI	10wM
Test	3	4	0	38	37	9.50	-	-	10	1							
All First	41	64	9	1269	160	23.07	1	3	116	6							
1-day Int																	
NatWest	8	7	2	103	37	20.60	-	-	8	2							
B & H																	
1-day Lge	26	21	3	441	62	24.50	-	1	28	3							

RENSHAW, S. J.　　　　　Hampshire

Name: Simon John Renshaw
Role: Right-hand bat, right-arm
fast-medium bowler
Born: 6 March 1974, Bebington, Wirral
Height: 6ft 3in **Weight:** 14st 4lbs
Nickname: Rennie Arnoux, Toady
County debut: 1996
1st-Class 50s: 1
1st-Class 5 w. in innings: 1
1st-Class catches: 13
One-Day 5 w. in innings: 1
Place in batting averages:
247th av. 14.42
Place in bowling averages:
123rd av. 37.50
Strike rate: 76.30 (career 69.89)
Parents: Michael and Barbara
Wife and date of marriage:
Tracy, 26 September 1998

Family links with cricket: Father and brother play in local league competitions
Education: Birkenhead Prep School; Birkenhead; Leeds University
Qualifications: 9 GCSEs, 4 A-levels, BSc Microbiology, Grade 1 coach
Career outside cricket: Coaching
Off-season: Coaching in Southampton
Overseas teams played for: Mulgrave, Melbourne 1995-96; Ashwood, Melbourne
1996-97
Cricketers particularly admired: Ian Botham, Viv Richards
Players to look out for: 'Peter Hartley'
Other sports followed: Football (Everton FC)
Relaxations: 'Away trips'
Extras: His 6-25 against Surrey in 1997 is the best bowling by a Hampshire bowler in
the Benson and Hedges Cup
Opinions on cricket: 'Pitches around the country need to be better. From 2nd XI one-
day to 1st XI four-day, at out-grounds or Test grounds, there are too many sub-
standard pitches.'
Best batting: 56 Hampshire v Surrey, Guildford 1997
Best bowling: 5-110 Hampshire v Derbyshire, Chesterfield 1997

1999 Season

	M	Inns	NO	Runs	HS	Avge	100s	50s	Ct	St	O	M	Runs	Wkts	Avge	Best	5wI	10wM
Test																		
All First	12	13	6	101	28	14.42	-	-	7	-	381.3	93	1125	30	37.50	4-43	-	-
1-day Int																		
NatWest																		
B & H																		
1-day Lge	13	6	5	66	27 *	66.00	-	-	1	-	88	7	442	13	34.00	4-40	-	

Career Performances

	M	Inns	NO	Runs	HS	Avge	100s	50s	Ct	St	Balls	Runs	Wkts	Avge	Best	5wI	10wM
Test																	
All First	35	41	19	390	56	17.72	-	1	13	-	6011	3361	86	39.08	5-110	1	-
1-day Int																	
NatWest	4	2	0	5	4	2.50	-	-	1	-	186	133	4	33.25	2-20	-	
B & H	12	8	3	28	23	5.60	-	-	2	-	708	532	21	25.33	6-25	1	
1-day Lge	36	20	14	177	27 *	29.50	-	-	2	-	1404	1216	42	28.95	4-40	-	

RHODES, S. J. Worcestershire

Name: Steven John Rhodes
Role: Right-hand bat, wicket-keeper
Born: 17 June 1964, Bradford,
West Yorkshire
Height: 5ft 8in **Weight:** 12st 4lbs
Nickname: Bumpy, Wilf
County debut: 1981 (Yorkshire),
1985 (Worcestershire)
County cap: 1986 (Worcestershire)
Benefit: 1996
Test debut: 1994
Tests: 11
One-Day Internationals: 9
1000 runs in a season: 2
1st-Class 50s: 64
1st-Class 100s: 10
1st-Class catches: 914
1st-Class stumpings: 112
Place in batting averages: 167th av. 23.64 (1998 60th av. 35.71)
Parents: William Ernest and Norma Kathleen
Wife and date of marriage: Judy Ann, 6 March 1993

Children: Holly Jade, 20 August 1985; George Harry, 26 October 1993; Lily Amber, 3 March 1995
Family links with cricket: Father played for Nottinghamshire 1959-64
Education: Bradford Moor Junior School; Lapage St Middle; Carlton-Bolling Comprehensive, Bradford
Qualifications: 4 O-levels, advanced coach
Career outside cricket: Marketing department at Worcestershire CCC
Overseas tours: England A to Sri Lanka 1986; England A to Zimbabwe and Kenya 1989-90, to Pakistan 1990-91, to West Indies 1991-92, to South Africa 1993-94; England to Australia 1994-95; MCC to Kenya 1999
Overseas teams played for: Past Bros, Bundaberg, Queensland; Avis Vogeltown, New Plymouth, New Zealand; Melville, Perth, Australia
Cricketers particularly admired: Graeme Hick, Richard Hadlee, Courtney Walsh
Young players to look out for: Paul Franks
Other sports followed: Horse racing and golf
Relaxations: Horse racing
Extras: Played for England YC v Australia YC in 1983 and set record for most victims in an innings for England YC. Youngest wicket-keeper to play for Yorkshire. Released by Yorkshire to join Worcestershire at end of 1984 season. Selected for cancelled England tour to India 1988-89 and was one of four players put on stand-by as reserves for 1992 World Cup squad. Writes a weekly cricket column for a Birmingham newspaper. One of *Wisden*'s Five Cricketers of the Year 1995. Overtook David Bairstow as the wicket-keeper with the most dismissals in the Sunday League. Made 1000th first-class dismissal of his career when he caught Graeme Swann off Alamgir Sheriyar v Northants at Northampton 1999
Opinions on cricket: 'As long as English cricket is tough and competitive I see no reason why England shouldn't be one of the top two Test-playing cricketing nations. To be this, we must remain fresh with the right balance between rest and competition.'
Best batting: 122* Worcestershire v Young Australia, Worcester 1995

1999 Season

	M	Inns	NO	Runs	HS	Avge	100s	50s	Ct	St	O	M	Runs	Wkts	Avge	Best	5wI	10wM
Test																		
All First	18	30	5	591	74	23.64	-	1	51	2								
1-day Int																		
NatWest	2	2	1	19	14 *	19.00	-	-	4	-								
B & H																		
1-day Lge	15	10	5	101	25 *	20.20	-	-	14	8								

Career Performances

	M	Inns	NO	Runs	HS	Avge	100s	50s	Ct	St	Balls	Runs	Wkts	Avge	Best	5wI	10wM
Test	11	17	5	294	65 *	24.50	-	1	46	3							
All First	364	513	136	12428	122 *	32.96	10	64	914	112	6	30	0	-	-	-	-
1-day Int	9	8	2	107	56	17.83	-	1	9	2							
NatWest	42	33	12	419	61	19.95	-	2	52	7	6	1	0	-	-	-	
B & H	66	47	8	575	51 *	14.74	-	1	90	10							
1-day Lge	229	140	39	1801	48 *	17.83	-	-	239	72							

RICHARDSON, A.　　　　Warwickshire

Name: Alan Richardson
Role: Right-hand bat, right-arm
medium-fast bowler
Born: 6 May 1975, Newcastle-under-Lyme
Height: 6ft 2in **Weight:** 13st
Nickname: Richo
County debut: 1995 (Derbyshire),
1999 (Warwickshire)
1st-Class 5 w. in innings: 1
1st-Class 10 w. in match: 1
1st-Class catches: 1
Place in bowling averages: 45th av. 23.43
Strike rate: 49.69 (career 48.34)
Parents: Roy and Sandra
Marital status: Single
Family links with cricket: 'Dad captained
Little Stoke 3rd XI'

Education: Manor Hill First School; Walton
Priory Middle School; Alleyne's High School, Stone; Stafford College of Further
Education
Qualifications: 8 GCSEs, 2 A-levels, 2 AS-levels, qualified senior cricket coach
Career outside cricket: 'Very bad landscape gardening'
Off-season: 'Playing for Northern Districts, Sydney; joining Warwickshire pre-season
tour in South Africa'
Overseas teams played for: Northern Natal, South Africa 1994-96; Hawkesbury CC,
Sydney 1997-99; Northern Districts, Sydney 1999-2000
Cricketers particularly admired: Angus Fraser, Tim Munton, Denton Brock ('for his
strict flexibility programme'), Jarred Hodges, John Allen
Young players to look out for: Ian Bell, Darren Altree, Jamie Spires, 'anyone from
Staffordshire'
Other sports played: Football ('play sweeper for the young "Bears"')

Other sports followed: Football (Stoke City 'through thin and thin'), rugby league (Parramatta Eels), rugby union (Parramatta Two Blues)

Relaxations: 'Socialising, going to the football, odd game of golf'

Extras: *The Cricketer*/Slazenger Cricketer of the Month June 1991. *Cricket World* award for best bowling performance in Oxford U19 Festival (8-60 v Devon). Topped Minor Counties bowling averages 1998 and won Minor Counties bowling award. Most Improved 2nd XI Player 1999. Outstanding Performance of the Year 1999 for his 8-51 v Gloucestershire on home debut; besides being the season's best analysis, it was the best return by a Warwickshire player on debut at Edgbaston

Opinions on cricket: 'We may play a bit too much, but I'm not complaining. It's far better than cutting grass.'

Best batting: 4 Derbyshire v Oxford University, The Parks 1995
                   4 Warwickshire v Durham, Chester-le-Street 1999

Best bowling: 8-51 Warwickshire v Gloucestershire, Edgbaston 1999

1999 Season

	M	Inns	NO	Runs	HS	Avge	100s	50s	Ct	St	O	M	Runs	Wkts	Avge	Best	5wI	10wM
Test																		
All First	6	8	3	9	4	1.80	-	-	1	-	190.3	45	539	23	23.43	8-51	1	1
1-day Int																		
NatWest																		
B & H																		
1-day Lge	2	1	1	11	11 *	-	-	-	-	-	-	12.1	0	44	3	14.66	2-16	-

Career Performances

	M	Inns	NO	Runs	HS	Avge	100s	50s	Ct	St	Balls	Runs	Wkts	Avge	Best	5wI	10wM
Test																	
All First	7	9	3	13	4	2.16	-	-	1	-	1257	599	26	23.03	8-51	1	1
1-day Int																	
NatWest	3	3	0	3	3	1.00	-	-	-	-	168	116	1	116.00	1-48	-
B & H	3	2	1	2	1 *	2.00	-	-	-	-	72	48	1	48.00	1-16	-
1-day Lge	3	1	1	11	11 *	-	-	-	-	-	109	85	3	28.33	2-16	-

RIDGWAY, P. M.   Lancashire

Name: Paul Mathew Ridgway
Role: Right-hand bat, right-arm fast-medium bowler
Born: 13 February 1977, Keighley, Yorkshire
Height: 6ft 3in **Weight:** 15st 2lbs
Nickname: Ridgeback
County debut: 1997

Strike rate: (career 66.00)
Parents: Peter and Judith
Marital status: Single
Family links with cricket: Father is first cousin to Don Wilson (Yorkshire and England)
Education: Hellifield Primary School; Settle High School
Qualifications: GCSEs, BTEC Business and Finance
Off-season: 12-month contract with Lancashire
Cricketers particularly admired: Ian Austin, Wasim Akram
Young players to look out for: 'All Lancashire 2nd XI'
Other sports followed: Motorcycle racing, rugby, football (Bradford City FC)
Relaxations: Motorbikes
Extras: Awarded 2nd XI cap 1998

Opinions on cricket: 'Longer break at tea. More music and fun for the crowd.'
Best batting: 35 Lancashire v Durham, Riverside 1998
Best bowling: 3-51 Lancashire v Durham, Riverside 1998

1999 Season

	M	Inns	NO	Runs	HS	Avge	100s	50s	Ct	St	O	M	Runs	Wkts	Avge	Best	5wl	10wM
Test																		
All First	2	3	2	9	8 *	9.00	-	-	-	-	9	1	55	0	-	-	-	-
1-day Int																		
NatWest																			
B & H																			
1-day Lge																			

Career Performances

	M	Inns	NO	Runs	HS	Avge	100s	50s	Ct	St	Balls	Runs	Wkts	Avge	Best	5wl	10wM
Test																	
All First	5	7	3	48	35	12.00	-	-	-	-	396	301	6	50.16	3-51	-	-
1-day Int																	
NatWest	2	1	1	47	47 *	-	-	-	1	-	120	103	5	20.60	4-62	-
B & H																	
1-day Lge																	

RIPLEY, D.   Northamptonshire

Name: David Ripley
Role: Right-hand bat, wicket-keeper,
county vice-captain
Born: 13 September 1966, Leeds
Height: 5ft 11in **Weight:** 11st 7lbs
Nickname: Spud, Rips, Austin
County debut: 1984
County cap: 1987
1st-Class 50s: 29
1st-Class 100s: 8
1st-Class 200s: 1
1st-Class catches: 596
1st-Class stumpings: 77
Place in batting averages: 21st av. 42.68
(1998 39th av. 40.25)
Strike rate: (career 30.00)
Parents: Arthur and Brenda
Wife and date of marriage: Jackie, 24
September 1988
Children: Joe David, 11 October 1989; George William, 5 March 1994
Education: Woodlesford Primary; Royds High, Leeds
Qualifications: 5 O-levels, staff coach
Career outside cricket: Cricket development officer for Northampton
Off-season: Working for the club in youth development
Overseas tours: England YC to West Indies 1984-85; Northants to Durban 1991-92, to
Cape Town 1992-93, to Zimbabwe 1994-95, 1998, to Johannesburg 1996
Overseas teams played for: Marists and Poverty Bay, New Zealand 1985-87
Cricketers particularly admired: Alan Knott, Bob Taylor 'and many other keepers',
Clive Radley, Ian Botham, Geoff Boycott, Dennis Lillee
Young players to look out for: 'Sales, Davies, Swann'
Other sports played: Football (locally), golf
Other sports followed: Football (Leeds United), rugby league (Castleford), golf
Injuries: Out for three weeks with a broken thumb
Relaxations: 'Eating out, and sampling different bitters'
Extras: Finished top of wicket-keepers' dismissals list for 1988 and 1992 and was
voted Wombwell Cricket Lovers' Society Best Wicket-keeper 1992. Played for
England YC v Sri Lanka 1986. Northamptonshire Player of the Year in 1988 and 1997.
Put on 401 for the fifth wicket with Mal Loye v Glamorgan 1998, setting a new fifth
wicket partnership record for first-class cricket in England and registering a career best
209. Put on 293 for the seventh wicket with David Sales v Essex 1999, setting a new
seventh wicket partnership record for the county. Also shared in county record

partnership for the eighth wicket, 164 v Lancashire in 1987 with Nick Cook. Lies second, behind K. V. Andrew, in county wicket-keeping dismissals list. Vice-captain of Northants since 1999

Opinions on cricket: 'Enjoyed the season with extra competitive edge. Wickets still not good enough for four days. England have a good team; get behind them.'
Best batting: 209 Northamptonshire v Glamorgan, Northampton 1998
Best bowling: 2-89 Northamptonshire v Essex, Ilford 1987

1999 Season

	M	Inns	NO	Runs	HS	Avge	100s	50s	Ct	St	O	M	Runs	Wkts	Avge	Best	5wl	10wM
Test																		
All First	15	22	6	683	107	42.68	2	3	40	3								
1-day Int																		
NatWest	3	1	0	13	13	13.00	-	-	4	-								
B & H																		
1-day Lge	10	6	3	65	33	21.66	-	-	10	2								

Career Performances

	M	Inns	NO	Runs	HS	Avge	100s	50s	Ct	St	Balls	Runs	Wkts	Avge	Best	5wl	10wM
Test																	
All First	279	367	95	7737	209	28.44	9	29	596	77	60	103	2	51.50	2-89	-	-
1-day Int																	
NatWest	38	21	9	143	27 *	11.91	-	-	40	3							
B & H	47	31	12	383	36 *	20.15	-	-	51	6							
1-day Lge	152	91	40	966	52 *	18.94	-	1	108	15							

70. Which Welsh international rugby player captained Glamorgan to their first County Championship in 1948?

ROBERTS, D. J.   Northamptonshire

Name: David James Roberts
Role: Right-hand bat
Born: 29 December 1976, Truro, Cornwall
Height: 5ft 11in **Weight:** 13st
Nickname: Chips, Maverick, Robbo
County debut: 1996
1st-Class 50s: 2
1st-Class 100s: 1
1st-Class catches: 8
Place in batting averages: 270th av. 10.42
Parents: Dennis and Pam
Marital status: Engaged to Becky Williams
Family links with cricket: Cousin, Chris
Bullen, played for Surrey. Father played
cricket for local club and is also a youth
coach. 'Mother is a keen supporter!'
Education: Mullion County Primary;
Mullion Comprehensive
Qualifications: 9 GCSEs, senior cricket coach
Career outside cricket: Coaching
Off-season: Playing and coaching in South Africa
Overseas tours: West of England to Barbados, Trinidad and Tobago 1990-91
and 1991-92 (captain)
Cricketers particularly admired: Graeme Hick, Mal Loye, David Gower
Young players to look out for: Richard Logan, John Blain, Mark Powell
Other sports followed: Football (Manchester United), NBA basketball and all sports
Relaxations: Watching television, listening to music, playing football
Extras: Played for English Schools from the age of 14, including matches against
South Africa in 1992. Represented England U17 against India U17 in 1994
Opinions on cricket: 'Tea is too short. 2nd XI cricket should be played at first-class
grounds instead of club grounds.'
Best batting: 117 Northamptonshire v Essex, Northampton 1997

1999 Season

	M	Inns	NO	Runs	HS	Avge	100s	50s	Ct	St	O	M	Runs	Wkts	Avge	Best	5wl	10wM
Test																		
All First	5	8	1	73	34 *	10.42	-	-	4	-								
1-day Int																		
NatWest																		
B & H																		
1-day Lge																		

	M	Inns	NO	Runs	HS	Avge	100s	50s	Ct	St	Balls	Runs	Wkts	Avge	Best	5wI	10wM
Test																	
All First	17	30	1	751	117	25.89	1	2	8	-							
1-day Int																	
NatWest																	
B & H																	
1-day Lge																	

ROBERTS, G. M.   Derbyshire

Name: Glenn Martin Roberts
Role: Left-hand bat, slow left-arm bowler
Born: 4 November 1973, Huddersfield
Height: 5ft 11in **Weight:** 12st
Nickname: Robbo
County debut: 1996
1st-Class 50s: 1
1st-Class catches: 8
Place in batting averages: (1998 156th av. 23.70)
Strike rate: (career 136.20)
Parents: Tony and Margaret
Marital status: Single
Family links with cricket: 'Major influence was my grandfather who played Huddersfield League cricket. My parents took me everywhere to play and support me'
Education: King James's School; Greenhead College, Huddersfield; Carnegie College, Leeds Metropolitan University
Qualifications: 8 GCSEs, 4 A-levels, BEd (Hons) Physical Education, FA Teaching Certificate, NCA advanced coach
Career outside cricket: PE teacher
Overseas tours: Roses CC (Yorkshire) to Menorca 1995, 1996
Overseas teams played for: Easts, Brisbane 1997-98
Cricketers particularly admired: Kim Barnett, Phil DeFreitas, Phil Carrick
Other sports followed: Rugby league (Huddersfield Giants) and football
Relaxations: Jogging, fitness, gym work, socialising
Extras: Played for Yorkshire from U14 to U19 and captained the U16s and the U19s. Was a member of the Yorkshire Academy for two years. Scored 50 batting at No. 9 on his Championship debut for Derbyshire in 1996 and featured in a then-record eighth-wicket stand for Derbyshire of 118 with Karl Krikken. Released by Derbyshire at end of 1999 season

Best batting: 52 Derbyshire v Somerset, Taunton 1996
Best bowling: 4-105 Derbyshire v Durham, Derby 1998

1999 Season

	M	Inns	NO	Runs	HS	Avge	100s	50s	Ct	St	O	M	Runs	Wkts	Avge	Best	5wI	10wM
Test																		
All First																		
1-day Int																		
NatWest	1	0	0	0	0	-	-	-	-	-	8	0	37	0	-		-	-
B & H																		
1-day Lge	7	5	2	68	27	22.66	-	-	2	-	52.3	0	239	10	23.90	4-23	-	

Career Performances

	M	Inns	NO	Runs	HS	Avge	100s	50s	Ct	St	Balls	Runs	Wkts	Avge	Best	5wI	10wM
Test																	
All First	11	17	4	334	52	25.69	-	1	8	-	1362	810	10	81.00	4-105	-	-
1-day Int																	
NatWest	4	0	0	0	0	-	-	-	-	-	180	78	1	78.00	1-30	-	
B & H	5	3	1	15	12	7.50	-	-	2	-	276	228	9	25.33	3-45	-	
1-day Lge	28	17	7	107	27	10.70	-	-	7	-	1152	937	33	28.39	4-23	-	

ROBINSON, D. D. J.   Essex

Name: Darren David John Robinson
Role: Right-hand opening bat, occasional right-arm medium bowler
Born: 2 March 1973, Braintree, Essex
Height: 5ft 11in **Weight:** 14st
Nickname: Pie Shop, Robbo
County debut: 1993
County cap: 1997
1st-Class 50s: 15
1st-Class 100s: 6
1st-Class 200s: 1
1st-Class catches: 70
One-Day 100s: 3
Place in batting averages: 120th av. 28.07 (1998 213th av. 17.84)
Parents: David and Dorothy
Marital status: Single
Children: Kalli, 20 July 1998

Family links with cricket: Father plays club cricket for Halstead
Education: Tabor High School, Braintree; Chelmsford College of Further Education
Qualifications: 5 GCSEs, BTEC National Diploma in Building and Construction
Career outside cricket: Civil engineering and surveying
Off-season: Coaching in the indoor school at Chelmsford
Overseas tours: England U18 to Canada 1991; England U19 to Pakistan 1991-92
Overseas teams played for: Waverley, Sydney 1992-94; Eden Roskill CC, Auckland 1995-96
Cricketers particularly admired: David Denny
Young players to look out for: James Foster, Tim Phillips
Other sports followed: Golf, football, rugby, swimming
Relaxations: Reading crime novels, music, eating out, pubs
Extras: *Daily Telegraph* batting award 1988 and International Youth Tournament in Canada batting award 1991. Scored maiden first-class 200 v New Zealand at Chelmsford 1999
Opinions on cricket: 'Cricket's a great game when everything is going well, but a pain in the arse when it's not.'
Best batting: 200 Essex v New Zealand, Chelmsford 1999

1999 Season

	M	Inns	NO	Runs	HS	Avge	100s	50s	Ct	St	O	M	Runs	Wkts	Avge	Best	5wI	10wM
Test																		
All First	17	29	1	786	200	28.07	3	1	12	-	2	1	6	0	-	-	-	-
1-day Int																		
NatWest	1	1	0	8	8	8.00	-	-	1	-								
B & H																		
1-day Lge	9	9	1	260	74 *	32.50	-	2	3	-								

Career Performances

	M	Inns	NO	Runs	HS	Avge	100s	50s	Ct	St	Balls	Runs	Wkts	Avge	Best	5wI	10wM
Test																	
All First	77	136	4	3567	200	27.02	7	15	70	-	48	37	0	-	-	-	-
1-day Int																	
NatWest	14	12	1	247	62	22.45	-	2	5	-							
B & H	17	15	3	451	137 *	37.58	2	-	2	-							
1-day Lge	67	66	8	1584	129 *	27.31	1	7	20	-	17	26	1	26.00	1-7	-	

ROBINSON, M. A.   Sussex

Name: Mark Andrew Robinson
Role: Right-hand bat, right-arm
fast-medium bowler
Born: 23 November 1966, Hull
Height: 6ft 3in **Weight:** 13st
Nickname: Jessy, Coddy, Scoope, Tiger,
Stormy, Storm
County debut: 1987 (Northamptonshire),
1991 (Yorkshire), 1996 (Sussex)
County cap: 1990 (Northamptonshire),
1992 (Yorkshire)
1st-Class 5 w. in innings: 10
1st-Class 10 w. in match: 2
1st-Class catches: 37
Place in batting averages: 296th av. 4.84
(1998 297th av. 3.07)
Place in bowling averages: 95th av. 29.95
(1998 61st av. 26.80)
Strike rate: 65.08 (career 66.24)
Parents: Malcolm and Joan
Wife and date of marriage: Julia, 8 October 1994
Children: Samuel Lewes, 11 January 1996
Family links with cricket: Grandfather a prominent local cricketer and 'father was
hostile bowler in the back garden'
Education: Fifth Avenue Primary; Endike Junior High; Hull Grammar School
Qualifications: 6 O-levels, 2 A-levels, advanced cricket coach, badminton coach,
rugby union coach
Career outside cricket: Self-employed cricket coach
Overseas tours: England U19 North to Bermuda; Yorkshire to Cape Town 1991-92,
1992-93, to West Indies 1993-94
Overseas teams played for: East Shirley, Canterbury, New Zealand 1987-89;
Canterbury, New Zealand 1989-98
Cricketers particularly admired: Dennis Lillee
Young players to look out for: Dave Barrick, Steve Patterson, Yaniv Judah, Simon
Tennant 'and all the boys of Hull CC'
Injuries: 'Usual aches and pains but stayed fit throughout – thanks Tim and Stu'
Extras: Took hat-trick with first three balls of innings in Yorkshire League playing for
Hull v Doncaster. First player to win Yorkshire U19 Bowler of the Season in two
successive years. Northamptonshire Uncapped Player of the Year in 1989. Endured a
world record 12 innings without scoring a run in 1990. Currently trying to open an
eight-lane indoor cricket stadium. Sussex Clubman of the Year 1997 and 1998. Scored

500th first-class run on the same day as he took 500th first-class wicket – 20 August 1999, v Surrey at Hove; the 500th run prevented Saqlain Mushtaq taking four wickets in four balls, having just claimed a hat-trick

Opinions on cricket: 'Give a batter three warnings for running down the wicket, the same as a bowler. Bad luck Dennis. Toby, get that £5 ready.'

Best batting: 27 Sussex v Lancashire, Old Trafford 1997

Best bowling: 9-37 Yorkshire v Northamptonshire, Harrogate 1993

1999 Season

	M	Inns	NO	Runs	HS	Avge	100s	50s	Ct	St	O	M	Runs	Wkts	Avge	Best	5wI	10wM
Test																		
All First	17	24	11	63	10	4.84	-	-	1	-	520.4	140	1438	48	29.95	6-88	1	-
1-day Int																		
NatWest	2	0	0	0	0	-	-	-	-	-	20	3	54	2	27.00	1-15	-
B & H	2	1	1	0	0 *	-	-	-	-	-	20	2	63	2	31.50	2-21	-
1-day Lge	14	2	0	1	1	0.50	-	-	-	-	121	5	468	17	27.52	4-34	-

Career Performances

	M	Inns	NO	Runs	HS	Avge	100s	50s	Ct	St	Balls	Runs	Wkts	Avge	Best	5wI	10wM
Test																	
All First	205	231	96	529	27	3.91	-	-	37	-	33587	16049	507	31.65	9-37	10	2
1-day Int																	
NatWest	25	9	6	11	4	3.66	-	-	3	-	1680	923	35	26.37	4-32	-
B & H	29	13	7	6	3 *	1.00	-	-	5	-	1636	977	35	27.91	4-53	-
1-day Lge	141	52	22	88	9 *	2.93	-	-	14	-	6125	4411	128	34.46	4-23	-

71. In which season were four-day County Championship matches introduced?

ROBINSON, P. E.   Leicestershire

Name: Phillip Edward Robinson
Role: Right-hand bat, left-arm
fast bowler, occasional wicket-keeper
Born: 3 August 1963, Keighley, West Yorks
Height: 5ft 9in **Weight:** 14st 7lbs
Nickname: Brigadier, Robbo, FB, Billy
County debut: 1984 (Yorkshire),
1992 (Leicestershire)
County cap: 1988 (Yorkshire)
1000 runs in a season: 3
1st-Class 50s: 51
1st-Class 100s: 7
1st-Class catches: 130
One-Day 100s: 1
Strike rate: (career 98.66)
Parents: Keith and Lesley
Wife and date of marriage: Jane,
19 September 1986

Family links with cricket: Brothers play in Bradford League. Father umpires in
Bradford League. Mother secretary of Heavy Woollen Cup
Education: Long Lee County Primary; Hartington Middle; Greenhead GS
Qualifications: 2 O-levels, senior coaching award, 'degree in University of Life'
Off-season: St Andrew's School, Bloemfontein, South Africa
Overseas tours: Southland CC to Tasmania 1987; Yorkshire to St Lucia and Barbados
1988; Leicestershire to Jamaica 1993, to South Africa 1994-95
Overseas teams played for: Southland, New Zealand 1987; Eastern Southland cricket
coach 1987; Eden Roskill, Auckland 1989-90; Riverside, Wellington 1990-91
Cricketers particularly admired: Geoff Boycott, Richard Hadlee, Michael Holding
Young players to look out for: Ashley Wright
Other sports played: Golf ('got a hole in one'), football, kabaddi, touch rugby
Other sports followed: Football (Manchester United), rugby league (Keighley Cougars)
Relaxations: War-gaming, playing on computer
Extras: Made the highest score by a Yorkshire 2nd XI player with 233 in 1983. Scored
most runs by an overseas player in the Auckland Cricket League for Eden Roskill
1989-90 (1200 runs). Hit the fastest televised 50 in the Sunday League (19 balls) v
Derbyshire at Chesterfield 1991. Released by Yorkshire at his own request at the end
of the 1991 season. Played for Cumberland in 1992 and could play only limited-overs
for Leicestershire in 1992 (apart from one match) but on full contract from 1993.
Captain of Leicestershire 2nd XI. Led the team to Bain Hogg win in 1995
Opinions on cricket: 'Cricket should be played on uncovered pitches over three days.
Alternatively, four-day games should be played Wednesday to Saturday, with the
Sunday League game after. Also, second-class cricket should be played Wednesday to

Friday to allow the younger players to work with the senior players during the season.'
Best batting: 189 Yorkshire v Lancashire, Scarborough 1991
Best bowling: 1-10 Yorkshire v Somerset, Scarborough 1990

1999 Season

	M	Inns	NO	Runs	HS	Avge	100s	50s	Ct	St	O	M	Runs	Wkts	Avge	Best	5wl	10wM
Test																		
All First																		
1-day Int																		
NatWest																		
B & H																		
1-day Lge	1	1	0	1	1	1.00	-	-	-	-								

Career Performances

	M	Inns	NO	Runs	HS	Avge	100s	50s	Ct	St	Balls	Runs	Wkts	Avge	Best	5wl	10wM
Test																	
All First	159	261	35	7617	189	33.70	7	51	130	-	296	329	3	109.66	1-10	-	-
1-day Int																	
NatWest	17	13	0	421	73	32.38	-	3	5	-							
B & H	33	29	4	684	73 *	27.36	-	4	12	-							
1-day Lge	146	141	14	3112	104	24.50	1	14	59	-							

ROBINSON, R.   Durham

Name: Ryan Robinson
Role: Right-hand bat, right-arm medium bowler
Born: 19 October 1976, Huddersfield, West Yorkshire
Height: 6ft 1in **Weight:** 13st
Nickname: Robbo
County debut: 1999 (one-day)
Parents: Peter and Jennifer
Marital status: Single
Family links with cricket: 'Cousin coaches local Stiffs CC'
Education: Emley First; Kirkburton Middle; Shelley High and Sixth Form
Qualifications: 9 GCSEs
Career outside cricket: 'Working for Chopper's Electrical Contractors'

Off-season: Working and playing football
Overseas teams played for: Darling, Cape Town 1994-95
Cricketers particularly admired: Jacques Kallis
Young players to look out for: Nicky Peng
Other sports played: Football (Emley FC – Unibond Premier)
Other sports followed: Rugby league (Thornhill RLFC)
Injuries: No bowling in last month of season because of intercostal injury
Relaxations: Golf and fishing
Opinions on cricket: 'If floodlights and coloured clothes are needed to encourage more spectators, then they should continue being used.'

1999 Season

	M	Inns	NO	Runs	HS	Avge	100s	50s	Ct	St	O	M	Runs	Wkts	Avge	Best	5wI	10wM
Test																		
All First																		
1-day Int																		
NatWest																		
B & H																		
1-day Lge	9	8	0	52	33	6.50	-	-	2	-	42	1	214	4	53.50	2-22	-	

Career Performances

	M	Inns	NO	Runs	HS	Avge	100s	50s	Ct	St	Balls	Runs	Wkts	Avge	Best	5wI	10wM
Test																	
All First																	
1-day Int																	
NatWest																	
B & H																	
1-day Lge	9	8	0	52	33	6.50	-	-	2	-	252	214	4	53.50	2-22	-	

ROBINSON, R. T.   Nottinghamshire

Name: Robert Timothy Robinson
Role: Right-hand opening bat
Born: 21 November 1958, Sutton-in-Ashfield, Nottinghamshire
Height: 6ft **Weight:** 12st 7lbs
Nickname: Robbo
County debut: 1978
County cap: 1983
Benefit: 1992 (£90,040)
Test debut: 1984-85
Tests: 29

One-Day Internationals: 26
1000 runs in a season: 14
1st-Class 50s: 141
1st-Class 100s: 60
1st-Class 200s: 3
1st-Class catches: 257
One-Day 100s: 9
Place in batting averages: 151st av. 25.00
(1998 65th av. 34.56)
Strike rate: (career 64.75)
Parents: Eddy and Christine
Marital status: Separated
Children: Philip Thomas; Alex James
Family links with cricket: Father, uncle,
cousin and brother all played or play local
cricket
Education: Dunstable Grammar School;
High Pavement College, Nottingham;
Sheffield University
Qualifications: BA (Hons) Accountancy and Financial Management
Career outside cricket: Director of sports retail business
Overseas tours: England to India and Sri Lanka 1984-85, to West Indies 1985-86, to
India and Pakistan (World Cup) 1987-88, to New Zealand 1987-88; to Australia
1987-88; unofficial English XI to South Africa 1989-90
Cricketers particularly admired: Clive Rice, Geoffrey Boycott
Young players to look out for: Matt Whiley
Other sports played: Golf, squash
Other sports followed: Football (Nottingham Forest, Notts County)
Relaxations: 'Spending time with my children'
Extras: Played for Northamptonshire 2nd XI in 1974-75 and for Nottinghamshire 2nd
XI in 1977. Had soccer trials with Portsmouth, Chelsea and QPR. One of *Wisden*'s
Five Cricketers of the Year 1986. Banned from Test cricket for joining 1989-90 tour of
South Africa; remitted in 1992. Scored two 100s (119 and 139*) v Glamorgan at
Swansea 1993. Handed over county captaincy to Paul Johnson in 1995 to give more
time to business. Is second in the list of Notts leading run-scorers behind George
Gunn. Retired from county cricket at end of 1999 season
Opinions on cricket: 'Decision-makers should listen to the views of the participants
and the spectators!!'
Best batting: 220* Nottinghamshire v Yorkshire, Trent Bridge 1990
Best bowling: 1-22 Nottinghamshire v Northamptonshire, Northampton 1982

1999 Season

	M	Inns	NO	Runs	HS	Avge	100s	50s	Ct	St	O	M	Runs	Wkts	Avge	Best	5wI	10wM
Test																		
All First	12	22	1	525	80	25.00	-	4	10	-								
1-day Int																		
NatWest	2	2	0	56	36	28.00	-	-	-	-								
B & H																		
1-day Lge	6	6	0	92	29	15.33	-	-	-	-								

Career Performances

	M	Inns	NO	Runs	HS	Avge	100s	50s	Ct	St	Balls	Runs	Wkts	Avge	Best	5wI	10wM
Test	29	49	5	1601	175	36.38	4	6	8	-	6	0	0	-	-	-	-
All First	425	739	85	27571	220 *	42.15	63	141	257	-	259	289	4	72.25	1-22	-	-
1-day Int	26	26	0	597	83	22.96	-	3	6	-							
NatWest	45	45	3	1708	139	40.66	2	8	17	-							
B & H	78	75	9	2567	120	38.89	3	18	17	-							
1-day Lge	239	232	27	6695	119 *	32.65	4	44	75	-							

ROLLINS, A. S.   Northamptonshire

Name: Adrian Stewart Rollins
Role: Right-hand bat, right-arm medium bowler, occasional wicket-keeper
Born: 8 February 1972, Barking, Essex
Height: 6ft 5in **Weight:** 'Heavy – like Lennox Lewis'
Nickname: Rollie
County debut: 1993 (Derbyshire)
County cap: 1995 (Derbyshire)
1000 runs in a season: 3
1st-Class 50s: 33
1st-Class 100s: 10
1st-Class 200s: 1
1st-Class catches: 81
1st-Class stumpings: 1
One-Day 100s: 1
Place in batting averages: 43rd av. 38.60 (1998 74th av. 32.52)
Strike rate: (career 90.00)
Parents: Marva
Marital status: Engaged to Debbie

Children: Stepdaughter Gemma, 6 yrs; son, Jared Terrell, 1 June 1999
Family links with cricket: 'Brother [Robert] just retired; played for Essex 1991-99. Brother Gary should be playing. Uncles played in Essex League'
Education: Avenue Primary, Manor Park, London; Little Ilford Comprehensive, Manor Park, London
Qualifications: 10 GCSEs, 4 A-levels, NCA coaching award, Diploma in Sports Psychology, 'I am also doing a course in business management at present'
Career outside cricket: 'Not sure; salesman for the Bad Apple Corporation'
Off-season: 'Signing for Northants; chilling out; yoga'
Overseas tours: London Federation of Boys Clubs to Barbados 1987
Overseas teams played for: Kaponga, New Zealand 1993-94
Cricketers particularly admired: Phillip DeFreitas, Malcolm Marshall, David Gower, Viv Richards, Gordon Greenidge, Desmond Haynes, Michael Holding
Young players to look out for: Ben Spendlove, Ian Blackwell, Vikram Solanki, Trevor Smith, Paul Franks, Robin Weston
Other sports played: Basketball, badminton (played for New Ham Schools), football, 'racketball master'
Other sports followed: Football (West Ham United), basketball
Injuries: 'Conspiracyitis'
Relaxations: 'Looking after my baby boy; looking after my family. Having a net'
Extras: Made Championship debut on same day as brother. Became 500th first-class player for Derbyshire, for whom he was named Young Player of the Year 1993. Was the 100th Derbyshire player to score a hundred. In 1995 set record for the highest score by a Derbyshire opener to carry his bat, and his 200 not out against Gloucestershire was the longest innings by a Derbyshire player. He became the youngest English-qualified Derbyshire double centurion. Voted Derbyshire Player of the Year for 1995. Took part in record third wicket partnership for Derbyshire (316*) with Kim Barnett against Leicestershire 1997. Scored century before lunch against Glamorgan at Chesterfield August 1997. Scored 111 not out in one-day match v New Zealand 1999. Left Derbyshire at end of 1999 season and has joined Northamptonshire for 2000
Opinions on cricket: 'Groundsmen should be contracted to ECB. ECB should have a management staff of batting, bowling and wicket-keeping coaches, preferably ex-players, who should tour the country and help clubs raise the standard of their players (e.g., if Ian Botham, David Gower, Allan Lamb etc were regularly making contact with players of today and pointed out the technical and mental requirements to be successful, English cricket could only get better).'
Best batting: 210 Derbyshire v Hampshire, Chesterfield 1997
Best bowling: 1-19 Derbyshire v Essex, Chelmsford 1995

1999 Season

	M	Inns	NO	Runs	HS	Avge	100s	50s	Ct	St	O	M	Runs	Wkts	Avge	Best	5wl	10wM
Test																		
All First	15	28	3	965	113	38.60	2	5	9	-								
1-day Int																		
NatWest	2	2	0	88	80	44.00	-	1	3	-								
B & H																			
1-day Lge	10	10	1	198	31	22.00	-	-	3	-								

Career Performances

	M	Inns	NO	Runs	HS	Avge	100s	50s	Ct	St	Balls	Runs	Wkts	Avge	Best	5wl	10wM
Test																	
All First	101	187	18	6021	210	35.62	11	33	81	1	90	122	1	122.00	1-19	-	-
1-day Int																	
NatWest	11	11	0	278	80	25.27	-	3	8	-							
B & H	11	11	1	262	70 *	26.20	-	2	2	-							
1-day Lge	64	58	5	1013	126 *	19.11	1	1	26	-	12	15	0	-	-	-

ROLLINS, R. J.   Essex

Name: Robert John Rollins
Role: Right-hand bat, wicket-keeper
Born: 30 January 1974, Plaistow, London
Height: 5ft 9in **Weight:** 14st
Nickname: Walter, Rollie
County debut: 1992
County cap: 1995
1st-Class 50s: 11
1st-Class 100s: 1
1st-Class catches: 158
1st-Class stumpings: 21
Place in batting averages: (1998 249th av. 14.25)
Parents: 'Mrs Marva Rollins BEd, MA'
Marital status: Engaged to Kerry-Ann
Children: Lawren and Ellisee
Family links with cricket: Elder brother (Adrian) played for Derbyshire and now

Northamptonshire, 'middle brother (Gary) is an aspiring fast bowler (if anyone is interested, please call me)'
Education: Avenue Primary School, Manor Park; Little Ilford Comprehensive School; 'School of Hard Knocks'

Qualifications: 6 GCSEs, senior coach NVQ Level 2
Overseas tours: England U18 to Canada 1991; England U19 to Pakistan 1991-92, to India 1992-93
Overseas teams played for: MOB Pietermaritzburg, South Africa 1995-96; Shell Harbour, New South Wales 1996-97
Cricketers particularly admired: Adrian Rollins, Gary Rollins, Ash, Keith Hurst, John French
Young players to look out for: Ryan Hurst, Carl Hurst, Benjamin Hurst, Dominic Hurst ('my little cousins')
Other sports played: Loxford Youth Club pool team – district winners 1992
Other sports followed: Football (West Ham United)
Relaxations: Reading, playing golf, playing on PlayStation
Extras: Named Essex Young Player of the Year 1992 and awarded his 2nd XI cap in September of that year. Made Championship debut on the same day as his brother Adrian. Both kept wicket in the same Sunday League game. Forced to retire from first-class cricket at end of 1999 season because of knee injury
Opinions on cricket: 'The game continues to be a great leveller.'
Best batting: 133* Essex v Glamorgan, Swansea 1995

1999 Season

	M	Inns	NO	Runs	HS	Avge	100s	50s	Ct	St	O	M	Runs	Wkts	Avge	Best	5wl	10wM
Test																		
All First	3	4	1	65	33	21.66	-	-	6	1								
1-day Int																		
NatWest																		
B & H																		
1-day Lge	4	4	0	189	87	47.25	-	2	4	2								

Career Performances

	M	Inns	NO	Runs	HS	Avge	100s	50s	Ct	St	Balls	Runs	Wkts	Avge	Best	5wl	10wM
Test																		
All First	69	111	10	2258	133 *	22.35	1	11	158	21								
1-day Int																		
NatWest	14	11	4	258	67 *	36.85	-	3	8	3								
B & H	19	11	2	89	28	9.88	-	-	17	4								
1-day Lge	70	55	9	705	87	15.32	-	2	59	18								

ROSE, G. D.   Somerset

Name: Graham David Rose
Role: Right-hand bat, right-arm
fast-medium bowler, first slip
Born: 12 April 1964, Tottenham
Height: 6ft 4in **Weight:** 15st 7lbs
Nickname: Rosie, Hagar, Yid
County debut: 1985 (Middlesex),
1987 (Somerset)
County cap: 1988 (Somerset)
Benefit: 1997 (£91,500)
1000 runs in a season: 1
50 wickets in a season: 5
1st-Class 50s: 40
1st-Class 100s: 9
1st-Class 5 w. in innings: 14
1st-Class 10 w. in match: 1
1st-Class catches: 112
One-Day 100s: 2

Place in batting averages: 46th av. 38.00 (1998 140th av. 25.25)
Place in bowling averages: 126th av. 38.64 (1998 62nd av. 26.90)
Strike rate: 77.41 (career 55.70)
Parents: William and Edna
Wife and date of marriage: Teresa Julie, 19 September 1987
Children: Georgina Charlotte, 6 December 1990; Felix William Michael, 11 August 1997
Family links with cricket: Father and brothers have played club cricket
Education: Northumberland Park School, Tottenham
Qualifications: 6 O-levels, 4 A-levels, NCA coaching certificate
Career outside cricket: 'Would like to have some idea!'
Off-season: 'Coaching, training and recharging mental and physical batteries'
Overseas teams played for: Carey Park, Bunbury, Western Australia 1984-85;
Fremantle, Perth 1986-87; Paarl, Cape Town 1988-89
Cricketers particularly admired: Andrew Caddick, Jimmy Cook, Richard Hadlee,
Malcolm Marshall, Mushtaq Ahmed
Young players to look out for: Matthew Bulbeck, Peter Trego
Other sports followed: Football, rugby, golf
Injuries: Out for eight weeks on and off with cartilage and bone removed from
right knee
Relaxations: Wine, golf, 'Georgina and Felix'
Extras: Played for England YC v Australia YC 1983. Took 6-41 on Middlesex debut
in 1985, then scored 95 on debut for Somerset in 1987. Completed double of 1000
runs and 50 wickets in first-class cricket in 1990 and set records for fastest recorded

centuries in NatWest Trophy (36 balls v Devon) and Sunday League (46 balls v Glamorgan; since bettered). Cricket Society's All-rounder of the Year 1997

Opinions on cricket: 'The structure of the game is not far off being good enough to bring success internationally. I wonder if the national team would be more relaxed and more likely to win if we didn't have such a frenzied and acidic press who seem to delight in its many failings. It is no coincidence and it is an attitude that will have to change.'

Best batting: 191 Somerset v Sussex, Taunton 1997
Best bowling: 7-47 Somerset v Nottinghamshire, Taunton 1996

1999 Season

	M	Inns	NO	Runs	HS	Avge	100s	50s	Ct	St	O	M	Runs	Wkts	Avge	Best	5wI	10wM
Test																		
All First	9	11	2	342	123 *	38.00	1	1	2	-	219.2	61	657	17	38.64	4-14	-	-
1-day Int																		
NatWest	1	1	0	24	24	24.00	-	-	-	-	10	3	38	2	19.00	2-38	-	
B & H																		
1-day Lge	10	6	0	101	41	16.83	-	-	2	-	70	7	311	9	34.55	2-26	-	

Career Performances

	M	Inns	NO	Runs	HS	Avge	100s	50s	Ct	St	Balls	Runs	Wkts	Avge	Best	5wI	10wM
Test																	
All First	230	321	58	8118	191	30.86	9	40	112	-	31863	16805	572	29.37	7-47	14	1
1-day Int																	
NatWest	25	21	3	372	110	20.66	1	1	4	-	1366	889	29	30.65	3-11	-	
B & H	54	48	4	911	79	20.70	-	4	12	-	2932	1950	67	29.10	4-21	-	
1-day Lge	191	164	32	3535	148	26.78	1	18	48	-	7454	5537	189	29.29	4-26	-	

72. Which current county wicket-keeper scored a Championship 100 in 1990 entirely with the aid of a runner?

ROSEBERRY, M. A.   Middlesex

Name: Michael Anthony Roseberry
Role: Right-hand bat, right-arm
medium-fast bowler
Born: 28 November 1966,
Houghton-le-Spring, Sunderland
Height: 6ft 2in **Weight:** 14st 7lbs
Nickname: Micky
County debut: 1985 (Middlesex),
1995 (Durham)
County cap: 1990 (Middlesex), 1998
(Durham)
1000 runs in a season: 4
1st-Class 50s: 54
1st-Class 100s: 20
1st-Class catches: 153
One-Day 100s: 6
Place in batting averages: 161st av. 24.15
(1998 123rd av. 26.81)
Strike rate: (career 127.75)
Parents: Matthew and Jean
Wife and date of marriage: Helen Louise, 22 February 1991
Children: Jordan Louise, 29 May 1992; Lauren Ella, 19 February 1994
Family links with cricket: Brother Andrew played for Glamorgan and Leicestershire;
father is director of Durham CCC
Education: Tonstall Preparatory School, Sunderland; Durham School
Qualifications: 5 O-levels, 1 A-level, advanced cricket coach
Career outside cricket: 'Coaching cricket. Director in our business'
Overseas tours: England YC to West Indies 1984-85; England A to Australia 1992-93;
England XI and Lord's Taverners to Hong Kong 'on numerous occasions'; MCC
to West Africa 1993-94; Durham CCC to South Africa 1994-95
Overseas teams played for: Fremantle, Western Australia 1986; Melville, Perth 1988;
Alberton, Johannesburg 1994-96
Cricketers particularly admired: 'Desmond Haynes for the obvious and his
generosity on the golf course'
Other sports played: 'Played rugby union at a good level when at school,
representing Durham County at all levels except the senior side'
Other sports followed: 'Follow golf and very loyal supporter of Sunderland FC'
Relaxations: 'Eating out and spending time with my family, which is limited during
the summer'
Extras: Won Lord's Taverners/MCC Cricketer of the Year 1983, Cricket Society award
for Best Young Cricketer of the Year 1984 and twice won Cricket Society award for

best all-rounder in schools cricket. Played in Durham League as a professional while still at school. At age 16, playing for Durham School v St Bees, he hit 216 in 160 minutes. In 1992 scored 2044 runs – joint highest in first-class cricket with Peter Bowler – and was named Middlesex Player of the Year and Lucozade Player of the Year. Left Middlesex at end of 1994 to return to his native Durham as captain for the 1995 season but relinquished the captaincy during the 1996 season. Rejoined Middlesex for 1999 season

Best batting: 185 Middlesex v Leicestershire, Lord's 1993
Best bowling: 1-1 Middlesex v Sussex, Hove 1988

1999 Season

	M	Inns	NO	Runs	HS	Avge	100s	50s	Ct	St	O	M	Runs	Wkts	Avge	Best	5wI	10wM
Test																		
All First	12	21	1	483	116	24.15	1	1	7	-								
1-day Int																		
NatWest	1	1	0	0	0	0.00	-	-	-	-								
B & H																		
1-day Lge	13	13	2	423	91 *	38.45	-	5	3	-								

Career Performances

	M	Inns	NO	Runs	HS	Avge	100s	50s	Ct	St	Balls	Runs	Wkts	Avge	Best	5wI	10wM
Test																	
All First	214	364	38	10981	185	33.68	20	54	153	-	511	406	4	101.50	1-1	-	-
1-day Int																	
NatWest	18	18	1	703	121	41.35	3	1	7	-	36	42	1	42.00	1-22	-	
B & H	33	31	3	707	84	25.25	-	6	7	-	6	2	0	-	-	-	
1-day Lge	139	133	17	3740	119 *	32.24	3	28	50	-	4	7	0	-	-	-	

73. Which West Indies fast bowler scored the fastest 100
of the 1981 season and for which county?

RUSSELL, R. C. Gloucestershire

Name: Robert Charles Russell
Role: Left-hand bat, wicket-keeper
Born: 15 August 1963, Stroud
Height: 5ft 8¹/₄in **Weight:** 9st 9lbs
Nickname: Jack
County debut: 1981
County cap: 1985
Benefit: 1994
Test debut: 1988
Tests: 54
One-Day Internationals: 40
1000 runs in a season: 1
1st-Class 50s: 77
1st-Class 100s: 7
1st-Class catches: 1028
1st-Class stumpings: 115
One-Day 100s: 2
Place in batting averages: 82nd av. 32.91
(1998 187th av. 20.26)
Strike rate: (career 56.00)
Parents: John and Jennifer
Wife and date of marriage: Aileen Ann, 6 March 1985
Children: Stepson, Marcus Anthony 1980; Elizabeth Ann, March 1988;
Victoria, 1989; Charles David, 1991; Katherine Jane, 1996
Education: Uplands County Primary School; Archway Comprehensive School;
Bristol Polytechnic ('walked out after two months of accountancy course. Couldn't
understand the sociology and economics – wanted to play cricket instead')
Qualifications: 7 O-levels, 2 A-levels
Career outside cricket: Professional artist
Overseas tours: England A to Australia 1992-93; England to Pakistan 1987-88, to
India and West Indies 1989-90, to Australia 1990-91, to New Zealand 1991-92, to West
Indies 1993-94, to Australia 1994-95, to South Africa 1995-96, to Pakistan and India
(World Cup) 1995-96, to Zimbabwe and New Zealand 1996-97, to West Indies 1997-
98, to Bangladesh (Wills International Cup) 1998-99
Cricketers particularly admired: Alan Knott, Bob Taylor, Ian Botham,
Rodney Marsh 'and other greats'
Other sports followed: Football (Tottenham Hotspur), rugby (England), snooker,
'anything competitive'
Relaxations: Playing cricket and painting pictures. 'I love comedians and comedies.
Life is too short, you need to laugh as much as you can'
Extras: Spotted at age nine by Gloucestershire coach, Graham Wiltshire. Became

youngest Gloucestershire wicket-keeper (17 years 307 days) and set record for most dismissals in a match on first-class debut: 8 (7 caught, 1 stumped) for Gloucestershire v Sri Lankans at Bristol, 1981. Hat-trick of catches v Surrey at The Oval 1986. Represented England YC v West Indies YC in 1982. Was chosen as England's Man of the Test Series, England v Australia 1989 and was one of *Wisden*'s Five Cricketers of the Year 1990. Appointed vice-captain to Martyn Moxon on the England A tour to Australia 1992-93. Called up as stand-by wicket-keeper for the England tour to Australia 1994-95 when Alec Stewart broke his finger for the second time on the tour. Opened Jack Russell Gallery in Chipping Sodbury, South Gloucestershire, in 1995 where he displays original oil paintings and limited edition prints of cricketing scenes, landscapes, wildlife etc. Books of his that have been published include *A Cricketer's Art – Sketches by Jack Russell* (1988), *Sketches of a Season – illustrated by Jack Russell* (1989), *Jack Russell's Sketch Book* (1996) and *Jack Russell – Unleashed*, an autobiography which made the top ten bestsellers in 1997. Commissioned by Dean of Gloucester to do a drawing of Gloucester Cathedral to raise funds for 900th Anniversary. Still turns out for his original club, Stroud CC, whenever he can. Keen military enthusiast, 'We must never forget'. His paintings are sold and displayed in museums and private collections all around the world. Loves England, 'To me, it's the greatest place of all to play and paint.' Captain of Gloucestershire and Player of the Year 1995. Broke Bob Taylor's long-standing world record for the number of dismissals in a Test match with 11 (all caught) in the second Test v South Africa at Johannesburg 1995-96; his 27 Test dismissals in the series is a record for England. Awarded MBE in 1996 for services to cricket. Was the Whyte and Mackay wicket-keeper/batsman of the year 1995, 1996, 1997. He also has his own website: http://www.jackrussell.co.uk. Announced his retirement from international cricket in October 1998 after the Wills International Cup in Bangladesh. Became seventh wicket-keeper to take 1000 first-class catches when he caught Tim Robinson v Notts at Bristol 1999. Set a new NatWest dismissals record by claiming his 67th victim (Adrian Rollins) v Derbyshire at Bristol 1999. Man of the Match in Gloucestershire's NatWest final victory over Somerset 1999. Leading wicket-keeper in the single-division four-day County Championship era with 356 victims (335 caught/21 stumped) 1993-99
Best batting: 129* England v Boland, Paarl 1995-96
Best bowling: 1-4 Gloucestershire v West Indians, Bristol 1991

1999 Season

	M	Inns	NO	Runs	HS	Avge	100s	50s	Ct	St	O	M	Runs	Wkts	Avge	Best	5wI	10wM
Test																		
All First	17	30	6	790	94 *	32.91	-	5	55	5								
1-day Int																		
NatWest	5	5	2	109	38	36.33	-	-	7	2								
B & H	3	3	1	81	50 *	40.50	-	1	3	1								
1-day Lge	16	16	4	409	91 *	34.08	-	4	13	6								

Career Performances

	M	Inns	NO	Runs	HS	Avge	100s	50s	Ct	St	Balls	Runs	Wkts	Avge	Best	5wI	10wM
Test	54	86	16	1897	128 *	27.10	2	6	153	12							
All First	409	609	129	14438	129 *	30.07	7	77	1028	115	56	68	1	68.00	1-4	-	-
1-day Int	40	31	7	423	50	17.62	-	1	41	6							
NatWest	45	33	10	639	59 *	27.78	-	1	64	11							
B & H	69	52	18	1088	119 *	32.00	1	4	70	13							
1-day Lge	225	175	38	3206	108	23.40	1	14	182	37							

SACHDEVA, A. — Leicestershire

Name: Atul Sachdeva
Role: Right-hand bat, leg-spin bowler
Born: 22 August 1980, Preston, Lancs
Height: 5ft 9in **Weight:** 10st 7lbs
Nickname: Sach
County debut: 1999
Strike rate: 72.00 (career 72.00)
Parents: Anju and Surendra
Marital status: Single
Education: Queen's Drive County Primary, Preston; St Pius X School, Preston; King Edward VII School, Lytham; Lancaster RGS; Leicester University
Qualifications: 10 GCSEs, 4 A-levels
Career outside cricket: Medical student
Overseas tours: Lancaster RGS to Barbados 1998; Leicestershire to Holland 1998
Cricketers particularly admired:
Viv Richards, Shane Warne

Young players to look out for: Chris Schofield
Other sports played: Rugby union, badminton, golf
Other sports followed: Rugby, football, golf
Relaxations: Sport – golf
Extras: Represented Lancashire at U15, U17, U19 level. Played for Northern League U18 representative side
Opinions on cricket: 'In favour of two divisions.'
Best bowling: 1-32 Leicestershire v Derbyshire, Leicester 1999

1999 Season

	M	Inns	NO	Runs	HS	Avge	100s	50s	Ct	St	O	M	Runs	Wkts	Avge	Best	5wI	10wM
Test																		
All First	1	2	1	0	0 *	0.00	-	-	-	-	12	1	54	1	54.00	1-32	-	-
1-day Int																		
NatWest																		
B & H																		
1-day Lge																		

Career Performances

	M	Inns	NO	Runs	HS	Avge	100s	50s	Ct	St	Balls		Runs	Wkts	Avge	Best	5wI	10wM
Test																		
All First	1	2	1	0	0 *	0.00	-	-	-	-	72		54	1	54.00	1-32	-	-
1-day Int																		
NatWest																		
B & H																		
1-day Lge																		

SAGGERS, M. J.   Kent

Name: Martin John Saggers
Role: Right-hand bat, right-arm
fast-medium bowler
Born: 23 May 1972, King's Lynn
Height: 6ft 2in **Weight:** 13st 10lbs
Nickname: Saggs, Saggsy, Saggy Bits,
Sagaloo, Pony, Bruv, Wibs
County debut: 1996 (Durham), 1999 (Kent)
1st-Class 5 w. in innings: 2
1st-Class catches: 3
Place in bowling averages: 3rd av. 16.00
Strike rate: 29.91 (career 43.56)
Parents: Brian and Edna
Marital status: Single
Family links with cricket: Grandfather
played in the Essex League
Education: Roseberry Avenue Primary
School; Springwood High School;
University of Huddersfield
Qualifications: BA (Hons) Architectural Studies International
Career outside cricket: Architectural technician/consultant

Off-season: Coaching and training in South Africa
Overseas teams played for: Randburg CC, Johannesburg 1996-98; Southern Suburbs, Johannesburg 1998-99
Cricketers particularly admired: Allan Donald, Neil Foster, Darren Gough, Kevin Lacy
Young players to look out for: Robert Ferley, James Hockley, Graeme Fox
Other sports played: Golf
Other sports followed: Football (Tottenham Hotspur), British Touring Car Championship, Formula 1
Injuries: Out from beginning of June to end of season with stress fracture to lower back
Relaxations: 'Going to the "Bat and Ball" for dinner. Beating Hockers and Kriss at golf on the PlayStation. Annoying my housemates by listening to loud music'
Extras: Released by Durham at end of 1998 season and joined Kent
Opinions on cricket: 'Best game in the world.'
Best batting: 18 Durham v Somerset, Weston-super-Mare 1996
Best bowling: 6-65 Durham v Glamorgan, Chester-le-Street 1996

1999 Season

	M	Inns	NO	Runs	HS	Avge	100s	50s	Ct	St	O	M	Runs	Wkts	Avge	Best	5wI	10wM
Test																		
All First	2	1	0	0	0	0.00	-	-	-	-	59.5	13	192	12	16.00	4-26	-	-
1-day Int																		
NatWest																		
B & H																		
1-day Lge																		

Career Performances

	M	Inns	NO	Runs	HS	Avge	100s	50s	Ct	St	Balls	Runs	Wkts	Avge	Best	5wI	10wM
Test																	
All First	12	18	5	128	18	9.84	-	-	3	-	1699	961	39	24.64	6-65	2	-
1-day Int																	
NatWest	2	1	0	0	0	0.00	-	-	-	-	118	98	2	49.00	2-42	-	
B & H	5	5	3	58	34 *	29.00	-	-	2	-	246	247	5	49.40	2-49	-	
1-day Lge	13	6	4	31	13	15.50	-	-	3	-	522	367	17	21.58	4-35	-	

74. Which batsman scored 100s before lunch in each innings of the match between Gloucestershire and Yorkshire at Bradford in 1900?

SALES, D. J. G.   Northamptonshire

Name: David John Grimwood Sales
Role: Right-hand bat, right-arm
occasional bowler
Born: 3 December 1977, Carshalton, Surrey
Height: 6ft **Weight:** 13st
Nickname: Jumble
County debut: 1994 (one-day),
1996 (first-class)
County cap: 1999
1000 runs in a season: 1
1st-Class 50s: 9
1st-Class 100s: 3
1st-Class 200s: 1
1st-Class 300s: 1
1st-Class catches: 38
Place in batting averages: 8th av. 51.64
(1998 219th av. 17.30)
Strike rate: 23.62 (career 33.66)
Parents: John and Daphne
Marital status: Single
Family links with cricket: Father played club cricket
Education: Cumnor House Prep School, Croydon; Caterham Boys' School
Qualifications: 7 GCSEs, cricket coach
Off-season: England A tour to Bangladesh and New Zealand
Overseas tours: England U15 to South Africa 1993; England U19 to West Indies
1994-95, to Zimbabwe 1995-96, to Pakistan 1996-97; England A to Kenya and Sri Lanka
1997-98, to Bangladesh and New Zealand 1999-2000
Cricketers particularly admired: Graham Gooch
Young players to look out for: Owais Shah
Other sports followed: Football (Crystal Palace), golf
Relaxations: Golf and fishing
Extras: In 1994, became youngest batsman (16 years 289 days) to score a 50 in the
Sunday League with his 56-ball 70* v Essex at Chelmsford. Scored 210* v Worcs
1996 to become first Englishman to score a double century on his Championship debut
and the youngest ever to score a double century. Became the youngest Englishman to
score a first-class 300 (303*) v Essex at Northampton 1999 aged 21 years 240 days
(and became the first Englishman to 1000 runs for 1999 in the process); the record was
previously held by Sir Leonard Hutton, who scored his 364 v Australia at The Oval in
1938 aged 22 years and two months. Awarded Northants cap 1999. PCA/CGU Young
Player of the Year 1999
Best batting: 303* Northamptonshire v Essex, Northampton 1999
Best bowling: 4-25 Northamptonshire v Sri Lanka A, Northampton 1999

1999 Season

	M	Inns	NO	Runs	HS	Avge	100s	50s	Ct	St	O	M	Runs	Wkts	Avge	Best	5wI	10wM
Test																		
All First	18	29	4	1291	303 *	51.64	3	5	15	-	31.3	7	99	8	12.37	4-25	-	-
1-day Int																		
NatWest	3	3	0	92	53	30.66	-	1	2	-								
B & H																		
1-day Lge	14	14	0	288	54	20.57	-	1	8	-								

Career Performances

	M	Inns	NO	Runs	HS	Avge	100s	50s	Ct	St	Balls	Runs	Wkts	Avge	Best	5wI	10wM
Test																	
All First	55	86	9	2643	303 *	34.32	5	9	38	-	303	163	9	18.11	4-25	-	-
1-day Int																	
NatWest	6	6	0	187	53	31.16	-	2	3	-							
B & H	5	5	0	67	26	13.40	-	-	2	-							
1-day Lge	47	43	5	803	70 *	21.13	-	2	16	-							

SALISBURY, I. D. K.   Surrey

Name: Ian David Kenneth Salisbury
Role: Right-hand bat, leg-break bowler
Born: 21 January 1970, Moulton,
Northampton
Height: 5ft 11in **Weight:** 12st 7lbs
Nickname: Solly, Dingle, Sals
County debut: 1989 (Sussex), 1997 (Surrey)
County cap: 1991 (Sussex), 1998 (Surrey)
Test debut: 1992
Tests: 12
One-Day Internationals: 4
50 wickets in a season: 5
1st-Class 50s: 14
1st-Class 100s: 1
1st-Class 5 w. in innings: 30
1st-Class 10 w. in match: 4
1st-Class catches: 144
One-Day 5 w. in innings: 1
Place in batting averages: 197th av. 20.76 (1998 195th av. 19.62)
Place in bowling averages: 32nd av. 21.91 (1998 54th av. 25.89)
Strike rate: 55.83 (career 63.63)

Parents: Dave and Margaret

Wife and date of marriage: Emma Louise, 25 September 1993

Family links with cricket: 'Dad is vice-president of my first club, Brixworth. He also re-lays cricket squares (e.g. Lord's, Northampton, Leicester)'

Education: Moulton Primary; Moulton Comprehensive (both Northampton)

Qualifications: 7 O-levels, NCA coaching certificate, 'Life'

Off-season: 'Captaining University of NSW, Sydney, in grade cricket'

Overseas tours: England A to Pakistan 1990-91, to Bermuda and West Indies 1991-92, to India 1994-95, to Pakistan 1995-96; England to India and Sri Lanka 1992-93, to West Indies 1993-94; World Masters XI v Indian Masters XI November 1996 ('Masters aged 26?')

Overseas teams played for: University of New South Wales, Sydney 1997-2000

Cricketers particularly admired: 'Any that keep performing day in, day out, for both country and county (e.g. Saqlain, Martin Bicknell, Andrew Caddick, Steve Waugh)'

Young players to look out for: Ben Hollioake, Owais Shah, Alex Tudor, David Sales, Paul Franks, Steve Harmison, Luke Sutton

Other sports played: 'Most sports'

Other sports followed: Football (Southampton FC, Northampton Town FC), rugby union (Northampton Saints), 'any England team'

Relaxations: 'Spending time with wife, Emma; meeting friends and relaxing with them and eating out with good wine. Also, Sydney has its moments!!'

Extras: Picked to play two Tests for England against Pakistan in 1992, 'proudest moments of my career'. Originally selected for England A tour to Australia 1992-93 but was asked to stay on in India and played in the first two Tests of the series. In 1992 was named Young Player of the Year by both the Wombwell Cricket Lovers and the Cricket Writers. One of *Wisden*'s Five Cricketers of the Year 1993. Left Sussex during the 1996-97 off-season to join Surrey. Scored maiden first-class 100 (100*) v Somerset at The Oval 1999

Opinions on cricket: 'Improve the standard of cricket pitches (e.g. ECB-contract groundsmen, so no doctoring of pitches). If possible improve media's view of our game – rather than constantly criticising, maybe praise and be constructive in criticism (for example, Channel 4 "refreshing").'

Best batting: 100* Surrey v Somerset, The Oval 1999

Best bowling: 8-75 Sussex v Essex, Chelmsford 1996

1999 Season

	M	Inns	NO	Runs	HS	Avge	100s	50s	Ct	St	O	M	Runs	Wkts	Avge	Best	5wI	10wM
Test																		
All First	17	19	2	353	100 *	20.76	1	1	5	-	558.2	145	1315	60	21.91	5-44	2	-
1-day Int																		
NatWest	4	1	0	3	3	3.00	-	-	-	-	36	3	155	6	25.83	3-29	-	
B & H	1	1	0	15	15	15.00	-	-	-	-	6	0	36	0	-	-	-	
1-day Lge	10	9	0	57	19	6.33	-	-	2	-	58.2	0	297	3	99.00	1-25	-	

Career Performances

	M	Inns	NO	Runs	HS	Avge	100s	50s	Ct	St	Balls	Runs	Wkts	Avge	Best	5wl	10wM
Test	12	22	2	284	50	14.20	-	1	5	-	2078	1346	19	70.84	4-163	-	
All First	210	271	54	4002	100 *	18.44	1	14	144	-	38560	19558	606	32.27	8-75	30	4
1-day Int	4	2	1	7	5	7.00	-	-	1	-	186	177	5	35.40	3-41	-	
NatWest	25	16	4	143	34 *	11.91	-	-	5	-	1529	875	32	27.34	3-28	-	
B & H	34	20	7	169	19	13.00	-	-	13	-	1845	1311	43	30.48	4-53	-	
1-day Lge	122	81	21	767	48 *	12.78	-	-	39	-	4532	3801	105	36.20	5-30	1	

SAMPSON, P. J. Surrey

Name: Philip James Sampson
Role: Right-hand bat, right-arm fast bowler
Born: 6 September 1980, Manchester, England
Height: 6ft 2in **Weight:** 12st 7lbs
Nickname: Philo, Sammo
County debut: No first-team appearance
Parents: Les and Kay
Marital status: Single
Family links with cricket: Father played league cricket and was chairman of the Harlequins club, Pretoria, in their South African National Club Championship winning season 1996
Education: Waterkloof House Preparatory School, Pretoria; Pretoria Boys High School
Qualifications: Matriculation (A-level equivalent)
Off-season: Playing for Harlequins, Pretoria, in Northerns Premier League
Overseas teams played for: Harlequins, Pretoria 1999, 2000
Other sports followed: Football (Manchester United)
Extras: Captain of school 1st XI 1998. Represented Northerns at U15, U18, U19. Played for Buckinghamshire in the Minor Counties 1999

75. Who captained Surrey to the County Championship in 1971?

SAQLAIN MUSHTAQ   Surrey

Name: Saqlain Mushtaq
Role: Right-hand bat, off-spin bowler
Born: 27 November 1976, Lahore, Pakistan
County debut: 1997
County cap: 1998
Test debut: 1995-96
Tests: 22
One-Day Internationals: 108
50 wickets in a season: 2
1st-Class 50s: 4
1st-Class 5 w. in innings: 31
1st-Class 10 w. in match: 10
1st-Class catches: 33
One-Day 5 w. in innings: 5
Place in batting averages: (1998 217th av. 17.60)
Place in bowling averages: 1st av. 11.37 (1998 8th av. 17.76)
Strike rate: 30.08 (career 49.62)

Overseas tours: Pakistan to Australia 1995-96, to Sharjah 1995-96, 1996-97, 1997-98, to Singapore 1995-96, to England 1996, to Sri Lanka 1996-97, to Toronto and Nairobi 1996-97, to Australia 1996-97, to India 1996-97, to South Africa 1997-98, to Zimbabwe 1997-98, to Sri Lanka 1997-98, to Toronto 1997-98, 1998-99, to Bangladesh 1998-99, to India 1998-99, to UK, Ireland and Holland (World Cup) 1999, to Australia 1999-2000
Overseas teams played for: PIA, Islamabad 1994-1998
Extras: Has reportedly developed a 'mystery ball' – a leg break bowled with an off-break action. Won Man of the Series award in 1998-99 Test series v India. Took only the second hat-trick in World Cup cricket, v Zimbabwe at The Oval 1999; his victims were Olonga, Huckle and Mbangwa; it was his second hat-trick in One-Day Internationals v Zimbabwe. Featured in the Vodafone World Cup XI, a 'dream team' selected by journalists after the 1999 tournament. Took the fifth hat-trick of his career, for Surrey v Sussex at Hove 1999. Topped the first-class bowling averages in 1999, taking 58 wickets at an astonishing average of 11.37 in the seven games he played for Surrey; the last bowler to record an average of less than 11.50 in an English season was Derbyshire's Harold Rhodes (11.04) in 1965
Best batting: 79 Pakistan v Zimbabwe, Shekhupura 1996-97
Best bowling: 8-65 Surrey v Derbyshire, The Oval 1998

1999 Season

	M	Inns	NO	Runs	HS	Avge	100s	50s	Ct	St	O	M	Runs	Wkts	Avge	Best	5wI	10wM
Test																		
All First	7	8	5	46	25 *	15.33	-	-	1	-	290.5	90	660	58	11.37	7-19	7	2
1-day Int	10	7	4	40	21	13.33	-	-	3	-	83.4	4	379	17	22.29	5-35	1	
NatWest	4	1	1	3	3 *	-	-	-	-	-	39	4	107	15	7.13	4-17	-	
B & H	1	1	1	1	1 *	-	-	-	-	-	10	3	19	1	19.00	1-19	-	
1-day Lge	3	3	1	9	5 *	4.50	-	-	1	-	23	3	80	4	20.00	2-28	-	

Career Performances

	M	Inns	NO	Runs	HS	Avge	100s	50s	Ct	St	Balls	Runs	Wkts	Avge	Best	5wI	10wM
Test	22	34	7	372	79	13.77	-	2	8	-	6389	2868	97	29.56	5-32	8	2
All First	79	113	34	1168	79	14.78	-	4	33	-	18359	7734	370	20.90	8-65	31	10
1-day Int	108	63	23	509	30 *	12.72	-	-	29	-	5639	4012	204	19.66	5-29	5	
NatWest	8	3	2	15	6 *	15.00	-	-	-	-	493	257	22	11.68	4-17	-	
B & H	7	3	1	18	11	9.00	-	-	2	-	382	247	10	24.70	4-46	-	
1-day Lge	18	11	3	84	29 *	10.50	-	-	4	-	706	522	21	24.85	3-31	-	

SAVIDENT, L.   Hampshire

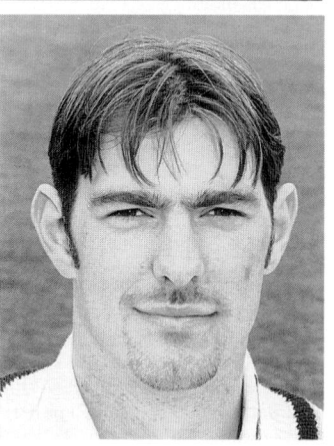

Name: Lee Savident
Role: Right-hand bat, right-arm
medium bowler
Born: 22 October 1976, Guernsey
Height: 6ft 5in **Weight:** 15st 10lbs
Nickname: Sav, Frenchman
County debut: 1997
1st-Class catches: 1
Strike rate: (career 84.00)
Parents: Nev and Sue
Marital status: Single ('occupied')
Education: Castel Primary School; Grammar
School, Guernsey; Guernsey College of
Further Education
Qualifications: 5 GCSEs and 1 A-level
Off-season: 'Relaxing, training, spending
time with Vicki'
Overseas teams played for: Glenwood Old
Boys, Durban, South Africa 1997-99
Cricketers particularly admired: Malcolm Marshall, Darren Gough
Young players to look out for: Si Francis, James Adams

Other sports played: Football, golf
Other sports followed: Football (Tottenham Hotspur)
Injuries: Out for one week with back and shoulder injuries
Relaxations: Playing golf; watching football
Extras: First person from the Channel Islands to play first-class cricket
Opinions on cricket: 'Changing.'
Best batting: 6 Hampshire v Yorkshire, Portsmouth 1997
Best bowling: 2-86 Hampshire v Yorkshire, Portsmouth 1997

1999 Season (did not make any first-class or one-day appearances)

Career Performances

	M	Inns	NO	Runs	HS	Avge	100s	50s	Ct	St	Balls	Runs	Wkts	Avge	Best	5wI	10wM
Test																	
All First	3	4	1	15	6	5.00	-	-	1	-	336	247	4	61.75	2-86	-	-
1-day Int																	
NatWest																	
B & H																	
1-day Lge	5	4	2	60	39	30.00	-	-	1	-	115	104	6	17.33	3-41	-	

SCHOFIELD, C. P.   Lancashire

Name: Chris Paul Schofield
Role: Left-hand bat, leg-break bowler
Born: 6 October 1978, Birch Hill,
Wardle, Rochdale
Height: 6ft 1in **Weight:** 11st 5lbs
Nickname: Scoey, Junior, Scoffer
County debut: 1998
1st-Class 5 w. in innings: 1
1st-Class catches: 9
Place in batting averages: 198th av. 20.50
Place in bowling averages: 109th av. 32.79
(1998 84th av. 29.90)
Strike rate: 67.03 (career 62.10)
Parents: David and Judith
Marital status: Single
Family links with cricket: Father played
with local club team Whittles and brother
plays with local team Littleborough
Education: St John's; Wardle High School

Qualifications: 4 GCSEs, NVQ Levels 2 and 3 in Information Technology

Off-season: Touring Bangladesh and New Zealand with England A
Overseas tours: England U17 to Bermuda 1997; England U19 to South Africa 1997-98; England A to Bangladesh and New Zealand 1999-2000
Cricketers particularly admired: Shane Warne, Stuart Law
Young players to look out for: Graeme Swann, Robert Key
Other sports played: Football (Littleborough FC, Whittles FC), snooker (Wardle Con Club – Littleborough League champions; individual knockout semi-finalist; handicap of four)
Other sports followed: Football ('like watching Liverpool FC')
Relaxations: Listening to music, playing snooker, socialising
Extras: Was on England U17 unbeaten tour to Bermuda. Was part of England U19 World Cup winning set-up 1998. Won double twice in two years with Littleborough CC (Wood Cup and Lancashire Cup 1997; League and Wood Cup 1998). Awarded 2nd XI cap 1998. Was employed as net leg-spinner by England party touring Australia 1998-99
Best batting: 39* Lancashire v Leicestershire, Leicester 1999
Best bowling: 5-66 Lancashire v Durham, Old Trafford 1999
Stop press: Awarded England contract (Band D) for 2000; the only uncapped player to be contracted for this season

1999 Season

	M	Inns	NO	Runs	HS	Avge	100s	50s	Ct	St	O	M	Runs	Wkts	Avge	Best	5wl	10wM
Test																		
All First	10	14	4	205	39 *	20.50	-	-	8	-	324	82	951	29	32.79	5-66	1	-
1-day Int																		
NatWest																		
B & H																		
1-day Lge	2	2	0	33	28	16.50	-	-	-	-	9	0	32	2	16.00	2-32	-	

Career Performances

	M	Inns	NO	Runs	HS	Avge	100s	50s	Ct	St	Balls	Runs	Wkts	Avge	Best	5wl	10wM
Test																	
All First	12	17	6	210	39 *	19.09	-	-	9	-	2422	1250	39	32.05	5-66	1	-
1-day Int																	
NatWest																	
B & H																	
1-day Lge	2	2	0	33	28	16.50	-	-	-	-	54	32	2	16.00	2-32	-	

SCOTT, D. A.   Kent

Name: Darren Anthony Scott
Role: Left-hand bat, off-spin bowler
Born: 26 August 1973, Canterbury
Height: 6ft 2in **Weight:** 13st
Nickname: Stavros, Bubble
County debut: 1998
1st-Class catches: 1
Strike rate: 71.50 (career 95.55)
Parents: Linda and Tony
Marital status: Engaged to Julia Skeet
Education: St Stephens Primary School,
Canterbury; Chaucer Technology School,
Canterbury; Canterbury Christ Church
University College, Canterbury
Qualifications: 7 GCSEs, A-levels, BSc
(Hons) Business Studies and Sports Science
(2:1), AAT, Level 2 cricket coach
Career outside cricket: Accountant/sports
trader
Off-season: 'Working for IG Index plc in London as a sports trader'
Overseas teams played for: Fish Hoek CC, Cape Town 1991-92
Cricketers particularly admired: David Gower, Graeme Fowler
Young players to look out for: Rob Key, James Hockley, Chris Schofield
Other sports played: Badminton, football
Other sports followed: Football (Nottingham Forest), American football
(San Francisco 49ers)
Relaxations: Reading, watching sport, gardening
Extras: Represented the ECB in the Triple Crown and European Championships 1998.
Awarded 2nd XI cap 1998
Opinions on cricket: 'Wickets need drastically improving to ensure players are
prepared for Test cricket.'
Best batting: 17* Kent v Oxford University, Canterbury 1998
Best bowling: 4-151 Kent v New Zealand, Canterbury 1999

> 76. Which innovative Middlesex all-rounder
> scored hundreds in each innings and had a match return of 11-128
> v Sussex at Lord's in 1905?

1999 Season

	M	Inns	NO	Runs	HS	Avge	100s	50s	Ct	St	O	M	Runs	Wkts	Avge	Best	5wI	10wM
Test																		
All First	3	4	3	16	12 *	16.00	-	-	1	-	95.2	18	332	8	41.50	4-151	-	-
1-day Int																		
NatWest																		
B & H																		
1-day Lge	2	0	0	0	0	-	-	-	-	-	9	0	57	0	-		-	-

Career Performances

	M	Inns	NO	Runs	HS	Avge	100s	50s	Ct	St	Balls	Runs	Wkts	Avge	Best	5wI	10wM
Test																	
All First	5	7	6	38	17 *	38.00	-	-	1	-	860	456	9	50.66	4-151	-	-
1-day Int																	
NatWest																	
B & H																	
1-day Lge	2	0	0	0	0	-	-	-	-	-	54	57	0	-		-	-

SCUDERI, J. C.   Lancashire

Name: Joseph Charles Scuderi
Role: Right-hand bat, right-arm medium bowler
Born: 24 December 1968, Ingham, Queensland, Australia
Height: 5ft 11in **Weight:** 11st 7lbs
Nickname: Scud
County debut: No first-team appearance
Parents: Nalda and Enrico
Marital status: Single
Education: Macknade State Primary; Ingham State High (both Queensland)
Overseas tours: Australia U19 to New Zealand 1987
Overseas teams played for: South Australia 1988-89 – 1998-99
Cricketers particularly admired: Jeff Thomson, Ian Botham
Players to look out for: Brad Young (South Australia)
Other sports followed: Rugby league (Sydney City), football (Manchester United)
Injuries: Out for one week with back spasm

Relaxations: Listening to and playing music

Extras: South Australia Player of the Year 1991-92. Was in Australia squad of 20 for World Cup 1992. Played for Prime Minister's XI v Pakistan and England. Has played for Italy since 1998 and is an Italian passport holder. Has satisfied criteria for EU nationals in county cricket and is not considered an overseas player

Opinions on cricket: 'Fitness is becoming more important, sometimes at the expense of the skills.'

Best batting: 125* South Australia v Western Australia, Adelaide 1991-92

Best bowling: 7-79 South Australia v New South Wales, Adelaide 1991-92

1999 Season (did not make any first-class or one-day appearances)

Career Performances

	M	Inns	NO	Runs	HS	Avge	100s	50s	Ct	St	Balls	Runs	Wkts	Avge	Best	5wl	10wM
Test																	
All First	61	100	14	2667	125*	31.01	3	13	24	-	11776	5422	156	34.75	7-79	8	1
1-day Int																	
NatWest																	
B & H																	
1-day Lge																	

SHAH, O. A.　　　　　　　　　　　　Middlesex

Name: Owais Alam Shah

Role: Right-hand bat, off-spin bowler

Born: 22 October 1978, Karachi, Pakistan

Height: 6ft 1in **Weight:** 12st

Nickname: Ace

County debut: 1995 (one-day), 1996 (first-class)

1st-Class 50s: 11

1st-Class 100s: 6

1st-Class catches: 35

One-Day 100s: 2

Place in batting averages: 125th av. 27.63 (1998 47th av. 39.30)

Place in bowling averages: 92nd av. 29.63

Strike rate: 54.09 (career 57.23)

Parents: Jamshed and Mehjabeen

Marital status: Single

Family links with cricket: Father played for his college side

Education: Berkley's Junior School; Isleworth and Syon School; Lampton School; part-time course at Westminster University, Harrow
Qualifications: 7 GCSEs, 2 A-levels, studying for Business Administration degree
Overseas tours: England U19 to Zimbabwe 1995-96, to South Africa 1997-98; England A to Australia 1996-97, to Kenya and Sri Lanka 1997-98
Cricketers particularly admired: Viv Richards, Wasim Akram
Young players to look out for: Stephen Peters, Paul Franks, Robert Key, Matthew Wood, Graeme Swann
Other sports played: Snooker
Other sports followed: Football (Manchester United)
Relaxations: 'Spend time with friends. Gym. Music'
Extras: Middlesex Sports Federation Award winner. Man of the Series in U17 'Test' series against India 1994. Played for Middlesex U13, Ken Barrington Trophy (national champions) winners, and Middlesex U15, county competition winners, as captain. Scored record 232 for England U15 against England U16. Man of the Series for England U17 against India U17. Awarded 2nd XI cap in 1996. Captained the England U19 side to success in the U19 World Cup in South Africa, scoring 54 not out in the final in 1997-98. Captain of England U19 against Pakistan U19 (one-day and 'Test' matches) 1998
Opinions on cricket: 'There is too much cricket played in this country. This is the reason why all county cricketers love the sight of rain.'
Best batting: 140 Middlesex v Yorkshire, Lord's 1998
Best bowling: 3-33 Middlesex v Gloucestershire, Bristol 1999

1999 Season

	M	Inns	NO	Runs	HS	Avge	100s	50s	Ct	St	O	M	Runs	Wkts	Avge	Best	5wI	10wM
Test																		
All First	17	32	2	829	110 *	27.63	3	3	9	-	99.1	14	326	11	29.63	3-33	-	-
1-day Int																		
NatWest	1	1	0	36	36	36.00	-	-	1	-								
B & H																		
1-day Lge	15	14	0	487	134	34.78	2	1	2	-	9	0	54	0	-		-	-

Career Performances

	M	Inns	NO	Runs	HS	Avge	100s	50s	Ct	St	Balls	Runs	Wkts	Avge	Best	5wI	10wM
Test																	
All First	51	85	8	2462	140	31.97	6	11	35	-	744	448	13	34.46	3-33	-	-
1-day Int																	
NatWest	8	8	1	137	37	19.57	-	-	2	-							
B & H	8	7	1	126	43	21.00	-	-	5	-	8	2	2	1.00	2-2	-	
1-day Lge	52	48	7	1241	134	30.26	2	6	13	-	103	122	2	61.00	1-4	-	

SHAHID, N. Surrey

Name: Nadeem Shahid
Role: Right-hand bat, leg-spin bowler
Born: 23 April 1969, Karachi
Height: 6ft **Weight:** 12st
Nickname: Nad, Gonads etc
'too many to mention'
County debut: 1989 (Essex), 1995 (Surrey)
1000 runs in a season: 1
1st-Class 50s: 26
1st-Class 100s: 7
1st-Class catches: 104
One-Day 100s: 1
Place in batting averages: (1998 58th
av. 35.94)
Strike rate: (career 70.00)
Parents: Ahmed and Salma
Marital status: Single
Family links with cricket: Brother plays
cricket in Suffolk
Education: Stoke High; Northgate High; Ipswich School; Plymouth Polytechnic
Qualifications: 6 O-levels, 1 A-level, coaching certificate
Off-season: 'Selling Xmas trees with the Honourable Ed Giddins. Travelling through the Amazon rainforest, fighting the crocodiles and catching piranhas, swimming among them. Getting a six pack, and working on my cricket. Getting my footwork to be more nimble, precise, accurate, like a boxer. Working on my diet, cutting all fats out and increasing my intake of carbohydrates and polyunsaturates. Absolutely no intake of alcohol'
Overseas tours: Ipswich School to Barbados (Sir Garfield Sobers Trophy) 1987; England (South) to N Ireland (Youth World Tournament) 1988
Overseas teams played for: Gosnells, Perth, Western Australia 1989-91; Fairfield, Sydney 1992-93
Cricketers particularly admired: Ian Botham, Shane Warne, Graham Thorpe and Nasser Hussain
Young players to look out for: 'Every one'
Other sports followed: Golf, tennis, badminton, squash, 'most ball sports'
Injuries: Out for most of the season with a broken left wrist
Relaxations: 'Sleeping in hammocks with the natives in the Amazon'
Extras: Youngest Suffolk player, aged 17. Played for HMC, MCC Schools, ESCA U19, NCA Young Cricketers (Lord's and International Youth tournament in Belfast), England U25 and at every level for Suffolk. TSB Young Player of the Year 1987, winner of the *Daily Telegraph* Bowling Award 1987 and 1988, Cricket Society's

All-rounder of the Year 1988 and Laidlaw Young Player of the Year for Essex 1993. Essex Society Player of the Year 1993. Released by Essex at end of 1994 season and signed for Surrey. Member of the Surrey Sunday League winning side of 1996. Member of Surrey County Championship winning squad of 1999

Opinions on cricket: 'The two-divisional system will be a success. To improve the state of the pitches, as so much now depends on every game (due to promotion/relegation) centrally contracting the groundsmen may be the answer.'

Best batting: 139 Surrey v Yorkshire, The Oval 1995
Best bowling: 3-91 Essex v Surrey, The Oval 1990

1999 Season

	M	Inns	NO	Runs	HS	Avge	100s	50s	Ct	St	O	M	Runs	Wkts	Avge	Best	5wI	10wM
Test																		
All First	2	3	1	36	23	18.00	-	-	2	-								
1-day Int																		
NatWest																		
B & H																		
1-day Lge	1	1	0	24	24	24.00	-	-	1	-	1	0	9	0	-	-	-

Career Performances

	M	Inns	NO	Runs	HS	Avge	100s	50s	Ct	St	Balls	Runs	Wkts	Avge	Best	5wI	10wM
Test																	
All First	112	179	25	4914	139	31.90	7	26	104	-	3010	1993	43	46.34	3-91	-	-
1-day Int																	
NatWest	9	7	1	163	85 *	27.16	-	1	5	-	72	30	4	7.50	3-30	-	
B & H	22	15	5	271	65 *	27.10	-	2	3	-	150	131	1	131.00	1-59	-	
1-day Lge	91	78	12	1557	101	23.59	1	4	28	-	66	72	0	-	-	-	

SHARIF, Z.   Essex

Name: Zoheb Sharif
Role: Left-hand bat, leg-spin bowler
Born: 22 February 1983, Leytonstone
Height: 5ft 10in **Weight:** 11st 2lbs
Nickname: Omar
County debut: No first-team appearance
Parents: Khalid and Robina
Marital status: Single
Education: Henry Maynard Junior School; Warwick Boys School; Chigwell School; The Coopers Company and Coborn School
Qualifications: 9 GCSEs

Off-season: Studying for three A-levels
Overseas teams played for: PNT CC, Pakistan
Cricketers particularly admired: Sachin Tendulkar, Saeed Anwar, Wasim Akram
Young players to look out for: Owais Shah, Vikram Solanki, Yousuf Youhana
Other sports followed: Football (Manchester United)
Relaxations: Watching movies, reading sports books
Extras: Won the MCC Lord's Taverners' Trophy a record three times. Was in England U17 squad. Had contract with MCC Young Cricketers at Lord's

SHAW, A. D. Glamorgan

Name: Adrian David Shaw
Role: Right-hand bat, off-spin ('dangerously unpredictable'), wicket-keeper
Born: 17 February 1972, Neath
Height: 5ft 11in **Weight:** 12st 12lbs
Nickname: Shawsy, Redknapp, Midfield General, Dale, John Inman, Barrymore, George Michael, Shawmeister, Shawster
County debut: 1992 (one-day), 1994 (first-class)
1st-Class 50s: 5
1st-Class 100s: 1
1st-Class catches: 140
1st-Class stumpings: 10
Place in batting averages: 196th av. 20.80 (1998 229th av. 16.53)
Parents: David Colin and Christina
Marital status: Single
Education: Catwg Primary; Llangatwg Comprehensive; Neath Tertiary College
Qualifications: 9 O-levels, 3 A-levels, advanced cricket coach
Off-season: 'Staying as far away from the female species as possible, living my life on a higher plane, both physically and spiritually. There is more, much more, to life than the

mere pursuit of physical gratification. Isn't there??? And a bit of coaching and training'

Overseas tours: Welsh Schools U17 to Barbados 1987; England YC to New Zealand 1990-91; Glamorgan to Cape Town 1999

Overseas teams played for: Welkom Police, Orange Free State 1995-96

Cricketers particularly admired: 'I admire any player who, having played a reasonable amount of first-team cricket, has the professionalism to abuse young players in the opposition as a "test" of character. Outstanding!!'

Young players to look out for: 'The man they couldn't hang – the one, the only Owen Parkin (only 28)'

Other sports played: Rugby (formerly centre with Neath RFC; Welsh U19 and U21 squad member)

Other sports followed: Rugby (Neath RFC, 'whoever's top of the Premiership', 'Cardiff RFC, 'cause they produce all their own players and never, ever poach off any other club!')

Injuries: Out for two weeks because of illness ('contrary to Glamorgan players' opinion, not the "Slimming Disease"')

Relaxations: 'I am so totally focused on my sole mission in life, which is to enjoy it, I have no time whatsoever for interests or relaxations'

Extras: One of youngest players (18 years 7 days) to play first-class rugby for Neath. Played for Neath against Swansea six days after playing against Zimbabwe for Glamorgan, and had the 'pleasure' of marking Scott Gibbs. Neath RFC Back of the Year 1993-94. 'Hoping to be awarded Glamorgan 2nd XI's first benefit after 10 years in the "Stiffs"!' Voted Glamorgan 2nd XI Player of the Year and Glamorgan Young Player of the Year in 1995. 2nd XI Player of the Month, June 1996. Claimed 12 victims in 2nd XI game v Gloucestershire at Usk in 1998, a record for 2nd XI cricket. Awarded county Young Player of the Month for August 1999 'at the geriatric age of 27'. Struck maiden first-class 100 (140) v Oxford University at The Parks 1999

Opinions on cricket: 'I am consistently staggered by the apparent ease with which some people perform in this sport of ours. For me it is like a life-time habit of finding a brick wall and banging my nut as hard as possible against it. When I think it's going well, something always happens to kick me in the ... well, where it hurts!! Never mind, I'll keep plugging away.'

Best batting: 140 Glamorgan v Oxford University, The Parks 1999

1999 Season

	M	Inns	NO	Runs	HS	Avge	100s	50s	Ct	St	O	M	Runs	Wkts	Avge	Best	5wl	10wM
Test																		
All First	12	16	1	312	140	20.80	1	-	25	1								
1-day Int																		
NatWest																		
B & H																		
1-day Lge	9	6	1	75	21	15.00	-	-	10	2								

Career Performances

	M	Inns	NO	Runs	HS	Avge	100s	50s	Ct	St	Balls	Runs	Wkts	Avge	Best	5wI	10wM
Test																	
All First	59	78	10	1268	140	18.64	1	5	140	10	6	7	0	-	-	-	-
1-day Int																	
NatWest	6	6	1	112	47	22.40	-	-	8	-							
B & H	8	7	1	64	25	10.66	-	-	9	4							
1-day Lge	43	30	8	366	48	16.63	-	-	24	7							

SHEIKH, M. A. Warwickshire

Name: Mohammed Avez Sheikh
Role: Left-hand bat, right-arm
medium bowler
Born: 2 July 1973, Birmingham
Nickname: Sheikhy
Education: Broadway School
County debut: 1997
Strike rate: (career 51.83)
Overseas teams played for:
Western Province CC 1997-98
Extras: Has also played for Warwickshire
U19 and played for both Worcestershire and
Essex 2nd XIs in 1995
Best batting: 30 Warwickshire v Oxford
University, The Parks 1998
Best bowling: 2-14 Warwickshire v
Middlesex, Edgbaston 1997

1999 Season

	M	Inns	NO	Runs	HS	Avge	100s	50s	Ct	St	O	M	Runs	Wkts	Avge	Best	5wI	10wM
Test																		
All First	1	2	1	19	12	19.00	-	-	-	-	6	0	21	0	-	-	-	-
1-day Int																		
NatWest	1	1	1	12	12*	-	-	-	2	-	7	1	18	2	9.00	2-18	-	
B & H	2	0	0	0	0	-	-	-	-	-	19	1	69	2	34.50	1-31	-	
1-day Lge	3	1	0	0	0	0.00	-	-	2	-	22	1	90	4	22.50	2-28	-	

Career Performances

	M	Inns	NO	Runs	HS	Avge	100s	50s	Ct	St	Balls	Runs	Wkts	Avge	Best	5wI	10wM
Test																	
All First	4	6	1	99	30	19.80	-	-	-	-	311	119	6	19.83	2-14	-	-
1-day Int																	
NatWest	2	2	1	17	12*	17.00	-	-	2	-	108	56	2	28.00	2-18	-	
B & H	2	0	0	0	0	-	-	-	-	-	114	69	2	34.50	1-31	-	
1-day Lge	10	6	1	14	8	2.80	-	-	4	-	354	234	16	14.62	3-28	-	

SHERIYAR, A. Worcestershire

Name: Alamgir Sheriyar
Role: Right-hand bat, left-arm fast bowler
Born: 15 November 1973, Birmingham
Height: 6ft 1in **Weight:** 13st
Nickname: Sheri
County debut: 1993 (one-day, Leics),
1994 (first-class, Leics), 1996 (Worcs)
County cap: 1997 (Worcs)
50 wickets in a season: 2
1st-Class 5 w. in innings: 11
1st-Class 10 w. in match: 3
1st-Class catches: 15
Place in batting averages: 285th av. 7.16
(1998 268th av. 11.00)
Place in bowling averages: 57th av. 24.70
(1998 130th av. 40.08)
Strike rate: 39.73 (career 49.13)
Parents: Mohammed Zaman (deceased) and
Safia Sultana
Marital status: Single

Family links with cricket: Brothers play a bit
Education: George Dixon Secondary School, Birmingham; Joseph Chamberlain Sixth
Form College, Birmingham; Oxford Brookes University
Qualifications: 6 O-levels, studying for BEng (Hons) Combined Engineering
Off-season: England A tour to Bangladesh and New Zealand
Overseas tours: Leicestershire to South Africa 1995; Worcestershire to
Barbados 1996; England A to Bangladesh and New Zealand 1999-2000
Cricketers particularly admired: Wasim Akram
Other sports followed: Football, basketball
Relaxations: Time at home, music
Extras: Played for English Schools U17 and has also played in the Indoor National

League. Became only the second player to take a hat-trick on his first-class debut. Asked to be released by Leicestershire at the end of the 1995 season and joined Worcestershire for 1996. Became first bowler to reach 50 first-class wickets in 1999 when he dismissed Matthew Hayden v Northants at Northampton; ended season as leading wicket-taker with 92. Took second first-class hat-trick of his career v Kent at Worcester 1999

Opinions on cricket: 'It's a batsman's game.'
Best batting: 21 Worcestershire v Pakistan A, Worcester 1997
Best bowling: 7-130 Worcestershire v Hampshire, Southampton 1999

1999 Season

	M	Inns	NO	Runs	HS	Avge	100s	50s	Ct	St	O	M	Runs	Wkts	Avge	Best	5wI	10wM
Test																		
All First	19	26	8	129	18	7.16	-	-	3	-	609.2	119	2273	92	24.70	7-130	4	1
1-day Int																		
NatWest	2	1	1	0	0*	-	-	-	-	-	16.5	4	85	2	42.50	2-52	-	
B & H																		
1-day Lge	15	2	0	3	3	1.50	-	-	2	-	104.5	6	540	26	20.76	4-42	-	

Career Performances

	M	Inns	NO	Runs	HS	Avge	100s	50s	Ct	St	Balls	Runs	Wkts	Avge	Best	5wI	10wM
Test																	
All First	77	79	28	414	21	8.11	-	-	15	-	12530	7670	255	30.07	7-130	11	3
1-day Int																	
NatWest	5	3	1	10	10	5.00	-	-	-	-	221	194	4	48.50	2-52	-	
B & H	8	4	2	28	15	14.00	-	-	-	-	355	275	8	34.37	3-40	-	
1-day Lge	51	15	9	52	19	8.66	-	-	5	-	1608	1431	56	25.55	4-18	-	

77. What is the lowest completed innings total by a team in the County Championship?

SHOAIB AKHTAR Nottinghamshire

Name: Shoaib Akhtar
Role: Right-hand bat, right-arm fast bowler
Born: 13 June 1975, Rawalpindi, Pakistan
Height: 6ft
County debut: No first-team appearance
Test debut: 1997-98
Tests: 10
One-Day Internationals: 26
1st-Class 5 w. in innings: 15
1st-Class catches: 22
Strike rate: (career 45.76)
Education: Elliot High School, Rawalpindi;
Asgar Mal Government College, Rawalpindi
Overseas tours: Pakistan to South Africa
1997-98, to Zimbabwe 1997-98, to UK,
Ireland and Holland (World Cup) 1999, to
Australia 1999-2000
Overseas teams played for: Rawalpindi;
ADBP

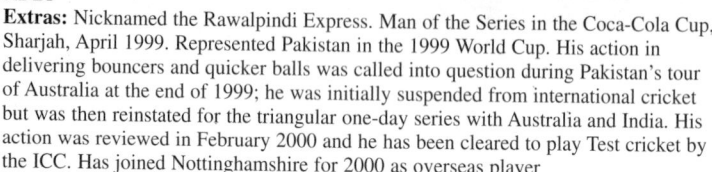

Extras: Nicknamed the Rawalpindi Express. Man of the Series in the Coca-Cola Cup,
Sharjah, April 1999. Represented Pakistan in the 1999 World Cup. His action in
delivering bouncers and quicker balls was called into question during Pakistan's tour
of Australia at the end of 1999; he was initially suspended from international cricket
but was then reinstated for the triangular one-day series with Australia and India. His
action was reviewed in February 2000 and he has been cleared to play Test cricket by
the ICC. Has joined Nottinghamshire for 2000 as overseas player
Best batting: 23 Rawalpindi v Karachi Whites, Karachi 1996-97
Best bowling: 6-69 Rawalpindi B v Lahore City 1994-95

1999 Season

	M	Inns	NO	Runs	HS	Avge	100s	50s	Ct	St	O	M	Runs	Wkts	Avge	Best	5wI	10wM
Test																		
All First																		
1-day Int	10	4	4	4	2 *	-	-	-	1	-	80.5	6	391	16	24.43	3-11	-	
NatWest																		
B & H																		
1-day Lge																		

Career Performances

	M	Inns	NO	Runs	HS	Avge	100s	50s	Ct	St	Balls	Runs	Wkts	Avge	Best	5wI	10wM
Test	10	12	4	47	11	5.87	-	-	4	-	1871	969	28	34.60	5-43	1	-
All First	62	77	31	377	23	8.19	-	-	22	-	9518	5995	208	28.82	6-69	15	-
1-day Int	26	11	8	56	36	18.66	-	-	4	-	1247	917	43	21.32	4-37	-	
NatWest																	
B & H																	
1-day Lge																	

SIDEBOTTOM, R. J.   Yorkshire

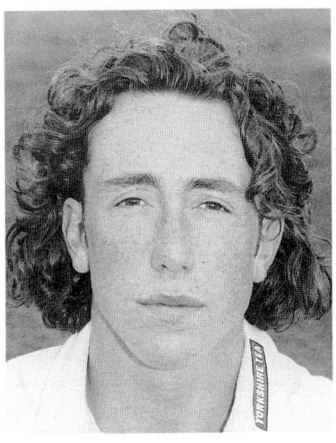

Name: Ryan Jay Sidebottom
Role: Left-hand bat, left-arm
fast-medium bowler
Born: 15 January 1978, Huddersfield
Height: 6ft 4in **Weight:** 13st
Nickname: Sexual Chocolate,
Ginger Spice, Curly
County debut: 1997
1st-Class 50s: 1
1st-Class catches: 9
One-Day 5 w. in innings: 1
Place in batting averages: 275th av. 9.73
Place in bowling averages: 111th av. 32.87
Strike rate: 68.87 (career 68.52)
Parents: Arnie and Gillian
Marital status: Single
Family links with cricket: Father played for
Yorkshire and England and football for
Manchester United and Huddersfield Town
Education: Almondbury Primary, Huddersfield; Lepton Middle; King James Grammar
School, Almondbury
Qualifications: 5 GCSEs
Career outside cricket: Promoting cricket in schools around Yorkshire
Overseas tours: England U17 to Holland 1995; MCC to Bangladesh 1999-2000
Overseas teams played for: Ringwood, Melbourne
Cricketers particularly admired: Darren Gough, Wayne Morton, Bradley Parker
Young players to look out for: John Inglis, Paul Hutchison, Matthew Wood,
Gary Fellows
Other sports played: Football (once with Sheffield United), 'all sports'
Other sports followed: Football (Huddersfield Town FC)
Injuries: Hernia and groin injury

Best batting: 54 Yorkshire v Glamorgan, Cardiff 1998
Best bowling: 3-13 Yorkshire v Durham, Riverside 1998

1999 Season

	M	Inns	NO	Runs	HS	Avge	100s	50s	Ct	St	O	M	Runs	Wkts	Avge	Best	5wI	10wM
Test																		
All First	12	20	5	146	48 *	9.73	-	-	6	-	275.3	70	789	24	32.87	3-16	-	-
1-day Int																		
NatWest	4	1	1	7	7 *	-	-	-	1	-	32	7	143	3	47.66	1-2	-	
B & H	3	2	1	1	1 *	1.00	-	-	1	-	27.4	0	113	3	37.66	2-26	-	
1-day Lge	16	7	2	41	24 *	8.20	-	-	1	-	134	14	541	20	27.05	3-14	-	

Career Performances

	M	Inns	NO	Runs	HS	Avge	100s	50s	Ct	St	Balls	Runs	Wkts	Avge	Best	5wI	10wM
Test																	
All First	18	25	8	232	54	13.64	-	1	9	-	2467	1250	36	34.72	3-13	-	-
1-day Int																	
NatWest	5	1	1	7	7 *	-	-	-	1	-	216	158	6	26.33	3-15	-	
B & H	4	3	1	5	4	2.50	-	-	1	-	226	155	5	31.00	2-26	-	
1-day Lge	30	11	5	43	24 *	7.16	-	-	3	-	1294	952	35	27.20	6-40	1	

SIERRA, R.   Warwickshire

Name: Ryan Sierra
Role: Left-hand bat (No. 3), left-arm medium
bowler, cover fielder
Born: 8 September 1980
Height: 5ft 9in   **Weight:** 12st 7lbs
Nickname: Teddy
County debut: No first-team appearance
Parents: John and Margaret
Marital status: Single
Family links with cricket: 'Both my father
and grandfather played representative cricket
and are passionate about the game'
Education: St John's College, Johannesburg;
Wits University, Johannesburg (studying
BComm degree)
Overseas tours: South Africa U15 to
England (U15 World Cup)

Cricketers particularly admired: Daryll Cullinan
Other sports played: Rugby (1st team at St John's College)
Other sports followed: International rugby
Relaxations: Listening to music ('groups like Counting Crows are favourites at the moment but I have wide-ranging tastes')
Extras: Represented South Africa U15 in inaugural U15 World Cup. Played for Gauteng Colts, South Africa 1996-99, South Africa Schools U19 1997 and South Africa Schools Colts 1999. Played against touring Nottinghamshire side 1998-99, scoring 86. Has satisfied criteria for EU nationals in county cricket and is not considered an overseas player

---

SILVERWOOD, C. E. W.   Yorkshire

Name: Christopher Eric Wilfred Silverwood
Role: Right-hand bat, right-arm fast-medium bowler
Born: 5 March 1975, Pontefract
Height: 6ft 1in **Weight:** 12st 9lbs
Nickname: Spoons, Silvers, Chubby
County debut: 1993
Test debut: 1996-97
Tests: 1
One-Day Internationals: 6
50 wickets in a season: 1
1st-Class 50s: 4
1st-Class 5 w. in innings: 14
1st-Class 10 w. in match: 1
1st-Class catches: 19
One-Day 5 w. in innings: 1
Place in batting averages: 249th av. 14.38

(1998 154th av. 23.90)
Place in bowling averages: 19th av. 20.40 (1998 37th av. 23.39)
Strike rate: 41.22 (career 48.37)
Parents: Brenda
Wife and date of marriage: Emma, 3 October 1997
Family links with cricket: 'Dad played a bit'
Education: Gibson Lane School, Kippax; Garforth Comprehensive
Qualifications: 8 GCSEs, City and Guilds in Leisure and Recreation
Off-season: To Bangladesh and New Zealand with England A tour
Overseas tours: England A to Kenya and Sri Lanka 1997-98, to Bangladesh and New Zealand 1999-2000; England to Zimbabwe and New Zealand 1996-97, to West Indies 1997-98, to Bangladesh (Wills International Cup) 1998-99, to South Africa 1999-2000
Overseas teams played for: Wellington, Cape Town 1993-94, 1995-96

Cricketers particularly admired: Ian Botham, Allan Donald
Other sports played: Karate
Other sports followed: Rugby league (Castleford)
Relaxations: Listening to music, watching videos, 'riding my motorbike'
Extras: Black belt in karate. Attended the Yorkshire Cricket Academy. Represented Yorkshire at athletics. Played for England U19 in the home series against India in 1994. Called up to the England tour of West Indies 1997-98 after the withdrawal of Darren Gough through injury
Best batting: 58 Yorkshire v Lancashire, Old Trafford 1997
Best bowling: 7-93 Yorkshire v Kent, Headingley 1997
Stop press: Called up from England A tour to England tour of South Africa as injury cover. Took his first five-wicket haul in Test cricket (5-91) in South Africa's only innings in the fourth Test at Cape Town, January 2000

1999 Season

	M	Inns	NO	Runs	HS	Avge	100s	50s	Ct	St	O	M	Runs	Wkts	Avge	Best	5wl	10wM
Test																		
All First	13	20	2	259	53 *	14.38	-	1	3	-	405.2	87	1204	59	20.40	5-28	3	-
1-day Int																		
NatWest	2	0	0	0	0	-	-	-	1	-	18	0	80	1	80.00	1-33	-	
B & H	3	2	0	12	8	6.00	-	-	-	-	27	2	124	3	41.33	2-44	-	
1-day Lge	12	9	6	34	11 *	11.33	-	-	1	-	101.5	13	361	24	15.04	4-44	-	

Career Performances

	M	Inns	NO	Runs	HS	Avge	100s	50s	Ct	St	Balls	Runs	Wkts	Avge	Best	5wl	10wM
Test	1	1	0	0	0	0.00	-	-	1	-	150	71	4	17.75	3-63	-	-
All First	83	112	24	1327	58	15.07	-	4	19	-	13449	7331	278	26.37	7-93	14	1
1-day Int	6	4	0	17	12	4.25	-	-	-	-	252	201	3	67.00	2-27	-	
NatWest	12	4	3	23	12 *	23.00	-	-	4	-	635	381	12	31.75	3-24	-	
B & H	20	7	0	29	8	4.14	-	-	4	-	994	729	35	20.82	5-28	1	
1-day Lge	70	37	21	154	14 *	9.62	-	-	6	-	2894	2087	94	22.20	4-26	-	

SINGH, A.   Warwickshire

Name: Anurag Singh
Role: Right-hand bat, right-arm 'everything'
Born: 9 September 1975, Kanpur, India
Height: 5ft 11in **Weight:** 11st
Nickname: Ragi
County debut: 1995
1st-Class 50s: 6

1st-Class 100s: 4
1st-Class catches: 14
One-Day 100s: 1
Place in batting averages: 242nd av. 15.40
(1998 57th av. 36.16)
Parents: Vijay and Rajul
Marital status: Single
Family links with cricket: Brother plays for
Warwickshire juniors
Education: Mayfield Prep, Walsall/Bishop
Gilpin, Wimbledon; King Edward's School,
Birmingham; Gonville and Caius College,
Cambridge
Qualifications: 12 GCSEs, 4 A-levels,
qualified solicitor
Career outside cricket: Solicitor
Off-season: With law firm; in Australia
playing cricket
Overseas tours: England U19 to West Indies 1994-95; Warwickshire U21 to
South Africa; Warwickshire CCC to South Africa
Overseas teams played for: Gordon CC, Sydney
Cricketers particularly admired: Allan Donald, Brian Lara, Sachin Tendulkar,
Steve Waugh, David Gower
Young players to look out for: 'My brother Rudi', Ian Bell, Alan Richardson,
Nick Warren
Other sports played: Hockey
Other sports followed: Football (Aston Villa FC)
Relaxations: Music, reading, films
Extras: Broke school record for number of runs in a season (1102). *Daily Telegraph*
regional award for batting (twice) and bowling (once). Tiger Smith Memorial Award
for Warwickshire Most Promising Young Cricketer 1994, Coney Edmonds Trophy for
Warwickshire Best U19 Cricketer 1994, Lord's Taverners' Trophy for Best Young
Cricketer 1994, Gray-Nicolls Len Newbery Award for ESCA U19 Best Player 1994.
Scored two centuries for England U19 against India U19 in 1994. Scored one century
against West Indies U20 and was Man of the Series 1994-95. Awarded 2nd XI cap in
1995. Cambridge Blue 1996-98; captain of Cambridge University 1997-98. Struck 36-
ball Championship 50 v Derbyshire at Edgbaston 1999
Opinions on cricket: 'Too many matches – not enough time to work on technique.'
Best batting: 157 Cambridge University v Sussex, Hove 1996

1999 Season

	M	Inns	NO	Runs	HS	Avge	100s	50s	Ct	St	O	M	Runs	Wkts	Avge	Best	5wI	10wM
Test																		
All First	5	10	0	154	69	15.40	-	2	-	-								
1-day Int																		
NatWest	2	2	0	51	46	25.50	-	-	-	-								
B & H	2	2	0	14	13	7.00	-	-	1	-								
1-day Lge	9	9	1	215	76	26.87	-	2	3	-								

Career Performances

	M	Inns	NO	Runs	HS	Avge	100s	50s	Ct	St	Balls	Runs	Wkts	Avge	Best	5wI	10wM
Test																		
All First	38	60	3	1673	157	29.35	4	6	14	-	54	45	0	-		-	-	-
1-day Int																		
NatWest	2	2	0	51	46	25.50	-	-	-	-								
B & H	17	17	1	446	123	27.87	1	3	4	-								
1-day Lge	16	16	1	329	86	21.93	-	3	4	-								

SLATER, M. J. Derbyshire

Name: Michael Jonathon Slater
Role: Right-hand bat, leg-spin bowler
Born: 21 February 1970,
Wagga Wagga, New South Wales
Height: 5ft 9in
Nickname: Slats
County debut: 1998
County cap: 1998
Test debut: 1993
Tests: 49
One-Day Internationals: 42
1st-Class 50s: 54
1st-Class 100s: 27
1st-Class 200s: 2
1st-Class catches: 85
One-Day 100s: 1
Place in batting averages: 93rd av. 31.76
(1998 61st av. 35.33)
Strike rate: (career 66.00)
Education: Wagga Wagga High School, NSW
Overseas tours: Australia to England 1993, to Sharjah 1993-94, to South Africa

1993-94, to Sri Lanka 1994-95, to Pakistan 1994-95, to West Indies 1994-95, to Sri Lanka 1996-97, to India 1996-97, to England 1997, to India 1997-98, to Pakistan 1998-99, to West Indies 1998-99, to Sri Lanka 1999, to Zimbabwe 1999

Overseas teams played for: University of New South Wales; New South Wales 1991-92 –

Extras: Has published autobiography – *Slats Opens Up*. Joined Derbyshire in 1998 as overseas player. Scored three Test 100s against the 1998-99 England tourists, his 123 at Sydney (the third) accounting for 66 per cent of Australia's second innings total of 184; only Australia's Charles Bannerman made a higher percentage of a side's innings total in a Test match. Released by Derbyshire at end of 1999 season

Best batting: 221 Australia v Karachi, Karachi 1998-99

Best bowling: 1-4 Australia v Pakistan, Rawalpindi 1994-95

Stop press: Second in list of leading Test run-scorers of 1999 with 1051 (av. 45.70). Selected for Australia's tour of New Zealand 1999-2000

1999 Season

	M	Inns	NO	Runs	HS	Avge	100s	50s	Ct	St	O	M	Runs	Wkts	Avge	Best	5wl	10wM
Test																		
All First	10	18	1	540	171	31.76	1	2	9	-	4	0	23	0	-	-	-	-
1-day Int																		
NatWest	2	2	0	43	22	21.50	-	-	-	-								
B & H																		
1-day Lge	10	10	0	232	59	23.20	-	3	3	-								

Career Performances

	M	Inns	NO	Runs	HS	Avge	100s	50s	Ct	St	Balls	Runs	Wkts	Avge	Best	5wl	10wM
Test	49	88	3	3792	219	44.61	12	12	20	-	7	4	1	4.00	1-4	-	-
All First	154	273	12	11400	221	43.67	29	54	85	-	66	57	1	57.00	1-4	-	-
1-day Int	42	42	1	987	73	24.07	-	9	9	-	12	11	0	-	-	-	
NatWest	7	7	0	189	82	27.00	-	1	1	-							
B & H																	
1-day Lge	20	20	0	661	110	33.05	1	6	6	-							

78. Which England cricketer averaged 100.91 for his 1211 Championship runs in 1985?

SMALL, G. C.   Warwickshire

Name: Gladstone Cleophas Small
Role: Right-hand bat, right-arm
fast-medium bowler
Born: 18 October 1961, St George, Barbados
Height: 5ft 11in **Weight:** 12st
Nickname: Gladys, Glad, Stoney
County debut: 1980
County cap: 1982
Benefit: 1992 (£129,500)
Test debut: 1986
Tests: 17
One-Day Internationals: 53
50 wickets in a season: 6
1st-Class 50s: 7
1st-Class 5 w. in innings: 29
1st-Class 10 w. in match: 2
1st-Class catches: 93
One-Day 5 w. in innings: 5
Strike rate: (career 58.17)
Parents: Chelston and Gladys
Wife and date of marriage: Lois, 19 September 1987
Children: Zak, Marcus and Zoe
Family links with cricket: Cousin Milton Small toured England with West Indies in 1988
Education: Moseley School; Hall Green Technical College, Birmingham
Qualifications: 2 O-levels, NCA senior coaching award
Career outside cricket: Sports marketing consultant
Overseas tours: Warwickshire to Cape Town, to Zimbabwe, to Trinidad; England YC to New Zealand 1979-80; England to Australia 1986-87, to India and Pakistan (World Cup) 1987-88, to India and West Indies 1989-90, to Australia 1990-91, to Australia and New Zealand (World Cup) 1991-92
Overseas teams played for: Balwyn, Melbourne 1982-83, 1984-85; West Torrens, Adelaide 1985-86; South Australia 1985-86
Cricketers particularly admired: Malcolm Marshall, Richard Hadlee, Allan Donald, Brian Lara, Robin Smith
Other sports followed: Golf, tennis, football (Aston Villa FC)
Relaxations: 'Home with family, tending my vegetable garden, wining and dining with friends'
Extras: Was called up for England Test squad v Pakistan at Edgbaston, July 1982, but did not play. Bowled 18-ball over v Middlesex in August 1982, with 11 no-balls. Grandfather watched him take eight wickets in the Barbados Test v West Indies in 1989-90 on his return to the land of his birth. Was Andy Lloyd's best man. Retired at the end of the 1999 season

Best batting: 70 Warwickshire v Lancashire, Old Trafford 1988
Best bowling: 7-15 Warwickshire v Nottinghamshire, Edgbaston 1988

1999 Season

	M	Inns	NO	Runs	HS	Avge	100s	50s	Ct	St	O	M	Runs	Wkts	Avge	Best	5wI	10wM
Test																		
All First																		
1-day Int																		
NatWest																		
B & H																		
1-day Lge	6	2	0	9	5	4.50	-	-	1	-	44	3	211	7	30.14	2-16	-

Career Performances

	M	Inns	NO	Runs	HS	Avge	100s	50s	Ct	St	Balls	Runs	Wkts	Avge	Best	5wI	10wM
Test	17	24	7	263	59	15.47	-	1	9	-	3927	1871	55	34.01	5-48	2	-
All First	314	403	97	4409	70	14.40	-	7	93	-	49411	24324	851	28.58	7-15	29	2
1-day Int	53	24	9	98	18 *	6.53	-	-	7	-	2793	1942	58	33.48	4-31	-	
NatWest	50	30	9	256	33	12.19	-	-	9	-	2931	1550	54	28.70	3-22	-	
B & H	68	40	12	210	22	7.50	-	-	11	-	3764	2194	81	27.08	5-23	1	
1-day Lge	208	90	32	461	40 *	7.94	-	-	45	-	8592	6342	261	24.29	5-18	4	

SMETHURST, M. P.   Lancashire

Name: Michael Paul Smethurst
Role: Right-hand bat, right-arm
fast-medium bowler
Born: 11 October 1976, Oldham
Height: 6ft 5in **Weight:** 13st 7lbs
County debut: 1999
1st-Class catches: 1
Place in bowling averages: 85th av. 29.00
Strike rate: 58.23 (career 58.23)
Parents: Julie Martin ('Mum')
Marital status: Single
Education: Middleton Parish Primary
School; Hulme Grammar School, Oldham;
University of Salford
Qualifications: 9 GCSEs, 4 A-levels,
BA (Hons) Leisure Management
Off-season: 12-month contract with
Lancashire

Other sports followed: Football (Manchester United)
Best batting: 3 Lancashire v Leicestershire, Leicester 1999
Best bowling: 4-44 Lancashire v Cambridge University, Fenner's 1999

1999 Season

	M	Inns	NO	Runs	HS	Avge	100s	50s	Ct	St	O	M	Runs	Wkts	Avge	Best	5wI	10wM
Test																		
All First	5	4	0	5	3	1.25	-	-	1	-	126.1	29	377	13	29.00	4-44	-	-
1-day Int																		
NatWest	1	1	1	4	4*	-	-	-	-	-	10	1	46	4	11.50	4-46	-	
B & H																		
1-day Lge	4	2	0	1	1	0.50	-	-	-	-	19.2	0	111	5	22.20	2-13	-	

Career Performances

	M	Inns	NO	Runs	HS	Avge	100s	50s	Ct	St	Balls	Runs	Wkts	Avge	Best	5wI	10wM
Test																	
All First	5	4	0	5	3	1.25	-	-	1	-	757	377	13	29.00	4-44	-	-
1-day Int																	
NatWest	1	1	1	4	4*	-	-	-	-	-	60	46	4	11.50	4-46	-	
B & H																	
1-day Lge	4	2	0	1	1	0.50	-	-	-	-	116	111	5	22.20	2-13	-	

SMITH, A. M. Gloucestershire

Name: Andrew Michael Smith
Role: Right-hand bat, left-arm fast-medium swing bowler
Born: 1 October 1967, Dewsbury, West Yorks
Height: 5ft 9in **Weight:** 12st 3lbs
Nickname: Smudge
County debut: 1991
Test debut: 1997
Tests: 1
50 wickets in a season: 5
1st-Class 50s: 4
1st-Class 5 w. in innings: 19
1st-Class 10 w. in match: 5
1st-Class catches: 24
One-Day 5 w. in innings: 1
Place in batting averages: 287th av. 6.75 (1998 167th av. 22.58)
Place in bowling averages: 20th av. 20.49 (1998 22nd av. 21.17)
Strike rate: 47.38 (career 49.15)

Parents: Hugh and Margaret

Wife and date of marriage: Sarah, 2 October 1993

Children: William James, 9 October 1994; Amelia Lucy, 14 June 1997

Family links with cricket: Father (Birstall club) and brother (East Ardsley club) local league cricketers in Yorkshire

Education: Queen Elizabeth Grammar School, Wakefield; Exeter University; University of the West of England, Bristol

Qualifications: 9 O-levels, 4 A-levels, BA (Hons) French and German

Career outside cricket: 'Father!'

Off-season: 'Studying law at UWE, Bristol; keeping fit; looking after kids'

Overseas tours: Queen Elizabeth Grammar School to Holland 1985; Bradford Junior Cricket League to Barbados 1986; Exeter University to Barbados 1987; Gloucestershire to Kenya 1990, to Sri Lanka 1992-93, to Zimbabwe 1996; England A to Pakistan 1995-96; MCC to New Zealand 1999

Overseas teams played for: Waimea, New Zealand 1990; WTTU, New Zealand 1991

Cricketers particularly admired: Richard Hadlee, Allan Donald, Jonty Rhodes, Sanath Jayasuriya, Wasim Akram, Courtney Walsh

Young players to look out for: Owais Shah, Michael Gough

Other sports played: Football, golf

Other sports followed: Football (Leeds United)

Injuries: Out for three weeks with hairline fracture of fibula

Relaxations: Looking after the kids ('hardly relaxing!'). Crosswords. Computers

Extras: Played for English Schools U19, NAYC and represented Combined Universities in the B&H Cup in 1988 and 1990. Persistent side strain forced him to fly home from the England A tour of Pakistan in 1995-96. Finished the 1997 season as leading first-class wicket-taker with 83 first-class wickets. Gloucestershire Player of the Year 1997. Took 400th first-class wicket when Jack Russell caught Keith Parsons v Somerset at Bath 1999

Opinions on cricket: 'Two divisions have increased competition but haven't yet raised the standard and have led to a deterioration in the standard of pitches as teams look for a definite and guaranteed result. So one problem solved, but many more created.'

Best batting: 61 Gloucestershire v Yorkshire, Gloucester 1998

Best bowling: 8-73 Gloucestershire v Middlesex, Lord's 1996

1999 Season

	M	Inns	NO	Runs	HS	Avge	100s	50s	Ct	St	O	M	Runs	Wkts	Avge	Best	5wI	10wM
Test																		
All First	14	21	5	108	14	6.75	-	-	4	-	450.1	127	1168	57	20.49	5-41	2	-
1-day Int																		
NatWest	4	0	0	0	0	-	-	-	-	-	38	10	83	8	10.37	3-25	-	
B & H	1	1	1	1	1 *	-	-	-	1	-	8	0	28	1	28.00	1-28	-	
1-day Lge	14	8	6	13	8 *	6.50	-	-	5	-	118.2	18	409	11	37.18	2-25	-	

Career Performances

	M	Inns	NO	Runs	HS	Avge	100s	50s	Ct	St	Balls	Runs	Wkts	Avge	Best	5wI	10wM
Test	1	2	1	4	4 *	4.00	-	-	-	-	138	89	0	-	-	-	-
All First	124	166	42	1536	61	12.38	-	4	24	-	20842	10524	424	24.82	8-73	19	5
1-day Int																	
NatWest	20	9	5	51	13	12.75	-	-	5	-	1141	644	29	22.20	4-46	-	
B & H	38	22	12	91	15 *	9.10	-	-	8	-	2174	1471	49	30.02	6-39	1	
1-day Lge	121	60	36	302	26 *	12.58	-	-	20	-	4842	3662	124	29.53	4-29	-	

SMITH, B. F.   Leicestershire

Name: Benjamin Francis Smith
Role: Right-hand bat, right-arm medium bowler
Born: 3 April 1972, Corby
Height: 5ft 8in **Weight:** 11st
Nickname: Smudge, The Ferret
County debut: 1990
County cap: 1995
1000 runs in a season: 2
1st-Class 50s: 29
1st-Class 100s: 12
1st-Class 200s: 1
1st-Class catches: 64
One-Day 100s: 1
Place in batting averages: 72nd av. 34.85 (1998 6th av. 62.00)
Strike rate: (career 130.50)
Parents: Keith and Janet
Wife and date of marriage: Lisa, 10 October 1998
Family links with cricket: 'Dad, grandad and both uncles played club, colts and England U15s'

Education: Tugby Primary; Kibworth High; Robert Smyth, Market Harborough
Qualifications: 5 O-levels, NCA coaching certificate
Overseas tours: England YC to New Zealand 1990-91; Rutland Tourists to South Africa 1992; MCC to Bangladesh 1999-2000
Overseas teams played for: Alexandria, Zimbabwe 1990; Bankstown Canterbury, Sydney 1993-96; Central Hawke's Bay CC, New Zealand 1997-98
Cricketers particularly admired: David Gower, Viv Richards
Other sports played: Tennis, golf
Other sports followed: Football (Leicester City), rugby union (Leicester Tigers)
Relaxations: 'Eating out. Nights in. Nights out. Watching films. Listening to good music'
Extras: Played tennis for Leicestershire aged 12. Cricket Society Young Player of the Year 1991. Took part in Leicestershire record fifth-wicket partnership (322) with Phil Simmons v Notts at Worksop 1998
Best batting: 204 Leicestershire v Surrey, The Oval 1998
Best bowling: 1-5 Leicestershire v Essex, Ilford 1991

1999 Season

	M	Inns	NO	Runs	HS	Avge	100s	50s	Ct	St	O	M	Runs	Wkts	Avge	Best	5wI	10wM
Test																		
All First	14	21	0	732	154	34.85	2	2	10	-								
1-day Int																		
NatWest	2	2	0	54	27	27.00	-	-	2	-								
B & H	1	1	0	0	0	0.00	-	-	1	-								
1-day Lge	12	12	1	369	74	33.54	-	3	3	-								

Career Performances

	M	Inns	NO	Runs	HS	Avge	100s	50s	Ct	St	Balls	Runs	Wkts	Avge	Best	5wI	10wM
Test																	
All First	142	212	29	6698	204	36.60	13	29	64	-	261	205	2	102.50	1-5	-	-
1-day Int																	
NatWest	15	14	1	344	63 *	26.46	-	2	7	-							
B & H	28	26	1	666	90	26.64	-	5	13	-							
1-day Lge	124	122	13	3007	115	27.58	1	14	32	-	18	15	0	-		-	-

SMITH, E. T.   Kent

Name: Edward Thomas Smith
Role: Right-hand bat
Born: 19 July 1977, Pembury, Kent
Height: 6ft 2in   **Weight:** 12st 10lbs
Nickname: Smudger, Hughie
County debut: 1996
1000 runs in a season: 1
1st-Class 50s: 17
1st-Class 100s: 5
1st-Class catches: 11
Place in batting averages: 34th av. 40.47
(1998 144th av. 24.82)
Parents: Jonathan and Gillie
Marital status: Single
Family links with cricket: Father wrote
Good Enough? with Chris Cowdrey
Education: Tonbridge School; Peterhouse,
Cambridge University
Qualifications: 11 GCSEs, 3 A-levels, degree in History
Career outside cricket: Journalist
Cricketers particularly admired: Martin Crowe, Greg Chappell
Young players to look out for: Andrew Symonds, Robert Key, James Hockley,
Matt Banes
Other sports followed: Football (Arsenal FC)
Relaxations: Reading, socialising, listening to music
Extras: Scored a century (101) on his first-class debut against Glamorgan in 1996 and
in doing so became the youngest player to score a century on debut for Cambridge
University. He was also the first person to score 50 or more in each of his first five
first-class games. Cambridge Blue in 1996. Played for England U19 against New
Zealand U19 in 1996
Opinions on cricket: 'Everyone knows we should play less, practise with more intensity
and in better facilities, and play on much better wickets. So why don't we do it?'
Best batting: 190 Cambridge University v Leicestershire, Fenner's 1997

---

79. At Birmingham in 1922, Hampshire defeated Warwickshire by 155 runs,
having scored 521 in their second innings. Besides the fact that 521
is a large total, what was unusual about Hampshire's performance?

	M	Inns	NO	Runs	HS	Avge	100s	50s	Ct	St	O	M	Runs	Wkts	Avge	Best	5wl	10wM
Test																		
All First	14	25	2	931	111	40.47	1	6	2	-	1	0	3	0	-	-	-	-
1-day Int																		
NatWest	3	3	0	33	19	11.00	-	-	-	-								
B & H																		
1-day Lge	8	7	0	52	34	7.42	-	-	-	-								

Career Performances

	M	Inns	NO	Runs	HS	Avge	100s	50s	Ct	St	Balls	Runs	Wkts	Avge	Best	5wl	10wM
Test																		
All First	50	85	6	3092	190	39.13	5	17	11	-	18	25	0	-	-	-	-
1-day Int																		
NatWest	3	3	0	33	19	11.00	-	-	-	-							
B & H	4	4	0	61	43	15.25	-	-	3	-							
1-day Lge	17	14	2	287	72 *	23.91	-	2	2	-							

SMITH, N. M. K.   Warwickshire

Name: Neil Michael Knight Smith
Role: Right-hand bat, off-spin bowler
('occasional on our wickets'),
county captain
Born: 27 July 1967, Solihull
Height: 6ft **Weight:** 14st
Nickname: Gert
County debut: 1987
County cap: 1993
One-Day Internationals: 7
1000 runs in a season: 1
1st-Class 50s: 27
1st-Class 100s: 4
1st-Class 5 w. in innings: 16
1st-Class catches: 54
One-Day 100s: 2
One-Day 5 w. in innings: 3
Place in batting averages: 164th av. 24.00
(1998 34th av. 41.75)
Place in bowling averages: 114th av. 33.75 (1998 129th av. 39.87)
Strike rate: 71.43 (career 75.58)

Parents: Mike (M.J.K.) and Diana
Wife and date of marriage: Rachel, 4 December 1993
Family links with cricket: Father captained Warwickshire and England
Education: Warwick School
Qualifications: 3 O-levels, cricket coach Grade 1
Career outside cricket: Sports teacher
Off-season: Hosting tour to Zimbabwe in February for One-day Internationals
Overseas tours: England to South Africa 1995-96, to India and Pakistan (World Cup) 1995-96
Overseas teams played for: Phoenix, Perth, Western Australia 1989-90
Cricketers particularly admired: David Gower, Ian Botham, Allan Donald
Young players to look out for: Ian Bell, Tony Frost, Alan Richardson
Other sports played: Golf
Other sports followed: Rugby union, football
Injuries: Out for three and a half weeks with an intercostal rib muscle injury
Relaxations: Sport
Extras: Played for England in the one-day series against South Africa in 1995-96 and was then selected for the squad to play in the World Cup in India and Pakistan. Followed in his father's footsteps when he led the Warwickshire side out against Northamptonshire in the Sunday League 1997 – the first time both father and son have captained Warwickshire. Played for an England XI in the Cricket Max tournament in New Zealand in 1997-98. Reached 100 v Durham at Edgbaston at 4.09pm on 17 April 1998, thereby scoring the earliest century in County Championship history; record passed to team-mate Dougie Brown on 15 April 1999. Was selected to represent England in the cancelled World Super Max 8s originally scheduled to take place in Perth in October 1998. Was appointed Warwickshire captain for the 1999 season
Opinions on cricket: 'Pitches are the main fault in English cricket. Two divisions will work if the game is played hard but true and fair.'
Best batting: 161 Warwickshire v Yorkshire, Headingley 1989
Best bowling: 7-42 Warwickshire v Lancashire, Edgbaston 1994

1999 Season

	M	Inns	NO	Runs	HS	Avge	100s	50s	Ct	St	O	M	Runs	Wkts	Avge	Best	5wl	10wM
Test																		
All First	15	21	0	504	71	24.00	-	3	8	-	190.3	47	540	16	33.75	4-90	-	-
1-day Int																		
NatWest	1	1	0	24	24	24.00	-	-	-	-	8	0	27	1	27.00	1-27	-	
B & H	1	1	0	9	9	9.00	-	-	-	-	5	0	27	0	-	-	-	
1-day Lge	14	14	0	174	61	12.42	-	1	6	-	76	8	340	12	28.33	3-27	-	

Career Performances

	M	Inns	NO	Runs	HS	Avge	100s	50s	Ct	St	Balls	Runs	Wkts	Avge	Best	5wI	10wM
Test																	
All First	160	232	30	5590	161	27.67	4	27	54	-	23053	11461	305	37.57	7-42	16	-
1-day Int	7	6	1	100	31	20.00	-	-	1	-	261	190	6	31.66	3-29	-	
NatWest	36	32	6	560	72	21.53	-	4	11	-	1474	911	39	23.35	5-17	1	
B & H	36	30	2	589	125	21.03	1	3	5	-	1337	1014	34	29.82	3-29	-	
1-day Lge	168	141	18	2914	111 *	23.69	1	17	61	-	5358	4128	154	26.80	6-33	2	

SMITH, R. A. Hampshire

Name: Robin Arnold Smith
Role: Right-hand bat, slip fielder, county captain
Born: 13 September 1963, Durban, South Africa
Height: 6ft **Weight:** 15st
Nickname: The Judge
County debut: 1982
County cap: 1985
Benefit: 1996
Test debut: 1988
Tests: 62
One-Day Internationals: 71
1000 runs in a season: 11
1st-Class 50s: 119
1st-Class 100s: 55
1st-Class 200s: 1
1st-Class catches: 211
One-Day 100s: 27
Place in batting averages: 20th av. 42.69 (1998 53rd av. 37.08)
Strike rate: (career 77.64)
Parents: John and Joy
Wife and date of marriage: Katherine, 21 September 1988
Children: Harrison Arnold, 4 December 1991; Margaux Elizabeth, 28 July 1994
Family links with cricket: Grandfather played for Natal in Currie Cup. Brother Chris played for Natal, Hampshire and England
Education: Northlands Boys High, Durban
Qualifications: Matriculation, '62 England caps'
Career outside cricket: Director of Judge Tours. Set up Masuri Helmets and Chase Bats with former county cricketer Jon Hardy. Is partner in a chain of sports theme bars
Overseas tours: England to India and West Indies 1989-90, to Australia 1990-91,

to Australia and New Zealand (World Cup) 1991-92, to India and Sri Lanka 1992-93, to West Indies 1993-94, to South Africa 1995-96, to India and Pakistan (World Cup) 1995-96

Overseas teams played for: Natal 1980-84; Perth, Australia 1984-85 (grade cricket)
Cricketers particularly admired: Malcolm Marshall, Brian Lara, Graeme Hick, Graham Gooch, Allan Lamb
Other sports followed: Soccer, athletics, rugby, golf, racing
Relaxations: 'Reading (Leslie Thomas in particular), trout fishing, assembling a good wine cellar, keeping fit and spending as much time as possible with my lovely wife Katherine and my children'
Extras: Played rugby for Natal Schools and for Romsey RFC as a full-back. Held 19 school athletics records and two South African schools records in shot putt and 100-metre hurdles. One of *Wisden*'s Five Cricketers of the Year 1990. First child was born while he was on tour in Australia. Played for an England XI in the Cricket Max tournament in New Zealand in 1997-98. Was appointed Hampshire captain for the 1998 season. Raises funds for physically handicapped children at Cedar School, Nursling. Passed 6000 runs in Sunday/National League v Gloucestershire at Southampton 1999
Opinions on cricket: 'I enjoy playing cricket for Hampshire and particularly enjoy the camaraderie of the county circuit.'
Best batting: 209* Hampshire v Essex, Southampton 1987
Best bowling: 2-11 Hampshire v Surrey, Southampton 1985

1999 Season

	M	Inns	NO	Runs	HS	Avge	100s	50s	Ct	St	O	M	Runs	Wkts	Avge	Best	5wl	10wM
Test																		
All First	18	29	3	1110	96	42.69	-	10	9	-	1	0	2	0	-		-	-	-
1-day Int																		
NatWest	2	2	0	99	68	49.50	-	1	1	-								
B & H	1	1	0	13	13	13.00	-	-	-	-								
1-day Lge	14	14	3	290	97 *	26.36	-	1	3	-								

Career Performances

	M	Inns	NO	Runs	HS	Avge	100s	50s	Ct	St	Balls	Runs	Wkts	Avge	Best	5wl	10wM
Test	62	112	15	4236	175	43.67	9	28	39	-	24	6	0	-		-	-
All First	368	622	83	23608	209 *	43.79	56	119	211	-	1087	967	14	69.07	2-11	-	-
1-day Int	71	70	8	2419	167 *	39.01	4	15	26	-							
NatWest	40	40	11	2205	158	76.03	8	9	21	-	17	13	2	6.50	2-13	-	
B & H	58	55	8	2199	155 *	46.78	5	9	22	-	6	2	0	-		-	-
1-day Lge	183	176	20	6058	131	38.83	10	36	71	-	2	0	1	0.00	1-0	-	

SMITH, T. M.   Derbyshire

Name: Trevor Mark Smith
Role: Left-hand 'No. 11' bat, right-arm
fast-medium bowler
Born: 18 January 1977, Derby
Height: 6ft 3in **Weight:** 14st
Nickname: Tricky
County debut: 1997
1st-Class 5 w. in innings: 5
1st-Class 10 w. in match: 1
1st-Class catches: 4
Place in batting averages: (1998 270th
av. 10.44)
Place in bowling averages: 22nd av. 20.83
(1998 35th av. 23.04)
Strike rate: 35.54 (career 39.86)
Parents: Graham and Marilyn
Marital status: Single
Family links with cricket: Three brothers all
play for Sandiacre Town CC; dad umpires in local league
Education: Cloudside Junior School, Sandiacre; Friesland Comprehensive School,
Sandiacre; Broxtowe College of Further Education, Chilwell, Notts
Qualifications: 9 GCSEs, BTEC National Diploma in Business and Finance,
Level II coach
Career outside cricket: '*Still* working on it'
Off-season: Playing club cricket in South Africa
Overseas teams played for: Alma Marist CC, Cape Town 1999-2000
Cricketers particularly admired: Allan Donald, Ian Botham, Phillip DeFreitas,
Michael Slater
Young players to look out for: Ben Spendlove, Ian Blackwell, Robin Weston
Other sports played: Football, golf, tennis
Other sports followed: Football (Derby County; Blue Eagles – 'brother's team')
Injuries: Out for two and a half months with a stress fracture of the shin
Relaxations: Playing golf, reading; 'spending time with friends, family and one
special person!! (you know who you are!!!)'
Extras: Had three five-wicket hauls in four innings during 1999 season
Opinions on cricket: 'It will be interesting to see if splitting the Championship will
actually raise the standard. Better wickets will make for better players and better
cricket. Oh … and it is a nice way to make a living.'
Best batting: 29 Derbyshire v Essex, Derby 1998
Best bowling: 6-32 Derbyshire v Essex, Derby 1998

1999 Season

	M	Inns	NO	Runs	HS	Avge	100s	50s	Ct	St	O	M	Runs	Wkts	Avge	Best	5wI	10wM
Test																		
All First	8	9	6	52	20 *	17.33	-	-	3	-	183.4	34	646	31	20.83	5-63	3	1
1-day Int																		
NatWest																			
B & H																			
1-day Lge	6	5	4	13	8 *	13.00	-	-	2	-	41	2	259	11	23.54	4-38	-	

Career Performances

	M	Inns	NO	Runs	HS	Avge	100s	50s	Ct	St	Balls	Runs	Wkts	Avge	Best	5wl	10wM
Test																	
All First	16	19	7	146	29	12.16	-	-	4	-	2113	1181	53	22.28	6-32	5	1
1-day Int																	
NatWest																		
B & H																		
1-day Lge	7	6	4	19	8 *	9.50	-	-	3	-	273	290	11	26.36	4-38	-	

SNAPE, J. N.　　　　　　Gloucestershire

Name: Jeremy Nicholas Snape
Role: Right-hand bat, off-spin bowler;
all-rounder
Born: 27 April 1973, Stoke-on-Trent,
Staffordshire
Height: 5ft 8in **Weight:** 12st
Nickname: Coot, Jez, Snapper
County debut: 1992 (Northamptonshire),
1999 (Gloucestershire)
County cap: 1999 (Gloucestershire)
1st-Class 50s: 10
1st-Class 5 w. in innings: 1
1st-Class catches: 42
One-Day 5 w. in innings: 1
Place in batting averages:
177th av. 22.52
Place in bowling averages:
150th av. 67.00
Strike rate: 138.58 (career 93.00)
Parents: Keith and Barbara
Marital status: Single
Family links with cricket: 'Brother Jonathan plays league cricket for Rode Park CC

in Cheshire. Dad loves cricket now, and Mum hates the sweep shot!'
Education: Denstone College, Staffordshire; Durham University
Qualifications: 8 GCSEs, 3 A-levels, BSc Natural Science
Career outside cricket: Director of travel company
Off-season: Working for Cape Tours hosting holiday/sports groups in South Africa
Overseas tours: England U18 to Canada 1991 (captain); England U19 to Pakistan 1991-92; Durham University to South Africa 1993; Northamptonshire to Cape Town 1993; Durham University to Vienna (Indoor European Championships) 1994; Christians in Sport to Zimbabwe 1994-95; Troubadours to South Africa 1997; Gloucestershire to Kimberley, South Africa 1999
Overseas teams played for: Petone, Wellington, New Zealand 1994-95; Wainuiamata, Wellington, New Zealand 1995-96; Techs CC, Cape Town 1996-99
Cricketers particularly admired: Allan Lamb, Anil Kumble, Jack Russell
Young players to look out for: Graeme Swann, Chris Taylor
Relaxations: Good food and drink, listening to music, travelling
Extras: Sir Jack Hobbs award (U15 Schoolboy 1988). B&H Gold Award winner for Combined Universities v Worcestershire 1992 (3-34) at The Parks. Player of the Tournament at European Indoor 6-a-side Championships in 1994. Left Northants at end of 1998 season and joined Gloucestershire for 1999; awarded cap 1999
Opinions on cricket: 'Definitely in favour of four-day cricket as it induces a more disciplined approach, although I equally enjoy the challenges of one-day cricket. Counties should work harder to maximise the potential of their individual players while encouraging the teamwork essential to competition.'
Best batting: 98* Gloucestershire v Essex, Gloucester 1999
Best bowling: 5-65 Northamptonshire v Durham, Northampton 1995

1999 Season

	M	Inns	NO	Runs	HS	Avge	100s	50s	Ct	St	O	M	Runs	Wkts	Avge	Best	5wl	10wM
Test																		
All First	17	29	6	518	98 *	22.52	-	3	8	-	277.1	71	804	12	67.00	3-67	-	-
1-day Int																		
NatWest	5	4	2	63	28 *	31.50	-	-	2	-	16	1	75	3	25.00	2-19	-	
B & H	3	2	0	53	50	26.50	-	1	1	-	14	0	52	1	52.00	1-20	-	
1-day Lge	16	15	2	256	56	19.69	-	1	7	-	80.5	2	338	17	19.88	4-27	-	

Career Performances

	M	Inns	NO	Runs	HS	Avge	100s	50s	Ct	St	Balls	Runs	Wkts	Avge	Best	5wl	10wM
Test																	
All First	56	85	17	1657	98 *	24.36	-	10	42	-	7161	3735	77	48.50	5-65	1	-
1-day Int																	
NatWest	13	11	4	197	54	28.14	-	1	5	-	451	310	9	34.44	2-19	-	
B & H	23	19	4	317	52	21.13	-	2	10	-	1116	766	24	31.91	5-32	1	
1-day Lge	70	50	17	740	77 *	22.42	-	2	24	-	2223	1758	71	24.76	4-27	-	

SOLANKI, V. S. — Worcestershire

Name: Vikram Singh Solanki
Role: Right-hand bat, off-spin bowler
Born: 1 April 1976, Udaipur, India
Height: 6ft 1in **Weight:** 12st
Nickname: Mowgli, Vik
County debut: 1993 (one-day),
1995 (first-class)
County cap: 1998
1000 runs in a season: 1
1st-Class 50s: 20
1st-Class 100s: 6
1st-Class 5 w. in innings: 3
1st-Class 10 w. in match: 1
1st-Class catches: 85
One-Day 100s: 1
Place in batting averages: 33rd av. 40.57
(1998 113th av. 28.54)
Place in bowling averages: 97th av. 30.23
Strike rate: 55.94 (career 69.77)
Parents: Vijay Singh and Florabell
Marital status: Single

Family links with cricket: 'Father played in India. Brother Vishal (10 yrs) is keen
cricketer'
Education: St Luke's, Udaipur; Merridale, Wolverhampton; Regis School,
Wolverhampton
Qualifications: 9 GCSEs, 3 A-levels
Off-season: England A tour to Bangladesh and New Zealand; England one-day squad
to South Africa and Zimbabwe
Overseas tours: England U18 to South Africa 1992-93, to Denmark 1994 (ICC Youth
Tournament); England U19 to West Indies 1994-95; Worcestershire CCC to Barbados
1996, to Zimbabwe 1997; England A to Zimbabwe and South Africa 1998-99, to
Bangladesh and New Zealand 1999-2000; England to South Africa and Zimbabwe
1999-2000 (one-day series)
Overseas teams played for: Midland Guildford, Perth, Western Australia
Cricketers particularly admired: Sachin Tendulkar, Graeme Hick, Tom Moody
Other sports played: 'Enjoy playing most sports'
Relaxations: 'Spending time with friends and family'
Extras: Scored more first-class runs in 1999 season than any other English player
Opinions on cricket: 'Clubs should prepare wickets to produce good cricket and good
cricketers and not "result wickets" which often see games over in two or three days.
This defeats the object of four-day cricket.'

Best batting: 171 Worcestershire v Gloucestershire, Cheltenham 1999
Best bowling: 5-69 Worcestershire v Middlesex, Lord's 1996
Stop press: Topped batting averages with 597 first-class runs (av. 59.70) on England A tour of Bangladesh and New Zealand 1999-2000. Made One-Day International debut v South Africa at Bloemfontein, January 2000

1999 Season

	M	Inns	NO	Runs	HS	Avge	100s	50s	Ct	St	O	M	Runs	Wkts	Avge	Best	5wI	10wM
Test																		
All First	19	35	2	1339	171	40.57	3	6	21	-	158.3	47	514	17	30.23	4-41	-	-
1-day Int																		
NatWest	2	2	0	33	21	16.50	-	-	-	-	2	0	7	0	-		-	-
B & H																		
1-day Lge	15	14	2	368	63	30.66	-	2	8	-								

Career Performances

	M	Inns	NO	Runs	HS	Avge	100s	50s	Ct	St	Balls	Runs	Wkts	Avge	Best	5wI	10wM
Test																	
All First	77	130	9	4024	171	33.25	6	20	85	-	3977	2450	57	42.98	5-69	3	1
1-day Int																	
NatWest	8	7	0	128	50	18.28	-	1	1	-	195	149	2	74.50	1-48	-	
B & H	9	9	0	131	25	14.55	-	-	4	-	18	17	1	17.00	1-17	-	
1-day Lge	71	57	9	1247	120 *	25.97	1	5	24	-	132	141	4	35.25	1-9	-	

80. What was unusual about K. Ibadulla's dismissal
for Warwickshire v Hampshire at Coventry in 1963?

SPEAK, N. J.   Durham

Name: Nicholas Jason Speak
Role: Right-hand bat,
leg-spin bowler, county captain
Born: 21 November 1966, Manchester
Height: 6ft **Weight:** 12st 4lbs
Nickname: Speaky
County debut: 1986-87 (Lancashire),
1997 (Durham)
County cap: 1992 (Lancashire),
1998 (Durham)
1000 runs in a season: 3
1st-Class 50s: 52
1st-Class 100s: 14
1st-Class 200s: 1
1st-Class catches: 105
One-Day 100s: 1
Place in batting averages: 55th av. 37.40
(1998 131st av. 26.32)
Strike rate: (career 90.50)
Parents: John and Irene

Wife and date of marriage: Michele Frances, 29 March 1993
Children: Kenneth John, 24 September 1995; Ella Frances, 13 July 1997
Family links with cricket: Father and uncle were league professionals in Lancashire and Yorkshire
Education: Broad Oak, Didsbury; Parrs Wood High School, Manchester; Sixth Form College, Didsbury, Manchester
Qualifications: 5 O-levels, Levels 1 and 2 coaching
Off-season: In Durham
Overseas tours: Lancashire to Jamaica 1986-87, 1993, to Zimbabwe 1989, to Tasmania 1990, to Perth 1991, to Johannesburg 1992
Overseas teams played for: Maroochydore, Queensland 1988-89; South Canberra 1989-90; North Canberra 1990-91, 1992-93; Hawthorn, Melbourne 1994-96; Dandenong, Melbourne 1997-98
Cricketers particularly admired: Mark Waugh, Shane Warne, Sachin Tendulkar
Young players to look out for: Chris Schofield, Stephen Harmison
Other sports played: Golf, football, lacrosse
Other sports followed: Football (Manchester City FC)
Injuries: Out for three months with nerve damage in left leg and foot
Relaxations: Golf (Brancepeth Castle GC)
Extras: Scored century for Australian Capital Territories v England A at Canberra 1992-93. Released by Lancashire at the end of the 1996 season and joined Durham for

1997. Appointed Durham vice-captain for 1999. Succeeds David Boon as Durham captain for 2000

Opinions on cricket: 'Hopefully things are heading in the right direction.'

Best batting: 232 Lancashire v Leicestershire, Leicester 1992

Best bowling: 1-0 Lancashire v Warwickshire, Old Trafford 1991

1999 Season

	M	Inns	NO	Runs	HS	Avge	100s	50s	Ct	St	O	M	Runs	Wkts	Avge	Best	5wI	10wM
Test																		
All First	10	17	2	561	110	37.40	2	2	6	-								
1-day Int																		
NatWest	1	1	0	1	1	1.00	-	-	1	-								
B & H																			
1-day Lge	8	6	1	159	53	31.80	-	1	-	-								

Career Performances

	M	Inns	NO	Runs	HS	Avge	100s	50s	Ct	St	Balls	Runs	Wkts	Avge	Best	5wI	10wM
Test																	
All First	160	279	28	9045	232	36.03	15	52	105	-	181	191	2	95.50	1-0	-	-
1-day Int																	
NatWest	11	11	1	354	83	35.40	-	4	3	-	24	31	0	-		-	-
B & H	25	23	2	587	82	27.95	-	4	1	-							
1-day Lge	94	86	10	2069	102 *	27.22	1	9	20	-							

81. Who broke his uncle's record score for Sussex of 285 by amassing 333 v Northamptonshire at Brighton in 1930?

SPEIGHT, M. P.   Durham

Name: Martin Peter Speight
Role: Right-hand middle-order bat, wicket-keeper
Born: 24 October 1967, Walsall
Height: 5ft 10in **Weight:** 12st 7lbs
Nickname: Speighty, Sprog, Badger, Ginger, Hoover, Raghead, Mophead, Rastaman
County debut: 1986 (Sussex), 1997 (Durham)
County cap: 1991 (Sussex), 1998 (Durham)
1000 runs in a season: 2
1st-Class 50s: 46
1st-Class 100s: 13
1st-Class catches: 260
1st-Class stumpings: 5
One-Day 100s: 3
Place in batting averages: 143rd av. 25.72
(1998 145th av. 24.56)

Strike rate: (career 10.50)
Parents: Peter John and Valerie
Wife and date of marriage: Lisa Irene, 27 September 1997
Education: The Windmills School, Hassocks; Hurstpierpoint College Junior and Senior Schools; Durham University (St Chad's College)
Qualifications: 13 O-levels, 3 A-levels, BA (Hons) Ancient History/Archaeology
Career outside cricket: Artist
Off-season: 'Various commissioned paintings; painting set of all six English Test match venues. Building up a small painting/art company (www.martinspeight.co.uk) to include the development of a gift collection. Playing a bit of golf! Walking the dog!'
Overseas tours: NCA U19 to Bermuda 1984; Hurstpierpoint to India 1985-86; England YC to Sri Lanka 1986-87
Overseas teams played for: Karori, Wellington, New Zealand 1989-90; University CC, Wellington 1990-93; North City, Wellington 1995-96; Wellington CA 1989-90, 1992-93, 1995-96
Cricketers particularly admired: Paul Parker, Viv Richards, Malcolm Marshall, Martin Crowe
Young players to look out for: Stephen Harmison, John Collingwood
Other sports played: Hockey, squash, golf
Other sports followed: Football (Walsall FC), 'most sports especially if England are playing'
Injuries: Out for one week with fractured and dislocated finger
Relaxations: Painting, art, pet dog ('a Weimaraner called Cloudy Bay'), wine ('especially New World reds'), eating out at nice restaurants, golf

Extras: Member of Durham University UAU winning side 1987; played for Combined Universities in B&H Cup 1987 and 1988; Sussex Most Promising Player 1989. Walter Lawrence Trophy for fastest first-class 100 of 1992 – 62 balls v Lancashire at Hove. Scored 47-ball Sunday League 100 v Somerset at Taunton 1993. Has won two Gold Awards in the Benson and Hedges competition. Painted an oil painting of the maiden first-class game at Arundel Castle between Sussex and Hampshire which was later auctioned to raise £1200 for the Sussex YC tour to India 1990-91, and of which a limited edition has also been printed and sold. Has done paintings of Hove, Southampton and The Oval for the benefits of Messrs Pigott, Parks and Greig. Member of Durham University's men's hockey team to Barbados 1988. Book of his paintings, *A Cricketer's View*, a collection of 54 paintings and commentary, published in 1995. Various commissions and a print of Abergavenny CC published in 1997. His paintings have also been reproduced on greetings cards and mugs, and as wooden jigsaws. Joined Durham from Sussex for the 1997 season
Opinions on cricket: 'Pitch standards poor. Vital to our game that these improve.'
Best batting: 184 Sussex v Nottinghamshire, Eastbourne 1993
Best bowling: 1-2 Sussex v Middlesex, Hove 1988

1999 Season

	M	Inns	NO	Runs	HS	Avge	100s	50s	Ct	St	O	M	Runs	Wkts	Avge	Best	5wl	10wM
Test																		
All First	17	27	5	566	97 *	25.72	-	4	48	2								
1-day Int																		
NatWest	1	1	0	60	60	60.00	-	1	-	-								
B & H																		
1-day Lge	14	13	1	302	60	25.16	-	1	14	4								

Career Performances

	M	Inns	NO	Runs	HS	Avge	100s	50s	Ct	St	Balls	Runs	Wkts	Avge	Best	5wl	10wM
Test																	
All First	174	290	27	8567	184	32.57	13	46	260	5	21	32	2	16.00	1-2	-	-
1-day Int																	
NatWest	20	18	1	451	60	26.52	-	2	10	1							
B & H	40	37	1	820	83	22.77	-	4	31	2							
1-day Lge	140	129	7	3405	126	27.90	3	16	60	11							

SPENDLOVE, B. L.   Derbyshire

Name: Benjamin Lee Spendlove
Role: Right-hand bat
Born: 4 November 1978, Derby City Hospital
Height: 6ft 1in   **Weight:** 13st
Nickname: Silky
County debut: 1997
1st-Class 50s: 2
1st-Class catches: 8
Place in batting averages: 189th av. 21.46 (1998 199th av. 19.44)
Parents: Lee and Christine
Marital status: Engaged to Beckie
Children: Zack Benjamin Spendlove, 8 September 1999
Family links with cricket: Father played local leagues and was coach of Trent College first team

Education: Harrington Junior School, Long Eaton; Trent College, Long Eaton
Qualifications: 9 GCSEs, coaching awards
Career outside cricket: 'Dad'
Off-season: 'Coaching and taking care of my family'
Overseas tours: England U17 to Holland (International Youth Tournament) 1995
Overseas teams played for: Gold Coast CC, Queensland, Australia 1995-96
Cricketers particularly admired: 'Daffy', Chris Adams, Adrian Rollins
Young players to look out for: 'Daffy', Ian Blackwell, Robin Weston, AJ Harris
Other sports played: Hockey (Derbyshire U15), rugby (Midlands U16)
Other sports followed: Football (Derby County)
Injuries: Out for five weeks with torn tendon in little finger
Relaxations: Golf, music, eating out
Extras: Represented England at U15, U17 and U19. Fielded as 12th man for England in Test match v South Africa at Edgbaston 1998, taking two catches (Gerry Liebenberg and Hansie Cronje) off bowling of Dominic Cork. Played in a Lord's final aged 19 ('I really enjoyed that')
Opinions on cricket: 'Good to see some young blood finally given the chance to represent their country.'
Best batting: 63 Derbyshire v Warwickshire, Edgbaston 1999

1999 Season

	M	Inns	NO	Runs	HS	Avge	100s	50s	Ct	St	O	M	Runs	Wkts	Avge	Best	5wI	10wM
Test																		
All First	7	13	0	279	63	21.46	-	2	2	-								
1-day Int																		
NatWest	1	1	0	23	23	23.00	-	-	-	-								
B & H																		
1-day Lge	3	3	0	42	26	14.00	-	-	-	-								

Career Performances

	M	Inns	NO	Runs	HS	Avge	100s	50s	Ct	St	Balls	Runs	Wkts	Avge	Best	5wI	10wM
Test																	
All First	19	35	2	656	63	19.87	-	2	8	-							
1-day Int																	
NatWest	6	5	0	142	58	28.40	-	1	1	-							
B & H	2	2	0	16	11	8.00	-	-	1	-							
1-day Lge	12	11	0	128	26	11.63	-	-	3	-							

SPIRING, K. R. Worcestershire

Name: Karl Reuben Spiring
Role: Right-hand middle-order bat
Born: 13 November 1974, Southport
Height: 5ft 11in **Weight:** 13st
Nickname: Spud, Ginga
County debut: 1993 (one-day),
1994 (first-class)
1000 runs in a season: 1
1st-Class 50s: 13
1st-Class 100s: 4
1st-Class catches: 22
Place in batting averages: 286th av. 6.90
Parents: Pete and June
Marital status: Single
Education: St Paul's, Hereford; Bishops of
Bluecoat, Hereford/Monmouth School;
Durham University
Qualifications: 9 GCSEs, 3 A-levels, NCA
Senior Coach, helicopter private pilot's licence – PPL(H)
Career outside cricket: 'Ideally, to fly helicopters for a living'
Off-season: 'Playing and coaching in Australia, and raising money to start a
commercial pilot's licence course'

Overseas tours: Worcestershire to Barbados 1996
Overseas teams played for: Fremantle-Mosman Park Pirates, Perth, Western Australia 1995-97
Cricketers particularly admired: Peter Carlstein
Young players to look out for: Vikram 'Solankipose', Chris 'Liprot'
Injuries: Out 'for an annoying amount of time' with 'every knee injury possible'
Relaxations: 'Taking people up for helicopter pleasure flights'
Extras: Father was a professional footballer. Rapid Cricketline 2nd XI Player of the Month June 1994. Worcestershire Uncapped Player of the Year 1994
Opinions on cricket: 'Far too much played. Players' opinions on the game are completely disregarded by the people in charge.'
Best batting: 150 Worcestershire v Essex, Chelmsford 1997

1999 Season

	M	Inns	NO	Runs	HS	Avge	100s	50s	Ct	St	O	M	Runs	Wkts	Avge	Best	5wI	10wM
Test																		
All First	5	10	0	69	18	6.90	-	-	3	-								
1-day Int																		
NatWest	1	1	0	57	57	57.00	-	1	-	-								
B & H																		
1-day Lge	4	4	0	121	56	30.25	-	1	1	-								

Career Performances

	M	Inns	NO	Runs	HS	Avge	100s	50s	Ct	St	Balls	Runs	Wkts	Avge	Best	5wI	10wM
Test																	
All First	42	74	9	2141	150	32.93	4	13	22	-	12	10	0	-	-	-	-
1-day Int																	
NatWest	5	5	0	198	57	39.60	-	2	2	-							
B & H	12	10	1	202	35	22.44	-	-	4	-							
1-day Lge	33	29	10	639	58 *	33.63	-	2	10	-							

STEAD, R. A.   Yorkshire

Name: Roger Alexander Stead
Role: Right-hand bat, right-arm medium bowler
Born: 18 April 1980, Dewsbury
Height: 6ft 1in **Weight:** 13st
Nickname: Zani, Steady
County debut: No first-team appearance
Parents: Roger and Linda
Marital status: Single

Education: Lightcliffe Church of England School; Hipperholme and Lightcliffe High School; University of Durham
Qualifications: 10 GCSEs, 4 A-levels
Career outside cricket: Student at University of Durham
Off-season: 'Training with the University of Durham School of Excellence; travelling to South Africa with University 1st XI on tour; studying for Sports degree'
Cricketers particularly admired: Jacques Kallis, Steve Waugh
Young players to look out for: John Sadler ('Yorks Academy and England U19')
Other sports played: Football (Calderdale district and local team), athletics (200m – Calderdale district)
Other sports followed: Football ('mad Leeds United supporter since early age')

Extras: Scored 88* on 2nd XI debut v Warwicks at Edgbaston 1998. Took 4-29 first time he bowled for 2nd XI, v Notts at Trent Bridge 1999
Opinions on cricket: 'Good to see more and more young players playing at a higher level and producing good performances. Glad to see two-division system in both leagues to increase competition.'

---

82. Who scored 108 in Gloucestershire's only innings
and returned match figures of 13-73 in the county's defeat
of Worcestershire at Cheltenham in 1977?

STELLING, W. F.　　　　　　　　Leicestershire

Name: William Frederick Stelling
Role: Right-hand bat, right-arm
medium-fast bowler
Born: 30 June 1969, Johannesburg
Height: 6ft 4in　**Weight:** 13st 6lbs
Nickname: Will, Stealth
County debut: No first-team appearance
1st-Class 50s: 1
1st-Class catches: 8
Strike rate: (career 78.68)
Parents: Bill and Kathy
Marital status: Engaged to Kerrie Anne
Muldoon (date of wedding 11 March 2000)
Education: St Peters Preparatory School;
Michaelhouse and St Stithians College;
University of Cape Town
Career outside cricket: Freelance journalist
(cricket and rugby)
Off-season: 'Relaxing in the Caribbean or
Thailand, Mexico or anywhere else warm, cheap and tropical'
Overseas teams played for: Western Province B and Western Province 1991-92,
1993-94; Boland 1994-96
Cricketers particularly admired: Steve Waugh, Kepler Wessels, Malcolm Marshall,
Dale Benkenstein
Young players to look out for: Michael Lumb (Yorks), Ben Phillips (Kent)
Other sports played: Rugby (Transvaal U20), golf, gym, cycling, beach bats
Other sports followed: Football (Liverpool, AC Milan), rugby (Canterbury Crusaders,
South Africa and New Zealand)
Injuries: Damaged ligaments in left ankle; no time off required
Relaxations: Crossword puzzles, mystery puzzles and films
Extras: Made highest score of 162* in 25-over game when ten years old. Played for
Transvaal Schools 1986-87. Made first-class debut for Western Province B v Natal B at
Pietermaritzburg in 1991-92. Played for Holland in 1995 NatWest Trophy and is a Dutch
passport holder. Played for East Lancs in the Lancashire League. Played for the Berkshire
club Finchampstead. Won Thames Valley League Batting Award 1998. Represented Berkshire
in the NatWest Trophy in 1999 and also played for them against Bangladesh in a World Cup
warm-up match, taking 7-32. Scored 412 runs (av. 68.70) for Leics 2nd XI 1999 with a top
score of 130 v Yorks. Has satisfied criteria for EU nationals in county cricket and is not
considered an overseas player; has joined Leicestershire for 2000 on a two-year contract
Opinions on cricket: 'Too much domestic cricket in the UK. Must be strength versus
strength as in Australia. Not enough recognition in club cricket and too little interest in
schools to produce good cricketers. Good competition produces good players.'

Best batting: 53 Western Province B v KwaZulu-Natal B, Pietermaritzburg 1991-92
Best bowling: 4-12 Boland v Border, Paarl 1994-95

1999 Season (did not make any first-class or one-day appearances)

Career Performances

	M	Inns	NO	Runs	HS	Avge	100s	50s	Ct	St	Balls	Runs	Wkts	Avge	Best	5wI	10wM
Test																	
All First	17	28	2	475	53	18.26	-	1	8	-	2203	980	28	35.00	4-12	-	-
1-day Int																	
NatWest	3	3	2	85	76 *	85.00	-	1	-	-	162	87	3	29.00	3-18	-	
B & H																		
1-day Lge																		

STEMP, R. D.　　　　　Nottinghamshire

Name: Richard David Stemp
Role: Right-hand bat, slow left-arm bowler
Born: 11 December 1967, Erdington, Birmingham
Height: 6ft **Weight:** 12st 4lbs
Nickname: Stempy, Sherriff, Badger
County debut: 1990 (Worcestershire), 1993 (Yorkshire), 1999 (Nottinghamshire)
County cap: 1996 (Yorkshire)
1st-Class 50s: 2
1st-Class 5 w. in innings: 13
1st-Class 10 w. in match: 1
1st-Class catches: 60
Place in batting averages: 290th av. 6.16 (1998 205th av. 19.00)
Place in bowling averages: 148th av. 60.87 (1998 122nd av. 37.07)
Strike rate: 122.18 (career 82.09)
Parents: Arnold and Rita Homer
Marital status: Single
Family links with cricket: Father played Birmingham League cricket for Old Hill
Education: Britannia High School, Rowley Regis
Qualifications: NCA coaching award
Overseas tours: England A to India 1994-95, to Pakistan 1995-96
Overseas teams played for: Pretoria Technikon 1988-89
Cricketers particularly admired: Ian Botham, Phil Tufnell

Other sports followed: Indoor cricket, American football (New England Patriots)
Relaxations: Ornithology, music, driving
Extras: Played for England indoor cricket team v Australia in ManuLife 'Test' series 1990. Moved to Yorkshire at end of 1992 season (first English non-Yorkshireman to be signed for the county). Included in England Test squad against New Zealand in 1994. Left Yorkshire at the end of the 1998 season and joined Notts for 1999
Opinions on cricket: 'Groundsmen should prepare cricket wickets, not wickets made for corporate hospitality.'
Best batting: 65 Yorkshire v Durham, Chester-le-Street 1996
Best bowling: 6-37 Yorkshire v Durham, Durham University 1994

1999 Season

	M	Inns	NO	Runs	HS	Avge	100s	50s	Ct	St	O	M	Runs	Wkts	Avge	Best	5wI	10wM
Test																		
All First	13	17	5	74	18	6.16	-	-	1	-	325.5	88	974	16	60.87	4-114	-	-
1-day Int																		
NatWest	2	1	0	12	12	12.00	-	-	-	-	20	2	80	3	26.66	2-28	-	
B & H																		
1-day Lge	14	5	3	49	29 *	24.50	-	-	4	-	108	4	490	13	37.69	3-15	-	

Career Performances

	M	Inns	NO	Runs	HS	Avge	100s	50s	Ct	St	Balls	Runs	Wkts	Avge	Best	5wI	10wM
Test																	
All First	149	178	58	1499	65	12.49	-	2	60	-	27503	11842	335	35.34	6-37	13	1
1-day Int																	
NatWest	13	4	2	13	12	6.50	-	-	1	-	786	486	17	28.58	4-45	-	
B & H	19	4	1	3	2	1.00	-	-	-	-	1062	679	19	35.73	3-22	-	
1-day Lge	83	28	11	167	29 *	9.82	-	-	20	-	3315	2680	86	31.16	4-25	-	

STEPHENSON, J. P.   Hampshire

Name: John Patrick Stephenson
Role: Right-hand bat, right-arm medium bowler
Born: 14 March 1965, Stebbing, Essex
Height: 6ft 1in **Weight:** 12st 7lbs
Nickname: Stan
County debut: 1985 (Essex), 1995 (Hants)
County cap: 1989 (Essex), 1995 (Hants)
Test debut: 1989
Tests: 1
1000 runs in a season: 5

1st-Class 50s: 71
1st-Class 100s: 23
1st-Class 200s: 1
1st-Class 5 w. in innings: 10
1st-Class catches: 166
One-Day 100s: 7
One-Day 5 w. in innings: 3
Place in batting averages: 209th av. 19.31
(1998 104th av. 29.60)
Place in bowling averages: 88th av. 29.35
(1998 98th av. 32.08)
Strike rate: 50.27 (career 61.14)
Parents: Pat and Eve
Wife and date of marriage: Fiona Maria,
24 September 1994
Children: Emma-Lydia, 19 May 1997
Family links with cricket: Father was
member of Rugby Meteors Cricketer Cup-
winning side in 1973. Three brothers played in Felsted 1st XI; Guy played for Essex
2nd XI and now plays for Teddington
Education: Felsted Prep School; Felsted Senior School; Durham University
Qualifications: 7 O-levels, 3 A-levels, BA General Arts, Level 3 coaching award
Overseas tours: English Schools U19 to Zimbabwe 1982-83; England A to Kenya and
Zimbabwe 1989-90, to Bermuda and West Indies 1991-92; MCC to Kenya 1999
Overseas teams played for: Fitzroy, Melbourne 1982-83, 1987-88; Boland, South
Africa 1988-89; Gold Coast Dolphins and Bond University, Australia 1990-91;
St George's, Argentina 1994-95; Belgrano, Argentina 1994-95; Victoria CC, South
Africa 1995-96
Cricketers particularly admired: Brian Hardie
Young players to look out for: Matthew Wood
Injuries: Out for one month with a foot injury
Relaxations: Watching cricket, reading (*Sunday Telegraph, Wisden, The Cricketer*),
alternative music
Extras: Awarded 2nd XI cap in 1984 when leading run-scorer with Essex 2nd XI.
Essex Young Player of the Year 1985. Captained Durham University to victory in UAU
Championship 1986 and was captain of Combined Universities team 1987 in the first
year that it was drawn from all universities. Called up to replace the injured Michael
Atherton on England A tour to Bermuda and West Indies 1991-92 and was leading
wicket-taker. Scored two not out centuries v Somerset at Taunton in 1992 and was on
the field for the whole game (the first Essex player to achieve this). First Essex player
to achieve 500 runs and 20 wickets in Sunday League season 1993. Took over the
captaincy of Hampshire in 1996, but relinquished it at the end of the 1997 season.
Founded the One Test Wonder Club in 1996
Opinions on cricket: 'Let's have more day/night cricket. Identify the class players in
ability and attitude and stick with them.'

Best batting: 202* Essex v Somerset, Bath 1990
Best bowling: 7-51 Hampshire v Middlesex, Lord's 1995

1999 Season

	M	Inns	NO	Runs	HS	Avge	100s	50s	Ct	St	O	M	Runs	Wkts	Avge	Best	5wI	10wM
Test																		
All First	15	24	2	425	136	19.31	1	1	17	-	310	57	1086	37	29.35	5-60	1	-
1-day Int																		
NatWest	2	2	0	14	14	7.00	-	-	-	-	16	1	80	2	40.00	2-20	-	
B & H	1	1	1	39	39 *	-	-	-	-	-	4	0	29	0	-	-	-	
1-day Lge	11	11	2	365	96	40.55	-	2	7	-	55.5	1	277	6	46.16	2-26	-	

Career Performances

	M	Inns	NO	Runs	HS	Avge	100s	50s	Ct	St	Balls	Runs	Wkts	Avge	Best	5wI	10wM
Test	1	2	0	36	25	18.00	-	-	-	-							
All First	268	453	44	13623	202 *	33.30	24	71	166	-	19262	10627	315	33.73	7-51	10	-
1-day Int																	
NatWest	29	27	1	820	107	31.53	1	7	11	-	1093	855	27	31.66	5-34	1	
B & H	46	41	6	1510	142	43.14	2	11	11	-	1528	1089	42	25.92	3-22	-	
1-day Lge	174	156	21	3906	110 *	28.93	4	18	72	-	5131	4048	160	25.30	6-33	2	

STEVENS, D. I. Leicestershire

Name: Darren Ian Stevens
Role: Right-hand bat, right-arm medium bowler
Born: 30 April 1976, Leicester
Height: 5ft 11in **Weight:** 12st 7lbs
Nickname: Beetroot, JJ Junior
County debut: 1997
1st-Class 50s: 3
1st-Class 100s: 1
1st-Class catches: 13
Place in batting averages: 119th av. 28.10
Strike rate: (career 19.00)
Parents: Robert and Madeleine
Marital status: Single
Family links with cricket: Father and grandfather played club cricket in local leagues
Education: Richmond Primary School; Mount Grace High School; John Cleavland College, Hinckley
Qualifications: 4 GCSEs, BTEC in Sports Studies
Overseas tours: Leicestershire U19 to South Africa 1994-95
Overseas teams played for: Wanderers CC, Johannesburg, South Africa 1995-97;

Rhodes University, Grahamstown, South Africa 1997-98
Cricketers particularly admired: Ian Botham, Graham Thorpe, David Gower
Young players to look out for: Darren Maddy, Tim 'Biffa' Mason, Jon 'Babe Ruth' Dakin, Dominic 'Yoda' Williamson
Other sports followed: Football (Leicester City), rugby (Leicester Tigers), golf, squash
Relaxations: Socialising, going out with friends, clubbing, spending time with girlfriend Clare. 'Having a round of golf – not walking around but on a buggy'
Extras: Scored maiden first-class 100 (130) in fourth Championship match, v Sussex at Arundel 1999
Opinions on cricket: 'Great game.'
Best batting: 130 Leicestershire v Sussex, Arundel 1999
Best bowling: 1-5 Leicestershire v Sussex, Eastbourne 1997

1999 Season

	M	Inns	NO	Runs	HS	Avge	100s	50s	Ct	St	O	M	Runs	Wkts	Avge	Best	5wI	10wM
Test																		
All First	11	20	0	562	130	28.10	1	3	12	-	1.1	0	6	0	-	-	-	-
1-day Int																		
NatWest	2	2	0	37	24	18.50	-	-	-	-								
B & H	1	1	0	16	16	16.00	-	-	-	-								
1-day Lge	10	10	0	270	82	27.00	-	2	2	-								

Career Performances

	M	Inns	NO	Runs	HS	Avge	100s	50s	Ct	St	Balls	Runs	Wkts	Avge	Best	5wI	10wM
Test																	
All First	14	24	0	600	130	25.00	1	3	13	-	19	11	1	11.00	1-5	-	-
1-day Int																	
NatWest	2	2	0	37	24	18.50	-	-	-	-							
B & H	1	1	0	16	16	16.00	-	-	-	-							
1-day Lge	16	16	1	316	82	21.06	-	2	3	-							

STEWART, A. J.   Surrey

Name: Alec James Stewart
Role: Right-hand bat, wicket-keeper,
honorary club captain
Born: 8 April 1963, Merton
Height: 5ft 11in **Weight:** 13st 2lbs
Nickname: Stewie, Ming
County debut: 1981
County cap: 1985
Benefit: 1994 (£202,187)
Test debut: 1989-90
Tests: 90
One-Day Internationals: 125
1000 runs in a season: 8
1st-Class 50s: 126
1st-Class 100s: 42
1st-Class 200s: 2
1st-Class catches: 535
1st-Class stumpings: 19
One-Day 100s: 16
Place in batting averages: 117th av. 28.38 (1998 24th av. 43.77)
Strike rate: (career 160.33)
Parents: Michael and Sheila
Wife and date of marriage: Lynn, 28 September 1991
Children: Andrew James, 21 May 1993; Emily Elizabeth, 6 September 1996
Family links with cricket: Father played for England (1962-64), Surrey (1954-72)
and Malden Wanderers. Brother Neil captains Malden Wanderers
Education: Tiffin Boys School
Qualifications: 'Streetwise'
Off-season: England tour of South Africa
Overseas tours: England to India (Nehru Cup) 1989-90, to West Indies 1989-90, to
Australia 1990-91, to Australia and New Zealand (World Cup) 1991-92, to India and
Sri Lanka 1992-93, to West Indies 1993-94, to Australia 1994-95, to South Africa
1995-96, to Pakistan and India (World Cup) 1995-96, to Zimbabwe and New Zealand
1996-97, to Sharjah 1997-98 (Champions Trophy), to West Indies 1997-98, to
Australia 1998-99 (captain), to Sharjah (Coca-Cola Cup) 1998-99, to South Africa
1999-2000
Overseas teams played for: Midland Guildford, Perth, Western Australia 1981-89
Cricketers particularly admired: Graham Monkhouse, Graham Gooch, Alan Knott,
Geoff Arnold, K. Gartrell
Young players to look out for: Ben Hollioake
Other sports followed: Football (Chelsea)

Relaxations: 'Spending as much time with my family as possible'
Extras: Captained England in a Test match for the first time v India at Madras 1992-93 and acted as vice-captain to both Graham Gooch and Mike Atherton. One of *Wisden*'s Five Cricketers of the Year 1993. First Englishman to score a century in each innings against West Indies, at Barbados 1994. He was the leading scorer in Test cricket in the 1996 calendar year (with 793 runs) ahead of Saeed Anwar (701). Appointed captain of England 1998. Awarded MBE in HM The Queen's birthday honours list 1998. His 164 in England's second innings v South Africa at Old Trafford in 1998 was a record by a captain/wicket-keeper in Tests. Captained England in the 1999 World Cup; stood down as captain afterwards. Is contracted to Surrey until 2003
Opinions on cricket: 'Improve the level of pitches and practice pitches.'
Best batting: 271* Surrey v Yorkshire, The Oval 1997
Best bowling: 1-7 Surrey v Lancashire, Old Trafford 1989
Stop press: Leading run-scorer in world Test cricket in the 1990s with 6407 runs (av. 40.81). Awarded England contract (Band A) for 2000

1999 Season

	M	Inns	NO	Runs	HS	Avge	100s	50s	Ct	St	O	M	Runs	Wkts	Avge	Best	5wI	10wM
Test	4	8	1	215	83*	30.71	-	2	4	-								
All First	12	20	2	511	95	28.38	-	3	15	2	2	0	6	0	-	-	-	-
1-day Int	5	5	0	125	88	25.00	-	1	7	-								
NatWest	4	4	0	123	64	30.75	-	1	4	3								
B & H	1	1	0	17	17	17.00	-	-	1	-								
1-day Lge	8	8	0	231	76	28.87	-	1	4	1								

Career Performances

	M	Inns	NO	Runs	HS	Avge	100s	50s	Ct	St	Balls	Runs	Wkts	Avge	Best	5wI	10wM
Test	90	164	12	6183	190	40.67	12	32	159	7	20	13	0	-	-	-	-
All First	376	626	68	22507	271*	40.33	44	126	535	19	481	423	3	141.00	1-7	-	-
1-day Int	125	120	8	3378	116	30.16	2	19	111	11							
NatWest	43	40	6	1668	125*	49.05	3	12	52	5							
B & H	66	66	10	2615	167*	46.69	4	18	48	11							
1-day Lge	176	160	16	4442	125	30.84	7	25	136	12	4	8	0	-	-	-	

83. Which county won the last pre-World War II Championship and the first of the post-war era, and who was their captain on both occasions?

STRAUSS, A. J. Middlesex

Name: Andrew John Strauss
Role: Left-hand bat, left-arm swing bowler
Born: 2 March 1977, Johannesburg,
South Africa
Height: 5ft 11in **Weight:** 13st
Nickname: Johann, Mousey, Jazzer, Mareman
County debut: 1997 (one-day),
1998 (first-class)
1st-Class 50s: 5
1st-Class catches: 6
Place in batting averages: 104th av. 30.50
(1998 149th av. 24.33)
Parents: David and Dawn
Marital status: Single
Education: Caldicott Prep School;
Radley College; Durham University
Qualifications: 4 A-levels, BA (Hons)
Economics
Off-season: Playing for Mosman CC in Sydney
Overseas tours: Durham University to Zimbabwe 1997-98
Overseas teams played for: Sydney University 1998-99; Mosman, Sydney 1999-2000
Cricketers particularly admired: Brian Lara, Allan Donald
Young players to look out for: Ed 'Gower' Joyce
Other sports played: Rugby (Durham University 1996-97), golf (Durham
University 1998)
Other sports followed: Any sport
Injuries: 'Backache from picking up all the names dropped by David "Big Gun" Nash'
Relaxations: Macroeconomics, economic data analysis, contemporary economies
Extras: Opened for Middlesex v Essex at Southend 1999 with Ben Hutton, his former
opening partner at Radley
Opinions on cricket: 'Too much talk, not enough action!'
Best batting: 98 Middlesex v Surrey, Lord's 1999

1999 Season

	M	Inns	NO	Runs	HS	Avge	100s	50s	Ct	St	O	M	Runs	Wkts	Avge	Best	5wl	10wM
Test																		
All First	9	17	1	488	98	30.50	-	4	3	-								
1-day Int																		
NatWest																		
B & H																		
1-day Lge	6	5	2	33	19	11.00	-	-	1	-								

Career Performances

	M	Inns	NO	Runs	HS	Avge	100s	50s	Ct	St	Balls	Runs	Wkts	Avge	Best	5wl	10wM
Test																	
All First	12	23	1	634	98	28.81	-	5	6	-							
1-day Int																	
NatWest																		
B & H	3	3	1	48	29	24.00	-	-	-	-							
1-day Lge	11	10	2	64	19	8.00	-	-	3	-							

STRONG, M. R.   Northamptonshire

Name: Michael Richard Strong
Role: Left-hand bat, right-arm
fast-medium bowler
Born: 28 June 1974, Cuckfield, West Sussex
Height: 6ft 1in **Weight:** 12st 10lbs
Nickname: Strongbow, Stronglager,
Stella, Bill
County debut: 1997 (one-day, Sussex),
1998 (first-class, Sussex)
1st-Class catches: 1
Parents: David and Gillian
Marital status: Single ('just')
Family links with cricket: Father and
brother both played club cricket in Sussex
Education: St Peter's School, Burgess Hill;
Brighton College; Brunel University College
(formerly West London Institute)
Qualifications: 9 GCSEs, 3 A-levels,
BA/BSc (QTS) PE and Geography, various coaching awards
Career outside cricket: 'PE teacher and lager drinker'
Off-season: Playing and coaching in South Africa
Overseas tours: Brighton College to India 1991-92
Overseas teams played for: Umbilo CC, Durban 1992-93, 1997-2000
Cricketers particularly admired: 'WG', Ranjitsinhji
Young players to look out for: William Lewry
Other sports played: Football, hockey, golf
Other sports followed: Football (Brighton and Chelsea), rugby (Saracens)
Injuries: Out for eight weeks with a torn intercostal muscle
Relaxations: 'Going out with the boys; lying on a beach with a cold beer'
Extras: 'Would like to thank the master in charge of cricket at Brighton College, John
Spencer, for all the time he spent coaching me from the age of ten.' 'Caused much

amusement in an AON Trophy match at The Oval when going for an important caught-and-bowled chance. Having flattened all three stumps, fallen over, dived and got one hand to the ball, I dropped it! Roy Palmer found it particularly amusing. Luckily we went on to win the match.' Most Improved Sussex Player 1998. 'Most Underused Sussex Player 1999.' Left Sussex in 1999-2000 off-season and has joined Northants
Opinions on cricket: 'May the seeds of today be the fruits of tomorrow – as the phrase above says, counties should be prepared to be brave and bold enough to back younger players more than they do now.'
Best batting: 35* Sussex v Leicestershire, Arundel 1999

1999 Season

	M	Inns	NO	Runs	HS	Avge	100s	50s	Ct	St	O	M	Runs	Wkts	Avge	Best	5wI	10wM
Test																		
All First	1	2	1	51	35 *	51.00	-	-	1	-	31	5	124	0	-		-	-	-
1-day Int																		
NatWest																		
B & H																		
1-day Lge																		

Career Performances

	M	Inns	NO	Runs	HS	Avge	100s	50s	Ct	St	Balls	Runs	Wkts	Avge	Best	5wI	10wM
Test																	
All First	2	3	2	53	35 *	53.00	-	-	1	-	252	165	0	-		-	-
1-day Int																	
NatWest																	
B & H																	
1-day Lge	3	3	1	4	2 *	2.00	-	-	-	-	92	97	0	-		-	-

STUBBINGS, S. D.   Derbyshire

Name: Stephen David Stubbings
Role: Left-hand bat
Born: 31 March 1978, Huddersfield
Height: 6ft 4in   **Weight:** 14st 1lb
Nickname: Stubbo
County debut: 1997
1st-Class catches: 3
Place in batting averages: 190th av. 21.30
Parents: David and Marie-Anne
Marital status: Single
Family links with cricket: 'Father played the odd game'

Education: Frankston High School, Victoria
Qualifications: Completed Year 12
Overseas teams played for: Frankston-Finchley CC, Victoria 1993-1998
Cricketers particularly admired:
Mark Taylor, Ricky Ponting, Steve Waugh, Michael Atherton
Young players to look out for:
Ian Blackwell, Kevin Dean, Ben Spendlove
Other sports followed: Aussie Rules (Essendon Bombers), football (Cambridge United)
Relaxations: Golf, eating, drinking and television
Extras: Has also played for Victoria at U17, Colts and U21 level
Best batting: 45 Derbyshire v Leicestershire, Leicester 1999

1999 Season

	M	Inns	NO	Runs	HS	Avge	100s	50s	Ct	St	O	M	Runs	Wkts	Avge	Best	5wI	10wM
Test																		
All First-	5	10	0	213	45	21.30	-	-	3	-	5	0	41	0	-	-	-	-
1-day Int																		
NatWest																		
B & H																		
1-day Lge	6	6	0	98	37	16.33	-	-	1	-								

Career Performances

	M	Inns	NO	Runs	HS	Avge	100s	50s	Ct	St	Balls	Runs	Wkts	Avge	Best	5wI	10wM
Test																	
All First	6	12	0	240	45	20.00	-	-	3	-	30	41	0	-	-	-	-
1-day Int																	
NatWest																	
B & H	2	2	0	8	7	4.00	-	-	-	-							
1-day Lge	7	7	0	102	37	14.57	-	-	1	-							

SUCH, P. M.   Essex

Name: Peter Mark Such
Role: Right-hand bat, off-spin bowler
Born: 12 June 1964, Helensburgh, Scotland
Height: 6ft **Weight:** 11st 7lbs
Nickname: Suchy
County debut: 1982 (Nottinghamshire),
1987 (Leicestershire), 1990 (Essex)
County cap: 1991 (Essex)
Test debut: 1993
Tests: 11
50 wickets in a season: 6
1st-Class 50s: 2
1st-Class 5 w. in innings: 44
1st-Class 10 w. in match: 8
1st-Class catches: 109
One-Day 5 w. in innings: 3
Place in batting averages: 271st av. 10.30
(1998 204th av. 19.00)
Place in bowling averages: 100th av. 31.09 (1998 126th av. 38.81)
Strike rate: 76.58 (career 67.57)
Parents: John and Margaret
Wife and date of marriage: Nicola Jane, 25 September 1999
Family links with cricket: Father and brother both village cricketers
Education: Lantern Lane Primary; Harry Carlton Comprehensive, East Leake, Notts
Qualifications: 9 O-levels, 3 A-levels, advanced cricket coach
Overseas tours: England A to Australia 1992-93, 1996-97, to South Africa 1993-94;
England to Australia 1998-99
Overseas teams played for: Kempton Park, South Africa 1982-83; Bathurst, Australia
1985-86; Matabeleland, Zimbabwe 1989-92
Cricketers particularly admired: Bob White, Eddie Hemmings, Graham Gooch,
John Childs
Young players to look out for: Paul Franks, Michael Davies, Graeme Swann,
Matthew Wood
Other sports played: Golf
Other sports followed: Rugby union
Relaxations: 'Music, playing golf, socialising with mates, reading'
Extras: Played for England YC v Australian YC 1983 and for TCCB XI v New
Zealand 1985. Left Nottinghamshire at end of 1986 season; joined Leicestershire in
1987 and was released at end of 1989; signed by Essex for 1990. Played in one-day
games for England A v Sri Lanka 1991. Joint winner with J.H. Childs of the Essex
Player of the Year Award 1992 and shared the award again in 1993. Took 6-67 on Test

debut v Australia 1993 – best figures by England Test debutant since John Lever in India 1976-77. Set record for the most overs bowled in a County Championship innings – 86 overs against Leicestershire in August 1997; he ended up with figures of 4 for 96. Set the unenviable record of having scored the longest duck in English Test history with his 72-minute innings in the third Test v New Zealand at Old Trafford 1999. Is vice-chairman of the Professional Cricketers' Association

Best batting: 54 Essex v Worcestershire, Chelmsford 1993

54 Essex v Nottinghamshire, Chelmsford 1996

Best bowling: 8-93 Essex v Hampshire, Colchester 1995

1999 Season

	M	Inns	NO	Runs	HS	Avge	100s	50s	Ct	St	O	M	Runs	Wkts	Avge	Best	5wl	10wM
Test	1	1	0	0	0	0.00	-	-	1	-	41	11	114	4	28.50	4-114	-	-
All First	20	24	11	134	22 *	10.30	-	-	5	-	702	192	1710	55	31.09	7-136	2	1
1-day Int																		
NatWest	1	0	0	0	0	-	-	-	1	-	7	0	44	0	-		-	-
B & H																		
1-day Lge	13	9	6	24	5 *	8.00	-	-	5	-	97	3	426	16	26.62	3-26	-	

Career Performances

	M	Inns	NO	Runs	HS	Avge	100s	50s	Ct	St	Balls	Runs	Wkts	Avge	Best	5wl	10wM
Test	11	16	5	67	14 *	6.09	-	-	4	-	3124	1242	37	33.56	6-67	2	-
All First	279	294	112	1475	54	8.10	-	2	109	-	53314	23519	789	29.80	8-93	44	8
1-day Int																	
NatWest	25	9	5	21	8 *	5.25	-	-	4	-	1554	872	25	34.88	3-56	-	
B & H	38	14	8	46	10 *	7.66	-	-	7	-	1947	1207	32	37.71	4-43	-	
1-day Lge	139	58	34	208	19 *	8.66	-	-	37	-	5507	4240	144	29.44	5-29	3	

84. What feat did A.E. Trott perform for Middlesex v Somerset at Lord's in 1907?

SUTCLIFFE, I. J.   Leicestershire

Name: Iain John Sutcliffe
Role: Left-hand bat, leg-spin bowler
Born: 20 December 1974, Leeds
Height: 6ft 1in **Weight:** 12st
Nickname: Sooty, Bertie, Ripper
County debut: 1995
1st-Class 50s: 17
1st-Class 100s: 5
1st-Class catches: 38
One-Day 100s: 2
Place in batting averages: 181st av. 21.85
(1998 85th av. 31.72)
Strike rate: (career 51.60)
Parents: John and Valerie
Marital status: Single
Education: Leeds Grammar School;
Oxford University
Qualifications: 10 GCSEs, 4 A-levels,
2:1 PPE degree
Overseas tours: Leeds GS to Kenya
Cricketers particularly admired: David Gower, Brian Lara, Saeed Anwar
Other sports followed: Boxing (Mike Tyson), football (Liverpool)
Relaxations: Listening to music, eating out
Extras: Played NCA England U14 and NCA Development Team U18/U19. Oxford
boxing Blue 1994 and 1995, British Universities Light-middleweight Champion 1993.
In 1995, took part (with C. Gupte) in record partnership for Oxford University against
a first-class county (283 v Hampshire at The Parks), in which he scored 163*
Best batting: 167 Leicestershire v Middlesex, Leicester 1998
Best bowling: 2-21 Oxford University v Cambridge University, Lord's 1996

1999 Season

	M	Inns	NO	Runs	HS	Avge	100s	50s	Ct	St	O	M	Runs	Wkts	Avge	Best	5wl	10wM
Test																		
All First	16	27	0	590	110	21.85	1	2	9	-	1	1	0	0	-	-	-	-
1-day Int																		
NatWest	1	1	0	23	23	23.00	-	-	-	-								
B & H	1	1	0	0	0	0.00	-	-	-	-								
1-day Lge	9	9	0	105	40	11.66	-	-	1	-								

Career Performances

	M	Inns	NO	Runs	HS	Avge	100s	50s	Ct	St	Balls	Runs	Wkts	Avge	Best	5wI	10wM
Test																	
All First	76	115	11	3324	167	31.96	5	17	38	-	258	200	5	40.00	2-21	-	-
1-day Int																	
NatWest	8	8	2	377	103 *	62.83	1	2	2	-							
B & H	15	15	1	425	105 *	30.35	1	3	2	-							
1-day Lge	21	21	1	343	96	17.15	-	1	5	-							

SUTCLIFFE, R. V.   Northamptonshire

Name: Robin Victor Sutcliffe
Role: Right-hand bat, right-arm medium-fast bowler
Born: 10 July 1980, Hemel Hempstead
Height: 6ft 8in **Weight:** 12st
Nickname: Suts, Sticks, Long Bones, Sutty, McGrath (Glenn)
County debut: 1999
Strike rate: 82.50 (career 82.50)
Parents: Angeline Reader and Trevor Sutcliffe
Marital status: Single
Family links with cricket: Father played for Blackpool. 'Brother and I played Test matches in front drive; he plays for Abbots Langley'
Education: Two Waters JMI; Cavendish Comprehensive; Cassio Campus (Watford); Greenhill College (Harrow)
Qualifications: 9 GCSEs, 2 A-levels
Off-season: 'Playing in Australia/holiday'
Overseas teams played for: Red Banks, Ipswich, Queensland 1999-2000
Cricketers particularly admired: Glenn McGrath, Steve Waugh, Lance Klusener, Jason Gillespie
Young players to look out for: Mark Powell, Richard Logan, Jeff Cook
Other sports played: Golf
Other sports followed: Golf, football (Man Utd – 'for financial reasons')
Injuries: Out for three weeks with tendonitis of right knee
Relaxations: 'Golf; listening to Pink Floyd, Verve, Radiohead; watching videos, drinking, night clubs, pubs'
Extras: 'Making my first-class debut was my best achievement.' Has received bowling awards for Abbots Langley

Opinions on cricket: 'Far too much cricket is played for the game to be competitive enough in this country.'
Best batting: 9* Northamptonshire v Sri Lanka A, Northampton 1999
Best bowling: 2-88 Northamptonshire v Sri Lanka A, Northampton 1999

1999 Season

	M	Inns	NO	Runs	HS	Avge	100s	50s	Ct	St	O	M	Runs	Wkts	Avge	Best	5wI	10wM
Test																		
All First	2	2	1	9	9*	9.00	-	-	-	-	55	14	164	4	41.00	2-88	-	-
1-day Int																		
NatWest																			
B & H																			
1-day Lge																			

Career Performances

	M	Inns	NO	Runs	HS	Avge	100s	50s	Ct	St	Balls	Runs	Wkts	Avge	Best	5wI	10wM
Test																	
All First	2	2	1	9	9*	9.00	-	-	-	-	330	164	4	41.00	2-88	-	-
1-day Int																	
NatWest																		
B & H																		
1-day Lge																		

SUTTON, L. D.   Derbyshire

Name: Luke David Sutton
Role: Right-hand bat, 'right-arm filth – on a par with Rob "The Dentist" Turner', wicket-keeper
Born: 4 October 1976, Keynsham
Height: 5ft 11in **Weight:** 12st 7lbs – 'less than "Sumo" Kerr'
Nickname: Sutts, Duke, 'others that cannot be printed'
County debut: 1997 (Somerset)
1st-Class catches: 10
Parents: David and Molly
Marital status: Single
Family links with cricket: 'None spring to mind'
Education: Edgarley Hall (Millfield Junior School); Millfield School; Durham University 'and Kevin Shine's School of Life'
Qualifications: 9 GCSEs, 4 A-levels, 2:1 degree in Economics, various cricket coaching awards

Career outside cricket: 'None yet'

Off-season: Playing club cricket in Port Elizabeth, South Africa. 'Recovering from captaining Pete Trego for a season'

Overseas tours: Various Somerset Schools tours to Holland; West of England U15 to West Indies 1991; Millfield School to Zimbabwe 1993, to Sri Lanka 1994; Durham University to Zimbabwe 1997

Overseas teams played for: UNSW, Sydney 1998-99

Cricketers particularly admired: Ian Healy, Steve Waugh, Paul Nixon, Adrian Pierson, Anthony Wilcox, Tom Paltridge

Young players to look out for: Matt Bulbeck, Mark Chilton, Toby Southgate, Paul Gillmon, Graham Quilliam, Nick Hoyle

Other sports played: Football, hockey, 'Temper-Temper Trophy golf'; 'I'll give any sport a go'

Other sports followed: Football (Newcastle United), 'every England team in any sport'

Injuries: Out for six weeks with torn medial meniscus in left knee; for eight weeks with broken left thumb

Relaxations: Keeping fit; going to the beach; socialising with friends

Extras: Captain of the England U15 side that played against South Africa and also played for England U18 and U19. Won John Hobbs Award for the U16 Cricketer of the Year in 1992 and the Gray Nicolls Award for the English Schools Cricketer of the Year in 1995. Left Somerset at the end of the 1999 season and has joined Derbyshire for 2000

Opinions on cricket: 'We continuously talk about improving the Test side's results, and I don't disagree that this should be a priority. But let's not just talk about it; let's get serious about it. We need to improve the type of cricket played, the standard of balls and pitches, monitor the standard of umpiring and the quality and attitude of coaches used. I'm not denying the ECB are trying to do this already to some extent, but the solution doesn't just lie in the hands of the ECB. Cricket at all levels needs to accept some responsibility for improving the game. The sooner we can get rid of selfish attitudes, from chief executives to U11 club coaches, the better. English cricket from the lowest to the highest level needs to appreciate the big picture.'

Best batting: 16* Somerset v Sri Lanka, Taunton 1998

Career Performances

	M	Inns	NO	Runs	HS	Avge	100s	50s	Ct	St	Balls	Runs	Wkts	Avge	Best	5wI	10wM
Test																	
All First	3	6	3	41	16 *	13.66	-	-	10	-							
1-day Int																		
NatWest																		
B & H	4	4	1	105	60	35.00	-	1	-	-							
1-day Lge																		

SWANN, A. J. Northamptonshire

Name: Alec James Swann
Role: Right-hand opening bat, occasional
off-spin bowler, occasional wicket-keeper
Born: 26 October 1976, Northampton
Height: 6ft 2in **Weight:** 12st 7lbs
Nickname: Ron
County debut: 1996
1st-Class 50s: 4
1st-Class 100s: 3
1st-Class catches: 18
Place in batting averages: 91st av. 31.83
(1998 244th av. 14.70)
Strike rate: 120.00 (career 189.00)
Parents: Ray and Mavis
Marital status: Single
Family links with cricket: Dad played for
Northumberland, Bedfordshire, Northants II
and England Amateurs. Still plays local
league cricket. Brother Graeme plays for Northants and toured South Africa and
Zimbabwe with England 1999-2000
Education: Sponne School, Towcester
Qualifications: 9 GCSEs, 4 A-levels, NCA coaching award
Off-season: Coaching and playing golf
Overseas tours: Northants to Zimbabwe 1998
Overseas teams played for: Wallsend, NSW, Australia 1995-96, 1997-98;
Montrose CC, Cape Town 1998-99
Cricketers particularly admired: Mark and Steve Waugh, Robin Smith,
Russell Warren
Young players to look out for: Richard Logan, Derek Kenway

Other sports played: Golf
Other sports followed: Football (Newcastle United)
Relaxations: 'I enjoy gambling on horses and sometimes on football or cricket', reading political thrillers, watching films
Extras: Played for England Schools U15 and U19. Opened batting for Bedfordshire (with father in Minor Counties game). *Daily Telegraph* U15 Young Cricketer of the Year 1992. Midlands Club Cricket Conference Young Cricketer of the Year 1992. Played for England U19 against New Zealand in 1996
Opinions on cricket: 'Floodlit cricket is worth continuing with. We play too much cricket. I don't know how some bowlers play all season.'
Best batting: 154 Northamptonshire v Nottinghamshire, Northampton 1999
Best bowling: 1-19 Northamptonshire v Sri Lanka A, Northampton 1999

1999 Season

	M	Inns	NO	Runs	HS	Avge	100s	50s	Ct	St	O	M	Runs	Wkts	Avge	Best	5wI	10wM
Test																		
All First	12	18	0	573	154	31.83	2	2	11	-	20	3	80	1	80.00	1-19	-	-
1-day Int																		
NatWest	2	2	0	109	74	54.50	-	1	1	-								
B & H																		
1-day Lge	8	8	0	180	60	22.50	-	1	2	-								

Career Performances

	M	Inns	NO	Runs	HS	Avge	100s	50s	Ct	St	Balls	Runs	Wkts	Avge	Best	5wI	10wM
Test																	
All First	28	43	1	1085	154	25.83	3	4	18	-	189	154	1	154.00	1-19	-	-
1-day Int																	
NatWest	2	2	0	109	74	54.50	-	1	1	-							
B & H																	
1-day Lge	8	8	0	180	60	22.50	-	1	2	-							

85. Name the three companies that have sponsored
the County Championship to date.

SWANN, G. P.   Northamptonshire

Name: Graeme Peter Swann
Role: Right-hand bat, off-spin bowler
Born: 24 March 1979, Northampton
Height: 6ft **Weight:** 11st 7lbs
Nickname: G-spot, Swanny
County debut: 1997 (one-day),
1998 (first-class)
County cap: 1999
50 wickets in a season: 1
1st-Class 50s: 6
1st-Class 100s: 2
1st-Class 5 w. in innings: 4
1st-Class 10 w. in match: 1
1st-Class catches: 28
One-Day 5 w. in innings: 1
Place in batting averages: 95th av. 31.60
(1998 67th av. 34.25)
Place in bowling averages: 83rd av. 28.78
(1998 86th av. 30.27)
Strike rate: 58.96 (career 57.70)
Parents: Raymond and Mavis
Marital status: Single
Family links with cricket: Dad has played Minor Counties cricket for Bedfordshire and Northumberland and also for England Amateurs. Brother is contracted to Northants. 'Cat is named after Gus Logie'
Education: Abington Vale Lower School; Sponne School, Towcester
Qualifications: 10 GCSEs, 4 A-levels, NCA coaching award
Off-season: England tour to South Africa
Overseas tours: England U19 to South Africa 1997-98; England A to Zimbabwe and South Africa 1998-99; England to South Africa 1999-2000
Cricketers particularly admired: Don Bradman, Devon Malcolm, Neil Foster, Shane Warne, the Waugh brothers
Young players to look out for: John Blain, Richard Logan, Monty Panesar, Rob Key, Michael Davies, Alec Swann
Other sports played: Golf
Other sports followed: Football (Newcastle United, Northampton Town)
Relaxations: 'Working out with the girls from the gym; watching TV and videos; studying Chaucer'
Extras: Played for England U14, U15, U17 and U19. *Daily Telegraph* regional bowling award winner in 1994. Gray-Nicolls Len Newbery Schools Cricketer of the Year in 1996. Took 8-118 for England U19 in second 'Test' v Pakistan U19 1998, the

best ever figures in an U19 'Test'. Scored 92 and 111 in Championship match
v Leicestershire at Grace Road in 1998. Drafted into England 13 for the fourth Test
v New Zealand 1999. Completed Championship double of 500 runs and 50 wickets
1999. Awarded Northants cap 1999

Opinions on cricket: 'Too much cricket. Quality is definitely compromised for
quantity. Floodlit cricket is a must. Wickets should be better to bat on – however, they
should also rag square!'

Best batting: 130* Northamptonshire v Sri Lanka A, Northampton 1999

Best bowling: 6-41 Northamptonshire v Leicestershire, Northampton 1999

Stop press: Retained temporarily for one-day series v South Africa 1999-2000 as
cover for the injured Ashley Giles; made One-Day International debut v South Africa
at Bloemfontein, January 2000

1999 Season

	M	Inns	NO	Runs	HS	Avge	100s	50s	Ct	St	O	M	Runs	Wkts	Avge	Best	5wI	10wM
Test																		
All First	18	27	4	727	130 *	31.60	1	4	13	-	560.1	131	1641	57	28.78	6-41	2	1
1-day Int																		
NatWest	3	3	0	105	42	35.00	-	-	1	-	18.5	0	91	3	30.33	2-40	-	
B & H																		
1-day Lge	14	13	1	295	63	24.58	-	2	3	-	89	1	413	17	24.29	5-35	1	

Career Performances

	M	Inns	NO	Runs	HS	Avge	100s	50s	Ct	St	Balls	Runs	Wkts	Avge	Best	5wI	10wM
Test																	
All First	37	54	7	1451	130 *	30.87	2	6	28	-	5770	2845	100	28.45	6-41	4	1
1-day Int																	
NatWest	3	3	0	105	42	35.00	-	-	1	-	113	91	3	30.33	2-40	-	
B & H	1	0	0	0	0	-	-	-	-	-	36	14	1	14.00	1-14	-	
1-day Lge	24	17	3	311	63	22.21	-	2	4	-	837	687	27	25.44	5-35	1	

---

86. Which by-word for bowling accuracy took five wickets in nine balls
for Hampshire v Leicestershire at Leicester in 1950?

SYMINGTON, M. J.   Durham

Name: Marc Joseph Symington
Role: Right-hand bat, right-arm medium bowler
Born: 10 January 1980, Newcastle-upon-Tyne
Height: 5ft 9in **Weight:** 11st 4lbs
Nickname: Simo
County debut: 1998
1st-Class catches: 1
Strike rate: (career 36.33)
Parents: Keith and Sheila
Marital status: Single
Family links with cricket: Grandfather (Ron Symington) played 24 years in Northumberland League, then umpired in same league for 21 years. Father currently plays for Norton CC in NYSD League. Brother (Craig) plays for Norton CC and Cleveland county U15. Mother is fixtures secretary for Norton CC
Education: St Joseph's, Norton, Stockton-on-Tees; St Michael's, Billingham, Stockton-on-Tees; Stockton Sixth Form College
Qualifications: 6 GCSEs, cricket coaching award
Career outside cricket: Student
Off-season: Practising
Overseas tours: Durham U21 to Sri Lanka 1996; England U19 to New Zealand 1998-99
Cricketers particularly admired: Graham Thorpe, Alec Stewart, Shaun Pollock
Young players to look out for: Graeme Bridge, Ian Bell
Other sports played: Football ('played for Middlesbrough U16')
Other sports followed: Football (Middlesbrough)
Injuries: Out for 12 weeks with a groin injury
Relaxations: Playing snooker and golf
Opinions on cricket: 'The two divisions in both competitions have made a big difference, and everything should be left the way it is for the time being.'
Best batting: 8* Durham v Cambridge University, Fenner's 1998
Best bowling: 3-55 Durham v Derbyshire, Derby 1998

1999 Season

	M	Inns	NO	Runs	HS	Avge	100s	50s	Ct	St	O	M	Runs	Wkts	Avge	Best	5wl	10wM
Test																		
All First																		
1-day Int																		
NatWest																		
B & H																		
1-day Lge	3	2	0	13	10	6.50	-	-	-	-	26	0	163	2	81.50	1-39	-	

Career Performances

	M	Inns	NO	Runs	HS	Avge	100s	50s	Ct	St	Balls	Runs	Wkts	Avge	Best	5wl	10wM
Test																	
All First	2	1	1	8	8 *	-	-	-	1	-	218	148	6	24.66	3-55	-	-
1-day Int																	
NatWest																	
B & H																	
1-day Lge	5	3	0	20	10	6.66	-	-	1	-	198	214	3	71.33	1-39		

SYMONDS, A.   Kent

Name: Andrew Symonds
Role: Right-hand bat, right-arm
medium or off-spin bowler
Born: 9 June 1975, Birmingham
Height: 6ft 1in **Weight:** 13st 5lbs
Nickname: Roy
County debut: 1995 (Gloucestershire),
1999 (Kent)
County cap: 1999 (Kent)
One-Day Internationals: 1
1000 runs in a season: 2
1st-Class 50s: 25
1st-Class 100s: 17
1st-Class 200s: 1
1st-Class catches: 56
Place in batting averages: 31st av. 40.86
Place in bowling averages: 149th av. 63.41
Strike rate: 103.58 (career 69.01)
Parents: Ken and Barbara
Marital status: Single
Family links with cricket: Father played Minor Counties cricket

Education: All Saints Anglican School, Gold Coast, Australia; Ballarat and Clarondon College, Gold Coast, Australia
Qualifications: Level 2 coaching, professional fisherman
Off-season: Playing cricket in Australia
Overseas tours: Australia A to Los Angeles 1999; Australia to Pakistan 1998-99 (one-day series), to Sri Lanka and Zimbabwe 1999-2000 (one-day series)
Overseas teams played for: Australian Cricket Academy 1993-94; Queensland Colts 1993-94; Queensland 1993-94 –
Cricketers particularly admired: Viv Richards, Shane Warne, Michael Holding
Other sports followed: Hockey, rugby, football
Relaxations: Fishing, camping and hunting
Extras: In his first season of first-class cricket he scored a century for Queensland against England on their 1994-95 tour of Australia. Born in England, he was brought up in Australia and attended the Australian Cricket Academy. Hit a world record number of sixes (16) during his innings of 254* for Gloucestershire v Glamorgan 1995. Professional Cricketers' Association Young Player of the Year 1995. Turned down the invitation to tour with England A in 1995 so that he could remain eligible to play for Australia. Made One-Day International debut for Australia v Pakistan, Lahore 1998. Scored 113 off 116 balls and took 4-83 for Queensland v Western Australia in the 1998-99 Sheffield Shield final. Joined Kent for 1999 as overseas player. Awarded Kent cap 1999; released by Kent at end of 1999 season
Best batting: 254* Gloucestershire v Glamorgan, Abergavenny 1995
Best bowling: 4-39 Queensland v Western Australia, Perth 1998-99
Stop press: Named in Australia squad for one-day series in New Zealand 1999-2000

1999 Season

	M	Inns	NO	Runs	HS	Avge	100s	50s	Ct	St	O	M	Runs	Wkts	Avge	Best	5wl	10wM
Test																		
All First	14	25	2	940	177	40.86	3	4	15	-	207.1	37	761	12	63.41	2-48	-	-
1-day Int																		
NatWest	3	3	0	117	52	39.00	-	1	2	-	10.2	0	56	1	56.00	1-42	-	
B & H																		
1-day Lge	9	9	0	248	95	27.55	-	2	3	-	31.1	0	165	2	82.50	1-24	-	

Career Performances

	M	Inns	NO	Runs	HS	Avge	100s	50s	Ct	St	Balls	Runs	Wkts	Avge	Best	5wl	10wM
Test																	
All First	97	165	14	6047	254 *	40.04	18	25	56	-	4900	2612	71	36.78	4-39	-	-
1-day Int	1	0	0	0	0	-	-	-	-	-	12	14	0	-	-	-	
NatWest	8	8	0	283	87	35.37	-	2	2	-	164	119	2	59.50	1-18	-	
B & H	11	11	0	291	95	26.45	-	2	4	-	24	23	0	-	-	-	
1-day Lge	38	37	2	1004	95	28.68	-	6	21	-	499	443	15	29.53	3-34	-	

TAYLOR, B. V.   Sussex

Name: Billy Victor Taylor
Role: Left-hand bat, right-arm
medium-fast bowler
Born: 11 January 1977, Southampton
Height: 6ft 3in **Weight:** 13st 4lbs
Nickname: Crusty, BT, Crusty One
County debut: 1999
Strike rate: 75.00 (career 75.00)
Parents: Vic and Jackie
Marital status: 'Single?'
Family links with cricket: 'Both my
brothers, Martin and James, play for
Winchester KS in the Southern League, and
James plays Minor Counties cricket for
Wiltshire'
Education: Townhill Park; Bitterne Park;
So Tec College

Qualifications: 5 GCSEs, NVQ 2 Carpentry
and Joinery
Career outside cricket: Carpenter
Off-season: 'Going to the gym, playing golf off 28, and watching my brother James
play football for Havant FC; watching *The Simpsons* ("which I star in")'
Overseas tours: Sussex/Hampshire to Cyprus 1999
Overseas teams played for: Central Hawke's Bay, New Zealand 1996-97; Manawatu
Foxton, New Zealand 1998-99; Horowhenua Reps, New Zealand 1998-99
Cricketers particularly admired: Clive Lloyd, Robin Smith, Mark Robinson,
Chris Adams, James Taylor, Martin Taylor and Steve Perrin
Young players to look out for: Oli Green, Pop Morley
Other sports played: Golf ('28'), 'spoof'
Other sports followed: Football (Havant FC, West Ham)
Relaxations: 'Falconry, fishing, walking the dog ("Storm"), and going to the tapas
bar; playing spoof'
Extras: Played Minor Counties cricket for Wiltshire 1996-98 and has played club
cricket for Winchester KS since 1993. Took 98 wickets in New Zealand club cricket in
1998-99
Opinions on cricket: 'Bigger drinks lists, so we can have more than one free drink
after the game. More day/night cricket games because everyone loves watching them.
Better TV coverage, so we can all earn more money. Every county should be made to
have ra-ra girls at all matches.'
Best batting: 14 Sussex v Derbyshire, Derby 1999
Best bowling: 1-54 Sussex v Derbyshire, Derby 1999

1999 Season

	M	Inns	NO	Runs	HS	Avge	100s	50s	Ct	St	O	M	Runs	Wkts	Avge	Best	5wI	10wM
Test																		
All First	1	2	0	14	14	7.00	-	-	1	-	25	4	108	2	54.00	1-54	--	
1-day Int																		
NatWest	1	0	0	0	0	-	-	-	-	-	-	10	2	43	0	-		-	-
B & H																		
1-day Lge	9	2	2	22	21 *	-	-	-	1	-	61	4	312	11	28.36	3-22	-	

Career Performances

	M	Inns	NO	Runs	HS	Avge	100s	50s	Ct	St	Balls	Runs	Wkts	Avge	Best	5wI	10wM
Test																	
All First	1	2	0	14	14	7.00	-	-	1	-	150	108	2	54.00	1-54	-	-
1-day Int																	
NatWest	1	0	0	0	0	-	-	-	-	-	60	43	0	-		-	-
B & H																	
1-day Lge	9	2	2	22	21 *	-	-	-	1	-	366	312	11	28.36	3-22	-	

TAYLOR, C. G.   Gloucestershire

Name: Chris Glyn Taylor
Role: Right-hand bat, right-arm
off-spin bowler
Born: 27 September 1976, Bristol
Height: 5ft 8in   **Weight:** 10st
Nickname: Tales, Tootsie
County debut: No first-team appearance
Parents: Chris and Maggie
Marital status: Girlfriend Sarah
Family links with cricket: Father and
grandfather both played local club cricket
Education: Brentry Primary School;
Colston's Collegiate School
Qualifications: GCSEs and A-levels
Off-season: Australia – playing and travelling
Overseas teams played for: Harbord CC,
Manly, Australia 2000
Cricketers particularly admired:
Jonty Rhodes, Mark Waugh
Young players to look out for: Ben Burton, Richard Cook, Andy Bennett
Other sports played: Rugby, hockey

Other sports followed: Rugby
Injuries: Out for most of the winter with a dislocated shoulder
Relaxations: Fishing, playing on PlayStation
Extras: Represented England Schools U18. In 1995-96 won the Cricket Society's
A. A. Thomson Fielding Prize and Wetherell Award. Set school record of 278* v
Hutton Grammar School. Made his highest score of 300* for Gloucestershire 2nd XI
v Somerset 1999
Opinions on cricket: The standards, competitiveness and entertainment of the game
need to improve so that the interest, support and success of cricket excel in the future.'

1999 Season (did not make any first-class or one-day appearances)

Career Performances

	M	Inns	NO	Runs	HS	Avge	100s	50s	Ct	St	Balls	Runs	Wkts	Avge	Best	5wI	10wM
Test																	
All First																	
1-day Int																	
NatWest	1	1	0	0	0	0.00	-	-	1	-							
B & H																	
1-day Lge																	

TAYLOR, J. P.　　　　　Northamptonshire

Name: Jonathan Paul Taylor
Role: Left-hand bat, left-arm
fast-medium bowler
Born: 8 August 1964, Ashby-de-la-Zouch,
Leicestershire
Height: 6ft 2in **Weight:** 14st
Nickname: Roadie, PT
County debut: 1984 (Derbyshire),
1991 (Northamptonshire)
County cap: 1992 (Northamptonshire)
Test debut: 1992-93
Tests: 2
One-Day Internationals: 1
50 wickets in a season: 6
1st-Class 50s: 8
1st-Class 5 w. in innings: 17
1st-Class 10 w. in match: 3
1st-Class catches: 55
One-Day 5 w. in innings: 1

Place in batting averages: 232nd av. 16.63 (1998 173rd av. 21.82)
Place in bowling averages: 93rd av. 29.72 (1998 45th av. 24.75)
Strike rate: 63.41 (career 56.29)
Parents: Derek (deceased) and Janet
Wife and date of marriage: Elaine Mary, 30 July 1993
Children: Christopher Paul, 8 July 1994; Danny Michael, 6 February 1997
Family links with cricket: Father and brother played local league cricket
Education: Pingle School, Swadlincote, Derbyshire
Qualifications: 6 O-levels, NCA senior coach
Off-season: Northamptonshire CCC marketing department and organising benefit 2000
Overseas tours: Midland Club Cricket Conference to Australia 1990-91; England to India and Sri Lanka 1992-93; England A to South Africa 1993-94; Northamptonshire to Natal 1993, to Zimbabwe 1995, 1998, to Johannesburg 1996
Overseas teams played for: Papakura, New Zealand 1984-85; Napier High School Old Boys, New Zealand 1985-86; North Kalgoorlie, Western Australia 1990-91; Great Boulder, Western Australia 1991-92; Montrose CC, Cape Town 1998-99
Cricketers particularly admired: Dennis Lillee, Courtney Walsh, Curtly Ambrose
Young players to look out for: Jason Brown, Michael Davies, Graeme Swann ('the Spin Triplets'), Richard Logan
Other sports followed: Soccer, rugby, basketball
Relaxations: 'Looking after two hyperactive little lads. Relaxing … I think not; enjoyable … definitely!!!'
Extras: Spent four seasons on the staff at Derbyshire 1984-87 and played Minor Counties cricket for Staffordshire 1989-90. Won Man of the Match in the Bain Clarkson Final in 1987 for Derbyshire, after being released. Played first game at Lord's in NatWest Trophy final 1992. Was voted Northamptonshire's Player of the Year in 1992. Called up as replacement during England A tour to South Africa 1993-94. Selected for England Indoor World Cup squad 1995. Granted a benefit for 2000
Opinions on cricket: 'Even more cricket this year!!!! Central contracts – great idea!! About time – keep our top players fresh.'
Best batting: 86 Northamptonshire v Durham, Northampton 1995
Best bowling: 7-23 Northamptonshire v Hampshire, Bournemouth 1992

1999 Season

	M	Inns	NO	Runs	HS	Avge	100s	50s	Ct	St	O	M	Runs	Wkts	Avge	Best	5wl	10wM
Test																		
All First	17	21	2	316	71	16.63	-	1	5	-	507.2	119	1427	48	29.72	5-105	1	-
1-day Int																		
NatWest	3	1	0	6	6	6.00	-	-	-	-	19	3	112	2	56.00	1-25	-	
B & H																		
1-day Lge	13	6	4	49	19*	24.50	-	-	4	-	89.5	6	421	15	28.06	4-41	-	

Career Performances

	M	Inns	NO	Runs	HS	Avge	100s	50s	Ct	St	Balls	Runs	Wkts	Avge	Best	5wI	10wM
Test	2	4	2	34	17 *	17.00	-	-	-	-	288	156	3	52.00	1-18	-	-
All First	164	186	61	1884	86	15.07	-	8	55	-	28487	14733	506	29.11	7-23	17	3
1-day Int	1	1	0	1	1	1.00	-	-	-	-	18	20	0	-	-	-	-
NatWest	30	12	6	40	9	6.66	-	-	6	-	1767	1182	39	30.30	4-34	-	
B & H	32	14	7	62	14	8.85	-	-	6	-	1797	1101	42	26.21	5-45	1	
1-day Lge	121	42	21	229	24	10.90	-	-	27	-	5195	4018	136	29.54	4-41	-	

THEWLIS, M. Yorkshire

Name: Matthew Thewlis
Role: Right-hand bat, wicket-keeper
Born: 16 July 1981, Barnsley
Height: 5ft 7in **Weight:** 9st 8lbs
Nickname: Twitlips
County debut: No first-team appearance
Parents: Janice and John
Marital status: Single
Education: Highfields School, Wombwell;
Wombwell High School
Qualifications: Coaching awards 1 and 2
Off-season: 'On standby for England U19
tour to Sri Lanka; if not needed, playing
cricket in Australia with a club in Sydney'
Cricketers particularly admired: Jack
Russell, Alan Knott
Young players to look out for: John Inglis
Other sports played: Football
Other sports followed: Rugby league (Leeds
Rhinos), football (Barnsley FC)
Relaxations: Socialising with friends
Extras: Made debut for Yorkshire 2nd XI aged 14

87. Which former Test Match Special regular took eight wickets
before lunch on the first day v Kent at Dover in 1954?

THOMAS, P. A. Derbyshire

Name: Paul Anthony Thomas
Role: Right-hand bat, right-arm fast bowler
Height: 5ft 9in **Weight:** 11st 8lbs
Born: 3 June 1971, Dudley
Nickname: Thommo
County debut: 1995 (Worcestershire),
1999 (Derbyshire)
1st-Class 5 w. in innings: 1
1st-Class catches: 1
Strike rate: 48.00 (career 66.66)
Parents: Clifford and Myrtle
Marital status: Single
Family links with cricket: Father is a great
fan of the game. Brothers play
Education: Broadway School
Extras: Awarded Worcestershire 2nd XI cap
1995. Released by Worcestershire at the end
of the 1997 season. Registered by Derbyshire

in 1999 as injury cover for current players. Played for Herefordshire v Yorkshire in
NatWest 1999
Best batting: 25 Worcestershire v Warwickshire, Edgbaston 1995
Best bowling: 5-70 Worcestershire v West Indies, Worcester 1995

1999 Season

	M	Inns	NO	Runs	HS	Avge	100s	50s	Ct	St	O	M	Runs	Wkts	Avge	Best	5wI	10wM
Test																		
All First	1	2	0	1	1	0.50	-	-	-	-	16	1	74	2	37.00	2-54	-	-
1-day Int																		
NatWest	1	0	0	0	0	-	-	-	-	-	10	0	48	1	48.00	1-48	-	
B & H																		
1-day Lge																		

Career Performances

	M	Inns	NO	Runs	HS	Avge	100s	50s	Ct	St	Balls	Runs	Wkts	Avge	Best	5wI	10wM
Test																		
All First	22	26	5	120	25	5.71	-	-	1	-	3400	2369	51	46.45	5-70	1	-
1-day Int																		
NatWest	2	0	0	0	0	-	-	-	-	-	120	78	3	26.00	2-30	-	
B & H	2	1	0	3	3	3.00	-	-	-	-	112	85	1	85.00	1-34	-	
1-day Lge	1	0	0	0	0	-	-	-	-	-	36	30	0	-	-	-	-

THOMAS, S. D.   Glamorgan

Name: Stuart Darren Thomas
Role: Left-hand bat, right-arm
fast-medium bowler
Born: 25 January 1975, Morriston
Height: 6ft **Weight:** 13st
Nickname: Thommo, Teddy, Daz
County debut: 1992
County cap: 1997
50 wickets in a season: 3
1st-Class 50s: 8
1st-Class 5 w. in innings: 13
1st-Class catches: 36
One-Day 5 w. in innings: 3
Place in batting averages: 245th av. 14.66
(1998 169th av. 22.04)
Place in bowling averages: 55th av. 24.26
(1998 43rd av. 24.63)
Strike rate: 44.00 (career 49.56)
Parents: Stuart and Anne
Marital status: 'Engaged to lovely Claire Jones'
Family links with cricket: 'Dad used to give it a lick for Llanelli; Mum likes hurling abuse at the opposition'
Education: Old Road: Graig Comprehensive; Neath Tertiary College
Qualifications: 4 GCSEs, BTEC National Diploma in Sports Science, advanced cricket coach
Career outside cricket: 'Starting my own holiday TV programme with the missus'
Off-season: 'Building my house, holidaying around the globe, watching Sky TV, and a bit of fitness'
Overseas tours: England U18 to South Africa 1992-93; Glamorgan to South Africa 1992-93, 1996, 1998, to Portugal 1995, to Zimbabwe 1996; England U19 to Sri Lanka 1993-94; England A to Zimbabwe and South Africa 1998-99
Overseas teams played for: Rovers CC, Welkom, Orange Free State 1995
Cricketers particularly admired: Matthew Maynard, Duncan Fletcher, Waqar Younis, 'and you got to listen to the Croftster'
Young players to look out for: Mark Wallace, 'the youthful Robert Croft', Wayne Law
Other sports played: Rugby (New Dock Stars)
Injuries: 'White ball fever (or so the boys say)'
Relaxations: 'Watching movies or Sky TV, wining and dining, holidaying – all with my darling fiancée Claire'
Extras: Became youngest player (17 years 217 days) to take five wickets on debut, v Derbyshire in 1992, and finished eighth in national bowling averages. BBC Welsh

Young Sports Personality 1992. Played last U19 'Test' against India at Edgbaston 1994. Broke Alan Wilkins' (Glamorgan) best Benson and Hedges bowling record on his debut in the competition with 6 for 20 in 1995. Took 7-16 v Surrey in the Sunday League in 1998, the best analysis by a Glamorgan bowler in the competition. Glamorgan Player of the Year 1998. Took 8-50 for England A v Zimbabwe A at Harare on 1998-99 tour – the first eight-wicket haul by an England A tourist

Opinions on cricket: 'The season is very demanding. But a brilliant way to earn a living!'

Best batting: 78* Glamorgan v Gloucestershire, Abergavenny 1995

Best bowling: 8-50 England A v Zimbabwe A, Harare 1998-99

Stop press: Called up for England A tour of Bangladesh and New Zealand 1999-2000 as replacement for Chris Silverwood, who was added to the senior tour party in South Africa

1999 Season

	M	Inns	NO	Runs	HS	Avge	100s	50s	Ct	St	O	M	Runs	Wkts	Avge	Best	5wI	10wM
Test																		
All First	18	26	2	352	54	14.66	-	1	9	-	447.2	78	1480	61	24.26	5-64	1	-
1-day Int																		
NatWest	3	3	0	66	40	22.00	-	-	-	-	30	1	152	6	25.33	3-35	-	
B & H																		
1-day Lge	13	13	3	153	38 *	15.30	-	-	1	-	80.5	4	418	20	20.90	4-33	-	

Career Performances

	M	Inns	NO	Runs	HS	Avge	100s	50s	Ct	St	Balls	Runs	Wkts	Avge	Best	5wI	10wM
Test																	
All First	93	127	26	1837	78 *	18.18	-	8	36	-	14821	8812	299	29.47	8-50	13	-
1-day Int																	
NatWest	10	8	1	120	40	17.14	-	-	2	-	615	486	18	27.00	5-74	1	
B & H	13	8	3	95	29	19.00	-	-	5	-	560	502	20	25.10	6-20	1	
1-day Lge	45	36	6	353	38 *	11.76	-	-	6	-	1555	1350	55	24.54	7-16	1	

THOMPSON, D. J.   Essex

Name: David James Thompson
Role: Right-hand bat, right-arm fast bowler
Born: 11 March 1976, Wandsworth, London
Height: 6ft 3in
Nickname: Thommo
County debut: 1994 (Surrey), 1999 (Essex)
1st-Class catches: 1

Place in batting averages: 292nd av. 5.50
Place in bowling averages: 78th av. 28.54
Strike rate: 46.00 (career 46.88)
Marital status: Single
Education: Ernest Bevin School, Wandsworth; Westminster School
Overseas tours: England U19 to West Indies 1994-95
Cricketers particularly admired: Michael Holding
Young players to look out for: Tim Phillips
Other sports played: Football
Other sports followed: Football (Liverpool)
Relaxations: Music, socialising
Extras: Left Surrey after 1994 season and joined Lancashire. Joined Essex for 1999
Best batting: 22 Essex v Northamptonshire, Northampton 1999
Best bowling: 4-46 Essex v Somerset, Chelmsford 1999

1999 Season

	M	Inns	NO	Runs	HS	Avge	100s	50s	Ct	St	O	M	Runs	Wkts	Avge	Best	5wI	10wM
Test																		
All First	8	10	0	55	22	5.50	-	-	1	-	184	30	685	24	28.54	4-46	-	-
1-day Int																		
NatWest																		
B & H																		
1-day Lge	3	2	1	2	1*	2.00	-	-	-	-	13.3	1	67	2	33.50	2-34	-	

Career Performances

	M	Inns	NO	Runs	HS	Avge	100s	50s	Ct	St	Balls	Runs	Wkts	Avge	Best	5wI	10wM
Test																	
All First	9	12	0	94	22	7.83	-	-	1	-	1266	808	27	29.92	4-46	-	-
1-day Int																	
NatWest																	
B & H																	
1-day Lge	3	2	1	2	1*	2.00	-	-	-	-	81	67	2	33.50	2-34	-	

THOMPSON, J. B. de C.　　　　Kent

Name: Julian Barton de Courcy Thompson
Role: Right-hand bat, right-arm
fast-medium bowler
Born: 28 October 1968, Cape Town
Height: 6ft 5in **Weight:** 14st
Nickname: Doc, Bambi, Geri
County debut: 1994
County cap: 1999
50 wickets in a season: 1
1st-Class 50s: 2
1st-Class 5 w. in innings: 5
1st-Class catches: 5
Place in batting averages: 228th av. 17.60
Place in bowling averages: 15th av. 19.76
(1998 90th av. 30.45)
Strike rate: 40.70 (career 45.02)
Parents: John and Joyce
Wife and date of marriage: Tanya,
4 October 1997
Children: Jack, 7 September 1999
Family links with cricket: Father and brother used to play club cricket. 'Wife a keen
and avid follower and supporter(!)'
Education: Holmewood House School, Tunbridge Wells, Kent; The Judd School,
Tonbridge, Kent; Guy's Hospital Medical School, University of London
Qualifications: MBBS, basic coaching certificate
Career outside cricket: Doctor
Off-season: General Practice training, Canterbury
Overseas tours: University of London to India 1992; 'Kent Cultural Tour to
Amsterdam 1999'
Overseas teams played for: Northern Districts CC, Sydney 1987-88
Cricketers particularly admired: Allan Donald, David Boon, Stuart Law,
Chris Silverwood, Martin Bicknell, Glenn McGrath
Young players to look out for: Ricky Anderson, Matt Banes
Other sports played: Golf, squash
Other sports followed: Football (Liverpool)
Injuries: Out for one week with a slight groin strain
Relaxations: 'Cooking and eating; spending time with wife and new baby son;
changing nappies'
Extras: Dismissed Brian Lara twice for a duck in Kent's game against the West Indies
in 1995 – Brian Lara's first pair in first-class cricket. Dismissed three England captains
in first month of the 1996 season – Atherton, Gatting and Gooch. His 6-27 v Northants

at Canterbury 1999 included a spell of 6-2 in 23 balls. Awarded county cap at home ground (Tunbridge Wells) June 1999. Kent Player of the Year 1999

Opinions on cricket: 'There's too much cricket. The workload results in games not being "special", less time and energy for good quality practice, more injuries etc. Two divisions is great, but we should only play each other once.'

Best batting: 65* Kent v Oxford University, Canterbury 1998

Best bowling: 7-89 Kent v Durham, Stockton 1999

1999 Season

	M	Inns	NO	Runs	HS	Avge	100s	50s	Ct	St	O	M	Runs	Wkts	Avge	Best	5wI	10wM
Test																		
All First	14	19	9	176	44	17.60	-	-	1	-	434.1	106	1265	64	19.76	7-89	3	-
1-day Int																		
NatWest	2	1	1	0	0*	-	-	-	-	-	20	3	80	1	80.00	1-22	-	
B & H																		
1-day Lge	15	5	5	3	2*	-	-	-	3	-	107	14	382	18	21.22	3-16	-	

Career Performances

	M	Inns	NO	Runs	HS	Avge	100s	50s	Ct	St	Balls	Runs	Wkts	Avge	Best	5wI	10wM
Test																	
All First	36	48	19	546	65*	18.82	-	2	5	-	5493	3103	122	25.43	7-89	5	-
1-day Int																	
NatWest	2	1	1	0	0*	-	-	-	-	-	120	80	1	80.00	1-22	-	
B & H	4	3	2	17	12*	17.00	-	-	-	-	180	114	6	19.00	3-29	-	
1-day Lge	44	21	14	78	30	11.14	-	-	6	-	1570	1105	40	27.62	3-16	-	

88. Which two England Test players shared the Middlesex captaincy in the 1951 and 1952 seasons?

THORPE, G. P. Surrey

Name: Graham Paul Thorpe
Role: Left-hand bat, occasional
right-arm medium bowler
Born: 1 August 1969, Farnham
Height: 5ft 10in **Weight:** 12st 4lbs
Nickname: Chalky
County debut: 1988
County cap: 1991
Test debut: 1993
Tests: 57
One-Day Internationals: 53
1000 runs in a season: 8
1st-Class 50s: 91
1st-Class 100s: 32
1st-Class 200s: 3
1st-Class catches: 208
One-Day 100s: 6
Place in batting averages: 27th av. 41.64
(1998 134th av. 26.16)
Strike rate: (career 92.36)
Parents: 'Mr and Mrs Thorpe'
Wife: Nicola

Children: Henry and Amelia
Family links with cricket: Both brothers play for Farnham, father also plays cricket
and mother is 'professional scorer'
Education: Weydon Comprehensive; Farnham Sixth Form College
Qualifications: 7 O-levels, PE Diploma
Career outside cricket: 'None as yet'
Off-season: 'At home'
Overseas tours: England A to Zimbabwe and Kenya 1989-90, to Pakistan 1990-91,
to Bermuda and West Indies 1991-92, to Australia 1992-93; England to West Indies
1993-94, to Australia 1994-95, to South Africa 1995-96, to India and Pakistan
(World Cup) 1995-96, to Zimbabwe and New Zealand 1996-97, to Sharjah
(Champions Trophy) 1997-98, to West Indies 1997-98, to Australia 1998-99, to
Sharjah (Coca-Cola Cup) 1998-99
Cricketers particularly admired: Grahame Clinton, Waqar Younis, Ian Botham,
Viv Richards
Young players to look out for: Ian Ward, Ben Hollioake
Other sports followed: Football (Chelsea FC), golf
Relaxations: Sleeping
Extras: Played for English Schools cricket U15 and U19 and England Schools

football U18. Scored a century against Australia on his Test debut at Trent Bridge 1993. Arrived a few days late for the Zimbabwe leg of England's 1996-97 tour to attend the birth of his son. Scored hundreds in successive Tests during the tour to New Zealand 1996-97. England's Player of the Series and leading run scorer in the 1997 Ashes campaign with 453 runs at an average of 50.33. Shared in a record England v West Indies sixth wicket Test partnership (205) with Mark Ramprakash at Bridgetown 1997-98. A back injury suffered during the 1997-98 West Indies tour affected his availability for England in the 1998 season. One of *Wisden*'s Five Cricketers of the Year 1998. Named Cornhill England Player of the Year 1998. During 1998-99 Ashes tour, put on 377 for England with Mark Ramprakash in an unbroken fifth wicket stand v South Australia in Adelaide, finishing with a new career best 223*. Forced to return early from the 1998-99 Ashes tour with recurrence of back injury. Represented England in the 1999 World Cup. Granted a benefit for 2000. Made himself unavailable for the England tour of South Africa and Zimbabwe 1999-2000 to remain at home with his family

Best batting: 223* England v South Australia, Adelaide 1998-99
Best bowling: 4-40 Surrey v Australians, The Oval 1993

1999 Season

	M	Inns	NO	Runs	HS	Avge	100s	50s	Ct	St	O	M	Runs	Wkts	Avge	Best	5wI	10wM
Test	4	8	2	147	44	24.50	-	-	5	-								
All First	13	21	4	708	164	41.64	2	2	18	-	13	0	42	0	-	-	-	-
1-day Int	5	4	1	125	62	41.66	-	1	6	-								
NatWest	4	4	3	234	91 *	234.00	-	2	4	-								
B & H	1	1	0	84	84	84.00	-	1	-	-								
1-day Lge	8	8	0	364	84	45.50	-	3	2	-								

Career Performances

	M	Inns	NO	Runs	HS	Avge	100s	50s	Ct	St	Balls	Runs	Wkts	Avge	Best	5wI	10wM
Test	57	105	13	3599	138	39.11	6	24	53	-	138	37	0	-	-	-	-
All First	250	419	61	16111	223 *	45.00	35	91	208	-	2309	1290	25	51.60	4-40	-	-
1-day Int	53	52	8	1786	89	40.59	-	17	32	-	120	97	2	48.50	2-15	-	
NatWest	28	27	7	1058	145 *	52.90	1	8	17	-	13	12	0	-	-	-	
B & H	44	43	4	1616	103	41.43	1	12	20	-	168	131	4	32.75	3-35	-	
1-day Lge	121	111	14	3487	115 *	35.94	4	24	44	-	318	307	8	38.37	3-21	-	

TITCHARD, S. P.   Derbyshire

Name: Stephen Paul Titchard
Role: Right-hand bat, right-arm
medium bowler
Born: 17 December 1967,
Warrington, Cheshire
Height: 6ft 3in **Weight:** 15st
Nickname: Titch, Stainy, Tyrone
County debut: 1990 (Lancs), 1999 (Derbys)
1st-Class 50s: 27
1st-Class 100s: 5
1st-Class catches: 54
Place in batting averages:
122nd av. 27.85
Strike rate: (career 90.00)
Parents: Alan and Margaret
Marital status: Single
Family links with cricket: Father, uncle and

two brothers have played for Grappenhall 1st
XI in the Manchester Association League. Father also represented the Army
Education: Lymm County High School; Priestley College
Qualifications: 3 O-levels, NCA senior coaching award
Career outside cricket: Coach
Overseas tours: Lancashire to Tasmania and Western Australia 1990, to Western
Australia 1991, to Johannesburg 1992
Overseas teams played for: South Canberra, Australia 1991-92
Cricketers particularly admired: Graham Gooch, Malcolm Marshall
Other sports followed: Football (Manchester City) and rugby league (Warrington)
Relaxations: Snooker, golf, 'most sports'
Extras: Played for England U19. Made record scores for Manchester Association U18
(200*) and Cheshire Schools U19 (203*). Released by Lancashire at end of 1998
season and joined Derbyshire
Best batting: 163 Lancashire v Essex, Chelmsford 1996
Best bowling: 1-11 Lancashire v Northamptonshire, Old Trafford 1997
                 1-11 Lancashire v Kent, Old Trafford 1997

1999 Season

	M	Inns	NO	Runs	HS	Avge	100s	50s	Ct	St	O	M	Runs	Wkts	Avge	Best	5wI	10wM
Test																		
All First	17	31	4	752	136	27.85	1	2	2	-	8	3	19	0	-		-	-	-
1-day Int																		
NatWest	2	2	1	13	7	13.00	-	-	-	-								
B & H																		
1-day Lge	14	13	1	240	44 *	20.00	-	-	1	-	9	0	48	1	48.00	1-19	-	

Career Performances

	M	Inns	NO	Runs	HS	Avge	100s	50s	Ct	St	Balls	Runs	Wkts	Avge	Best	5wI	10wM
Test																	
All First	93	162	12	4697	163	31.31	5	27	54	-	360	190	4	47.50	1-11	-	-
1-day Int																	
NatWest	5	5	1	129	92	32.25	-	1	1	-							
B & H	3	3	0	101	82	33.66	-	1	1	-							
1-day Lge	43	42	4	945	96	24.86	-	3	5	-	54	48	1	48.00	1-19	-	

TOLLEY, C. M. — Nottinghamshire

Name: Christopher Mark Tolley
Role: Right-hand bat, left-arm medium bowler
Born: 30 December 1967, Kidderminster
Height: 5ft 9in **Weight:** 11st 12lbs
Nickname: Red Dog, Red'uns, Ginger Warrior
County debut: 1989 (Worcestershire), 1996 (Nottinghamshire)
County cap: 1993 (Worcestershire), 1997 (Nottinghamshire)
1st-Class 50s: 11
1st-Class 5 w. in innings: 5
1st-Class catches: 40
One-Day 5 w. in innings: 1
Place in batting averages: 256th av. 13.25 (1998 170th av. 22.00)
Place in bowling averages: (1998 72nd av. 28.23)
Strike rate: 102.00 (career 72.27)
Parents: Ray and Liz

Wife and date of marriage: Simone, 12 December 1998
Family links with cricket: Brother Richard plays in the Birmingham League for Stourbridge
Education: Oldswinford Primary School; Redhill Comprehensive School; King Edward VI College, Stourbridge; Loughborough University
Qualifications: 9 O-levels, 3 A-levels, BSc (Hons) PE, Sports Science & Recreation Management, Dip SMT. Qualified teacher and level 2 hockey coach
Career outside cricket: PE teacher
Overseas tours: British Universities Sports Federation tour to Barbados, October 1989; Worcestershire to Zimbabwe and South Africa
Overseas teams played for: Lancaster Park, Christchurch, New Zealand 1996-97
Cricketers particularly admired: Ian Botham, Graeme Hick
Young players to look out for: Andy Oram
Other sports followed: Hockey
Relaxations: Food and wine
Extras: Played for English Schools U19 in 1986 and for the Combined Universities in B&H Cup. Asked to be released by Worcestershire at the end of the 1995 season and joined Nottinghamshire for the 1996 season. Took first-class hat-trick against Leicestershire in 1997
Best batting: 84 Worcestershire v Derbyshire, Derby 1994
Best bowling: 7-45 Nottinghamshire v Worcestershire, Kidderminster 1998

1999 Season

	M	Inns	NO	Runs	HS	Avge	100s	50s	Ct	St	O	M	Runs	Wkts	Avge	Best	5wI	10wM
Test																		
All First	4	8	0	106	51	13.25	-	1	-	-	85	20	199	5	39.80	3-15	-	-
1-day Int																		
NatWest	2	2	0	24	20	12.00	-	-	-	-	15	0	77	1	77.00	1-15	-	
B & H																		
1-day Lge	9	7	1	96	39	16.00	-	-	-	-	52	1	223	11	20.27	4-34	-	

Career Performances

	M	Inns	NO	Runs	HS	Avge	100s	50s	Ct	St	Balls	Runs	Wkts	Avge	Best	5wI	10wM
Test																	
All First	100	139	30	2443	84	22.41	-	11	40	-	13370	6516	185	35.22	7-45	5	-
1-day Int																	
NatWest	13	10	3	182	77	26.00	-	1	1	-	708	427	16	26.68	3-21	-	
B & H	20	17	2	355	77	23.66	-	3	3	-	978	633	9	70.33	1-12	-	
1-day Lge	81	51	12	649	44	16.64	-	-	24	-	2728	2185	86	25.40	5-16	1	

TREGO, P. D.   Somerset

Name: Peter David Trego
Role: Right-hand bat, right-arm
'quickish' bowler
Born: 12 June 1981, Weston-super-Mare
Height: 6ft **Weight:** 12st 7lbs
Nickname: Tregs 'and many more'
County debut: No first-team appearance
Parents: Carol and Paul
Marital status: Single
Family links with cricket: 'Brother Sam
played for Somerset; Dad plays for Uphill
Castle – both strong batsmen'
Education: St Martins, Weston-super-Mare;
Wyvern Comprehensive
Qualifications: Lifeguard (at Hutton Moor
Leisure Centre)
Career outside cricket: Training with father
as a financial adviser
Off-season: 'Maybe go to Australia or South Africa'
Cricketers particularly admired: Ian Botham and Graham Rose - 'they have both
been huge inspirations to me'
Young players to look out for: Mathew Gitcham, Michael Coles (Somerset),
Ian Flanagan, James Adams
Other sports played: Football ('I had a winter contract with Weston-super-Mare; now
playing for Torrington FC')
Other sports followed: Football (Man Utd), darts, golf
Relaxations: Golf, snooker, music, socialising with friends, shopping
Extras: Won Best Batsman award at U16 – averaged 137 in nine games. Scored
century for Somerset 2nd XI v Glos 1999. Attended Lilleshall with England U17
Opinions on cricket: 'Cricket today in my opinion has to be taken very seriously to
achieve even an average standard of play. The great thing about cricket for me is that
there is always a challenge around the corner. You can never relax or lose
concentration; you must always strive to better your game.'

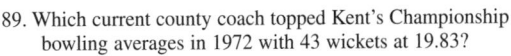

89. Which current county coach topped Kent's Championship
bowling averages in 1972 with 43 wickets at 19.83?

1999 Season (did not make any first-class or one-day appearances)

Career Performances

	M	Inns	NO	Runs	HS	Avge	100s	50s	Ct	St	Balls	Runs	Wkts	Avge	Best	5wl	10wM
Test																	
All First																	
1-day Int																	
NatWest	1	1	0	0	0	0.00	-	-	-	-	42	42	2	21.00	2-42	-	
B & H																	
1-day Lge																	

TRESCOTHICK, M. E. Somerset

Name: Marcus Edward Trescothick
Role: Left-hand bat, right-arm swing bowler, reserve wicket-keeper, county vice-captain
Born: 25 December 1975, Keynsham, Bristol
Height: 6ft 3in **Weight:** 14st 7lbs
Nickname: Banger
County debut: 1993
County cap: 1999
1st-Class 50s: 24
1st-Class 100s: 6
1st-Class catches: 95
One-Day 100s: 3
Place in batting averages: 54th av. 37.41 (1998 89th av. 31.37)
Place in bowling averages: (1998 124th av. 38.47)
Strike rate: 45.60 (career 64.82)
Parents: Martyn and Lin
Marital status: Single
Family links with cricket: Father played for Somerset 2nd XI; uncle played club cricket; girlfriend plays for Taunton Ladies and Somerset Ladies CC
Education: Sir Bernard Lovell School
Qualifications: 7 GCSEs
Career outside cricket: Playing abroad
Off-season: 'Touring with England A, then training in the gym with Daz and Shiney Boy'
Overseas tours: England U18 to South Africa 1992-93; England U19 to Sri Lanka 1993-94, to West Indies 1994-95 (captain); England A to Bangladesh and New Zealand 1999-2000
Overseas teams played for: Melville CC, Perth 1997-99

Cricketers particularly admired: Andrew Caddick
Young players to look out for: Luke Sutton, Joe Tucker, Pete Trego
Other sports followed: Golf, football (Bristol City FC)
Injuries: Out for one month with torn lower right thigh; for one week with torn ligament in ankle
Relaxations: 'Spending time with my girlfriend, Hayley; playing golf, repairing and renovating cricket bats and listening to music'
Extras: Member of England U19 squad for home series against West Indies 1993. Man of the Series against India U19 in 1994, scoring most runs in the series. Whittingdale Young Player of the Month, August 1994. Took a hat-trick against Young Australia in 1995. Scored more than 1000 runs for England U19. Scored 322 in the second innings of a 2nd XI game against Warwickshire in 1997 – Somerset were chasing a target of 612 and Trescothick was the last man out with the score on 605! Vice-captain of Somerset since 1999. Awarded Somerset cap 1999
Opinions on cricket: 'If we want to produce better Test players, we have to start producing better wickets for first-class matches and also be realistic about fining or deducting points from teams.'
Best batting: 190 Somerset v Middlesex, Taunton 1999
Best bowling: 4-36 Somerset v Young Australia, Taunton 1995

1999 Season

	M	Inns	NO	Runs	HS	Avge	100s	50s	Ct	St	O	M	Runs	Wkts	Avge	Best	5wI	10wM
Test																		
All First	15	24	0	898	190	37.41	2	3	27	-	38	8	127	5	25.40	2-26	-	-
1-day Int																		
NatWest	3	3	0	70	38	23.33	-	-	-	-								
B & H																		
1-day Lge	13	12	3	351	110	39.00	1	-	5	-	4	0	19	1	19.00	1-19	-	

Career Performances

	M	Inns	NO	Runs	HS	Avge	100s	50s	Ct	St	Balls	Runs	Wkts	Avge	Best	5wI	10wM
Test																	
All First	87	146	4	4210	190	29.64	6	24	95	-	1815	1090	28	38.92	4-36	-	-
1-day Int																	
NatWest	9	8	0	281	116	35.12	1	-	2	-	108	92	2	46.00	2-49	-	
B & H	11	11	2	350	122	38.88	1	2	7	-	180	134	8	16.75	3-46	-	
1-day Lge	70	61	9	1217	110	23.40	1	3	23	-	570	494	15	32.93	2-14	-	

TUCKER, J.   Somerset

Name: Joseph Tucker
Role: Right-hand bat, right-arm fast-medium
bowler, occasional wicket-keeper
Born: 14 September 1979, Bath
Height: 6ft 3in **Weight:** 13st 7lbs
Nickname: Tucks, Cheeky Tucker, My Boy
County debut: No first-team appearance
Parents: Geoff and Chris
Marital status: Single
Family links with cricket: Father, brother
and grandfather all played good club cricket.
'Family played in the back garden'
Education: Pensford Primary School,
Bristol; Chew Valley and Colston's Collegiate
School, Bristol; Richard Huish Sixth Form
College, Taunton
Qualifications: 11 GCSEs, 3 A-levels, NCA
coaching awards

Career outside cricket: 'Erecting steelwork
and riding motocross for Team Red Bull Yamaha'
Off-season: 'Getting fit for 2000 season and eating lots!'
Overseas tours: West of England U15 to West Indies 1996; England U17 to Bermuda
(International Youth Tournament) 1997; England U19 to South Africa (Youth World
Cup) 1997-98, to New Zealand 1998-99
Cricketers particularly admired: Steve Waugh, Glenn McGrath, Allan Donald,
Shoaib Akhtar, Andy Caddick, Jason Kerr, W.G. Grace
Young players to look out for: Michael Gough, Matt Bulbeck, Ian Bell,
Geoff Tucker, 'my nephew Jacob and my son'
Other sports played: Motocross (Red Bull Yamaha), football ('back garden')
Other sports followed: Motocross ('my cousin Martyn on Team Yamaha'), football
(Man Utd, Bristol City, Clevedon Town)
Injuries: Out for the entire 1999 season with a stress fracture of the back
Relaxations: 'Eating out at steak houses and curry houses; riding my bike and keeping
fit; seeing friends and family; sleeping!'
Extras: Recorded the best bowling for Somerset 2nd XI in 1997 with 5 for 41 in the
Bain Hogg Trophy against Worcestershire. Recorded the best bowling figures for
England U17 in the International Youth Tournament in Bermuda in 1997 with 4 for 41
against Holland. Made his 2nd XI debut for Somerset at the age of 15. Has attended
Dennis Lillee coaching school, Madras
Opinions on cricket: 'It's good to see day/night cricket now; it's bringing more
crowds in. We need longer for lunch and tea to recharge the batteries. I love it.'

TUDOR, A. J. Surrey

Name: Alexander Jeremy Tudor
Role: Right-hand bat, right-arm fast bowler
Born: 23 October 1977,
West Brompton, London
Height: 6ft 4in **Weight:** 13st 7lbs
Nickname: Big Al, Bambi, Tudes
County debut: 1995
County cap: 1999
Test debut: 1998-99
Tests: 3
1st-Class 50s: 2
1st-Class 5 w. in innings: 6
1st-Class catches: 8
Place in batting averages: 157th av. 24.66
(1998 26th av. 16.70)
Place in bowling averages: 37th av. 22.37
(1998 51st av. 25.41)
Strike rate: 44.62 (career 45.00)
Parents: Daryll and Jennifer
Marital status: Single
Family links with cricket: Brother was on the staff at The Oval
Education: Wandle Primary, Earlsfield; St Mark's C of E, Fulham; City of
Westminster College
Off-season: England tour of South Africa
Overseas tours: England U15 to South Africa 1992-93; England U19 to Zimbabwe
1995-96, to Pakistan 1996-97; England to Australia 1998-99, to South Africa 1999-2000
Cricketers particularly admired: Curtly Ambrose, Brian Lara
Other sports followed: Basketball, football (QPR)
Relaxations: Listening to music
Extras: Played for London Schools at all ages from U8. Played for England U17
against India in 1994. MCC Young Cricketer. Had to return home from the England
U19 tour to Zimbabwe in 1995-96 through injury and subsequently missed the
majority of the 1996 season through injury. He toured Pakistan with England U19
in 1996-97. Made Test debut at Perth during 1998-99 Ashes tour, taking 4-89 in
Australia's first innings; his victims included both Waugh twins. Scored 99* in second
innings of first Test v New Zealand at Edgbaston 1999, bettering the highest score by a
nightwatchman for England (Harold Larwood's 98 v Australia at Sydney 1932-33) and
winning the Man of the Match award; in total he scored 131 unbeaten runs in the
match. Awarded Surrey cap 1999
Best batting: 99* England v New Zealand, Edgbaston 1999
Best bowling: 7-77 Surrey v Leicestershire, Leicester 1999

1999 Season

	M	Inns	NO	Runs	HS	Avge	100s	50s	Ct	St	O	M	Runs	Wkts	Avge	Best	5wI	10wM
Test	1	2	2	131	99*	-	-	1	-	-	16	4	59	1	59.00	1-44	-	-
All First	10	13	4	222	99*	24.66	-	1	3	-	297.3	70	895	40	22.37	7-77	3	-
1-day Int																		
NatWest	1	0	0	0	0	-	-	-	-	-	9	2	34	1	34.00	1-34	-	
B & H	1	1	0	0	0	0.00	-	-	-	-	9	1	41	2	20.50	2-41	-	
1-day Lge	6	6	1	55	28	11.00	-	-	-	-	43.2	2	222	8	27.75	2-26	-	

Career Performances

	M	Inns	NO	Runs	HS	Avge	100s	50s	Ct	St	Balls	Runs	Wkts	Avge	Best	5wI	10wM
Test	3	6	3	166	99*	55.33	-	1	-	-	350	239	8	29.87	4-89	-	-
All First	38	51	14	689	99*	18.62	-	2	8	-	4861	2912	108	26.96	7-77	6	-
1-day Int																	
NatWest	3	1	0	1	1	1.00	-	-	-	-	177	100	6	16.66	4-39	-	
B & H	1	1	0	0	0	0.00	-	-	-	-	54	41	2	20.50	2-41	-	
1-day Lge	14	11	2	103	29*	11.44	-	-	5	-	470	431	17	25.35	3-38	-	

TUFNELL, P. C. R.   Middlesex

Name: Philip Clive Roderick Tufnell
Role: Right-hand bat, slow left-arm spinner
Born: 29 April 1966, Hadley Wood, Hertfordshire
Height: 6ft **Weight:** 12st 7lbs
Nickname: The Cat
County debut: 1986
County cap: 1990
Benefit: 1999
Test debut: 1990-91
Tests: 38
One-Day Internationals: 20
50 wickets in a season: 7
1st-Class 50s: 1
1st-Class 5 w. in innings: 43
1st-Class 10 w. in match: 5
1st-Class catches: 99
One-Day 5 w. in innings: 1
Place in batting averages: 265th av. 11.64 (1998 276th av. 9.68)
Place in bowling averages: 61st av. 25.47 (1998 132nd av. 41.07)
Strike rate: 72.18 (career 72.80)

Parents: Sylvia and Alan
Marital status: Divorced
Education: Highgate School; Southgate School
Qualifications: O-level in Art; City & Guilds Silversmithing
Off-season: England tour to South Africa
Overseas tours: England YC to West Indies 1984-85; England to Australia 1990-91, to New Zealand and Australia (World Cup) 1991-92, to India and Sri Lanka 1992-93, to West Indies 1993-94, to Australia 1994-95, to Zimbabwe and New Zealand 1996-97, to West Indies 1997-98, to South Africa 1999-2000
Overseas teams played for: Queensland University, Australia
Cricketers particularly admired: Jason Pooley
Other sports followed: American football
Relaxations: Sleeping
Extras: MCC Young Cricketer of the Year 1984 and Middlesex Uncapped Bowler of the Year 1987. Was originally a seam bowler and gave up cricket for three years in his mid-teens. Recalled to the England squad for winter tours to Zimbabwe and New Zealand in 1996-97 after an absence of two years and ensured himself a place on England's tour to West Indies with match figures of 11 for 93 in the final Test against Australia at The Oval in 1997 – picking up the Man of the Match award in the process
Best batting: 67* Middlesex v Worcestershire, Lord's 1996
Best bowling: 8-29 Middlesex v Glamorgan, Cardiff 1993

1999 Season

	M	Inns	NO	Runs	HS	Avge	100s	50s	Ct	St	O	M	Runs	Wkts	Avge	Best	5wI	10wM
Test	4	6	3	14	6	4.66	-	-	-	-	132.2	36	317	14	22.64	3-22	-	-
All First	16	21	4	198	48	11.64	-	-	3	-	577.3	155	1223	48	25.47	5-61	2	-
1-day Int																		
NatWest																		
B & H																		
1-day Lge	1	1	1	1	1*	-	-	-	1	-	4	1	29	1	29.00	1-29	-	

Career Performances

	M	Inns	NO	Runs	HS	Avge	100s	50s	Ct	St	Balls	Runs	Wkts	Avge	Best	5wI	10wM
Test	38	53	26	137	22*	5.07	-	-	12	-	10024	3953	114	34.67	7-47	5	2
All First	264	287	108	1809	67*	10.10	-	1	99	-	63775	25796	876	29.44	8-29	43	5
1-day Int	20	10	9	15	5*	15.00	-	-	4	-	1020	699	19	36.78	4-22	-	
NatWest	8	1	0	8	8	8.00	-	-	4	-	570	323	10	32.30	3-29	-	
B & H	15	8	4	56	18	14.00	-	-	2	-	809	591	15	39.40	3-32	-	
1-day Lge	37	13	7	36	13*	6.00	-	-	5	-	1548	1192	45	26.48	5-28	1	

TURNER, R. J. Somerset

Name: Robert Julian Turner
Role: Right-hand bat, wicket-keeper
Born: 25 November 1967, Worcester
Height: 6ft 2in **Weight:** 13st 11lbs
Nickname: Noddy, Turns
County debut: 1991
County cap: 1994
1000 runs in a season: 2
1st-Class 50s: 33
1st-Class 100s: 8
1st-Class catches: 382
1st-Class stumpings: 38
Place in batting averages: 6th av. 52.91
(1998 119th av. 27.90)
Parents: Derek Edward and Doris Lilian
Wife and date of marriage: Lucy,
25 September 1999
Family links with cricket: 'My father and

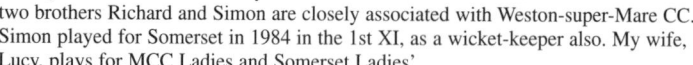

two brothers Richard and Simon are closely associated with Weston-super-Mare CC.
Simon played for Somerset in 1984 in the 1st XI, as a wicket-keeper also. My wife,
Lucy, plays for MCC Ladies and Somerset Ladies'
Education: Uphill Primary School; Broadoak School, Weston-super-Mare; Millfield
School; Magdalene College, Cambridge University
Qualifications: B Eng (Hons) Engineering, Diploma in Computer Science,
NCA coaching award, SFA securities representative of the London Stock Exchange
Career outside cricket: Stockbroker with Rowan Dartington & Co in Bristol
Off-season: England A tour to Bangladesh and New Zealand ('and hopefully a
honeymoon!')
Overseas tours: Millfield School to Barbados, 1985; Combined Universities to
Barbados 1989; Qantas Airlines Tournament, Kuala Lumpur, Malaysia 1992-93;
English Lions Cricket Max tour to New Zealand 1997; MCC to New Zealand 1999;
England A to Bangladesh and New Zealand 1999-2000 (vice-captain)
Overseas teams played for: Claremont-Nedlands, Perth, Western Australia 1991-93
Cricketers particularly admired: Mushtaq Ahmed, Jack Russell
Young players to look out for: Mark Wallace
Other sports followed: Football ('The Villa')
Relaxations: Eating and drinking with friends, 'sleeping a lot'
Extras: Captain of Cambridge University (Blue 1988-91) and Combined Universities
1991. Equalled Somerset record of six catches in an innings in 1995 against West
Indies and eight dismissals in a match against West Indies and Durham. Set Somerset
record seventh-wicket partnership with Shane Lee of 278 against Worcestershire in

1996. Wombwell Cricket Lovers' Society Wicket-keeper of the Year 1999. Played for an England XI in the Cricket Max tournament in New Zealand in 1997-98. In 1997 became first wicket-keeper in 26 years to score 1000 runs in a season for Somerset. Highest-placed Englishman in the 1999 batting averages. Had to cancel honeymoon since it coincided with departure of 1999 England A tour for Bangladesh and New Zealand. Was on stand-by for England tours of West Indies 1997-98 and South Africa and Zimbabwe 1999-2000. Nominated for PCA Players' Player of the Year 1999
Opinions on cricket: 'Splitting the Championship into two divisions has already proved exciting and I'm sure it will improve the state of the English game, with more competitive cricket throughout the whole of the season.'
Best batting: 144 Somerset v Kent, Taunton 1997

1999 Season

	M	Inns	NO	Runs	HS	Avge	100s	50s	Ct	St	O	M	Runs	Wkts	Avge	Best	5wl	10wM
Test																		
All First	19	27	4	1217	138 *	52.91	2	10	67	2								
1-day Int																		
NatWest	5	5	1	130	52	32.50	-	2	9	1								
B & H																		
1-day Lge	16	15	3	297	63	24.75	-	2	19	1								

Career Performances

	M	Inns	NO	Runs	HS	Avge	100s	50s	Ct	St	Balls	Runs	Wkts	Avge	Best	5wl	10wM
Test																		
All First	152	235	46	6206	144	32.83	8	33	382	38	19	29	0	-	-	-	-
1-day Int																		
NatWest	15	12	3	230	52	25.55	-	2	27	2								
B & H	25	23	9	516	70	36.85	-	1	24	1								
1-day Lge	92	78	22	1239	67	22.12	-	4	87	11								

90. Who was the first captain to lead his county to the Championship and England to a Test series victory in the same season?

TWEATS, T. A.   Derbyshire

Name: Timothy Andrew Tweats
Role: Right-hand bat, off-spin bowler
Born: 18 April 1974, Stoke-on-Trent
Height: 6ft 3in **Weight:** 13st
County debut: 1992
1st-Class 50s: 4
1st-Class 100s: 2
1st-Class catches: 29
Place in batting averages: 301st av. 3.00
(1998 210th av. 18.44)
Strike rate: (career 74.50)
Parents: Malcolm and Linda
Marital status: Single
Family links with cricket: Father and two
brothers, Jon and Simon, play for the local
club, Leek, for whom he played before
joining Derbyshire
Education: Endon High School; Stoke-on-
Trent Sixth Form College; Staffordshire University
Qualifications: 5 GCSEs, 2 A-levels
Overseas tours: Kidsgrove and District Junior Cricket League to Australia 1991
Cricketers particularly admired: Robin Smith, Phil Tufnell
Other sports followed: Football
Extras: Retired from first-class cricket at end of 1999 season
Best batting: 189 Derbyshire v Yorkshire, Derby 1997
Best bowling: 1-23 Derbyshire v Surrey, Derby 1995

1999 Season

	M	Inns	NO	Runs	HS	Avge	100s	50s	Ct	St	O	M	Runs	Wkts	Avge	Best	5wl	10wM
Test																		
All First	4	7	0	21	10	3.00	-	-	2	-								
1-day Int																		
NatWest																		
B & H																		
1-day Lge																		

Career Performances

	M	Inns	NO	Runs	HS	Avge	100s	50s	Ct	St	Balls	Runs	Wkts	Avge	Best	5wI	10wM
Test																	
All First	33	62	5	1405	189	24.64	2	4	29	-	298	237	4	59.25	1-23	-	-
1-day Int																	
NatWest	4	3	1	26	16	13.00	-	-	1	-							
B & H	6	5	1	92	42 *	23.00	-	-	-	-							
1-day Lge	22	17	2	185	35	12.33	-	-	9	-	24	27	0	-		-	-

UDAL, S. D. Hampshire

Name: Shaun David Udal
Role: Right-hand bat, off-spin bowler,
county vice-captain
Born: 18 March 1969, Farnborough, Hants
Height: 6ft 3in **Weight:** 13st 6lbs
Nickname: Shaggy
County debut: 1989
County cap: 1992
One-Day Internationals: 10
50 wickets in a season: 5
1st-Class 50s: 17
1st-Class 100s: 1
1st-Class 5 w. in innings: 23
1st-Class 10 w. in match: 4
1st-Class catches: 70
One-Day 5 w. in innings: 1
Place in batting averages: 231st av. 17.40
(1998 95th av. 31.07)
Place in bowling averages: 66th av. 26.72 (1998 117th av. 34.31)
Strike rate: 59.70 (career 71.01)
Parents: Robin Francis and Mary Elizabeth
Wife and date of marriage: Emma Jane, 4 October 1991
Children: Katherine Mary, 26 August 1992; Rebecca Jane, 17 November 1995
Family links with cricket: Father played for Camberley for 42 years, and also for
Surrey Colts; brother is Camberley 1st XI captain. Grandfather played for
Leicestershire and Middlesex
Education: Tower Hill Infant and Junior Schools; Cove Secondary Modern
Qualifications: 8 CSEs, qualified print finisher
Career outside cricket: 'Work in sales for the 7 Corners Printing Group'
Off-season: 'Working, going to South Africa with Judge Tours, and reintroducing
myself to my family'

Overseas tours: England to Australia 1994-95; England A to Pakistan 1995-96; England Cricket Max XI to New Zealand 1997
Overseas teams played for: Hamilton Wickham, Newcastle, NSW 1990-91
Cricketers particularly admired: Ian Botham, Robin Smith
Young players to look out for: Andy Flintoff, Derek Kenway
Other sports played: Football, golf (handicap of 14)
Other sports followed: Football (Aldershot Town, West Ham Utd)
Injuries: Out for four weeks with a broken ankle
Relaxations: 'Pubs, going out, enjoying myself and relaxing with the family'
Extras: Has taken two hat-tricks in club cricket. Has scored a double hundred (202) in a 40-over club game. Man of the Match on NatWest debut against Berkshire 1991. Took 8-50 v Sussex in the first game of 1992 season, his seventh Championship match. Named Hampshire Cricket Association Player of the Year 1993. Played for an England XI in the Cricket Max tournament in New Zealand in 1997-98. Vice-captain of Hampshire since 1998 season
Opinions on cricket: 'I've had enough of ex-players slagging off the county game. If it's that bad then why do they stay involved in it? And also it still provides them with a living, so it can't be that bad, can it! Get behind the players and back them for once.'
Best batting: 117* Hampshire v Warwickshire, Southampton 1997
Best bowling: 8-50 Hampshire v Sussex, Southampton 1992

1999 Season

	M	Inns	NO	Runs	HS	Avge	100s	50s	Ct	St	O	M	Runs	Wkts	Avge	Best	5wI	10wM
Test																		
All First	15	21	6	261	40	17.40	-	-	1	-	497.3	124	1336	50	26.72	6-47	3	-
1-day Int																		
NatWest	2	1	0	3	3	3.00	-	-	1	-	19	0	93	5	18.60	3-32	-	
B & H	1	1	0	17	17	17.00	-	-	-	-	7	0	38	0	-	-	-	
1-day Lge	15	12	2	103	20	10.30	-	-	3	-	84.4	3	393	11	35.72	2-17	-	

Career Performances

	M	Inns	NO	Runs	HS	Avge	100s	50s	Ct	St	Balls	Runs	Wkts	Avge	Best	5wI	10wM
Test																	
All First	155	219	41	4017	117 *	22.56	1	17	70	-	29969	14819	422	35.11	8-50	23	4
1-day Int	10	6	4	35	11 *	17.50	-	-	1	-	570	371	8	46.37	2-37	-	
NatWest	23	11	5	128	39 *	21.33	-	-	12	-	1377	790	33	23.93	4-20	-	
B & H	36	21	5	205	34	12.81	-	-	10	-	2118	1381	42	32.88	4-40	-	
1-day Lge	143	94	26	1010	78	14.85	-	5	45	-	5928	4876	163	29.91	5-43	1	

VAN DER GUCHT, C. G.   Hampshire

Name: Charlie Graham van der Gucht
Role: Left-hand bat, left-arm spin bowler
Born: 14 January 1980, London
Height: 6ft **Weight:** 12st 1lb
Nickname: Gucht, Chilli
County debut: No first-team appearance
Parents: Nicola and Mike
Marital status: Single
Family links with cricket: Grandfather
played/kept wicket for Gloucestershire and
Bengal in the 1930s
Education: Cothill House; Radley College;
Durham University
Qualifications: 10 GCSEs, 3 A-levels
Off-season: 'Studying at Durham; getting
work experience'
Overseas tours: West of England to West
Indies 1995; British Universities to South
Africa 1999
Overseas teams played for: Gordon DCC, Sydney 1998-99
Cricketers particularly admired: Phil Tufnell, Muttiah Muralitharan, Gary Sobers,
Henry Fitz
Young players to look out for: John Francis, Gav Franklin, James Bruce,
Mark Hardinges
Other sports played: Rackets, golf (12 handicap)
Other sports followed: Football (Southampton), horse racing
Relaxations: Keeping fit, playing golf, reading, 'going to "Klute"'
Extras: Leading wicket-taker at Gordon club in Sydney 1998-99. Played for
Hampshire Board XI in 1999 NatWest, winning Man of the Match award in fourth
round v Glamorgan at Southampton
Opinions on cricket: 'Too many first-class teams. Not enough cricket in schools.
Staffs are too big.'

> 91. Which cricketing brothers were the only batsmen to pass
> 1000 Championship runs for Sussex in 1987?

1999 Season (did not make any first-class or one-day appearances)

Career Performances

	M	Inns	NO	Runs	HS	Avge	100s	50s	Ct	St	Balls	Runs	Wkts	Avge	Best	5wl	10wM
Test																	
All First																	
1-day Int																	
NatWest	3	2	0	4	3	2.00	-	-	-	-	144	95	5	19.00	3-35	-	
B & H																	
1-day Lge																	

VAUGHAN, M. P. Yorkshire

Name: Michael Paul Vaughan
Role: Right-hand bat, off-spin bowler
Born: 29 October 1974, Eccles, Manchester
Height: 6ft 2in **Weight:** 11st 7lbs
Nickname: Virgil, Frankie, Chippo
County debut: 1993
County cap: 1995
1000 runs in a season: 4
1st-Class 50s: 32
1st-Class 100s: 16
1st-Class catches: 46
Place in batting averages: 129th av. 27.12
(1998 35th av. 41.46)
Place in bowling averages: 137th av. 42.40
Strike rate: 82.30 (career 86.71)
Parents: Graham John and Dee
Marital status: Single
Family links with cricket: Father played
league cricket for Worsley CC. Brother plays for Sheffield Collegiate. Mother is
related to the famous Tyldesley family (Lancashire and England)
Education: St Marks, Worsley, Manchester; Dore Juniors, Sheffield; Silverdale
Comprehensive, Sheffield
Qualifications: 7 GCSEs
Off-season: Touring South Africa with England
Overseas tours: England U19 to India 1992-93, to Sri Lanka 1993-94; Yorkshire to
West Indies 1994, to South Africa 1995, to Zimbabwe 1996; England A to India
1994-95, to Australia 1996-97, to Zimbabwe and South Africa 1998-99 (captain);
England to South Africa 1999-2000
Cricketers particularly admired: Glenn Chapple, Graham Lloyd, 'all the present
Yorkshire team'

Young players to look out for: Matthew Wood, Matthew Hoggard
Other sports played: Football (Baslow FC), golf
Other sports followed: Football (Sheffield Wednesday), all golf
Relaxations: Most sports. 'Enjoy a good meal with friends'
Extras: Played club cricket for Sheffield Collegiate in the Yorkshire League. *Daily Telegraph* U15 Batsman of the Year, 1990. Maurice Leyland Batting Award 1990. Rapid Cricketline Player of the Month, June 1993. The Cricket Society's Most Promising Young Cricketer 1993. A. A. Thompson Memorial Trophy – The Roses Cricketer of the Year 1993. Whittingdale Cricketer of the Month, July 1994. Scored 1066 runs in first full season of first-class cricket in 1994. Captained England U19 in home series against India 1994. Scored two 100s (100 and 151) v Essex at Chelmsford 1999; Stuart Law scored two 100s for Essex in the same match
Best batting: 183 Yorkshire v Glamorgan, Cardiff 1996
Best bowling: 4-39 Yorkshire v Oxford University, The Parks 1994
Stop press: Made Test debut v South Africa in the first Test at Johannesburg, November 1999. Struck 69 in England's only innings of the rain-shortened fifth Test at Centurion, January 2000, a match-winning maiden Test 50 that earned him the Man of the Match award. Awarded England contract (Band C) for 2000

1999 Season

	M	Inns	NO	Runs	HS	Avge	100s	50s	Ct	St	O	M	Runs	Wkts	Avge	Best	5wl	10wM
Test																		
All First	17	34	1	895	153	27.12	3	3	5	-	137.1	26	424	10	42.40	2-19	-	-
1-day Int																		
NatWest	4	4	0	166	85	41.50	-	2	2	-	32	2	107	3	35.66	1-19	-	
B & H	3	2	0	53	29	26.50	-	-	1	-	24	0	82	4	20.50	2-28	-	
1-day Lge	16	16	1	425	72	28.33	-	2	10	-	97.3	4	420	17	24.70	4-31	-	

Career Performances

	M	Inns	NO	Runs	HS	Avge	100s	50s	Ct	St	Balls	Runs	Wkts	Avge	Best	5wl	10wM
Test																	
All First	121	219	10	7071	183	33.83	16	32	46	-	6937	3989	80	49.86	4-39	-	-
1-day Int																	
NatWest	17	17	1	397	85	24.81	-	3	4	-	258	152	4	38.00	1-17	-	
B & H	25	24	1	775	88	33.69	-	6	5	-	477	319	10	31.90	2-28	-	
1-day Lge	77	75	4	1728	72	24.33	-	8	23	-	909	743	26	28.57	4-31	-	

WAGH, M. A. Warwickshire

Name: Mark Anant Wagh
Role: Right-hand bat, off-spin bowler
Born: 20 October 1976, Birmingham
Height: 6ft 2in **Weight:** 12st 7lbs
Nickname: Waggy
County debut: 1997
1st-Class 50s: 9
1st-Class 100s: 7
1st-Class catches: 27
Place in batting averages: 88th av. 32.15
(1998 73rd av. 32.66)
Strike rate: 25.40 (career 102.73)
Parents: Mohan and Rita
Marital status: Single
Education: Harborne Junior School;
King Edward's School, Birmingham;
Keble College, Oxford
Qualifications: 12 GCSEs, 4 A-levels,
basic coaching

Overseas tours: Warwickshire U19 to South Africa 1992
Cricketers particularly admired: Carl Hooper, Brian Lara, David Gower,
Daryll Cullinan
Other sports followed: Hockey, snooker, football
Relaxations: Snooker and going out with friends
Extras: Oxford Blue 1996-98; Oxford University captain 1997
Best batting: 216* Warwickshire v Oxford University, The Parks 1999
Best bowling: 4-11 Warwickshire v Middlesex, Lord's 1998

1999 Season

	M	Inns	NO	Runs	HS	Avge	100s	50s	Ct	St	O	M	Runs	Wkts	Avge	Best	5wI	10wM
Test																		
All First	13	21	1	643	216*	32.15	1	1	3	-	21.1	4	66	5	13.20	4-33	-	-
1-day Int																		
NatWest																		
B & H																		
1-day Lge	3	3	0	38	27	12.66	-	-	-	-								

Career Performances

	M	Inns	NO	Runs	HS	Avge	100s	50s	Ct	St	Balls	Runs	Wkts	Avge	Best	5wI	10wM
Test																	
All First	57	90	8	2702	216 *	32.95	7	9	27	-	3082	1671	30	55.70	4-11	-	-
1-day Int																	
NatWest																	
B & H	3	3	1	36	23	18.00	-	-	-	-	174	119	3	39.66	1-39	-	
1-day Lge	3	3	0	38	27	12.66	-	-	-	-							

WALKER, M. J.   Kent

Name: Matthew Jonathan Walker
Role: Left-hand bat, right-arm
medium bowler
Born: 2 January 1974, Gravesend, Kent
Height: 5ft 6in **Weight:** 13st 2lbs
Nickname: Walks, Walkdog,
Pumba, Dicky Neurerker, Merse
County debut: 1992-93
1st-Class 50s: 10
1st-Class 100s: 2
1st-Class 200s: 1
1st-Class catches: 35
One-Day 100s: 1
Place in batting averages: 139th av. 26.33
(1998 133rd av. 26.23)
Parents: Richard and June
Wife and date of marriage: Claudia,
25 September 1999
Family links with cricket: Grandfather Jack played for Kent as a wicket-keeper.
Father played for Kent and Middlesex 2nd XIs and was on Lord's groundstaff.
Mother taught ex-England Ladies captain Megan Lear
Education: Shorne CE Primary School; King's School, Rochester
Qualifications: 9 GCSEs, 2 A-levels, advanced cricket coach
Career outside cricket: 'Yet to be decided'
Off-season: Coaching cricket, playing hockey for Gore Court, getting fit
Overseas tours: Kent U17 to New Zealand 1991; England U19 to Pakistan 1991-92,
to India 1992-93 (captain); Kent to Zimbabwe 1992-93
Cricketers particularly admired: Aravinda De Silva, John Crawley,
Mark Ramprakash
Young players to look out for: James Watson, Bob Key
Other sports played: Hockey (England U14-U18 [captain U15-U17], Kent U14-U21,

South East U16-U18), rugby (Kent U18), football (trials for Chelsea and Gillingham), athletics (Kent U15 javelin champion)

Other sports followed: Football (Charlton Athletic), hockey (Gore Court HC), rugby (Gravesend RFC)

Injuries: Out for five weeks with shoulder ligament damage

Relaxations: Music and films ('avid collector of both'). 'Spending as much time as I can with my family'

Extras: Captained England U19 on tour to India 1992-93 and v West Indies in 1993 home series which England U19 won 2-0 in one-day matches and 1-0 in 'Test' series. Received Sir Jack Hobbs award for best young cricketer 1989, and *Daily Telegraph* U15 batting award 1989. Woolwich Kent League's Young Cricketer of the Year 1994. Scored 275 not out against Somerset in 1996 – the highest ever individual score by a Kent batsman at Canterbury – and was on the pitch for the whole game. Became an eminent Ruffensian in 1995

Opinions on cricket: 'You've got to be fit!!'

Best batting: 275* Kent v Somerset, Canterbury 1996

1999 Season

	M	Inns	NO	Runs	HS	Avge	100s	50s	Ct	St	O	M	Runs	Wkts	Avge	Best	5wI	10wM
Test																		
All First	14	23	2	553	103*	26.33	1	3	13	-	19.1	3	64	0	-		-	-	-
1-day Int																		
NatWest	2	2	0	86	73	43.00	-	1	-	-	10	2	33	1	33.00	1-33	-	
B & H																		
1-day Lge	13	12	0	153	39	12.75	-	-	3	-	6	0	26	0	-		-	-

Career Performances

	M	Inns	NO	Runs	HS	Avge	100s	50s	Ct	St	Balls	Runs	Wkts	Avge	Best	5wI	10wM
Test																	
All First	55	92	8	2309	275*	27.48	3	10	35	-	193	134	0	-		-	-
1-day Int																	
NatWest	5	5	1	191	73	47.75	-	2	-	-	60	33	1	33.00	1-33	-	
B & H	22	21	3	709	117	39.38	1	5	9	-							
1-day Lge	71	66	8	1197	80	20.63	-	6	16	-	36	26	0	-		-	-

WALLACE, M. A.   Glamorgan

Name: Mark Alex Wallace
Role: Left-hand bat, wicket-keeper
Born: 19 November 1981, Abergavenny,
South Wales
Height: 5ft 10in **Weight:** 11st
Nickname: Grom, Wally, Marcellus
County debut: 1999
1st-Class 50s: 1
1st-Class catches: 12
Parents: Ryland and Alvine
Marital status: Single
Family links with cricket: Father plays for
Abergavenny
Education: Crickhowell Primary School;
Crickhowell High School; 'listening to
Browny and "The Wasp"'
Qualifications: 10 GCSEs
Career outside cricket: Studying for A-levels

Off-season: 'Going on England U19 tour to Malaysia and to Sri Lanka for Youth
World Cup; studying for A-levels'
Overseas tours: Gwent U15 to South Africa 1996; Wales U16 to Jersey 1996, 1997;
England U19 to New Zealand 1998-99, to Malaysia and (Youth World Cup) Sri Lanka
1999-2000; England U17 to Ireland (International Youth Tournament) 1999
Cricketers particularly admired: Ian Healy, Chris Read, Adrian Shaw, Steve James,
Chris Brown
Young players to look out for: Mike Powell, Ian Bell, John Maunders, Graeme
Bridge, David Harrison, Owen Parkin ('still only 27')
Other sports played: Football, rugby, golf ('Glamorgan 2nd team golf days')
Other sports followed: Football (Merthyr Tydfil FC), rugby
Relaxations: Sleep, golf, Merthyr Tydfil FC
Extras: Represented England U19 in home matches against Pakistan 1998 and
Australia 1999. Made first-class debut v Somerset 1999 aged 17 years 287 days –
youngest ever Glamorgan wicket-keeper
Opinions on cricket: 'Tea break should be extended by ten minutes to allow players
time to recuperate for final session. England A sides should be picked on merit, not
just on age and potential.'
Best batting: 64* Glamorgan v Yorkshire, Headingley 1999

1999 Season

	M	Inns	NO	Runs	HS	Avge	100s	50s	Ct	St	O	M	Runs	Wkts	Avge	Best	5wl	10wM
Test																		
All First	3	4	1	98	64 *	32.66	-	1	12	-								
1-day Int																		
NatWest																		
B & H																		
1-day Lge	3	2	0	3	2	1.50	-	-	4	2								

Career Performances

	M	Inns	NO	Runs	HS	Avge	100s	50s	Ct	St	Balls	Runs	Wkts	Avge	Best	5wl	10wM
Test																		
All First	3	4	1	98	64 *	32.66	-	1	12	-							
1-day Int																		
NatWest																		
B & H																		
1-day Lge	3	2	0	3	2	1.50	-	-	4	2							

WALTON, T. C.   Essex

Name: Timothy Charles Walton
Role: Right-hand bat, right-arm
medium bowler
Born: 8 November 1972, Low Lead,
North Yorkshire
Height: 6ft **Weight:** 12st 10lbs
Nickname: TC, Spadge
County debut: 1992 (one-day,
Northamptonshire), 1994 (first-class,
Northamptonshire), 1999 (Essex)
1st-Class 50s: 8
1st-Class catches: 12
Place in batting averages:
207th av. 19.37
Strike rate: 45.00 (career 87.00)
Parents: Alan Michael and Sally Ann
Marital status: Single
Family links with cricket: Younger brother

Adam played Yorkshire Schools cricket and is a good prospect
Education: Leeds Grammar School; University of Northumbria, Newcastle
Qualifications: 7 GCSEs, 3 A-levels

Overseas tours: England U19 to Pakistan 1991-92
Overseas teams played for: Woolston Workingmens CC, New Zealand
Cricketers particularly admired: Viv Richards, Greg Blewett
Young players to look out for: David Sales, Jason Brown
Other sports followed: Rugby union ('long ago I played for England U16 at full-back') and league
Relaxations: Sketching and impersonating
Extras: Released by Northamptonshire at end of 1998 season. Joined Essex for 1999; released by Essex at end of 1999 season
Opinions on cricket: 'Still too stiff. Needs loosening to make it interesting for all people, e.g. Cricket Max in New Zealand.'
Best batting: 71 Northamptonshire v Somerset, Taunton 1995
71 Essex v Gloucestershire, Gloucester 1999
Best bowling: 1-8 Essex v Oxford University, Chelmsford 1999

1999 Season

	M	Inns	NO	Runs	HS	Avge	100s	50s	Ct	St	O	M	Runs	Wkts	Avge	Best	5wI	10wM
Test																		
All First	6	8	0	155	71	19.37	-	1	7	-	7.3	2	28	1	28.00	1-8	-	-
1-day Int																		
NatWest	1	1	0	8	8	8.00	-	-	-	-								
B & H																		
1-day Lge	7	7	1	75	23	12.50	-	-	1	-								

Career Performances

	M	Inns	NO	Runs	HS	Avge	100s	50s	Ct	St	Balls	Runs	Wkts	Avge	Best	5wI	10wM
Test																		
All First	25	37	3	808	71	23.76	-	8	12	-	435	310	5	62.00	1-8	-	-
1-day Int																		
NatWest	5	4	0	29	15	7.25	-	-	2	-							
B & H	13	10	2	266	70 *	33.25	-	1	6	-	36	27	1	27.00	1-27	-	
1-day Lge	66	58	11	1105	72	23.51	-	6	16	-	240	197	6	32.83	2-27	-	

92. In which season was the Championship reduced
from 28 to 22 matches?

WARD, I. J.   Surrey

Name: Ian James Ward
Role: Left-hand bat, right-arm
'very low' bowler
Born: 30 September 1973, Plymouth
Height: 5ft 8in ('taller than G. Thorpe')
Weight: 13st
Nickname: Wardy, Cocker, Son of Baboon,
Dwarf, Stumpy, Pig in a Passage, Warley
('courtesy of Henry Thorpe')
County debut: 1996
1000 runs in a season: 1
1st-Class 50s: 15
1st-Class 100s: 1
1st-Class catches: 23
Place in batting averages: 51st av. 37.70
(1998 93rd av. 31.11)

Parents: Tony and Mary
Wife and date of marriage:
Joanne, 15 February 1998
Children: Robert
Family links with cricket: Grandfather and father played for Devon. 'Mother thinks anything Mark Butcher does is "sexy". Wife hates cricket ("Footballers are paid better")'
Education: Valley End; Millfield School; 'Ben Hollioake's School of Life'; 'wife's cooking'
Qualifications: 8 GCSEs, 3 A-levels, NCA coaching award
Career outside cricket: 'John Wayne impersonator'
Off-season: 'On tour with England A; New Year training in Perth'
Overseas tours: Surrey U19 to Barbados 1990; Millfield to Barbados and Jamaica 1991; Malden Wanderers to Jersey 1994; England A to Bangladesh and New Zealand 1999-2000
Overseas teams played for: North Perth CC, Western Australia 1996-97; Perth CC, Western Australia
Cricketers particularly admired: Graham Thorpe, Greg Kennis, Mark Wasley (North Perth CC), Saqlain Mushtaq, Martin Bicknell
Young players to look out for: Jon Batty, Mike Johnson (North Perth CC)
Other sports played: Golf
Other sports followed: Football (Liverpool), rugby (Richmond), golf
Relaxations: 'Spending time with my wife; running, golf'
Extras: Surrey 2nd XI cap at the age of 23. Scored maiden first-class century v Derbyshire at Derby 1999

Opinions on cricket: 'Two divisions a step in the right direction, as are ECB contracts (but should be for 12 months). Pitches and nets must improve. Must find a way to reduce amount played; players must have more time to prepare and rest. Most overseas players say we play too much; why do we not listen?'
Best batting: 103 Surrey v Derbyshire, Derby 1999

1999 Season

	M	Inns	NO	Runs	HS	Avge	100s	50s	Ct	St	O	M	Runs	Wkts	Avge	Best	5wI	10wM
Test																		
All First	18	30	3	1018	103	37.70	1	9	7	-	4	2	8	0	-		-	-	-
1-day Int																		
NatWest	4	3	1	62	26	31.00	-	-	-	-								
B & H	1	1	0	1	1	1.00	-	-	-	-								
1-day Lge	15	15	2	332	80	25.53	-	1	3	-	3	0	18	0	-		-	-

Career Performances

	M	Inns	NO	Runs	HS	Avge	100s	50s	Ct	St	Balls	Runs	Wkts	Avge	Best	5wI	10wM
Test																	
All First	33	56	5	1668	103	32.70	1	15	23	-	126	92	0	-		-	-	-
1-day Int																	
NatWest	8	7	1	120	27	20.00	-	-	-	-							
B & H	1	1	0	1	1	1.00	-	-	-	-							
1-day Lge	40	38	7	766	91	24.70	-	4	8	-	53	84	0	-		-	-

93. Which batsman scored the most Championship runs
from 1993, when the four-day Championship began, to the end of the
single-division era in 1999?

WARD, T. R.   Leicestershire

Name: Trevor Robert Ward
Role: Right-hand bat, occasional
off-spin bowler
Born: 18 January 1968, Farningham, Kent
Height: 5ft 11in **Weight:** 13st
Nickname: Wardy, Chikka
County debut: 1986 (Kent)
County cap: 1989 (Kent)
Benefit: 1999 (Kent)
1000 runs in a season: 6
1st-Class 50s: 70
1st-Class 100s: 23
1st-Class 200s: 1
1st-Class catches: 197
One-Day 100s: 7
Place in batting averages: 218th av. 18.46
(1998 207th av. 18.90)
Strike rate: (career 135.37)
Parents: Robert Henry and Hazel Ann
Wife and date of marriage: Sarah Ann, 29 September 1990
Children: Holly Ann, 23 October 1995; Samuel Joseph, 25 April 1998
Family links with cricket: Father played club cricket
Education: Anthony Roper County Primary; Hextable Comprehensive
Qualifications: 7 O-levels, NCA coaching award
Overseas tours: NCA to Bermuda 1985; England YC to Sri Lanka 1986-87,
to Australia (Youth World Cup) 1987-88
Overseas teams played for: Scarborough, Perth, Western Australia 1985;
Gosnells, Perth 1993
Cricketers particularly admired: Ian Botham, Graham Gooch, Robin Smith
Other sports followed: Most sports
Relaxations: Fishing, watching television, golf
Extras: Was awarded £1000 for becoming the first player to score 400 runs in the
Benson and Hedges Cup in 1995. Released by Kent at end of 1999 season and has
joined Leicestershire for 2000 on a three-year contract
Best batting: 235* Kent v Middlesex, Canterbury 1991
Best bowling: 2-10 Kent v Yorkshire, Canterbury 1996

1999 Season

	M	Inns	NO	Runs	HS	Avge	100s	50s	Ct	St	O	M	Runs	Wkts	Avge	Best	5wI	10wM
Test																		
All First	8	13	0	240	101	18.46	1	-	9	-								
1-day Int																		
NatWest	2	2	0	19	16	9.50	-	-	-	-	3	0	25	2	12.50	2-25	-	
B & H																		
1-day Lge	11	11	0	318	70	28.90	-	2	2	-								

Career Performances

	M	Inns	NO	Runs	HS	Avge	100s	50s	Ct	St	Balls	Runs	Wkts	Avge	Best	5wI	10wM
Test																		
All First	206	355	19	11897	235 *	35.40	24	70	197	-	1083	647	8	80.87	2-10	-	-
1-day Int																		
NatWest	24	24	1	934	120	40.60	1	8	4	-	174	154	4	38.50	2-25	-	
B & H	50	50	3	1647	125	35.04	2	12	11	-	12	10	0	-	-	-	-
1-day Lge	171	166	6	4838	131	30.23	4	30	37	-	228	187	6	31.16	3-20	-	

WARNE, S. K.   Hampshire

Name: Shane Keith Warne
Role: Right-hand bat, leg-spin bowler
Born: 13 September 1969, Upper Ferntree Gully, Victoria
Height: 6ft
County debut: No first-team appearance
Test debut: 1991-92
Tests: 71
One-Day Internationals: 125
1st-Class 50s: 4
1st-Class 5 w. in innings: 24
1st-Class 10 w. in match: 4
1st-Class catches: 89
One-Day 5 w. in innings: 1
Strike rate: (career 62.92)
Parents: Keith and Brigitte
Wife: Simone
Children: Brooke and Jackson
Education: Hampton High School; Mentone Grammar School
Overseas tours: Australia to Sri Lanka 1992-93, to New Zealand 1992-93, to England 1993, to South Africa 1993-94, to Pakistan 1994-95, to West Indies 1994-95, to India,

Pakistan and Sri Lanka (World Cup) 1995-96, to South Africa 1996-97, to England 1997, to India 1997-98, to West Indies 1998-99, to UK, Ireland and Holland (World Cup) 1999, to Sri Lanka and Zimbabwe 1999-2000

Overseas teams played for: St Kilda, Victoria; Victoria 1990-91 –

Cricketers particularly admired: Dennis Lillee, Ian Botham, Ian Chappell, Mark Waugh, Sachin Tendulkar, Brett Lee

Players to look out for: Brad Hodge, Michael Clinger, Darren Berry

Other sports played: Tennis, golf

Other sports followed: Football (Chelsea), Australian Rules (St Kilda), snooker (Jimmy White)

Extras: One of *Wisden*'s Five Cricketers of the Year 1993. Is vice-captain of Australia and has captained his country in One-Day Internationals. Took Test hat-trick v England at Melbourne 1994-95. Took 300th Test wicket (Jacques Kallis) v South Africa at Sydney 1998. Man of the Match in 1999 World Cup semi-final v South Africa and final v Pakistan. Shares record (with Geoff Allott of New Zealand) for the number of wickets in a World Cup tournament (20 in 1999). Lies second, behind Dennis Lillee, in the list of Australian Test wicket-takers. Has joined Hampshire for 2000 as overseas player

Opinions on cricket: 'I think that the captains have taken a more positive attitude to Test matches and first-class cricket. Cricketers should think of themselves as entertainers for the public. They pay the money to watch cricket, then they're entitled to watch exciting cricket. So the responsibility has to be with the captains. In Australia it is working, with nearly every game coming down to the last day.

'I'm looking forward to county cricket with Hampshire, seeing how every team plays cricket. I'm really looking forward to getting to know the Hampshire guys and hopefully winning some trophies.

'All in all we need to be aware of responsibilities to the game and the public. Cricket is in good shape – let's enjoy it.'

Best batting: 74* Australia v New Zealand, Brisbane 1993-94

Best bowling: 8-71 Australia v England, Brisbane 1994-95

Stop press: Leading wicket-taker in world Test cricket in the 1990s with 351 wickets (av. 25.67). Selected for Australia's tour of New Zealand 1999-2000

1999 Season

	M	Inns	NO	Runs	HS	Avge	100s	50s	Ct	St	O	M	Runs	Wkts	Avge	Best	5wl	10wM
Test																		
All First																		
1-day Int	10	4	1	34	18	11.33	-	-	1	-	94.2	13	361	20	18.05	4-29	-	
NatWest																		
B & H																		
1-day Lge																		

Career Performances

	M	Inns	NO	Runs	HS	Avge	100s	50s	Ct	St	Balls	Runs	Wkts	Avge	Best	5wI	10wM
Test	71	101	11	1378	74 *	15.31	-	2	51	-	20528	8134	317	25.65	8-71	14	4
All First	134	177	25	2429	74 *	15.98	-	4	89	-	34668	14773	551	26.81	8-71	24	4
1-day Int	125	73	22	630	55	12.35	-	1	41	-	7018	4851	202	24.01	5-33	1	
NatWest																	
B & H																	
1-day Lge																	

WARREN, N. A.   Warwickshire

Name: Nick Alexander Warren
Role: Right-hand bat, right-arm
medium-fast bowler
Born: 26 June 1982, Moseley
Height: 5ft 10in   **Weight:** 11st 4lbs
Nickname: Waz
County debut: No first-team appearance
Parents: Lesley
Marital status: Single
Education: Wheelers Lane Boys School;
Solihull Sixth Form College
Off-season: England U19 to Malaysia and
Sri Lanka; at college
Overseas tours: Warwickshire U19 to South
Africa 1998-99; England U17 to Ireland
1999; England U19 to Malaysia and (Youth
World Cup) Sri Lanka 1999-2000
Cricketers particularly admired:
Ed Giddins, Mike Atherton, Allan Donald
Other sports played: Football
Other sports followed: Football (Birmingham City)
Relaxations: Listening to music, socialising with friends

---

94. In the Somerset v Essex match at Taunton in 1985,
the first eight Somerset batsmen out were all caught at the wicket.
Name the Essex wicket-keeper involved.

WARREN, R. J.   Northamptonshire

Name: Russell John Warren
Role: Right-hand bat, wicket-keeper
Born: 10 September 1971, Northampton
Height: 6ft 2in **Weight:** 13st 7lbs
Nickname: Rabbit, Rabbs
County debut: 1992
County cap: 1995
1st-Class 50s: 21
1st-Class 100s: 3
1st-Class 200s: 1
1st-Class catches: 94
1st-Class stumpings: 3
One-Day 100s: 1
Place in batting averages: 56th av. 37.40
(1998 294th av. 3.75)
Parents: John and Sally
Marital status: Single
Family links with cricket: 'Dad likes a bet.
Mum follows scores on Teletext'
Education: Whitehills Lower School; Kingsthorpe Middle and Upper Schools
Qualifications: 8 O-levels, 2 A-levels
Overseas tours: England YC to New Zealand 1990-91; Northamptonshire to Cape
Town 1993, to Zimbabwe 1995, to Johannesburg 1996
Overseas teams played for: Lancaster Park, Christchurch, and Canterbury B, New
Zealand 1991-93; Riverside CC, Lower Hutt, New Zealand 1994-95; Petone CC,
Wellington, New Zealand 1995-96; Alma Marist CC, Cape Town, South Africa
1997-98
Cricketers particularly admired: Wayne Larkins, Allan Lamb, Malachy Loye
Young players to look out for: David Roberts, Alec Swann, Graeme Swann, David
Sales, Richard Logan, John Blain, Richard Montgomerie, Tim Walton
Other sports followed: Football (Manchester United and Northampton Town), rugby
(Northampton Saints), golf, snooker and horse racing ('mostly Nick Cook and John
Hughes tips!')
Relaxations: Sky television, fashion and training
Opinions on cricket: 'Fewer games, smaller staffs and increased wages. Too many
"ra-ras" in the game.'
Best batting: 201* Northamptonshire v Glamorgan, Northampton 1996

1999 Season

	M	Inns	NO	Runs	HS	Avge	100s	50s	Ct	St	O	M	Runs	Wkts	Avge	Best	5wI	10wM
Test																		
All First	18	29	4	935	110	37.40	1	6	12	-								
1-day Int																		
NatWest	3	3	0	89	53	29.66	-	1	2	-								
B & H																		
1-day Lge	14	14	1	389	61	29.92	-	1	11	-								

Career Performances

	M	Inns	NO	Runs	HS	Avge	100s	50s	Ct	St	Balls	Runs	Wkts	Avge	Best	5wI	10wM
Test																	
All First	79	129	16	3678	201 *	32.54	4	21	94	3							
1-day Int																	
NatWest	16	14	2	347	100 *	28.91	1	1	20	1							
B & H	12	11	1	95	23	9.50	-	-	11	-							
1-day Lge	77	66	10	1300	71 *	23.21	-	4	65	9							

WATKIN, S. L. Glamorgan

Name: Steven Llewellyn Watkin
Role: Right-hand bat, right-arm
fast-medium bowler
Born: 15 September 1964, Dyffryn, Rhondda
Height: 6ft 3in **Weight:** 12st 8lbs
Nickname: Watty, Banger
County debut: 1986
County cap: 1989
Benefit: 1998
Test debut: 1991
Tests: 3
One-Day Internationals: 4
50 wickets in a season: 9
1st-Class 5 w. in innings: 28
1st-Class 10 w. in match: 4
1st-Class catches: 65
One-Day 5 w. in innings: 1
Place in batting averages:
279th av. 8.60
Place in bowling averages: 59th av. 25.27 (1998 29th av. 21.83)
Strike rate: 58.81 (career 57.78)

Parents: John (deceased) and Sandra
Marital status: Single
Family links with cricket: One brother plays local cricket; 'older brother a good watcher'
Education: Cymer Afan Comprehensive; Swansea College of Further Education; South Glamorgan Institute of Higher Education
Qualifications: 8 O-levels, 2 A-levels, BA (Hons) Human Movement Studies
Career outside cricket: Cricket development officer
Off-season: 'Coaching, DIY, car restoration'
Overseas tours: British Colleges to West Indies 1987; England A to Kenya and Zimbabwe 1989-90, to Pakistan and Sri Lanka 1990-91, to Bermuda and West Indies 1991-92; England to West Indies 1993-94
Overseas teams played for: Potchefstroom University, South Africa 1987-88; Aurora, Durban 1991-92
Cricketers particularly admired: Richard Hadlee, Dennis Lillee, Ian Botham
Young players to look out for: Mark Wallace, Dave Harrison
Other sports played: Football (Welsh Boys' Clubs cap as goalkeeper)
Other sports followed: Football ('all Welsh football clubs'), rugby (Neath and Maesteg)
Injuries: Out for one game with cricked neck; for one game with back spasm
Relaxations: Watching television, music, DIY, motor mechanics, 'a quiet pint'
Extras: Joint highest wicket-taker in English first-class cricket 1989 with 94 wickets and took most (92) in 1993. Sister Lynda has played for Great Britain at hockey. Players' Player of the Year and Glamorgan Player of the Year 1993. One of *Wisden*'s Five Cricketers of the Year 1994. Began Glamorgan's match v Notts at Colwyn Bay 1999 with a spell of 5-0 off 17 balls, passing 800 first-class wickets in the process
Opinions on cricket: 'Enough tinkering with the structure. Now is the time to let the changes work and produce more quality rather than quantity.'
Best batting: 41 Glamorgan v Worcestershire, Worcester 1992
Best bowling: 8-59 Glamorgan v Warwickshire, Edgbaston 1988

1999 Season

	M	Inns	NO	Runs	HS	Avge	100s	50s	Ct	St	O	M	Runs	Wkts	Avge	Best	5wI	10wM
Test																		
All First	15	19	9	86	16 *	8.60	-	-	7	-	421.3	121	1087	43	25.27	6-75	3	-
1-day Int																		
NatWest	3	2	1	0	0 *	0.00	-	-	1	-	29	4	117	2	58.50	1-31	-	
B & H																		
1-day Lge	13	7	3	10	5	2.50	-	-	2	-	103.3	17	401	21	19.09	3-15	-	

Career Performances

	M	Inns	NO	Runs	HS	Avge	100s	50s	Ct	St	Balls	Runs	Wkts	Avge	Best	5wl	10wM
Test	3	5	0	25	13	5.00	-	-	1	-	534	305	11	27.72	4-65	-	-
All First	238	267	96	1724	41	10.08	-	-	65	-	46861	22724	811	28.01	8-59	28	4
1-day Int	4	2	0	4	4	2.00	-	-	-	-	221	193	7	27.57	4-49	-	
NatWest	32	15	5	53	13	5.30	-	-	3	-	2058	1090	43	25.34	4-26	-	
B & H	37	21	11	89	15	8.90	-	-	8	-	2133	1417	48	29.52	4-31	-	
1-day Lge	146	60	22	262	31 *	6.89	-	-	23	-	6433	4603	177	26.00	5-23	1	

WATKINSON, M. Lancashire

Name: Michael Watkinson
Role: Right-hand bat, right-arm
medium or off-spin bowler
Born: 1 August 1961, Westhoughton
Height: 6ft 1½in **Weight:** 13st
Nickname: Winker
County debut: 1982
County cap: 1987
Benefit: 1996 (£209,000)
Test debut: 1995
Tests: 4
One-Day Internationals: 1
1000 runs in a season: 1
50 wickets in a season: 7
1st-Class 50s: 50
1st-Class 100s: 11
1st-Class 5 w. in innings: 27
1st-Class 10 w. in match: 3
1st-Class catches: 156
One-Day 100s: 2
One-Day 5 w. in innings: 3

Place in batting averages: 115th av. 28.75 (1998 109th av. 28.90)
Place in bowling averages: 116th av. 34.41 (1998 112th av. 33.72)
Strike rate: 68.50 (career 64.69)
Parents: Albert and Marian
Wife and date of marriage: Susan, 12 April 1986
Children: Charlotte, 24 February 1989; Liam, 27 July 1991
Education: Rivington and Blackrod High School, Horwich
Qualifications: 8 O-levels, HTC Civil Engineering
Career outside cricket: Draughtsman
Overseas tours: England to South Africa 1995-96

Cricketers particularly admired: Clive Lloyd, Imran Khan
Other sports followed: Football
Relaxations: Watching Bolton Wanderers
Extras: Played for Cheshire in Minor Counties Championship and in NatWest Trophy (v Middlesex) 1982. Man of the Match in the first Refuge Assurance Cup final 1988 and in B&H Cup final 1990. Resigned the Lancashire captaincy during the 1997-98 off-season. Scored maiden NatWest 100 (130) v Hertfordshire at Radlett 1999. 2nd XI captain and coach for 2000
Best batting: 161 Lancashire v Essex, Old Trafford 1995
Best bowling: 8-30 Lancashire v Hampshire, Old Trafford 1994

1999 Season

	M	Inns	NO	Runs	HS	Avge	100s	50s	Ct	St	O	M	Runs	Wkts	Avge	Best	5wI	10wM
Test																		
All First	8	13	1	345	116	28.75	1	-	4	-	137	30	413	12	34.41	3-43	-	-
1-day Int																		
NatWest	3	3	0	159	130	53.00	1	-	-	-	21	1	96	3	32.00	2-44	-	
B & H	1	1	0	10	10	10.00	-	-	-	-	9	0	45	1	45.00	1-45	-	
1-day Lge	11	10	0	194	49	19.40	-	-	3	-	53	5	187	9	20.77	3-25	-	

Career Performances

	M	Inns	NO	Runs	HS	Avge	100s	50s	Ct	St	Balls	Runs	Wkts	Avge	Best	5wI	10wM
Test	4	6	1	167	82 *	33.40	-	1	1	-	672	348	10	34.80	3-64	-	-
All First	308	459	49	10939	161	26.68	11	50	156	-	47806	24960	739	33.77	8-30	27	3
1-day Int	1	0	0	0	0	-	-	-	-	-	54	43	0	-	-	-	
NatWest	46	40	7	1064	130	32.24	1	7	12	-	2681	1751	46	38.06	3-14	-	
B & H	72	52	12	829	76	20.72	-	4	22	-	3710	2610	87	30.00	5-44	2	
1-day Lge	233	187	38	3220	121	21.61	1	9	58	-	8586	6991	222	31.49	5-46	1	

WATSON, J. D.   Kent

Name: James David Watson
Role: Right-hand bat, right-arm fast bowler
Born: 21 April 1981, Ashford, Kent
Height: 6ft 7in **Weight:** 18st 7lbs
Nickname: Watto
County debut: No first-team appearance
Parents: David and Caroline
Marital status: Single
Family links with cricket: Grandfather Watson comes from famous Watson cricketing family of Hertfordshire. Father played Kent League cricket for Ashford and Wye CC.

Grandfather Ireland played for Thornton
Heath in the Surrey Championship
Education: Willesborough Junior School;
Sutton Valence School
Qualifications: 5 GCSEs, 2 A-levels
Off-season: Playing for Sutherland CC,
Sydney, Australia
Overseas tours: Kent U14 to Holland 1993;
Sutton Valence to Barbados 1997
Cricketers particularly admired:
Viv Richards, Richard Hadlee
Young players to look out for: 'My brother
Alex', Leo Taylor
Other sports played: Rugby (school 1st
XV), hockey (school 1st XI)
Other sports followed: Football (Arsenal)
Relaxations: Music, reading
Extras: U17 Kent county cap. Number of
club awards. Played in Kent 2nd XI AON Trophy winning side
Opinions on cricket: 'Should be a Test match league.'

WEEKES, P. N.   Middlesex

Name: Paul Nicholas Weekes
Role: Left-hand bat, off-spin bowler
Born: 8 July 1969, Hackney, London
Height: 5ft 10in **Weight:** 12st 10lbs
Nickname: Weekesy, Twiddles
County debut: 1990
County cap: 1993
1000 runs in a season: 1
1st-Class 50s: 29
1st-Class 100s: 10
1st-Class 5 w. in innings: 3
1st-Class catches: 123
One-Day 100s: 3
Place in batting averages: 73rd av. 34.50
(1998 28th av. 43.00)
Place in bowling averages: 128th av. 38.69
(1998 140th av. 54.00)
Strike rate: 82.47 (career 87.39)
Parents: Robert and Carol
Marital status: 'Partner Christine'

Children: Cherie, 4 September 1993; Shyann, 3 May 1998
Family links with cricket: Father played club cricket
Education: Homerton House Secondary School, Hackney; Hackney College
Qualifications: 3 O-levels, NCA and senior cricket coach
Career outside cricket: Coach for Middlesex MCB
Overseas tours: England A to India 1994-95; BWIA to Trinidad 1999
Overseas teams played for: Newcastle University, NSW 1989; Sunrise, Zimbabwe 1990
Cricketers particularly admired: Courtney Walsh
Young players to look out for: Stephen Peters
Other sports played: 'Try to play football. Best goal-hanger in the country – strike rate fantastic'
Other sports followed: Boxing
Relaxations: 'Don't get much time to relax. If possible, listening to music; having a good time with friends'
Extras: Scored 50 in debut innings for both 2nd and 1st teams. Took two catches whilst appearing as 12th man for England in the second Test against West Indies at Lord's in 1995. Scored unbeaten century for Middlesex v South Africans in 1999 World Cup warm-up match
Opinions on cricket: 'The game needs to be televised more. Needs more games under lights; something to boost the interest of youngsters.'
Best batting: 171* Middlesex v Somerset, Uxbridge 1996
Best bowling: 8-39 Middlesex v Glamorgan, Lord's 1996

1999 Season

	M	Inns	NO	Runs	HS	Avge	100s	50s	Ct	St	O	M	Runs	Wkts	Avge	Best	5wI	10wM
Test																		
All First	16	28	4	828	140 *	34.50	1	6	19	-	316.1	68	890	23	38.69	4-50	-	-
1-day Int																		
NatWest	1	1	0	6	6	6.00	-	-	-	-	10	0	43	3	14.33	3-43	-	
B & H																		
1-day Lge	16	15	1	299	80	21.35	-	1	9	-	114	4	564	18	31.33	4-43	-	

Career Performances

	M	Inns	NO	Runs	HS	Avge	100s	50s	Ct	St	Balls	Runs	Wkts	Avge	Best	5wI	10wM
Test																	
All First	135	211	24	6156	171 *	32.91	10	29	123	-	13633	6497	156	41.64	8-39	3	-
1-day Int																	
NatWest	16	16	2	417	143 *	29.78	2	1	4	-	911	649	19	34.15	3-35	-	
B & H	31	28	6	723	77	32.86	-	5	9	-	1400	1009	28	36.03	3-32	-	
1-day Lge	138	115	15	2502	119 *	25.02	1	11	57	-	4744	4042	147	27.49	4-29	-	

WELCH, G.   Warwickshire

Name: Graeme Welch
Role: Right-hand bat, right-arm medium-fast bowler
Born: 21 March 1972, County Durham
Height: 6ft **Weight:** 13st
Nickname: Pop
County debut: 1992 (one-day), 1994 (first-class)
50 wickets in a season: 1
1st-Class 50s: 7
1st-Class 5 w. in innings: 4
1st-Class 10 w. in match: 1
1st-Class catches: 29
Place in batting averages: 185th av. 21.73 (1998 198th av. 19.52)
Place in bowling averages: 94th av. 29.90 (1998 128th av. 39.84)
Strike rate: 52.16 (career 56.37)
Parents: Jean and Robert
Wife and date of marriage: Emma, 4 October 1997
Family links with cricket: Father Robert plays club cricket in Durham. Brother Barrie plays club cricket in Leeds
Education: Hetton Primary; Hetton Comprehensive
Qualifications: 9 GCSEs, City & Guilds in Sports and Leisure, senior coaching award
Career outside cricket: 'Anything'
Overseas tours: Warwickshire to Cape Town 1992 and 1993
Overseas teams played for: Avendale, Cape Town 1991-93; Wellington Collegians 1994-95; Johnsonville CC, New Zealand 1995-96; Wellington 1997
Cricketers particularly admired: Allan Donald, Andy Moles, Brian Lara, Dominic Ostler, Tim Munton
Young players to look out for: Mark Wagh, Tony Frost
Other sports played: Football, 'PlayStation'
Other sports followed: Football (Newcastle United)
Relaxations: 'Few beers in "The Brook". Playing PlayStation. Spending time with wife Emma'
Extras: Played for England YC v Australian YC 1991. Has taken two hat-tricks in the 2nd XI against Durham in 1992 and against Worcestershire. Axa Equity and Law Winner's Medal 1994. Britannic Assurance Winner's Medal 1994. Warwickshire's most improved player in 1994. Played for an England XI in the Cricket Max tournament in New Zealand in 1997-98
Best batting: 84* Warwickshire v Nottinghamshire, Edgbaston 1994
Best bowling: 6-115 Warwickshire v Lancashire, Blackpool 1997

1999 Season

	M	Inns	NO	Runs	HS	Avge	100s	50s	Ct	St	O	M	Runs	Wkts	Avge	Best	5wl	10wM
Test																		
All First	14	21	6	326	48 *	21.73	-	-	5	-	269.3	45	927	31	29.90	5-47	1	-
1-day Int																		
NatWest	2	2	0	10	9	5.00	-	-	-	-	16	2	68	1	68.00	1-34	-	
B & H	2	1	0	1	1	1.00	-	-	-	-	11.1	1	61	3	20.33	2-28	-	
1-day Lge	12	11	3	208	71	26.00	-	1	3	-	75.4	8	379	11	34.45	2-15	-	

Career Performances

	M	Inns	NO	Runs	HS	Avge	100s	50s	Ct	St	Balls	Runs	Wkts	Avge	Best	5wl	10wM
Test																	
All First	71	101	17	1779	84 *	21.17	-	7	29	-	10204	5672	181	31.33	6-115	4	1
1-day Int																	
NatWest	13	9	2	87	25	12.42	-	-	-	-	678	370	9	41.11	4-31	-	
B & H	21	15	4	212	55 *	19.27	-	1	1	-	883	695	20	34.75	3-20	-	
1-day Lge	62	47	19	653	71	23.32	-	2	12	-	2137	1736	44	39.45	3-37	-	

WELLS, A. P.   Kent

Name: Alan Peter Wells
Role: Right-hand bat, right-arm medium bowler
Born: 2 October 1961, Newhaven
Height: 6ft **Weight:** 13st 3lbs
Nickname: Godfrey – 'the really old one in *Dad's Army*!'
County debut: 1981 (Sussex), 1997 (Kent)
County cap: 1986 (Sussex), 1997 (Kent)
Benefit: 1995 (Sussex)
Test debut: 1995
Tests: 1
One-Day Internationals: 1
1000 runs in a season: 11
1st-Class 50s: 99
1st-Class 100s: 45
1st-Class 200s: 1
1st-Class catches: 224
One-Day 100s: 8
Place in batting averages: 84th av. 32.66 (1998 120th av. 27.36)
Strike rate: (career 115.30)

Parents: Ernest William Charles and Eunice Mae

Wife and date of marriage: Melanie Elizabeth, 26 September 1987

Children: Luke William Peter, 29 December 1990; Daniel Allan Christian, 24 June 1995

Family links with cricket: Father, Billy, played for many years for local club and had trial for Sussex. Eldest brother Ray plays club cricket; brother Colin played for Sussex, Derbyshire and Somerset and is now cricket manager at Derbyshire

Education: Tideway Comprehensive, Newhaven

Qualifications: 5 O-levels, NCA coaching certificate

Career outside cricket: Family packaging business

Overseas tours: Unofficial England XI to South Africa 1989-90; England A to South Africa 1993-94, to India 1994-95 (captain)

Overseas teams played for: Border, South Africa 1981-82

Cricketers particularly admired: Graham Gooch

Young players to look out for: James Hockley

Other sports followed: Football (Tottenham Hotspur)

Injuries: Out for 10-12 weeks – knee operation

Relaxations: Good wine, cooking, spending time with family, reading books and articles on wine

Extras: Played for England YC v India 1981. Banned from Test cricket for five years in 1990 for joining tour of South Africa; suspension remitted in 1992. Scored a century in each of his first two matches as acting-captain of Sussex and won both matches. Won top batting award for Sussex 1989-93, 'much to David Smith's annoyance'. Vice-captain on England A tour to South Africa 1993-94 and captain for the highly successful tour to India 1994-95. Scored a century in both innings against Kent at Hove in 1995, the first Sussex player to do so since C.B. Fry. This was followed by a pair against Glamorgan at Swansea ('Funny old game!'). Left Sussex after 15 years during the 1996-97 off-season and joined Kent in 1997. Struck six sixes off successive deliveries v Durham in the AXA League at Canterbury 1998, of which five came from an over by Jon Lewis

Opinions on cricket: 'Everyone saw how the two-divisional structure improved the competitiveness of the first-class game right up until the last day of the season. Perhaps in future the powers be will move and change things quicker when something as obvious as two divisions is going to improve our game. How long will it be before they reduce the amount of cricket played by reducing the number of counties? Another decade? When will they centrally employ groundsmen? Wickets will not improve until they do. This will always hinder our chances at Test level.'

Best batting: 253* Sussex v Yorkshire, Middlesbrough 1991

Best bowling: 3-67 Sussex v Worcestershire, Worcester 1987

1999 Season

	M	Inns	NO	Runs	HS	Avge	100s	50s	Ct	St	O	M	Runs	Wkts	Avge	Best	5wI	10wM
Test																		
All First	10	15	0	490	111	32.66	2	1	1	-								
1-day Int																		
NatWest																		
B & H																		
1-day Lge	2	2	0	41	23	20.50	-	-	-	-								

Career Performances

	M	Inns	NO	Runs	HS	Avge	100s	50s	Ct	St	Balls	Runs	Wkts	Avge	Best	5wI	10wM
Test	1	2	1	3	3 *	3.00	-	-	-	-							
All First	364	609	79	20802	253 *	39.24	46	99	224	-	1153	820	10	82.00	3-67	-	-
1-day Int	1	1	0	15	15	15.00	-	-	-	-							
NatWest	37	34	7	1038	119	38.44	3	5	13	-	6	1	0	-		-	-
B & H	67	63	8	1667	111 *	30.30	1	14	17	-	60	72	3	24.00	1-17	-	
1-day Lge	246	226	26	6121	127	30.60	4	36	72	-	62	69	4	17.25	1-0	-	

WELLS, C. M. Derbyshire

Name: Colin Mark Wells
Role: Right-hand bat, right-arm medium bowler
Born: 3 March 1960, Newhaven
Height: 6ft **Weight:** 13st
Nickname: Bomber, Dougie
County debut: 1979 (Sussex), 1994 (Derbyshire)
County cap: 1982 (Sussex)
Benefit: 1993 (Sussex; £50,353)
One-Day Internationals: 2
1000 runs in a season: 6
50 wickets in a season: 2
1st-Class 50s: 67
1st-Class 100s: 24
1st-Class 200s: 1
1st-Class 5 w. in innings: 7
1st-Class catches: 110
One-Day 100s: 4
Strike rate: (career 73.03)
Parents: Ernest William Charles and Eunice Mae

Marital status: Divorced
Children: Jessica Louise, 2 October 1987
Family links with cricket: Father, Billy, had trials for Sussex and played for Sussex Cricket Association. Elder brother Ray plays club cricket and younger brother Alan was captain of Sussex and now plays for Kent
Education: Tideway Comprehensive School, Newhaven
Qualifications: 9 O-levels, 2 CSEs, 1 A-level, senior coaching award
Overseas tours: England to Sharjah 1984-85
Overseas teams played for: Border, South Africa 1980-81; Western Province, South Africa 1984-85
Other sports followed: Football, rugby, hockey, basketball, tennis, table tennis
Relaxations: Sea-angling, philately, listening to music
Extras: Played in three John Player League matches in 1978. Was recommended to Sussex by former Sussex player Ian Thomson. Appointed vice-captain of Sussex in 1988 and captain in 1992. Joined Derbyshire in 1994 but left at the end of the 1996 season to become 2nd XI coach at Somerset. Is now cricket manager at Derbyshire but played one National League game in 1999 because of injuries to current players
Best batting: 203 Sussex v Hampshire, Hove 1984
Best bowling: 7-42 Sussex v Derbyshire, Derby 1991

1999 Season

	M	Inns	NO	Runs	HS	Avge	100s	50s	Ct	St	O	M	Runs	Wkts	Avge	Best	5wI	10wM
Test																		
All First																		
1-day Int																		
NatWest																		
B & H																		
1-day Lge	1	0	0	0	0	-	-	-	1	-	4	0	7	2	3.50	2-7	-	

Career Performances

	M	Inns	NO	Runs	HS	Avge	100s	50s	Ct	St	Balls	Runs	Wkts	Avge	Best	5wI	10wM
Test																	
All First	318	510	78	14289	203	33.07	24	67	112	-	31197	14748	428	34.45	7-42	7	-
1-day Int	2	2	0	22	17	11.00	-	-	-	-							
NatWest	37	30	4	545	76	20.96	-	2	8	-	1737	855	22	38.86	3-16	-	
B & H	60	57	8	1442	117	29.42	3	5	13	-	2148	1390	44	31.59	4-21	-	
1-day Lge	217	188	30	4102	104 *	25.96	1	21	54	-	7329	4812	158	30.45	4-15	-	

WELLS, V. J.   Leicestershire

Name: Vincent John Wells
Role: Right-hand bat, right-arm medium
bowler, occasional wicket-keeper,
county captain
Born: 6 August 1965, Dartford
Height: 6ft **Weight:** 13st 7lbs
Nickname: Vinny, Both
County debut: 1987 (Kent),
1992 (Leicestershire)
County cap: 1994 (Leicestershire)
One-Day Internationals: 9
1000 runs in a season: 2
1st-Class 50s: 35
1st-Class 100s: 11
1st-Class 200s: 3
1st-Class 5 w. in innings: 3
1st-Class catches: 98
One-Day 100s: 3
One-Day 200s: 1
One-Day 5 w. in innings: 2
Place in batting averages: 85th av. 32.66 (1998 56th av. 36.34)
Place in bowling averages: 142nd av. 47.30 (1998 2nd av. 14.27)
Strike rate: 105.60 (career 53.70)
Parents: Pat and Jack
Wife and date of marriage: Deborah Louise, 14 October 1989
Children: Harrison John, 25 January 1995; Molly Louise, 2 June 1996
Family links with cricket: Brother plays Kent league cricket
Education: Downs School, Dartford; Sir William Nottidge School, Whitstable
Qualifications: 1 O-level, 8 CSEs, junior and senior coaching certificates
Off-season: 'Having a break; maybe some cricket after Christmas'
Overseas tours: Leicestershire to Jamaica 1993, to Bloemfontein 1994 and 1995,
to Western Transvaal 1996, to Durban 1997, to Barbados 1998; England to Australia
(CUB Series) 1998-99, to Sharjah (Coca-Cola Cup) 1998-99
Overseas teams played for: Parnell, Auckland 1986; Avendale, Cape Town 1986-89,
1990-91; Potchefstroom University, North West Transvaal 1996-97; Cornwall CC,
Auckland 1998-99
Cricketers particularly admired: Phil Simmons, James Whitaker, Robin Smith,
Mike Kasprowicz
Young players to look out for: James Ormond
Other sports followed: Most sports especially football
Injuries: Out for a total of 15 days with injuries to eye and neck

Relaxations: 'Spending time with family, pint of Guinness and good food'
Extras: Was a schoolboy footballer with Leyton Orient. Scored 100 not out on
NatWest debut v Oxfordshire. Left Kent at the end of 1991 season to join
Leicestershire. Missed 1992 NatWest final owing to viral infection. Hat-trick against
Durham, 1994. Scored 201 not out against Berkshire in the 1996 NatWest Trophy.
Was selected to represent England in the cancelled World Super Max 8s originally
scheduled to take place in Perth in October 1998. Member of England's 1999 World
Cup squad. Appointed captain of Leicestershire during 1999 season after retirement of
James Whitaker
Opinions on cricket: 'Wickets need to improve greatly to encourage batters to play
longer innings and also make the bowlers do more with the ball to get their wickets, as
in Test cricket. Perhaps abolish toss of coin and let opposing captain have choice to try
and promote good pitches, or all groundsmen employed by ECB. Pitches a big worry
with promotion and relegation as they may become even worse.'
Best batting: 224 Leicestershire v Middlesex, Lord's 1997
Best bowling: 5-18 Leicestershire v Nottinghamshire, Worksop 1998

1999 Season

	M	Inns	NO	Runs	HS	Avge	100s	50s	Ct	St	O	M	Runs	Wkts	Avge	Best	5wI	10wM
Test																		
All First	13	20	2	588	109 *	32.66	2	3	13	-	176	47	473	10	47.30	2-2	-	-
1-day Int																		
NatWest	2	2	0	110	84	55.00	-	1	-	-	17	0	63	3	21.00	2-23	-	
B & H	1	1	0	17	17	17.00	-	-	1	-	9	0	39	1	39.00	1-39	-	
1-day Lge	13	13	0	195	43	15.00	-	-	3	-	68.4	3	293	8	36.62	2-19	-	

Career Performances

	M	Inns	NO	Runs	HS	Avge	100s	50s	Ct	St	Balls	Runs	Wkts	Avge	Best	5wI	10wM
Test																	
All First	145	227	18	7159	224	34.25	14	35	98	-	11814	5838	220	26.53	5-18	3	-
1-day Int	9	7	0	141	39	20.14	-	-	7	-	220	189	8	23.62	3-30	-	
NatWest	19	18	4	593	201	42.35	2	2	1	-	845	505	22	22.95	3-30	-	
B & H	36	30	3	664	90	24.59	-	3	12	-	1510	1100	38	28.94	6-25	1	
1-day Lge	121	115	12	2609	101	25.33	2	10	27	-	3820	3022	107	28.24	5-10	1	

WELTON, G. E.   Nottinghamshire

Name: Guy Edward Welton
Role: Right-hand opening bat
Born: 4 May 1978, Grimsby
Height: 6ft 1in   **Weight:** 13st 7lbs
Nickname: Trigger, Giggs, Welts
County debut: 1997
1st-Class 50s: 3
1st-Class catches: 8
One-Day 100s: 1
Place in batting averages: 205th av. 19.75
(1998 225th av. 16.88)
Parents: Robert and Diana
Marital status: Single
Family links with cricket: Father is a
qualified cricket coach and keen club
cricketer

Education: Keelby Primary; Healing
Comprehensive; Grimsby College of
Technology; Nottingham Trent University
Qualifications: 9 GCSEs, BTEC in Business and Finance, senior level cricket coach
Off-season: Studying for BA (Hons) Humanities; working on fitness and technique
Overseas tours: England U17 to Holland 1995; Nottinghamshire to South Africa 1998
Overseas teams played for: Randfontein CC, Johannesburg, South Africa 1996-97;
Willetton CC, Perth, Western Australia 1997-98; Coolbinia CC, Perth 1998-99
Cricketers particularly admired: David Gower, Viv Richards, Steve Waugh,
Sachin Tendulkar, Mark Lavender
Young players to look out for: Scott Meuleman, Shane Lavender
Other sports played: Football ('youth trainee at Grimsby Town Football Club 1994-96')
Injuries: Out for four weeks with a cracked rib; for two weeks with a fractured hand
Relaxations: Music and going to the gym
Extras: Completed a two-year YTS with Grimsby Town Football Club where he made
one first-team appearance as a substitute. Played cricket for England U14, U15 and
U17. Won the Lord's Taverners' Young Player Award in 1993 and was MCC Young
Cricketer from 1994-95. Was 12th man for England at Lord's and The Oval against
West Indies in 1995
Opinions on cricket: 'The elite players need to be segregated into a smaller
competition (maybe the divisional structure will do this) and less cricket should be
played.'
Best batting: 95 Nottinghamshire v Sussex, Hove 1997

1999 Season

	M	Inns	NO	Runs	HS	Avge	100s	50s	Ct	St	O	M	Runs	Wkts	Avge	Best	5wI	10wM
Test																		
All First	9	17	1	316	76	19.75	-	1	4	-								
1-day Int																		
NatWest																		
B & H																		
1-day Lge	9	9	1	201	104 *	25.12	1	-	2	-								

Career Performances

	M	Inns	NO	Runs	HS	Avge	100s	50s	Ct	St	Balls	Runs	Wkts	Avge	Best	5wI	10wM
Test																		
All First	20	37	1	763	95	21.19	-	3	8	-								
1-day Int																		
NatWest																		
B & H																		
1-day Lge	15	15	1	299	104 *	21.35	1	1	4	-								

WESTON, R. M. S.   Middlesex

Name: Robin Michael Swann Weston
Role: Right-hand bat, leg-break bowler
Born: 7 June 1975, Durham
Height: 6ft **Weight:** 12st 6lbs
County debut: 1995 (Durham);
1998 (Derbyshire)
1st-Class 50s: 6
1st-Class 100s: 3
1st-Class catches: 25
Place in batting averages: 71st av. 34.91
(1998 87th av. 31.58)
Strike rate: 36.00 (career 93.50)
Parents: Michael Philip and Kathleen Mary
Marital status: Single
Family links with cricket: Father played for
Durham (and played rugby union for
England); brother Philip plays for
Worcestershire
Education: Bow School; Durham School; Loughborough University
Qualifications: 10 GCSEs, 4 A-levels, degree in Economics with Accountancy, basic
cricket coaching certificate

Overseas tours: England U18 to South Africa 1992-93, to Denmark 1993; England U19 to Sri Lanka 1993-94

Overseas teams played for: Fremantle, Western Australia 1996-98

Cricketers particularly admired: 'Anyone at the highest level'

Young players to look out for: Kevin Dean, Melvyn Betts

Other sports played: Golf, rugby union (Loughborough Students 1994-96, England U18 1993)

Other sports followed: Football (Sunderland AFC)

Relaxations: Most sports, listening to music and socialising with friends

Extras: Became youngest to play for Durham 1st XI, in Minor Counties competition, aged 15 in 1991. Played rugby for England U18. Released by Durham at the end of the 1997 season and joined Derbyshire. Scored maiden first-class century v Essex at Chelmsford 1999 and followed up with centuries in the next two Championship matches. Left Derbyshire at the end of 1999 season and has joined Middlesex for 2000

Opinions on cricket: 'Structure the season so that teams play no more than four Championship games without a decent rest (four to five days). That way people will stay fitter and still play the same number of games.'

Best batting: 156 Derbyshire v Somerset, Derby 1999

Best bowling: 1-15 Derbyshire v Hampshire, Derby 1999

1999 Season

	M	Inns	NO	Runs	HS	Avge	100s	50s	Ct	St	O	M	Runs	Wkts	Avge	Best	5wI	10wM
Test																		
All First	15	26	2	838	156	34.91	3	2	9	-	6	1	23	1	23.00	1-15	-	-
1-day Int																		
NatWest	2	2	0	2	2	1.00	-	-	-	-								
B & H																		
1-day Lge	13	12	1	277	56	25.18	-	2	2	-								

Career Performances

	M	Inns	NO	Runs	HS	Avge	100s	50s	Ct	St	Balls	Runs	Wkts	Avge	Best	5wI	10wM
Test																	
All First	35	62	2	1556	156	25.93	3	6	25	-	187	104	2	52.00	1-15	-	-
1-day Int																	
NatWest	6	6	1	103	56	20.60	-	1	1	-							
B & H																	
1-day Lge	22	21	2	408	56	21.47	-	2	4	-							

WESTON, W. P. C.   Worcestershire

Name: William Philip Christopher Weston
Role: Left-hand bat, left-arm medium bowler
Born: 16 June 1973, Durham
Height: 6ft 4in **Weight:** 14st
Nickname: Sven, Junior, Reverend
County debut: 1991
County cap: 1995
1000 runs in a season: 3
1st-Class 50s: 35
1st-Class 100s: 14
1st-Class 200s: 1
1st-Class catches: 70
One-Day 100s: 1
Place in batting averages: 138th av. 26.38
(1998 105th av. 29.60)
Strike rate: (career 229.75)
Parents: Michael Philip and Kathleen Mary
Marital status: Engaged to Sarah

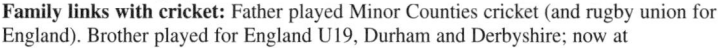

Family links with cricket: Father played Minor Counties cricket (and rugby union for England). Brother played for England U19, Durham and Derbyshire; now at Middlesex
Education: Bow School, Durham; Durham School
Qualifications: 9 GCSEs, 4 A-levels, NCA coaching award
Off-season: 'Working as a coach for the club – travelling into schools in the county'
Overseas tours: England U18 to Canada 1991; England YC to New Zealand 1990-91; England U19 to Pakistan 1991-92 (captain); Worcestershire to Zimbabwe 1996
Overseas teams played for: Melville, Perth 1992-94 and 1996-97; Swanbourne, Perth 1995-96
Cricketers particularly admired: 'Everyone who makes the most of their talent'
Young players to look out for: Vikram Solanki, Depesh Patel
Other sports followed: Rugby union, football (Sunderland AFC)
Injuries: Out for a total of 13 weeks with torn ankle ligaments
Relaxations: 'Socialising, travelling, spending time with my girlfriend; films, sport'
Extras: Scored century for England YC v Australian YC 1991. Was appointed captain of England U19 for their tour to Pakistan 1991-92 and told by Keble College, Oxford, that he would not be accepted if he decided to tour; he chose to sacrifice his place at Oxford. Downing College, Cambridge, offered him a place the following year, but by then he was so disillusioned with universities that he turned down the offer and decided to concentrate on his cricket. Played for Northants 2nd XI and Worcs 2nd XI in 1989. Cricket Society's Most Promising Young Cricketer 1992. Worcestershire Uncapped Player of the Year 1992. Member of Whittingdale Fringe Squad 1993. In

1999, returned from eight weeks out with injury to score 100s in two consecutive Championship matches

Opinions on cricket: 'County cricket does not need a major upheaval, but attitudes do. People need to realise that the pitches on which we play and, just as importantly, train must be of the highest quality to allow both batters and bowlers to develop as well as they need to to reach the highest level. Talk is cheap – action is long overdue. Centrally employ groundsmen if necessary!'

Best batting: 205 Worcestershire v Northamptonshire, Northampton 1997
Best bowling: 2-39 Worcestershire v Pakistanis, Worcester 1992

1999 Season

	M	Inns	NO	Runs	HS	Avge	100s	50s	Ct	St	O	M	Runs	Wkts	Avge	Best	5wl	10wM
Test																		
All First	11	21	0	554	157	26.38	2	1	3	-								
1-day Int																		
NatWest																		
B & H																		
1-day Lge	8	7	0	184	125	26.28	1	-	1	-								

Career Performances

	M	Inns	NO	Runs	HS	Avge	100s	50s	Ct	St	Balls	Runs	Wkts	Avge	Best	5wl	10wM
Test																	
All First	134	234	23	7416	205	35.14	15	35	70	-	919	599	4	149.75	2-39	-	-
1-day Int																	
NatWest	8	8	0	103	31	12.87	-	-	1	-							
B & H	21	20	2	234	54 *	13.00	-	1	9	-							
1-day Lge	72	60	8	1242	125	23.88	1	4	14	-	6	2	1	2.00	1-2	-	

WHARF, A. G.   Glamorgan

Name: Alexander George Wharf
Role: Right-hand bat, right-arm fast-medium bowler, all-rounder
Born: 4 June 1975, Bradford
Height: 6ft 4in **Weight:** 15st 7lbs
Nickname: Gangster, River
County debut: 1994 (Yorks), 1998 (Notts)
1st-Class 50s: 3
1st-Class catches: 16
Place in batting averages: 235th av. 16.08
Place in bowling averages: 131st av. 39.22
Strike rate: 64.93 (career 64.03)

Parents: Derek and Jane
Marital status: Lives with partner
Children: Tristan Jack Busfield Wharf, 15 November 1997
Family links with cricket: Father played local league cricket
Education: Marshfields First School; Preistman Middle School; Buttershaw Upper School; Thomas Danby College
Qualifications: 6 GCSEs, City and Guilds in Sports Management, NCA coaching award, junior football coaching award
Career outside cricket: 'Not really known but working on it!'
Off-season: 'Having a good break, then back to it; training; spending time with family'
Overseas tours: Varous pre-season tours with Yorkshire and Notts, including Yorkshire to Cape Town 1994-95, to Guernsey 1996

Overseas teams played for: Somerset West, Cape Town 1993-95; Johnsonville CC, Wellington, New Zealand 1996-97; Universities, Wellington 1998-99
Cricketers particularly admired: Ian Botham, Steve Waugh, Glenn McGrath, Vasbert Drakes
Young players to look out for: David Lucas, Guy Welton
Other sports played: Football
Other sports followed: Football (Manchester United)
Injuries: Out for two weeks with a side strain
Relaxations: 'Relaxing with family; watching the little one grow'
Extras: Attended Dennis Lillee coaching school, Madras, during winter 1997-98. Scored 78 for Notts v Glamorgan at Colwyn Bay 1999, having arrived at the wicket with his side on 9 for 6. Left Nottinghamshire at end of 1999 season and joined Glamorgan for 2000 on a three-year contract
Opinions on cricket: 'I try to keep my opinions to myself and just get on with it!'
Best batting: 78 Nottinghamshire v Glamorgan, Colwyn Bay 1999
Best bowling: 4-29 Yorkshire v Lancashire, Old Trafford 1996

1999 Season

	M	Inns	NO	Runs	HS	Avge	100s	50s	Ct	St	O	M	Runs	Wkts	Avge	Best	5wI	10wM
Test																		
All First	16	26	3	370	78	16.08	-	2	8	-	335.3	65	1216	31	39.22	4-30	-	-
1-day Int																		
NatWest	1	1	0	12	12	12.00	-	-	-	-	8	0	38	0	-		-	-
B & H																		
1-day Lge	14	11	7	175	38 *	43.75	-	-	3	-	95.4	3	489	8	61.12	3-26	-	

Career Performances

	M	Inns	NO	Runs	HS	Avge	100s	50s	Ct	St	Balls	Runs	Wkts	Avge	Best	5wl	10wM
Test																	
All First	28	41	5	564	78	15.66	-	3	16	-	3266	2003	51	39.27	4-29	-	-
1-day Int																	
NatWest	1	1	0	12	12	12.00	-	-	-	-	48	38	0	-		-	-
B & H	6	4	0	48	20	12.00	-	-	2	-	354	321	9	35.66	4-29	-	
1-day Lge	21	15	8	197	38 *	28.14	-	-	4	-	772	655	15	43.66	3-26	-	

WHILEY, M. J. A. Nottinghamshire

Name: Matthew Jeffrey Allen Whiley
Role: Right-hand bat, left-arm
fast bowler
Born: 6 May 1980, Nottingham
Height: 6ft 4in **Weight:** 14st
Nickname: Ding, Shadow, Hank Marvin
County debut: 1998
Strike rate: 72.00 (career 123.00)
Parents: Paul and Barbara
Marital status: Single
Family links with cricket: 'Dad played club
cricket for Notts Harrington CC'
Education: Whitegate Primary School,
Clifton; Harry Carlton Comprehensive
School, East Leake
Qualifications: 8 GCSEs
Career outside cricket: 'None yet'
Off-season: 'Coaching on the Trent Bridge
coaching scheme; Wayne Noon's shadow (Hank Marvin)'
Overseas tours: England U19 to New Zealand 1998-99; Nottinghamshire to
Johannesburg 1999
Overseas teams played for: Manawatu-Foxton CC and Horowhenua District Cricket
Association, both New Zealand 1997-98
Cricketers particularly admired: Shoaib Akhtar, Vasbert Drakes, Paul Franks,
Chris Read, Tim Robinson
Young players to look out for: Stephen Randall, Ian Bell
Other sports followed: Football (Man Utd), rugby (Wellington Hurricanes –
Super 12)
Injuries: Out for three weeks with an Achilles tendon injury
Relaxations: 'Shopping, listening to music, spending time with girlfriend'
Opinions on cricket: 'Central contracts for England players plus an England

Academy for the best youngsters in the country is a must.'
Best bowling: 1-44 Nottinghamshire v Oxford University, The Parks 1999

1999 Season

	M	Inns	NO	Runs	HS	Avge	100s	50s	Ct	St	O	M	Runs	Wkts	Avge	Best	5wI	10wM
Test																		
All First	1	0	0	0	0	-	-	-	-	-	12	3	44	1	44.00	1-44	-	-
1-day Int																		
NatWest																		
B & H																		
1-day Lge																		

Career Performances

	M	Inns	NO	Runs	HS	Avge	100s	50s	Ct	St	Balls	Runs	Wkts	Avge	Best	5wI	10wM
Test																	
All First	2	2	1	0	0 *	0.00	-	-	-	-	246	168	2	84.00	1-44	-	-
1-day Int																	
NatWest																	
B & H																	
1-day Lge																	

WHITAKER, J. J.   Leicestershire

Name: John James Whitaker
Role: Right-hand bat, off-spin bowler
Born: 5 May 1962, Skipton, North Yorkshire
Height: 6ft **Weight:** 13st
Nickname: Jimmy
County debut: 1983
County cap: 1986
Benefit: 1993
Test debut: 1986-87
Tests: 1
One-Day Internationals: 2
1000 runs in a season: 10
1st-Class 50s: 80
1st-Class 100s: 36
1st-Class 200s: 2
1st-Class catches: 172
One-Day 100s: 6
Place in batting averages: 215th av. 18.57

Strike rate: (career 89.00)
Parents: John and Ann
Marital status: Single
Family links with cricket: Father is a local league player
Education: Malsis Hall Prep School, Crosshills, Yorks; Uppingham School, Leics
Qualifications: 7 O-levels
Overseas tours: Uppingham to Australia 1980-81; England to Australia 1986-87, to Sharjah 1987; England A to Zimbabwe and Kenya 1989-90; Hong Kong Sixes 1991, 1992
Overseas teams played for: Glenelg, Australia 1982-83; Old Scotch, Tasmania 1983-84; Somerset West, Cape Town 1984-85
Cricketers particularly admired: Geoff Boycott, Dennis Amiss, Brian Davison, Maurice Hallam
Other sports played: Squash, tennis
Other sports followed: Rugby (Leicester Tigers), football (Leicester City)
Relaxations: Eating out, movies, watching sport
Extras: One of *Wisden*'s Five Cricketers of the Year 1987. Second in batting averages in 1986. Young Cricketer Award jointly in 1986. Appointed Leics captain 1996 and won the Championship twice. Voted the Brian Sellars County Captain of the Year by the Wombwell Cricket Lovers' Society in 1996. His 218 v Yorkshire in 1996 at Bradford was the highest score by a Yorkshireman against his native county. Forced to retire during the 1999 season by persistent knee injury. Appointed manager of 1999-2000 England U19 tour to Malaysia and to Sri Lanka for the Youth World Cup
Opinions on cricket: 'Get better pitches, more practice time, better practice facilities.'
Best batting: 218 Leicestershire v Yorkshire, Bradford 1996
Best bowling: 1-29 Leicestershire v Somerset, Leicester 1992
Stop press: Appointed Leicestershire's secretary and general manager in January 2000

1999 Season

	M	Inns	NO	Runs	HS	Avge	100s	50s	Ct	St	O	M	Runs	Wkts	Avge	Best	5wl	10wM
Test																		
All First	5	7	0	130	44	18.57	-	-	1	-								
1-day Int																		
NatWest																		
B & H																		
1-day Lge																		

Career Performances

	M	Inns	NO	Runs	HS	Avge	100s	50s	Ct	St	Balls	Runs	Wkts	Avge	Best	5wI	10wM
Test	1	1	0	11	11	11.00	-	-	1	-							
All First	315	497	51	17198	218	38.56	38	80	172	-	178	268	2	134.00	1-29	-	-
1-day Int	2	2	1	48	44 *	48.00	-	-	1	-							
NatWest	30	29	2	1077	155	39.88	1	6	1	-	24	9	0	-		-	-
B & H	58	53	3	1490	100	29.80	1	10	10	-							
1-day Lge	184	172	18	5035	132	32.69	4	31	53	-	2	4	0	-		-	-

WHITE, C. Yorkshire

Name: Craig White
Role: Right-hand bat, right-arm
fast-medium bowler, cover fielder
Born: 16 December 1969, Morley, Yorkshire
Height: 6ft 1in **Weight:** 11st 11lbs
Nickname: Chalky, Bassey
County debut: 1990
County cap: 1993
Test debut: 1994
Tests: 8
One-Day Internationals: 15
1st-Class 50s: 33
1st-Class 100s: 8
1st-Class 5 w. in innings: 7
1st-Class catches: 115
One-Day 100s: 2
Place in batting averages: 226th av. 17.96
(1998 44th av. 39.58)
Place in bowling averages: 63rd av. 25.80 (1998 3rd av. 15.64)
Strike rate: 51.80 (career 50.29)
Parents: Fred Emsley and Cynthia Anne
Wife and date of marriage: Elizabeth Anne, 19 September 1992
Family links with cricket: Father played for Pudsey St Lawrence
Education: Kennington Primary; Flora Hill High School; Bendigo Senior High School
(all Victoria, Australia)
Overseas tours: Australian YC to West Indies 1989-90; England A to Pakistan
1995-96, to Australia 1996-97; England to Australia 1994-95, to India and Pakistan
(World Cup) 1995-96, to Zimbabwe and New Zealand 1996-97, to South Africa and
Zimbabwe 1999-2000 (one-day series)
Overseas teams played for: Victoria, Australia 1990-94
Cricketers particularly admired: Graeme Hick, Mark Waugh, Brian Lara

Other sports followed: Leeds RFC, motocross, golf, tennis
Relaxations: Playing guitar, reading, gardening and socialising
Extras: Recommended to Yorkshire by Victorian Cricket Academy, being eligible to play for Yorkshire as he was born in the county. 'Fred Trueman and I are the only Yorkshire players to debut in the 1st XI before the 2nd XI.' Formerly bowled off-spin. Had to fly home from the World Cup in 1995-96 with a side strain and was replaced by Dermot Reeve. After a successful A tour to Australia, called up to England's tour to Zimbabwe and New Zealand in 1996-97 as cover for the injured Ronnie Irani
Best batting: 181 Yorkshire v Lancashire, Headingley 1996
Best bowling: 8-55 Yorkshire v Gloucestershire, Gloucester 1998
Stop press: Called up for one-day series v South Africa and Zimbabwe 1999-2000 after injury to Andrew Flintoff. Took 5-21 and scored 26 in second One-Day International v Zimbabwe at Bulawayo in February 2000, winning the Man of the Match award. Awarded England contract (Band C) for 2000

1999 Season

	M	Inns	NO	Runs	HS	Avge	100s	50s	Ct	St	O	M	Runs	Wkts	Avge	Best	5wl	10wM
Test																		
All First	17	31	2	521	52	17.96	-	1	12	-	354	69	1058	41	25.80	4-32	-	-
1-day Int																		
NatWest	4	4	0	111	50	27.75	-	1	1	-	27	2	112	3	37.33	2-24	-	
B & H	3	3	1	93	55	46.50	-	1	2	-	28	2	122	7	17.42	4-51	-	
1-day Lge	15	15	0	318	67	21.20	-	1	1	-	114.1	18	437	26	16.80	4-25	-	

Career Performances

	M	Inns	NO	Runs	HS	Avge	100s	50s	Ct	St	Balls	Runs	Wkts	Avge	Best	5wl	10wM
Test	8	12	0	166	51	13.83	-	1	3	-	811	452	11	41.09	3-18	-	-
All First	162	250	35	6578	181	30.59	8	33	115	-	13629	7351	271	27.12	8-55	7	-
1-day Int	15	13	0	187	38	14.38	-	-	2	-	608	446	15	29.73	4-37	-	
NatWest	22	19	5	680	113	48.57	1	5	9	-	1007	623	20	31.15	3-38	-	
B & H	31	27	6	474	57 *	22.57	-	2	11	-	1356	1003	32	31.34	4-29	-	
1-day Lge	115	102	14	2206	148	25.06	1	7	36	-	3490	2589	105	24.65	4-18	-	

WHITE, G. W.   Hampshire

Name: Giles William White
Role: Right-hand bat, leg-break bowler
Born: 23 March 1972, Barnstaple, Devon
Height: 6ft **Weight:** 12st
Nickname: Chalky, Chilli
County debut: 1991 (Somerset), 1994 (Hampshire)

County cap: 1998 (Hampshire)
1000 runs in a season: 1
1st-Class 50s: 24
1st-Class 100s: 7
1st-Class catches: 70
Place in batting averages: 105th av. 30.29
(1998 33rd av. 41.75)
Strike rate: 45.20 (career 79.42)
Parents: John and Tina
Marital status: Engaged (Samantha Donald)
Family links with cricket: Father played
club cricket for Exeter CC
Education: Sandford Primary School,
Devon; Exeter Cathedral School; Millfield
School; Loughborough University
Qualifications: 10 O-levels, 3 A-levels,
BA (Hons) Sports Management, Computing
diploma

Career outside cricket: 'Trying to find that out'
Overseas tours: Millfield School to Australia 1989; Hampshire to Anguilla, Cork and
Guernsey
Overseas teams played for: Waverley, Sydney 1990-91; Tigers Parrow, Cape Town
1994-95; Techs Mutual CC, Cape Town 1995-96; Rygersdaal, Cape Town 1996-97;
Waneroo, Perth 1997-98
Cricketers particularly admired: Wayne Larkins, Paul Terry, Cardigan Connor,
Peter Hartley
Young players to look out for: Simon Francis, Derek Kenway, 'Bernard and Dimi'
Other sports played: Golf, football
Other sports followed: Football (Chelsea FC), golf (Fred Couples)
Relaxations: Pubs, restaurants, travelling, painting, money-making schemes
Extras: Hants Exiles Young Player of the Year 1997. Played for Somerset before
joining Hants. 'Beat "The Judge" in "Down a Stella Competition" – Bushwhackers,
Worcs, 1998'
Opinions on cricket: 'Should be a greater/stricter control on the state of wickets.
Surely the purpose of introducing four-day cricket was to play on wickets as close to
Test quality as possible. I know everyone wants a result, but too many of the wickets
have been "shockers". Still think tea should be 30 minutes.'
Best batting: 156 Hampshire v Sri Lanka, Southampton 1998
Best bowling: 3-23 Hampshire v Nottinghamshire, Trent Bridge 1999

1999 Season

	M	Inns	NO	Runs	HS	Avge	100s	50s	Ct	St	O	M	Runs	Wkts	Avge	Best	5wI	10wM
Test																		
All First	16	28	1	818	121	30.29	1	4	11	-	37.4	2	158	5	31.60	3-23	-	-
1-day Int																		
NatWest																		
B & H																		
1-day Lge	13	13	0	223	51	17.15	-	1	4	-								

Career Performances

	M	Inns	NO	Runs	HS	Avge	100s	50s	Ct	St	Balls	Runs	Wkts	Avge	Best	5wI	10wM
Test																	
All First	85	145	11	4425	156	33.02	7	24	70	-	556	398	7	56.85	3-23	-	-
1-day Int																	
NatWest	7	7	0	92	69	13.14	-	1	6	-	72	45	1	45.00	1-45	-	
B & H	12	11	0	187	56	17.00	-	1	1	-							
1-day Lge	64	62	5	1403	76	24.61	-	9	20	-	12	14	0	-		-	-

WHITE, R. A.   Northamptonshire

Name: Robert Allan White
Role: Right-hand bat, occasional
leg-break bowler
Born: 15 October 1979, Chelmsford
Height: 5ft 11in **Weight:** 11st 5lbs
County debut: No first-team appearance
Parents: Dennis and Ann
Marital status: Single
Family links with cricket: 'Dad was keen
club player; grandfather was on Essex
committee'
Education: Spratton Hall; Stowe School; St
John's College, Durham University
Qualifications: 9 GCSEs, 3 A-levels
Off-season: Studying at Durham
Cricketers particularly admired:
Ian Botham, Steve Waugh, Shane Warne,
Sachin Tendulkar
Other sports played: Football, snooker, tennis
Other sports followed: Football (West Ham)
Relaxations: Relaxing with friends

Extras: Northamptonshire County League Young Player of the Year 1999
Opinions on cricket: 'Play too much cricket. Not enough time for quality practice.'

WHITTICASE, P. Leicestershire

Name: Philip Whitticase
Role: Right-hand bat, wicket-keeper
Born: 15 March 1965, Wythall, Birmingham
Height: 5ft 8in **Weight:** 11st
Nickname: Jasper, Tracy, Boggy, Rat
County debut: 1984
County cap: 1987
Benefit: 1997
1st-Class 50s: 17
1st-Class 100s: 1
1st-Class catches: 309
1st-Class stumpings: 14
Parents: Larry Gordon and Ann
Marital status: Single
Family links with cricket: Grandfather and
father played local club cricket (both were
wicket-keepers)
Education: Belle Vue Junior and Middle
School; Buckpool Secondary; Crestwood Comprehensive
Qualifications: 5 O-levels, 4 CSEs, senior coaching certificate
Overseas teams played for: South Bunbury, Western Australia 1983-85
Cricketers particularly admired: Bob Taylor, Alan Knott, Dennis Amiss
Other sports followed: Football, rugby
Relaxations: Playing soccer, watching rugby and 'a good night out'
Extras: Played schoolboy football for Birmingham City. Was Derek Underwood's last
first-class victim. Lost seven teeth after being struck in the mouth by a bouncer from
Neil Williams in Leicestershire's game against Essex in April 1995
Best batting: 114* Leicestershire v Hampshire, Bournemouth 1991

---

95. Which overseas player carried his bat twice for centuries in the
same match for Somerset v Notts at Trent Bridge in 1989?

Career Performances

	M	Inns	NO	Runs	HS	Avge	100s	50s	Ct	St	Balls	Runs	Wkts	Avge	Best	5wI	10wM
Test																	
All First	132	174	40	3113	114 *	23.23	1	17	309	14	5	7	0	-	-	-	-
1-day Int																	
NatWest	13	6	1	67	32	13.40	-	-	14	-							
B & H	29	19	7	313	45	26.08	-	-	29	4							
1-day Lge	69	45	9	413	38	11.47	-	-	56	4							

WIDDUP, S.   Yorkshire

Name: Simon Widdup
Role: Right-hand bat, right-arm bowler,
occasional wicket-keeper
Born: 10 November 1977, Doncaster,
South Yorks
Height: 6ft **Weight:** 11st 11lbs
Nickname: Widds, Posh Spice, Reardo
County debut: No first-team appearance
Parents: Eric and Maggie
Marital status: Single
Family links with cricket: Great uncle
Richard Knowles Tyldesley played for
Lancashire in 1920s and was *Wisden*
Cricketer of the Year 1925
Education: Saltersgate Infants/Middle
School, Doncaster; Ridgewood
Comprehensive School, Doncaster;
Danum Sixth Form School, Doncaster

Qualifications: 11 GCSEs, 1 A-level, Level 1 and 2 coaching awards
Career outside cricket: Barman
Off-season: Playing football and training
Overseas tours: England Schools U15 to South Africa 1993; England U17 to Holland
(ICC Youth Tournament) 1995
Overseas teams played for: Curtin University CC, Perth 1997-98
Cricketers particularly admired: Graeme Hick, Steve Waugh, Gary Fellows
Young players to look out for: John Sadler
Other sports played: Golf (16 handicap)
Other sports followed: Football (Doncaster Rovers FC, Arsenal FC)
Relaxations: 'Music (Stereophonics, Stone Roses), eating out, spending time with my
girlfriend'

Extras: Young *Telegraph* Cricketer of the Year 1992. Set Yorkshire League opening partnership record 1994. Set Yorkshire 2nd XI opening partnership record 1998. Abbot Ale Cup winner with Doncaster Town CC 1998

Opinions on cricket: 'Better pitches for batters to play. Game is bowler-friendly. Need this to improve technique and strokemaking to take into the Test arena.'

WILLIAMS, R. C. J.   Gloucestershire

Name: Richard Charles James Williams
Role: Left-hand bat, wicket-keeper
Born: 8 August 1969, Bristol
Height: 5ft 10in **Weight:** 11st
Nickname: Reg
County debut: 1990
County cap: 1996
1st-Class 50s: 5
1st-Class catches: 97
1st-Class stumpings: 15
Parents: Michael (deceased) and Angela
Marital status: Single
Family links with cricket: Father played local club cricket
Education: Clifton College Preparatory School; Millfield School
Qualifications: PE Diploma, NCA junior coaching award

Overseas tours: Gloucestershire to Namibia 1990, to Kenya 1991, to Sri Lanka 1992-93; Romany CC to Durban & Cape Town 1993; Gloucestershire Gypsies to Zimbabwe 1994-95, to South Africa 1995-96
Overseas teams played for: Manicaland, Zimbabwe 1990-91
Cricketers particularly admired: Andy Brassington, Jack Russell, David Gower
Other sports followed: Football, hockey, squash, snooker
Relaxations: 'Eating out, pubs and clubs, strutting my funky stuff'
Best batting: 90 Gloucestershire v Oxford University, Bristol 1995

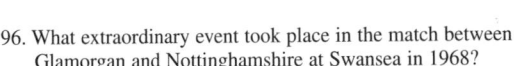

96. What extraordinary event took place in the match between Glamorgan and Nottinghamshire at Swansea in 1968?

Career Performances

	M	Inns	NO	Runs	HS	Avge	100s	50s	Ct	St	Balls	Runs	Wkts	Avge	Best	5wI	10wM
Test																	
All First	37	47	8	712	90	18.25	-	5	97	15							
1-day Int																	
NatWest																	
B & H	1	0	0	0	0	-	-	-	1	-							
1-day Lge	19	7	2	76	19	15.20	-	-	20	4							

WILLIAMSON, D. Leicestershire

Name: Dominic Williamson
Role: Right-hand bat, right-arm
medium bowler
Born: 15 November 1975, Durham City
Height: 6ft 2in **Weight:** 11st
Nickname: Woky, Midge, Burt Picker, Watto
County debut: 1996
1st-Class catches: 5
One-Day 5 w. in innings: 2
Strike rate: (career 75.88)
Parents: Dorothy and Gerard
Marital status: Single
Family links with cricket: Father and brother
Mark play/played for Kimblesworth CC
Education: Easington C of E Primary
School, Co. Durham; St Leonards RC
Comprehensive, Co. Durham; Durham Sixth
Form Centre
Qualifications: 9 GCSEs, 3 A-levels
Career outside cricket: 'Property developer'
Overseas tours: Leicestershire CCC to Holland 1996, 1998, to Guernsey 1997, 1998
('returned home early to sort club house out'), to Barbados 1998
Overseas teams played for: Ashburton CC, Australia 1994, 1996; Klerksdorp CC,
South Africa 1996-97
Cricketers particularly admired: Brian McMillan, Shane Warne, Steve Waugh,
Glenn McGrath, Stuart Smith ('The Walrus')
Young players to look out for: Robson Smith ('slip fielder'), Totty and Michael Carr,
Mark Williamson ('left-arm tweaker'), 'Fitt Smitt'
Other sports played: Squash, golf, football 'and PlayStation'

Other sports followed: Football (Newcastle United)

Relaxations: 'Mark, Bill and myself spending an evening chilling together'

Extras: Winner of the Leicestershire 2nd XI Bowler of the Year award in 1997. Most Improved Uncapped Player of the Year award 1998. Received the first 'free hit' for a no-ball bowled in National League, v Hampshire at Leicester 1999; he despatched John Stephenson's delivery for four

Opinions on cricket: 'Coaching and facilities must be improved in primary and secondary schools.'

Best batting: 41* Leicestershire v Hampshire, Leicester 1998

Best bowling: 3-19 Leicestershire v Glamorgan, Leicester 1997

1999 Season

	M	Inns	NO	Runs	HS	Avge	100s	50s	Ct	St	O	M	Runs	Wkts	Avge	Best	5wl	10wM
Test																		
All First	2	4	0	59	19	14.75	-	-	2	-	16	3	33	0	-		-	-	-
1-day Int																		
NatWest	1	1	1	17	17 *	-	-	-	-	-	6	0	36	0	-		-	-
B & H																		
1-day Lge	10	9	1	121	39	15.12	-	-	1	-	53	1	255	10	25.50	3-28	-	

Career Performances

	M	Inns	NO	Runs	HS	Avge	100s	50s	Ct	St	Balls	Runs	Wkts	Avge	Best	5wl	10wM
Test																	
All First	6	8	1	157	41 *	22.42	-	-	5	-	683	351	9	39.00	3-19	-	-
1-day Int																	
NatWest	5	2	2	36	19 *	-	-	-	-	-	252	179	8	22.37	5-37	1	
B & H	5	2	0	17	11	8.50	-	-	-	-	198	203	3	67.66	2-49	-	
1-day Lge	44	34	11	300	39	13.04	-	-	13	-	1406	1064	48	22.16	5-32	1	

97. Which of these three counties did not take part
in the first 'official' County Championship in 1890:
Sussex, Gloucestershire, Somerset?

WILLIS, S. C. Kent

Name: Simon Charles Willis
Role: Right-hand bat, wicket-keeper
Born: 19 March 1974, Greenwich, London
Height: 5ft 8in **Weight:** 12st 7lbs
Nickname: Wilco
County debut: 1993
1st-Class 50s: 5
1st-Class catches: 37
1st-Class stumpings: 3
Parents: Ray and Janet
Wife and date of marriage:
Louise Clare, 12 October 1996
Family links with cricket: Father played in
Kent League. Father-in-law Alan Ealham
played for Kent 1962-82. Brother-in-law
Mark Ealham plays for Kent and England
Education: Fleetdown Primary School;
Wilmington Grammar School
Qualifications: 9 GCSEs, advanced coach
Overseas tours: Kent U17 to New Zealand 1990-91; Kent to Zimbabwe 1993
Overseas teams played for: Scarborough, Western Australia 1992-93
Cricketers particularly admired: Alan Knott, Robin Smith, Carl Hooper, Jack Russell
Young players to look out for: Richard Clinton, Rob Key, Ed Smith
Other sports followed: Golf, soccer (Arsenal FC), horse racing, squash
Relaxations: 'Playing golf, spending time with my wife'
Extras: Retired at end of 1999 season
Best batting: 82 Kent v Cambridge University, Folkestone 1995

1999 Season

	M	Inns	NO	Runs	HS	Avge	100s	50s	Ct	St	O	M	Runs	Wkts	Avge	Best	5wl	10wM
Test																		
All First	4	6	2	117	67	29.25	-	1	10	1								
1-day Int																		
NatWest																		
B & H																		
1-day Lge	1	1	0	3	3	3.00	-	-	-	-								

Career Performances

	M	Inns	NO	Runs	HS	Avge	100s	50s	Ct	St	Balls	Runs	Wkts	Avge	Best	5wl	10wM
Test																	
All First	16	21	6	506	82	33.73	-	5	37	3							
1-day Int																	
NatWest	3	2	1	22	19 *	22.00	-	-	4	-							
B & H	1	0	0	0	0	-	-	-	-	-							
1-day Lge	9	7	2	83	31 *	16.60	-	-	11	1							

WILSON, E. J. Worcestershire

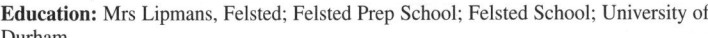

Name: Elliott James Wilson
Role: Right-hand bat
Born: 3 November 1976, London
Height: 6ft 3in **Weight:** 13st 7lbs
Nickname: Ness, Jocky, Wils, Lotty
County debut: 1998
1st-Class 50s: 3
1st-Class 100s: 1
1st-Class catches: 9
Place in batting averages: 64th av. 35.73
(1998 273rd av. 10.10)
Parents: Alec and Faye
Marital status: Single
Family links with cricket: 'Father is keen cricket fan and is chairman of my club at home (Saffron Walden). Rest of family wanted me to play rugby (they're New Zealanders)'
Education: Mrs Lipmans, Felsted; Felsted Prep School; Felsted School; University of Durham
Qualifications: 10 GCSEs, 3 A-levels
Career outside cricket: 'Studying hard for Politics, Business and Geography degree (need to)'
Off-season: 'Doing finals at Uni; three-week British Universities tour at Christmas to South Africa (if selected); devising interesting way to see the New Millennium in without getting hurt'
Overseas tours: Felsted to Australia 1996-97; Essex U14 to Amsterdam ('excellent trip to be selected for even if only 14')
Overseas teams played for: Pinetown CC, Durban 1995-96; Claremont, Cape Town
Cricketers particularly admired: Nick Knight, John Stephenson, Steve Waugh, Frank Hayes, Gordon Barker, 'Tom and Hicky this year'

Young players to look out for: Vikram Solanki 'and all the up-and-coming Worcester freaks', Tim Phillips

Other sports played: Rugby (Eastern Counties) and hockey (East of England) while at school; darts ('Hild Bede College v Trevelyan College at Durham Uni being an interesting fixture due to the particularly attractive nature of the opposition')

Other sports followed: Rugby, athletics

Relaxations: 'Enjoy running, bad dancing, and people willing to make idiots of themselves for general amusement'

Extras: Broke Nick Knight's school record at Felsted with 1200 runs in 16 innings at an average of 120 in 1995 ('but that's now been beaten'). Scored 950 runs in ten 2nd XI Championship games in 1996, while scoring more than 3000 runs in the season. Essex League Batsman of the Year in 1996. Worcestershire Uncapped Player of the Year 1999. Art scholar at Felsted School. Broke National Prep School javelin record. Made a national LTA junior tennis final ('my doubles partner was a very good French player; I wasn't'). Uncle Neville Crichton won yachting two-tonne world championship and was New Zealand touring car champion. Aunt is chair of Variety Charity Club in New Zealand. Great-grandfather went to the South Pole with Shackleton in 1907-09. 'Caught' by Stuart Law off a no-ball bowled by Ashley Cowan in National League match v Essex at Chelmsford 1999; then 'caught' again off the ensuing 'free hit'. Played in Durham University's BUSA Championship winning side 1999

Opinions on cricket: 'The sooner cricket evolves into a game run on principles similar to those on which the football Premiership is run, the sooner English cricket will realise its potential. Groundsmen should be centrally employed by the ECB, attempting to provide good cricket wickets every game – this will help the spectacle and therefore popularity no end. A cricketer's quality of life is unrivalled, except perhaps by a well-endowed rock star, and I wholeheartedly recommend this livelihood to any aspiring youth.'

Best batting: 116 Worcestershire v Middlesex, Worcester 1999

1999 Season

	M	Inns	NO	Runs	HS	Avge	100s	50s	Ct	St	O	M	Runs	Wkts	Avge	Best	5wI	10wM
Test																		
All First	9	17	2	536	116	35.73	1	3	6	-								
1-day Int																		
NatWest																		
B & H																		
1-day Lge	7	7	0	227	62	32.42	-	2	5	-								

Career Performances

	M	Inns	NO	Runs	HS	Avge	100s	50s	Ct	St	Balls	Runs	Wkts	Avge	Best	5wI	10wM
Test																	
All First	14	27	2	637	116	25.48	1	3	9	-							
1-day Int																	
NatWest																	
B & H																	
1-day Lge	12	11	0	255	62	23.18	-	2	6	-							

WILTON, N. J. Sussex

Name: Nicholas James Wilton
Role: Right-hand bat, wicket-keeper
Born: 23 September 1978, Pembury
Height: 6ft **Weight:** 12st
Nickname: Pops
County debut: 1998
1st-Class 50s: 1
1st-Class catches: 18
1st-Class stumpings: 2
Place in batting averages: 241st av. 15.60
Parents: Graham Robert and Susan Dawn
Marital status: 'Girlfriend Amy'
Family links with cricket:
Dad played local club cricket. Brother plays
for school
Education: St Johns C of E Primary School,
Crowborough; Beacon Community College,
Crowborough; Beacon Sixth Form College;
City of Westminster College
Qualifications: 5 GCSEs, CFS in Sports Studies, Pitman Computer Course Level 1,
Level 1 coaching award
Career outside cricket: Coach
Off-season: 'Recovering after shoulder operation and getting fit and ready for next
year'
Overseas tours: England U19 to South Africa (inc Youth World Cup) 1997-98
Cricketers particularly admired: Alan Knott, Mark and Steve Waugh, Ian Healy
Young players to look out for: Michael Gough, Graeme Swann
Other sports played: Football (Sussex U10 and U11)
Other sports followed: Football (Arsenal FC)
Injuries: Out for last three weeks of season with dislocation of left shoulder
Relaxations: 'Music, cinema, eating out'

Extras: Played for Sussex Colts from the age of ten (U11 to U19). Retained and registered by Sussex in 1997 while spending a season with the MCC Young Cricketers. Has represented England at U14, U17 and U19 levels. Part of the England U19 squad which won the Youth World Cup in South Africa 1998

Opinions on cricket: 'Introduction of day/night cricket has proved to be a massive success and more should be played, maybe a separate league. All 2nd XI cricket should be four days and played at first-class grounds to narrow gap between the two standards of 1st and 2nd XI. Change needed in amount of cricket played, allowing quality practice time and rest so players can be at the top of their game.'

Best batting: 55 Sussex v Leicestershire, Arundel 1999

1999 Season

	M	Inns	NO	Runs	HS	Avge	100s	50s	Ct	St	O	M	Runs	Wkts	Avge	Best	5wI	10wM
Test																		
All First	6	10	0	156	55	15.60	-	1	13	2								
1-day Int																		
NatWest																		
B & H																		
1-day Lge	2	1	0	7	7	7.00	-	-	2	-								

Career Performances

	M	Inns	NO	Runs	HS	Avge	100s	50s	Ct	St	Balls	Runs	Wkts	Avge	Best	5wI	10wM
Test																	
All First	8	14	2	202	55	16.83	-	1	18	2							
1-day Int																	
NatWest																	
B & H																	
1-day Lge	3	2	0	10	7	5.00	-	-	5	-							

WINDOWS, M. G. N.   Gloucestershire

Name: Matthew Guy Newman Windows
Role: Right-hand bat, left-arm medium bowler
Born: 5 April 1973, Clifton, Bristol
Height: 5ft 6in **Weight:** 11st 7lbs
Nickname: Steamy, Maggot
County debut: 1992
County cap: 1998
1000 runs in a season: 1
1st-Class 50s: 23
1st-Class 100s: 8

1st-Class catches: 56
Place in batting averages: 65th av. 35.55
(1998 26th av. 43.44)
Strike rate: (career 52.50)
Parents: Tony and Carolyn
Marital status: Single
Family links with cricket: Father (A.R.)
played for Gloucestershire (1960-69) and
Cambridge University. 'Brother is backbone
of Clifton Nomads'
Education: Clifton Primary; Clifton College;
Durham University
Qualifications: 9 GCSEs, 3 A-levels,
BA (Hons) Sociology
Career outside cricket: Works for Sporting
Index spread-betting firm
Overseas tours: Clifton College to Barbados
1991; England U19 to Pakistan 1991-92;
Durham University to South Africa 1992-93; England A to Zimbabwe and South
Africa 1998-99
Overseas teams played for: Gold Coast Dolphins, Queensland 1996-97
Cricketers particularly admired: Robin Smith, Mike Procter
Young players to look out for: Vikram Solanki
Other sports played: Rugby, rackets (British Open runner-up 1997)
Other sports followed: Football (Arsenal), rugby
Relaxations: Travel, keeping fit, 'having an ale'
Extras: Played for Lincolnshire and in England U19 home series v Sri Lanka 1992.
Scored 71 on county debut v Essex in 1992. Public schools rackets and fives
champion. 1994 Gloucestershire Young Player of the Year. Set record for highest
individual score for Durham University (218 not out). Gloucestershire Player of the
Year 1998. First Gloucestershire batsman to 1000 runs in 1998 season
Opinions on cricket: 'We have to bowl too many overs in a day resulting in a heavy
fine rate. The county circuit offers us great camaraderie.'
Best batting: 184 Gloucestershire v Warwickshire, Cheltenham 1996
Best bowling: 1-6 Combined Universities v West Indies, The Parks 1995

1999 Season

	M	Inns	NO	Runs	HS	Avge	100s	50s	Ct	St	O	M	Runs	Wkts	Avge	Best	5wl	10wM
Test							*											
All First	17	30	3	960	118	35.55	2	5	5	-	1	0	7	0	-		-	-	-
1-day Int																		
NatWest	5	5	3	115	43 *	57.50	-	-	2	-								
B & H	3	3	1	84	39	42.00	-	-	1	-								
1-day Lge	16	16	1	325	48 *	21.66	-	-	9	-								

Career Performances

	M	Inns	NO	Runs	HS	Avge	100s	50s	Ct	St	Balls	Runs	Wkts	Avge	Best	5wl	10wM
Test																	
All First	77	140	9	4414	184	33.69	8	23	56	-	105	104	2	52.00	1-6	-	-
1-day Int																	
NatWest	10	10	3	186	43 *	26.57	-	-	3	-							
B & H	7	7	2	147	39	29.40	-	-	1	-							
1-day Lge	65	59	5	1120	72	20.74	-	3	23	-	48	49	0	-		-	-

WOOD, J. Durham

Name: John Wood
Role: Right-hand bat, right-arm fast-medium bowler
Born: 22 July 1970, Crofton, Wakefield
Height: 6ft 3in **Weight:** 16st
Nickname: Woody
County debut: 1992
County cap: 1998
50 wickets in a season: 1
1st-Class 50s: 2
1st-Class 5 w. in innings: 8
1st-Class catches: 21
Place in batting averages: 274th av. 9.92 (1998 269th av. 10.72)
Place in bowling averages: 36th av. 22.36 (1998 92nd av. 30.80)
Strike rate: 41.27 (career 52.69)
Parents: Brian and Anne
Wife and date of marriage: Emma Louise, 30 October 1994
Children: Alexandra Mae, 7 April 1996; Joseph Samuel, 3 July 1998
Family links with cricket: 'Father played local league cricket for many years; brother plays for Spen Victoria in Bradford League'
Education: Crofton Junior School; Crofton High School; Wakefield District College; Leeds Polytechnic
Qualifications: 6 O-levels, BTEC Diploma Electronic Engineering, HND Electrical and Electronic Engineering, senior cricket coach
Career outside cricket: 'At the moment cricket coach'
Off-season: Coaching at Durham
Overseas tours: Durham CCC to South Africa 1994-95
Overseas teams played for: Griqualand West Cricket Union, South Africa 1990-91; TAWA, Wellington and Wellington B, New Zealand 1993-95

Cricketers particularly admired: Wasim Akram, David Boon, Wayne Larkins
Young players to look out for: Steve Harmison, David Sales, Darren Stevens
Other sports played: Golf
Other sports followed: Football (Newcastle United, Leeds United), rugby league (Wakefield Trinity)
Injuries: Out for three weeks with a hamstring injury
Relaxations: Golf, swimming
Extras: Played in the Bradford League. Made his debut for Durham (Minor Counties) in 1991. Durham Players' Player of the Year 1998
Opinions on cricket: 'Just improve the wickets and all will be fine.'
Best batting: 63* Durham v Nottinghamshire, Chester-le-Street 1993
Best bowling: 7-58 Durham v Yorkshire, Headingley 1999

1999 Season

	M	Inns	NO	Runs	HS	Avge	100s	50s	Ct	St	O	M	Runs	Wkts	Avge	Best	5wl	10wM
Test																		
All First	10	15	1	139	49 *	9.92	-	-	4	-	247.4	57	805	36	22.36	7-58	2	-
1-day Int																		
NatWest																			
B & H																			
1-day Lge	14	9	4	60	16	12.00	-	-	6	-	106	5	487	15	32.46	3-43	-	

Career Performances

	M	Inns	NO	Runs	HS	Avge	100s	50s	Ct	St	Balls	Runs	Wkts	Avge	Best	5wl	10wM
Test																	
All First	78	117	20	1154	63 *	11.89	-	2	21	-	11962	7601	227	33.48	7-58	8	-
1-day Int																	
NatWest	7	2	1	9	8 *	9.00	-	-	-	-	366	252	6	42.00	2-22	-	
B & H	11	6	2	48	27	12.00	-	-	1	-	607	411	10	41.10	3-50	-	
1-day Lge	60	41	14	258	28	9.55	-	-	10	-	2559	2172	58	37.44	4-17	-	

98. Who completed a match double of 100 runs and 10 wickets for Yorkshire v Glamorgan at Cardiff in 1998?

WOOD, M. J.   Somerset

Name: Matthew James Wood
Role: Right-hand bat, right-arm
off-spin bowler
Born: 30 September 1980, Exeter
Height: 5ft 11in **Weight:** 11st 5lbs
Nickname: Woody
County debut: No first-team appearance
Parents: James and Trina
Marital status: Single
Education: St Joseph's Primary, Exmouth;
Exmouth Community College; Exeter
University
Qualifications: 8 GCSEs, 2 A-levels, Level 2
cricket coach
Career outside cricket: University student
Overseas tours: West of England U15 to
West Indies 1995
Cricketers particularly admired:
Nick Folland, Saeed Anwar
Other sports played: Football
Other sports followed: Football (Liverpool FC)
Injuries: Out for three weeks with broken right index finger
Relaxations: Music
Extras: Has played for Devon

WOOD, M. J.   Yorkshire

Name: Matthew James Wood
Role: Right-hand bat, off-spin bowler
Born: 6 April 1977, Huddersfield
Height: 5ft 9in **Weight:** 12st
Nickname: Chud, Ronnie
County debut: 1997
1000 runs in a season: 1
1st-Class 50s: 6
1st-Class 100s: 3
1st-Class 200s: 1
1st-Class catches: 28
Place in batting averages: 253rd av. 13.66 (1998 19th av. 46.95)

Parents: Roger and Kathryn
Marital status: Single
Family links with cricket: 'Father played for local team Emley. Mum made the teas and sister Caroline scored'
Education: Emley First School; Kirkburton Middle School; Shelley High School and Sixth Form Centre
Qualifications: 9 GCSEs, 2 A-levels, NCA coaching award
Career outside cricket: 'None at the moment'
Off-season: 'Plenty of DIY on my new home and training and preparing for next summer by playing abroad after Christmas'
Overseas tours: England U19 to Zimbabwe 1995-96; Yorkshire CCC to West Indies 1996-97, to Cape Town 1997, 1998; MCC to Kenya 1999, to Bangladesh 1999-2000

Overseas teams played for: Somerset West CC, Cape Town 1994-95, Upper Hutt United CC, Wellington, New Zealand 1997-98
Cricketers particularly admired: Martyn Moxon, Darren Lehmann, Matthew Maynard, Michael Slater, 'Yorkshire CCC staff'
Young players to look out for: David Sales, Ryan Sidebottom, Matthew Hoggard
Other sports played: Football (Kirkburton FC), 'occasional golfer'
Other sports followed: Football (Emley FC, Liverpool FC)
Relaxations: Watching films, socialising with friends, eating out
Extras: Played for England U17 against India 1994. Spent two years at the Yorkshire Academy before graduating to the full staff in 1996. Scored 81 on first-class debut v Lancashire at Headingley in 1997. Scored 1000 runs in first full season 1998
Opinions on cricket: 'Neutral groundsmen employed by the ECB to prevent doctored pitches to suit home team. Hopefully this would see better pitches and games going into day four. Two divisions has certainly spiced up county cricket and provided more interest and should continue.'
Best batting: 200* Yorkshire v Warwickshire, Headingley 1998

1999 Season

	M	Inns	NO	Runs	HS	Avge	100s	50s	Ct	St	O	M	Runs	Wkts	Avge	Best	5wI	10wM
Test																		
All First	17	33	0	451	53	13.66	-	1	10	-								
1-day Int																		
NatWest																		
B & H																		
1-day Lge	7	4	1	73	48*	24.33	-	-	2	-								

Career Performances

	M	Inns	NO	Runs	HS	Avge	100s	50s	Ct	St	Balls	Runs	Wkts	Avge	Best	5wI	10wM
Test																	
All First	37	64	6	1633	200 *	28.15	4	6	28	-							
1-day Int																	
NatWest	1	1	1	25	25 *	-	-	-	-	-							
B & H																		
1-day Lge	16	11	2	234	65 *	26.00	-	2	4	-							

WOOD, N. T. Lancashire

Name: Nathan Theodore Wood
Role: Left-hand opening bat
Born: 4 October 1974, Dewsbury, Yorkshire
Height: 5ft 7in **Weight:** 10st 5lbs
Nickname: Rodders, Woderwick, Hot Rod
County debut: 1996
1st-Class 50s: 5
1st-Class 100s: 1
1st-Class catches: 5
Place in batting averages: 152nd av. 25.00
(1998 112th av. 28.56)
Parents: Barry and Janet
Marital status: Single
Family links with cricket: Father played
first-class and Test cricket (Yorkshire,
Derbyshire, Lancashire and England). Uncle
(Ron) played first-class cricket
(for Yorkshire)
Education: Altrincham Prep School; William Hulme's Grammar School; 'The Stiffs'
Qualifications: 8 GCSEs, cricket coaching award
Career outside cricket: 'Chauffeur to "the wife"'
Off-season: 'Travelling to the moon to visit Richard Green'
Overseas tours: England U18 to South Africa 1992-93, to Denmark 1993; England
U19 to Sri Lanka 1993-94; Lancashire CCC to India and South Africa 1997, to South
Africa 1998, 1999
Cricketers particularly admired: Sir Don Bradman, Sir Garfield Sobers,
Viv Richards
Young players to look out for: Owais Shah
Other sports played: Football
Other sports followed: Football (Manchester United)
Relaxations: 'Getting some TLC'

Extras: Played in junior One-Day Internationals against Zimbabwe, India, South Africa and Sri Lanka. Played in U19 'Tests' against West Indies and Sri Lanka. Set opening partnership record for Lancashire 2nd XI of 340 with P.C. McKeown. Shared in first-wicket record partnership for Lancashire in matches against Surrey (259 with M.A. Atherton) 1997

Opinions on cricket: 'Poor man management can lead to serious disillusionment.'

Best batting: 155 Lancashire v Surrey, The Oval 1997

1999 Season

	M	Inns	NO	Runs	HS	Avge	100s	50s	Ct	St	O	M	Runs	Wkts	Avge	Best	5wI	10wM
Test																		
All First	6	9	0	225	82	25.00	-	1	1	-	6	0	36	0	-	-	-	-
1-day Int																		
NatWest																			
B & H																			
1-day Lge																			

Career Performances

	M	Inns	NO	Runs	HS	Avge	100s	50s	Ct	St	Balls	Runs	Wkts	Avge	Best	5wI	10wM
Test																	
All First	29	44	5	1152	155	29.53	1	5	5	-	92	154	0	-	-	-	-
1-day Int																	
NatWest																		
B & H																		
1-day Lge	1	1	0	23	23	23.00	-	-	-	-							

99. Whose 316* for Surrey v Middlesex in 1926 is still the highest individual Championship score registered at Lord's?

WOOLLEY, A. P. Derbyshire

Name: Anthony Paul Woolley
Role: Right-hand bat, right-arm
medium bowler
Born: 4 December 1971, Derby
Height: 6ft 2in **Weight:** 14st
Nickname: Gus
County debut: 1999
Parents: Gerry and Jean
Marital status: Single ('girlfriend Annie')
Education: St Werburgh's Primary, Spondon,
Derby; Spondon School, Spondon, Derby;
Broomfield College, Morley, Derby
Qualifications: 4 GCSEs, Phase I and II
Greenkeeping
Career outside cricket: Engineering –
machinist
Cricketers particularly admired:
Ian Botham, Viv Richards

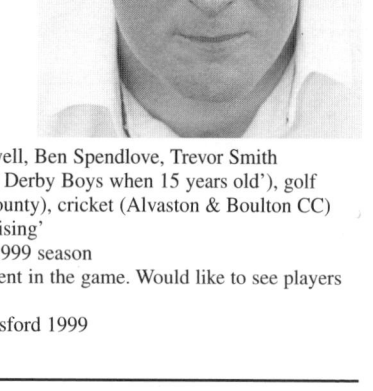

Young players to look out for: Ian Blackwell, Ben Spendlove, Trevor Smith
Other sports played: Football ('played for Derby Boys when 15 years old'), golf
Other sports followed: Football (Derby County), cricket (Alvaston & Boulton CC)
Relaxations: 'Golf, football, general socialising'
Extras: Released by Derbyshire at end of 1999 season
Opinions on cricket: 'Not enough investment in the game. Would like to see players
better rewarded financially.'
Best batting: 8 Derbyshire v Essex, Chelmsford 1999

1999 Season

	M	Inns	NO	Runs	HS	Avge	100s	50s	Ct	St	O	M	Runs	Wkts	Avge	Best	5wl	10wM
Test																		
All First	1	2	0	9	8	4.50	-	-	-	-	11	1	61	0	-		-	-
1-day Int																		
NatWest																		
B & H																		
1-day Lge	5	3	1	2	1 *	1.00	-	-	-	-	31	1	181	5	36.20	4-61	-	

	M	Inns	NO	Runs	HS	Avge	100s	50s	Ct	St	Balls	Runs	Wkts	Avge	Best	5wI	10wM
Test																	
All First	1	2	0	9	8	4.50	-	-	-	-	66	61	0	-	-	-	-
1-day Int																	
NatWest																	
B & H																	
1-day Lge	5	3	1	2	1 *	1.00	-	-	-	-	186	181	5	36.20	4-61	-	

WRIGHT, A. S.   Leicestershire

Name: Ashley Spencer Wright
Role: Right-hand opening bat, right-arm medium bowler
Born: 21 October 1980, Grantham
Height: 5ft 11in **Weight:** 11st 7lbs
Nickname: Ash
County debut: No first-team appearance
Parents: Keith and Anna
Marital status: Single
Family links with cricket: Father very keen cricketer and senior coach; brother Luke plays for Leicester U15
Education: Redmile Primary School; Belvoir High School; King Edward VII, Melton Mowbray
Qualifications: 10 GCSEs, coaching award
Career outside cricket: 'Cricket is the only thing I want to do'
Off-season: 'Keeping fit; going to South Africa'
Cricketers particularly admired: 'All the Leicestershire players'
Young players to look out for: Darren Stevens
Other sports played: Squash
Other sports followed: Football (Leicester City, Notts County, Notts Forest)
Relaxations: Music, cinema, going to gym, going out
Extras: Hit a highest score of 158 against Staffordshire U15. Was in pre-Christmas squad of 22 for England U19 tour to New Zealand 1998-99. Won the Livingstone Cup for outstanding batting performance in the 2nd XI 1999
Opinions on cricket: 'Pleased to see more younger players given a chance to play at higher levels.'

Career Performances

	M	Inns	NO	Runs	HS	Avge	100s	50s	Ct	St	Balls	Runs	Wkts	Avge	Best	5wl	10wM
Test																	
All First																	
1-day Int																	
NatWest	1	1	0	63	63	63.00	-	1	-	-							
B & H																		
1-day Lge																		

YARDY, M. H. Sussex

Name: Michael Howard Yardy
Role: Left-hand bat, left-arm medium bowler
Born: 27 November 1980, Pembury, Kent
Height: 6ft
Nickname: Yards, Cyril
County debut: 1999 (one-day)
Marital status: Single
Family links with cricket: Brother plays club cricket for Hastings
Education: William Parker, Hastings
Qualifications: 5 GCSEs, 1 A-level
Off-season: Playing club cricket in Cape Town
Overseas tours: Sussex U19 to Barbados 1997
Cricketers particularly admired: Jacques Kallis, Ian Harvey, Raj Rao, Steve Waugh
Young players to look out for: Jon Snashall, Mark Hazelton, Andrew Hodd, Nick Wilton, Matt Prior, 'and every Sussex youngster!'
Other sports played: Football, golf
Other sports followed: Football (West Ham)
Relaxations: 'Drinking with mates'
Extras: Played in the Sussex U15 side that won the U15 County Championship 1996, the U16 side that won the U16 County Championship in 1997 and the U19 side that were runners-up in the NAYC Two-Day Cup 1997. Represented England U17 1998. Played in the William Parker school side that won the Goodyear National Cup (U16 football) 1997. Played for Sussex Board XI in 1999 NatWest. Made debut for Sussex in one-day match v Sri Lanka A at Hove 1999
Opinions on cricket: '2nd XI should be split into two divisions for one-day and

Championship cricket, making eight one-day and Championship games. Four-day 2nd XI games. Two overseas players per county for 1st-class cricket. Transfer systems. Hastings should hold a lot of first-class games.'

1999 Season (did not make any first-class or one-day competition appearances)

Career Performances

	M	Inns	NO	Runs	HS	Avge	100s	50s	Ct	St	Balls	Runs	Wkts	Avge	Best	5wI	10wM
Test																	
All First																	
1-day Int																	
NatWest	1	1	0	0	0	0.00	-	-	-	-	12	14	0	-		-	-
B & H																	
1-day Lge																	

YATES, G.   Lancashire

Name: Gary Yates
Role: Right-hand bat, off-spin bowler
Born: 20 September 1967,
Ashton-under-Lyne
Height: 6ft 1in   **Weight:** 12st 10lbs
Nickname: Sweaty, Yugo, Pearly,
Backyard, Zippy
County debut: 1990
County cap: 1994
1st-Class 50s: 4
1st-Class 100s: 3
1st-Class 5 w. in innings: 5
1st-Class catches: 32
Place in batting averages: 297th av. 4.16
Place in bowling averages: 39th av. 22.50
(1998 39th av. 24.00)
Strike rate: 56.21 (career 74.78)
Parents: Alan and Patricia
Marital status: Single
Children: Francis Leonard George, 1 May 1999
Family links with cricket: Father played in Lancashire Leagues
Education: Manchester Grammar School
Qualifications: 6 O-levels, Australian Cricket Coaching Council coach
Career outside cricket: 'Rep with family business (Digical Ltd), selling diaries, calendars and business gifts'

Off-season: 'Working at Digical. Start back with Lancashire in December'
Overseas tours: Lancashire to Tasmania and Western Australia 1990, to Western Australia 1991, to Johannesburg 1992, to Barbados and St Lucia 1992, to Cape Town 1997-98, to Calcutta 1997; MCC to Bangladesh 1999-2000
Overseas teams played for: South Barwon, Geelong, Australia 1987-88; Johnsonville, Wellington, New Zealand 1989-90; Western Suburbs, Brisbane 1991-92; Old Selbornian, East London, South Africa 1992-93; Hermanus CC, South Africa 1995-96
Cricketers particularly admired: Michael Atherton, Ian Botham, John Emburey
Young players to look out for: Chris Schofield
Other sports followed: All sports, especially football (Manchester City), golf, motor rallying
Relaxations: Playing golf, watching football and good films, eating
Extras: Played for Worcestershire 2nd XI in 1987. Made debut for Lancashire 2nd XI in 1988 and taken on to county staff in 1990. Scored century on Championship debut v Nottinghamshire at Trent Bridge. Rapid Cricketline Player of the Month April/May 1992
Opinions on cricket: 'Would like to see more points awarded for rained-off games or draws. This would hopefully help to abolish contrived matches. Hope four-day cricket is here to stay.'
Best batting: 134* Lancashire v Northamptonshire, Old Trafford 1993
Best bowling: 6-64 Lancashire v Kent, Old Trafford 1999

1999 Season

	M	Inns	NO	Runs	HS	Avge	100s	50s	Ct	St	O	M	Runs	Wkts	Avge	Best	5wI	10wM
Test																		
All First	5	6	0	25	21	4.16	-	-	4	-	131.1	42	315	14	22.50	6-64	2	-
1-day Int																		
NatWest																			
B & H																			
1-day Lge	7	3	1	34	22 *	17.00	-	-	-	-	58	0	232	9	25.77	3-36	-	

Career Performances

	M	Inns	NO	Runs	HS	Avge	100s	50s	Ct	St	Balls	Runs	Wkts	Avge	Best	5wI	10wM
Test																	
All First	75	99	35	1695	134 *	26.48	3	4	32	-	12638	6568	169	38.86	6-64	5	-
1-day Int																	
NatWest	17	9	5	82	34 *	20.50	-	-	1	-	1038	594	12	49.50	2-15	-	
B & H	32	14	3	134	26	12.18	-	-	6	-	1548	1081	35	30.88	3-42	-	
1-day Lge	96	42	22	339	38	16.95	-	-	23	-	3414	2827	96	29.44	4-34	-	

ZUIDERENT, B.   Sussex

Name: Bas Zuiderent
Role: Right-hand bat, right-arm
medium bowler
Born: 3 March 1977, Utrecht, Holland
Height: 6ft 3in   **Weight:** 14st 4lbs
Nickname: Diggler, Bazler, Dirk
County debut: 1999 (one-day)
One-Day Internationals: 5
Parents: Eduard Zuiderent and Jaqueline
Zuiderent-Sluyter
Marital status: Single
Family links with cricket: Cousin J.J. plays
for Excelsior 20 in Holland and for the
Holland national side
Education: Van Oldebarnevelt School,
Rotterdam; Erasmiaans Gymnasium,
Rotterdam; University of Amsterdam
('studied Economics')

Off-season: 'Playing overseas and spending time with my family and friends'
Overseas tours: Tours with various Holland sides – to Kenya (twice), Pakistan,
Malaysia, South Africa (four times); Holland to India and Pakistan (World Cup) 1995-96
Overseas teams played for: VOC Rotterdam 1989-97; Wits Technicon, Johannesburg
1996-97; VRA Amsterdam 1998
Cricketers particularly admired: Martin Crowe, Hansie Cronje, Steven Lubbers
Young players to look out for: Tjade Groot (Holland), Grant Morrish (Sussex)
Other sports played: Golf, tennis, football, squash, skiing
Other sports followed: Football (PSV Eindhoven, Arsenal)
Injuries: Out for four weeks with intercostal damage caused by bowling
Relaxations: 'Music, being a lounge lizard, watching movies'
Extras: Has represented Holland at various levels since the age of 12. Player of the
Tournament, International Youth Tournament, Denmark 1993. Scored 54 v England in
1995-96 World Cup. Scored 99 (run out) v Worcestershire in NatWest Trophy 1997
Opinions on cricket: 'Still too much cricket played in England. Reduce the amount of
games, which would make players more eager and hungrier to play and perform.'

1999 Season

	M	Inns	NO	Runs	HS	Avge	100s	50s	Ct	St	O	M	Runs	Wkts	Avge	Best	5wI	10wM
Test																		
All First																		
1-day Int																		
NatWest	1	1	0	2	2	2.00	-	-	-	-								
B & H	1	1	0	1	1	1.00	-	-	1	-								
1-day Lge	2	2	0	24	24	12.00	-	-	2	-								

Career Performances

	M	Inns	NO	Runs	HS	Avge	100s	50s	Ct	St	Balls	Runs	Wkts	Avge	Best	5wI	10wM
Test																	
All First																	
1-day Int	5	5	1	91	54	22.75	-	1	4	-							
NatWest	4	4	0	133	99	33.25	-	1	1	-	12	15	0	-		-	-
B & H	1	1	0	1	1	1.00	-	-	1	-							
1-day Lge	2	2	0	24	24	12.00	-										

100. Which West Indies fast bowler took
134 Championship wickets for Hampshire in 1982?

THE UMPIRES

BENSON, M. R.

Name: Mark Richard Benson
Born: 6 July 1958, Shoreham, Sussex
Height: 5ft 10in
Nickname: Benny, Beefy
Appointed to 1st-Class list: 2000
County as player: Kent
Role: Left-hand bat, off-spin bowler
County debut: 1980
County cap: 1981
Benefit: 1991 (£174,619)
Test debut: 1986
Tests: 1
One-Day Internationals: 1
1000 runs in a season: 11
1st-Class 50s: 99
1st-Class 100s: 47
1st-Class 200s: 1
1st-Class catches: 140
One-Day 100s: 5

Wife and date of marriage: Sarah, 20 September 1986
Children: Laurence Mark Edward, 16 October 1987; Edward, 23 June 1990
Family links with cricket: Father played for Ghana
Education: Sutton Valence School
Cricketers particularly admired: Malcolm Marshall, Jimmy Cook, Chris Tavaré
Other sports followed: Golf, football (Charlton)
Extras: Scored 1000 runs in first full season. Record for most runs in career and season at Sutton Valence School. Kent captain 1991-95. Captained England in two one-day matches against Holland in 1993
Best batting: 257 Kent v Hampshire, Southampton 1991
Best bowling: 2-55 Kent v Surrey, Dartford 1986

First-Class Career Performances

	M	Inns	NO	Runs	HS	Avge	100s	Ct	St	Runs	Wkts	Avge	Best	5wl	10wM
Test	1	2	0	51	30	25.50	-	-	-						
All First	292	491	34	18387	257	40.23	48	140	-	493	5	98.60	2-55	-	-

BURGESS, G. I.

Name: Graham Iefvion Burgess
Born: 5 May 1943,
Glastonbury, Somerset
Appointed to 1st-Class list: 1991
County as player: Somerset
Role: Right-hand bat, right-arm
medium bowler
County debut: 1966
County cap: 1968
Testimonial: 1977
1st-Class 100s: 2
1st-Class 5 w. in innings: 18
1st-Class 10 w. in match: 2
1st-Class catches: 120
Education: Millfield School
Extras: Played Minor Counties cricket for
Wilts 1981-82 and for Cambs 1983-84
Best batting: 129 Somerset v
Gloucestershire, Taunton 1973
Best bowling: 7-43 Somerset v Oxford University, The Parks 1975

First-Class Career Performances

	M	Inns	NO	Runs	HS	Avge	100s	Ct	St	Runs	Wkts	Avge	Best	5wI	10wM
Test															
All First	252	414	37	7129	129	18.90	2	120	-	13543	474	28.57	7-43	18	2

CLARKSON, A.

Name: Anthony Clarkson
Born: 5 September 1939, Killinghall, North Yorkshire
Height: 6ft
Appointed to 1st-Class list: 1996
Counties as player: Yorkshire, Somerset
Role: Right-hand bat, right-arm off-spin bowler
County debut: 1963 (Yorkshire), 1965 (Somerset)
County cap: 1969 (Somerset)
1000 runs in a season: 2
1st-Class 100s: 2
1st-Class catches: 52
Wife's name: Cheryl
Children: André, 5 September 1964; Chantal, 27 May 1967; Pierre, 1 May 1969
Family links with cricket: Father was a league professional

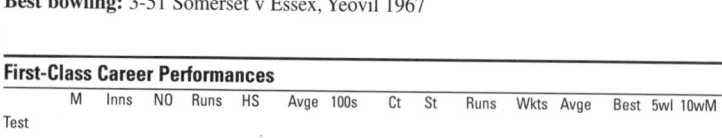

Education: Killinghall C of E; Harrogate Grammar School; Leeds College of Building; Bradford Polytechnic; Brunel College, Bristol
Career outside cricket: Architectural, civil engineering and surveying consultant
Off-season: Working and completing the renovation of house
Other sports followed: Golf and rugby ('especially league')
Relaxations: Golf, DIY, and gardening
Extras: First English player to score a century in the Sunday League
Best batting: 131 Somerset v Northamptonshire, Northampton 1969
Best bowling: 3-51 Somerset v Essex, Yeovil 1967

First-Class Career Performances

	M	Inns	NO	Runs	HS	Avge	100s	Ct	St	Runs	Wkts	Avge	Best	5wI	10wM
Test															
All First	110	189	12	4458	131	25.18	2	52	-	367	13	28.23	3-51	-	-

CONSTANT, D. J.

Name: David John Constant
Born: 9 November 1941,
Bradford-on-Avon, Wiltshire
Height: 5ft 7in
Nickname: Connie
Appointed to 1st-Class list: 1969
First appointed to Test panel: 1971
Tests umpired: 36
One-Day Internationals umpired: 31
Counties as player: Kent, Leicestershire
Role: Left-hand bat, slow left-arm bowler
County debut: 1961 (Kent),
1965 (Leicestershire)
1st-Class 50s: 6
1st-Class catches: 33
Wife's name: Rosalyn
Children: Lisa, 6 July 1966;
Julie, 21 February 1969

Family links with cricket: Father-in-law, G.E.E. Lambert, played for Gloucestershire
Education: Grove Park Secondary Modern
Off-season: Bowls
Other sports followed: Football (Millwall)
Interests/relaxations: 'Six grandchildren and bowls'
Extras: County bowls player for Gloucestershire 1984-86 (outdoors). Also represented Somerset at indoor version of the game in the Liberty Trophy
Best batting: 80 Leicestershire v Gloucestershire, Bristol 1966
Best bowling: 1-28 Leicestershire v Surrey, The Oval 1968

First-Class Career Performances

	M	Inns	NO	Runs	HS	Avge	100s	Ct	St	Runs	Wkts	Avge	Best	5wI	10wM
Test															
All First	61	93	14	1517	80	19.20	-	33	-	36	1	36.00	1-28	-	-

COWLEY, N. G.

Name: Nigel Geoffrey Cowley
Born: 1 March 1953, Shaftesbury, Dorset
Height: 5ft 6½in
Appointed to 1st-Class list: 2000
Counties as player: Hampshire, Glamorgan
Role: Right-hand bat, off-spin bowler
County debut: 1974 (Hampshire),
1990 (Glamorgan)
County cap: 1978 (Hampshire)
Benefit: 1988 (£88,274)
1000 runs in a season: 1
50 wickets in a season: 2
1st-Class 50s: 36
1st-Class 100s: 2
1st-Class 5 w. in innings: 5
1st-Class catches: 105
Marital status: Divorced
Children: Mark Antony, 14 June 1973;
Darren James, 30 October 1976
Family links with cricket: Darren played Hampshire Schools U11, U12, U13; Natal Schools 1993, 1994, 1995; and toured India with South Africa U19 1996
Education: Duchy Manor, Mere, Wilts
Off-season: Cricket coach at Durban High School
Overseas tours: Hampshire to Barbados 1985, 1986, 1987, to Dubai 1989
Overseas teams played for: Paarl CC, 1982-83; Amanzimtoti, 1984-96 (both South Africa)
Young players to look out for: Graeme Swann
Other sports played: Golf (8 handicap)
Other sports followed: Football (Liverpool FC)
Extras: Played for Dorset 1972. NatWest Man of the Match award
Best batting: 109* Hampshire v Somerset, Taunton 1977
Best bowling: 6-48 Hampshire v Leicestershire, Southampton 1982

First-Class Career Performances

	M	Inns	NO	Runs	HS	Avge	100s	Ct	St	Runs	Wkts	Avge	Best	5wI	10wM
Test															
All First	271	375	62	7309	109*	23.35	2	105	-	14879	437	34.04	6-48	5	-

DUDLESTON, B.

Name: Barry Dudleston
Born: 16 July 1945, Bebington, Cheshire
Height: 5ft 9in
Nickname: Danny
Appointed to 1st-Class list: 1984
First appointed to Test panel: 1991
Tests umpired: 2
One-Day Internationals umpired: 2
Counties as player: Leicestershire,
Gloucestershire
Role: Right-hand opening bat, occasional
slow left-arm bowler, occasional
wicket-keeper
County debut: 1966 (Leicestershire),
1981 (Gloucestershire)
County cap: 1969 (Leicestershire)
Benefit: 1980 (£25,000)
1000 runs in a season: 8
1st-Class 100s: 31
1st-Class 200s: 1
1st-Class catches: 234
One-Day 100s: 4
Wife and date of marriage: Louise Wendy, 19 October 1994
Children: Sharon Louise, 29 October 1968; Matthew Barry, 12 September 1988;
Jack Nicholas, 29 April 1998
Family links with cricket: Father was a club cricketer
Education: Stockport School
Career outside cricket: Managing director of Sunsport Tours & Travel
(sports travel company)
Off-season: In South Africa, Sri Lanka and Zimbabwe on business
Overseas tours: Kent (as guest player) to West Indies 1972; D.H. Robins' XI
to West Indies 1973; Wisden XI to West Indies 1984; MCC to Kenya 1993
Overseas teams played for: Rhodesia 1975-80
Cricketers particularly admired: Gary Sobers, Tom Graveney
Cricketers particularly learnt from: Vinoo Mankad
Young players to look out for: Vikram Solanki
Other sports played: Golf
Other sports followed: 'Follow all sports. Don't laugh – support Stockport County
and Manchester City'
Relaxations: 'TV, bridge, good red wine'
Extras: Played for England U25. Suffered badly from broken fingers, breaking fingers
on the same hand three times in 1978. Holder with John Steele of the highest first

wicket partnership for Leicestershire, 390 v Derbyshire at Leicester in 1979. Fastest player in Rhodesian cricket history to 1000 first-class runs in Currie Cup; second fastest ever in Currie Cup. Has acted as third umpire in 15 Tests

Opinions on cricket: 'Too much emphasis on blanket fitness rather than being able to do your job mentally and physically. Too little attention to playing straight and bowling straight. A fear that if Colin Cowdrey and Colin Milburn turned up for a trial today, they would be sent away without ever holding a bat.'

Best batting: 202 Leicestershire v Derbyshire, Leicester 1979
Best bowling: 4-6 Leicestershire v Surrey, Leicester 1972

First-Class Career Performances

	M	Inns	NO	Runs	HS	Avge	100s	Ct	St	Runs	Wkts	Avge	Best	5wl	10wM
Test															
All First	295	501	47	14747	202	32.48	32	234	7	1365	47	29.04	4-6	-	-

HAMPSHIRE, J. H.

Name: John Harry Hampshire
Born: 10 February 1941, Thurnscoe, Yorkshire
Height: 6ft
Nickname: Hamp
Appointed to 1st-Class list: 1985
First appointed to Test panel: 1989
International panel: 1999-
Tests umpired: 11
One-Day Internationals umpired: 8
Counties as player: Yorkshire, Derbyshire
Role: Right-hand bat, leg-spin bowler
County debut: 1961 (Yorkshire), 1982 (Derbyshire)
County cap: 1963 (Yorkshire), 1982 (Derbyshire)
Benefit: 1976
Test debut: 1969
Tests: 11
1000 runs in a season: 15
1st-Class 50s: 142
1st-Class 100s: 43
1st-Class 5 w. in innings: 2
1st-Class catches: 445
One-Day 100s: 7
Wife and date of marriage: Judith Ann, 5 September 1964

Children: Ian Christopher, 6 January 1969; Paul Wesley, 12 February 1972
Family links with cricket: Father (J.) and brother (A.W.) both played for Yorkshire
Education: Oakwood Technical High School, Rotherham
Overseas tours: MCC (England) to Australia and New Zealand 1970-71; MCC to Bangladesh 1999-2000 (as umpire)
Overseas teams played for: Tasmania, 1966-69, 1977-79
Cricketers particularly admired: Peter May, Gary Sobers
Other sports followed: Most sports
Relaxations: Gardening and cooking
Extras: Captained Yorkshire 1979-80. Scored a century (107) at Lord's in his first Test match (against West Indies 1969); the only England player to have done so. Appointed manager/coach of the Zimbabwe Test squad for their first Test matches against India and New Zealand 1992-93. Umpired four Tests in Pakistan 1989-90. Appointed to the ICC international panel 1999
Best batting: 183* Yorkshire v Surrey, Hove 1971
Best bowling: 7-52 Yorkshire v Glamorgan, Cardiff 1963

First-Class Career Performances

	M	Inns	NO	Runs	HS	Avge	100s	Ct	St	Runs	Wkts	Avge	Best	5wl	10wM
Test	8	16	1	405	107	26.86	1	9	-						
All First	577	924	112	28059	183	*34.55	43	445	-	1637	30	54.56	7-52	2	-

HARRIS, J. H.

Name: John Henry Harris
Born: 13 February 1936, Taunton
Height: 5ft 11in
Nickname: Arry, Boater, JH
Appointed to 1st-Class list: 1983
County as player: Somerset
Role: Left-hand bat, right-arm fast-medium bowler
County debut: 1952
1st-Class catches: 6
Wife and date of marriage: Morag Elspeth Jane, 20 October 1984
Children: Karen, Andrew, Mark and Tim
Family links with cricket: 'Grandfather (Harry Jernie) was head groundsman at Somerset CCC for 25 years'
Education: Priory School, Taunton; Coopers Lane, Grove Park, London

Career outside cricket: Devon League cricket inspector of grounds
Other sports played/followed: Golf ('poorly') and squash
Relaxations: DIY, Glenn Miller music, Bournemouth Symphony Orchestra, television 'and a few drinks with my friends at the D&E squash club'
Extras: Made his debut for Somerset aged 16 years 99 days. Played Minor Counties cricket for Suffolk (1960-62) and Devon (1975). Two overseas tours with the MCC as umpire. Umpired the first Masters World Cup in Bombay. Was Chairman of the First-Class Cricket Umpires' Association for five years
Best batting: 41 Somerset v Worcestershire, Taunton 1957
Best bowling: 3-29 Somerset v Worcestershire, Bristol 1959

First-Class Career Performances

	M	Inns	NO	Runs	HS	Avge	100s	Ct	St	Runs	Wkts	Avge	Best	5wI	10wM
Test															
All First	15	18	4	154	41	11.00	-	6	-	609	19	32.05	3.29	-	-

HARRIS, M. J.

Name: Michael John Harris
Born: 25 May 1944, St Just-in-Roseland, Cornwall
Height: 6ft 1in
Nickname: Pasty
Appointed to 1st-Class list: 1998
Counties as player: Middlesex, Nottinghamshire
Role: Right-hand bat, leg-break bowler, wicket-keeper
County debut: 1964 (Middlesex), 1969 (Nottinghamshire)
County cap: 1967 (Middlesex), 1970 (Notts)
1000 runs in a season: 11
1st-Class 50s: 98
1st-Class 100s: 40
1st-Class 200s: 1
1st-Class catches: 288
1st-Class stumpings: 14

Wife and date of marriage: Danielle Ruth, 10 September 1969
Children: Jodie, Richard
Education: Gerrans Comprehensive
Career outside cricket: Sports teacher
Cricketers particularly admired: Gary Sobers, Clive Rice

Cricketers particularly learnt from: Eric Russell (Middlesex)
Other sports followed: Squash, golf
Extras: Shared Middlesex then-record first wicket partnership of 312 with Eric Russell v Pakistanis at Lord's 1967. Played for Eastern Province in the Currie Cup 1971-72 and for Wellington in the Shell Trophy 1975-76. Scored nine centuries in 1971 to equal Nottinghamshire county record, scoring two centuries in a match twice and totalling 2238 for the season at an average of 50.86
Best batting: 201* Nottinghamshire v Glamorgan, Trent Bridge 1973
Best bowling: 4-16 Nottinghamshire v Warwickshire, Trent Bridge 1969

First-Class Career Performances

	M	Inns	NO	Runs	HS	Avge	100s	Ct	St	Runs	Wkts	Avge	Best	5wl	10wM
Test															
All First	344	581	58	19196	201*	36.70	41	288	14	3459	79	43.78	4-16	-	-

HOLDER, J. W.

Name: John Wakefield Holder
Born: 19 March 1945,
St George, Barbados
Height: 6ft
Nickname: Benson, Hod
Appointed to 1st-Class list: 1983
First appointed to Test panel: 1988
Tests umpired: 10
One-Day Internationals umpired: 15
County as player: Hampshire
Role: Right-hand bat, right-arm
fast bowler
County debut: 1968
50 wickets in a season: 1
1st-Class 5 w. in innings: 5
1st-Class 10 w. in match: 1
1st-Class catches: 12
Wife's name: Glenda
Children: Christopher 1968; Nigel 1970
Family links with cricket: None
Education: St Giles Boys School; Combermere High School, Barbados;
Rochdale College
Off-season: 'Idling'
Young players to look out for: Alex Tudor
Other sports followed: Football (Manchester United)

Relaxations: Keeping fit and watching wildlife documentaries
Extras: Umpired four Tests in Pakistan 1989-90
Best batting: 33 Hampshire v Sussex, Hove 1971
Best bowling: 7-79 Hampshire v Gloucestershire, Gloucester 1972

First-Class Career Performances

	M	Inns	NO	Runs	HS	Avge	100s	Ct	St	Runs	Wkts	Avge	Best	5wI	10wM
Test															
All First	47	49	14	374	33	10.68	-	12	-	3415	139	24.56	7-79	5	1

HOLDER, V. A.

Name: Vanburn Alonza Holder
Born: 8 October 1945,
St Michael, Barbados
Height: 6ft 3in
Nickname: Van
Appointed to 1st-Class list: 1991
County as player: Worcestershire
Role: Right-hand bat, right-arm
fast-medium bowler
County debut: 1968
County cap: 1970
Test debut: 1969
Tests: 40
1st-Class 50s: 4
1st-Class 100s: 1
1st-Class 5 w. in innings: 38
1st-Class 10 w. in match: 3
1st-Class catches: 98
Wife's name: Christine
Children: James Vanburn, 2 September 1981
Education: St Leonard's Secondary Modern; Community High
Off-season: 'Working'
Overseas tours: West Indies to England 1969, 1973, 1975 (World Cup), to India,
Sri Lanka and Pakistan 1974-75, to Australia 1975-76, to England 1976, to India and
Sri Lanka 1978-79 (as vice-captain); Rest of the World to Pakistan 1973-74
Overseas teams played for: Barbados 1966-78
Young players to look out for: Ben Hollioake, Alex Tudor, Steve Harmison
Other sports followed: Football (Liverpool)
Relaxations: Music. Doing crosswords
Extras: Made his debut for Barbados in the Shell Shield competition in 1966-67. Won

John Player League with Worcestershire 1973 and County Championship 1974. Played in West Indies 1975 World Cup winning side
Opinions on cricket: 'The English players have got to learn to back themselves.'
Best batting: 122 Barbados v Trinidad, Bridgetown 1973-74
Best bowling: 7-40 Worcestershire v Glamorgan, Cardiff 1974

First-Class Career Performances

	M	Inns	NO	Runs	HS	Avge	100s	Ct	St	Runs	Wkts	Avge	Best	5wI	10wM
Test	40	59	11	682	42	14.20	-	16	-	3627	109	33.27	6-28	3	-
All First	311	354	81	3559	122	13.03	1	98	-	23183	948	24.45	7-40	38	3

JESTY, T. E.

Name: Trevor Edward Jesty
Born: 2 June 1948, Gosport, Hampshire
Height: 5ft 9in
Nickname: Jets
Appointed to 1st-Class list: 1994
Counties as player: Hampshire, Surrey, Lancashire
Role: Right-hand bat, right-arm medium bowler
County debut: 1966 (Hampshire), 1985 (Surrey), 1988 (Lancashire)
County cap: 1971 (Hampshire), 1985 (Surrey), 1990 (Lancashire)
Benefit: 1982 (Hampshire)
One-Day Internationals: 10
1000 runs in a season: 10
50 wickets in a season: 2
1st-Class 50s: 110
1st-Class 100s: 33
1st-Class 200s: 2
1st-Class 5 w. in innings: 19
1st-Class catches: 265
1st-Class stumpings: 1
One-Day 100s: 7

Wife and date of marriage: Jacqueline, 12 September 1970
Children: Graeme Barry, 27 September 1972; Lorna Samantha, 7 November 1976
Education: Privett County Secondary Modern, Gosport
Off-season: Coaching for Hampshire CCC from January to March
Overseas tours: International XI to West Indies 1982; joined England tour to Australia

and New Zealand 1982-83; Lancashire to Zimbabwe 1989

Overseas teams played for: Border, South Africa 1973-74; Griqualand West 1974-76, 1980-81; Canterbury, New Zealand 1979-80

Cricketers particularly admired: Sir Garfield Sobers, Barry Richards

Young players to look out for: Graeme Swann, Alec Swann, Robert Key

Other sports followed: Football (Arsenal)

Relaxations: Gardening, reading

Extras: One of *Wisden*'s Five Cricketers of the Year 1983. Left Hampshire at end of 1984. Captain of Surrey for 1985 season

Best batting: 248 Hampshire v Cambridge University, Fenner's 1984

Best bowling: 7-75 Hampshire v Worcestershire, Southampton 1976

First-Class Career Performances

	M	Inns	NO	Runs	HS	Avge	100s	Ct	St	Runs	Wkts	Avge	Best	5wl	10wM
Test															
All First	490	777	107	21916	248	32.71	35	265	1	16075	585	27.47	7-75	19	-

JONES, A. A.

Name: Alan Arthur Jones

Born: 9 December 1947, Horley, Surrey

Height: 6ft 3in

Nickname: Jonah, Buckets

Appointed to 1st-Class list: 1985

One-Day Internationals umpired: 1

Counties as player: Sussex, Somerset, Middlesex, Glamorgan

Role: Right-hand bat, right-arm fast-medium bowler

County debut: 1964 (Sussex), 1970 (Somerset), 1976 (Middlesex), 1980 (Glamorgan)

County cap: 1972 (Somerset), 1976 (Middlesex), 1980 (Glamorgan)

50 wickets in a season: 4

1st-Class 5 w. in innings: 23

1st-Class 10 w. in match: 3

1st-Class catches: 50

Education: St John's College, Horsham

Overseas teams played for: Northern Transvaal 1971-72; Orange Free State 1976-77

Cricketers particularly admired: Tom Cartwright, Brian Close

Young players to look out for: Ian Blackwell, Matt Bulbeck

Other sports followed: All sports
Relaxations: Reading, cooking and travel
Extras: Won two Championship medals with Middlesex (1976 and 1977). He was the first person to play for four counties
Best batting: 33 Middlesex v Kent, Canterbury 1978
Best bowling: 9-51 Somerset v Sussex, Hove 1976

First-Class Career Performances

	M	Inns	NO	Runs	HS	Avge	100s	Ct	St	Runs	Wkts	Avge	Best	5wI	10wM
Test															
All First	214	216	68	799	33	5-39	-	50	-	15414	549	28.07	9-51	23	3

JULIAN, R.

Name: Raymond Julian
Born: 23 August 1936,
Cosby, Leicestershire
Height: 5ft 11in
Nickname: Julie
Appointed to 1st-Class list: 1972
International panel: 1996
One-Day Internationals umpired: 3
County as player: Leicestershire
Role: Right-hand bat, wicket-keeper
County debut: 1953
County cap: 1961
1st-Class 50s: 2
1st-Class catches: 381
1st-Class stumpings: 40
Wife and date of marriage:
Megan, 3 April 1993
Children: Peter Raymond, 1 February 1958;
John Kelvin, 13 October 1960; David Andrew, 15 October 1963; Paul Anthony,
22 September 1967
Family links with cricket: Father and two brothers all played local cricket. Two sons play local cricket
Education: Cosby Primary School, Leicestershire; Wigston Secondary Modern
Career outside cricket: Cricket coach, decorator and gardener
Off-season: Watching Zimbabwe v Australia in Harare and watching England A tour in New Zealand
Overseas tours: MCC to West Africa, 1975
Cricketers particularly admired: Gary Sobers, Keith Andrew

Young players to look out for: James Ormond, Paul Hutchison
Other sports followed: Football (Leicester City FC), boxing, rugby (Leicester Tigers)
Relaxations: Gardening, holidays, travel
Extras: Youngest wicket-keeper to make debut in first-class cricket, Leicestershire v Gloucestershire, Bristol 1953, aged 16. Took six catches in an innings, Leicestershire v Northants, Kettering 1965. Played for the Army 1955-57. Gave eight lbw decisions in succession, Glamorgan v Sussex at Cardiff 1986. Stood in 1998 B&H final and 1999 B&H Super Cup final and has umpired three B&H semi-finals and one Gillette Cup semi-final. Has just completed 27 years on the first-class list. Has been the stand-by umpire in four Tests, has acted as third umpire in seven Tests and has umpired three One-Day Internationals. Captained Leicestershire 2nd XI from 1968 to 1971. First-class football referee. One FA Cup match. Linesman in old Southern League 1960-72. Recipient of the Professional Cricketers' Association's Umpires' Cup in 1998 and 1999
Opinions on cricket: 'Good to have two divisions.'
Best batting: 51 Leicestershire v Worcestershire, Worcester 1962

First-Class Career Performances

	M	Inns	NO	Runs	HS	Avge	100s	Ct	St	Runs	Wkts	Avge	Best	5wI	10wM
Test															
All First	192	288	23	2581	51	9.73	-	381	40						

KITCHEN, M. J.

Name: Mervyn John Kitchen
Born: 1 August 1940,
Nailsea, Somerset
Appointed to 1st-Class list: 1982
First appointed to Test panel: 1990
International panel: 1995-99
Tests umpired: 19
One-Day Internationals umpired: 25
County as player: Somerset
Role: Left-hand bat, right-arm
medium bowler
County debut: 1960
County cap: 1966
Testimonial: 1973
1000 runs in a season: 7
1st-Class 50s: 68
1st-Class 100s: 17
1st-Class catches: 157
One-Day 100s: 1

Education: Blackwell Secondary Modern, Nailsea
Extras: Was third umpire for two Tests in 1994
Best batting: 189 Somerset v Pakistanis, Taunton 1967
Best bowling: 1-4 Somerset v Sussex, Taunton 1969

First-Class Career Performances

	M	Inns	NO	Runs	HS	Avge	100s	Ct	St	Runs	Wkts	Avge	Best	5wI	10wM
Test															
All First	354	612	32	15230	189	26.25	17	157	-	109	2	54.50	1-4	-	-

LEADBEATER, B.

Name: Barrie Leadbeater
Born: 14 August 1943, Leeds
Height: 6ft
Nickname: Leady
Appointed to 1st-Class list: 1981
One-Day Internationals umpired: 4
County as player: Yorkshire
Role: Right-hand opening bat, right-arm medium bowler, slip fielder
County debut: 1966
County cap: 1969
Benefit: 1980 (joint benefit with G.A. Cope)
1st-Class 50s: 27
1st-Class 100s: 1
1st-Class catches: 82
Marital status: Widowed
Wife and date of marriage: Jacqueline (deceased 1997), 18 September 1971
Children: Richard Barrie, 23 November 1972; Michael Spencer, 21 March 1976; Daniel Mark Ronnie, 19 June 1981
Education: Brownhill County Primary; Harehills Secondary Modern, Leeds
Career outside cricket: HGV driver
Overseas tours: Duke of Norfolk's XI to West Indies 1970
Overseas teams played for: Johannesburg Municipals 1978-79
Cricketers particularly admired: Colin Cowdrey, Clive Rice, Richard Hadlee, Gary Sobers, Michael Holding
Cricketers particularly learnt from: Brian Close, Willie Watson, Arthur Mitchell, Maurice Leyland
Other sports followed: Table tennis, golf, snooker, football (Leeds United)
Relaxations: 'Taking care of my family'

Extras: Took part in London Marathon 1997, 1998, 2000
Opinions on cricket: 'Disappointed in players who lack self-control and professional pride and set bad examples to young players and public alike. Public should be regularly and properly informed during stoppages in play. Stoppages for bad light cause more frustration for public, players and, not least, umpires and a change in regulations may be needed soon if the game is to retain its support and credibility. The recent theory of the wicket-keeper standing between the leg stump and the return crease when the slow left-arm bowler is operating over the wicket should be made illegal. It is grossly negative and against the spirit of the game.'
Best batting: 140* Yorkshire v Hampshire, Portsmouth 1976
Best bowling: 1-1 Yorkshire v Middlesex, Headingley 1971

First-Class Career Performances

	M	Inns	NO	Runs	HS	Avge	100s	Ct	St	Runs	Wkts	Avge	Best	5wI	10wM
Test															
All First	147	241	29	5373	140*	25.34	1	82	-	5	1	5.00	1-1	-	-

LLOYDS, J. W.

Name: Jeremy William Lloyds
Born: 17 November 1954, Penang, Malaya
Height: 5ft 11in
Nickname: Jerry
Appointed to 1st-Class list: 1998
Counties as player: Somerset, Gloucestershire
Role: Left-hand bat, off-spin bowler
County debut: 1979 (Somerset), 1985 (Gloucestershire)
County cap: 1982 (Somerset), 1985 (Gloucestershire)
1000 runs in a season: 3
1st-Class 50s: 62
1st-Class 100s: 10
1st-Class 5 w. in innings: 13
1st-Class 10 w. in match: 1
1st-Class catches: 229

Wife and date of marriage: Janine, 16 September 1997
Children: Kaeli, 16 November 1991
Family links with cricket: Father played cricket in Malaya. Brother Chris played for Somerset 2nd XI

Education: Curry Rivel Primary School; St Dunstan's Prep School; Blundell's School, Tiverton

Career outside cricket: Coaching and setting up Western Province Youth Programme 1992-95 in South Africa. Coach at St Stithian's, Johannesburg, 1995-98

Off-season: Working at home in Cape Town

Overseas tours: Somerset to Antigua 1982; Gloucestershire to Barbados 1985, to Sri Lanka 1987

Overseas teams played for: St Stithian's Old Boys, Johannesburg 1978-79; Toombull DCC, Brisbane 1980-82; North Sydney District 1982-83; Alberton, Johannesburg 1984; Preston CC, Melbourne 1986; Orange Free State 1987; Fish Hoek CC, Cape Town 1988-92

Young players to look out for: Chris Read

Other sports played: Golf (6 handicap)

Other sports followed: Golf, football (Tottenham Hotspur), American football (San Francisco 49ers), Formula 1 and saloon car racing, rugby (Bath)

Relaxations: 'Reading, music and spending time at home with my family'

Extras: Highest score in Brisbane Premier League 1980-81 (165). Britannic Player of the Month July 1987. Gloucestershire Player of the Year 1987. Leading run-scorer in Western Province Cricket League 1988, 1989

Opinions on cricket: 'The only way to produce good players is to play on good wickets. Maybe one way to stop wicket tampering is to let the away team have the choice of batting or bowling first.'

Best batting: 132* Somerset v Northamptonshire, Northampton 1982

Best bowling: 7-88 Somerset v Essex, Chelmsford 1982

First-Class Career Performances

	M	Inns	NO	Runs	HS	Avge	100s	Ct	St	Runs	Wkts	Avge	Best	5wl	10wM
Test															
All First	267	408	64	10679	132*	31.04	10	229	-	12943	333	38.86	7-88	13	1

MALLENDER, N. A.

Name: Neil Alan Mallender
Born: 13 August 1961, Doncaster
Height: 6ft
Appointed to 1st-Class list: 1999
Counties as player: Northamptonshire, Somerset
Role: Right-hand bat, right-arm fast-medium bowler
County debut: 1980 (Northamptonshire), 1987 (Somerset)
County cap: 1984 (Northamptonshire), 1987 (Somerset)
Test debut: 1992
Tests: 2
50 wickets in a season: 6
1st-Class 50s: 10
1st-Class 100s: 1
1st-Class 5 w. in innings: 36
1st-Class 10 w. in match: 5
1st-Class catches: 111
One-Day 5 w. in innings: 3

Children: Kirstie, 11; Dominic, 8; Jacob 3
Family links with cricket: Brother Graham used to play good representative cricket before joining the RAF
Education: Beverley Grammar School
Overseas tours: England YC to West Indies 1979-80
Overseas teams played for: Kaikorai, Dunedin, New Zealand; University, Wellington, New Zealand; Otago, New Zealand 1983-93
Young players to look out for: Marcus Trescothick, Simon Francis
Other sports played: Golf
Other sports followed: Most sports
Relaxations: Golf
Extras: Took 5-50 on Test debut v Pakistan at Headingley in 1992
Best batting: 100* Otago v Central Districts, Palmerston North 1991-92
Best bowling: 7-27 Otago v Auckland, Auckland 1984-85

First-Class Career Performances

	M	Inns	NO	Runs	HS	Avge	100s	Ct	St	Runs	Wkts	Avge	Best	5wI	10wM
Test	2	3	0	8	4	2.66	-	-	-	215	10	21.50	5-50	1	-
All First	345	396	122	4709	100*	17.18	1	111	-	24654	937	26.31	7-27	36	5

PALMER, K. E.

Name: Kenneth Ernest Palmer
Born: 22 April 1937, Winchester
Height: 5ft 10in
Nickname: Pedlar
Appointed to 1st-Class list: 1972
First appointed to Test panel: 1978
International panel: 1994
Tests umpired: 22
One-Day Internationals umpired: 20
County as player: Somerset
Role: Right-hand bat, right-arm
fast-medium bowler
County debut: 1955
County cap: 1958
Testimonial: 1968
Test debut: 1965
Tests: 1
1000 runs in a season: 1
50 wickets in a season: 2
100 wickets in a season: 4
1st-Class 50s: 27
1st-Class 100s: 2
1st-Class 5 w. in innings: 46
1st-Class 10 w. in match: 5
1st-Class catches: 156

Wife and date of marriage: Jacqueline, 24 September 1994
Children: Gary Vincent, 6 September 1961
Family links with cricket: Father played club cricket and did the cricketer's double
13 times. Son played for Somerset, as did brother Roy, also a Test umpire
Education: Southbroom Secondary Modern, Devizes
Overseas tours: Commonwealth XI to Pakistan 1962; International Cavaliers
to West Indies 1963-64
Cricketers particularly admired: Gary Sobers, Richard Hadlee, Viv Richards,
David Gower, Michael Holding, Malcolm Marshall
Cricketers particularly learnt from: Father and Maurice Tremlett
Other sports followed: Football (Manchester United) and rugby (Bath and England)
Relaxations: Car enthusiast
Extras: Won Carling Single Wicket Competition 1961. Did the 'double' in 1961 (114
wickets, 1036 runs). With Bill Alley holds the Somerset record for sixth-wicket
partnership – 265 v Northants at Northampton 1961. Called into Test side while
coaching in South Africa 1964-65. Won Man of the Match Award for Somerset v

Lancashire 1967. Was twice on World Cup panel in England. Has umpired four Benson and Hedges finals and four NatWest finals
Best batting: 125* Somerset v Northamptonshire, Northampton 1961
Best bowling: 9-57 Somerset v Nottinghamshire, Trent Bridge 1963

First-Class Career Performances

	M	Inns	NO	Runs	HS	Avge	100s	Ct	St	Runs	Wkts	Avge	Best	5wl	10wM
Test	1	1	0	10	10	10.00	-	-	-	189	1	189.00	1-113	-	-
All First	314	481	105	7771	125*	20.66	2	156	-	18485	866	21.34	9-57	46	5

PALMER, R.

Name: Roy Palmer
Born: 12 July 1942, Hampshire
Height: 6ft 3in
Nickname: Arp
Appointed to 1st-Class list: 1980
First appointed to Test panel: 1992
Tests umpired: 2
One-Day Internationals umpired: 8
County as player: Somerset
Role: Right-hand bat, right-arm fast-medium bowler
County debut: 1965
50 wickets in a season: 1
1st-Class 50s: 1
1st-Class 5 w. in innings: 4
1st-Class catches: 25
Wife and date of marriage: Alyne, 5 November 1983

Children: Nick, 7 October 1968
Family links with cricket: Brother of Ken Palmer, Test umpire and former Somerset player; nephew Gary also played for Somerset
Education: Southbroom Secondary Modern, Devizes
Young players to look out for: Dean Cosker
Relaxations: DIY, reading, golf
Extras: Won two Man of the Match Awards in the Gillette Cup
Best batting: 84 Somerset v Leicestershire, Taunton 1967
Best bowling: 6-45 Somerset v Middlesex, Lord's 1967

	M	Inns	NO	Runs	HS	Avge	100s	Ct	St	Runs	Wkts	Avge	Best	5wI	10wM
Test															
All First	74	110	32	1037	84	13.29	-	25	-	5439	172	31.62	6-45	4	-

SHARP, G.

Name: George Sharp
Born: 12 March 1950,
Hartlepool, County Durham
Height: 5ft 11in
Nickname: Blunt, Razor, Sharpie
Appointed to 1st-Class list: 1991
International panel: 1996-
Tests umpired: 9
One-Day Internationals umpired: 12
County as player: Northamptonshire
Role: Right-hand bat, wicket-keeper
County debut: 1967
County cap: 1972
1st-Class catches: 565
1st-Class stumpings: 90
Wife and date of marriage:
Audrey, 14 September 1974
Children: Gareth James, 27 June 1985
Education: Elwick Road, Hartlepool

Career outside cricket: Director of GSB Loams Ltd, suppliers of top dressings for all types of sports fields
Off-season: Working for GSB Loams Ltd. Umpiring as part of international panel (overseas)
Overseas tours: England Counties XI to Barbados and Trinidad 1975
Cricketers particularly admired: Alan Knott, Bob Taylor, Keith Andrew
Other sports played: Golf
Other sports followed: Football (Newcastle Utd), rugby league and union
Relaxations: Golf and watching most sports
Extras: Has acted as third umpire in one Test. Has umpired two B&H finals and one NatWest final. Stood in Singer Trophy (India, Sri Lanka, Pakistan), Singapore 1996. Umpired in tournament between Pakistan, Sri Lanka and New Zealand in Sharjah 1997
Best batting: 98 Northamptonshire v Yorkshire, Northampton 1983
Best bowling: 1-47 Northamptonshire v Yorkshire, Northampton 1980

First-Class Career Performances

	M	Inns	NO	Runs	HS	Avge	100s	Ct	St	Runs	Wkts	Avge	Best	5wI	10wM
Test															
All First	306	396	81	6254	98	19.85	-	565	90	70	1	70.00	1-47	-	-

SHEPHERD, D. R.

Name: David Robert Shepherd
Born: 27 December 1940,
Bideford, Devon
Height: 5ft 10in
Nickname: Shep
Appointed to 1st-Class list: 1981
First appointed to Test panel: 1985
International panel: 1994-
Tests umpired: 47
One-Day Internationals umpired: 84
County as player: Gloucestershire
Role: Right-hand bat, right-arm
medium bowler
County debut: 1965
County cap: 1969
Benefit: 1978 (joint benefit with J. Davey)
1000 runs in a season: 2
1st-Class 50s: 55
1st-Class 100s: 12
1st-Class catches: 95
One-Day 100s: 2
Marital status: Single
Family links with cricket: Brother played for MCC Young Professionals and Devon
Education: Barnstaple Grammar School; St Luke's College, Exeter
Career outside cricket: Teacher. Family business – post office/newsagent
Off-season: ICC umpiring abroad
Cricketers particularly admired: Gary Sobers, Mike Procter
Other sports followed: Rugby, football
Relaxations: Stamp collecting
Extras: Played Minor Counties cricket for Devon 1959-64. Only Gloucestershire
player to score a century on his first-class debut. Umpired the MCC Bicentenary Test,
England v Rest of the World, at Lord's in 1987. With Dickie Bird and Steve Bucknor
was one of the first umpires officially sponsored by the ICC. Known for his
superstition regarding 'Nelson' score 111, and multiples – 222, 333 etc. Has stood in
each World Cup since 1983, including the 1996 final between Australia and Sri Lanka

in Lahore and the 1999 final between Australia and Pakistan at Lord's. Has umpired numerous domestic finals. Was awarded the MBE in 1997 for services to cricket. Received National Grid/ICC 'bronze award' in March 1998 for long-service as a Test umpire
Best batting: 153 Gloucestershire v Middlesex, Bristol 1968
Best bowling: 1-1 Gloucestershire v Northamptonshire, Gloucester 1968
Stop press: Umpired 50th Test, India v South Africa, Mumbai (Bombay) February 2000, receiving ICC 'silver award' to acknowledge this achievement

First-Class Career Performances

	M	Inns	NO	Runs	HS	Avge	100s	Ct	St	Runs	Wkts	Avge	Best	5wI	10wM
Test															
All First	282	476	40	10672	153	24.47	12	95	-	106	2	53.00	1-1	-	-

STEELE, J. F.

Name: John Frederick Steele
Born: 23 July 1946, Stafford
Height: 5ft 10in
Nickname: Steely
Appointed to 1st-Class list: 1997
Counties as player: Leicestershire, Glamorgan
Role: Right-hand bat, slow left-arm bowler
County debut: 1970 (Leicestershire), 1984 (Glamorgan)
County cap: 1971 (Leicestershire), 1984 (Glamorgan)
1000 runs in a season: 6
1st-Class 100s: 21
1st-Class 5 w. in innings: 16
1st-Class catches: 414
Wife and date of marriage:
Susan, 17 April 1977
Children: Sarah Jane, 2 April 1982; Robert Alfred, 10 April 1985
Family links with cricket: Uncle Stan played for Staffordshire. Brother David played for Northamptonshire, Derbyshire and England. Cousin Brian Crump played for Northamptonshire and Staffordshire
Education: Endon School, Stoke-on-Trent; Stafford College
Career outside cricket: Work study officer. Fireman with Staffordshire Fire Brigade
Overseas teams played for: Springs HSOB, Northern Transvaal 1971-73; Pine Town CC, Natal 1973-74, 1982-83; Natal 1975-76, 1978-79

Other sports followed: Soccer (Stoke City, Port Vale), golf
Relaxations: Music and walking
Extras: Played for England U25. First wicket record partnership for Leics of 390 with Barry Dudleston versus Derbyshire at Leicester in 1979. Won two Man of the Match Awards in the Gillette Cup and four in the Benson and Hedges Cup. Won the award for the most catches in a season in 1984 and was voted Natal's Best Bowler in 1975-76
Best batting: 195 Leicestershire v Derbyshire, Leicester 1971
Best bowling: 7-29 Natal B v Griqualand West, Umzinto 1973-74
7-29 Leicestershire v Gloucestershire, Leicester 1980

First-class career performances

	M	Inns	NO	Runs	HS	Avge	100s	Ct	St	Runs	Wkts	Avge	Best	5wI	10wM
Test															
All First	379	605	85	15053	195	28.94	21	414	-	15793	584	27.04	7-29	16	-

WHITE, R. A.

Name: Robert Arthur White
Born: 6 October 1936, Fulham
Height: 5ft 9in
Nickname: Knocker
Appointed to 1st-Class list: 1982
Counties as player: Middlesex, Nottinghamshire
Role: Left-hand bat, off-break bowler
County debut: 1958 (Middlesex), 1966 (Nottinghamshire)
County cap: 1963 (Middlesex), 1966 (Nottinghamshire)
Benefit: 1974
1000 runs in a season: 1
50 wickets in a season: 2
1st-Class 50s: 50
1st-Class 100s: 5
1st-Class 5 w. in innings: 28
1st-Class 10 w. in match: 4
1st-Class catches: 190

Wife: Janice – 'still married, must be a record in the modern game'
Children: Robin and Vanessa
Education: Chiswick Grammar School
Career outside cricket: Fireworks salesman
Off-season: Working

Cricketers particularly admired: 'Gary Sobers more than anyone else'
Cricketers particularly learnt from: 'I tried to learn from everyone I encountered'
Young players to look out for: 'All of them'
Other sports followed: All sports – golf, football, ice hockey and horse racing in particular
Relaxations: Theatre-going
Extras: Made independent coaching trips to South Africa 1959, 1960, 1966, 1967, 1968. Together with M.J. Smedley, put on 204 for the seventh wicket, then a Nottinghamshire record, v Surrey at The Oval 1967
Opinions on cricket: 'There is so much verbal noise on the field these days (mainly in my opinion to distract the batsman), that I, if still a player, would wear earphones and carry a Walkman so that I could listen to soothing music and obliterate the verbals. Those people who saw me play would no doubt say that I would have had time just to hear the "Minute Waltz".'
Best batting: 116* Nottinghamshire v Surrey, The Oval 1967
Best bowling: 7-41 Nottinghamshire v Derbyshire, Ilkeston 1971

First-Class Career Performances

	M	Inns	NO	Runs	HS	Avge	100s	Ct	St	Runs	Wkts	Avge	Best	5wl	10wM
Test															
All First	413	642	105	12452	116*	23.18	5	190	-	21138	693	30.50	7-41	28	4

WHITEHEAD, A. G. T.

Name: Alan Geoffrey Thomas Whitehead
Born: 28 October 1940,
Butleigh, Somerset
Appointed to 1st-Class list: 1970
First appointed to Test panel: 1982
Tests umpired: 5
One-Day Internationals umpired: 13
County as player: Somerset
Role: Left-hand bat, slow left-arm bowler
County debut: 1957
1st-Class 5 w. in innings: 3
1st-Class catches: 20
Extras: Acted as third umpire in the fifth Test against Australia at Edgbaston 1993 and in two Tests in 1994
Best batting: 15 Somerset v Hampshire, Southampton 1959
Best bowling: 6-74 Somerset v Sussex, Eastbourne 1959

First-Class Career Performances

	M	Inns	NO	Runs	HS	Avge	100s	Ct	St	Runs	Wkts	Avge	Best	5wl	10wM
Test															
All First	38	49	25	137	15	5.70	-	20	-	2306	67	34.41	6-74	3	

WILLEY, P.

Name: Peter Willey
Born: 6 December 1949, Sedgefield, County Durham
Height: 6ft 1in
Nickname: Will, 'many unprintable'
Appointed to 1st-Class list: 1993
International panel: 1996-
Tests umpired: 15
One-Day Internationals umpired: 16
Counties as player: Northamptonshire, Leicestershire
Role: Right-hand bat, off-break bowler
County debut: 1966 (Northamptonshire), 1984 (Leicestershire)
County cap: 1971 (Northamptonshire), 1984 (Leicestershire)
Benefit: 1981 (£31,400)
Test debut: 1976
Tests: 26
One-Day Internationals: 26
1000 runs in a season: 10
50 wickets in a season: 2
1st-Class 50s: 101
1st-Class 100s: 43
1st-Class 200s: 1
1st-Class 5 w. in innings: 26
1st-Class 10 w. in match: 3
1st-Class catches: 235
One-Day 100s: 9
Wife and date of marriage: Charmaine, 23 September 1971
Children: Heather Jane, 11 September 1985; David, 28 February 1990
Family links with cricket: Father played local club cricket in County Durham
Education: Seaham Secondary School, County Durham
Overseas tours: England to Australia and India 1979-80, to West Indies 1980-81, 1985-86; with unofficial England XI to South Africa 1981-82

Overseas teams played for: Eastern Province, South Africa 1982-85
Cricketers particularly admired: Malcolm Marshall
Other sports followed: All sports
Relaxations: Gardening, dog walking
Extras: With Wayne Larkins, received 2016 pints of beer (seven barrels) from a brewery in Northampton as a reward for their efforts in Australia with England in 1979-80. Became youngest player ever to play for Northamptonshire at 16 years 180 days v Cambridge University in 1966. Banned from Test cricket for three years for joining England rebel tour of South Africa in 1982. Left Northamptonshire at end of 1983 and moved to Leicestershire as vice-captain. Appointed Leicestershire captain for 1987, but resigned after only one season. Released by Leicestershire at end of 1991 season to play for Northumberland in 1992. He was appointed to the first-class umpires list in 1993 and to the international panel in 1996. Umpired the 1996-97 Australia v West Indies series in Australia. Stood in the 1999 World Cup and in the 1999 Benson and Hedges Super Cup final
Opinions on cricket: 'I think the fun has gone out of the game for many of the players. Not enough hard work and practice is done to improve playing standards throughout the first-class game. Players of average ability are being paid silly money in the modern game, by clubs, so they may not need to try and improve their standards. Why does the English game need overseas coaches? Why do we also need team managers?'
Best batting: 227 Northamptonshire v Somerset, Northampton 1976
Best bowling: 7-37 Northamptonshire v Oxford University, The Parks 1975

First-Class Career Performances

	M	Inns	NO	Runs	HS	Avge	100s	Ct	St	Runs	Wkts	Avge	Best	5wI	10wM
Test	26	50	6	1184	102	*26.90	2	3	-	456	7	65.14	2-73	-	-
All First	559	918	121	24361	227	30.56	44	235	-	23400	756	30.95	7-37	26	3

THE 1999 SEASON

Roll of Honour and Averages

ROLL OF HONOUR 1999

PPP HEALTHCARE CHAMPIONSHIP

		P	W	L	D	T	Bt	Bl	Pts
1	Surrey (5)	17	12	0	5	0	36	64	264
2	Lancashire (2)	17	8	4	5	0	37	55	208
3	Leicestershire (1)	17	5	3	9	0	43	61	200
4	Somerset (9)	17	6	4	7	0	38	56	194
5	Kent (11)	17	6	4	7	0	34	60	194
6	Yorkshire (3)	17	8	6	3	0	21	64	193
7	Hampshire (6)	17	5	5	7	0	45	58	191
8	Durham (14)	17	6	7	4	0	34	66	188
9	Derbyshire (10)	17	7	8	2	0	34	61	187
10	Warwickshire (8)	17	6	5	6	0	35	56	187
11	Sussex (7)	17	6	5	6	0	29	60	185
12	Essex (18)	17	5	7	5	0	38	63	181
13	Northamptonshire (15)	17	4	7	6	0	35	64	171
14	Glamorgan (12)	17	5	7	5	0	26	57	163
15	Worcestershire (13)	17	4	6	7	0	18	65	159
16	Middlesex (17)	17	4	5	8	0	24	53	157
17	Nottinghamshire (16)	17	4	11	2	0	27	57	140
18	Gloucestershire (4)	17	2	9	6	0	26	62	136

1998 positions in brackets. The top nine counties make up the first division in 2000

NATWEST TROPHY

Winners: Gloucestershire
Runners-up: Somerset

BENSON AND HEDGES SUPER CUP

Winners: Gloucestershire
Runners-up: Yorkshire

CGU NATIONAL LEAGUE DIVISION ONE

		P	W	L	T	NR	Pts
1	Lancashire	16	11	2	0	3	50
2	Worcestershire	16	10	4	0	2	44
3	Kent	16	8	6	0	2	36
4	Gloucestershire	16	8	8	0	0	32
5	Yorkshire	16	8	8	0	0	32
6	Leicestershire	16	6	8	0	2	28
7	Warwickshire	16	6	8	0	2	28
8	Hampshire	16	5	9	0	2	24
9	Essex	16	3	12	0	1	14

The bottom three counties were relegated to Division Two for the 2000 season

CGU NATIONAL LEAGUE DIVISION TWO

		P	W	L	T	NR	Pts
1	Sussex	16	13	2	0	1	54
2	Somerset	16	13	3	0	0	52
3	Northamptonshire	16	9	5	0	2	40
4	Glamorgan	16	8	7	1	0	34
5	Nottinghamshire	16	6	8	0	2	28
6	Surrey	16	5	9	1	1	24
7	Middlesex	16	5	10	1	0	22
8	Derbyshire	16	4	10	1	1	20
9	Durham	16	3	12	0	1	14

The top three counties were promoted to Division One for the 2000 season

1999 AVERAGES (all first-class matches)

BATTING AVERAGES - including fielding
Qualifying requirements : 6 completed innings

Name	Matches	Inns	NO	Runs	HS	Avge	100s	50s	Ct	St
S.G.Law	17	29	4	1833	263	73.32	8	6	29	-
T.M.Dilshan	5	10	1	562	127	62.44	2	3	8	1
J.L.Langer	12	22	4	1048	241*	58.22	4	2	12	-
J.Cox	18	30	2	1617	216	57.75	6	6	7	-
M.L.Hayden	9	15	2	745	170	57.30	4	1	6	-
R.J.Turner	19	27	4	1217	138*	52.91	2	10	67	2
N.Hussain	12	20	1	988	143	52.00	2	8	13	-
D.J.G.Sales	18	29	4	1291	303*	51.64	3	5	15	-
A.D.Brown	17	26	4	1127	265	51.22	4	2	31	1
D.J.Nash	8	11	3	395	135*	49.37	1	2	1	-
P.D.Bowler	17	27	8	931	149	49.00	4	-	8	-
G.A.Hick	13	22	0	1063	150	48.31	4	6	18	-
M.J.Powell	16	26	4	1060	164	48.18	2	5	5	-
C.C.Lewis	10	13	2	520	139	47.27	2	2	7	-
G.M.Hamilton	11	20	8	567	94*	47.25	-	4	3	-
M.J.Horne	9	15	0	670	172	44.66	3	1	4	-
M.A.Atherton	9	15	2	578	268*	44.46	1	2	4	-
N.J.Astle	10	15	1	617	121	44.07	3	2	17	-
G.R.Loveridge	7	10	0	427	126	42.70	1	2	7	-
R.A.Smith	18	29	3	1110	96	42.69	-	10	9	-
D.Ripley	15	22	6	683	107	42.68	2	3	40	3
G.D.Lloyd	17	26	1	1066	144	42.64	3	6	7	-
P.Johnson	16	29	3	1104	126	42.46	1	10	11	-
S.P.James	16	25	1	1017	259*	42.37	4	3	9	-
M.R.Ramprakash	16	28	3	1056	209*	42.24	2	7	11	-
D.A.Kenway	19	31	6	1055	102	42.20	1	7	13	-
G.P.Thorpe	13	21	4	708	164	41.64	2	2	18	-
B.W.Byrne	6	11	2	374	94	41.55	-	2	1	-
M.J.DiVenuto	16	28	2	1067	162	41.03	3	5	20	-
J.J.B.Lewis	16	28	0	1146	132	40.92	2	8	7	-
A.Symonds	14	25	2	940	177	40.86	3	4	15	-
A.Habib	18	29	3	1055	160*	40.57	3	6	2	-
V.S.Solanki	19	35	2	1339	171	40.57	3	6	21	-
E.T.Smith	14	25	2	931	111	40.47	1	6	2	-
M.P.Maynard	13	18	1	685	186	40.29	2	2	9	-
J.H.Kallis	6	9	0	362	101	40.22	1	2	3	-
M.A.Butcher	16	28	1	1077	259	39.88	2	4	15	-
S.P.Fleming	9	15	3	476	127	39.66	1	2	20	-
Q.J.Hughes	8	13	2	435	101	39.54	1	3	2	-
W.S.Kendall	19	32	2	1186	201	39.53	2	7	25	-
M.V.Fleming	17	25	4	830	138	39.52	1	4	4	-
R.C.Irani	21	34	5	1121	153	38.65	4	3	12	-

Name	Matches	Inns	NO	Runs	HS	Avge	100s	50s	Ct	St
A.S.Rollins	15	28	3	965	113	38.60	2	5	9	-
J.S.Laney	11	19	1	691	99	38.38	-	6	7	-
A.Flintoff	13	21	2	727	160	38.26	2	2	25	-
G.D.Rose	9	11	2	342	123*	38.00	1	1	2	-
D.L.Maddy	18	30	2	1060	158*	37.85	2	4	18	-
M.P.L.Bulbeck	15	15	8	265	76*	37.85	-	1	1	-
J.P.Crawley	15	25	2	870	158	37.82	2	6	10	-
D.L.Vettori	10	14	2	453	112	37.75	1	4	4	-
I.J.Ward	18	30	3	1018	103	37.70	1	9	7	-
G.J.Kennis	3	6	0	225	175	37.50	1	-	2	-
C.D.McMillan	10	16	2	525	121	37.50	2	1	4	-
M.E.Trescothick	15	24	0	898	190	37.41	2	3	27	-
N.J.Speak	10	17	2	561	110	37.40	2	2	6	-
R.J.Warren	18	29	4	935	110	37.40	1	6	12	-
I.Mohammed	9	16	2	520	110	37.14	1	2	1	-
R.R.Montgomerie	15	27	1	962	113*	37.00	2	6	19	-
D.C.Nash	17	27	8	696	92	36.63	-	4	46	4
A.P.Grayson	20	32	2	1083	159*	36.10	3	6	8	-
A.N.Aymes	18	27	5	791	115*	35.95	2	5	51	2
T.M.Moody	5	10	2	286	63*	35.75	-	3	5	-
K.D.M.Walker	7	8	0	286	132	35.75	1	1	2	-
E.J.Wilson	9	17	2	536	116	35.73	1	3	6	-
M.G.N.Windows	17	30	3	960	118	35.55	2	5	5	-
R.J.Bailey	14	23	2	743	113*	35.38	1	3	9	-
J.A.Claughton	7	13	4	318	85	35.33	-	3	3	-
M.J.Powell	9	14	0	494	136	35.28	2	1	5	-
M.Burns	19	27	1	915	109	35.19	2	5	11	-
D.L.Hemp	18	29	0	1014	144	34.96	2	6	11	-
R.M.S.Weston	15	26	2	838	156	34.91	3	2	9	-
B.F.Smith	14	21	0	732	154	34.85	2	2	10	-
P.N.Weekes	16	28	4	828	140*	34.50	1	6	19	-
M.P.Dowman	9	15	3	412	67*	34.33	-	3	6	-
N.V.Knight	14	23	2	719	94	34.23	-	6	30	-
R.P.Arnold	5	10	1	307	70	34.11	-	2	5	-
D.C.Boon	16	27	2	839	139	33.56	1	7	8	-
C.L.Cairns	7	10	1	302	80	33.55	-	2	1	-
A.J.Hollioake	13	18	2	534	116	33.37	1	3	8	-
M.P.Bicknell	15	17	4	432	69	33.23	-	3	5	-
C.J.Adams	17	31	2	956	130	32.96	1	5	23	-
R.C.Russell	17	30	6	790	94*	32.91	-	5	55	5
P.J.Prichard	16	26	0	852	110	32.76	2	6	6	-
A.P.Wells	10	15	0	490	111	32.66	2	1	1	-
V.J.Wells	13	20	2	588	109*	32.66	2	3	13	-
R.J.Cunliffe	7	13	0	421	108	32.38	1	2	8	-
P.C.L.Holloway	19	32	5	869	114*	32.18	2	5	9	-
M.A.Wagh	13	21	1	643	216*	32.15	1	1	3	-
D.A.Gunawardene	4	8	0	257	77	32.12	-	3	1	-
W.K.Hegg	16	24	3	670	94	31.90	-	3	45	4
A.J.Swann	12	18	0	573	154	31.83	2	2	11	-

Name	Matches	Inns	NO	Runs	HS	Avge	100s	50s	Ct	St
J.E.R.Gallian	19	34	3	985	120*	31.77	2	5	19	-
M.J.Slater	10	18	1	540	171	31.76	1	2	9	-
J.E.Morris	15	25	0	792	119	31.68	2	4	7	-
G.P.Swann	18	27	4	727	130*	31.60	1	4	13	-
D.J.Bicknell	11	17	1	504	115	31.50	2	1	3	-
A.L.Penberthy	18	25	2	718	123*	31.21	1	4	6	-
G.S.Blewett	12	23	2	655	190	31.19	1	2	5	-
A.Dale	16	26	0	809	113	31.11	3	1	4	-
P.C.McKeown	5	8	1	216	75	30.85	-	2	4	-
M.A.Ealham	13	22	3	585	88*	30.78	-	5	3	-
P.A.Nixon	18	29	2	828	121	30.66	1	3	46	4
M.J.Chilton	18	30	3	827	106*	30.62	2	4	21	-
A.J.Strauss	9	17	1	488	98	30.50	-	4	3	-
G.W.White	16	28	1	818	121	30.29	1	4	11	-
U.B.A.Rashid	10	18	3	454	73	30.26	-	3	5	-
A.McGrath	16	30	2	831	142*	29.67	1	6	15	-
M.T.E.Peirce	17	31	0	919	123	29.64	1	6	5	-
U.Afzaal	16	30	2	828	104	29.57	1	6	4	-
S.R.Lampitt	14	19	5	413	66*	29.50	-	2	7	-
M.Keech	8	13	1	353	50	29.41	-	1	8	-
N.W.Ashley	5	9	0	264	96	29.33	-	2	4	-
K.J.Barnett	15	26	1	727	125	29.08	2	4	15	-
S.D.Peters	11	15	2	374	99	28.76	-	2	13	-
M.Watkinson	8	13	1	345	116	28.75	1	-	4	-
T.H.C.Hancock	17	30	0	858	71	28.60	-	7	7	-
A.J.Stewart	12	20	2	511	95	28.38	-	3	15	2
J.M.Dakin	11	18	2	454	124	28.37	1	3	2	-
D.I.Stevens	11	20	0	562	130	28.10	1	3	12	-
D.D.J.Robinson	17	29	1	786	200	28.07	3	1	12	-
P.A.Cottey	17	29	1	780	126	27.85	1	4	11	-
S.P.Titchard	17	31	4	752	136	27.85	1	2	2	-
D.R.Brown	16	25	1	666	142	27.75	1	3	13	-
K.A.Parsons	15	21	3	499	80	27.72	-	3	12	-
O.A.Shah	17	32	2	829	110*	27.63	3	3	9	-
R.J.Harden	10	19	0	438	69	27.37	-	3	2	-
D.Byas	17	34	2	875	95	27.34	-	8	24	-
K.J.Innes	8	11	3	217	47*	27.12	-	-	4	-
M.P.Vaughan	17	34	1	895	153	27.12	3	3	5	-
R.W.T.Key	19	33	2	836	125	26.96	1	5	18	-
B.C.Hollioake	13	20	0	538	71	26.90	-	4	12	-
D.G.Cork	14	22	2	535	82	26.75	-	4	18	-
D.P.Fulton	17	29	2	722	126*	26.74	1	3	18	-
M.S.Kasprowicz	16	23	4	507	73	26.68	-	5	3	-
W.L.Law	5	9	0	240	64	26.66	-	2	3	-
J.A.Daley	14	24	1	609	105	26.47	1	3	7	-
N.H.Fairbrother	12	19	0	503	83	26.47	-	4	17	-
W.P.C.Weston	11	21	0	554	157	26.38	2	1	3	-
M.J.Walker	14	23	2	553	103*	26.33	1	3	13	-
R.G.Twose	8	13	0	341	91	26.23	-	3	7	-

Name	Matches	Inns	NO	Runs	HS	Avge	100s	50s	Ct	St
P.A.J.DeFreitas	13	18	1	441	105	25.94	1	2	7	-
A.D.Mascarenhas	14	20	2	465	62	25.83	-	2	4	-
M.P.Speight	17	27	5	566	97*	25.72	-	4	48	2
S.J.Lacey	6	8	2	154	42	25.66	-	-	5	1
P.S.Jones	9	14	3	281	105	25.54	1	-	3	-
A.R.Danson	6	10	4	153	31	25.50	-	-	2	-
R.J.Blakey	17	31	4	684	123	25.33	1	4	41	-
J.N.Batty	15	20	5	379	64	25.26	-	1	49	7
G.Chapple	13	18	2	402	83	25.12	-	2	2	-
S.Kalavitigoda	6	11	0	276	73	25.09	-	2	10	-
R.T.Robinson	12	22	1	525	80	25.00	-	4	10	-
N.T.Wood	6	9	0	225	82	25.00	-	1	1	-
G.P.Butcher	5	8	0	199	70	24.87	-	2	2	-
I.D.Blackwell	10	16	2	347	62*	24.78	-	2	6	-
M.J.McCague	10	13	2	272	53	24.72	-	1	7	-
P.D.Collingwood	17	28	0	692	106	24.71	1	4	25	-
A.J.Tudor	10	13	4	222	99*	24.66	-	1	3	-
T.L.Penney	15	24	3	517	73	24.61	-	3	6	2
A.W.Evans	15	24	3	512	88*	24.38	-	2	10	-
K.M.Krikken	12	19	3	389	88	24.31	-	3	30	1
M.A.Roseberry	12	21	1	483	116	24.15	1	1	7	-
A.C.Parore	6	8	0	193	80	24.12	-	2	23	-
M.W.Alleyne	17	29	1	672	76	24.00	-	3	20	-
N.M.K.Smith	15	21	0	504	71	24.00	-	3	8	-
N.R.G.Perera	3	6	0	144	49	24.00	-	-	3	-
I.D.Fisher	11	16	5	261	51	23.72	-	1	-	-
S.J.Rhodes	18	30	5	591	74	23.64	-	1	51	2
G.F.Archer	15	28	1	635	132	23.51	1	2	27	-
J.P.Pyemont	11	19	2	398	90*	23.41	-	3	6	-
B.J.Hyam	18	26	4	514	51	23.36	-	1	46	1
S.A.Marsh	15	22	2	466	73*	23.30	-	2	28	7
M.B.Loye	13	20	1	433	102*	22.78	2	-	4	-
D.P.Ostler	7	11	0	250	87	22.72	-	2	5	-
D.J.Millns	6	9	3	136	47	22.66	-	-	5	-
M.D.Bell	8	13	1	272	83	22.66	-	1	9	-
I.J.Harvey	12	19	0	429	123	22.57	1	-	6	-
J.N.Snape	17	29	6	518	98*	22.52	-	3	8	-
D.A.Leatherdale	19	34	3	693	85	22.35	-	3	9	-
M.C.J.Ball	12	19	4	333	70*	22.20	-	1	11	-
B.L.Hutton	8	15	0	331	59	22.06	-	2	5	-
I.J.Sutcliffe	16	27	0	590	110	21.85	1	2	9	-
I.Dawood	7	12	0	262	102	21.83	1	1	20	-
C.M.W.Read	19	31	1	653	160	21.76	1	1	59	2
R.K.Illingworth	16	26	5	457	91*	21.76	-	1	5	-
G.Welch	14	21	6	326	48*	21.73	-	-	5	-
K.Newell	8	11	0	239	46	21.72	-	-	2	-
K.J.Piper	5	7	0	152	66	21.71	-	1	8	1
H.P.W.Jayawardene	4	8	0	173	89	21.62	-	1	14	4
B.L.Spendlove	7	13	0	279	63	21.46	-	2	2	-

Name	Matches	Inns	NO	Runs	HS	Avge	100s	50s	Ct	St
S.D.Stubbings	5	10	0	213	45	21.30	-	-	3	-
M.A.Gough	12	20	0	424	67	21.20	-	4	17	-
J.I.D.Kerr	14	19	1	381	64	21.16	-	2	5	-
J.D.Ratcliffe	13	20	1	402	91	21.15	-	2	6	-
I.D.Austin	5	8	2	125	45*	20.83	-	-	2	-
A.F.Giles	16	23	5	375	123*	20.83	1	-	6	-
A.D.Shaw	12	16	1	312	140	20.80	1	-	25	1
I.D.K.Salisbury	17	19	2	353	100*	20.76	1	1	5	-
C.P.Schofield	10	14	4	205	39*	20.50	-	-	8	-
T.Frost	12	18	1	348	66	20.47	-	1	23	1
P.J.Hartley	12	15	6	183	58	20.33	-	1	3	-
N.E.Batson	5	10	1	181	72	20.11	-	1	5	-
R.A.Kettleborough	8	15	0	300	93	20.00	-	2	4	-
P.R.Pollard	11	21	2	377	60	19.84	-	3	2	-
T.C.Hicks	7	10	1	178	54	19.77	-	1	4	-
G.E.Welton	9	17	1	316	76	19.75	-	1	4	-
R.G.Halsall	7	9	1	157	76	19.62	-	1	4	-
T.C.Walton	6	8	0	155	71	19.37	-	1	7	-
J.P.B.Barnes	6	9	0	174	45	19.33	-	-	6	-
J.P.Stephenson	15	24	2	425	136	19.31	1	1	17	-
S.H.Khan	6	6	0	115	34	19.16	-	-	2	-
J.J.Bates	6	10	0	190	57	19.00	-	1	2	-
R.D.B.Croft	15	21	4	322	58*	18.94	-	2	5	-
R.S.C.Martin-Jenkins	14	24	2	413	70	18.77	-	2	2	-
M.E.Cassar	14	24	3	393	42	18.71	-	-	5	-
J.J.Whitaker	5	7	0	130	44	18.57	-	-	1	-
D.W.Headley	14	19	3	297	72	18.56	-	1	9	-
W.G.Khan	5	9	0	167	88	18.55	-	2	1	-
T.R.Ward	8	13	0	240	101	18.46	1	-	9	-
P.J.Newport	11	19	3	295	65*	18.43	-	1	3	-
A.R.Caddick	17	23	5	331	45	18.38	-	-	7	-
S.J.Cook	10	16	3	237	51	18.23	-	1	3	-
M.C.Ilott	12	17	1	290	44	18.12	-	-	5	-
M.J.Cawdron	6	9	2	126	42	18.00	-	-	1	-
S.P.Griffiths	5	7	1	108	35	18.00	-	-	15	1
D.J.Eadie	4	8	2	108	52*	18.00	-	1	1	-
C.White	17	31	2	521	52	17.96	-	1	12	-
G.R.Haynes	8	12	2	177	60*	17.70	-	1	-	-
J.B.D.Thompson	14	19	9	176	44	17.60	-	-	1	-
J.J.Bull	6	11	0	193	49	17.54	-	-	1	-
J.P.Hewitt	13	21	1	350	49*	17.50	-	-	6	-
S.D.Udal	15	21	6	261	40	17.40	-	-	1	-
J.P.Taylor	17	21	2	316	71	16.63	-	1	5	-
I.N.Flanagan	6	10	0	165	52	16.50	-	1	3	-
A.F.Gofton	5	8	1	115	37*	16.42	-	-	-	-
A.G.Wharf	16	26	3	370	78	16.08	-	2	8	-
V.C.Drakes	17	30	3	427	80	15.81	-	2	5	-
A.P.Cowan	17	24	3	332	52*	15.80	-	1	10	-
P.J.Martin	14	19	5	220	30*	15.71	-	-	2	-

Name	Matches	Inns	NO	Runs	HS	Avge	100s	50s	Ct	St
N.Killeen	12	19	3	251	46	15.68	-	-	1	-
B.J.Collins	7	11	2	141	46	15.66	-	-	4	-
N.J.Wilton	6	10	0	156	55	15.60	-	1	13	2
A.Singh	5	10	0	154	69	15.40	-	2	-	-
J.H.Louw	7	13	1	183	82	15.25	-	2	5	-
D.A.Cosker	13	18	4	212	49	15.14	-	-	14	-
S.D.Thomas	18	26	2	352	54	14.66	-	1	9	-
P.J.Franks	16	27	3	348	61	14.50	-	1	2	-
S.J.Renshaw	12	13	6	101	28	14.42	-	-	7	-
D.R.Hewson	5	10	0	144	40	14.40	-	-	3	-
C.E.W.Silverwood	13	20	2	259	53*	14.38	-	1	3	-
C.G.Liptrot	11	16	6	142	61	14.20	-	1	-	-
M.M.Patel	18	24	3	290	67	13.80	-	1	6	-
H.Boteju	4	7	0	96	31	13.71	-	-	3	-
M.J.Wood	17	33	0	451	53	13.66	-	1	10	-
J.D.Lewry	12	19	7	163	30*	13.58	-	-	2	-
J.Lewis	14	23	3	266	62	13.30	-	1	2	-
C.M.Tolley	4	8	0	106	51	13.25	-	1	-	-
J.Ormond	13	17	3	183	50*	13.07	-	1	2	-
A.R.C.Fraser	12	16	5	142	56*	12.90	-	1	-	-
A.R.K.Pierson	13	13	3	129	66	12.90	-	1	5	-
N.A.M.McLean	14	19	3	206	70	12.87	-	1	6	-
M.T.Brimson	14	16	6	127	36*	12.70	-	-	2	-
K.P.Dutch	6	10	0	119	23	11.90	-	-	2	-
N.C.Phillips	6	9	0	105	42	11.66	-	-	5	-
S.J.W.Lewis	4	6	0	70	17	11.66	-	-	3	-
P.C.R.Tufnell	16	21	4	198	48	11.64	-	-	3	-
S.Humphries	11	18	2	176	57	11.00	-	1	18	2
R.J.Kirtley	15	23	5	194	32	10.77	-	-	2	-
R.L.Johnson	6	8	0	86	39	10.75	-	-	1	-
S.J.E.Brown	15	23	8	160	29*	10.66	-	-	3	-
D.J.Roberts	5	8	1	73	34*	10.42	-	-	4	-
P.M.Such	20	24	11	134	22*	10.30	-	-	5	-
M.N.Bowen	11	21	8	130	19	10.00	-	-	2	-
T.F.Bloomfield	11	17	9	80	17*	10.00	-	-	1	-
J.Wood	10	15	1	139	49*	9.92	-	-	4	-
R.J.Sidebottom	12	20	5	146	48*	9.73	-	-	6	-
P.W.Jarvis	7	8	0	73	20	9.12	-	-	2	-
M.S.Villavarayan	4	6	0	54	28	9.00	-	-	-	-
B.W.Gannon	11	12	4	70	18	8.75	-	-	4	-
S.L.Watkin	15	19	9	86	16*	8.60	-	-	7	-
E.S.H.Giddins	15	20	11	76	18	8.44	-	-	2	-
R.S.G.Anderson	15	20	2	147	44	8.16	-	-	5	-
P.Aldred	12	17	2	122	29*	8.13	-	-	4	-
M.K.Davies	13	18	4	110	32*	7.85	-	-	3	-
S.P.Jones	10	13	3	77	19*	7.70	-	-	2	-
A.Sheriyar	19	26	8	129	18	7.16	-	-	3	-
K.R.Spiring	5	10	0	69	18	6.90	-	-	3	-
A.M.Smith	14	21	5	108	14	6.75	-	-	4	-

Name	Matches	Inns	NO	Runs	HS	Avge	100s	50s	Ct	St
M.J.Hoggard	8	11	3	53	21	6.62	-	-	2	-
A.D.Mullally	9	12	4	50	13	6.25	-	-	2	-
R.D.Stemp	13	17	5	74	18	6.16	-	-	1	-
M.M.Betts	7	11	2	55	19*	6.11	-	-	4	-
D.J.Thompson	8	10	0	55	22	5.50	-	-	1	-
A.Hafeez	4	8	0	43	32	5.37	-	-	2	-
S.J.Harmison	17	24	9	79	14*	5.26	-	-	4	-
T.A.Munton	13	19	3	80	24	5.00	-	-	5	-
M.A.Robinson	17	24	11	63	10	4.84	-	-	1	-
G.Yates	5	6	0	25	21	4.16	-	-	4	-
M.Muralitharan	7	9	1	30	10	3.75	-	-	2	-
O.T.Parkin	7	9	3	21	11	3.50	-	-	2	-
D.E.Malcolm	15	16	6	32	10*	3.20	-	-	4	-
T.A.Tweats	4	7	0	21	10	3.00	-	-	2	-

BOWLING AVERAGES
Qualifying requirements : 10 wickets taken

Name	Overs	Mdns	Runs	Wkts	Avge	Best	5wI	10wM
Saqlain Mushtaq	290.5	90	660	58	11.37	7-19	7	2
M.Muralitharan	386.2	122	777	66	11.77	7-39	8	5
M.J.Saggers	59.5	13	192	12	16.00	4-26	-	-
D.J.Nash	232	84	548	34	16.11	7-39	2	-
D.J.Millns	142.3	35	372	23	16.17	5-62	1	-
K.J.Dean	66.4	14	198	12	16.50	4-34	-	-
M.J.Cawdron	101.5	30	266	16	16.62	5-35	3	-
A.C.Morris	172	51	497	28	17.75	5-52	3	1
J.D.Ratcliffe	99	27	269	15	17.93	6-48	1	-
N.Killeen	411.3	114	1070	58	18.44	7-85	4	-
J.M.de la Pena	63.5	19	240	13	18.46	6-18	1	1
D.Gough	96.5	20	319	17	18.76	4-27	-	-
M.P.Bicknell	545.4	157	1346	71	18.95	4-32	-	-
G.M.Hamilton	277.1	64	825	43	19.18	5-30	1	-
J.B.D.Thompson	434.1	106	1265	64	19.76	7-89	3	-
T.A.Munton	409.1	107	1028	52	19.76	7-36	3	-
P.M.Hutchison	65.5	16	263	13	20.23	6-35	1	-
R.Herath	168	46	448	22	20.36	6-45	1	-
C.E.W.Silverwood	405.2	87	1204	59	20.40	5-28	3	-
A.M.Smith	450.1	127	1168	57	20.49	5-41	2	-
P.J.Martin	446.4	134	1028	50	20.56	5-43	4	-
T.M.Smith	183.4	34	646	31	20.83	5-63	3	1
A.R.Caddick	763.5	249	1900	91	20.87	8-113	5	-
C.G.Greenidge	76.4	20	231	11	21.00	5-60	1	-
R.C.Irani	395.2	101	1084	51	21.25	4-29	-	-
P.Aldred	362.4	85	1063	50	21.26	7-101	5	1
M.K.Davies	423.3	137	857	40	21.42	6-49	3	-
D.L.Maddy	85.4	22	260	12	21.66	3-5	-	-
P.A.J.DeFreitas	477.2	123	1284	59	21.76	6-41	4	-
P.J.Hartley	393	93	1176	54	21.77	8-65	2	1

Name	Overs	Mdns	Runs	Wkts	Avge	Best	5wI	10wM
C.L.Cairns	234.2	56	701	32	21.90	7-46	3	1
I.D.K.Salisbury	558.2	145	1315	60	21.91	5-44	2	-
E.S.H.Giddins	381.3	102	1142	52	21.96	6-90	2	-
M.J.Hoggard	215.1	58	619	28	22.10	5-47	1	-
D.G.Cork	427.3	95	1229	55	22.34	6-113	4	-
J.Wood	247.4	57	805	36	22.36	7-58	2	-
A.J.Tudor	297.3	70	895	40	22.37	7-77	3	-
V.C.Drakes	586.2	131	1794	80	22.42	6-39	5	2
G.Yates	131.1	42	315	14	22.50	6-64	2	-
S.R.Lampitt	287.1	70	888	39	22.76	4-28	-	-
S.J.E.Brown	475	112	1448	63	22.98	6-25	5	-
A.S.A.Perera	66.5	9	253	11	23.00	7-73	1	-
R.J.Kirtley	514.3	133	1504	65	23.13	7-21	3	-
O.T.Parkin	155.4	39	491	21	23.38	4-38	-	-
A.Richardson	190.3	45	539	23	23.43	8-51	1	1
I.S.Gallage	80.5	24	235	10	23.50	3-18	-	-
S.B.O'Connor	134.2	32	447	19	23.52	6-65	2	-
M.N.Bowen	264	53	872	37	23.56	5-66	1	-
P.J.Franks	513	124	1489	63	23.63	5-52	1	-
M.C.Ilott	310.4	85	900	38	23.68	6-38	1	-
J.D.Lewry	381.4	84	1330	56	23.75	7-38	4	1
M.A.Ealham	339.2	73	981	41	23.92	6-35	2	-
A.F.Giles	447.4	145	938	39	24.05	5-28	2	-
P.J.Newport	274.4	77	747	31	24.09	4-57	-	-
S.D.Thomas	447.2	78	1480	61	24.26	5-64	1	-
J.Ormond	406.1	88	1283	52	24.67	5-63	3	-
A.Sheriyar	609.2	119	2273	92	24.70	7-130	4	1
M.M.Patel	674.3	209	1568	63	24.88	8-115	3	1
S.L.Watkin	421.3	121	1087	43	25.27	6-75	3	-
R.S.G.Anderson	378.2	84	1273	50	25.46	5-36	2	-
P.C.R.Tufnell	577.3	155	1223	48	25.47	5-61	2	-
R.S.C.Martin-Jenkins	370.2	99	1074	42	25.57	4-50	-	-
C.White	354	69	1058	41	25.80	4-32	-	-
M.A.Butcher	180	49	445	17	26.17	4-30	-	-
D.S.Lucas	103.5	21	394	15	26.26	5-104	1	-
S.D.Udal	497.3	124	1336	50	26.72	6-47	3	-
A.Dale	136.5	46	407	15	27.13	3-29	-	-
G.Keedy	265.4	73	711	26	27.34	5-67	1	-
M.S.Kasprowicz	485.5	112	1458	53	27.50	5-42	2	-
A.D.Mullally	310.4	93	771	28	27.53	5-106	1	-
A.P.Cowan	393.1	66	1267	46	27.54	6-47	1	-
D.R.Brown	232.5	57	717	26	27.57	7-66	1	-
S.J.Harmison	565.5	120	1775	64	27.73	5-76	1	-
A.Flintoff	145.4	30	419	15	27.93	5-24	1	-
S.M.Sheikh	96.5	18	338	12	28.16	4-25	-	-
I.J.Harvey	296.1	77	876	31	28.25	5-76	1	-
R.L.Johnson	133.3	30	453	16	28.31	4-50	-	-
D.J.Thompson	184	30	685	24	28.54	4-46	-	-
M.P.L.Bulbeck	425.4	101	1456	51	28.54	5-45	3	1

Name	Overs	Mdns	Runs	Wkts	Avge	Best	5wI	10wM
K.J.Innes	137	37	429	15	28.60	4-85	-	-
A.R.C.Fraser	435.1	113	1093	38	28.76	5-63	1	-
D.E.Malcolm	485.1	90	1726	60	28.76	6-39	3	-
G.P.Swann	560.1	131	1641	57	28.78	6-41	2	1
A.J.Harris	229.3	44	752	26	28.92	5-63	2	-
M.P.Smethurst	126.1	29	377	13	29.00	4-44	-	-
M.M.Betts	175.1	41	583	20	29.15	4-34	-	-
J.P.Hewitt	311.1	69	1022	35	29.20	5-50	1	-
J.P.Stephenson	310	57	1086	37	29.35	5-60	1	-
K.A.Parsons	285.2	80	823	28	29.39	5-57	1	-
J.Lewis	492.2	134	1444	49	29.46	7-56	2	1
M.E.Cassar	164	34	562	19	29.57	5-51	1	-
O.A.Shah	99.1	14	326	11	29.63	3-33	-	-
J.P.Taylor	507.2	119	1427	48	29.72	5-105	1	-
G.Welch	269.3	45	927	31	29.90	5-47	1	-
M.A.Robinson	520.4	140	1438	48	29.95	6-88	1	-
B.W.Gannon	259.3	47	992	33	30.06	6-80	2	-
V.S.Solanki	158.3	47	514	17	30.23	4-41	-	-
J.M.Dakin	219.1	61	575	19	30.26	4-27	-	-
T.F.Bloomfield	266.3	45	1007	33	30.51	5-36	1	-
P.M.Such	702	192	1710	55	31.09	7-136	2	1
J.H.Kallis	95	12	345	11	31.36	3-52	-	-
R.D.B.Croft	521.4	135	1412	45	31.37	7-70	4	1
M.V.Fleming	266.3	64	726	23	31.56	3-59	-	-
C.D.Crowe	92	14	348	11	31.63	3-63	-	-
J.J.Bates	141	46	356	11	32.36	5-154	1	-
N.A.M.McLean	471	105	1489	46	32.36	4-63	-	-
P.W.Jarvis	201.2	43	619	19	32.57	4-76	-	-
M.T.Brimson	316.5	98	784	24	32.66	5-51	1	-
C.P.Schofield	324	82	951	29	32.79	5-66	1	-
D.L.Vettori	469	155	1051	32	32.84	5-80	2	-
R.J.Sidebottom	275.3	70	789	24	32.87	3-16	-	-
C.G.Liptrot	194.1	49	665	20	33.25	5-51	1	-
C.J.Adams	120	28	333	10	33.30	3-37	-	-
N.M.K.Smith	190.3	47	540	16	33.75	4-90	-	-
I.D.Fisher	162	42	476	14	34.00	5-73	1	-
M.Watkinson	137	30	413	12	34.41	3-43	-	-
R.J.Green	212.2	46	692	20	34.60	4-21	-	-
J.I.D.Kerr	305.2	68	1075	31	34.67	7-23	1	-
B.C.Hollioake	249.5	49	801	23	34.82	5-51	1	-
S.J.Cook	276.4	60	954	27	35.33	4-83	-	-
M.J.McCague	235	44	754	21	35.90	4-36	-	-
C.C.Lewis	191.1	51	585	16	36.56	3-18	-	-
S.J.Renshaw	381.3	93	1125	30	37.50	4-43	-	-
N.C.Phillips	212	41	677	18	37.61	6-97	2	1
A.P.Grayson	319.2	98	849	22	38.59	4-16	-	-
G.D.Rose	219.2	61	657	17	38.64	4-14	-	-
A.L.Penberthy	266.5	89	735	19	38.68	3-13	-	-
P.N.Weekes	316.1	68	890	23	38.69	4-50	-	-

Name	Overs	Mdns	Runs	Wkts	Avge	Best	5wI	10wM
D.W.Headley	457.5	93	1442	37	38.97	4-74	-	-
D.P.Mather	142.2	26	469	12	39.08	3-44	-	-
A.G.Wharf	335.3	65	1216	31	39.22	4-30	-	-
G.I.Allott	163.1	32	593	15	39.53	3-22	-	-
K.D.M.Walker	142	31	479	12	39.91	3-65	-	-
G.Chapple	338	92	964	24	40.16	5-92	1	-
P.S.Jones	255.2	50	845	21	40.23	4-126	-	-
S.P.Jones	208	31	776	19	40.84	5-31	1	-
M.P.Vaughan	137.1	26	424	10	42.40	2-19	-	-
M.W.Alleyne	367	109	1000	23	43.47	3-36	-	-
U.B.A.Rashid	218.3	67	664	15	44.26	4-41	-	-
D.A.Cosker	321	81	844	19	44.42	3-100	-	-
R.G.Halsall	168	35	491	11	44.63	3-64	-	-
V.J.Wells	176	47	473	10	47.30	2-2	-	-
I.D.Blackwell	250.1	69	595	12	49.58	3-30	-	-
A.D.Mascarenhas	308	98	868	17	51.05	2-2	-	-
R.K.Illingworth	336.4	92	767	15	51.13	3-58	-	-
M.C.J.Ball	266	69	723	13	55.61	3-38	-	-
A.R.K.Pierson	271.2	52	789	13	60.69	4-131	-	-
R.D.Stemp	325.5	88	974	16	60.87	4-114	-	-
A.Symonds	207.1	37	761	12	63.41	2-48	-	-
J.N.Snape	277.1	71	804	12	67.00	3-67	-	-
T.C.Hicks	181.1	28	672	10	67.20	2-61	-	-
G.R.Loveridge	209.4	25	830	11	75.45	2-59	-	-

PCA AWARD WINNERS

HAYTER CUP
PCA PLAYER OF THE YEAR

1970	Mike Procter and Jack Bond
1971	Lance Gibbs
1972	Andy Roberts
1973	Peter Lee
1974	Barry Stead
1975	Zaheer Abbas
1976	Peter Lee
1977	Mike Procter
1978	John Lever
1979	John Lever
1980	Robin Jackman
1981	Richard Hadlee
1982	Malcolm Marshall
1983	Ken McEwan
1984	Richard Hadlee
1985	Neal Radford
1986	Courtney Walsh
1987	Richard Hadlee
1988	Graeme Hick
1989	Jimmy Cook
1990	Graham Gooch
1991	Waqar Younis
1992	Courtney Walsh
1993	Steve Watkin
1994	Brian Lara
1995	Dominic Cork
1996	Phil Simmons
1997	Steve James
1998	Mal Loye
1999	Stuart Law

ARLOTT CUP
PCA YOUNG PLAYER OF THE YEAR

1990	Mike Atherton
1991	Dominic Cork
1992	Mark Lathwell
1993	Malachy Loye
1994	John Crawley
1995	Andy Symonds
1996	Chris Silverwood
1997	Ben Hollioake
1998	Andrew Flintoff
1999	David Sales

HAROLD GOLDBLATT UMPIRES' CUP

1997	Peter Willey
1998	Ray Julian
1999	Ray Julian

WATERFORD CRYSTAL
PCA SPECIAL MERIT AWARD

1997	Lord Cowdrey
1998	Dickie Bird
1999	David English

SLAZENGER SHEER INSTINCT
INDIVIDUAL PERFORMANCE AWARD

1997	Alistair Brown
1998	Graeme Hick
1999	Mark Alleyne

THE PRIMARY CLUB

PO Box 12121
London NW1 9WS
Tel: 0171 267 3316
Fax: 0171 485 6808

Derek Underwood, the patron of the Primary Club, qualified for membership in some style in 1965. Playing for Kent against the South Africans he was out first ball twice in the same match.

However, members do not have to be playing Test or county cricket when the ultimate disaster strikes in order to qualify for the club. As long as you are out first ball at ANY level of cricket you are eligible to join The Primary Club.

Why join? The Primary Club is a charity (Registered Charity No. 285285) and all profits from subscriptions, donations and the range of items for sale (ties, sweaters, shirts, mugs, umbrellas, etc.) go to pay for sporting and recreational facilities for the blind and partially sighted. All the club's workers are volunteers.

For many of us sport is an important part of our every day lives; for the blind and partially sighted, sport can mean so much more. The confidence and sense of achievement they get from mastering a physical skill helps them a great deal in tackling the problems of their lives.

MEMBERSHIP APPLICATION

Name

Address

Joining subscription:	
To include City tie – £15	
To include Club tie – £15	
To include City & Club tie – £25	
To include Bow tie – £15	
Lady, to include brooch – £10	
DONATION	
TOTAL REMITTANCE TO: 'THE PRIMARY CLUB' £	

Please photocopy this form rather than spoil the book

TIES AND OTHER ITEMS FOR MEMBERS

The City tie has several small reproductions of the club emblem embroidered on navy blue fabric – the Club tie has a single larger one on green. A colour leaflet of the full range of clothing and other items will be sent to members.

DEED OF COVENANT

If you wish to consider making a donation under a 4 year (or more) charitable deed of covenant, please tick the box, but do not include this donation in your present remittance. Further details and a form of deed will then be sent to you. Such a deed does not increase the cost to you of your donation but enables the Club to recover income tax. [ ]

INDEX OF PLAYERS BY COUNTY

*denotes not registered for the 2000 season. Where a player is known to have moved in the off-season he is listed under his new county.

INDEX OF PLAYERS BY COUNTY

INDEX OF PLAYERS BY COUNTY

SCHOFIELD, C.P.
SCUDERI, J.C.
SMETHURST, M.P.
WATKINSON, M.
WOOD, N.T.
YATES, G.

INDEX OF PLAYERS BY COUNTY

INDEX OF PLAYERS BY COUNTY

HEMP, D.L.
KNIGHT, N.V.
OSTLER, D.P.
PENNEY, T.L.
PIPER, K.J.
POWELL, M.J.
RICHARDSON, A.
SHEIKH, M.A.
SIERRA, R.
SINGH, A.
SMALL, G.C.*
SMITH, N.M.K.
WAGH, M.A.
WARREN, N.A.
WELCH, G.

WORCESTERSHIRE

ATHEY, C.W.J.
BATSON, N.E.*
CATTERALL, D.N.
DE LA PENA, J.M.*
DRIVER, R.C.
HAFEEZ, A.*
HAYNES, G.R.
HICK, G.A.
ILLINGWORTH, R.K.
KABIR ALI
KADEER ALI
LAMPITT, S.R.
LEATHERDALE, D.A.
LIPTROT, C.G.
MCGRATH, G.D.
MIRZA, M.M.
MOODY, T.M.*
NEWPORT, P.J.*
PATEL, D.
PIPE, D.J.
POLLARD, P.R.

RAWNSLEY, M.J.
RHODES, S.J.
SHERIYAR, A.
SOLANKI, V.S.
SPIRING, K.R.
WESTON, W.P.C.
WILSON, E.J.

YORKSHIRE

BLAKEY, R.J.
BLEWETT, G.S.*
BYAS, D.
CRAVEN, V.J.
DAWSON, R.K.J.
ELLISON, C.J.
FELLOWS, G.M.
FISHER, I.D.
GOUGH, D.
GUY, S.M.
HAMILTON, G.M.
HARDEN, R.J.
HOGGARD, M.J.
HUTCHISON, P.M.
INGLIS, J.W.
LEHMANN, D.S.
MCGRATH, A.
MIDDLEBROOK, J.D.
PARKER, B.*
SIDEBOTTOM, R.J.
SILVERWOOD, C.E.W.
STEAD, R.A.
THEWLIS, M.
VAUGHAN, M.P.
WHITE, C.
WIDDUP, S.
WOOD, M.J.

QUIZ ANSWERS

1. 1992; D.A. Graveney
2. Leicestershire in 1998
3. S.P. James
4. W. Rhodes (Yorkshire) with 762 (1898-1930)
5. W.R. Hammond (Gloucestershire)
6. M.E. Waugh
7. Eight
8. Glamorgan; 1921
9. 1977; Kent and Middlesex
10. They were all against Notts; at Nottingham in 1951, at Scarborough in 1955, and at Bradford in 1963
11. Middlesex; M.W. Gatting
12. R.C. Russell (Gloucestershire); 356 (335/21)
13. Against Somerset at Taunton
14. R.J. Hadlee; 1075 runs (av. 53.75), 97 wickets (av.11.89)
15. The Quaifes were father and son; likewise the Bestwicks
16. G.M. Turner
17. D. Kenyon
18. B.A. Richards, R.E. Marshall, C.G. Greenidge
19. Five in both cases
20. Surrey
21. J.A. Jameson (240*) and R.B. Kanhai (213*)
22. Lord Hawke
23. Surrey
24. He took all ten wickets in an innings (10-45)
25. A. Symonds, then of Gloucestershire, scored 16 sixes in his 254*
26. Against Durham at Edgbaston
27. Zaheer Abbas between 1976 and 1981
28. R.B. Kanhai, A.I. Kallicharran, D.L. Murray, L.R. Gibbs. Note: Besides these and numerous England Test players, Warwicks also had K. Ibadulla of Pakistan
29. M.J. Stewart for Surrey v Northants at Northampton; A.S. Brown for Glos v Notts at Trent Bridge
30. P.I. Pocock. Note: All told, Pocock took seven wickets in eleven balls in this burst
31. A.C.D. Ingleby-Mackenzie
32. Waqar Younis
33. F.D. Stephenson
34. C.L. Cairns
35. A.A. Donald
36. J.G. Binks (412 consecutive appearances)
37. T.W. Spencer (Kent 1935-46); 569 matches 1950-80
38. D.C.S. Compton; these were the best all-round figures of his career
39. Yorkshire; 29 times
40. W.E. Alley
41. J.M. Brearley; he made one first-class appearance in 1983
42. C.W.J. Athey (then of Glos; now coach at Worcs)
43. R. Illingworth
44. Essex
45. J.D. Carr (then of Middlesex; now ECB director of cricket operations)
46. J.E. Morris (204)
47. I.D. Austin
48. D.G. Cork (Derbyshire and England)
49. P.A. Cottey (now of Sussex)
50. 1989; Essex
51. S.R. Tendulkar; 1992

52. C.C. Inman (against declaration bowling)
53. A.C. MacLaren
54. He scored it (115*) batting at No. 11
55. K.S. Ranjitsinhji (100 and 125*) v Yorkshire at Hove on 22 August; he was in overnight on 0*
56. G. MacGregor
57. P.A. Neale (101*)
58. G.A.R. Lock (10-54)
59. Nottinghamshire
60. A.E. Fagg (244 and 202*)
61. I.V.A. Richards
62. A.R. Caddick (Somerset); 422 (av. 22.48)
63. K.G. Suttle (Sussex) with 423 (1954-69)
64. Sussex (at Hove)
65. Essex (at Leyton)
66. They scored 554; it was this record that Holmes and Sutcliffe bettered in 1932
67. A.C. Smith (Warwickshire)
68. H.Verity
69. C.E.B. Rice of South Africa
70. W. Wooller
71. 1988, although the four-day Championship was not inaugurated until 1993
72. M.P. Speight (then of Sussex; now of Durham) scored 131 v Glamorgan at Hove
73. S.T. Clarke; 100* in 62 minutes for Surrey v Glamorgan at Swansea
74. G.L. Jessop (Gloucestershire); 104 and 139 on the second and third mornings of the match
75. M.J. Stewart
76. B.J.T. Bosanquet, inventor of the googly, or 'Bosie'
77. 12 by Northamptonshire v Gloucestershire at Gloucester in 1907
78. I.T. Botham
79. They made the 521 following on, having been bowled out for 15 in their first innings (at one point they had also been 186 for 6 in their second)
80. He was out obstructing the field
81. K. S. Duleepsinhji, nephew of K.S. Ranjitsinhji
82. M.J. Procter
83. Yorkshire (in 1939 and 1946); A. B. Sellers
84. He took two hat-tricks in Somerset's second innings, one consisting of four wickets in four balls
85. Schweppes (1977-83), Britannic Assurance (1984-98) and PPP healthcare (1999 –)
86. D. Shackleton
87. F.S. Trueman
88. W.J. Edrich and D.C.S. Compton
89. R.A. Woolmer; now at Warwickshire
90. P.B.H. May led Surrey to the Championship and England to victory over West Indies in 1957
91. C.M. (1411 runs) and A.P. (1003 runs) Wells
92. 1969
93. M.R. Ramprakash (Middlesex); 8392 (av. 56.32)
94. D.E. East
95. S.J. Cook
96. G.S. Sobers (Nottinghamshire) scored 36 (6 x 6) off a six-ball over bowled by M.A. Nash
97. Somerset; they joined the Championship in 1891
98. G.M. Hamilton; 79, 70, 5-69, 5-43
99. J.B. Hobbs's
100. M.D. Marshall